T4-ADC-309

Aspects of Rationality

Reflections on What It Means
to Be Rational and
Whether We Are

Raymond S. Nickerson

Psychology Press
Taylor & Francis Group
New York Hove

Psychology Press
Taylor & Francis Group
270 Madison Avenue
New York, NY 10016

Psychology Press
Taylor & Francis Group
27 Church Road
Hove, East Sussex BN3 2FA

© 2008 by Taylor & Francis Group, LLC

Printed in the United States of America on acid-free paper
10 9 8 7 6 5 4 3 2 1

International Standard Book Number-13: 978-1-84169-487-0 (Hardcover)

Except as permitted under U.S. Copyright Law, no part of this book may be reprinted, reproduced, transmitted, or utilized in any form by any electronic, mechanical, or other means, now known or hereafter invented, including photocopying, microfilming, and recording, or in any information storage or retrieval system, without written permission from the publishers.

Trademark Notice: Product or corporate names may be trademarks or registered trademarks, and are used only for identification and explanation without intent to infringe.

Library of Congress Cataloging-in-Publication Data

Nickerson, Raymond S.
　　Aspects of rationality : reflections on what it means to be rational and whether we are / Raymond S. Nickerson.
　　　　p. cm.
　　Includes bibliographical references.
　　ISBN 978-1-84169-487-0 (alk. paper)
　　1. Rationalism--Psychological aspects. 2. Psychology--Philosophy. I. Title.

BF441.N49 2007
153.4'3--dc22
　　　　　　　　　　　　　　　　　　　　　　　　　　　　　　　　　　2007041450

Visit the Taylor & Francis Web site at
http://www.taylorandfrancis.com

and the Psychology Press Web site at
http://www.psypress.com

CONTENTS

Preface — vii

1. What Is Rationality? — 1

2. The Search for Standards of Rationality — 37

3. Intelligence and Knowledge — 71

4. Beliefs — 113

5. Goals, Values, and Affect — 175

6. Explanations — 209

7	**Preference and Judgment**	253
8	**Decision and Choice**	285
9	**Understanding and Wisdom**	323
10	**The Relativity of Rationality**	357
11	**Conclusions and a View**	389

References 421
Index 489

PREFACE

I suspect that everyone who reads these words considers himself or herself to be rational. But all of us probably can think of people whom we consider to be irrational, or at least to behave irrationally on occasion. These surmises imply the existence of some concept of rationality in terms of which such judgments are made, but that does not mean that we would find it easy to articulate that concept precisely, if asked.

What does it mean to be rational—to reason well and effectively? How does rationality, broadly conceived, relate to the knowledge one acquires, the beliefs one forms, the explanations one constructs or appropriates, the judgments and decisions one makes, the values one adopts? If you find the question of what it means to be rational difficult to answer precisely, you are in good company. Philosophers, among others, have debated it for many centuries.

A closely related question is: What is the character of human reasoning, and, in particular, does it tend to be rational? The second question presupposes an answer to the first. If we cannot say what rationality is, or what we intend to mean when we use the word, we cannot hope to determine whether any particular instance of reasoning or behavior is rational or not.

Much has been written about human rationality—or lack thereof. In recent years, some psychologists have focused attention on numerous ways in which people appear not to be rational, at least if being rational is taken to mean thinking or behaving in accordance with some normative standard. Others have argued that if human reasoning is as flawed as this work suggests, it is a wonder that we, as a species, are still around to notice the fact.

In this book, I discuss much of the experimental research on reasoning as it relates to the question of human rationality, in the context of a variety of conceptions of rationality, not limited to conformity of thought and behavior to the dictates of one or another normative system.

Ideas from beyond psychological research are included when deemed appropriate. The discussion focuses on specific topics that seem to me to represent essential aspects of any adequately inclusive concept of rationality: intelligence and knowledge; beliefs; goals, values and affect; explanations; judgment and choice; understanding and wisdom.

The target reader is anyone interested in the question of what it means to be rational and in reflecting on the various claims that have been made regarding the extent to which people meet, or fail to meet, the standards that one or another view of rationality entails. This includes, first and foremost, investigators and students of human reasoning, but my intent was, and sincere hope is, that the presentation be readily accessible to the interested layperson who is not an expert on human cognition. It is not intended to be a textbook, but I hope it will prove to be a suitable supplementary text, or resource book, for courses in reasoning, decision making, problem solving, and related aspects of cognition.

I am grateful to the National Science Foundation for project support during part of the time this book was in process. Of course, none of the views expressed in the book represent official positions of the Foundation.

I want to express my thanks also to Tufts University for providing me a congenial working environment since retiring from Bolt Beranek and Newman Inc. (BBN Technologies) several years ago, and to colleagues in the psychology department—especially Susan Butler, Michael Carlin, Richard Chechile, and Robert Cook—for many stimulating conversations on a wide range of topics, including several that are touched on in this book. I recall with pleasure also many spirited talks with Salvatore Soraci, and feel a great sense of loss from his untimely death.

Tufts connects with this book in several ways, a fact that dawned on me only as I began to write this preface. My interest in the question of what it means to be rational goes as far back as I can remember, but it was intensified by participation in several research projects during twenty-five years at BBN. One that stands out in my memory as being especially pertinent was a review of theoretical and empirical studies of decision making and their implications for the training of decision makers, done in collaboration with BBN colleague and one-time fellow Tufts graduate student Carl Feehrer, for the Naval Training Equipment Center. This review and our struggles to organize the sizeable literature impressed me with the variety of views that existed regarding what constituted rational choice behavior. I mention this project to acknowledge my debt to Carl for stoking my interest in the subject in the course of our discussions and collaborative effort.

Other Tufts connections include numerous talks on matters germane to this book with son Nathan, a Tufts graduate whose reflectiveness is a continuing source of parental pride and a prod to my own thinking, and granddaughter Amara Nickerson, also a Tufts graduate, who again (she has done this before) organized references for me (pulling out those cited in the text from a master list of several thousand entries) and otherwise helped to get the final manuscript in shape. And then there is Doris, wife, mother, and grandmother of Tufts graduates, whose constant love, patience, and support make everything else worthwhile.

My thinking about the various subtopics of this book has been influenced by numerous colleagues outside of Tufts with whom I have had the good fortune to collaborate over the years. It would be folly to try to mention them all, but a few who have made an especially deep impression by their commitment to science and their standards of scholarship include Ruma Falk, Thomas Landauer, Neville Moray, Richard Pew, Kenneth Stevens, and John Swets.

It is a great pleasure for me to dedicate this book to Philip Sampson, long-time chairman of the Psychology Department at Tufts and holder of the Moses Hunt Chair until his retirement in 1992. Phil's outstanding qualities as a mentor and advisor have been recognized formally by his receipt of the Seymour O. Simches Award for Distinguished Teaching and Advising from Tufts and the Paul M. Fitts Award from the Human Factors and Ergonomics Society, but they can only be fully appreciated by the fortunate students he advised, of whom I was one. I am immensely grateful for his support of my unorthodox combining of a stretched-out PhD program with a full-time job, and his ready accessibility and encouragement.

The range of Phil's academic interests is seen in the fact that he taught both engineering psychology and cognition. His appreciation of the importance of issues relating to both "knobs-and-dials" design and matters of cognition perhaps came as much from his hands-on experiences as a WWII bomber pilot and later avid recreational sailor (reliable rumor has it that his favorite weather condition for sailing is just-below-hurricane wind) as from academically acquired knowledge. From what I have gleaned from his colleagues and other graduate students, affection and admiration for him are universal among those who know him. With apologies for its shortcomings, I offer this book as a token of appreciation for Phil, an inspiring mentor and friend.

Raymond S. Nickerson

CHAPTER 1

What Is Rationality?

> Rationality....is a crucial component of the self-image of the human species, not simply a tool for gaining knowledge or improving our lives and society. Understanding our rationality brings deeper insight into our nature and into whatever special status we possess. (Nozick, 1993, p. xii)

What is rationality? Is it best thought of as a property of individuals? Can it also be a property of groups? Of nations? Of a species? Is rationality a mark of humanity? Does our ability to reason set us apart from other species, as Aristotle claimed? If we are rational, why do we find ourselves so frequently in great difficulties that seem to be largely our own doing?

What is the relationship between rationality and intelligence, or knowledge? How does—how should—rationality constrain beliefs? How does rationality relate to goals, values and affect? To attitudes and motivation? To understanding and wisdom? What constitutes a rational explanation? A rational judgment or decision?

This book is motivated by these and similar questions. For the most part, the specific questions are all subsumed, however, under two generic ones: one normative and one empirical. The first is "What constitutes rationality?" The second is "What is the character of human reasoning, and, in particular, is it rational?"

The normative question has to do with reasoning standards. I assume that most of us view rationality as a worthy goal for human beings and aspire to reason well ourselves. We criticize patterns of thought or behavior that appear to us to be irrational and do not give them the respect that we give to patterns that appear to have the force of sound reason behind them. But what are the criteria by which what is rational can be distinguished from what is not? And from where did they come? What gives them their authority? Can we hope to find an answer to the question of what constitutes rationality that is more than an expression

2 Aspects of Rationality

of a specific opinion on the matter? Can we expect to be able to do more than learn what it means to be rational from a particular point of view?

"Rationality" may be used to convey different ideas by different people and by the same people in different contexts. It is safe to assume, too, that some people who use the word would be able to give only a vague explanation of what they mean by it. Inasmuch as words do not have intrinsic meanings, the best we can aspire to is to discover the various connotations that have been given to the word, perhaps to see if usage reflects a high degree of consensus regarding what it should be taken to mean. When, in this book, I speak of the meaning of rationality, I shall have in mind the question of what ideas the term has been used to convey, and that of what people who have thought much about it might or might not agree it should be taken to mean.

The question of how people reason is an empirical one. In attempting to address it, I shall look, among other places, to the results of psychological experimentation. Human reasoning was a major focus of attention in the early days of experimental psychology and, while the subject suffered some neglect in the heyday of behaviorism, it is once again the subject of experimental investigation and has been for several decades. Much has been learned from this research, but with increased knowledge has come a greater appreciation of the complexity of the subject and a keener awareness of how incompletely we understand it still.

The normative question of what it means to be rational and the empirical one of how people reason are not independent, and they have been closely coupled in both philosophical and psychological work. A common motivation for normative studies has been to improve human reasoning by prescribing how it should be done. Empirical investigations of reasoning have often resulted, whether by intention or not, in discovering ways in which human reasoning appears to fail to measure up to specific norms. The findings from these studies raise questions both about the characteristics of human reasoning and about what should be considered normative.

I do not expect to be able to answer definitively either the normative or the empirical question in this book. What I wish to do is to discuss them in a useful way, to consider what various writers have said about them, and to see what light the results of empirical research can shed on them. I will venture opinions and tentative conclusions, and will present my own perspective, which I believe to be consistent with such relevant scientific evidence as there is, but not forced by it. My hope is that readers will find what follows helpful in their own thinking about what constitutes rationality and what it might mean to lead an acceptably rational life.

☐ Is it Rational to...?

> In our daily lives we all have a definite idea of what it means to be rational, and, no doubt, we would insist quite strenuously that we have the ability to think and act rationally. However, when we come to the philosopher's task of pinpointing precisely what makes the thought or action rational—or of discerning general principles upon which rationality operates—the situation gets a bit more difficult. (Levinson, 1988, p. 17)

The question of what constitutes rationality is a disarmingly simple one, but the answer is not simple at all. Like many other concepts that we use more or less effectively in our own thinking and for purposes of communication, we assume we understand what it means until we have occasion to be explicit about it. One way to begin thinking about what constitutes rationality is to consider some specific types of behavior or patterns of thought. Is it rational, for example, to work against one's own self-interest? To believe uncritically what others say? To fail to discount sunk costs? To play long odds? To discount the future sharply? To behave by rule? These types of questions will motivate much of the discussion in this book. Here I want to linger on them long enough to note that the answers to few, if any, of them are likely to be an unqualified yes or no.

Is it rational to work against one's self-interest?

Is it rational to engage willingly in behavior one knows is likely to do one harm? Why, if they are rational, do people do things that are known to be detrimental to their health—smoke, overeat, bake their skin in the sun, toy with addictive drugs? Why do they take unnecessary risks? Is it possible, as Aristotle believed it to be, for one knowingly to act contrary to what one considers best? Or is it the case, as Plato argued, that all such behavior must be attributed to ignorance, because no one deliberately acts contrary to one's own judgment of what is best?

Sometimes people are unaware of potentially harmful effects of specific behaviors in which they engage. It is clear, however, that awareness of the harmful effects of a particular type of behavior does not guarantee abstinence from it (Schacter, 1982; Stewart & Brook, 1983). There is also the possibility that people generally underestimate risks to themselves individually; they may assume that they are less at risk than other people. One might be less inclined to consider smoking to be an instance of irrational behavior when done by individuals who believe that smoking does not increase the risk of cancer than when done by people who acknowledge the increased risk, but what is one to say about the rationality of the belief itself?

Is it rational to build homes in flood plains, on earthquake faults, or on the sides of mountains subject to mud slides? Is it rational to choose to remain in an area that people have been warned to evacuate because of a predicted hurricane, typhoon, volcanic eruption, or other natural disaster? Many people refused to leave the vicinity of Mt. Saint Helens when warned to do so before its May 1980 eruption (Saarinen, 1980). Can such behavior be considered rational on the part of people who believed the prediction of the coming eruption? What about the people who did not believe the prediction? Was it rational for them to disbelieve it?

People seem to be willing to trade the risk of future problems for the certainty of present pleasures. Such trading can be seen as reasonable in terms of the economics of hedonism if the value of assured present pleasures exceeds the cost of possible consequential future problems weighted by their believed probability of occurrence. But people may misjudge either the magnitude of risks or the probability of their realization. Of particular interest is the possibility that people may tend systematically to overestimate the probability of desired events and underestimate that of events they would like to avoid. If there is such a tendency, should this be considered a manifestation of irrationality?

Why do we fail to do things we believe would be beneficial to us (e.g., get periodic medical examinations, get regular exercise, save money, voluntarily use automobile seat belts)? Here again, the question of greatest interest is why people who genuinely believe that certain actions or behaviors would be good for them fail to do them. And, again, one can construct a plausible answer similar to the one proposed above as to why people do things they consider to be bad for them. They may be willing to accept the risk of a future problem in exchange for avoiding a present inconvenience; but suppose they tend to underestimate the possible seriousness of the future problem or the probability that it will develop. How rational then should we consider their willingness to make such trades to be?

The phenomenon of working against one's self-interest can be seen not only in the behavior of individuals, but in that of corporate and political entities as well. Why do governments so frequently and independently of place or period pursue policies that are contrary to their own interests? In Tuchman's (1984) words, "Why do holders of high office so often act contrary to the way reason points and enlightened self interest suggests.... Why.... did the Trojan rulers drag that suspicious looking wooden horse inside their walls despite every reason to suspect the Greek trick? Why did successive ministries of George III insist on coercing rather than conciliating the American Colonies, though repeatedly advised by many counselors that the harm done must be greater than any possible gain? Why did Charles XII and Napoleon and successively Hitler invade Russia despite the disasters incurred by each predecessor...." (p. 4).

Tuchman's illustrations of governmental folly at various times in history provide food for thought for anyone who would like to understand human reasoning and especially its operation in the complex arena of governmental policy and decision making. For her purposes, Tuchman defines folly as a policy that was perceived as counterproductive in its own time and not merely by hindsight, that was the policy of a group rather than of just an individual ruler and that was adopted even though a peaceful alternative course of action was available. The general question of why people—as individuals, groups, or nations—sometimes behave in ways that are clearly not in their own best interests remains to be explained and its implications for our notions of human rationality understood.

Is it rational to believe uncritically what others say?

There have long been people who are gullible to the point of being easy prey to others who are able and willing to turn this trait to personal gain. Mackay (1841/1932) describes the crazes that afflicted France and England during the early part of the 18th century for stock-buying schemes into which people put life savings in the hope of becoming wealthy very rapidly. My favorite scheme, which Mackay characterizes as "the most absurd and preposterous of all," and which showed most completely the utter madness of the people, was entitled "a company for carrying on an undertaking of great advantage, but nobody to know what it is" (p. 55).

"The man of genius who essayed this bold and successful inroad upon public credulity, merely stated in his prospectus that the required capital was half a million, in 5,000 shares of 100 pounds each, deposit 2 pounds per share. Each subscriber, paying his deposit, would be entitled to 100 pounds per annum per share. How this immense profit was to be obtained, he did not condescend to inform them at that time, but promised that in a month full particulars should be duly announced, and a call made for the remaining 98 pounds of the subscription" (p. 55). MacKay reports that this man opened an office in Cornhill for a few hours on a single day, just long enough to relieve the first 500 people who beset his door of 2,000 pounds, whereupon he departed for the Continent, never to be heard from again.

Despite the fact that such fraudulent ventures were condemned by the government and ridiculed by the press, many people were taken in by them. Alas, in this respect, the situation seems little different today. As of the late 1980s and early 1990s Americans were being relieved of an estimated $10 billion to $15 billion annually by scams communicated by telephone (Harris, 1989; Lombino, 1993). Scammer utilization of the Internet can only have increased the annual losses between then and now. Solicitations from total strangers to invest savings in real estate ventures, mining operations, oil exploration, art, new franchises, communication frequency bands, rare coins, windfall money transfers, and countless other schemes for turning a quick and large profit find a sufficiently receptive general public to ensure a flourishing industry.

The willingness to accept without question what other people say, seems clearly irrational; but we cannot question everything that everyone tells us. Both of these extremes seem objectionable on practical, if on no other, grounds. When does it make sense to be skeptical and when not? What distinguishes between reasonable trust that what someone is telling us is true and unreasonable gullibility? Like many questions regarding the nature of rationality, this one suggests the need to recognize that some criteria of rationality must be seen as matters of degree. What should determine precisely how accepting or how skeptical one should be in specific instances is one of the many challenges of understanding what rationality means.

Is it rational to fail to discount sunk costs?

"Imagine that you have decided to see a play and pay the admission price of $10.00 per ticket. As you enter the theater, you discover that you have lost the ticket. The seat was not marked, and the ticket cannot be recovered. Would you pay $10.00 for another ticket?" Fifty-four percent of 200 people who were asked this question by Kahneman and Tversky (1984) said no. Another group of 183 was given the following problem: "Imagine that you have decided to see a play where admission is $10.00 per ticket. As you enter the theater, you discover that you have lost a $10.00 bill. Would you still pay $10.00 for the ticket for the play?" In this case 88% said yes, and only 12% said no. It appears that people are less willing to spend $10.00 to see a play after having lost a ticket to the play worth that amount than after having lost the same amount of cash. Since the incremental out-of-pocket cost of seeing the play is the same in both cases, should the reluctance to spend the money in the one case coupled with the willingness to do so in the other be seen as evidence of irrationality?

Kahneman and Tversky (1984) attribute this behavior to *topical accounting* whereby the individual "relates the consequences of possible choices to a reference level that is determined by the context in which the decision arises" (p. 347). The expenditure of an extra $10.00 to replace the lost ticket is accounted as spending $20.00 to see the play, whereas the loss of $10.00 of cash is not so directly associated with theater going and not posted to that account. So purchasing the ticket in this case is not seen as paying double to get into the theater. Suppose this explanation of people's behavior in this choice situation is essentially correct; should the behavior be considered rational?

Consider a person who develops tennis elbow soon after joining a tennis club, and continues to play in agony because not to do so would be to waste the cost of membership (Thaler, 1980). How should we think of this behavior? One explanation is that *payments* are more acceptable to people than are *deadlosses* of the same amounts (Kahneman & Tversky, 1984). By continuing to play, one is able to perceive the cost of membership as a payment, whereas if one stops playing it would have to be viewed as a loss. But is this distinction a reasonable one; and does it permit us to view the person's decision to incur the additional cost of pain in order to feel better about the membership expenditure to be a rational one?

Problems of this sort are often discussed under the subject of *sunk costs*. The prevailing opinion among decision theorists and economists is that decisions about present or future behavior should ignore such costs (Arkes & Blumer, 1985; Dawes, 1988; Staw, 1976). Sunk costs are gone, irretrievably and, according to the prevailing view, they are irrelevant to decisions about present or future behavior; such decisions should take into account only those costs that have not yet been incurred and over which one still has some control.

The kind of predicament one can find oneself in if one fails to follow this principle is illustrated by the "dollar auction." In this game, a dollar bill is auctioned to the highest bidder and, unlike the case of conventional auctions, both the highest and the second-highest bidders must pay the amounts of their last bids (Shubik, 1971). When the bidding starts, say at a few cents, it looks like a good deal to everyone involved, but as the bid price gets closer to $1.00, the situation becomes less attractive to those still bidding. Anyone who drops out risks being the second-highest bidder and losing the amount of his last bid with nothing to show for it. For this reason, the bidding often continues even after the bid exceeds $1.00, and sometimes considerably beyond, so *both* the highest and second-highest bidder are assured of losing money.

The reasoning that might keep one bidding even when the bid is above $1.00 is easy to imagine. Suppose my last bid was $1.15, someone else topped my bid with $1.16, and no one else is bidding. My choice is to quit, pay my $1.15 and go away and reflect on the injustice of it all, or to increase the bid to $1.17, hoping this bid will take the dollar, thereby leaving me with a loss of 17 cents instead of $1.15 and making me a winner—of sorts. This is a particularly interesting example of how an unwillingness to cut one's losses—to discount sunk costs—can motivate behavior that ends up increasing those costs without increasing the value of what is realized for the expenditure. It illustrates what is sometimes described as "throwing good money after bad" (Garland, 1990).

Many situations involving sunk costs are considerably more complicated than this one. Decisions regarding what to do about them sometimes involve considerations of commitment, principled behavior, self-image, or other factors in addition to monetary worth. Such considerations have been the bases of arguments against the idea that rationality demands that sunk costs always be ignored (Nozick, 1993). On the other hand, one might argue that such considerations really have to do with anticipated future effects of present behavior—if I do not continue to support this lost cause, I will be reneging on a commitment and will suffer pangs of conscience for having done so—and anticipated future effects are not part of the sunk costs, so one can take them into account without violating the principle of discounting sunk costs. The situation can become murky rather quickly.

Is it rational to play long odds?

Is it rational to buy a ticket in a lottery when one knows the odds are overwhelmingly against the possibility of acquiring the winning one? Consider, for example, a lottery in which one's chance of winning is one in a million. Although it would be strange for the holder of a ticket in such a lottery to claim to *know* that that ticket was not the winning one, we are not surprised to hear people claim to know other things for which the degree of certitude is considerably less (Harman, 1986).

In some cases in which people play long odds, they may believe the probability of their winning to be much higher than it really is. It does not follow from one's ability to verbalize the fact that one's chances of winning a particular lottery are one in a million, that one understands what that means. One's psychological assessment of the odds may be more favorable than it should be. One reads frequently about lottery winners in the newspaper, seldom about losers. If for every article about a winner, there appeared also an article of equal length on every purchaser of a non-winning ticket in the same lottery, readers' psychological understanding of the odds of winning might be brought closer to reality.

But this issue aside—assuming a ticket buyer who does understand probabilities and who appreciates the fact that a one-in-a-million chance of winning is tantamount to near-certain failure—can the purchase of a long-shot ticket be seen as rational behavior? Or, to turn the question around, must such behavior be considered irrational? More generally, is it rational to gamble when one knows that the odds of winning are strongly against one, as many people who gamble apparently do (Wagenaar, Keren, & Pleit-Kuiper (1984)?

Suppose Jack believes in astrology and has learned from his horoscope that he can expect great good luck today; even if *we* consider the *belief* to be irrational, should we consider the purchase today of a lottery ticket by this person, who happens to hold this belief, to be rational, at least in a narrow sense, because it is consistent with his belief? Can there be rational reasons for a person who recognizes the probability of winning to be vanishingly small, to buy a ticket? What about people who happily buy tickets, fully expecting to lose, because they want to help a cause that the lottery's proceeds are used to support? Or suppose the sense of participation in the game, whatever the odds against winning, is more valued by the ticket purchaser than the price of the ticket. Would the purchase of a ticket by a person with this perspective be more rational than the purchase by one who bought it for no reason other than the hope of winning?

Although not exactly an analog of participating in a lottery, voting raises questions similar to those relating to the playing of long odds. Is it rational to vote in an election in which one can be as certain as one can be of not winning the lottery that the outcome of the election will be independent of whether one casts a ballot. Viewed from a narrow view, the cost of voting—time and effort spent educating oneself to the issues and doing whatever is necessary to vote responsibly—seem incommensurate with the benefit that is derived, at least if the latter is measured strictly in terms of probable effect on outcome. But who wants to make the argument that casting one's vote in a democratic election is an irrational act?

Is it rational to discount the future sharply?

Environmentalists often contend that the wasting of natural resources and spoilation of the environment are the direct consequences of a pervasive failure to give appropriate weight, in economic decision making, to costs and benefits that will accrue to future generations as a result of current actions. "Every economist and businessman is familiar with the distinction [between income and capital], and applies it conscientiously and with considerable subtlety to all economic affairs—except where it really matters: namely, the irreplaceable capital which man has not made, but simply found, and without which he can do nothing" (Schumacher, 1973, p. 14). This natural capital, Schumacher claims, is being used up by modern society at an alarming rate, but the cost of its depletion typically does not register in the calculations that guide economic decisions. Calculations of the costs of production include the costs of making natural resources available to the production process, but do not, in most cases, reflect those that can be expected as a consequence of future shortages.

Little interest is shown in the possibility of incurring present-day costs in order to ensure benefits to future generations. And polluting effects of current behavior are not perceived as unacceptable costs provided their impact is unlikely to be felt for many years. More generally, in considering costs and benefits that are relevant to today's choices, decision makers focus almost exclusively on short-term effects. They tend to consider only those costs and benefits that are to be borne or realized directly by the individuals (companies, industries, countries) currently involved.

Underlying many policies of corporations and governments alike is the assumption that unlimited economic growth is both possible and desirable. Corporate chief executive officers who announce to their boards of directors or stockholders that they intend to decrease the sizes of their corporations—except as a fat-trimming measure for the purpose of spurring further growth—had better be ready for retirement. The single statistic that is used above all others as a measure of the economic health of a country—even though economists are not of one mind regarding what it means—is gross national product (GNP) and, more especially, its change from year to year. If, in any given year, this number does not increase—and by at least as great an amount as it did the preceding year—the economy is considered to be in difficulty. Action must be taken to stimulate it—to get it moving faster. The idea that unlimited growth is desirable or even possible has been challenged (Beckerman, 1992; Cohen, 1995; Schumacher, 1973), but it persists nonetheless.

Is behavior that sharply discounts the future rational? Does rationality demand—does what we want to mean by rationality demand—an interest in and responsibility for the wellbeing of people other than ourselves and for that of generations other than our own?

Is it rational to behave by rule?

Much of human behavior is governed by complex rules that few people can articulate but that most of us understand in the sense that we govern our own behavior in accordance with them and we consider behavior that violates them to be unacceptable or somehow odd. One tends not to walk long in step on the sidewalk with a person with whom one is not acquainted. When two people happen to end up beside each other, for example, when they come together at converging crosswalks, if they are walking at the same pace, one or both will change pace enough to preclude the possibility of them walking beside each other for long. They may walk at the same pace, once they have established some distance between them, but they will do so with one person walking behind the other rather than walking two abreast.

We have rules for carrying on conversations, for distributing ourselves in elevators, for acknowledging the presence of others in a room, for occupying seats in a bus or train. One normally would not be expected to sit in the same seat as the only other passenger—a stranger—on a bus, for example, but if the bus were crowded and that seat was among the few that were only partially occupied, sitting in it would be perfectly acceptable. We know that it is against the rules to stare at strangers, to fail to return a greeting from an acquaintance, to change the topic of a conversation abruptly without warning or apology, and so on. The origins of such rules have been the basis of much speculation (Flew, 1967; Goffman, 1963; Wilson, 1978).

Sometimes the rules can be complex and we may be at a loss to make them explicit even when we think about them. I jog, and often come upon an individual or group of people waiting at a bus stop on my route. Sometimes I speak, wave, or nod—sometimes I do not. Upon reflection, whether I do seems to depend on a number of factors—do I know the person(s), is there only one person or a group, if the latter, are they are engaged in conversation, are they looking in my direction, how close do I come to them, and so forth. I am not able to state precisely the rule that takes these and probably other factors into account, but I am keenly aware that sometimes it seems appropriate to speak (wave, nod) whereas sometimes it does not; sometimes it would seem rude not to speak, sometimes it would seem intrusive to do so; sometimes speaking seems to be optional. Although I cannot articulate the rule, I have a strong sense that what constitutes appropriate behavior in this example is dictated by situational factors, some of which are quite subtle.

We live by such rules, typically unstated, and often unrecognized as rules. Some of these rules have been codified in books of etiquette; most have not. When we do try to articulate them and understand them, some appear to be functional and others arbitrary. In either case, guiding one's behavior by them has the effect, especially if they are simple, of limiting the need for deep thinking about situations and consequences. Sometimes this may be all right; on other occasions it can result in serious difficulties. Principled behavior is predictable behavior; it also can be rigid, inflexible behavior. Whether we find principled behavior admirable or offensive depends in part on the principles involved, but also in part on whether they are appropriated and applied in a thoughtful or an unthinking way. Is it rational to permit one's behavior to be governed by rules one does not understand or by rules that, to the extent that one does understand them, appear to have little or no logical or functional basis?

Or is it rational to....?

Questions regarding what is or is not rational are easily multiplied.

- Is it rational to take pride in things over which one has absolutely no control and for which one cannot justifiably take any credit? For example, is it rational for one to be proud of one's genetic endowment, whatever that may be? Of one's ethnicity? Of the fact that one was born in a particular country?

- Is it rational to wish to be ignorant in specific ways—to wish not to know what can be known? To wish, for example, not to know facts about a loved one that would make him less lovable? For a person who is at risk for Huntington's disease to wish not to know whether she has the gene that will determine whether she will certainly develop it?

- Is it rational to hold beliefs that are mutually inconsistent? What does rationality demand with respect to inconsistencies found among one's beliefs? Is it rational to hold beliefs that one has made no effort to justify?

- Is it rational to judge the quality of decisions by the desirability of their consequences? Decision makers in most walks of life are rewarded or punished in accordance with the success or failure that followed their decisions, irrespective of the bases on which the decisions were made. Is this rational behavior on the part of the individual, organization, or nation that determines the rewards or punishments that decision makers get?

- Does rationality imply some responsibility for giving thought to what one thinks about? Does it involve a principle of *clutter avoidance*, according to which one should not clutter one's mind with trivialities (Harman, 1986)?

- Is there one rationality or many? How does one balance the "good" of ethics with the "good" of economics when they come in conflict (Morowitz, 1991)?

Clearly, the question of what constitutes rationality spawns a host of more specific questions. I have mentioned only a few of them here. The reader will undoubtedly think of others that could be added to this partial list. The list is long enough, however, to make the point that the general question is a complicated one and unlikely to admit of a simple answer that will be embraced as obviously correct by everyone who thinks about it.

☐ Some Conceptions of Rationality

> Literally, "rational" means "capable of reasoning correctly." People are called "rational" if we think they reason well; arguments are called "rational" if we think they are logically correct; and logical principles are called "rational" if we think they are canons of correct logical argument. (Salmon, 1974c, p. 70)

Given the difficulty of getting a strong consensus regarding the answers to questions like those above among people who ponder such things, one might expect there to be more conceptions of rationality than one, as indeed there are. In an extensive discussion of epistemology and cognition, Goldman (1986) despairs of providing an account of the concept of rationality, beyond commenting on other writers' treatments of it. He takes the position that the notion of rationality "is so vague in ordinary usage, and so disparately employed by different philosophers and social scientists, that it has limited usefulness" (p. 27). Our challenge is to get a better understanding of the various ways in which the concept has been used and of how human reasoning does or does not measure up to them.

Rationality as consistency with self-interest

According to one conception, thinking and acting in accordance with one's own best interest are the essence of rationality (Giere, 1988), so from this point of view, the answer to the question that was raised above—whether it is rational to work against one's self-interest—is a definite no. What working in one's self-interest means, however, is less straightforward than might appear at first glance. Should I think of working in my self-interest as working toward what I wish for myself? Or working toward what is best for myself? Could I possibly want for myself something other than what is best for myself?

Certainly it is possible to want for myself something that I will recognize in retrospect, having obtained it, to be less than best for myself. I may wish for something now because I believe it will make me happy, and then discover, when I have it, that the belief was ill-founded. That being the case, should rational behavior be defined as behavior that is consistent with one's *perceived* self-interest? To define rational behavior as behavior that is consistent with one's *actual* self-interest would put it out of reach of mere mortals, since we often do not know what our real self-interest is.

But suppose we agree that what rationality requires is that one think and act in accordance with what one believes to be one's own best interest. How does this principle suggest we view acts of altruism or self-sacrifice? One possible answer to this question is that such acts are seen to be rational when we recognize the elasticity of the concept of *self*. Thus it may be in the interest of my self as a moral being (or in the interest of my self-respect) to do something that is harmful to my physical or financial well being. This sounds right, but we come close with this line of thinking to making the relationship a tautological one and seeing whatever one does as consistent with one's perceived self-interest on the grounds that one would not do it otherwise.

If self-interest is equated with personal happiness or contentment, and rationality is defined as working in the interest of maximizing that, we must admit that beliefs and behaviors that make some people happy can appear to be anything but rational to others. We cannot doubt, for example, that many people find personal satisfaction and contentment in belief systems that are commonly classified as cults. But one person's cult is another's religion. More disturbingly, some people derive pleasure from inflicting pain on others. Defining rationality in terms of the objective of maximizing one's own happiness would seem to make the concept so subjective as to strip it of much of its usefulness for either descriptive or (especially) prescriptive purposes.

Rationality as consistency of actions with preferences or goals

Some writers have stressed the correspondence between actions and goals or preferences, which is a somewhat more inclusive idea than consistency with self-interest, because one's preferences and goals need not be limited to those having to do with oneself. Bernstein (1996) characterizes what he calls the Victorian concept of rational behavior this way: "Measurement always dominates intuition: rational people make choices on the basis of information rather than of the basis of whim, emotion, or habit. Once they have analyzed all the available information, they make decisions in accord with well-defined preferences. They prefer more wealth to less and strive to maximize utility" (p. 246).

Allais (1979/1990) defines rational conduct as conduct that satisfies the general principle of not being self-contradictory, and sees in this definition two implications: "The first is that the ends pursued should be logically consistent; the second, that the means employed should be appropriate to these ends" (p. 115). Means that are appropriate presumably are means that are effective in realizing the desired ends. The second of Allais's implications is the essence of the *instrumentalist* conception of rationality, according to which rationality is judged solely in terms of effectiveness in realizing goals; in this view, rationality is a qualification that is applicable only to means and not to ends.

Hempel (1965) expresses a similar view: "To qualify a given action as rational is to put forward an *empirical hypothesis* and a *critical appraisal*. The hypothesis is to the effect that the action was done for certain reasons, that it can be explained as having been motivated by them. The reasons will include the ends that the agent presumably sought to attain, and the beliefs he presumably entertained concerning the availability, propriety, and probable effectiveness of alternative means of attaining those ends. The critical appraisal is to the effect that, judged in the light of the agent's beliefs, the action he decided upon constituted a *reasonable* or *appropriate* choice of means for achieving his end" (p. 463). It is not required, Hempel held, that there be good reasons for adopting the ends.

The principle of rationality stated by Newell (1982) reflects the instrumental view: "If an agent has knowledge that one of its actions will lead to one of its goals, then the agent will select that action" (p. 102). Baron (1988) also characterizes rational thinking as the kind of thinking that helps one fulfill one's personal goals. He argues that if one's goal is happiness, then it is rational to follow the laws of logic only if doing so promotes one's happiness; if violating those laws makes one happier than following them, then the rational thing to do is to violate them. This comes close to saying that it is rational to be irrational if that makes one happy.

Essentially the same position is taken by Harsanyi (1977/1990) who notes that, at least as the term is used in everyday language, rationality often connotes the selection of "the best *means* available for achieving a given *end*" (p. 272). To say that a person acted rationally is to say that her behavior should be explainable in terms of her goals; behavior that is rational to one who is seeking wealth or fame may be irrational to another who is seeking peace and anonymity. We must recognize too that sometimes it is very difficult, if not impossible, to determine what actions are most likely to attain one's goals. Evidence suggests, for example, that hormone replacement therapy for post-menopausal women decreases the risk of death from heart disease, bone loss, or colon cancer, but increases the risk of breast and uterine cancer (Davidson, 1996). Whether hormone replacement therapy is consistent with the goal of enjoying a long and healthy life, obviously, is not trivially easy to decide.

An instrumental conception of rationality has proved not to be satisfactory to everyone. Brandt (1979), for example, does not hesitate to speak of the rationality or irrationality of desires. Audi (1985) argues that a purely instrumental conception is not consistent with our common-sense views. Common sense tells us that it is not unreasonable to ask of goals and values, as well as of the means to attain them, whether they are rational. Most of us would perhaps be willing to say that certain goals that one might set—to learn to breathe under water without the help of equipment, to acquire the state of Nevada as a possession, to avoid all risk of death by accident—are not rational. This seems to me a very important point. Judging behavior to be rational to the extent that it is consistent with one's goals, taking the goals as given, is contingent rationality at best. Given goal X, behavior may be seen as rational to the extent that it is adaptive with respect to the realization of that goal. But surely we can ask—should ask—is it rational to have X as a goal?

One might object that this is not an appropriate question, that the evaluation of goals is a matter not of rationality but of ethics, or perhaps of esthetics. Goals may be evaluated on the basis of whether they are good or bad, relative to some principles of ethics or morality, or they may be assessed in terms of whether or not they are appealing, but rationality is strictly a matter of the efficiency and effectiveness of realizing goals, no matter what they are. I want to contend to the contrary that goals should be subjected to critical analysis and reflection just as should the possible means of realizing them. Critical scrutiny of goals is arguably more important than critical scrutiny of means. Part of what it means to be rational is pursuing defensible goals.

Rationality as optimal analytic choice behavior

> In my opinion, "rational" is an adjective meaningfully applicable only to the *principles* or *rules* under which a purposive system operates.... A princi-

ple or rule is rational if, and only if, it makes the system function (almost) optimally for a given context and under given constraints. (Toda, 1980, p. 139)

To many economists, being rational means making choices that are optimal in terms of specific criteria. These choices may involve the selection of action alternatives in the face of uncertainty about their consequences or the allocation of limited resources to competing demands. In the former case, rational behavior is sometimes defined as weighting the worth of each possible outcome of an action by the judged probability of its occurrence contingent upon that action, doing this for all possible actions, and then selecting the action that best fits one's purposes. Rational behavior, in this view, involves trying to think through the possible consequences of one's choices in a quantitative way, and then selecting among them so as to accomplish a specific objective.

A decision situation is conceptualized in terms of a set of action options available to the decision maker and a set of possible states of the world. The situation may be represented by a *payoff matrix*, the rows of which represent the decision or action alternatives and the columns of which represent the possible states of the world. Each cell of the matrix represents the value or *payoff* associated with a particular combination of decision option and world state.

To apply this structure to a specific decision situation, the decision maker must: (a) identify the action alternatives, (b) identify the possible states of the world, (c) assign to each possible state of the world a probability reflecting the likelihood of its occurrence, (d) assign to each combination of action alternative and possible world state a value or payoff, and (e) select an action according to some normative rule (e.g., maximization of expected gain; maximization of minimum possible gain; minimization of maximum possible loss).

Payoffs can be quantified in several ways. Decision theorists make distinctions among monetary value, utility, and expected utility. The distinction between monetary value and utility, which was made by Daniel Bernoulli in the 18th century, is necessary to take account of the fact that the importance people attach to possible decision outcomes is not necessarily accurately indicated by the monetary value of those outcomes, even when this is known. As Jevons (1871/1956) puts it, "*utility is not proportional to commodity*: the very same articles vary in utility according as we already possess more or less of the same article" (p. 1222). This reflects the common sense notion that the gain of a small amount of money is likely to have greater utility to a penniless person than to a wealthy one.

The concept of expected utility is used to deal with situations in which the state of the world, and, consequently, the outcome of a selected action can be known in advance only probabilistically; the expected utility of such a decision is said to be the sum of the utilities of the possible outcomes each weighted by the probability of occurrence of that outcome. A distinction is also made between expected utility and subjective expected utility, which is analogous to the distinction between probability and subjective probability. Sometimes the probabilities associated with uncertain events can be thought of as objective, because they are dictated by the physics or the mathematics of the situation, and most everyone will agree what they are. This would be true, for example, of the possible outcomes of the roll of a fair die. In other cases, it seems more appropriate to consider the probabilities to be more subjective in nature, as when one attempts to attach numbers to the possible outcomes of a complex political policy decision. In general, expected utility would be appropriate to use when the probabilities could be considered objective and subjective expected utilities would be the more appropriate construct when the probabilities are considered subjective. The distinction between objective and subjective probabilities is one that not all probability theorists recognize, however, and the distinction between expected utilities and subjective expected utilities is a vexed one in decision theory. Fortunately, it is not of great concern for present purposes, and I shall not make much of it.

The analytic view of what it means to be rational has proved to be a useful one in some contexts; it can predict or help explain choice behavior in specific instances and can sometimes serve as a normative model providing guidance—given certain assumptions—regarding what choices should be made (Morgenstern, 1949; Raiffa, 1968; Savage, 1954/1972). It is a demanding view, however, and its applicability to real-life problems that are difficult to cast neatly in the payoff-matrix structure is questionable (Elster, 1989). Each of the steps, except perhaps the last, assumes much on the part of the decision maker. Application of the choice rule is a minor aspect of the whole process; construction of the matrix—which can require a great deal of information finding as well as judgment and probability estimation—is the more demanding part of it.

Theories of decision making based on the assumption that people generally attempt to maximize subjective expected utility have come under criticism from several quarters. Much of the experimentation aimed at theory testing in this area has involved having people choose which of two gambles they would prefer to make, assuming they had to make one or the other. Of special interest has been the discovery of situations in which people's choices are not consistent with the hypothesis that they are attempting to maximize subjective expected utility. A case in point is the finding that many people make decisions that violate the principle of stochastic dominance, according to which if Gamble A always gives at least as good a prize as Gamble B, and sometimes a better one, the former should always be preferred to the latter (Birnbaum & Martin, 2003; Birnbaum & Navarrete, 1998; Birnbaum, Patton & Lott, 1999).

The idea that preferences among formal gambles adequately capture the essence of human decision making has been challenged. Rettinger and Hastie (2003), for example, argue that although the use of simple gambles as the prototype for studying decision making facilitates experimentation in much the way that the use of nonsense syllables once facilitated memory research, by controlling for the effects of world knowledge on performance, in doing so it limits the generalizability of any results to real-world situations, where world knowledge plays an important role. Rettinger and Hastie argue too that in the absence of auxiliary principles, expected utility models cannot accommodate the various content effects on decision making that research has revealed.

Luce (2003) points out that, although subjective expected utility theory has long been considered normative for rational decision making under uncertainty, it has been shown not to be descriptive of people's choices with gambles involving mixtures of gains and losses. He notes too that there is some question of the adequacy of subjective expected utility as a normative theory—as to whether it really captures what most people mean by rationality. He shows that a different but equally defensible theory of rational decision making can be constructed by distinguishing gains from losses and adding a binary operation of *joint receipt*, the implications of which he spells out in some detail. The predictions (or prescriptions) of the alternative theory differ from those of conventional subjective expected utility in specific instances. Luce raises the question of whether there is a deeper sense of rationality that permits one to select between the two formulations considered, but suggests that, pending research on that question, maybe "we simply have to live with the fact that what seems rational depends more on the formulation of the domain of study than we had previously acknowledged" (p. 81).

Rationality as satisficing

Many writers have argued that optimization—or maximization—is not a reasonable goal of decision making, or any other type of human behavior. The idea that good enough should be good enough was promoted effectively by Simon (1955, 1956, 1957) with his introduction of the notion of *satisficing*. Numerous others have endorsed a similar view and/ or presented evidence that people, in fact, tend to operate more like satisficers than like optimizers. Shaklee and Fischhoff (1982), for example, have shown that when searching for causes, people tend to stop as soon as they have found a sufficient one and not to go on to look for additional possibilities. Kruglanski and colleagues contend that people characteristically stop processing evidence as soon as they feel they have enough in hand to justify a conclusion they wish to draw (Kruglanski, & Klar, 1987; Kruglanski & Webster, 1996). On the basis of their experimental findings, Perkins and colleagues describe people as "make-sense epistemologists," the idea being that people content themselves with finding *a* view of things that makes sense to them and do not feel the need to assure themselves that it is the best possible view (Perkins, Allen, & Hafner, 1983; Perkins, Farady, & Bushey, 1991).

People's willingness to be satisfied with less than the best, when it comes to drawing conclusions or forming opinions, has been seen as a weakness by many. Baron (1985a, 1988), for example, identifies the tendency to do insufficient searches for information as the primary reason for the premature drawing of conclusions. Others who have made similar observations include Gettys and Fisher (1979), Oakhill and Johnson-Laird (1985a), Harris (1990), and Svenson (2003). The general notion that people are typically willing to expend only a relatively limited amount of cognitive effort on problems is captured in the characterization of people as "cognitive misers" (Fiske & Taylor, 1991; Taylor, 1981), in the notion of premature cognitive commitments (Chanowitz & Langer, 1981), and in the claim that we are intellectually lazy organisms (McGuire, 1969).

The amount of cognitive resources that can be devoted to the making of any decision is necessarily limited by virtue of the fact that the resources are themselves limited. The question is whether what is done in any particular instance is adequate to be considered rational. As I understand the writers who endorse the idea of satisficing, or something akin to it, their contention is that a decision need be neither optimal nor even as close to optimal as one is capable of achieving in order to meet the dictates of rationality. How close to optimal a decision must be to be considered rational appears to be an open question.

Rationality as conformity to norms

> Normative models of judgment have a limited range of application; they cannot be relied upon to produce correct judgments anywhere outside specific experimental contexts. (Funder, 1987, p. 86)

Much of the immediately foregoing discussion has centered on ideas usually encountered in the literature on decision making, which tends to represent rationality as enlightened self-interest—one is being rational when one is behaving in a way that will help one achieve one's goals. This literature provides structured techniques for doing just that. Some investigators distinguish between this conception of rationality and one that is more prominent in the literature on reasoning, which emphasizes the importance of reasoning in conformity with some putatively normative system such as logic or probability theory.

The distinction between normative and descriptive models of human reasoning, especially of reasoning as it pertains to decision making, is widely recognized in the literature. Among the earlier proposers of norms for decision making was Daniel Bernoulli (1738). Other notable treatments of normative decision theory include those of Neyman and Pearson (1933), von Neumann and Morgenstern (1944/1953), Wald (1950), Good (1952), Blackwell and Girshick (1954), Luce and Raiffa (1957), Schlaifer (1959, 1969), and Savage (1972). Many of these treatments were developed in the context of reasoning about economics and most are grounded in probability theory and mathematical statistics.

More or less concurrently with the development of normative decision theory, psychologists and other researchers interested in how people actually behave—as distinct from how they should behave—have studied people making decisions and proposed models intended to be descriptive of the behavior they have observed. Accounts of much of the early work of this type may be found in Edwards (1954, 1961, 1967), Thrall, Coombs, and Davis (1954), Davidson, Suppes, and Siegel (1957), Luce (1959), Estes (1961), Edwards and Tversky (1967), and Lee (1971).

Sometimes a distinction is made between normative and prescriptive models (Baron, 1985a; Bell, Raiffa, & Tversky, 1988; Simon, 1956; Stanovich, 1999). Normative models show what the ideal thinker would do in specific situations, without taking into account human limitations and constraints. Prescriptive models show what one should do, taking those limitations and constraints into account. One way to think of normative models, Baron (1985a) suggests, is as prescriptive models for idealized creatures, which is to say creatures that do not have the limitations that characterize human beings. Normative models are useful as standards against which to evaluate prescriptive models. A good prescriptive model maximizes conformity to a good normative model and following the rules of a good prescriptive model is what constitutes rationality, in his view.

Although I see the rationale for the distinction between descriptive theories or models on the one hand and normative and prescriptive theories or models on the other, the distinction between normativeness and prescriptiveness seems to me tenuous for three reasons. First, the perfect decision maker for whom the normative model is said to be appropriate is perfect only in some arbitrary sense, which is to say, it has its own limitations; presumably, for example, it is not held to be omniscient. The normative model turns out to be a prescriptive model for a decision maker with certain limitations that are less limiting than the limitations of human beings, but are limitations none the less. Second, human beings differ greatly among themselves with respect to the limitations they have—the limitations of children differ from those of adults, and the limitations of highly intelligent people presumably differ from those whose intelligence is not so high—what is appropriately considered prescriptive for one human being is not necessarily so for another. It seems to follow then that one needs not one prescriptive model, but many. Third, a normative model that assumes infinite memory and processing power, or sets a standard that is impossible to attain, is not really normative for human beings, in my view. It would be normative for beings with infinite memory and processing power, but for them it would also be prescriptive.

In short, I see the need for conceptualizing different standards for decision makers or reasoners with different capabilities, but I do not see the rationale for a binary distinction between normative and prescriptive models. If a model is not prescriptive for me, it is not normative for me. As Stich (1990) has put it, "when we ask whether subjects are reasoning well, perhaps what we really want to know is whether their cognitive system is at least as good as any *feasible* alternative, where an alternative is feasible if it can be used by people operating within some appropriate set of constraints... In order to sustain the charge that subjects in a given experiment are reasoning badly, we must show that there is some alternative to the cognitive system that the subjects are currently using that is both pragmatically superior and feasible" (pp. 154, 156). In this book, I shall use "normative" and "prescriptive" more or less interchangeably.

The question that immediately arises when rationality is defined as conformity to certain norms or standards is: what are the norms or standards by which it is to be determined (Macdonald, 1986)? What should the scope of those norms be? Should they, as Larrick, Nisbett, and Morgan (1993) suggest, encompass both moral and economic principles, and provide a basis for adjudicating "between cost-benefit reasoning and moral questions reflecting such considerations as the rights of particular individuals and the avoidance of exploitation" (p. 292)? On what basis are the norms themselves to be justified?

A closely related question, which MacLean (1990) raises, is that of determining what specific normative doctrines mean. "Does the principle of utility call for maximizing pleasure, as it did for Bentham, maximizing some more abstract good, as it did for Mill and G. E. Moore, or maximizing the satisfaction of preferences, as it has come to be interpreted frequently among economists? If one chooses libertarianism, what do rights entail, which rights are basic, and how should conflicts among rights be resolved?" (p. 91). These are difficult questions, and—in one form or another—they have challenged thinkers for a very long time.

Economists have given us the normative model of *economic man*, according to which rational behavior is defined as behavior in accordance with certain rules involving the costs and benefits, or estimated costs and benefits, of alternative courses of action (Becker, 1976; Friedman, 1953; Mishan, 1976; Morgan & Duncan, 1982). A basic prescriptive rule is that when faced with a choice among actions, one should select the one that maximizes the net positive difference between the total benefit of the outcome and the total cost of effecting it. Economic models of rationality usually make explicit reference to opportunity costs, prescribing that they be included in cost-benefit calculations for purposes of action selection, and sunk costs, prescribing that they be ignored.

The economist's model of rationality has sometimes been treated as not only prescriptive but also as descriptive of how people actually think. However, people do not always take adequate account of opportunity costs in their decision making (Hoskin, 1983) and often fail to ignore sunk costs (Arkes & Blumer, 1985). Evidence of other ways in which the reasoning and decision making of people differ from the prescriptions of the model has come from many sources (Herrnstein, 1990; Kahneman & Tversky, 1979a, Tversky & Kahneman, 1974; Payne, 1982).

Game theory is a branch of mathematics developed explicitly for studying the behavior of people in conflict (competitive) situations. It defines rationality in terms of certain concepts and principles that assume individuals' goals to be the advancement of self-interest. If one accepts the definitions, the theory provides an unambiguous standard against which to judge the rationality of the behavior of people in the situations to which it pertains. "The fundamental theorem of the theory of games is that for every two-person zero-sum game, no matter how complex the rules or how great the range of possible strategies open to each player, there always exists some specific pattern of probabilities of strategies which constitutes rational play. It minimizes the maximum loss that each player can sustain, not in every play of the game, but in the long run. And there is a mathematical solution that tells us what this strategy is" (Kaplan, 1956, p. 1311).

The theory, originally expounded by von Neumann and Morgenstern (1944/1953), has been widely applied in the social sciences, especially economics and psychology (Blackwell & Girshick, 1954; Luce & Raiffa, 1957; Rapoport, 1960; Poundstone, 1992). Smith (1982) has used it as a metaphor for natural selection. Its use to represent real-life decision tasks has been defended and criticized from a variety of points of view. Although the prescriptions of the theory are clear enough in most cases, the appropriateness of application in any particular instance is a judgment call. One well-known criticism is the assumption that one's opponent is infallible, and this is never true in real-life situations; another is that the sometimes-prescribed objective of minimizing one's maximum loss makes sense only on the assumption that one is really engaged in a conflict with an opponent whose preferences are the complement of one's own, and this also often is not the case in real life.

Although not widely promoted as appropriate in either the psychological or philosophical literature, what appears often to serve tacitly as a norm for rationality is one's own thinking and behavior. As Salmon (1974c) puts it, "To a significant extent 'rational' connotes basic agreement with the user. Those who are politically far right are likely to regard those of the far left as irrational and vice versa, while the moderate is likely to doubt seriously the rationality of all extremists (except, perhaps, those who carry moderation to an extreme)" (p. 70). Slightly more generally, norms may be based on widely accepted behavior; in this view, irrationality is equated, more or less, with deviance from "the usual." "We deny that people are rational (and derivatively, their practices and their thinking) if they are exceedingly drunk, under the influence of certain drugs, just coming out of certain anaesthetics, extremely young, psychotic, completely lacking in common sense and practicality, unaware of the most familiar matters of fact, or extremely deviant in belief or behaviour" (p. 70).

However normative rationality is defined or conceptualized, the question can always be asked, why should one wish to be normatively rational in that sense. From a pragmatic point of view, the answer might be: because that is how one maximizes the chances of realizing one's goals. But how strong is the evidence that this is true? Hardman (2000) suggests that the evidence is not compelling that correspondence to traditional norms brings any benefit outside the psychological laboratory. He points to several studies (Clemen, 1999; Galotti, 1995; Wilson & Schooler, 1991) that looked for such evidence in decision-making contexts and failed to find it.

Rationality as reflectiveness

> Apart from the things in which we are vitally interested, the more or less conscious objects on which our egotism concentrates without any outward

incentive, teacher, or advice, we spend our lives in vagueness. Most men and women die vague about life and death, religion or morals, politics or art. (Dimnet, 1928, p. 103)

Another conception of rationality makes it primarily a matter of attitude and intent—love of truth, willingness to examine issues from various points of view, active fair-mindedness that searches out evidence and attempts to weigh it fairly in drawing conclusions or forming opinions, a characteristically reflective approach to problems and to life more generally. Something close to this idea is encountered often in both the philosophical and the psychological literature. Dewey (1933) promotes reflective thinking and equates it with controlled deliberate critical thinking, the kind of thinking that does not jump to conclusions, but demands compelling justifications for conclusions that are drawn. He describes it also as the kind of thinking that is called for when one is faced with a problem for which one has no ready rule or formula to apply. Gauthier (1986/1990) expresses a similar view, but with an emphasis on critical reflection aimed at oneself: "At the core of our rational capacity is the ability to engage in self-critical reflection. The fully rational being is able to reflect on his standard of deliberation and to change that standard in the light of reflection" (p. 331).

Jaspers (1952) characterizes reason as constant inquiry. "Reason has no assured stability; it is constantly on the move. Once it has gained a position it presses on to criticize it and is therefore opposed to the tendency to free oneself from the necessity for all further thought by once and for all accepting irrevocably fixed ideas. It demands a careful thoughtfulness—it is therefore the opposite of mere capriciousness. It leads to self-knowledge and knowledge of limits, and therefore to humility—and it is opposed to intellectual arrogance" (p. 39). Truth lies, Jaspers contends, "in a process of continuous questioning and critical appropriation" (p. 52).

Latent in the view of rationality as reflectiveness is the idea of cognitive effort: to be rational requires the expenditure of intellectual energy; it means making an effort to go beyond the given, to look below the surface, to attempt not only to see clearly the shadows on the cave wall but to figure out what is casting them; it means being willing to try hard to figure out what to believe, and what to do in choice situations. Baron (1985a) defines rational beliefs as those beliefs having strength proportional to the evidence available, and cites as a requirement of good thinking active search for such evidence. The main cause of poor thinking, in his view, is insufficient search and a tendency to underutilize evidence that is contrary to possibilities that we initially favor.

Several proponents of a greater emphasis on the teaching of thinking in the classroom have stressed the importance of attitudes, dispositions, values, and styles as determinants of the quality of the thinking that we do (Baron, 1985b; Ennis, 1969, 1985, 1987; Newmann, 1991; Paul, 1992; Resnick, 1987b; Schrag, 1987). The cultivation of thoughtfulness or reflectiveness, as a pervasive cognitive style, is seen by some to be more important than the teaching of specific thinking skills. Impulsiveness, the opposite of reflectiveness, is considered a disposition or style that is especially antithetical to good thinking (Ault, 1973; Baron, Badgio, & Gaskins, 1986; Kagan, 1966; Kurtz & Borkowski, 1987).

Can one be too reflective? There is the view that excessive reflectiveness makes for indecisiveness, that the ability to see all sides of a controversial issue undercuts one's ability to decide which way to go. The view may have some truth. It may be that reflective people tend to be less decisive than people who are less inclined to consider various viewpoints on an issue. If that is the case, is it necessarily a bad thing? "Decisiveness" is a questionable virtue in the abstract. Decisions based on superficial analyses of choice situations often have undesirable consequences that could have been avoided and the decisions would have been better never made. The inability to come to a decision when the information at the decision maker's disposal does not justify a choice is no shame. On the other hand, there can be little doubt that it is possible to put more thought into a decision than a situation warrants.

How much effort does rationality require that one expend to try to determine what one's options are and to understand the implications of the various choices one can make? At least part of the answer to this must be that how much effort one should be prepared to devote to "doing it right" depends on the stakes. When mistakes do not matter much, it does not make sense to put a lot of energy into avoiding them; whereas, avoidance of disastrous mistakes is worth considerable effort. This suggests that an important aspect of rationality is the ability to evaluate situations for the purpose of determining how much thought they deserve.

Prescriptive theories of decision making often call for the cessation of information gathering under certain conditions and the selection of an action alternative. In general, further information gathering is viewed as a suboptimal strategy whenever the potential value of the information to be gathered is less than the cost of gathering it. Whether, from a more philosophical point of view, it is possible to be too reflective, probably is a matter of personal values. My own sense of balance leads me to believe it is possible to carry reflectiveness to an unreasonable extreme, but I suspect that the opposite problem is, by far, the more common one.

Much attention has been given to the question of how to evaluate explicit arguments, both formal and informal, and rightly so because it is a question that is fundamental to rationality. What is equally fundamental however, but much less frequently considered, is the importance of awareness of the various means, other than direct explicit argumentation, whereby we are "persuaded" to adopt certain beliefs or attitudes and to behave in certain ways. Television, radio, and theater are powerful media in this regard. Expectations, attitudes, opinions, and values are shaped, whether intentionally or not, by the role models that are found in these media. The actions of characters can be made more or less acceptable simply by making the characters themselves more or less likable. Certain lifestyles are promoted as desirable, exciting, and successful. Standards are set for clothing, for behavior, and for interpersonal relationships. Such effects can be extremely subtle and difficult to gauge. Recognition and evaluation of them are a far greater challenge to reflectiveness than is the assessment of explicit arguments.

Rationality as responsiveness to reasons

Closely related to the idea of rationality as reflectiveness is that of rationality as responsiveness to reasons. Nozick (1993) expresses this view. "The rationality of a belief or action is a matter of its responsiveness to the reasons for and against, and of the process by which those reasons are generated" (p. 107). "Reasons" here is synonymous with "sound arguments" and does not connote causes. All beliefs and actions have reasons, in the sense of causes, but not all have reasons in the sense of being justified by sound arguments. Nozick's account of why rationality involves reasons is an instrumental one. Beliefs and actions that are responsive to reasons are more likely, in his view, to have certain (presumably intrinsically valued) properties, such as truth or satisfaction of desire, than are beliefs and actions that are not responsive to reasons.

Truth, or true belief, is, in Nozick's view, a cognitive goal that we seek. True beliefs may, but need not, have both intrinsic and instrumental value. Some knowledge is intrinsically valuable—"the truth about how the universe originated;" some has instrumental benefit—"Truths serve us better than falsehoods and better than no beliefs at all in coping with the world's dangers and opportunities;" some has little value of either sort—"the precise number of grains of sand on each beach in the world" (pp. 67, 68).

Nozick stresses the importance of being responsive to *all* reasons pro and con. He pays considerable attention to the ease with which reasons *against* a belief or action that is being evaluated can be overlooked and the need for special vigilance for the various types of biases that can manifest themselves as a consequence. The idea that negative evidence—evidence that is counterindicative with respect to a particular hypothesis or belief that is being evaluated—is deserving of special attention will be encountered again in more than one context in this book. Seeking evidence that is counterindicative to what one believes appears to be something that most people do not naturally do (Nickerson, 1998).

Audi (1985) takes a position similar to Novick's in noting that the fact that one does a rational kind of thing does not entail that the doing of it is rational. For the *doing* to be rational requires that the doer do it for the right reasons. Audi points out that this distinction is analogous to one that Kant made with respect to morality: one is not acting morally, Kant held, when one does the (morally) right thing for the wrong reasons. Audi argues further that because language does not force a distinction between something done ("action-type") and the act of doing it ("action-token"), discussions of rationality are often confused, and confusing, in this regard.

Rationality as pragmatic adaptiveness

> The pragmatic social actor needs to behave in ways that minimize costly mistakes in the real world. Strategies that are well designed for truth detection, yet regularly lead people to make costly mistakes in their day-to-day functioning, can hardly be viewed as rational or prescriptive. (Friedrich, 1993, p. 301)

Many observers have held that human cognition is adaptive in the sense that it has evolved in a way that has assured the survival of the species. Wilson (1978) expresses this view in the following way: "the brain exists because it promotes the survival and multiplication of the genes that direct its assembly. The human mind is a device for survival and reproduction, and reason is just one of its various techniques" (p. 2). Views emphasizing the adaptiveness of human reasoning and decision making have been expressed by Quine (1969), Dennett, (1978), Fodor (1981), Lycan (1981, 1988), White (1984), Cooper (1989), Anderson (1990, 1991), Payne, Bettman, and Johnson (1990, 1993), Skyrms (1996), and Gigerenzer & Todd (1999a, b), among others.

One might assume that, in general, reasoning strategies that lead people to draw true conclusions, or at least approximately true conclusions, would have greater adaptive merit than reasoning strategies that lead people to draw conclusions that are inconsistent with reality. But some theorists have argued that reasoning that is well adapted for survival purposes is not bound to be optimized for truth finding (Cooper, 1989; Stich, 1990). Sometimes it may be more conducive to one's survival and well-being to use strategies that are more effective in guarding against certain types of errors than in maximizing the probability of discovering what is true (Friedrich, 1993; Funder, 1987). Further, to the extent that strategies aimed at avoiding specific types of errors require less time to effect or are less demanding of cognitive resources, their use may be justified on a cost-benefit basis in some instances.

Closely associated with the claim that rationality is the natural consequence of the pragmatic adaptiveness of cognition is the idea that human communication would not be possible apart from the assumption of the rationality of those who engage in it (Clark & Marshall, 1981; Grice 1975). Much of the substance of any conversation is contained in what is said only by implication, and if the speaker could not assume (not necessarily consciously) that the hearer would make the inferences necessary to derive the intended meaning, effective communication by conversation could not take place.

The idea that human cognition is compatible with human survival is obviously correct—if it were not, we would not be around to speculate about it. But equating rationality with whatever helps to increase the chances of survival, of the individual or the species, is likely to be unsatisfactory to many people. Even if one were willing to settle for such a connotation, it seems clear that some uses of our brains increase survivability considerably more than do others. The position, assuming one wished to take it, that our survival to date as a species is testimony to the effectiveness—or at least the non-fatalness—of our reasoning in the aggregate, is not inconsistent with the assumption that individuals differ in the degree of their rationality or that the same individual can be more rational in some circumstances than in others.

Stich (1985, 1990) argues that fitness for survival does not necessarily equate to rationality, unless one makes the equation by defining rationality as whatever contributes to survival, and that is not the connotation that is usually given to the term. Stich contends that there is little support for either the assumption that an optimally well-designed cognitive system is a rational one or for the assumption that evolution produces optimally designed systems in any case. He questions also the assumption that our inferential processes have been shaped exclusively by biological evolution, as opposed, say, to cultural influences. But, as in the case of biological evolution, there is no reason to expect cultural evolution to produce optimally well-designed cognitive systems either: "neither biological nor social evolution can be relied upon to produce the best of all possible options, or even one that is close to the best" (p. 97).

Margolis (1987) takes a somewhat similar position in arguing that the cognitive characteristics that have been produced by evolutionary forces are advantageous in some situations but produce irrational behavior in others. The basis of all thinking is pattern recognition, in his view, and the facility we have acquired for recognizing patterns quickly and efficiently has been effective in enabling our survival, but the same facility sometimes makes us appear to be impetuous and thoughtless in situations that call for reflection. Irrational behavior, according to this view, often stems from the application of usually effective pattern recognition skills to situations for which they are not appropriate.

Anderson (1990), a major proponent of rationality as pragmatic adaptiveness, hypothesizes a general principle of rationality according to which "the cognitive system operates at all times to optimize the adaptation of the behavior of the organism" (p. 28). Noting that the prevailing view in psychology is that people are not rational and that their thinking is fraught with fallacies, he proposes a counter view according to which people act to maximize the chances of obtaining their goals while minimizing the costs of doing so. The connotation that is given to rationality here is that of optimal behavior relative to human needs and desires.

Anderson argues that people have learned from experience how to behave rationally in simple choice situations involving preferences between gambles where probabilities, costs, and possible gains are directly manipulated. He contends that second-order complications on this general trend, which have often been taken as evidence of irrationality, are explainable in terms of certain plausible assumptions about how a rational agent should partially discount information about probability and the reasonableness of a negatively accelerated subjective function of any objective property such as money. He attributes many of the reported evidences of irrationality to differences between situations typically studied in the laboratory and those encountered in real life.

The idea that the information-processing mechanisms of the human mind are adaptations, shaped by selective forces over the entire course of human development has been articulated also by Cosmides (1985, 1989) and Tooby (Cosmides & Tooby, 1987, 1989, 1992). Understanding the human mind as the product of an evolutionary process leads to viewing it as consisting of a set of adaptations designed to solve the kinds of problems encountered during the life of the species. Cosmides argues that the adaptations that have been made have tended to be domain, or content, specific. The primary evidence of the existence of domain-specific mechanisms is the fact that people appear to reason differently depending on the content—as distinct from the logical structure—of the problem about which they are reasoning.

The domain-specificity of effective reasoning mechanisms is to be expected, Cosmides contends, because different domains would have proved to be differentially important to survival and the most effective mechanisms would have been shaped by those domains in which adaptation was most critical. An interesting implication of this view is that, given that the time from the beginning of agriculture to the present—about 10,000 years—is much too short for much evolutionary selection to have occurred, "our cognitive mechanisms should be adapted to the hunter-gatherer mode of life, and not to the twentieth century industrialized world" (p. 194, footnote 3).

The conception of mind that Cosmides and Tooby promote is explicitly modular. According to the model they have developed, the mind should contain specialized systems of inference for solving specific frequently encountered types of problems. This is not to deny the importance of learning and culture, but it is to identify content-specialized cognitive mechanisms that have been adaptively shaped as the underlying reality on which effects of learning and culture are superimposed. Cosmides and Tooby contrast this view with what they call the "Standard Social Science Model," according to which the mind consists of a single reasoning faculty, or a small number of general-purpose, content-independent mechanisms that effect learning, induction, rationality, and so on.

The idea of rationality as pragmatic adaptiveness is close to the notion that people's rationality is proved by the fact that they get along well in the world (which goes somewhat beyond observing that the species has survived). But the claim that people get along well in the world can be challenged, and has been: "I have read numerous times that people get along well in the world, but I have never seen anything remotely like good evidence for that statement. It is hand waving. It *may* be true that people, on the whole, get along well in the world, but I don't see serious scientific work to back that statement up; perhaps convincing evidence is not even possible, given the value-ladenness of the claim" (Doherty, 2003, p. 657). What is an acceptable criterion, Doherty asks, for getting along in the world?

Doherty's question is a good one. If the criterion is survival, we have been successful as a species, up until now at least—although it is not hard to find knowledgeable people who are less than optimistic about the long-term prospects for the future. As individuals, those of us who are currently alive have also been successful, so far. But if "getting along well in the world" is taken to mean living purposeful and fulfilling lives, getting along with each other, causing no harm to the environment, and leaving things in good shape for our progeny, how successful we are, as a species or as individuals, is much less apparent.

Wilson (1978) argues that "[h]uman emotional responses and the more general ethical practices based on them have been programmed to a substantial degree by natural selection over thousands of generations" (p. 6), but he contends too that we are faced with the challenge of choosing which of the "censors and motivators" that we have inherited we will obey and which of them we will curtail and sublimate. He sees the problem as stemming from the relatively short time that cultural evolution has had to modify traits and predilections that evolved over 5,000,000 years of existence before the first civilizations arose, traits and predilections that, in many cases, were functional in a precivilization era but are no longer so.

Are we to assume that there are some real options here and that we have the freedom to exercise some judgment and choice? Or must we assume that we will do whatever our genes—which are the ones that managed to get replicated—have already dictated that we will do? Wilson argues that we have to find a way to override the human nature that was shaped over such a long time, and not wait for genetic evolution to do it for us, if we wish to continue to survive now that the circumstances of our lives have changed. Neither the argument nor the fact that he takes the trouble to make it would make much sense apart from the assumption that we really do have a choice.

☐ Theoretical versus Practical Rationality

> Surely what is most important is to know what ways of thinking will provide effective solutions to real world problems. (Hardman, 2000, p. 678)

A distinction is sometimes made between rationality of belief and rationality of action, or what might be called theoretical or normative rationality and practical or pragmatic rationality (Anderson, 1990; Cooper, 1989; Skyrms, 1996). According to this distinction, rationality of belief has to do with the correspondence between beliefs and reality, whereas rationality of action has to do with the correspondence between actions and desires or goals. Rationality of the first type should lead to beliefs that are true, rationality of the second type should enable goals to be realized. Kant made such a distinction in partitioning his major critical work on reasoning into two parts, *The Critique of Pure Reason* (Kant, 1787) and *The Critique of Practical Reason* (Kant, 1788). Applying the distinction to philosophy more generally, he noted that philosophy is either theoretical or practical, depending on whether it concerns itself with knowledge or with conduct, and whether its object is theory or practice.

Anderson (1990) distinguishes between two meanings of the term as it is typically used by social scientists today: logically correct reasoning in decision making (normative-sense rationality) and optimality in the achieving of human goals (adaptive-sense rationality). Noting the possibility that human beings are rational in one of these senses and not in the other, he suggests that many of the purported demonstrations of human irrationality are demonstrations of irrationality in the former sense but not the latter, and he lays out a variety of ways in which the criteria of rationality in the two senses differ.

Essentially the same distinction is made by Audi (1989): "Historically the main point of the terminology is to suggest that practical problems are addressed to us as agents and concern what one is to do, whereas theoretical problems are addressed to us as knowers, or potential knowers, and concern questions of what is or is not true. The former are solved by one's practice, say by taking the right detour; the latter are solved by one's forming, or bringing to bear, the right belief, say by working out a sound proof that an axiom system is consistent" (p. 1). Practical reasoning, Audi contends, is guided by a search for appropriate action, while theoretical reasoning is guided by a search for appropriate knowledge. A practical syllogism, one might say, should end with a conclusion about what one is to do, whereas a theoretical one should end with a conclusion about what one is to believe. Although Audi notes that the response to a practical argument could be cognitive (recognition that one should do something), intentional (intending to do what one should), decisional (deciding to do it), or behavioral (doing it). He argues that, ideally, good practical reasoning resembles good theoretical reasoning in form, and that when it does so, one's behavior is rational if (and only if) it is based on that reasoning.

Albert (1985) suggests that in the classical phase of modern philosophy two views of rationality prevailed: "classical intellectualism, which took as its starting point the sovereignty of reason, of intellectual intuition, and the primacy of theoretical knowledge," and "classical empiricism, which emphasized the sovereignty of observation, of sense perception, and the primacy of facts" (p. 28). The best-known spokesman for classical intellectualism was René Descartes and for classical empiricism, Francis Bacon. These viewpoints have in common "the idea of an immediate access to truth through self-evident intellectual insight or careful observation" (p. 32). Albert considers both of these views to be untenable on the grounds that both intuitions and observations have often proved to be wrong. As this distinction relates to that between theoretical and practical rationality, both of the views mentioned by Albert fit better under the theoretical rubric than under the practical one.

Evans and his colleagues (Evans, 1993; Evans, Over, & Maktelow, 1993) argue that failure to distinguish between a conception of rationality that emphasizes behavior that is appropriate to one's goals and one that stresses conformity to norms has led to some confusion; on the other hand, recognition of the distinction helps to resolve the paradox that people can be intelligent and cognitively effective while, at the same time, being chronically biased in their reasoning. They refer to the first conception as rationality$_1$, and sometimes as personal rationality or rationality of purpose, and to the second type as rationality$_2$, and sometimes as impersonal rationality or rationality of process.

Rationality is axiomatic, Evans (1993) argues, but only in the sense of rationality$_1$, and not in that of rationality$_2$; and even in the sense of rationality$_1$, it is bounded by cognitive limitations and constraints. "Many experiments demonstrate illogicality which their authors assume—or so their critics allege—to be evidence of irrationality. It is not. It is evidence only against rationality$_2$" (p. 27). And it is rationality$_1$, not rationality$_2$, that really matters to people, Evans contends. "Any mechanism of deductive competence can account for little real-world reasoning" (p. 28).

The distinction between rationality$_1$ and rationality$_2$ is closely related to the distinction between practical and theoretical reasoning. "People use practical reasoning to try to achieve their goals in the actions they perform, and when they do this in the right way, they display rationality$_1$. They use so-called theoretical reasoning to try to acquire true beliefs about matters of fact, and they have rationality$_2$ when they do this in the right way" (Evans, Over, & Manktelow, 1993, p. 169).

Evans, Over, and Manktelow (1993) note that the reasoning and decision-making literatures have not had a lot of cross fertilization, so the two representations of rationality have developed somewhat independently. This is unfortunate, because in real-world situations it is hard to draw a sharp line between reasoning and decision making. Evans et al. suggest that an overemphasis on rationality$_2$ and the equating of logicality with rationality have been responsible for misinterpretation of data that have been taken to demonstrate biases and content effects. More research attention to problems of practical reasoning, they argue, could help link the two subjects and also increase the ecological validity of reasoning research.

Although the conceptions represented by rationality$_1$ and rationality$_2$ differ, they are not completely disconnected. Evans, Over, and Manktelow (1993) point out that it is assumed that rationality$_2$ serves rationality$_1$, which is to say that reasoning logically helps one achieve one's goals. It is also the case that being rational in the sense of rationality$_2$ may be among the goals that one would like to achieve.

Harman (1995) also makes a distinction between theoretical and practical rationality, defining theoretical rationality as rationality in belief and practical rationality as rationality in action. Arbitrary choices of what to intend can be practically rational, he argues, while arbitrary choices of what to believe are not theoretically rational. The reason for this difference is that one often finds oneself required to choose between alternative actions in an arbitrary way (because inaction is not an option), whereas in the case of competing beliefs, if one has no good reason for accepting one over another, one has the option of suspending judgment.

Wishful thinking also, Harman suggests, can be practically rational but not theoretically rational; it is rational to let one's desires affect one's reasoning about how to realize those desires, but, as a general rule one's desires should not influence the conclusions one draws regarding what one should believe. I say as a general rule, because Harman notes the possibility of having good practical reasons to believe something. He notes too that all reasoning, including theoretical reasoning, has a practical aspect. What theoretical inferences one finds it reasonable to make is likely to depend to some extent on one's needs and goals. In short, the distinction between practical and theoretical is not as sharp as it might at first appear to be.

****

There are many conceptions of rationality; those mentioned above are not all that could be noted, but they are representative of ideas that are prominent in the literature. As the term "rationality" is encountered throughout this book, it will be important to bear in mind that it can have different connotations in different contexts and that not all users may mean by it precisely the same thing even when using it in the same context. Moreover, there may be wisdom in recognizing different types of rationality, or at least that rationality is a many-faceted concept and that the claim that a belief, a behavior, a person, or a policy is rational (or irrational) is likely to require qualification if understanding of the intention of the claim is to be assured.

It will become obvious also, if it is not already so, that any conception of rationality that is not superficial is likely to be somewhat complex. The more one reads and thinks about the concept, the more ramifications of it one discovers. The following thoughtful attempt to craft an approximation to what it might mean to say "it would be rational for X to do A" makes the point: "'I hereby recommend that X do A, while taking as my objective maximizing satisfaction of the transitive mood-independent ultimate desires of X, as they would be if they had been subjected to repeated vivid reflection on relevant facts, and having as my beliefs about options for actions and consequences those which are justified on X's evidence—a recommendation made because A is that one among the options justifiably believed to be open, choice of which exemplifies a strategy for decision making which we know will in the long run satisfy the (as above) corrected desires of X as effectively as any other strategy can be known to do'" (Brandt, 1990, p. 414). This is a carefully reasoned definition, the justification of which is given in Brandt's article. My purpose for quoting it is not to endorse it, or to contest it, but simply to support the idea that precision about what it means to be rational is not likely to be easy to achieve.

CHAPTER 2

The Search for Standards of Rationality

> Rationality requires objective criteria so that it can be distinguished from mere opinions about what is best. If no such criteria are available, the rationality argument is likely to remain hopelessly moot. (Schneider, 2000, p. 695)

To say that this behavior (belief, person, society) is rational and that another is not implies the existence of standards on which such a distinction can be based. If there are such standards, what are they? From where do they come? What is the basis of their authority? What assures their authenticity?

These are difficult questions. We should not be surprised to find many different opinions concerning them. Nor should we expect that it will be easy to arrive at our own. They are the kinds of questions that demand consideration, however, by anyone who aspires to a more than superficial understanding of what rationality might mean.

☐ The Logical Imperative

Logic is a prescriptive discipline; it explicates the rules by which reasoning should be governed. As Lycan (1981) puts it, the key notions in logic are normative through and through: "To say that an inference is unjustified, unwarranted, illegitimate, illicit, impermissible, unreasonable, or irrational is to make a value judgment. It is to say precisely that the inference is one the subject *ought not* to have drawn" (p. 344). But what is the basis of this logical imperative? We appear to assume that there exists a set of rules of right reasoning by which the permissibility of a specific inference is to be judged. But what are these rules? What is their origin?

How are we to recognize them? And why should we feel compelled to obey them?

This book will not deal with the question of why we feel compelled to make certain types of inferences and not others, beyond confessing that it is, to me, a profound question and one for which we are far from having an adequate answer. It suffices for present purposes to take our sense of a *logical imperative* as a given. Making inferences seems to be as natural as breathing—we cannot not make them. And we know, without being told, that some inferences are valid and others are not—we appear to be wired this way. We do not all necessarily agree on how to tell the valid inferences from the invalid ones, which is to say we may have different opinions regarding precisely what the rules that should govern our reasoning are, but we do not doubt that there are such rules.

Perhaps there are people who have no interest in knowing these rules. Maybe there are some who even prefer to be irrational—to be free of the feeling of obligation to try to reason well. If there be such people, it is not clear how one would appeal to them, or even whether it would make sense to try. As Bartley (1984) puts it, "Anyone who wishes, or who is personally able to do so, may remain an irrationalist. And it may be difficult indeed to argue with any such person, for he will have abandoned argument" (p. 162).

☐ Who Sets the Standards?

> Axioms and inference rules together constitute the fulcrum on which the lever of reasoning rests; but the particular structure of that fulcrum cannot be justified by the methods of reasoning. For an attempt at such a justification would involve us in an infinite regress of logics, each as arbitrary in its foundations as the preceding one. (Simon, 1983/1990, p. 190)

Is it the epistemologist's job to *discover* the canons of rationality, or to *define* them? If the former is the case, where does one look in the hope of making the discovery? How does one know when one has made it? And if the task is to define what it means to be rational, who is going to pass judgment on the adequacy of the definitions that are proposed? It does not suffice simply to point to logic as the ultimate standard, because there are many different logics no single one of which is strong enough to serve as a foundation for human knowledge; and taken together they are not sufficiently coherent to do so. Even if it were claimed that a specific logic is strong enough to serve as a foundation for human knowledge, or that together the various logics are sufficiently coherent to do so, how do we judge the merits of that claim, or decide who is competent to make such a judgment?

Rationality and untutored intuition

> [A]t crucial nodes an appeal to ordinary people's intuitions is indispensable. (Cohen, 1981, p. 318)

There is a sense in which rationality must derive from human intuition, else how could anyone have an opinion on what is rational and what is not? Moreover, what is going to decide what constitutes rationality if human intuition does not? Logic is not an empirical science; logicians do not decide the validity or invalidity of inferences by collecting data. (When I speak of logic here and in what follows, I refer to classical categorical or propositional logic, which I believe to be what is usually meant when the term "logic" is used without qualification, and what is generally taught as logic in introductory courses.) The laws of logic have been articulated by human beings who have thought about such things and the only authority to which these thinkers could appeal for justification of the laws they expressed was their own and others' intuitions.

But people differ with respect to their intuitions on particular matters, and individuals sometimes find their own intuitions in conflict with each other. Moreover, on almost any intuitively based concept of rationality, it must be admitted that people often behave in ways that appear to be irrational. Writers who make human intuition the final court of appeal as to what constitutes rationality typically have denied neither that people's intuitions may differ nor that people are capable of engaging in irrational thought or behavior. The intuition that is assumed to yield rationality is intuition upon reflection or intuition upon critical analysis. Something of this idea is seen in the writings on the subject by Goodman (1954/1983, 1966) and Goldman (1986). Goodman holds that deductive and inductive inferences are justified if they yield conclusions that we, upon reflection, are willing to accept. Goldman argues, similarly, that rules of inference are deemed to be correct when they lead to judgments that analysis shows to be in accord with the common core idea of justifiedness reflected in everyday thought and language.

Stich (1990) refers to views of this sort, which take "the choice between competing justificational rules or competing criteria of rightness to turn on conceptual or linguistic analysis" as "analytic epistemology" (p. 91) and he judges them harshly: "when it comes to deciding among alternative systems of cognitive processes, the fact that a system accords with the standards embedded in everyday thought and language is not likely to be of much interest to anyone but an epistemic chauvinist" (p. 99).

In fact, people, including logicians, have different opinions regarding what is rational in specific instances, and a given individual may have different opinions at different times. We have all had the experience of changing our minds about the validity of some argument, upon reflection, perhaps even of alternating between positions more than once. Thus, if one accepts the idea that human intuition, tutored or untutored, is the final arbiter on questions of rationality, there remains the nontrivial problem of specifying what it is that human intuition says.

Are there principles that would be recognized by all, or very nearly all, people as appropriate bases for the derivation of standards of rationality? Are there certain concepts that are innate to all, or very nearly all, human beings? Is *truth* such a concept? What about the idea of consistency or that of *contradiction*? These concepts seem to be deeply intuitive ones, but people may have difficulty on occasion deciding whether two ideas are consistent or contradictory. Is it contradictory, for example, to assert, on the one hand, that the even integers comprise a subset of all integers while claiming, on the other, that there are as many even integers as there are even and odd integers combined? Mathematicians find nothing contradictory in such assertions and make them quite freely, although they have not always done so. Fractal geometry, an area of mathematics recently developed by Mandelbrot (1982) and others, provides other interesting examples of ideas that challenge some of our intuitive notions about consistency and contradiction. The idea that a finite area can have a perimeter of infinite length is a case in point.

It is easy to find examples of ideas that are likely to be counterintuitive to people encountering them for the first time, and easy also to find examples that are compatible with the intuitions of some well-informed people and incompatible with those of others. These facts, by themselves, do not disqualify human intuition as the basis for deciding what is rational and what is not. They force us to recognize, however, that intuitions can change as a consequence of learning, and what seems counterintuitive from one vantage point may be intuitively acceptable, or even compelling, from another.

In an extensive discussion of the possibility of identifying principles of rationality (or of justice) that would be universally recognized as valid, MacIntyre (1988) claims that the question "What are those principles governing action to which no rational human being can deny his or her assent?" has been the central concern of moral philosophers. Hume's appeal to consensus regarding the passions and Kant's formulations of the categorical imperative and the principle of utility are seen as efforts to answer it. But each of these answers, "turned out to be susceptible of rejection by the adherents of rival answers, whose claims to rational justification were as much and as little contestable as those of its opponents" (p. 176).

MacIntyre takes the position that universally recognized principles of rationality do not exist—that there are no nontrivial statements that *all* human beings of moderate intelligence would recognize as evidently true. "Even the law of non-contradiction as formulated by Aristotle has encountered thinkers both sufficiently ingenious and sufficiently wrong-headed to deny it" (p. 251). Competing theories that are organized as deductive structures dependent upon first principles can be evaluated only within the context of a coherent tradition that provides to the evaluators a shared conceptual framework. Even then the best one can do is to evaluate one theory relative to competing theories within the context of that framework.

MacIntyre's negative conclusion is unequivocal. There is no neutral ground, he insists, "no place for appeals to practical-rationality-as-such or a justice-as-such to which all rational persons would by their very rationality be compelled to give their allegiance. There is instead only the practical-rationality-of-this-or-that-tradition and the justice-of-this-or-that-tradition" (p. 346). He argues further that the first principles of any theory cannot be justified or unjustified independently of the theory as a whole; their evidentness or lack thereof is relative to the conceptual scheme embodied in the theory they are intended to support and their fate will depend on the success or failure of the theory in meeting objections that are posed to it. He argues that this is true equally of theories in the physical sciences and of those involving metaphysics or theology.

Note that MacIntyre's contention is against the possibility of finding a conception of rationality with which all *rational* persons would agree. Whether or not one accepts his position, it is not obvious that failure to do so would put us very far ahead. To define rationality in terms of principles that would be considered undeniably true by all *rational* persons is clearly circular. In the absence of a standard with which to distinguish between rational and irrational persons, we would have no way of knowing whose opinions to take seriously on this matter and whose to ignore.

Rationality and tutored intuition

If universal agreement, or universal agreement among all rational people—ignoring for the moment the circularity of this qualification—is too much to expect, might we hope at least to find a consensus among people who are especially well qualified to have an informed opinion on the matter? If we go down this path, the question becomes, what does it mean to be qualified to have an opinion that counts, and who is to pass judgment on this issue. If validity is to come from tutored intuition, who is to do the tutoring, and from where is the tutor's authority to come? There is an obvious danger of an infinite regress here.

One might argue that to be qualified to determine the canons of rationality means to have been trained in the appropriate disciplines. But here again there arises the question of who decides what the appropriate disciplines are and what their content should be. What seems to have happened, in fact, is that some individuals who call themselves logicians or epistemologists claim to have the necessary qualifications and have assumed the role of standard setters. And they are quite good at defending their qualifications and arguing the merits of the standards they set, using of course the rules of argument that they themselves have deemed to be appropriate.

But this, it seems to me, can be considered proof by blatant assertion. Moreover, there is the fact that logicians, epistemologists and others trained in the appropriate disciplines often do not agree on what constitutes rationality and what does not. Perusal of the extensive commentary on Cohen's (1981) article on the question of whether human irrationality can be demonstrated experimentally is compelling evidence of this claim. What one highly qualified individual considers to be an example of logically sound reasoning, another sees as the epitome of fallacious thinking.

Those who have studied human reasoning empirically are not agreed as to what constitutes rationality. Some (e.g., Gilovich, 1991; Kahane, 1984; Manktelow, 1999; Margolis, 1988; Nisbett & Ross, 1980; Piattelli-Palmarini, 1994; Slovic, Fischhoff, & Lichtenstein, 1977; Tversky & Kahneman, 1974/1986) have documented many ways in which human reasoning and behavior often appear to be irrational, while others (e.g., Ayton & Hardman, 1997; Gigerenzer, 1991a, 1991b, 2004c; Henle, 1962b; Levi, 1983; MacDonald & Gilhooly, 1990; Messer & Griggs, 1983) have argued that what appears to be irrational thinking or behavior often can be explained on some other basis, sometimes including an untenable view of rationality held by the investigator.

Even within a single discipline, unanimity is not to be found. Here is how MacIntyre describes the situation within philosophy: "Modern academic philosophy turns out by and large to provide means for a more accurate and informed definition of disagreement rather than for progress toward its resolution. Professors of philosophy who concern themselves with questions of justice and a practical rationality turn out to disagree with each other as sharply, as variously, and, so it seems, as irremediably upon how such questions are to be answered as anyone else" (p. 3).

Some writers have argued that investigators of human reasoning, especially those who have been most productive in amassing evidence of human irrationality, have often been insufficiently sensitive to the role that their own conception of rationality plays in their interpretation of their findings and of the fact that other conceptions may be possible (Cohen, 1979, 1981, 1982; Gigerenzer, 1991a; Gigerenzer & Murray, 1987). It is important to recognize, it seems to me, that rationality is, of necessity, rationality *from some point of view*. There is no escaping this. It does not follow that we cannot have strong opinions about what rationality is, or what it is best conceived to be, but in the final analysis, we, as individuals, have to decide in favor of whatever makes sense to us, precisely because—and only because—it makes sense to us.

Is circularity inevitable?

> To employ a rational argument to demonstrate the desirability of rationality is to assume before the argument that rationality is desirable, and to rationally argue for the existence of rationality is to already assume the existence of the very rational process whose existence is at issue. (Levinson, 1988, p. 18)

According to one view, rational beliefs and behavior are beliefs and behavior for which one can give a rational justification (Kekes, 1980). But the immediate question that arises, of course, is what constitutes a rational justification. Can rational justification be defined without recourse, direct or indirect, to the very concept that is in need of definition?

Consider Aristotle's law of contradiction, arguably the most intuitively compelling of all laws of logic, or, as Aristotle described it, the most indisputable of all principles: It is not possible for anything to be and not to be at the same time and in the same sense. How would one go about justifying this principle? One possibility is with a *reductio ad absurdum* argument: assume it to be false and see if that produces a problem. Let us assert that the law is false. For this assertion to be meaningful, given the normal use of language, it means that we would not also assert that the law is true. But in making this observation, we are implicitly acknowledging the very law we have just asserted to be false. Asserting the law to be false leads to a situation that probably most of us would consider absurd; in recognizing the absurdity, we have made use of the principle in question, but can it be said that we have justified it, beyond illustrating its intuitive compellingness?

Some argue that rationality is self justifying. Siegel (1988), for example, puts it this way: "in order to seriously question the worth of rationality, one must already be committed to it. For to ask 'Why be rational?' is to ask for *reasons* for and against being rational; to entertain the question seriously is to acknowledge the force of reasons in ascertaining the answer. The very raising of the question, in other words, commits one to a recognition of the force of reasons" (p. 132). Nagel (1995) says: "Reason is universal because no attempted challenge to its results can avoid appealing to reason in the end" (p. 213). Hauptli (1995) points out that such a *tu quoque* argument can cut two ways: when the fideists, for whom faith is more fundamental than reason, are confronted with the argument that reason is self-justifying, they may respond with an equally compelling claim: "They may say to the rationalists: 'Given your failure to provide a nonquestion-begging defense of your rational standards and commitment, you too manifest a fundamental non-rational commitment: your "faith in reason" shows that you too are fideists'" (p. 221).

Any normative theory of reasoning, judgment, decision making, or other form of intellective behavior purports to be a standard against which such behavior can be judged. But how does one judge the validity of any particular normative theory? If probability theory, or Bayesian decision theory, or the theory of expected utility is taken as a norm for decision making under uncertainty, decisions that are inconsistent with what the theory prescribes are considered faulty, but this is from the perspective of the theory. When we ask, is such and such a conception of rationality reasonable, are we not invoking some notion of rationality (reasonableness) to decide what constitutes rationality? This all seems very circular indeed.

Perhaps we should appeal to logic as the ultimate standard. But, as has already been noted, there are more logics than one, so to which one should we appeal? And even if there were only one, we would have to acknowledge that its development, or at least its explication, had occurred over many years and had been accomplished by human beings. Apparently, as Peirce (1902/1956) points out, "it is not necessary, in order to reason, to be in possession of the theory of reasoning. Otherwise, plainly, the science of logic could never be developed" (p. 1781).

In his inimitable style, Charles Dodgson (Lewis Carroll) (1895/1977) illustrated the ease with which an attempt to use logic to justify logic can lead one to an infinite regress. Achilles and the tortoise are having a philosophical discussion following their famous race. The gist of the discussion is as follows. Consider a syllogism with the two premises, A and B, and the conclusion, Z. The tortoise explains to Achilles that a person might refuse to accept the conclusion of this syllogism on either of two grounds: disbelief in the truth of one or more of the premises or refusal to accept the form of the argument as valid. In the latter case, one denies that Z follows from A and B; in other words, one rejects the claim, let us call it C, "If A and B are true, then Z must be true." Clearly the truth of Z cannot be inferred from the truth of A and B if one does not recognize the truth of C. But suppose one becomes convinced that C is true. Now it would seem that if one believes A to be true, B to be true, *and* C to be true, one *must* believe Z to be true. But, the pesky tortoise points out, one must believe Z only if one also believes the following claim, let us call it D, "If A and B and C are true, Z must be true." It is easy to see that the road down which the tortoise is leading Achilles has no end. Philosophers have disagreed as to how to think about what the tortoise had to say (Bartley, 1977).

Perhaps we need to try to ground reason on some basis that is independent of reason. We might take the position that reason has been shaped by evolution and that our success—or at least survival, so far—as a reasoning species proves the utility of this function. But, as Nozick (1993) points out, "the evolutionary explanation itself is something we arrive at, in part, by the use of reason to support evolutionary theory in general and also this particular application of it. Hence it does not provide a reason-independent justification of reason, and, although it grounds reason in facts independent of reason, this grounding is not accepted by us independently of our reason" (p. 112).

Perhaps we should look to mathematics for a basis on which to build that does not require any appeals to intuition. But here too we run into circularities. Probability theory has been held out by many as a reliable guide to reasoning under uncertainty ever since the beginnings of its formulation in the 17th century. However, the development of probability theory was guided by the beliefs of its developers regarding what constitutes rational thought. On more than one occasion, the early probability theorists discovered that what the emerging theory prescribed as rational behavior in specific instances violated the intuitions of individuals who considered themselves both rational and mathematically sophisticated—to wit the St. Petersburg paradox—and, in such instances, these individuals were inclined to desert the theory and follow their intuitions. Such discrepancies between the dictates of probability theory and intuitive notions of rationality led sometimes to modification of the theory, and to much debate, not yet ended, about what probability means and its implications for human judgment and behavior (Daston, 1980; David, 1962; Hacking, 1975, 1990; Nickerson, 2004; Stove, 1986).

MacIntyre's (1988) answer to the question of the possibility of establishing a theory on self-evident first principles is as follows: "It is a necessary condition for the truth of any such doctrine that of any allegedly self-evident first principle identified by that doctrine it is the case that *either* every intelligent and adequately reflective human being assents to it *or* those intelligent and adequately reflective individuals who withhold their assent can be shown by adequately good reasons to be guilty of either intellectual error or of bad faith" (p. 234). As he points out, some proponents of basing doctrines on self-evident first principles have simply dismissed people who failed to acknowledge the evidentness of those principles as in some way intellectually or morally deficient, but this is not acceptable in the absence of some basis for determining intelligence, adequate reflectiveness, and good faith. Again, we find ourselves in the position of a sausage maker who discovers that the first ingredient his recipe calls for is a bit of the very sausage he wants to make. Is circularity inevitable when it comes to setting standards for rationality? I see no way of escaping it.

☐ Assessing Rationality

Much of the experimental work on human reasoning has focused on deduction. This is due, in part perhaps, to the view of many investigators that the ability to make valid deductions is the *sine qua non* of rationality, and, in part, also to the fact that performance can be evaluated objectively against widely accepted rules of inference.

Uncertainty of inferences from outcomes to processes

One of the difficulties associated with the assessment of reasoning is that of determining the bases on which conclusions are drawn. What appears to be illogical reasoning has been attributed by some investigators to misinterpretation or transformation of one or more parts of an argument (Bucci, 1978; Henle, 1962b). According to this view, people often misinterpret one or more of the premises of an argument, and then reason logically from the premises as misinterpreted; if the conclusion follows from the premises *as misinterpreted or transformed* by the reasoner, the reasoning should be considered sound and the problem viewed as rooted in the fallible use of language. This position has been referred to as the *premise conversion* hypothesis, because the prototypical example that is used is that of interpreting the assertion "All A are B" as equivalent to its converse "All B are A."

The hypothesis that what appear to be errors in reasoning really result from misinterpretations of language or revisions of arguments has two serious weaknesses. First, inasmuch as any invalid argument can be made valid if suitably transformed, one can account for any reasoning error on this basis, so one cannot distinguish between the two possibilities by examining the errors. I call this a weakness, but it must be admitted that an argument can be made that it simply reflects the way things are. Smedslund (1970) has made an argument of this type in claiming that the study of the relationship between logic and understanding is constrained by an uncertainty principle of the following sort: to determine whether one's approach to a reasoning task is logical, it must be assumed that one understands the task; on the other hand, to determine whether one understands the task, it must be assumed that one's approach to it is logical. According to this view, in order to study one of these variables one must make an assumption about the other, and there is no way out of this bind.

Second, for practical purposes it makes little difference whether one arrives at a wrong conclusion because of faulty reasoning or as a consequence of taking the liberty of revising the argument: the important thing is that one arrives at the wrong place in either instance. Despite these problems, the distinction could have implications for teaching. If one assumes that a student's problem is basically linguistic, one is likely to take a different approach to remediation than if one believes it stems from a faulty understanding, or application, of logic.

What appears to be valid syllogistic reasoning can also result from an appeal to knowledge derived from experience, and not only from the drawing of inferences from premises, which is to say that people can come to conclusions that are deemed valid vis-à-vis rules of a logic by consulting memory for problem-related experiences. This idea has gained support from several experimental studies (Griggs & Cox, 1982; Manktelow & Evans, 1979; Reich & Ruth, 1982). One of the reasons for using abstract problems to study reasoning is to avoid confounding the roles of reasoning and memory, the assumption being that people cannot solve abstract problems by making use of their experience (except, possibly, experience they have had solving abstract reasoning problems). Inasmuch as most of the problems that people face in everyday life involve concrete situations, however, there is great interest in knowing how well they reason—as opposed to how effectively they consult memory—in those situations, and it cannot be assumed that what they do when trying to solve abstract problems is an accurate indication of how they approach concrete problems that are meaningful to them.

The riskiness of taking the production of the correct answer to a reasoning problem as evidence of one's ability to reason effectively is illustrated by Wason's (1966) well-known selection task and variants of it. In one version of this task, subjects see four cards, showing an A, a B, a 1, and a 2, say, and are asked to indicate which cards should be turned over in order to determine the truth or falsity of the claim that any card with a vowel on one side has an even number on the other. The performance of college students on this task is notoriously poor; typically a small minority gives the correct answer: the card showing the A and the one showing the 1.

Several investigators have found that the same formal problem is much more likely to be solved correctly when it is cast in a familiar concrete context. Johnson-Laird, Legrenzi, and Legrenzi (1972), for example, demonstrated this by having people indicate which of four envelopes (one sealed, one unsealed, one with a specified stamp, one without that stamp) would have to be examined in order to determine compliance with a rule specifying that if a letter is sealed, it must contain the specified stamp. In a later study with the same task, older British subjects who were familiar with an obsolete postal regulation relating postage and envelope sealing did better than did younger subjects not familiar with it (Golding, 1981). Such findings, which have been replicated in many studies, have been cited in support of the idea that what may appear to be effective use of rules of inference may sometimes be primarily a matter of recall (Cheng & Holyoak, 1985). Other explanations of performance on Wason's task that assume that choices are often based on something other than logic have been proposed.

Separating the roles of memory and reasoning in the performance of concrete tasks poses a nontrivial methodological problem. If it is always possible to explain performance on reasoning tasks involving semantic content on the basis of one's knowledge about the content, it can never be established that reasoning as such is occurring at all. However, it is possible to structure reasoning problems involving semantic content in such a way that the conclusions dictated by logic are not consistent with one's (presumed) knowledge of the world. In such cases, when logic prescribes one conclusion and knowledge another, *and* participants clearly understand their task to be to reach logically valid (as opposed to factually true) conclusions, it should be possible to tell which is playing the more influential role. At least one can say, when people draw logically valid (but factually false) conclusions in such cases, that those conclusions were not dictated by their knowledge of the facts. Similarly, when a conclusion is drawn that is inconsistent with logic, one knows that whatever the process that produced the conclusion was, it was not logically valid.

Another explanation of how people might solve reasoning problems without making use of traditional logic assumes the use of thought patterns, such as *pragmatic reasoning schemas*, that lead to the same conclusions that would have been reached had formal logic been used (Cheng & Holyoak, 1985; Cheng, Holyoak, Nisbett, & Oliver, 1986; Griggs & Cox,

1993). With respect to what is necessary to verify the accuracy of an assertion, the schema for a sufficient but not necessary cause, for example, is analogous to the conditional ("if A then B"), whereas the schema for a necessary and sufficient cause is analogous to the biconditional ("if and only if A then B"). The point here is not quite the same as that of the possible role of memory of problem-related experiences. At least in theory, schemas could be applied to abstract problems as well as to problems with semantic content.

Still another possibility that has been proposed is that people construct mental models or other cognitive means of representing situations. The fundamental assumption is that, when faced with a reasoning task like that of evaluating a syllogism, people try to imagine conditions under which the premises could be true and the conclusion false. This they do by laying out, in the mind's eye, as it were, specific representations of what the premises and conclusion assert, looking for inconsistencies among them; if no inconsistencies are found, the reasoning is deemed to be sound. This idea has been articulated most completely by Johnson-Laird (1983; Johnson-Laird & Bryne, 1991), but has been supported, in whole or in part, by others as well (Evans, 1982; Holyoak, 1985; Manktelow & Over, 1991).

The possibility that people sometimes approach experimental tasks in ways that differ from any of the alternatives considered by an experimenter is a serious problem in the study of cognition. An experiment designed to determine whether people typically do A or B, where A and B are considered the entire universe of possibilities, will not be very informative—or may produce misleading results—if what people actually do is C. Or if, on the assumption that people invariably approach a particular type of task in a specified way, one designs an experiment to discover how effectively or ineffectively they use that approach, what one learns will be of questionable value if people really approach the task in a way that differs from what the experimenter assumed to be the case.

What makes this problem insidious is that performance may be interpretable in terms of the assumed approach even if that approach is not used. Judgments of the worth of gambles are sometimes consistent, for example, with those implied by the products of subjective values and subjective probabilities, but this is not compelling evidence that people making the judgments actually perform such computations (Lopes, 1976; Lopes & Ekberg, 1980). Lopes suggests one way—which she refers to as serial fractionation—in which people could produce such judgments without performing the multiplications; if one wishes to believe, however, that the multiplications are actually performed, the results of the usual experiment will not force one to discard that belief, or even cause one to question it. Other examples are easily identified.

Making inferences from performance to process, from outcomes of efforts to solve reasoning problems to the details of the mental activity that produced those outcomes, is a tricky business. Many researchers believe that people sometimes draw logically incorrect conclusions despite reasoning logically (because of misinterpreting or transforming the problem as given), others believe they sometimes draw the right conclusions without reasoning, in the sense of making inferences, at all. The fact that people who have studied reasoning intensively have arrived at these conclusions is strong evidence that figuring out what is going on in the head of one who is presumably engaged in reasoning is not easy.

Uncertainty of introspective and retrospective descriptions

Both introspection and retrospection can be sources of interesting ideas, but neither is an ideal means of explicating reasoning processes. The fact that we are able to introspect on our thinking is itself of considerable interest. It is as though one can split oneself into two cognitive agents, the first to carry on some cognitive task and the second to observe the first doing so. How we manage this is not well understood. It is clear, however, that the act of introspecting requires some cognitive resources and it would be surprising if it did not interfere to some degree with the performance of the task on which the introspection is focused; at the very least, the quality of the experience must be different when one is introspecting from when one is not (Brentano, 1973).

Moreover, if the act of introspecting radically changes the nature of the thought process under observation, this cannot be detected through introspection, inasmuch as introspection can yield information only about the appearance of the process when introspection is going on. Trying to get an introspective glimpse of one's thinking when one is not introspecting is like trying to get a look at one's self in the mirror without seeing one's reflection looking back.

Retrospection is at least as mysterious a process as introspection. In this case one reflects on one's thinking after the fact. An obvious concern here is with the reliability of memory: how does one know that what one remembers is an accurate representation of what took place? There is a more subtle problem as well. What exactly is one remembering? If one was paying attention to what one was thinking when one was doing it (i.e., introspecting), we could see how there would be something to remember. But, as noted above, we cannot be sure that one's thought process is the same when one is introspecting as when one is not, so at best we would have a memory of thinking under introspection. And if one was not introspecting, how did the substance of the thought get committed to memory? There is even a question as to whether reasoning processes (as opposed to reasoning products) are open to introspection; when asked to describe the process by which one has arrived at some conclusion in a reasoning task, what one may do is construct an explanation that, in retrospect, seems to account for one's behavior (Evans, 1982).

I suspect that most of us believe we can indeed introspect on our thinking, and that we can remember what we have thought, whether or not we were introspecting about it at the time. We find nothing strange about the claim "I remember thinking thus and so." Of course, the fact that one is convinced that one can remember accurately what one has thought does not make it so; but perhaps we have to settle for our intuitions again. So far as I know, memory for thought has not been the focus of much research. It is not clear exactly how one would go about doing research on the subject, but it is an intriguing topic nonetheless.

These kinds of difficulties aside, the evidence is not very compelling that people are good at explaining their own thought processes after the fact (Ericsson & Simon, 1980; Nisbett & Wilson, 1977a). Retrospective accounts of the thinking involved in significant episodes of decision making or problem solving or invention are notoriously suspect as reliable sources of evidence of the details of the thought processes involved (Perkins, 1981). Explanations or descriptions of the processes by which one has arrived at conclusions or decisions may not be accurate representations of those processes, but after-the-fact constructions (Soelberg, 1967; Wason & Evans, 1975).

☐ Consistency as a *Sine Qua Non* of Rationality

> The sort of irrationality that makes conceptual trouble is not the failure of someone else to believe or feel or do what we deem reasonable, but rather the failure, within a single person, of coherence or consistency in the pattern of beliefs, attitudes, emotions, intentions and actions. (Davidson, 1982, p. 290)

One candidate for a principle that would be recognized widely, if not universally, as basic to rationality surely must be the principle of consistency. Even young children generally acknowledge the force of this principle whether or not they can verbalize it explicitly. They are quick to detect inconsistencies in arguments their parents make on issues that matter to them and may protest bitterly about the unfairness of it all with words like "but yesterday you said . . ." One would be hard pressed to find many adults of normal intelligence, I think, who would not acknowledge consistency to be a good and desirable thing and would view a tendency to be inconsistent as justification for not taking very seriously what one had to say.

Consistency seems also to carry considerable weight in ethics. We generally consider it to be unfair to demand a standard of conduct of others that one is not willing to apply to oneself. Similarly, we tend not to hold in high esteem one who adjusts his standards of conduct from time to time for purposes of convenience.

It is easy to speak of consistency as though there is no danger of confusion about what is meant by the term. In fact, we may distinguish several types of consistency, including consistency among beliefs, consistency among actions, consistency between beliefs and behavior, and consistency of beliefs with evidence or data. All of these types of consistency relate to common notions of rationality.

Internal consistency among beliefs

> [E]very reasonably sophisticated person realizes that he holds inconsistent beliefs. He can see that all his friends are vulnerable to that failing, so unless a person has managed to convince himself of his unique wisdom, he will have to allow that like everyone else he too presumably has inconsistent beliefs. But that does not imply he can give an example. For if he found an example, he would somehow adjust those beliefs, whose incompatibility would now no longer be successfully tamed. (Margolis, 1987, p. 221)

Consistency among personal beliefs is considered by some to be the hallmark of rationality, or at least an objective toward which rational people invariably strive (Abelson, 1959; Festinger, 1957; McGuire, 1966). Whether, in fact, people's beliefs tend to be internally consistent is a matter of some debate. According to one view, they tend to be *locally* consistent in an intuitively meaningful way—closely related beliefs are at least loosely consistent—but they lack *global* consistency and even the local consistency may not satisfy a strict logical criterion (Abelson, Aronson, McGuire, Newcomb, Rosenberg, & Tannenbaum, 1968). Beliefs often occur in clusters; a person's attitude—pro or con—toward a controversial issue such as the justifiability of the death penalty, for example, is a relatively good predictor of other related beliefs (Boehm, 1968; Jurow, 1971). According to the assumption of local consistency, beliefs within a cluster are likely to be more consistent than beliefs from different clusters.

Bem (1970) characterizes one prevailing view—not his own—as holding that the beliefs and attitudes to which people subscribe tend not to be random collections but rather coherent systems that are internally and psychologically consistent, and that when a person's beliefs and attitudes appear to be inconsistent, an underlying consistency can be found if one probes sufficiently deeply into the basic premises underlying them. Various stratagems may be used for reducing inconsistency (Abelson, 1959, McGuire, 1966), but the very existence of these stratagems can be taken as evidence of the importance the individual attaches to being consistent. Bem rejects the idea that people's belief systems are consistent: "My own suspicion is that inconsistency is probably our most enduring cognitive commonplace" (p. 34).

Albert (1985) argues that some people, especially those who have an authoritarian, dogmatically structured belief system, are likely to maintain a belief system that is compartmentalized in the sense that closely related beliefs are clustered in compartments that are relatively isolated from each other. Such people would have no incentive to revise beliefs that were inconsistent with beliefs in other compartments because they would not be aware of the incompatibilities. On the basis of experimental evidence, Lewandowsky, Kalish, and Ngang (2002) suggest that people may simplify the problem of acquiring knowledge by partitioning what they learn into independent parcels that can contain mutually contradictory information.

In the framework proposed by Holland, Holyoak, Nisbett, and Thagard (1986), a cognitive system represents its world with mental models organized into default hierarchies. The components of these models need not be consistent across different levels of the hierarchy. "People are not trying to develop coherent views of the world . . . They are merely attempting to generate accurate predictions for whatever portion of the world they are focusing on at the moment. Thus their beliefs at some higher level of a default hierarchy may be quite inconsistent with their beliefs at some lower level of the hierarchy" (p. 38).

A different position is taken by Macnamara (1986) who argues that consistency among beliefs is essential, because "if the mind formed a single logical system and if it were inconsistent, it would be a logical mess" (p. 180). He concedes the truth of the argument made by some, that if the mind had relatively isolated subsystems, it would not necessarily be a mess if there were inconsistencies across subsystems, but he contends that such inconsistency has not been demonstrated and that there is, therefore, no good reason to worry about it.

My sense is that few psychologists would strongly defend the claim that people only entertain internally consistent belief sets, but that most would see internal consistency as an ideal to which people should, and perhaps do, aspire. But how hard should one strive to achieve this ideal?

Cherniak (1986) distinguishes between the *ideal consistency condition*, whereby, "if A has a particular belief-desire set, then if any inconsistency arose in that set, A would eliminate it (p. 17)," and what he refers to as the *minimal consistency condition*, whereby "If A has a particular belief-desire set, then if any inconsistencies arose in that belief set, A would sometimes eliminate some of them" (p. 16).

The ideal condition, in Cherniak's view, is too strong to be descriptive of real human beings; moreover he rules it out as a prescriptive model by noting that there often are activities that are more epistemically desirable than maintaining perfect consistency. Sometimes, in other words, eliminating an inconsistency is not worth the effort—or opportunity cost—of doing so. Harman (1995) expresses a similar idea in his *general principle of clutter avoidance*: "It is not reasonable or rational to fill your mind with trivial consequences of your beliefs, when you have better things to do with your time, as you often do" (p. 186). Harman (1986) argues that under some conditions it is rational even to retain inconsistent beliefs after one has discovered that one has them, as, for example, when one has neither the time nor the ability to trace the sources of the inconsistency. In such a case, rationality does demand, however, as Harman sees it, that one try not to exploit the inconsistency.

Two assertions should be distinguished: (1) that human beings often entertain inconsistent beliefs, and, (2) that resolution of all the inconsistencies in one's belief set is not a requirement of rationality. The first assertion is an empirical one and considerable evidence can be cited in its support. The second assertion is a theoretical one that is motivated by a recognition of the finite cognitive resources of human beings; we will return to it at the end of this chapter.

Consistency among actions

Suppose you are about to purchase a household item costing on the order of $100 at a neighbourhood store and you discover that you can buy that item for about $25 less at a store across town. Would you make the trip? What if what you were buying were a "large-ticket" item, like a new car? Would you incur the same inconvenience to save the same $25? Thaler (1985) found that some people who would make the trip to realize the savings on a relatively inexpensive item would not do so to save the same amount on a much more expensive purchase. This is seen as an example of behavioral inconsistency. One might argue that this is not necessarily being inconsistent in specific cases because more may be at stake than what appears; in the above illustration, for example, the $25 saving in the case of the car purchase may be overwhelmed by other considerations, such as the anticipated convenience of obtaining future service from a nearby dealer. Nevertheless, the point of the illustration is intuitively compelling: the difference of a few dollars *seems* smaller—less worth worrying about—in the context of a large amount of money than in that of a small amount.

The concepts of personality and personality types rest in part on the assumption that a given individual behaves more or less the same way in similar situations. The evidence of consistency is not always as strong, however, as one might expect. We might consider a person brave, for example, who characteristically faces dangerous situations with equanimity. There undoubtedly are such people, but it may more commonly be the case that the same individuals are brave in some situations and not so brave in others. Evidence on the subject of risk-taking behavior seems to suggest that there is little intra-individual consistency here; the same people who are highly risk averse in some situations are risk seeking in others (Davidshofer, 1976; Slovic, 1962). Margolis (1987) notes that any given individual plays many roles in life—perhaps sibling, parent, employee, warrior, teacher, and so forth, and that when playing one role one may be largely unaware of contradictions between one's behavior in that role and the behavior in which one would engage when functioning in a different role.

Behavioral consistency is a complex issue. Grossly inconsistent behavior that has no identifiable cause—wildly different reactions to similar situations on different occasions—is likely to be seen as irrational behavior. A degree of consistency is essential to the concept of person and to the maintenance of stable interpersonal relationships; if people were sufficiently inconsistent in their behavior so that their reactions to events were totally unpredictable, interactions between people would be chaotic. Complete consistency is not to be expected, however, and given the impossibility of identifying all the causes of any particular bit of behavior, it is not clear that completely consistent behavior could be recognized as such if it occurred. How consistent behavior must be in order to be considered rational is an open question; we can say of some behavior that it is irrational on the basis of its gross inconsistency, but the dividing line between rational and irrational behavior on the dimension of consistency is not easy to locate precisely.

One can think of situations in which one might deliberately be inconsistent. If, for example, one wants one's behavior not to be predictable—as for example, when one is involved in certain types of competitive games or conflict situations—one may be inconsistent for the purpose of making it difficult for one's opponent. But these might be considered special cases, and ones that does not challenge the tenability of the notion that behavioral consistency is desirable, generally speaking.

Consistency between beliefs and behavior

> It is in some sense "irrational" to assent to "I should do M" and then fail to intend to do M. (Clarke, 1985, p. 20)

A given behavior can be consistent with incompatible beliefs. If I believed that I could fly, jumping out of a 10-story window would be a reasonable thing to do even if I wished myself no harm. If I believed that jumping from the window would result in striking the ground with great force, jumping would be a reasonable thing to do only if I wished to hasten my demise. But one would have to say that the act of jumping was consistent with my belief in both cases. If I believed that jumping would result in striking the ground with great force, and I wished myself no harm, jumping would be an unreasonable thing to do. One might say that jumping would be inconsistent with my belief given my intention not to harm myself, or that it would be inconsistent with my intention not to harm myself, given my belief. The point is that one must know both the belief and the intention in order to conclude that an act is unreasonable from the actor's point of view.

One might argue that it is not clear that "inconsistency between belief and behavior" is a meaningful concept, at least in this context. One believes what one believes; whatever one does must be consistent with those beliefs in the sense that the beliefs do not prevent one from doing it. If I believe that jumping out of window of a 10-story building is likely to end my life and I jump anyway, the act of jumping—while certainly bad for my health—is not inconsistent, operationally, with my belief.

An interpretation that can be put on the idea of behavior that is inconsistent with belief is behavior in which a rational person who held that belief would not engage. But this makes consistency a property of rationality as a matter of definition, and without some reliable way of determining what a rational person who believed X would and would not do, it does not help much. Another, and closely related, interpretation is behavior that would not be expected of a person who held that belief. In this case, we are saying that the behavior is inconsistent with prevailing assumptions about what kinds of behavior specific beliefs would lead to or permit. This seems to come close to taking the fact that one has behaved in a certain way as evidence that one must not hold a certain belief that is considered incompatible with that behavior, which is not necessarily to deny that one may profess to hold that belief—perhaps even to believe one holds that belief.

What about the possibility of unwittingly behaving in a way that is inconsistent with one's beliefs? Suppose behavior Y (smoking) is inconsistent—by some interpretation—with belief X (that one should not willfully do things that are injurious to one's health). Might it not be possible for one to believe X and do Y without seeing the connection between the belief and the behavior? My sense is that unwitting inconsistency between belief and behavior would not be considered evidence of irrationality by most of us, but that persistence in the behavior when the inconsistency is made clear would.

In the abstract, it is hard to imagine people who have no wish to harm themselves doing things that they *believe* will harm them. But people smoke, use addictive drugs, drive recklessly, and engage in many forms of behavior that are very likely to have harmful consequences. Are we obliged to assume that either they do not believe in the harmfulness of these forms of behavior, despite the fact that they sometimes claim they do, or that they really wish themselves harm? It seems to me possible for people to do things that they really believe are harmful to them, even while wishing not to harm themselves. Addiction is the prototypical example of this possibility, but it is not the only one. All of us, I suspect, knowingly do things on occasion that we realize are not in our own best long-term interest even while having our best long-term interest at heart. I see this as irrational behavior and believe that understanding it better is a major challenge to research.

A particularly interesting laboratory finding relating to consistency between beliefs and behavior is that when people are induced to act in certain ways, they tend to internalize attitudes or dispositions that are consistent with those actions (Fazio, Effrein, & Falender, 1981; Snyder & Swann, 1978). This suggests that we instinctively value consistency between what we believe and what we do, or that we are uncomfortable acting in ways that are inconsistent with our beliefs. As Koehler (1991) puts it, "[a] great deal of work in social psychology has demonstrated that people wish to be consistent in their attitudes and behavior and are willing to alter one or the other to attain a consistent state" (p. 508). There is some evidence, however, that the effort that will be made to attain consistency may vary inversely with the degree to which people consider themselves to have a real choice in the matter; they are less likely to strive to resolve the inconsistency, for example, when forced to act inconsistently than when they have the option not to do so (Collins & Hoyt, 1972; Holmes & Strickland, 1970; Linder, Cooper, & Jones, 1967).

Principled behavior

Closely related to the idea of consistency between beliefs and behavior is that of principled behavior. People are said, sometimes, to behave in accordance with certain principles. Nozick (1993) raises the question of why we have principles and discusses it at some length. He suggests that principles serve several functions. One of them is to make behavior more predictable—more dependable—than it otherwise would be, and this has certain benefits to individuals and to society in general. "Principles constitute a form of binding: we bind ourselves to act as the principles mandate. Others can depend upon this behavior, and we too can benefit from others' so depending, for the actions they thereby become willing to undertake can facilitate our social ease and interactions, and our own personal projects as well" (p. 10). The importance that we attach to this kind of predictability or dependability is reflected by the low esteem in which "unprincipled" people whose actions do not show it are held. People invest in principles, Nozick claims, by adhering to them, and the more they have invested in a principle, the greater the cost to them of violating it in any particular instance. Violation of a principle not only demonstrates an inability to adhere consistently to *that* principle, but raises the question of one's ability to adhere to principles in general in the face of strong temptation to violate them. Because violation is costly, one should be careful in deciding which principles to adopt.

Nozick sees principles as intimately connected with rationality. "To speak of something, an action or belief, as rational is to assess the reasons for which it was done or held (and also the way in which the person took account of the reasons against doing or believing that). If reasons are, by their nature, general, and if principles capture the notion of acting *for* such general reasons—so that the person is committed to acting thus in other relevantly similar circumstances also—then to act or think rationally, one must do so in accordance with principles" (p. 40).

Principles have the practical effect, important for a creature of limited rationality, of simplifying decisions by acting as filters, making it unnecessary for one to consider options the selection of which would violate them. Of course, this would be true of any principle and could simplify the making of poor decisions as well as good ones. If, for example, I were to operate on the principle that no philosopher is to be taken seriously, I would not have to weigh the pros and cons of committing time to the reading of Nozick's book; my decision making would be made simpler, but not necessarily better.

Acting in accordance with principles does not, in itself, guarantee consistency. There is always the possibility of applying a principle selectively—applying it when it suits one's purposes and ignoring it when it does not. And principles can be in conflict. One may sincerely espouse each of two principles, because one believes each of them to be laudable when considered separately, but then find oneself in a situation in which in order to honor one of the principles, one must violate the other. One way to resolve some of the conflicts that might arise is to recognize a hierarchy of principles in which those at any given level take precedence over those at a lower level. This does not solve the problem of resolving conflicts that might arise between principles that are deemed to be at the same level of precedence. Ethical dilemmas are often of this sort.

Sometimes a principle that seems compelling in the abstract can prove to be problematic when an attempt is made to apply it consistently in different contexts. Sniderman, Brody, and Tetlock (1991) illustrate the point with the principle that one should be tolerant of people with ideas different from one's own. "[I]t is intolerant to refuse to accept as legitimate a group merely because its ideas are different; it is by no means intolerant—indeed it may reflect an effort to defend tolerance—to refuse to accept as legitimate a group because its conduct is violent and illegal. It is thus intolerant to refuse to tolerate socialists, but tolerant to refuse to tolerate terrorists" (p. 136).

The idea of living by principles has much to recommend it, especially as a way of facilitating attainment of some measure of consistency of behavior, but it does not ensure avoidance of dilemmas and hard choices. Baron (1998) gives many examples of how decisions made by the inflexible application of principles can have effects unintended, and unwanted, by those who make them.

Consistency of beliefs with evidence

Surely everyone would agree that beliefs should be consistent with whatever evidence one has that is relevant to them. But if this principle is universally accepted, how is it that different people with access to the same evidence end up believing different things? There are at least two plausible answers to this question. First is the fact that evidence requires interpretation, and how one interprets evidence depends to no small degree on what one already believes. Second, having access to evidence and availing oneself of that access are not the same. What we read, what we listen to, what we watch on television are largely under our own control. Much research suggests that we are inclined to seek information that is consistent with our beliefs rather than information that would challenge them, and that we selectively process the information that presents itself to us, again so as to favor existing beliefs.

Our tendency to treat evidence selectively and partially is generally considered a major human failing—one of the more significant ways in which we fall short of being completely rational. I see it that way and believe to be in good company in doing so (Nickerson, 1998). However, it should not escape our notice that this tendency is, somewhat ironically perhaps, a testament to the high value we attach to consistency. If consistency between our beliefs and evidence were of no importance to us, we would have no reason to guard beliefs from information that is inconsistent with them.

Indeterminacy of consistency

In this discussion consistency has been treated as an intuitively meaningful concept and the question of whether the consistency of entities (beliefs, actions) nontrivial in number can be determined has not been raised. Something must be said on both of these issues. Let us consider the question of establishing the consistency among a set of assertions, each of which can be said to be true or false.

What does it mean for two assertions to be consistent? In the simplest terms I can imagine, it means the absence of contradiction—that the truth of either one of these assertions does not preclude the truth of the other. Beyond this, it has no implications for the truth of either assertion: both could be true, both could be false, or one could be true and the other false. However, for two assertions to be inconsistent means that they cannot both be true; if one of them is true, the other must be false.

To say that a given number, n, of assertions are consistent is to say that they all could be true. It is also the case that they all could be false or that some could be true and others false. No combination is ruled out. To say that n assertions are inconsistent, as a set, is to rule out only the possibility that they are all true. Suppose we had 1,000 assertions and we knew that the first 999 of them were all true. If we knew that the set was inconsistent, we would know that the 1,000th assertion was false. Note however that if we knew that some of the assertions were true and others were false, this would not suffice to let us conclude that the set was inconsistent.

From the foregoing it follows that to be sure that n assertions are consistent one must convince oneself that they all *could* be true, which is to say that none of them singly, or in combination, contradicts any of the others. I say "singly or in combination" because it is possible for an assertion to be consistent with each of two other assertions singly but inconsistent with them when combined. For example "All A are B" is consistent with "All C are A" and with "No C are B" individually, but not with "Some A are not B," which they jointly imply.

Now suppose one wished to determine the consistency of a given assertion with an existing set of n assertions, which we will presume to be consistent. What one would have to do is check the consistency of the new assertion with each of the n existing assertions, and also with each of the 2-way, 3-way, and n-way combinations of these assertions. There are $2^n - 1$ ways to partition a set of n items into subsets each of which contains one or more items, so one would have to make this number of checks. This number grows sufficiently rapidly with n to rule out the feasibility of such a checking process for sets of more than very modest size, even if it were a trivially easy matter to decide whether any given assertion is consistent with any other assertion, including those assertions that are implied by combinations of two or more assertions.

Suppose, for purposes of illustration, that one held 300 assertions. This would be a singularly unimpressive store of knowledge, at least as compared with some estimates of what the average person knows. But even such a small set would require more than 10^{100} checks to determine that a new assertion was consistent with the entire set that comprised the existing knowledge base. Assuming the universe is between 10^{10} and 10^{11} years old, a computer that could make a check every picosecond (10^{-12} second) and that had been checking continuously since the instant of the big bang would by now have made roughly 10^{30} checks, which is such a small fraction of 10^{100} that if it were subtracted from 10^{100}, there would be approximately 10^{100} left. In other words the progress made by our imaginary supercomputer toward its goal would be so small relative to the magnitude of the task that one would be justified in saying it had hardly begun.

This is a variation on the argument made by Stockmeyer and Meyer (described in Poundstone, 1990, p. 183 and following pages), who pointed out that if a sphere 100 billion light years in diameter (considerably larger than the known universe) were tightly packed with proton-sized (10^{-15} meter) computers, each capable of checking for a contradiction in 10^{-23} second (roughly the time required for light to travel a distance equal to a proton's diameter), and the resulting machine were to run non-stop at full tilt for 100 billion years or so, it could make on the order of 10^{168} checks, which would be enough to ensure the logical consistency of about 558 beliefs.

The moral of this little excursion into combinatorics is that, M. Descartes notwithstanding, it is not reasonable to require of human beings that they hold only beliefs that they can be sure are mutually consistent.

It is very doubtful whether any individual who was sufficiently committed to skepticism to hold only those beliefs that could be directly determined to be consistent could believe enough to survive in a physical world. Margolis (1987) puts it this way: "A brain that required global consistency—one able to act effectively only if it held globally consistent beliefs—would be doomed in Darwinian competition with brains that could act on the pattern cued now without self-defeating hesitation or vacillation" (p. 132).

Does this leave us in a hopeless situation with respect to consistency as a criterion of rationality? If there is no possibility of establishing the consistency of even a modest-sized set of beliefs, does it follow that consistency merits no concern? I think the answer to these questions is no for two reasons.

First, if we assume that truth is consistent—that the laws of nature are not self-contradictory—then we can also assume that our beliefs are consistent to the extent that they are true. Striving for truth then is tantamount to striving for consistency. Of course determining whether a belief is true is not necessarily easy to do, and the assumption that truth is consistent is just that—an assumption—but it is one that we can ill afford not to make. It appears also to be one that we very naturally make; in the preceding discussion, I made that assumption tacitly in defining consistency in terms of truth—by saying that two claims are consistent if the truth of one does not preclude the truth of the other.

We should not miss the powerfulness of the assumption that all true assertions are consistent with each other, or how squarely it rests on intuition. Why should reality be consistent? Is reality consistent? Is it the case that the laws of nature never contradict each other? What about those laws of nature implicit in relativity theory and those implicit in quantum mechanics? Are they mutually consistent? The appearance of inconsistencies here has disturbed some theorists greatly. But why should they be the source of discomfort and dissatisfaction? Because the assumption that truth is self-consistent is a very compelling one—one that we tend to believe to be logically necessary if sense is to be made of the world. So when what appear to be inconsistencies are detected within or between theories, we believe something about the theory(ies) must be wrong or incomplete, and the search continues for deeper insights that will make the inconsistencies go away.

The second reason for holding that consistency should be a criterion for rationality, despite its nondemonstrability, is the idea that we should not happily retain inconsistent beliefs when we discover specific instances of doing so. We should try to resolve inconsistencies of which we become aware. We are left with the question, however, of how hard we should try to identify inconsistencies and what should determine how much effort we should put into resolving those that come to light.

One might want to make it a condition of rationality that one attempt to identify and resolve inconsistencies "that matter," although what it means to "matter" would have to be sharpened for this notion to be of much use. Cherniak argues that in view of our relatively short life spans, "*not* making the vast majority of sound and feasible inferences is not irrational; it is rational" (p. 24). While that principle again is easy to accept, the question remains *what* sound and feasible inferences should a rational agent make.

It is in part to deal with this question that Cherniak introduces the notion of *minimal normative rationality*: "to be minimally normatively rational, we must take into account not only (1) the soundness of the inference, but also (2) its feasibility and (3) its apparent usefulness according to the agent's belief-desire set" (p. 24). The difficulty of an inference, Cherniak notes, is as much a function of the reasoner as of the syntactics of the inference itself. In elaborating his view of minimal rationality, Cherniak also argues the infeasibility of resolving all the inconsistencies that may exist among the countless beliefs in long-term memory, most of which we are totally unaware of most of the time.

Although internal consistency is a major concern of builders of mathematical systems and scientific theories, complete consistency is never assuredly attained in either case. Gödel (Nagel & Newman, 1958) convinced mathematicians of the unprovability of the consistency of any mathematical system sufficiently comprehensive to include all of arithmetic. Although Gödel's proof was considered by many to be a devastating blow to the integrity of mathematics, it does not appear to have dissuaded the vast majority of practicing mathematicians from doing mathematics. As King (1992) observes, "the typical practicing mathematician worries about specific theorems, not about the probability or consistency of *all* possible theorems" (p. 54). This is fortunate, because, as noted above, worrying about the consistency of the entire edifice would be futile, inasmuch as demonstration of the same is beyond human reach, and this would be true whether or not the logical impossibility of demonstrating the consistency of mathematics had been proved in the usual mathematical sense.

With respect to science, the general theory of relativity and the theory of quantum mechanics, which many scientists consider to be the most powerful and best-established theories of modern physics, are inconsistent with each other so cannot both be completely correct. Both of these theories are seen as partial theories, one dealing with gravity and the large-scale structure of the universe and the other with fundamental particles and ultra-small-scale phenomena. The current quest is for a new theory that will incorporate both general relativity and quantum mechanics in a quantum theory of gravity. Until such an integrative theory is forthcoming, however, relativity and quantum mechanics will continue to be used because they are the best we have and are quite good indeed. Moreover, although the emergence of a new and more encompassing theory could resolve the inconsistencies that are now known to exist, it could not guarantee the total consistency of the entire system, for the reasons noted above.

Insufficiency of consistency

Despite its nondemonstrability, and perhaps its unattainability, consistency of various sorts, at least in the sense of not willfully entertaining known inconsistencies that could be resolved, is, in my view, a necessary condition for rationality. The importance of consistency is something that we intuitively understand. It is not necessary that people *be* consistent in all the possible ways of doing so in order to recognize consistency as an essential condition of truth. That people do recognize this is seen in the fact that they place greater reliance on consistent than on inconsistent information in reasoning situations, at least when the inconsistencies are apparent (Manis, Dovalina, Avis, & Cardoze, 1980; Ginossar & Trope, 1980).

However, if a modicum of consistency of various types is a necessary condition of rationality, it is not a sufficient one. There is more to being rational than being consistent in one's beliefs and actions and even more than being fair in one's evaluation of the evidence that happens to be at hand on any particular issue, which is not to deny that being consistent in these ways would be a considerable accomplishment.

That internal consistency among beliefs is an inadequate criterion for rationality is clear from the fact that it is possible for two sets of beliefs that are mutually contradictory each to be internally consistent. Fictional fantasies that intentionally ignore the laws of physics can be internally consistent, as can delusions that individuals entertain. More generally, consistency does not guarantee truth; as noted above, while it is not possible to have any inconsistencies in a set of assertions all of which are true, it is possible to have a set of mutually consistent assertions some or all of which are false. As Goldman (1986) succinctly puts it: "Removal of inconsistency eliminates the guarantee of errors, but it does not guarantee the elimination of errors" (p. 314). Assuming that truth is an objective of rationality (not everyone makes this assumption), consistency alone does not assure us of realizing it.

A second problem with a view of rationality that emphasizes only consistency is its passivity. What also is required, some would claim, especially as the question relates to consistency between beliefs and evidence is an active search for evidence, including evidence that may be difficult to find and evidence that may be counter to favored beliefs. Baron (1985a, 1994), for example, has argued that consistency and active search are the two major requirements of good thinking, and has especially emphasized search because it does not usually get the attention that consistency does in discussions of what it means to think well.

This is an important perspective, in my view, because of the ease with which we overlook evidence—even evidence that resides in our heads—that is not only relevant but perhaps critical to the conclusions we draw or the decisions we make. Moreover, the failure to dig for evidence can bias our reasoning in various ways. For example, accepting an argument as valid (whether it is or not) is a relatively passive process, whereas rejecting an argument as invalid (whether it is or not) is a relatively active one, because it requires finding one or more reasons for rejection. Searching for reasons requires effort, and failure to make that effort leaves one with acceptance of the argument by default. One might claim that acceptance of an argument should be based on a rationale just as should rejection of an argument, but in normal discourse one usually is not expected to say why one accepts an argument that another has just made, whereas if one rejects such an argument, one is expected to explain why.

Before leaving the topic of consistency, it is important to be clear about one thing that consistency, as a requirement of rationality, does not mean. To be rational does not require that one's beliefs be consistent over time. A slavish compulsion to be consistent over time would preclude honest changes of mind, which would be antithetical to rationality. Unfortunately changing one's view is perceived in some circles as evidence of weakness, of lacking the strength of one's convictions, but it is important to distinguish between a change in view honestly derived and a willingness to act in a way that is inconsistent with one's beliefs in the interest of expediency. The topic of belief revision is discussed in chapter 4.

☐ Intuition Exposed to Scrutiny

I have been emphasizing the importance of standards and discussing the problem of determining what the standards should be. Underlying all of this discussion is the idea that rationality is determined by conformity to standards—that one judges a bit of reasoning to be rational by virtue of its consistency with certain rules that specify the conditions under which inferences can legitimately be drawn. And the question that has presented itself is that of where the rules originate or of the authority on which they rest. But one might ask, do we judge the reasoning to be rational because it conforms to the rules, or do we judge the rules to be binding because they yield what we recognize to be valid bits of reasoning?

According to one view, sometimes referred to as "appeal to the standard example or to the paradigm case," rules of inference and principles of validity are abstractions from examples of arguments that are judged to be valid (Urmson, 1953/1974). In this view, it is the example and not the rule that serves as the ultimate standard and court of appeal; a rule is rejected if its application validates what is recognized to be an example of an invalid argument, or invalidates an argument that is held to be valid. The idea that general rules of inference are abstractions from particular cases of reasoning that are directly recognized to be sound is a plausible one, but it leaves open the question of the basis, in the absence of the rules, of the judgment of soundness with respect to the cases.

Perhaps one can get around some of these difficulties by taking an axiomatic approach. If one begins by stating a set of axioms from which everything else can be derived, one can then finesse the question of why one should accept that particular set of axioms by simply taking the position that the view of rationality that is being proposed holds only for people who do accept it. Developers of theories of rational behavior for application in the context of economic decision making often have taken this approach. But does this really solve the problem? The rules whereby the implications of the axioms are derived, for example, lie outside the axiomatic system, so the question arises as to where they get their legitimacy. Also there is likely to be at least a tacit set of standards that the axiomatic system must meet in order to be taken seriously.

Claiming that all theories of rationality include *instrumental rationality* —"the efficient and effective achieving of goals"—Nozick (1993) suggests that the attractiveness of this idea stems in part from the fact that it appears to need no justification. But, he argues, this is a false appearance. "[L]et us ask why we should be *instrumentally* rational. Why should anyone pursue their desires or goals in the most efficient or effective way? Because then it is most likely that they will achieve their goals or satisfy their desires, at the least cost (and so be able to achieve the greatest overall goal and desire satisfaction). But why should they achieve their goals and satisfy their desires? Because that is what they want to do. But why should they satisfy *that* desire? Is there any noncircular answer, any answer that does not beg the question of justifying instrumental rationality? If other modes of rationality cannot satisfy themselves without circularity, the same can be said of instrumental rationality" (p. 134).

Things indeed seem hopelessly circular. If in order to evaluate a conception of rationality, one must, at least implicitly, appeal to a view of rationality the validity of which one has presupposed, are we not destined, all of us, to retain indefinitely whatever view of rationality we already happen to hold? To convince me that my view is wrong—should you wish to do so—you must make an argument that I will see as rational, according to my existing conception of what being rational means.

I believe this comes close to describing the situation in which we find ourselves. When all is said and done, each of us must judge the merits of arguments, and reasoning more generally, in terms of our intuitions, and this despite the fact that our intuitions are, as Tversky (1981) claims, "often incomplete, inconsistent, and context dependent" (p. 355). The point at which the description does not seem quite right—or not quite complete—is failure to recognize that one's intuitions can change. I must believe they can change, or at least that our understanding of them and the way in which they are expressed can change. Otherwise, learning would be futile, and there could be no useful dialog across traditions. Attempts to understand rationality would be pointless and it would be impossible to make progress toward achieving greater rationality in our lives as individuals or society as a whole. What does seem to be an inescapable conclusion, however, is that the court of last appeal on questions of criteria of rationality or reasonableness is our own minds; what we find credible we will believe, what seems to us untenable we will reject.

Must differences of opinion as to what constitutes rationality be considered irresolvable in principle? Given the objective of choosing among competing conceptions of rationality, one will naturally select a procedure for doing so that one considers to be rational and this presupposes a specific answer to the question that is being asked. Even when we attempt to evaluate rival claims about rationality by comparing those claims with what are considered to be "basic facts" about reasoning, the descriptions of the facts are themselves conditioned by one or another theoretical perspective.

Arguing that "progress in rationality is achieved only from a point of view," MacIntyre (1988) suggests that "it is achieved when the adherents of that point of view succeed to some significant degree in elaborating ever more comprehensive and adequate statements of their positions through the dialectical procedure of advancing objections which identify incoherences, omissions, explanatory failures, and other types of flaw and limitation in earlier statements of them, of finding the strongest arguments available for supporting those objections, and then of attempting to restate the position so that it is no longer vulnerable to those specific objections and arguments" (p. 144).

While this account of how progress in rationality is achieved is not free of circularity, inasmuch as it prescribes a procedure that involves a number of implicit criteria for rational argumentation, and it assumes the existence of agents capable of evaluating the strength of objections and arguments, presumably in terms of such criteria, it is perhaps the best we can hope for and maybe it is good enough. (For an opposing opinion see Nagel, 1995, who argues, contra MacIntyre, that "The aim is to construct gradually a point of view that all reasonable persons can be asked to share" [p. 206].) The test that MacIntyre proposes is that of survival under vigorous criticism: "The test of truth in the present, therefore, is always to summon up as many questions and as many objections of the greatest strength possible; what can be justifiably claimed as true is what has sufficiently withstood such dialectical questioning and framing of objections" (p. 358). This is very similar in spirit to Oliver Wendell Holmes's observation that "the best test of truth is the power of the thought to get itself accepted in the competition of the market" (quoted in Boorstin, 1958, p. 154), and also to the idea, championed by Popper (1959), that the most credible scientific theories are those that have best survived concerted efforts on the part of researchers to demonstrate them to be false. Ruse (1999) characterizes Popper's view of science as that of "a kind of Darwinian process, where ideas compete in the marketplace and where, after rigorous selection, the best ones survive" (p. 16). Survival in science, he notes, is likely to be temporary; "best" means best until a better idea comes along.

There are many conceptions of rationality, even as there are many systems of logic. Even if this were not the case, *any* system of thought is itself a product of human thinking and as such no more reliable than the intuitions that produced it. One must decide for oneself what one will consider to be rational and why. We garden-variety folk must appeal to our own intuitions no less than the logicians. We must do so, for example, in deciding whether to accept what the logicians say or in determining which, if any of them, to believe when they disagree. "We are," as Good (1983) says, "always thrown back on judgment" (p. 215). That is not to suggest that one must make decisions and judgments in a vacuum. Advocates of specific conceptions of rationality can give reasons for their views; one must decide for oneself, however, how convincing one finds the various views and the reasons given for their support.

All of us will find some conceptions of rationality more intuitively compelling than others. If we really are wired to be rational, it should be that most of us should be able to find a lot upon which to agree. In any case, the best we can do is expose ourselves to the various perspectives and arguments and judge on the basis of how persuasive we find them to be. As for circularity, which appears to be unavoidable, perhaps we just have to accept it, maybe even embrace it, as Goodman (1954/1983) seems to do: "I have said that deductive inferences are justified by their conformity to valid general rules, and that general rules are justified by their conformity to valid inferences. But this circle is a virtuous one. The point is that rules and particular inferences alike are justified by being brought into agreement with each other. *A rule is amended if it yields an inference we are unwilling to accept; an inference is rejected if it violates a rule we are unwilling to amend.* The process of justification is the delicate one of making mutual adjustments between rules and accepted inferences; and in the agreement achieved lies the only justification needed for either. All this applies equally well to induction" (p. 64).

Urmson (1953/1974) distinguishes between the problem of identifying the criteria for validity of arguments in a given field and that of deciding why we should employ these criteria. The first problem is an empirical one. Standards are developed by different fields (groups, cultures) and determining what they are is a matter of studying those fields. Even when the criteria have not been explicit, Urmson notes, people use the words "valid" and "invalid" in an intelligible way, which suggests that criteria are operative and therefore, identifiable by appropriate research.

Having identified the criteria that any group of people uses to distinguish valid from invalid reasoning, we are faced with the question of whether we should adopt those criteria. Such a decision should be based, of course, on the reasons that can be advanced pro and con, but to evaluate those reasons we—each of us—must appeal, in the final analysis, to what seems to us intuitively to be correct.

3
CHAPTER

Intelligence and Knowledge

Rationality presupposes an ability to reason. Reference to a doorknob as rational or irrational would be understood to be an observation on the quality of the thinking of the person who designed the knob or who decided to place it where it is. Moreover, we seem to reserve the term for agents whose reasoning ability is above some minimal level. We typically do not describe dogs, for example, as rational or complain of their irrationality when they do things we would rather they did not do, although dogs certainly are capable of learning and, perhaps by some definitions, of reasoning to a degree.

The situation with respect to children is less clear. It seems a stretch to refer to an infant as rational, no matter how bright he or she may be relative to other infants. Presumably children acquire the reasoning ability that is essential to rationality gradually over several years. How this happens and the time course on which it does so have been of great interest to developmental psychologists. These matters are outside the scope of this book; here we focus on what rationality might mean when the term is applied to human adults.

☐ What Is Intelligence?

Intelligence is an elusive and controversial concept. Although the term has been widely used for some time, it never has been defined to everyone's satisfaction. Resnick (1976) has pointed out that many definitions had been proposed at least as early as 1921 and has noted those that were offered by contributors to a symposium on the topic held during that year: "the ability to 'carry on abstract thinking' (Lewis Terman); 'the power of good response from the point of view of truth or fact' (E.

L. Thorndike); 'learning or the ability to learn to adjust oneself to the environment' (S. S. Colvin); 'general modifiability of the nervous system' (Rudolf Pintner); a 'biological mechanism by which the effects of a complexity of stimuli are brought together and given a somewhat unified effect in behavior' (Joseph Peterson); an 'acquiring capacity' (Herbert Woodrow); and a 'group of complex mental processes traditionally defined . . . as sensation, perception, association, memory, imagination, discrimination, judgment, and reasoning' (M. E. Haggerty)" (p. 2). Nickerson, Perkins, and Smith (1985) extended the list with a few additional definitions that have been proposed: "the ability to direct oneself and to learn in the absence of direct and complete instruction (Brown & French, 1979); a learned habitual approach to problem solving (Whimbey, 1975); skill in the analysis and mental reconstruction of relations (Bereiter & Engelmann, 1966); the ability to use knowledge effectively: 'what you can do with what you know' (De Avila & Duncan, 1985)" (p. 15).

The elusiveness of a definition of intelligence that is beyond challenge is illustrated by the sometimes equating of intelligence with adaptability. Bartlett (1958), for example, equated intelligence in skilled action with the ability to adopt a new response pattern quickly in order to maintain the function of a behavior when circumstances are altered. Gallistel (1980) points out that by this definition, if taken literally, a cockroach would have to be deemed capable of intelligent behavior. Normally the six-legged roach swings the front and rear legs of the same side in unison, supporting its weight on the middle leg while these are still in transit; however, following amputation of its middle legs, it immediately adapts by adopting the now-effective strategy of moving the front and rear legs of the same side 180 degrees out of phase. Gallistel credits von Buddenbrock (1921) and Bethe (1930) with the discovery of such apparently insightful behavior by insects and notes that the discovery prompted "a good deal of fanciful scientific prose in which whiffs of mysticism might be detected" (p. 404). He explains both the original leg motions of the intact organism and the adaptation to the missing legs in terms of oscillator-coupled circuitry that coordinates the motions of the legs and adjusts the pattern of movement when the center leg is missing by automatically delaying the triggering of the motion of one leg relative to the triggering of that of the other.

The inability of psychologists to agree on a definition of intelligence has not precluded the design of tests for measuring it, whatever it is, and the emergence of an industry for administering and interpreting such tests. The idea that the concept has been shaped by the nature of these tests, at least as much as the tests have been determined by the concept, is reflected in the well-known observation that intelligence is whatever intelligence tests measure.

Some theorists distinguish different kinds of intelligence. Levinson (1995), for example, distinguishes between interactional intelligence and analytic intelligence, the former having to do with facility in interpersonal communication and the latter with the types of tasks one finds on IQ tests. Sternberg and Wagner (1986) similarly distinguish between practical and academic intelligence. Gardner (1983) promotes the idea that there are several types of intelligence and that failure to recognize this limits the effectiveness of education.

There is also the idea that intelligence—or the enablement of intelligent behavior—is embodied, to a nonincidental degree, in artifacts (Norman, 1993, 1995; Salomon, 1993). As Gardner (1995) puts this idea, "The key concept here is the *distribution* of intelligence. On this account, intelligence inheres as much in the human and manmade artifacts that surround the individual as inside the head of the individual himself. Stripped of my notebooks, my pencil, my computer, and the persons with whom I customarily work, I lose much of my intelligence. My ability to perform intellectually is a function of how I am able to draw on these resources in order to help me solve problems or fashion products" (p. 72). Success in intellectual pursuits, Gardner contends, is likely to depend strongly on one's ease of access to intelligence-bearing artifacts.

The controversial nature of the concept of intelligence and of the uses to which attempts to measure intelligence have been put have been highlighted by critiques of the field (Gould, 1981; Resnick, 1976; Sternberg & Wagner, 1986). It was brought into sharp focus by the publication of *The Bell Curve* (Herrnstein & Murray, 1995), and the remarkable reaction that its appearance evoked, both in scientific publications and in the popular press.

The concept has sometimes been used as an explanatory construct: one is said to perform well or poorly on cognitively-demanding tasks *because* one is more or less intelligent. Given that intelligence is usually assessed in terms of one's ability to perform such tasks, this use is clearly circular.

Until recent years, intelligence was of concern primarily to psychologists and was thought of as an attribute unique to human beings, or possibly extending in some form to other higher species of the animal kingdom. Since computers appeared on the scene, there has been a growing interest in the question of the possibility of the expression of intelligent behavior by machines. Attempts to program computers to do things that are considered to be evidence of intelligence when done by people have influenced thinking about the concept of intelligence itself.

It has been pointed out, for example, that a desire to think of intelligence as something that cannot be mechanized has more than once forced a change of attitude regarding what should be considered evidence of intelligent behavior. Sometimes a particular ability has been considered to require intelligence only until it was understood well enough to be provided to a machine. Once the ability was understood sufficiently to be mechanized, the concept of intelligence was modified so that it no longer encompassed that particular ability, thus making it possible to continue to think of intelligence as something that a person can have but a machine cannot.

Intelligence and reasoning ability

I do not wish to enter here the debate about what intelligence really is, whether it is fixed or modifiable, how it can best be measured, or whether it is unique to human beings. I will use the word intelligence to mean the ability to do well on a wide variety of cognitive tasks, including, but not only, the types of tasks that one typically finds on intelligence tests. Perhaps most readers will grant the assumption that people differ from each other with respect to this ability; a question of interest is whether such differences have implications for what it means to be rational. Does rationality require a certain level of intellectual competence? Can an individual with severely limited cognitive ability be rational? As rational as the individual whose intellectual capability is much greater? Does, other things equal, the probability of rational belief or behavior increase with one's level of intelligence?

Commonsense conceptions of intelligence appear to encompass such characteristics as openmindedness or fairmindedness, thoughtfulness, willingness to admit mistakes, among others not measured by IQ tests (Sternberg, 1985, 1987; Sternberg, Conway, Ketron, & Bernstein, 1981). Researchers have noted that scores on standard tests of intelligence are not as good predictors of performance of specific reasoning tasks that are not typically encountered in school contexts as of those that are (Galotti, 1989). IQ scores are not good indicators, for example, of success as a horse-race handicapper (Ceci & Liker, 1986) or in more conventional vocations (Wagner & Sternberg, 1985, 1986). Studies of people, including children, performing cognitively demanding tasks in nonacademic contexts give credence to the idea that people may use different cognitive strategies in practical real-world contexts than in the classroom (Carraher, Carraher, & Schliemann, 1985; Lave, Murtaugh, & de la Rocha, 1984; Rogoff, 1984), and have led to a distinction between *academic* and *practical* intelligence (Sternberg & Wagner, 1986).

Although I agree that the accuracy with which IQ scores predict performance on cognitively-demanding tasks in nonacademic contexts is limited, I have reservations about the need for a distinction between kinds of intelligence like the distinction between academic and practical intelligence represents (Nickerson, 1988). If an existence proof is needed that it is possible to display great intelligence even in academic type achievements without displaying genius on intelligence tests, Henri Poincaré appears to have been one. According to the historian of mathematics, Eric Temple Bell (1937), "when Poincaré was acknowledged as the foremost mathematician and leading popularizer of science of his time he submitted to the Binet tests and made such a disgraceful showing that, had he been judged as a child instead of as the famous mathematician he was, he would have been rated—by the tests—as an imbecile" (p. 532). What seems to be indisputable is that people display considerable versatility in learning to cope with problems that are meaningful and important to them and that this versatility is not necessarily apparent in their performance of structured tasks in academic settings.

Disposition versus capacity

The position that intelligence, as conceptualized by psychologists and operationalized by standardized tests, has little connection with rationality is defended by Stanovich (1994a, b), who conceives of rationality as a *disposition* to shape one's beliefs by evidence and to strive to maintain consistency among those beliefs. Standard methods for assessing intelligence do not assess dispositions toward rational thought and behavior, Stanovich contends, although the vernacular use of intelligence does incorporate notions of rationality, as do conceptions of intelligence one encounters in philosophy, computer science and legal systems; the claim, in everyday language, that one is smart, bright, or intelligent typically means not only that one can do well on tasks such as those found in IQ tests, but that one is likely to have well-reasoned views and can be counted on to act rationally as a rule.

Stanovich argues that examples of a lack of the disposition for rationality among people who are demonstrably intelligent, as indicated by their ability to perform well on tests of intellectual capacity, are so common that they constitute grounds for recognition of a clinically distinct handicapping condition which he proposes to call *dysrationalia*, and to define as "the inability to think and behave rationally, despite adequate intelligence" (Stanovich, 1994a, p. 11). Stanovich cites many examples of famous individuals who, despite their obviously high intelligence, persistently displayed behavior that many would consider irrational. He argues that either psychologists should amend their conception of intelligence so that it subsumes rationality and modify tests of intelligence so they assess dispositions toward rational thought and behavior, or acknowledge intelligence to connote nothing more than cognitive capacity and to recognize the limitations of this construct as a predictor of rational—as distinct from clever—behavior. In particular, such a limited construct predicts little about the adequacy of belief forming processes or the likelihood of the justifiability of beliefs formed.

This much seems clear: having a high IQ does not make one incapable of behaving irrationally on occasion, or even on frequent occasions. Calne (1999) points out that the National Socialist movement that led to Nazi Germany was not conceived by ignorant people, but by the intelligentsia. The ability to detect inconsistencies among one's beliefs might well depend to some degree on intelligence as traditionally conceived, but the *disposition* to *search* for inconsistencies, as emphasized by Baron (1985b, 1994), is probably at least as important as this ability and may be largely independent of it. Evidence presented by Perkins, Farady, and Bushey (1991) suggests that high IQ does not inoculate one against bias in reasoning, but that it may make one more effective in arguing from one's own, perhaps biased, point of view.

Stanovich argues that failure of the educational system to put the emphasis on rationality that it puts on intelligence, narrowly conceived as cognitive capacity, has the effect of ensuring that elite schools and universities will graduate people with proven cognitive ability but not proven dispositions to rational thinking. And inasmuch as graduates of elite institutions are primary candidates for positions of leadership in industry, government and academia, these positions may be filled by people who have demonstrated their cognitive capabilities but whose rationality has never been assessed.

Sternberg (1994) sees some merit in the concept of dysrationalia, as proposed, but argues that if it is to serve a useful function as a scientific construct it must be operationalized so as to be measurable. In the absence of an objectively testable theory of dysrationalia, the concept lends itself too easily to abuse. Inasmuch as the main symptom of the condition is the holding of unjustified beliefs, a major problem is that of determining which beliefs are justified and which are not. But who is to make that judgment? The natural inclination, among scientists and non-scientists alike, seems to be to assume that those beliefs that correspond to one's own are justified—rational—and those that do not are not.

Intelligence and normative models of rationality

Empirical evidence on the question of the relationship between intelligence and rationality is meager. This may be a consequence, to a large degree, of the lack of a widely agreed-upon methodology for measuring or evaluating rationality. There are many tests of intelligence, controversial though they be, but there are no comparable instruments for measuring rationality.

One possible approach to the study of the relationship between intelligence and rationality is to investigate whether intelligence, as indicated by standard tests, is a good predictor of how people behave relative to normative models of rationality. There is some evidence of a positive correlation between intelligence, as indicated by SAT scores, and tendency to apply appropriate statistical principles when reasoning about uncertain situations (Jepson, Krantz,, & Nisbett, 1983). Positive correlations have also been found for the likelihood of students applying cost-benefit reasoning to economic problems and their SAT scores or grade-point averages (Larrick, Nisbett, & Morgan, 1993). Stanovich and West (1998a, 1998b, 1998c, 1998d) found positive correlations of moderate size between SAT scores and various types of reasoning performance (syllogism evaluation, Wason's [1960] selection task, the use of base-rate information in statistical reasoning), while finding little or no correlation between cognitive ability and susceptibility to the false consensus effect (for a review of the false consensus effect, see Krueger, 1998) or the tendency to be overconfident in assessing one's own knowledge. Stanovich (1999) also presents evidence that people who get higher scores on tests of cognitive ability or performance (e.g., SATs) tend also to be somewhat less susceptible to framing effects, more apt to discount sunk costs, less susceptible to the conjunction fallacy, and to perform more nearly in keeping with normative models of choice in other situations as well.

On the other hand, Hertwig (2000) argues that the finding that second graders are more likely than sixth graders to give the normatively correct response to an analog of the Linda-bank teller problem (Davidson, 1995) poses a difficulty for the idea that normativeness increases with increasing cognitive ability unless one is willing to assume that second graders are more cognitively able than sixth graders in general. Several other findings of nonnormative responding increasing with age (e.g., Brainerd, 1981; Jacobs & Potenza, 1991; Klaczynski & Narasimham, 1998; Reyna, 1996; Reyna & Ellis, 1994) reinforce the point (Klaczynski, 2000). Krueger (2000) notes that lack of a correlation between cognitive ability and false consensus or overconfidence is also problematic for the idea that normativeness increases with intelligence.

Investigators have related performance on a wide assortment of reasoning tasks to a variety of specific normative models. Results of experiments have sometimes been used to support the claim that people are basically rational and they sometimes have been interpreted as supportive of the contrary claim. But the use of normative models as standards for investigating the relationship between intelligence and rationality is complicated by the fact that investigators are far from agreed on the question of what constitutes normative rationality, and some (e.g., Larrick, Nisbett & Morgan, 1993; Slovic & Tversky, 1974) have suggested that the responses that more cognitively able people make to reasoning problems should play a role in selecting among proposed normative models. The idea is that, inasmuch as any normative model must find its ultimate justification in human intuitions, it would seem to make sense to rely most heavily on the intuitions of the most cognitively able (most intelligent?) individuals, at least if people in this category tend to agree as to what the correct answers to the reasoning problems are. But this approach seems to make the relationship between intelligence and rationality a strong one as a matter of definition.

Goodie and Williams (2000) point out the possibility of circularity in the relationship between aptitude and the probability of giving the normative response in reasoning tasks. "Aptitude test scores are, after all, based largely on the frequency with which one provides normatively correct answers to reasoning problems. Thus, smart people are those who provide normative answers, and normative answers are those provided by smart people. They are defined in terms of each other precisely because of the decision to credit the answers of smart people as being definitively normative" (p. 676). A related point is made by Jou (2000), who contends that problems on the SAT and those often used in experiments on judgment and reasoning are similar in that in both cases superficially plausible distracters are used (in multiple choices) to "entrap" the test takers and that it is therefore not surprising that performance on the two tasks turns out to be positively correlated. Jou argues further that while findings like those of Stanovich and West tend to support the idea that what have been deemed to be normatively incorrect responses on judgment and reasoning tasks may often be attributed to insufficient intelligence or information-computation capacity to come up with the normatively correct responses, they do not settle the question of whether more intelligent people are more rational in general.

Several investigators have attempted to determine the extent to which more intelligent people agree in their responses to problems of reasoning, or the extent to which they agree on whether an alleged normative response is justified. Stanovich (1999) and Stanovich and West (2000b) have reviewed work showing individual differences in the performance of reasoning tasks and in the understanding and acceptance of various normative models of reasoning in specific contexts. Much of this work suggests that people with greater cognitive ability are, in fact, likely to differ from those with less cognitive ability in what they see, or can come to see, as normative. ("Can come to see" refers to the idea, promoted by Slovic and Tversky [1974], that people are the more likely to accept a generally endorsed normative rule as normative the better they understand it; and understanding, of course, is likely to vary with cognitive ability.)

Stanovich and West (2000a) agree with other investigators, however, who stress the importance of dispositional variables, as well as capacity variables, as determinants of good reasoning, noting their own finding of the predictive value of dispositional variables even when controlling for cognitive ability (Stanovich & West, 1997, 1998c; Sá, West, & Stanovich, 1999). Stanovich (1999) recognizes this dual dependence in arguing that normative models of rationality should not be threatened by a "normative/descriptive gap that is disproportionately created by subjects with superficial understanding and/or low task engagement" (p. 96).

Krueger (2000) raises the thought-provoking questions: if norms are appropriate only for the brighter people among us, what is to serve as normative for the less bright, and how bright does a person have to be in order to be held to conventional norms? Sternberg (2000), who also notes that the finding of a correlation between performance on the SAT and on reasoning tasks is not surprising inasmuch as the SAT is, in large part, a test of reasoning, objects to the idea that the performance of high SAT scorers should be used to set the norm for what is true or right. He argues that the evidence shows that people can perform less than spectacularly on intelligence tests and still be excellent everyday reasoners, or do well on measures of intelligence and poorly in everyday reasoning.

Comment

The view that is taken here is that rationality presupposes some degree of intelligence, and so does irrationality. That is to say, the attribute of rationality or irrationality is appropriately applied only to an intelligent agent. An agent that lacks intellectual competence completely, according to this view, cannot be said to be either rational or irrational. Where intelligence is lacking—better, to the degree that intelligence is lacking—behavior and beliefs are best thought of as arational and therefore not appropriately evaluated by criteria of rationality. Given that intelligence is a matter of degree, so therefore is the extent to which an agent should be subject to the strictures of rationality; the more intelligent the agent the more appropriately can its beliefs and behavior be judged in these terms.

One thing we can be sure about with respect to the relationship between intelligence and rationality, whatever model of rationality is used, is that high intelligence, as evidenced by conventional indicators, is no guarantee of consistently rational beliefs or behavior. It is not the case that intelligent people are incapable of nonsense. They can produce the best nonsense of all. There are some types of folly that require a fair degree of ingenuity. It is easy to find examples of (what probably most readers would be willing to consider) irrational beliefs and behavior of people of intellectual renown in various fields.

In the context of a discussion of characteristics of pseudo-scientist cranks, Gardner (1957) points out that a crank whose intelligence is low is unlikely to achieve much of a following, but that cranks often do not lack intelligence and that the brighter ones may be able to defend their views effectively even against intelligent critics. "If he is a brilliant thinker, he is capable of developing incredibly complex theories. He will be able to defend them in books of vast erudition, with profound observations, and often liberal portions of sound science. His rhetoric may be enormously persuasive. All the parts of his world usually fit together beautifully, like a jigsaw puzzle. It is impossible to get the best of him in any type of argument. He has anticipated all of your objections. He counters them with unexpected answers of great ingenuity" (p. 14). Gardner notes a description, given by George Bernard Shaw in *Everybody's Political What's What*, of a meeting at which a proponent of the view that the earth is flat silenced his opponents who raised objections from the floor. "He," Shaw wrote, "having heard their arguments hundreds of times, played skittles with them, lashing the meeting into a sputtering fury as he answered easily what it considered unanswerable" (p. 14).

In sum, intelligence is a necessary but not sufficient condition of rationality. Rationality requires intelligence, but intelligence, by itself, does not guarantee rationality. Irrationality also requires intelligence; this is another way of saying that it does not make sense to consider an agent irrational unless it has the capacity to be rational. Whether exceptionally high intelligence is generally likely to be associated with an exceptionally high degree of rationality must be considered an open question. The answer to this question must depend in part on how both intelligence and rationality are defined, but even if we could agree on this matter, my sense is that there would be room for considerable debate regarding the relationship between the two constructs.

☐ What Is Knowledge?

Bertrand Russell (1948) once said, "In regard to human knowledge, there are two questions that may be asked: first, What do we know?, and second, How do we know it?" (p. 52). These undoubtedly are important questions, but there are others at least equally fundamental. What does it mean to know something? Can we ever know anything, of a certainty, as distinct from believing something to be true? If knowledge and belief are not the same, how can one tell the difference between what one knows and what one believes? Does rationality depend on knowledge or expertise, and if so, how? Do rational agents have a responsibility to become knowledgeable in certain ways?

Knowledge and belief

> [T]here is no such thing as a definite piece of indisputable knowledge about the world whose meaning is not in some way colored by preexisting belief about the world. (Bauer, 1994, p. 65)

Some writers have taken the position that it is impossible to make a sharp distinction between knowledge and belief. What usually counts as knowledge, according to this view, are beliefs that are (believed to be) justified on the evidence—beliefs in which we have very high confidence for (presumably) good reason—and that are, so far as we can determine, true. Lycan (1988) defends this position. "The overwhelming majority of what we ordinarily count as pieces of knowledge are beliefs that although they are conclusively well justified for all practical purposes and as well justified as are most of the beliefs used as examples of knowledge in philosophy books, admit nominal competitors that cannot possibly be assigned zero physical probability" (p. 104).

The requirement that a belief be justified in order to qualify as knowledge rules out the case of believing a fact for an inadequate reason. Suppose that I hold the belief that all graduates of Dogpatch University are Republicans, when in fact only half of them are. When I discover that J. D. is a graduate of Dogpatch, I say that I know he is a Republican, and my sole basis for saying that is my belief that all Dogpatch graduates are Republicans. Now suppose that J. D. *is* a Republican. Is it correct to say that I *know* his political persuasion? Given the characterization of knowledge as stated above, the answer is no. As Goldman (1986) puts it, "[t]rue belief is not sufficient for knowledge, at least not in the strict sense of 'know.' If it is just accidental that you are right about p, then you do not know that p, even if you are correct in believing it" (p. 42).

Just as truth is not a sufficient condition for knowledge, by itself—assuming one accepts the preceding argument—neither is (what is believed to be) evidentiary justification. The belief that a belief is justified on the evidence can be wrong; high confidence is not an infallible guide to truth. The history of science gives us many examples of beliefs that appeared to be justified on the evidence at one time and that were shown to be false at a later time. We might say that once people "knew" the earth to be flat, because the belief was supported by all the evidence at their disposal, but this seems inconsistent with what we usually mean by "know."

On this view, then, both truth and justification are necessary but not (individually) sufficient conditions for knowledge. It can be argued that even in combination they do not guarantee knowledge. Gettier (1963) has described conditions under which one could hold a true belief that is justified but we would be reluctant to call it knowledge. Poundstone (1990) refers to the essence of a Gettier counterexample to the justified-true-belief connotation of knowledge as "being right for the right reasons, but the reasons don't apply," and he gives the example of the visitor to the Louvre museum who, while viewing what he believes to be the *Mona Lisa*, experiences a thrill from knowing that he is in the same room with this renowned work of art. What the visitor does not realize is that the picture he is looking at is a very good reproduction that the museum staff put up in place of the original when they received a tip that a theft was being planned. The staff hid the original in this very room, however, behind another painting. So the visitor's belief that he is in the same room as the masterpiece is true, and it appears to be justified on the evidence that is available to him—this is the room where the *Mona Lisa* is always exhibited, what he is looking at appears to be that painting, he has no reason to suspect that it is not—but it does not seem quite right to give his belief (that he is in the same room as the *Mona Lisa*) the status of knowledge in this case.

I shall use the term "knowledge" in what follows to connote, as it usually does, justified true beliefs, but with the admission up front that what constitutes belief justification is a controversial issue and that one can never (justifiably) be absolutely certain that a particular belief is true. Even assuming the existence of criteria that would permit the establishment of the truth of a belief with certainty, one can never be certain beyond the tiniest doubt that one is sufficiently sane to apply the criteria correctly. I want to be clear here that my intent is to acknowledge the impossibility of being absolutely certain that one knows the truth, but not to endorse the postmodern idea that truth is contextually determined or that all knowledge is relative—a function of one's perspective, as it were. (We will return to the topic of belief justification in chapter 4.)

Despite this admission of fuzziness in the distinction between knowledge and belief, I want to argue that the distinction is a useful one for practical purposes. When I say that I know that the earth rotates on its axis as it revolves about the sun, or that water is made of hydrogen and oxygen, or that I have a cousin named Steven, I am expressing a different state of mind than when I say I believe that it will rain tomorrow, or that United Airlines flies into Bangor, Maine, or that *Homo sapiens* is the only species that really laughs.

Knowledge and faith

It is an oversimplification, no doubt, but a distinction may be made between first- and second-hand knowledge. First hand knowledge is knowledge we gain from experience and discovery. I know, for example, that ice cream tastes good, that hornets sting, that wood generally floats in water while stones do not, and that having a tooth filled is not terribly pleasant. I know these and many other things from personal experience. I know, too, or think I know, that George Washington was the first president of the United States, that salt is a compound of sodium and chlorine, that at one time dinosaurs roamed the earth, and that light travels at about 300,000 kilometers per second. The latter bits of knowledge differ from those mentioned first by virtue of the fact that none of them was acquired in a first-hand way; each of them was passed on to me from some other source—a parent, a teacher, a book, . . .

Faith, or trust, plays a critical role in the acquisition of knowledge of both types. In the case of first-hand knowledge, I trust my senses and my cognitive apparatus not to deceive me. If I found it difficult to distinguish between memories of actual experiences and memories of dreams, and realized that I had this difficulty, I might hesitate to trust what seemed to be remembered experiences as bases for first-hand knowledge. In the case of second-hand knowledge, I must have faith in the knowledgeability and integrity of the sources from which I acquire that knowledge. In claiming that I know that dinosaurs once roamed the earth, I am, in effect, indicating that I trust the various reports (more accurately, the authors of those reports) that tell me that this is a fact. I may never have explicitly acknowledged, even to myself, that my knowledge rests on such an act of faith, but it clearly does. I am exercising what Swinburne (1983) calls the *testimony principle,* according to which, "other things being equal, if someone tells you that *p,* then probably *p*" (p. 40). One might argue that this principle is one that should be exercised in moderation, but my sense is that we apply relatively uncritically in most contexts.

Much (most?) of the knowledge we acquire in the process of receiving a formal education is second-hand knowledge. So too is most of what we learn from reading books, newspapers and magazines, listening to the radio and watching television. And this is true of professionals (doctors, lawyers, teachers) and lay people alike. One might ask whether scientists who are in the business of developing new knowledge via experimentation and discovery are exempt from this rule, and the answer is definitely not. Most of what any scientist knows is knowledge that has been passed on from others. This is obviously true with respect to knowledge, even scientific knowledge, outside one's field, but it is true as well even with respect to knowledge in one's special area of interest. All scientists build on knowledge passed on to them by many generations of predecessors; no one starts from scratch and builds on only what one has discovered by oneself.

Types of knowledge

Philosophers and psychologists have made numerous distinctions regarding knowledge. Hume (1748/1939), for example distinguishes between *truths of reason* and *matters of fact*. The former are self-evident truths that we know directly; examples are the tautologies of mathematics: $2 + 2 = 4$. Matters of fact are empirical truths about the world: water changes from liquid to solid form as its temperature is lowered below 0 degrees Celsius. To Hume there were no other types of knowledge so a question that could not be answered either by a truth of reason or a fact was unanswerable. Nagel (1986) refers to truths of mathematics as a type of a priori knowledge and suggests that we may be able to develop a better understanding of how our thoughts can lead to this type of knowledge than of how they can lead to knowledge based on empirical observation—to truths of arithmetic versus truths of chemistry.

Adler (1981) makes a distinction between tautologies and self-evident truths. Tautologies, such as "All triangles have three sides," a triangle being defined as a three-sided polygon, are truths by definition. A self-evident truth that is not a tautology, in his view, is illustrated by the statement "No triangles have diagonals" (a diagonal being defined as a straight line drawn between two non-adjacent angles of a polygon). The claim is not simply a restatement of the definition of a triangle; it requires an inference, but an inference that anyone who understands the terms is compelled to make. Adler's notion of self-evident truths encompasses more than the kinds of assertions that can be derived from mathematical axioms. A truth is self-evident, in his view, if we acknowledge the impossibility of thinking the opposite. That all people need knowledge is one example Adler gives of a truth that is self-evident by this criterion; that we ought to desire what is good for us and not to desire what is bad for us is another.

The distinction between knowledge that is gained from experience with the world and knowledge that appears to be self-evident has been recognized by many philosophers in addition to Hume. Another example of the second type of knowledge that is sometimes seen to be universal is recognition of the force of the syllogism (Hamill, 1990). In all cultures, human beings of unimpaired intelligence, it is claimed, understand intuitively that if it is true that all A are B and that all B are C, it *must* be true as well that all A are C. This is not something that one learns from one's culture, but something that one knows without being told.

Another distinction that is commonly made is the distinction between declarative and procedural knowledge: knowing *that* and knowing *how* (Anderson, 1976; Ryle, 1949) or knowledge versus know-how (Polya, 1945/1957). Declarative knowledge, as the term has been used by psychologists, usually connotes knowledge of facts and relationships that one can articulate. The knowledge of history that one acquires through the reading of books would generally be considered declarative knowledge. Procedural knowledge is knowledge of how to do the various things that one has learned how to do—ride a bicycle, tie one's shoes, use an eating utensil. One may have either declarative knowledge or procedural knowledge, both, or neither, about the same subject. One may understand, from a theoretical point of view, all about what is involved in riding a bicycle but not be able to ride one; conversely, one may be an excellent bicycle rider without having a verbalizable understanding of how bicycle riding is done.

Having procedural knowledge without corresponding declarative knowledge is especially common. All of us are able to carry out many procedures effectively without understanding at a very deep level why those procedures work. In learning to do basic arithmetic, we learn procedures for multiplying two multi-digit numbers, dividing one multi-digit number by another, finding the square root of a number, and so on. If we use these procedures occasionally after having learned them, we may retain them indefinitely, but it does not follow that we understand them in more than a superficial way. The reader who is not convinced of this might wish to perform a long division computation in the presence of an observer who has been coached to ask for a clear explanation of the rationale for every step in the process. Procedural knowledge can be useful with or without understanding of the rationale behind the procedures; however, lack of understanding can complicate learning and limit the extendibility of the knowledge.

Unfortunately, it is easy to mistake procedural knowledge for knowledge that represents a deeper understanding of why procedures work, and as a consequence to overestimate one's grasp of a subject. This is perhaps especially the case in mathematics. Wallace (2003) notes that the sheer surface-level difficulty of mathematics "can fool us into thinking we really know something when all we really 'know' is abstract formulas and rules for their deployment" (p. 52). Not that such procedural knowledge is worthless, but it is easily mistaken for a deeper knowledge than it actually is. Wallace's assessment of the teaching of mathematics generally is rather harsh: "That we end up not even knowing that we don't know is the really insidious part of most math classes" (p. 52).

Other distinctions relating to knowledge that have been made include the distinctions between inert and active knowledge, between episodic and encyclopedic knowledge (from the distinction that many memory investigators make between episodic and semantic memory), between private and public (common) knowledge, and between knowledge and metaknowledge.

Fragmentary and implicit nature of knowledge

> And don't I know that there is no stairway in this house going six floors deep into the earth, even though I have never thought about it? (Wittgenstein, 1972, p. 51)

Two of the more striking characteristics of knowledge, in my view, are its fragmentary character and the fact that so much of it is implicit. As I reflect on what I know, or think I know, I am struck by the fact that what I know about almost any subject about which I know anything at all is fragmentary in the extreme. I know bits and pieces of this and that. This applies not only to subjects that I have encountered in one or another educational context but also to knowledge gained from personal experiences as well.

I remember fragments of what I have learned in school and of events that I have experienced or witnessed. Moreover, in recalling in either case, I may use my general knowledge to fill in many of the pieces that are missing from the memory without even being aware of the fact that I am doing so, so my memory, which appears to me to be fragmentary, may be even less complete than it appears to be. And none of us would have any difficulty coming up with countless examples of things we know implicitly—like the example provided by Wittgenstein—despite the fact that we have never learned them explicitly or even thought about them before.

That we have implicit knowledge has problematic implications for any attempts to estimate how much a person knows, or can know. Given a number—any number—I can say whether it is even or odd. This means that I have knowledge of an infinity of numbers, from which it follows that I have an infinite amount of knowledge. Such infinite knowledge is not very impressive, one may say, and I would not be inclined to argue, but the illustration makes the point that any attempt to estimate how much anyone knows must face the question of what should count as knowledge and, in particular, how to treat what one knows only implicitly.

Implicit knowledge is knowledge we have not because we acquired it explicitly but because we can infer it from other things we know. A closely related concept is that of tacit knowledge in the sense discussed by Polanyi (1967). One may have no difficulty in distinguishing cats from dogs but find it difficult to give a description that would suffice to make the distinction in all cases. Much of the knowledge that underlies pattern recognition is of this type.

Nagel (1995) notes that the ability to behave (e.g., to speak) in accordance with certain rules does not necessarily imply a conscious awareness of those rules, and raises the question of the conditions under which knowledge of a language could be considered knowledge of the rules that govern it. His answer is that when one would acknowledge a statement of a rule or principle to be an expression of what one believes to be true that it should be counted as knowledge "even in cases where the relevant principles or statements have not yet been consciously acknowledged, or even in cases where they will never be explicitly formulated" (p. 60). He rejects the idea, however, that one could have knowledge about which one could not, in principle, be made aware. "Knowledge need not be verbally expressible, but it should be either consciously exercised or capable of reaching consciousness upon adequate reflection" (p. 69).

Untapped knowledge

Possession of knowledge is not enough to ensure that that knowledge will be accessed and applied whenever it could be useful; conversely, the fact that one does not apply knowledge that would be useful in a particular situation is not conclusive evidence that one does not have that knowledge. This idea is closely related to the distinction between competence and performance (see chapter 11) and it has been expressed in many ways. It is implicit, for example, in Kahneman and Tversky's (1982b) distinction between errors of comprehension and errors of application. It is there in Bereiter and Scardamalia's (1981) suggestion that much of the knowledge that students acquire can remain inert—unaccessed—in situations in which it could be applied to good effect. Gick and Holyoak

(1983) argue that in a problem-solving situation, failure to apply knowledge that would help find a solution is not compelling evidence that the problem solver does not have that knowledge.

Nisbett and his colleagues have emphasized that it does not suffice to have effective schemas in one's repertory of reasoning skills; it is necessary that these schemas be evoked as appropriate in specific problem situations. The fact that performance on reasoning problems can be improved when cues are provided that will trigger the appropriate schemas has been shown for both deductive (Cheng & Holyoak, 1985), and inductive reasoning (Fong, Krantz, & Nisbett, 1986; Jepson, Krantz, & Nisbett, 1983; Nisbett, Krantz, Jepson, & Kunda, 1983). One cause for reasoning errors suggested by some of these studies is failure of the reasoner to see the relevance of a particular schema to a specific problem.

In short, the belief that one can have knowledge and sometimes fail to access it when it would be to one's advantage to do so is widely held among investigators of human cognition. This has implications both for those with an interest in determining what people know about specific topics and for those involved in teaching. The distinction between the existence of knowledge and its accessibility complicates the problem of assessing what one knows. For teachers the distinction means that, to the extent that the goals of education include increasing the practically useful knowledge that students have, it is necessary to be concerned not only that the desired knowledge be acquired but that it be acquired in such a way that it will be accessible for effective use.

Knowledge and knowers

Sometimes we speak of knowledge as though it could exist independently of a knower. For example, we refer to the knowledge that may be found in such and such a book, or to the knowledge that has been acquired over the centuries and is stored in the world's libraries. But knowledge, one might argue, implies a knower. Words in a book are not even words in any meaningful sense unless there is someone to read and comprehend them. They can convey knowledge from one mind to another, but they are only instruments of communication.

Sometimes too, we speak of knowledge as though it could be the possession of a group—a corporation, a profession, a culture. Thus a corporation is said to be careful to keep from its competitors knowledge that it considers privileged and especially important to its corporate goals. Some professions—medicine, paleontology, chemistry—are defined, in large measure, by the knowledge that is assumed to be more or less uniquely theirs. Cultures are said to differ from one another, in part, by the types of knowledge they have about the world and by the types of theories of cause and effect that such knowledge supports or permits.

But what does it mean to say that a corporation, a profession, a culture—any collective entity, any group—knows something? Suppose I say that a specific group knows X. Do I mean that every member of the group knows X? That a majority of the members knows X? That a nontrivial minority knows X? That at least one member knows X? Suppose that some proportion of the members of the group believes X (and that X happens to be true), and a similar proportion believes not-X; should one say that the group, as a group, knows X, that X is part of the group's knowledge?

It seems safe to assume of any real group that its members differ with respect to what they know. All the members may know some things in common, but individual members are likely also to know things that other members do not know. Should what a group knows, as a group, be considered what all the members know in common (the intersection of what the individual members know)? Should it be considered to include everything that at least one member knows (the union of what the individual members know)? The first possibility limits what a group knows to what its least knowledgeable member knows. In practical terms, the limitation is probably much more severe than that, because it reflects the intersection of what all of its less knowledgeable members know in common, which seems likely to be considerably less than what any of them knows individually. The second possibility has difficulties of a different kind. What do we do with the situation in which something that one member of the group "knows" contradicts something that another member "knows." We could resolve this problem by holding that the members, in such a case, do not know what they think they do, because knowledge—belief that is consistent with reality—presumably is not self-contradictory.

But even if we assume we can solve the nontrivial practical problem of distinguishing between true beliefs and false beliefs, we might still have some reluctance to consider that a group, as such, knows what at least one of its members knows. Suppose that one member knows X (X being true) and that all other members believe not-X. It seems ridiculous, in such an instance, to say that the group knows X. We can make the example less extreme by assuming that a minority of the group knows X while a majority believes not-X. Perhaps we should be willing to consider X to be part of what the group, as such, knows if that knowledge is possessed by a sufficient number, or percentage, of members to affect the behavior of the group as a whole. On the other hand, it is not clear that there is anything to be gained by ascribing knowledge to the group, as such, as opposed to ascribing it to the individuals who comprise it.

Suppose that some of the members of a group know X and believe not-Y and that other members know Y and believe not-X (X and Y both being true), and that no members know both X and Y. It would seem odd in this case also to say that the group, as such, knows X and Y, even though each of these bits of knowledge is contained in the union of what the individual members know. Again, one can modify this illustration to make it less extreme, but one is still left with the question of what is to be gained by ascribing knowledge to a group, as such, as opposed to considering it to be possessed only by the individual mind, and then accounting for the effects of knowledge on group behavior in terms of what the members of the group do or do not know. At the least, any conception of what it means for a group (organization, nation, culture) to know something must differ substantially from what it means for an individual to know something, enough perhaps to warrant representing the two states of affairs with different words.

Metaknowledge

Numerous studies have shown that when people feel they have knowledge in memory they cannot retrieve, the strength of this feeling is a reasonably good indication of the probability that they will be able to recall it eventually or to recognize what they could not produce (Blake, 1973; Read & Bruce, 1982; Smith & Clark, 1993), or to produce it with the help of additional retrieval cues (Gruneberg & Monks, 1974). The feeling of knowing and the closely related tip-of-the-tongue experience (Brown & McNeill, 1966) have been documented with a variety of experimental tasks, including paired associates learning (Hart, 1967; Leonesio & Nelson, 1990; Nelson, Leonesio, Shimamura, Landwehr, & Narens, 1982; Ryan, Petty, & Wenzlaff, 1982), cued recall (Gruneberg & Monks, 1974), stem completion (Lupker, Harbluk, & Patrick, 1991), and perceptual identification (Nelson, Gerler, & Narens, 1984; Yaniv & Meyer, 1987), among others. Much of the work on feeling of knowing has been done with general-knowledge questions (Hart, 1965; Metcalfe, 1986a; Nelson, Gerler, & Narens, 1984; Nelson & Narens, 1990; Smith & Clark, 1993). In a typical study of this type, participants would be asked to indicate their degree of confidence that they would be able to recognize (select from among alternatives) the correct answers to questions for which they had not been able to produce answers.

Smith and Clark (1993), like Nelson and Narens (1990), found a positive correlation between the speed with which answers to general knowledge questions were produced and people's confidence in those answers; they also found that when their participants were unable to answer a question, the stronger their feeling of knowing, the longer they took before giving up. Other investigators have also found a positive relationship between the feeling of knowing and the time that people spend searching for an answer (Gruneberg, Monks, & Sykes, 1977; Lachman & Lachman, 1980; Reder, 1987, 1988; Ryan, Petty, & Wenzlaff, 1982). This makes intuitive sense; as Smith and Clark point out, one should continue searching only if one believes the answer is likely to be found. In at least one instance, the strength of feeling of knowing was predictive of the length of time people would search for an answer but not of the probability that they would find it (Costermans, Lories, & Ansay, 1992).

Relatively few investigators have attempted to measure the time taken to make feeling-of-knowing judgments. Some who have done so have found feeling-of-knowing reaction times to be faster than the time required to produce answers to the questions, when they could be produced (Reder, 1988; Reder & Ritter, 1992). This finding is consistent with the possibility, which several investigators have found plausible, that the feeling of knowing is implicated in memory retrieval more generally than as an experience that can accompany failed efforts to retrieve. Some have conjectured that people automatically evaluate the likelihood of being able to answer a question, before attempting to retrieve the answer, but that they are generally not aware of the outcome of this process unless the subsequent retrieval attempt fails.

Reder and Ritter (1992) note a number of other reasons for supposing this to be a possibility. These include the fact that it is easy to identify questions ("What was Charles Dickens's phone number?") that people would presumably realize straightaway they could not answer—that a search of memory would not be necessary—the finding that people search longer for answers they believe they know, and evidence (Reder, 1982, 1987, 1988) that people make strategic decisions about how they will search memory, perhaps on the basis of the outcome of an initial evaluation.

Reder and Ritter (1992) gave people practice in solving arithmetic problems and then, during a test session, asked them with respect to specific problems to indicate, quickly and before attempting to provide answers, whether they would be able to answer from memory or would have to resort to computation. They found that feeling of knowing was more dependent on previous exposure to problem parts (e.g., one or the other of the operands) than on previous exposure to complete problems. They took this result as evidence that feeling of knowing does not depend on the same processes as those involved in retrieving an answer and that people are able to make an initial evaluation of a question before attempting to answer it.

There are several, not mutually exclusive, bases for the feeling of knowing, including the following:

- Direct metaknowledge of availability and accessibility. Conceivably people have explicit metaknowledge about the contents of their memories—that they know, for example, whether they have the answer to a particular question even before they attempt to bring the answer to mind. Early investigators of the feeling of knowing and tip-of-the-tongue experience may have assumed something of this sort, inasmuch as they did not discuss the possibility of more inferential bases for the feeling (Brown & McNeill, 1966; Hart, 1965).

- Retrieval of information *about* the sought item (Hart, 1967; Nelson & Narens, 1990). This is consistent with the finding that the feeling of knowing tends to be stronger when participants can produce partially correct responses than when they cannot do so (Blake, 1973; Nelson, Gerler, & Narens, 1984; Schacter & Worling, 1985).

- Familiarity with retrieval cues (Koriat & Lieblich, 1977; Metcalfe, 1986a; Nelson, Gerler, & Narens, 1984; Reder, 1987; Reder & Ritter, 1992; Schwartz & Metcalfe, 1992). Schwartz and Metcalfe (1992) found that priming the cue words in a paired-associate recall task increased participants' feeling of knowing the target word. Reder (1987) increased feeling of knowing the answers to general-knowledge questions, without increasing the probability of recall or recognition of the answers, by preexposing participants to words used to compose the questions. Koriat and Lieblich (1977) also found that the feeling of knowing could be strengthened by repeating questions, without repeating the answers to them.

- Beliefs about what one should know (Costermans, Lories, & Ansay, 1992). I believe I should know the capital cities of the states of the United States, or at least that I once knew them, which is not to say that I am sure I could give them all on demand.

- Nelson and colleagues distinguish two types of mechanisms that they believe to be involved in the feeling of knowing—trace access mechanisms and inferential mechanisms (Barnes, Nelson, Dunlosky, Mazzoni, & Narens, 1999; Nelson, Gerler, & Narens, 1984). Trace-access mechanisms are assumed to access stored aspects or associates of a sought item that are not sufficiently coupled with the item to cause its retrieval. Inferential mechanisms allow one to make inferences of the sort that something must be in memory, despite the fact that it cannot be retrieved. Both types of mechanisms are suggested in the bases for the feeling of knowing mentioned above.

Elsewhere (Nickerson, 1980), I have suggested several possible bases of the feeling of knowing that have some overlap with the preceding list:

- Knowledge that one once knew. Remembering knowing something (the name of an acquaintance) that one cannot now call to mind.

- Being able to infer that one once knew. I cannot remember the name of the family that lived in the apartment below that in which my family lived when I was 5 years old, and cannot even remember ever knowing the name. But I am quite sure I did—the inference is based on my model of what 5-year-olds are likely to know—and would not be surprised if I could pick it out from a small set of distracters if given the chance.

- Knowing that one should know. One might be unable to recall who was the first vice president of the United States, or even to recall having ever known, but feel that one must have learned that at some point during one's school years.

- Thinking one knows, but not being sure—Having an answer that one believes could be, but may not be, correct. This is not quite what is usually meant by the feeling of knowing—the term usually applies to cases in which one is unable to retrieve a plausible possibility—but it is an important state of mind to recognize because it represents the situation in which we often find ourselves.

Something analogous to the feeling of knowing has been observed in the context of problem solving. In this case, "feeling of warmth" judgments have sometimes been shown to increase with the time that one has worked on a problem. This relationship appears to be more likely to hold for problems that do not require an insight for solution than for those that do (Metcalfe, 1986b; Metcalfe & Weibe, 1987). Almost by definition problems that depend on an insight for solution tend to be solved abruptly when the insight is achieved, and the insight, if it occurs, does so without warning. This difference is a basis for believing that approaches to insight and analytic problems probably share some mental processes but not all (Schooler & Melcher, 1995).

The feeling of knowing has motivated much research. Most of that research has focused on people's ability to judge whether they have a specific bit of knowledge that they are unable to produce on demand. Perhaps more important in relation to the question of what it means to be rational is the ability to assess in a more general sense what one knows on a given topic relative to what there is to know, or relative to what others with whom one is likely to interact know. There is considerable evidence that people easily assume they know more than they actually do. This is seen in such well-documented phenomena as *hindsight bias* (Christensen-Szalanski & Fobian Willham, 1991; Fischhoff, 1975; Fischhoff & Beyth-Marom, 1975; Hawkins & Hastie, 1990) and a tendency to be overconfident of one's own opinions and beliefs (Keren, 1991; Lichtenstein, Fischhoff & Phillips, 1982; O'Connor, 1989; Wallsten & Budescu, 1983). Overconfidence appears not to be limited to people who are not highly knowledgeable in a field; it has been found among experts as well, in a variety of fields, including medicine (Lusted, 1977; Faust, Hart, & Guilmette, 1988), psychology (Oskamp, 1965), and engineering (Kidd, 1970). This is not to suggest that overconfidence is universal or that it is uncorrectable, but the evidence suggests that it is prevalent and not always readily remediated.

☐ The Solipsistic Predicament

> I once received a letter from an eminent logician, Mrs. Christine Ladd Franklin, saying that she was a solipsist, and was surprised that there were no others. (Russell, 1948, p. 180)

Clinicians tell us that persons suffering from certain types of neurological or mental dysfunction are unaware of their problems (Sacks, 1987). This is easy enough to believe, but it leads to the obvious question: If some mentally unbalanced people are unaware of their problem, then the fact that one is unaware of a problem is not compelling evidence that one does not have one. How do I know that I am not one of those individuals? How do you know that you are not? If some insane people believe they are sane, then the belief that one is sane does not suffice to establish that one is.

How does one know, at any given time, whether one is awake or asleep and dreaming? Dreams appear, in retrospect, to have been very realistic. When I believe I am awake and am reflecting on a dream, I believe that when in the dream state I did not consider it a dream state, which is to say I believed myself to be awake. If it is the case that when I dream I believe myself to be awake, should my belief that I am awake at any given time be taken (by myself) as good evidence that I am indeed so? John Wheeler's advice for answering such questions is to check with someone else. "If I see something, but I'm not sure whether it's a dream or reality, there's hardly a better test than to check whether somebody else is aware of it and can confirm my observations. That's essential in distinguishing between reality and dreams" (Davies & Brown, 1986, p. 62). But how do I know that the someone with whom I check is not a figment of my imagination? How can I rule out the possibility that the process of checking is part of my dream?

As I write these words, I believe I am awake. Moreover, I think I know the difference between being awake and dreaming. My perception of the world is much sharper and more continuous when awake than when dreaming; my thinking is more logical and the substance of my thought more "realistic." There are many other ways in which the state of being awake and the state of dreaming while asleep differ. So I have quite a lot of confidence in my assumption that I am awake at the moment.

But is this confidence justified? My assessment of what it is like to be asleep and dreaming is from the perspective of my present, presumably waking, state. It is based on memories of experiences I have had while asleep, but the memories themselves are waking-state—or what I assume to be waking-state—experiences. How can I be certain they accurately reflect what it is like to be asleep and dreaming? It is conceivable that when I am asleep and dreaming, the world appears much sharper and more continuous than it does in my memory of my dreams. Perhaps in my dreams I have fuzzy and discontinuous memories of waking-state experiences that seem less real than the experiences in the dream. In fact there is no way I can be absolutely sure that my dream life is not every bit as real as my waking life; and that being so, neither can I be certain that I am not dreaming when I believe myself to be awake. This is not a new thought. Descartes expressed it in 1641, and it is very doubtful that he was the first to have had it.

The process of distinguishing between a present perception and a present act of imagination is sometimes referred to as *reality testing* and that of distinguishing between memories of externally-caused events and memories of imagined events as *reality monitoring* (Johnson, 1988; Johnson, Foley, Suengas, & Raye, 1988; Suengas & Johnson, 1988;

Johnson & Raye, 1981). People with certain types of mental illness often cannot tell the difference between real and imagined events (McGuigan, 1966; Mintz & Alpert, 1972). But there is good evidence also that presumably perfectly sane people sometimes are unable to distinguish between real and imagined memories (Hyman, Husband, & Billings, 1995; Johnson, 1988; Johnson & Raye, 1981; Raye, Johnson, & Taylor, 1980; Mazzoni, Loftus, & Kirsch, 2001; Slusher & Anderson, 1987).

How can one *ever* be sure that what one "remembers" really happened? We know that memory is inaccurate at best, that two people can remember the same event quite differently, that memories themselves can change over time, that they can become embellished as a consequence of reporting and rehearsing, and that much of what we think we remember we actually construct from other knowledge that we have. I say we know these things; of course I mean we think we know them, because that knowledge rests on the assumption that our minds are not playing tricks on us in this instance.

The physical world around us, the various forms of energy that activate our sensory systems, the sensory systems themselves, all serve to get impulses to a brain that it, in some mysterious way, turns into conscious experience. Presumably if there were a way to get the same impulses to a disembodied but otherwise functioning brain, the same conscious experience would result. That being the case, how does one know that one's experience arises from interactions with the physical world and is not the consequence of an artificially maintained disembodied brain? This is the famous "brain-in-the-vat" puzzle, the image being that of a brain being kept alive in a vat of nutrients and stimulated electrically in such a way as to simulate the stimulation that a brain normally receives via the sensory systems that connect it to the outside world. If one accepts the possibility, in principle, of the brain-in-a-vat notion, then it is not clear how one can be certain that one is not, in reality, such a brain in a vat. A smorgasbord of ruminations on related ideas has been provided by Hofstadter and Dennet (1981).

The brain-in-the-vat image may strike many readers as ludicrous, but is it clearly more far-fetched than the idea, taken quite seriously by some theorists, that the universe as we know it is the consequence of a spontaneous "fluctuation" in an eternal state that is best described as nothingness. "[T]he most probable assumption, if fluctuation theory is to hold, is simply that my brain is a fluctuation out of the equilibrium, just at this moment and in this small region of space; while none of the familiar objects of the universe (stars, planets, other human beings) exist, and all my (illusory) perceptions and memories are simply encoded in the states of my neurons (a 'scientific' version of solipsism). However improbable such a fluctuation is, it is still far more probable than a fluctuation giving rise to the observed universe, of which my brain is a part" (Bricmont, 1996, p. 148).

These uncertainties are variations on the solipsistic predicament whereby one cannot be sure of the existence of any reality other than one's own consciousness. This is an idea that probably occurs to most of us during our formative years, and that we easily lay aside because of its impracticality, but that comes back, uninvited, from time to time in one or another guise. The prevailing attitude toward questions of this general sort, I believe, is that they are mainly academic, or recreational, and have little in the way of important practical implications. Macdonald (1952) reflects this attitude in the following observations: "it is true that no solipsist refuses to converse with others, unless he is also suffering from incipient schizophrenia. Nor does the skeptic about the existence of material objects sit down very gingerly on every chair for fear it isn't really there. For these problems have not, usually, been suggested by any practical difficulties about communication or knowledge in ordinary life. Nor will any answer which the philosopher gives to them be likely to alter his subsequent behavior" (p. 170).

This characterization of the solipsist's ability to distinguish between theoretical and practical reality may be fair, but it does not follow that solipsism should never be expected to influence one's behavior. If one really believes that other people are figments of one's own imagination, one might be less motivated than otherwise to be concerned for their welfare. In any case, the question of how one tells that one is sane—that one is not suffering from delusions of adequacy—*is* of some practical significance. And it differs only in degree from the question of how one knows whether one's thinking on any particular issue is sound.

☐ Limits of Knowledge

Any given individual can know only so much; no one can know everything, even about a given topic. Pais (1986) points out that, at the time of his writing, a high-energy physicist would had to have digested 17 publications every day in order to claim familiarity with the whole body of literature in the field. A similar observation could be made of many other fields. One must make choices regarding what is worth knowing. But that being said, it is also the case that no one, as far as I know, has come up with a compelling estimate of what the limits of individual human knowledge are. It is at least a plausible hypothesis that the fact that most of us learn as little as we do, relative to what there is to be learned, is due to factors other than that limit, whatever it is.

One obvious practical limitation on the amount of knowledge we acquire is motivational. Learning beyond what one must know to get along in one's day-to-day world appears not to be a high priority goal for many people. Holton (1973) argues that the pursuit of scientific knowledge is not highly valued by nonscientists in our society and that, as a consequence, such knowledge is not widely distributed throughout it, even among intellectuals. Holton's observation focuses on scientific knowledge because it was made in the context of a discussion of scientific thinking. A similar observation could be made, however, with respect to knowledge in other fields such as history, economics, or philosophy.

Another practical constraint on human learning is the limited effectiveness of the ways we have developed, to date, to inform ourselves. One hopes that, with the help of modern technology, we can find ways to do a better job of this; so far, evidence of success is sparse. The problem of ineffective educational techniques is exacerbated by the great rate at which information is being acquired at the present time especially through the scientific enterprise. This is the basis, it has been argued, for the necessity of increasing specialization in education (Gardner, 1988).

In addition to limits on knowledge that may derive from fundamental limitations of human beings to assimilate information, from the possibility that learning is not as high a priority for many of us as it might be, and from the limitations of our instructional techniques, there is the possibility also that sometimes we may prefer not to have certain knowledge even if it is, or could be, readily available to us. Perhaps there is such a thing as preferred ignorance. Wallace (2003) expresses this idea: "One thing is certain, though. It is a total myth that man is by nature curious and truth-hungry and wants, above all things, *to know*. Given certain recognized senses of 'to know,' there is in fact a great deal of stuff we do *not* want to know" (p. 12).

Given the option, not everyone would wish to know the time and cause of one's own death (or the future in general). Some scientists might prefer not to know all the uses to which their discoveries will be put. One might prefer not to know of unsavory things done by a loved one (a child, a parent, a spouse). One might wish not to be given information that one would have to feel obliged to safeguard (information classified as sensitive by the government, trade secrets, information of a personal nature that a friend or acquaintance may wish to protect.) One might prefer not to be aware of evidence or arguments that are damaging to a valued belief.

We sometimes may prefer not to be aware of difficulties that other people are facing, because such awareness would make us feel obliged to attempt to do something about it. If we did not really want to do what seemed appropriate, we then would face the dilemma of doing something we wished not to do (e.g., parting with some money or time) or suffering a guilty conscience for not doing it. More generally, we may sometimes wish not to know that certain decision alternatives are available to us because to have that knowledge would complicate our lives and give us a responsibility for choice that we might wish to avoid. A way to avoid the responsibility of choice is to remain ignorant of one's options, or even of the fact that one has any.

Assuming highly motivated and highly intelligent people who wish to know as much as they can about, say, the world in general and how it works, what they can know is limited by the time in which they live. Archhimedes could not know what Newton knew, and Newton could not know what Einstein did; each was limited by what had been discovered, or was discoverable, at the time of his existence. We cannot hope to know things about the world that may be common knowledge 100 or 1,000 years hence.

A qualitatively different type of limitation on what we know, or can know, is that which follows from the conceptual possibilities of the human mind. From Plato through Kant there runs the idea, which many find intuitively compelling, that our knowledge of the world is limited to how things appear to us; that we cannot hope to appear behind the appearances and see reality in the buff, as it were. Even with the help of technology, we see appearances—more detailed, to be sure, but appearances nonetheless. In addition to the problem of not being able to get behind the appearances, there may be aspects of reality that are simply beyond the ability of humans to conceive. Nagel (1986) puts it this way: "What there is and what we, in virtue of our nature, can think about are different things, and the latter may be smaller than the former" (p. 91). It would be the epitome of hubris, would it not, to assume otherwise.

Another limitation on our knowledge, as individuals, is related to the solipsistic predicament. I may find it easy to reject solipsism, and to be willing to believe that you exist, but what can I hope to know of your experience and can I ever be sure that it resembles mine to any degree? I cannot get inside your mind in any meaningful sense—to see the world through your eyes, to learn first hand whether what you experience when you see red, or feel pain, is what I experience when I see red or feel pain. I have no way of telling for sure how what you mean when you say that you find Mozart's music beautiful corresponds to what I mean when I make the same claim. Perhaps the best one can do is to apply what is sometimes referred to as the *principle of charity*, according to which one assumes that others are pretty much like oneself and that their experience corresponds closely to one's own—that what others see is more or less what I see, that how they respond in specific situation is more or less the same as I would respond in those situations, that they hurt much as I hurt, and get pleasure much as do I.

☐ Varieties of Ignorance

> The greatest of all the accomplishments of twentieth-century science has been the discovery of human ignorance. (Thomas, 1981, p. 49)

A distinction relating to knowledge that is not often made, but one that is relevant to the focus of this book, is the distinction between informed ignorance and uninformed ignorance. Informed ignorance is a knowledge-based state of mind. It is the kind of ignorance that only people who are knowledgeable in a field can have. It is an ignorance that can be articulated with precise questions about what has yet to be learned, and the formulation of such questions depends on being conversant with what is already known.

Major theoretical advances or reformulations of scientific knowledge, such as those produced by Copernicus, Newton, and Einstein, cause the asking of questions that could not have been asked before. Holton (1973) speaks of such advances as the breaking through to new areas of "fruitful ignorance." The effect of scientific growth is "not so much the escalation of knowledge as the escalation of ignorance—the sometimes discontinuous process of breaking into new areas of work where very little is yet known" (p. 15). Uninformed ignorance stems from lack of familiarity with what is known. To one whose ignorance of a field is uninformed, questions raised by informed ignorance are likely to be unintelligible.

A related distinction is made by Bauer (1994) who contrasts the "known unknown" with the "unknown unknown" in the context of scientific knowledge. The known unknown is the unknown that can be articulated by well-informed scientists. The unknown unknown is the unknown that is outside the awareness even of the most knowledgeable people. It is from the unknown unknown that the truly surprising discoveries come. Examples of discoveries from the unknown unknown that occurred during the latter part of the 19th century and the early part of the 20th that Bauer mentions are radioactivity, the necessity to describe radiation sometimes as particles and sometimes as waves, relativity, non-Euclidean space, and the uncertainty principle.

The relationship between knowledge and one's awareness of one's own ignorance is a paradox of sorts. The more one knows, the more basis one has for being aware of the extent of one's ignorance. People who know very little about, say, the composition of matter, of necessity have a limited appreciation of how much there is to be known on the topic. Conversely, people who have spent their lives studying the subject have discovered, for every answer they have found, a host of new questions that they originally did not know enough to ask. Autobiographical writings of the great scientists are replete with evidences of an extraordinary awareness of the limitations of their own knowledge, especially with respect to the aspects of nature on which their own work has focused.

Expressions of this awareness are often interpreted as evidence of self-effacing modesty on the part of those who have made them. And in some instances this may be an accurate perception. As a group, however, scientists are no more inclined to be modest than other folk; they typically have ample egos and are not in the habit of deferring intellectually to others. My sense is that when they have commented on the limitations of their knowledge, they have, more often than not, simply expressed the way they felt about how amazingly little they—or anyone else—knew about the world compared to what they would like to have known. They really have been impressed with the enormity of the difference. Roland-Robinson (1977) has expressed this sentiment rather well: "To be a true scientist is only to have an inkling of the full extent of man's ignorance" (p. 62).

☐ Measuring Knowledge

How might one determine what, or how much, an individual knows? The first problem one faces in any effort to address this question is that of deciding what it means to know something—which, we have already noted, is not an easy task. Consider the "straightforward" question of what it means to know a word. What might I mean, for example, by claiming to know the word "run?" I certainly do not mean that I could give all the dictionary definitions, of which there are well over one hundred in an unabridged dictionary—many as a transitive verb, many as an intransitive verb, many as a noun, and a few as an adjective. I do not even mean that I am confident I would recognize the word as appropriate in every context in which it might conceivably be used. What I do mean is that I am able to use the word with several of its connotations and to interpret it appropriately when I encounter it in a variety of contexts.

The view that a word either is or is not in one's vocabulary is a gross oversimplification of the range of possibilities with respect to what it means to know a word. It follows that determining the size of one's vocabulary is very difficult. It is not even clear what should count as a word. Is "run" one word? Or should "run_1" and "run_2" count as different words? Assuming the former, should a word be counted as part of my vocabulary if I recognize some of its connotations but not others? And even when we limit our attention to a single connotation of a word, two persons' grasp of that connotation may differ in important ways; one may be relatively concrete and narrowly bound to context while another is rich in metaphor and associative connections.

Finding a satisfactory answer to the question of what it means to know something is only the first step in determining what a person knows. Simply asking people what they know does not work. A major challenge that developers of knowledge-based "expert systems" for computers have faced is that of explicating what experts in specific domains of interest know about those domains, and the difficulty of the task stems in part from the fact that experts typically know much more than they can make explicit on demand. Surprisingly, it has turned out that the kind of specialized, domain-specific knowledge that an expert has acquired through explicit training is easier to explicate and codify than the commonsense knowledge of the world that all of us share and on which our ability to communicate with each other depends. It may be that what the expert knows that the nonexpert does not know pales in comparison to the knowledge they share, even though the differences in their respective knowledge bases may be more apparent to us than their commonalities.

How to quantify what a specific individual knows is a challenge that is beyond psychology's currently available techniques. Any description that is to come close to being adequate must take account of the fragmentary and implicit nature of much of what we know, of the fuzziness of the line between knowledge and belief, of the varying degrees of certainty with which we hold things to be true, of our inability to put into words all the concepts, principles, relationships, and processes that we understand well enough to use effectively, and a host of other obscurities and complexities about the representations of reality that we carry in our heads.

☐ Knowledge and Reasoning

The importance of knowledge to reasoning is arguably a fairly recent discovery. Mandler (1995) describes the view "that the main way children differ from adults is in the size and interrelatedness of their knowledge base" as a recent realization. "We know now, of course, that the ability to see patterns and relations among pieces of information in a problem is crucially dependent on how much you already know. Most of our most sophisticated and creative reasoning depends on that ability, rather than on the ability to form or follow chains of logical propositions" (p. 81).

One's reasoning might conceivably be affected either by what one knows about the subject on which the reasoning is focused or by what one knows about the process of reasoning itself. The first possibility is illustrated when one decides that a deductive argument is valid, whether or not it is so, because one knows its conclusion to be true. The second is illustrated by the case in which one avoids making the logical error of affirming the consequent when evaluating a hypothetical syllogism because one has learned to recognize this syllogistic form as an invalid one.

A substantial literature exists on the question of how one's reasoning about any given subject is likely to be affected by one's knowledge of that subject. Much debate has centered on the question of whether people reason in accordance with general principles and abstract rules of inference that apply in any context or depend primarily on knowledge and skills that pertain to specific contexts or domains. Reasoning that depends on specific domain knowledge is sometimes referred to as *experience-based* reasoning.

Approaches to the teaching of thinking or reasoning skills are sometimes divided into two groups on the basis of whether they emphasize general, domain-independent, skills, or domain-specific knowledge and know-how. The division can easily be characterized in an overly dichotomous way, in my view, because few, if any, proponents of the teaching of thinking argue for the exclusive focus on one type of capability to the total exclusion of the other; but there are definite differences of opinion as to the relative importance of the two. Among those who emphasize the importance of domain-specific knowledge and problem-solving skills are McPeck (1981), Glaser (1984, 1990), Stigler and Baranes (1988), Lave and Wenger (1991), and Ceci (1993). Domain knowledge is sometimes held to play a more important role in practical or everyday reasoning than in theoretical or formal reasoning. The objective of practical reasoning is to get the right answer—not to make only logically valid inferences—and, given this objective, it makes sense to draw on whatever knowledge one has that will improve one's chances of realizing it.

The application of knowledge of how particular types of problems have been solved in the past to the solution of similar problems in the present is sometimes referred to as case-based reasoning (Kolodner, 1993; Schank & Abelson, 1977). Case-based reasoning has been used to good effect in artificial-intelligence research, and there is little reason to doubt that people also sometimes are able to solve problems by remembering how similar problems were solved in the past. The justification for using case-based reasoning in artificial intelligence systems is the fact that it works and sometimes makes less demand on resources than alternative approaches.

One can argue, however, that we should distinguish between the application of domain knowledge in everyday situations and the reasoning that is going on in those situations, recognizing that the knowledge may sometimes complement the reasoning to good effect and sometimes work against it. Some studies have shown what appear to be detrimental effects of domain knowledge on reasoning—people may be misled about the soundness of an argument by what they know regarding the truth or falsity of its conclusion; other studies have found what appear to be facilitating effects—people sometimes solve reasoning problems more effectively when the problems involve situations with which they are familiar than when their content is unfamiliar or abstract, although in cases of the latter type it is often difficult to distinguish what should be attributed to reasoning per se and what is better attributed to recall.

Many of the findings regarding the relationship between content knowledge and reasoning are consistent with the idea that it is, to a large extent, a complementary one. When one knows the solution to a problem, because one has learned it or previously worked it out for oneself, one does not need to spend a lot of energy thinking about it. In contrast, given a problem about which one knows very little, one must think about it if one is to solve it. Some investigators hold that, as a matter of fact, people typically use domain-specific knowledge to solve problems when they can do so and fall back on more domain-independent heuristics when they cannot (Polson & Jeffries, 1982).

Such a complementary relationship makes sense from a cost-effectiveness point of view. Assuming that retrieval of a known problem solution from memory is generally less demanding of cognitive resources than is reasoning out a solution, resorting to memory when possible leaves one's cognitive resources more fully available for other uses. On the other hand, many of the problems that present themselves to us are not familiar, so complete dependency on memory is not possible. Moreover, for some types of problems, the expenditure of resources (energy, storage space) that would be required to memorize solutions would be greater than that required to memorize a procedure for inferring solutions. Memorizing procedures for multiplying or dividing multi-digit numbers, for finding square roots, or for determining other mathematical functions, is much less demanding of resources, for example, than would be memorizing all the products, quotients, square roots, and so on, that one might have occasion to use.

The fact that one may be misled about the soundness of an argument by what one knows about the truth or falsity of the argument's conclusion might be seen to be inconsistent with this cost-effectiveness view. But for most practical purposes, it is probably more important to judge correctly the truth or falsity of an argument's conclusion than to determine the validity or invalidity of the argument's form. If that is so, then when one has direct knowledge of the truth status of a conclusion, one may be wasting one's time to give much thought to whether or not the argument that supports it is sound.

The complementary interplay of reasoning and memory makes the distinction between the two types of processes very difficult in particular cases. Inasmuch as performance on a reasoning task involving a concrete situation can almost always be explained on the basis of one's knowledge about the situation, it may be difficult or impossible to establish that reasoning as such is occurring at all. This is one motivation for investigating reasoning ability with abstract reasoning tasks on which people cannot so easily make direct use of previous experience.

We may note, in passing, how the complementary relationship between reasoning and knowledge reveals itself in the history of efforts to build intelligent machines. The earliest attempts to build perceptrons and other machines that could acquire the ability to discriminate between different types of patterns relied almost entirely on general learning processes. The first efforts to develop computer programs that could do problem solving targeted "general problem solvers" and relied heavily on the codification of general reasoning principles. Later, the pendulum swung to the other extreme with most of the effort being directed at the development of knowledge-based systems that were intended to be applied in specific domains and were initially given large amounts of information about the domains of interest. Still later, the pendulum began to swing back toward center with the recognition of the need for both powerful reasoning heuristics *and* lots of domain knowledge as well.

A similar pattern can be seen in work aimed at developing approaches to the teaching of thinking, or higher-order cognitive skills (Nickerson, Perkins, & Smith, 1985). Some investigators have attempted to design techniques for teaching general principles, processes, skills, or strategies that would be applicable independently of domain. Others have taken the position that effective thinking is more domain-dependent than proponents of general domain-independent approaches assume and they have advocated the teaching of traditional subject matter and domain-specific problem solving techniques. Here too, one may see the importance of *both* general reasoning ability and domain-specific knowledge to good thinking in the broadest sense.

A distinction that was made at the beginning of this chapter that is especially germane to the relationship between knowledge and reasoning is that between declarative and procedural knowledge. If we accept this distinction, we might apply it to principles of sound reasoning in the following way. One might understand such principles in the sense of being able to describe them (one might have declarative knowledge of them) but be unable to apply them effectively (lack procedural knowledge of them); one might be able to apply the principles in situations that call for reasoning, but be unable to describe them; one might be able both to describe and apply them; or one might be unable either to describe or apply them.

The first of these possibilities—understanding principles of good reasoning but failing to apply them—may seem an unlikely combination; if one clearly understood how to reason well, why would one not do so? The idea that people can have inert knowledge—knowledge that is not accessed and used to advantage—is a familiar one in psychology and it has considerable experimental support (Broadbent, Fitzgerald, & Broadbent, 1986; Gick & Holyoak, 1983). The second possibility—that of being able to apply principles that one cannot articulate—is intuitively plausible and also has evidential support (Lewicki, 1986; Lewicki, Hill, & Bizot, 1988). The third and fourth possibilities are plausible if the first two are.

Finally, we should note that reasoning is itself a subject about which there exists a body of knowledge. In my view, the acquisition of at least some of this knowledge should be an objective of efforts to enhance the quality of thinking through instruction (Nickerson, 1994, 2000, 2004). I have in mind general knowledge about human cognition (the difference between reasoning and case building, the difference between reasoning and rationalizing, how emotions can affect reasoning), knowledge of common reasoning limitations, foibles and biases (the confirmation bias, the tendency to jump to conclusions, stereotyping), tools of thought (logic, problem-solving heuristics), and metacognitive knowledge (evaluating one's own thinking, managing one's cognitive resources). Having such knowledge does not guarantee good reasoning, but it is hard to see how it could hurt.

☐ Expertise

Until fairly recently, the term "expert" was reserved for people who have unusual knowledge or ability in a specific field. Today the term is also often used to refer to computer-based systems that have been given a great deal of information, usually encoded as sets of if-then condition-action rules, about particular domains. In either case, the connotation is of extensive knowledge of a well-defined and limited domain; the fact that one has great expertise with respect to a particular subject tells us little, if anything, about one's competence in unrelated domains.

The most obvious difference between experts and novices in domain-specific problem contexts is the amount of knowledge they have that relates directly to the problem domain. The contrast has been brought into stark relief in studies of expert and novice players of chess (DeGroot, 1965). Expert players have been estimated to have acquired a memory of as many as 50,000 board positions over years of play (Simon & Schaeffer, 1992). Evidence of the importance of experience-based knowledge as a defining aspect of expertise has been obtained for other areas as disparate as electronics (Egan & Schwartz, 1979), baseball (Voss, Vesonder, & Spilich, 1980) bridge (Charness, 1979; Engle & Bukstel, 1978), and medical diagnosis (Balla, Biggs, Gibson, & Chang, 1990; Elstein, Shulman, & Sprafka, 1978; Grant, 1989).

The importance of domain knowledge to expert problem solving is generally recognized among researchers and is not a matter of debate. Some make a distinction, however, between knowledge of a domain and mere experience in the domain (Neale & Bazerman, 1991; Neale & Northcraft, 1990). One would expect knowledge and experience to be highly correlated, but they are not the same thing; the kind of knowledge that is associated with expertise is assumed to include a relatively deep understanding not only of subject matter but of problem-solving strategies that are effective in the domain (Neale & Northcraft, 1990).

Evidence of the role of problem-solving know-how in expertise comes from studies like that of Chi, Feltovich, and Glaser (1981) who converted their participants' protocols into production rules (Newell, 1973) and found that the experts' production rules contained references to explicit methods, whereas those of the novices did not. They concluded from this that experts have stored in memory schemata that are associated with specific problem types and that these schemata are likely to include appropriate solution methods. The possibility that experts' knowledge helped them focus on the essentials of the problem and to not be distracted by less essential features is suggested by the fact that when asked to identify words in a problem statement that were helpful in deciding how a problem was to be solved, the words selected by experts were a subset of those selected by novices.

Another way in which the knowledge of experts may differ from that of novices is that experts may be able to judge the plausibility of a solution to a problem without working through the steps necessary to solve it precisely. That is to say, an expert may be able to decide whether a solution that has been proposed is the right *type* of solution on the basis of qualitative considerations. A novice is less likely to be able to do this.

That experts have a larger store of domain knowledge than do novices may mean that they can solve, without much thought, problems that will require a lot of thinking on the part of novices. If one overlooks this possibility, one can be misled by the results of studies of expert problem solving that were conducted for the purpose of finding clues to good reasoning. The obvious risk is that of attributing to good reasoning what may have been based largely on knowledge and required little reasoning at all. It has been suggested that the main difference between experts and lay people of comparable educational level may be in the amount of domain knowledge they have at their disposal and not in the way they think (Fischhoff, Slovic, & Lichtenstein, 1982).

Several investigators have emphasized the importance of metaknowledge in expertise. Not only do experts know more about their domain of expertise than do nonexperts, they appear to have a better understanding of the scope and limitations of their knowledge, although they are not immune to the tendency, which appears to be relatively universal, to overestimate how much they know (Odean, 1998). Expert problem solvers appear to be more aware of their own problem-solving processes than are novices (Champagne, Klopfer, & Anderson, 1980), and to give evidence of being better able to manage effectively their own cognitive resources (Schoenfeld, 1983).

That experts have a greater amount of knowledge about a problem domain than do novices permits them to classify problems as to types for which effective approaches are known, to make inferences from problem descriptions that novices are unable to make, to avoid being distracted by uncritical aspects of a problem description, to anticipate the types of solutions that must be obtained, and to judge the plausibility of solutions that are found. A question on which there is less agreement is whether experts differ from novices in ways other than the extent of their domain-specific knowledge bases. Do the processes they use differ in significant ways? Do experts have a more effective collection of domain-independent approaches to problem solving? How do the experts compare with the novices when working in an area that is unfamiliar to both? On these questions the data are not conclusive.

☐ Responsibility for Knowledge

All of us assume certain common knowledge on the part of other people, including strangers, and we find it odd when someone appears to lack some bit of knowledge that we assume everyone has. We are surprised, for example, to encounter an adult resident of an industrialized country who does not know how to use a telephone, or who is unaware that one must pay to ride on a bus, or who believes that potatoes grow on trees.

Of course, what constitutes common knowledge is not very precisely bounded and its edges are fuzzy. We would be less shocked to discover a city dweller who believed that potatoes grow on trees than to find one who is unaware that Wednesday follows Tuesday with some regularity.

Cherniak (1986) notes that society holds individuals responsible for knowing certain things. The principle that ignorance of the law usually is not a defensible excuse for breaking it illustrates the point. Should we take the position that the acquisition of certain types of knowledge is a requirement of rationality, independently of considerations of the law? Or to put the question another way, should we assume that rational people will, by virtue of their rationality, take the responsibility to acquire certain types of knowledge?

One might argue that a person who elects to embark on a particular course of action without making any effort to determine what the outcome of that course, or of alternative courses that could have been chosen, is likely to be is behaving irrationally. Or one might take a similar position with respect to the person who takes one or another side in a dispute without attempting to become informed with respect to the issues involved. We do see it as a requirement of rationality that one acquire, or at least attempt to acquire, certain types of knowledge in particular situations, or so it seems to me. Lack of knowledge—or at least lack of effort to acquire knowledge—can be considered evidence, in some cases, of irrationality; ignorance is not always a justifiable excuse, even when there is no question of whether one has explicitly broken a law.

Dawes (1988) takes the position that ignorance in certain situations is unethical. He illustrates the point by reference to the considerable amount of evidence that the future behavior of individuals, say in academic or job situations, is predicted better by objective data (test scores, actuarial statistics) than by opinions formed from brief unstructured interviews. He argues not only that "it is *unethical* for psychologists who know that unstructured interviews are generally not predictive of future behavior to decide to base a personnel or legal decision on a *particular* unstructured interview or set of interviews," but that it is "even unethical for a psychologist involved in such decision making to remain ignorant of the research literature concerning the invalidity of unstructured interviews—through intellectual laziness or a defensive attribution that the research is somehow 'irrelevant' to his or her particular practice" (p. 270). Strong words, but well said.

The question of what a rational person has a responsibility to learn, and of how that depends on the culture in which the person lives, is complex; the claim I wish to make here is that society has a right to expect its members to learn certain things—barring disabilities that would make it impossible to do so. One can only be expected to form opinions and make decisions within the scope of one's knowledge, but one can be expected to acquire specific types of knowledge and can reasonably be considered irresponsible for failing to make an effort to do so. How difficult the acquisition of specific types of knowledge may be depends, of course, on many factors, not the least of which are the information handling and dissemination capabilities of the society in which one lives.

Brown (1989) has given a fascinating account of how the ways in which information moved through society changed in America during the 18th and 19th centuries, and of the social significance that possession of various types of information had. The overall trend during this period, and indeed at least since the invention of print technology in 15th century, has been for information of all types to become increasingly available to everyone. Knowledge that would have been extremely difficult for the average colonial American to have acquired, and impossible for most 13th century Europeans, is readily available to us from a variety of sources and in several forms. (Brown provides the interesting statistic: in the latter part of the 18th century, a book cost from a day's to a week's wages for a common laborer in the United States.)

Should the requirements of rationality be different in a society in which information is abundant from what they are in a society in which information is scarce? Surely, when information is abundant and easily accessible, ignorance is less easy to excuse than when it is scarce. But when information is abundant, as it is today, one must choose what to pay attention to; there is far too much to permit one to assimilate it all. When information is scarce, as it was in 17th-century America—pre-television, pre-radio, pre-newspaper, pre-public library, pre-Internet, books in limited supply and costing a much larger percentage of a laborer's income—one does not have a selection problem, or at least not one of the same magnitude. When one does have the problem of choice, does one have a responsibility to choose well?

What are the implications of specialization—which seems not to be a matter of choice, given the disparity between what there is to know and the limitations of the individual mind—for rationality? How are we to think about the unhappy, but possibly unavoidable, tendency for the scope of specialties to become increasingly narrow. What are we to make, for example, of the schism that Kline (1980) claims has developed between mathematics and science? "In Bacon's time the concern of mathematicians with physical studies needed no prompting. But today the break from science is factual. In the last one hundred years, a schism has developed between those who would cleave to the ancient and honorable motivations for mathematical activity, the motivations which have thus far supplied the substance and fruitful themes, and those who sailing with the wind investigate what strikes their fancy. Today mathematicians and physical scientists go their separate ways. The newer mathematical creations have little application. Moreover, mathematicians and scientists no longer understand each other, and it is little comfort that, because of the intense specialization, mathematicians do not even understand other mathematicians" (p. 286).

There are examples of areas of science that were once considered relatively independent of each other that have recently been coming together over questions of common interest. The interaction of particle physicists and astronomers, in their mutual quest for information about the origin, early history and destiny of the universe, is a case in point. The discovery of each other by the sciences of the ultrasmall and the ultralarge and their synergetic exploration of questions of cosmology is an especially interesting aspect of the recent history of science.

This being said, however, there can be little doubt that most scientists (as well as most mathematicians) are forced to focus on a very narrow specialty if they are to hope to do original work in their field. And the demands of any given specialty are sufficiently great as to allow relatively little time to devote to learning a lot about specialties other than one's own or about the "larger picture." This is true not only in science and mathematics but more generally. As the amount of knowledge in nearly every field has expanded explosively, individual professionals have felt obliged to focus on ever more narrow subfields in order to remain current.

The need for specializing seems obvious, at least given the limitations of our current educational techniques. Nevertheless, excessive specialization is a serious problem for society. Given that the need for specialization can be expected to become increasingly acute, how are we to ensure that focusing on ever narrower domains does not lead to the development of very limited and biased perspectives? How are we to guard against the possibility that people working in different areas will have less and less to say to each other, that their understanding of each others' perspectives will diminish, along with their basis for common values? What does it mean to be rational in an age of specialization? Is it possible to have a rational society comprised of narrowly-focused specialists who are unable to understand the thinking of people outside their specialties? What obligation do the specialists have to know something about, and to think about, subjects that lie outside their areas of special interest?

Holton (1973) has expressed concern about the divisive and factious effect that increasing specialization can have on society. It can lead, as he puts it, to "increasing atomization of loyalties within the intelligentsia. The writer, the scholar, the scientist, the engineer, the teacher, the lawyer, the politician, the physician—each now regards himself first of all as a member of a separate, special group of fellow professionals to which he gives almost all of his allegiance and energy; only very rarely does the professional feel a sense of responsibility toward, or of belonging to, a larger intellectual community. This loss of cohesion is perhaps the most relevant symptom of the disease of our culture, for it points directly to one of its specific causes" (p. 448).

What should a rational person be expected to know, or to attempt to find out? When should ignorance be seen as irresponsible? These questions are highly relevant to an adequately substantive view of what it means to be rational, and they are not easy to answer. What seems clear however is that rationality involves accepting responsibility for one's own knowledge within the limits of one's capabilities to learn and to know. Ignorance is, in many instances, a lame excuse for opinions and behavior that would reasonably be judged to be irrational in light of information that is readily accessible to those who take the trouble to avail themselves of it.

4 Beliefs

Every human mind is a doctrine factory. (Keyser, 1926, p. 56)

Beliefs are indispensable to us; they play essential roles in our daily lives. Some beliefs we acquire through personal experience, some we adopt as a result of study and reflection, and some we appropriate uncritically from others who happen to hold them. Some are well-founded; others are not. However we get them, and however well or poorly justified they may be, they guide our behavior and, to a great degree, our reasoning as well. It must be the case that, on average, our beliefs are conducive to survival, inasmuch as we, as a species, have survived to the present time. One can make a convincing argument, however, that many problems—personal, national, global—have their roots in unfounded beliefs.

☐ The Nature of Beliefs

What beliefs are, how they are best represented, whether they should be treated as all-or-not-at-all affairs or as varying in degree, how they become established, and how they affect our reasoning are matters of some debate among psychologists and philosophers. Should we admit to the existence of beliefs that cannot be expressed in language? Can we be said to hold beliefs of which we are not aware? How do beliefs originate? How do beliefs affect the quality of one's reasoning; how does the quality of one's reasoning influence one's beliefs?

For present purposes, a belief can be thought of as an assertion that one considers, or would consider if asked to think about it, likely to be true. This is not to claim that all beliefs necessarily are represented as assertions but only that they could be. And by referring to assertions considered likely to be true rather than to assertions considered to be true, I mean to suggest that beliefs are not all-or-nothing affairs but can vary in degree.

Thus conceived, beliefs can differ from each other with respect to many characteristics. They may differ in accuracy, the degree to which they correspond to fact. They may differ in certainty, or the amount of confidence with which they are held. They may be malleable to differing degrees. Some beliefs are closely related in the sense that a change in one would necessitate a change in all; some bear so little relationship to each other that the truth or falsity of each may be considered irrelevant to the truth or falsity of the others. Some beliefs are very significant to the individual who holds them and their modification would have important implications for the individual's basic value system; others are incidental and their truth or falsity is of minor concern.

Explicit versus implicit beliefs

Harman (1986), among others, makes a distinction between explicit beliefs, which are beliefs for which one has explicit mental representations, and implicit beliefs, which can be inferred from one's explicit beliefs. According to some views of rationality, an ideally rational agent holds only *deductively closed* beliefs, beliefs that are "closed under logical implication," which means that anything that is logically implied by beliefs explicitly held by the agent is also believed (Harman, 1995). Presumably this includes beliefs that one does not realize one holds, because one has never thought explicitly of them and is unaware that the beliefs that one does explicitly hold implies them. Harman argues that ordinary rationality does not require deductive closure of beliefs and human limitations preclude it.

Counting implicit beliefs, or what philosophers have sometimes referred to as *dispositional beliefs*, as beliefs is controversial. Goldman (1986), for example, does not count as a belief an assertion to which one would give immediate assent—that fish do not eat eggs and toast for breakfast, say—but about which one had never before thought. Goldman does distinguish between activated and inactivated beliefs, the latter being beliefs in long-term memory when one is not aware of holding them. An assertion like the one about what fish do not eat for breakfast cannot be considered an inactivated belief in the sense of being in long-term memory, because presumably one cannot remember an idea that never before passed through one's mind. Audi (1982, 1985) takes a similar position, making a distinction between having a disposition to believe, which he allows, and dispositionally believing, which he does not. Dennett (1978), on the other hand, holds that there are indefinitely many assertions to which each of us would give immediate assent and that they should be counted as beliefs even though they are not stored explicitly in our memories.

My inclination is to consider such implicit beliefs as real, inasmuch as they can be accessed, just as can explicitly stored beliefs, and used for reasoning purposes in appropriate contexts. Moreover, one can give reasons for implicit beliefs as well as for explicit ones. If I were asked, for example, if I believe there is anyone alive today who is 10 feet tall, I would say no. Apparently I hold the belief that all living people are less than 10 feet tall, although until asked the question (in this case by myself) I was not aware of holding this belief. I certainly do not know for a fact that there is no one alive today who is 10 feet tall; however, I am confident enough that it is the case to be willing to bet on it at relatively large odds. My confidence rests on several considerations. I guess height to be more or less normally distributed around a mean close to 5 feet 6 inches with a standard deviation of perhaps about 6 inches, so a height of 10 feet would be 8 to 10 standard deviations above the mean—not impossible, but highly unlikely. Second, I assume that if there were such a person, it would be so unusual as to be newsworthy, so there is a good chance I would have heard about it. Third, there are reasons, I think, to believe that a height of 10 feet would be anatomically precarious for an organism with the structure of the human body (Haldane, 1928/1956; Thompson, 1917/1961).

Some time after writing the immediately preceding paragraph, it occurred to me to check my surmise, which I did by consulting *Guinness World Records* at www.guinnessworldrecords.com, where I found the claim that the "tallest man in medical history for whom there is irrefutable evidence is Robert Pershing Wadlow," (1918–1940) who measured 8 feet, 11.1 inches shortly before his death. This gave me some reassurance. However, I also learned from Wallechinsky, Wallace, and Wallace (1977, p. 308) that there are several other claimed instances of people (all deceased) who attained heights of 9 feet and a few inches. This discovery decreased the odds somewhat, but not greatly, at which I would wager that there is no one alive who is more than 10 feet tall.

In chapter 2 it was argued that, within the limits of practicality, one should attempt to hold beliefs that are internally consistent. If we include as part of one's belief corpus all that one believes only implicitly or dispositionally, it is too much to ask that one be sure that all such beliefs are consistent. Indeed, it is too much to ask that one even be aware of what they all are. It may happen, however, that when an implicit belief is made explicit, one becomes aware that it is inconsistent with one or more other beliefs that one explicitly holds. In this case, one is obliged, in my view, if the beliefs involved are significant, to try to reconcile the inconsistency, which means modifying either the implicit belief that just became explicit or the old belief(s) with which it is inconsistent. Modifying an implicit belief may be a nontrivial thing to do, inasmuch as it is likely to require modifying the belief(s) from which it is derived.

Degrees of belief

> There is a middle way between certainty and relativism, which corresponds to the critical adherence to rationally motivated belief, held with conviction but open to the possibility of correction. (Polkinghorne, 1998, p. 15)

Given that the evidence for some beliefs is much stronger than the evidence for others, should we not expect a rational agent to hold different beliefs to different degrees? Should it not be a requirement of rationality that the amount of credence one gives to a belief be proportional to the amount of evidential support one has for it? This principle is defended by Carnap (1950/1962), and Hempel (1965) among others. It has found an extreme expression in what Jeffrey (1992) calls *radical Bayesianism*, according to which all beliefs should be represented by probability statements. As to the practical significance of different degrees of belief, Ramsey (1931) suggests that one's degree of belief should be reflected in how willing one is to act on that belief—to act, in other words, as though the belief were true.

Stove (1986) defends a variant of this idea. "Where a conclusion is entailed by one's total evidence, rationality prescribes not only that one *believe* the conclusion: it prescribes a unique *degree* of belief in it, namely a degree of belief which is a fraction 1/1 of one's belief in the evidence.... If, for example, the conclusion has probability = 0.95 in relation to our total evidence, and we are certain of that evidence, rationality prescribes a degree of belief in the conclusion which is a fraction 0.95 of certainty" (p. 209). Stove is insistent that in the case in which a conclusion is merely probable in relation to one's total evidence, it is not enough to meet the requirements of rationality that one believe the conclusion with *some* degree of belief lower than that which the evidence indicates, if one believes the evidence completely and the evidence indicates the conclusion has probability = X, one's degree of belief in the conclusion should be X.

I refer to Stove's position as a variant of the idea that degree of belief should match strength of evidence because he considers the situation that one is certain of the evidence in hand and the evidence is probabilistic in nature. The situation is illustrated by the case in which one's total evidence is that 95% of ravens are black and that Abe is a raven. Rationality dictates, according to this view, that, if one is certain of the evidence, one's degree of belief that Abe is black should be 0.95 of certainty. The question of degree of belief pertains also to situations in which the evidence in hand is of uncertain reliability or open to more than one interpretation, but it is more difficult to be quantitative in such cases.

The idea that the credence one gives to a hypothesis should be proportional to the weight of evidence for it has been referred to as *evidence proportionalism*, and it has its critics. Goldman (1986) rejects the idea on the grounds of unworkability: for one to apply all the evidence available on any given issue would require more or less simultaneous activation of all one's beliefs that are relevant to that issue and this is psychologically impossible. As a matter of fact, Goldman argues, the human cognitive system tends to produce categorical, rather than graded, beliefs.

Harman (1986) too claims that belief tends to be an all-or-not-at-all matter; for practical purposes, we either believe something or we do not. "If one had unlimited powers of record keeping and an unlimited ability to survey ever more complex structures of argument, replies, rebuttal, and so on, it would be rational always to accept things only tentatively as working hypotheses, never ending inquiry. But since one does not have such unlimited powers of record keeping, and has a quite limited ability to survey reasons and arguments, one is forced to limit the amount of inquiry in which one is engaged and one must fully accept most of the conclusions one accepts, thereby ending inquiry. Tentative acceptance must remain a special case of acceptance. It cannot be the general rule" (p. 50). Levi (1980, 1991) also sees beliefs as essentially all-or-none; they may be changed, but while we hold them, we behave as though they were certain, in his view.

A middle-of-the-road position is taken by Lyttleton (1977), who suggests that we tend to accept or reject beliefs in an all-or-not-at-all fashion, but sees this as a reasoning fault that we should attempt to remedy, at least as it applies to our acceptance or rejection of scientific hypotheses. "It seems to be a common defect of human minds that they tend to crave for complete certainty of belief or disbelief in anything. Not only is this undesirable scientifically, but it must be recognized that no such state is obtainable in science. However successful and reliable a theory may be up to any point of time, further data may come along and show a need for adjustment of the theory, while at the other extreme, however little confidence one has in a hypothesis, new data may change the situation" (p. 14). Lyttleton's advice regarding the attitude one should adopt toward any scientific hypothesis is never to let one's estimate of the probability that it is correct get to either one or zero.

My own position is close to that of Lyttleton. We are inclined to accept or reject beliefs in an all-or-not-at-all way, and although doing so may conserve cognitive effort and may suffice for many purposes, it also gets us into difficulties. It makes us behave as though the grounds for many of our beliefs were stronger than they really are and, similarly, it leads us to underestimate—or to discredit entirely—whatever evidence may favor beliefs we do not hold. I want to argue that we may entertain beliefs in an all-or-not-at-all fashion for most everyday purposes, but that we should recognize that doing so is a matter of practical convenience and that when the justifiability of a particular belief is called into question, the all-or-not-at-all perspective is often less appropriate than one that recognizes degrees of certitude.

Failure to recognize degrees of belief can lead to the acceptance of mutually contradictory beliefs. For example, one might believe of each individual ticket in a fair lottery with one million tickets that that particular ticket will not win. On the other hand, one knows that one of those tickets will win, so one knows the conjunction of the individual beliefs to be untrue. Kyburg (1983) uses this example to illustrate the possibility of accepting each of several statements as true while believing the statement "all of these statements are true" to be false.

The only escape from this dilemma is recognition of degrees of belief—of probabilistic beliefs—and in particular acknowledgement of the difference between believing that a ticket has zero chance of winning and believing that it has an extremely small chance of winning. One might argue that such a distinction has no practical significance; one chance in a million is tantamount, for practical purposes, to a probability of zero. And this argument has some force: .000001 is indeed, for practical purposes, very close to 0. But people do buy tickets in million-to-one lotteries, which seems to be fairly compelling evidence that they do not consider their chances of winning to be nil. Of course, people may underestimate the odds against them. They know *someone* will win and they may well find it easier than is reasonable to imagine themselves as that person.

What should determine the strength of belief? The answer that comes immediately to mind is "the weight of the evidence for and against it," but a moment's reflection makes it clear that this will not do. The weight of what evidence? Certainly not all the evidence there is that is relevant to the belief in question. No finite being is likely ever to be aware of all the evidence that exists pertaining to anything. The evidence in hand? But what if that evidence was obtained by a biased search for evidence that supports the belief? And even if the process for gathering information was unbiased and yielded a representative sample of the evidence that exists, who is to decide the degree of relevance that various items of information have and who is to determine the weights that should be assigned?

Deciding how much weight should be given to evidence of various sorts involves a considerable degree of subjective judgment. Consider the question of whether there is intelligence in the universe other than what is to be found on earth. Among scientists, one can find a range of opinions on this question, including the opinion that the answer is not really a matter of opinion: "That other intelligences do not exist is so improbable as to be unworthy of further speculation" (Atkins, 1994, p. 87). The claim that the answer to the question is quite certain rests on assumptions that some people will accept without reservation, and therefore take as compelling evidence for it, but that others will not.

Again one is brought back to one's intuitions. The best one can hope to do, it seems to me, is to attempt to gather evidence that one considers to be relevant in an unbiased way and to weight it as objectively as one can. But having done this, one also must recognize the limitations that we all share in this regard, the likelihood that there is relevant evidence of which one is not aware, the difficulty we have in attaching as much significance to evidence that counts against a favored belief as we attach to evidence that counts for it, the necessary element of subjectivism in assessing relevance and evidentiary strength, and so on. The moral is not that we should not have strong beliefs, but that we should recognize our fallibility as holders of them.

Derivation of beliefs

Beliefs originate primarily in two ways, from direct experience and from instruction. I believe that I am allergic to poison ivy because of the unpleasant consequences of a couple of close encounters with this beautiful but pestiferous vine. I believe that my health would suffer if I were to ingest arsenic, not because I learned this from experience but because someone took the trouble to record this propensity of arsenic, thus making acquiring this belief from experience fortunately unnecessary.

That we are able to learn from the accumulated experiences of previous generations—that we have developed ways of representing knowledge so that it can be preserved, amended, refined, and passed from one generation to the next—is certainly one of the more important distinguishing features of humankind as a species. If each of us could know no more than what we could learn from personal experience, we would be very limited indeed.

But personal experiences and information obtained from others both must be interpreted and evaluated in the light of other things one knows or believes. My belief about the consequences of contact with poison ivy was not fully formed at the first scratch. And beliefs that derive from what others have had to say on various subjects often are a long time in the making.

The way in which a belief came to be what it is is at least as important a determinant of its rationality as is the substance of that belief. If I believe something for no better reason than the fact that someone told me I should do so, you probably would be reluctant to consider this to be an instance of a rational belief, even if you consider it to be well supported by evidence. On the other hand, if I arrive at a belief that you consider to be false, but do so because that belief is consistent with the relevant information that is available to me, you perhaps would not judge my thinking to be irrational simply because the belief at which I arrived is contrary to evidence of which you are aware but I am not.

Some people have held the view, uncomplimentary to humankind as a whole, that the beliefs of most people on many subjects are not well founded, but are simply appropriated uncritically from others. A contrasting view is that most of the beliefs that most of us hold, if not necessarily true, at least function to our benefit. According to one version of this view, we are predisposed to arrive at beliefs that are useful and consistent with our well-being as individuals and as a species. Lycan (1981), who holds this view, suggests that there are certain fundamental—as opposed to derived—rules of inference that we use to arrive at beliefs. Finding out what the rules are is an empirical task, but explaining why we ought to obey those particular rules rather than some others is not. "This [latter] question cannot properly be a request for a *proof* or derivation of the rules from any more fundamental principles, for by hypothesis the rules are themselves fundamental. The question must rather have the force of asking why it is good or desirable or useful for us to use those rules, to operate according to those principles, rather than others" (p. 345).

Lycan's own answer to this question invokes the idea that the cognitive propensities that we as a species have acquired are those that are conducive, given our limited cognitive resources, to the formation of useful beliefs. Useful beliefs are those that promote our survival and well being. Because our cognitive resources are limited, the set of basic principles on which we operate will have to be small and to gain efficiency at the cost of care and detail. We are built, Lycan argues, "to prefer simpler hypotheses to more complex ones because they are easier to work with and afford plenitude of prediction out of parsimonious means" (p. 345). And generally speaking, we do not change our minds without reason, because doing so would be inefficient and confusing.

On this view we would expect certain beliefs to be fairly universal and others to differ among different societies. The belief that one cannot fly simply by willing hard enough to do so, for example, would appear to be useful in any time and place. However, it is easy to think of specific beliefs that would be useful in a nontechnical society that would be dysfunctional in a technical society, and conversely.

Beliefs as causal factors in thinking

> The fact that a conviction is irrational doesn't diminish it; the fact that a probability is subjective doesn't mean it won't influence a decision. (Ekeland, 1993, p. 135)

Given the obvious strong causal connection between beliefs and behavior and the fact that reasoning—whatever else it may be—is a form of behavior, it would be surprising indeed if what we believe did not greatly influence how we reason. Precisely *how* beliefs influence reasoning has been a focus of some attention from researchers.

Baron (1985a, 1991) suggests that certain beliefs can enhance thinking while certain others can inhibit it. Within the former category he lists the following: "that thinking often leads to better results, that difficulties can often be overcome through thinking (rather than, say, through luck), that good thinkers are open to new possibilities and to evidence against possibilities they favor, and that there is nothing wrong (per se) with being undecided or uncertain for a while." Among beliefs that work against good thinking are these: "that changing one's mind is a sign of weakness, that being open to alternatives leads to confusion and despair, that quick decision making is a sign of strength or wisdom, that truth is determined by authority, that we cannot influence what happens to us by trying to understand things and weigh them, and that intuition is the best guide to the making of decisions" (1985a, p. 254). An important part of the teaching of thinking, Baron argues, is promotion of the former types of beliefs and discouragement of the latter.

Baron (1995) also presents evidence that people who believe that two-sided thinking (thinking that considers both sides of a controversial issue) is better than one-sided thinking (thinking that focuses primarily or exclusively on the reasons that support one side of the issue) are more likely to engage in the former. Interestingly, the majority of participants in his study judged one-sided arguments to be superior to two-sided arguments.

Beliefs that children hold about intelligence can influence the way they approach learning tasks. If, for example, children conceive of intelligence as an unchanging property of an individual, they will be motivated to display their intelligence by performing well and to avoid situations in which they would give evidence of lack of intelligence by making wrong responses. On the other hand, if they conceive of intelligence as a collection of skills that can be enhanced as a result of learning, this "incremental" conception will encourage them to attempt to learn not so much for the sake of displaying intelligence as for that of expanding it (Dweck, 1975; Dweck & Bempechat, 1983; Dweck & Elliott, 1983; Dweck & Leggett, 1988; Elliott & Dweck, 1988; Stevenson, Chen, & Lee, 1993; Torgeson & Licht, 1983). Beliefs about the usefulness, or uselessness, of what is being studied (Lampert, 1986; Schoenfeld, 1983) and beliefs about the causes of success and failure on cognitively demanding tasks (Andrews & Debus, 1978; Deci & Ryan, 1985; Dweck, 1975; Reid, 1987) have also been seen as important determinants of the quality of reasoning and of the effort that people are willing to put into improving it.

Beliefs about one's own knowledge—especially about its adequacy or inadequacy in specific domains—can inhibit or stimulate thinking about those domains. Boorstin (1985) points out that discovering the shape of the earth, the continents, and the ocean, was hindered less by ignorance than by the illusion of knowledge. The reference here is to the state of affairs that pertained before the sea-going explorations that accomplished the charting of the earth, but the observation applies much more generally. One is not inclined to ask the kinds of questions that lead to discovery if one believes one already knows the answers. At the other extreme is the possibility of being paralyzed by the belief that one is powerless to have any effect on one's circumstances or the world more generally; the idea that such beliefs can be acquired through early experiences is reflected in the concept of learned helplessness (Abramson, Seligman, & Teasdale, 1978; Dweck, 1975; Diener & Dweck, 1978; Seligman, 1975).

Among the better-documented effects of beliefs on reasoning are a number of phenomena that can be seen as manifestations of what has become known as the *confirmation bias* (Nickerson, 1998). This bias can be characterized in a variety of ways. One manifestation of it is as a tendency to seek and interpret evidence in ways that are supportive of preexisting beliefs. Beliefs that are widely held within a community can, and often do, constrain the reasoning of members of that community. As Himsworth (1986) puts it: "It would seem.... that any idea that comes to be held in common by a group of men will, *ipso facto*, acquire an ascendancy over their thought processes. Thereby, it is translated from the status of a concept to be considered in the light of the evidence to that of a belief which it is morally incumbent upon them to accept" (p. 81).

That beliefs influence reasoning in numerous ways can hardly be doubted, but just as surely, reasoning must influence beliefs. In particular, we must assume, reasoning well should help one arrive at true beliefs (although, for a contrary opinion, see Stich, 1990). There is a problem here, however, in figuring what is cause and what is effect. The quality of one's reasoning must be judged within the framework of the individual's belief system. What looks like careful insightful reasoning as judged within the frame of reference of one belief system may appear to be irrational or bizarre as judged within another, and conversely. On the other hand, the beliefs one holds are, to a large degree, a consequence of the quality of the reasoning that has produced them. We seem to be travelling in a small circle, but this may simply reflect the reality of the tight coupling between beliefs and thought.

Schwartz (1997) points out that ideas can permeate a culture and have profound effects on people's beliefs and behavior, and that this is the case for false ideas as well as true ones. He notes how, if specific ideas (e.g., about effects of aging on performance, about gender differences in mathematical ability, about race and intelligence) become part of the prevailing belief systems within a culture, they can, by affecting policies and practices, be causal agents in their own confirmation. Eccles and Robinson (1985) make the thought-provoking argument that human goals and actions are greatly influenced by our beliefs about ourselves, by the "sort of being" we think we are. "Indeed, to a striking degree the very character of laws, governments, educational institutions, and international relations has depended historically on fundamental notions about the nature of human nature" (p. 3).

☐ Justification of Beliefs

> The central problem of epistemology is the first-person problem of what to believe and how to justify one's beliefs. (Nagel, 1986, p. 69)

"Warranted belief," one definition goes, "is what a person should believe, given the available information. Thus, warranted belief is rational" (Frick, 1996, p. 384). Presumably most people want to hold warranted beliefs. Possibly, as Kuhn (1992) contends, generating justifications for beliefs is the most important way in which most people use higher-order thinking. But what constitutes a warrant? What justifies the holding of a particular belief?

Belief justification cannot be simply a matter of the truth or falsity of the beliefs in question; clearly it is possible to hold false beliefs for good reasons and to hold true beliefs for poor ones. Or to make the point in other words, a belief can be true without being justified, and because a belief is baseless does not necessarily mean that it is false. Many beliefs that once were consistent with the scientific understanding of the day are now known to be false, but we would not deny that people who held them on the strength of their scientific credibility held them for good reasons. We would say, perhaps, that such beliefs once were justified, but no longer are. On the other hand, if I hold a belief that happens to be true—say that world climate is warming as a consequence of human behavior is basically correct (assuming for the sake of argument that it is so)—but I believe it for the simple reason that an environmental activist of my acquaintance claims it to be so, should this belief be considered justified? If I have made no effort to examine the evidence and attempt to understand the arguments pro and con, am I entitled to claim that my personal belief with respect to this matter—even given that it is shared by many knowledgeable people—is justified? Latent in this question is the distinction between a belief being justified by evidence and the holder of a belief being justified in holding that belief by virtue of being aware of and accepting that evidence.

But one might argue that there may be good reasons for holding a belief apart from any evidence of its truth that may be at hand—that it is comforting, that it permits one to think well of one's friends or acquaintances, that it helps one to lead a good life or to preserve one's sanity. I find this argument quite compelling, but am inclined to consider such reasons for holding a belief to be non-rational—not irrational, but other than rational. I like Swinburne's (1983) definition of a rational belief as a belief that is justified for epistemological reasons—reasons that concern the probability that it is true.

The question of how beliefs are justified is also different from that of how they came to be formed. Some philosophers have held that the study of belief formation is the proper focus of psychology while consideration of matters of belief justification is the concern of epistemology (Carnap, 1937; Reichenbach, 1938). Although the distinction between belief formation and belief justification is clearly a valid one—who can deny the possibility of forming unjustified beliefs?—the defensibility of a sharp demarcation between the domains of psychology and epistemology is less clear. The probability that a particular belief will be formed is not, one hopes, completely independent of its logicality and evidentiary justification. And although justification may be primarily a matter of satisfying certain rules of evidence and inference, the question of what rules are to be followed is a matter of human judgment. In any case, the problem of evaluation of beliefs—of deciding what beliefs are warranted, of determining what *should* of *should not* be believed in any particular circumstance—is highly relevant to any inquiry into what it means to be rational.

Descartes's principle of universal doubt

> That nobody is *really* a skeptic—*even* while philosophizing—becomes clear if you watch what we philosophers do, not what we say. (Shatz, 1994, p. 268)

Skepticism has a long history and has been expressed in many forms. As an articulated philosophy of knowledge, it goes back at least to classical Greece. The idea that nothing can be known with certainty beyond what can be experienced directly is associated with the school of the Academics, and the suspending of judgment on questions of the nature of reality was made a virtue by the Pyrrhonians (Goldman, 1986).

This philosophy was expressed in a memorable way by Rene Descartes (1641/1950), who argued that the proper point of departure for the establishment of correct beliefs is universal—or nearly universal—doubt. He attempted to apply the axiomatic deductive approach of mathematics to all knowledge, claiming that the proper way to build knowledge was to start by doubting all that could be doubted and to build an epistemological edifice on the foundation of those self-evident truths that legitimately could be considered axiomatic. The recognition of some truths as self evident was essential to avoid the black hole of irremediable nihilism, the position that nothing can be known. Albert (1985) sums up his epistemology this way: "Basically, all truth is attainable through the joint action of self-evident intuition and necessary deduction" (p. 29).

Descartes's confidence in intuition, especially his own, was matched by his disdain for the traditional instructional methods of imparting knowledge to the young. One cannot help being impressed by the kind of ego that would permit a man, after receiving the best education his society had to offer, to declare "that he had derived no other benefit from his studies than the conviction of his utter ignorance and profound contempt for the systems of philosophy then in vogue" (Turnbull, 1929/1956, p. 129).

Hersh (1997) points out that Descartes ignored his own advice in his work in mathematics. Athough he embraced the Euclidean ideal of starting from self-evident axioms and proceeding by infallible deductions in his discussion of method in *Discourse on Method, Optics, Geometry, and Meteorology* (1637), he ignored it in his treatment of geometry. "It is strange that in the vast body of writing about Descartes accumulated in three centuries, almost no one seems to have called attention to this bizarre misfit—Euclidean certainty boldly advertised in the *Method* and shamelessly ditched in the *Geometry*....Maybe philosophers don't read the *Geometry*, and mathematicians don't read the *Method*" (p. 113). And perhaps total self-consistency is too much to expect even from the giants. Hersh notes too that Descartes was mistaken in his mathematics on several points, a fact that discredits his claim of certainty.

Related to Descartes's principle of universal doubt, but not quite as extreme, is the idea that all the beliefs one holds should be evaluated critically. Commenting on courses that are intended to teach critical thinking, Hatcher (1985) suggests that the goal should be to teach students to evaluate their own beliefs and those of others critically, before endorsing or acting upon them. He points out that this can be difficult, that it may involve the unpacking of arguments, the identifying of premises and conclusions, the detection of hidden assumptions or presuppositions, the disambiguation of language, and the determination of whether the beliefs or conclusions of interest are adequately supported by the premises from which they are derived. Reasonably held beliefs, he contends, are conclusions of arguments that have strong logical support.

Shermer (2002b) considers skepticism to be a vital part of science. "Science is a specific way of analyzing information with the goal of testing claims....The process is a constant interaction of making observations, drawing conclusions, making predictions, and checking them against evidence" (pp. 18, 19). He argues, however, that skepticism is to be indulged in moderation. Pure skepticism, taken to an extreme, cannot stand, because to be skeptical about everything is to be skeptical of one's own skepticism. Or to put it another way, the position that no statements are true or false, or that there is no such thing as truth, is self-defeating, because to take that position is to accept the idea that there is at least one thing that is true—namely the position itself—and one counterexample is enough to show the general claim that nothing is true is false.

Skepticism in moderation was also counseled by Hume. Adler (1981) approvingly describes Hume's position on the subject as consisting "in an ever-present tincture or tinge of doubt that should accompany all—or, if not all, most—of the judgments we make concerning what is true or false. It should arise from our acknowledgment of the infirmities—and the consequent fallibility—of the human mind. It holds a middle ground between what Hume calls excessive skepticism at one extreme and excessive dogmatism at the other, a dogmatism that claims certitude and infallibility about matters in which neither is attainable" (p. 40). Adler follows this description of Hume's attitude with his own view that one should adopt a form of skepticism that does not challenge the objectivity of truth, but recognizes the fallibility of human judgments and the rarity of beliefs about which one can be certain.

Alternative views

> We are, all of us....much more credulous creatures than we perhaps like to think. Even the most skeptical have to take many things on faith. (Young, 1978, p. 252)

Descartes's dictum, as well as less extreme forms of skepticism, has been rejected by some philosophers, notably Peirce and Quine, in favor of the idea that one should, for the most part, take the majority of one's belief's for granted (Cherniak, 1986). Swinburne (1996) expresses a similar view: "it is a basic principle of rationality, which I call the principle of credulity, that we ought to believe that things are as they seem to be (in the epistemic sense) unless and until we have evidence that we are mistaken....If you say the contrary—never trust appearances until it is proved that they are reliable—you will never have any beliefs at all. For what would show that appearances are reliable, except more appearances?" (p. 131).

Most psychologists, I assume, would reject the principle of universal doubt as a practical impossibility. We really have no choice but to accept many things on faith. The risk is that we will be misled to believe things that are not true, but to refuse to believe anything for which one lacks ironclad evidence is to make it impossible to learn from others or from the storehouse of accumulated human knowledge. There is the possibility, as Richards (1996) argues, that most of us, most of the time, will hold confused or wrong beliefs, at least in subjects in which we lack expertise. But inasmuch as we cannot be experts in everything, we have no choice but to rely on others for guidance regarding what we should believe on specific topics.

If we did not do this, we could not learn from others, because such learning is based on believing. Wittgenstein (1972) puts it this way: "I believe what people transmit to me in a certain manner. In this way I believe geographical, chemical, historical facts, etc. That is how I *learn* the sciences" (p. 25). This is not to say, of course, that one should never doubt what one is taught; but if one doubts *everything* one is taught, there is little hope of learning anything. Of course, one has the problem of deciding who is to be believed and who is not. But, generally speaking, we tend to believe people that we assume know what they are talking about and have no reason to wish to deceive us.

The role that Descartes gives to self-evident truths as the foundation on which beliefs were to be constructed has also been challenged. Albert (1985) aggressively attacks the philosophy of *foundationalism*. No belief, in his view, is self-evidently true and beyond critical evaluation. His criticist philosophy holds that knowledge progresses by the construction and criticism of ideas and that the criticism of *all* ideas is a moral obligation.

Opposing the view that all beliefs need to be justified is the view, sometimes known as *fideism*, according to which the justification of all beliefs is not possible; some beliefs, according to this view, must be taken as givens—accepted on faith. Hauptli (1995) distinguishes between fideists and justificatory rationalists, and notes that the former accept a limitation on human reason that the latter reject. In rejecting the fideists' position that the limitations of human reason dictate that certain beliefs must be accepted uncritically as basic and unchallengeable, justificatory rationalists obligate themselves to show that their beliefs are indeed justified. Hauptli points out that this demand opens justificatory rationalists to the question of how to justify their commitment to their rational standard without begging the question. One possible response to this question, he notes, is to redefine the rationalistic position so as to require justification for all beliefs, theories, etc, except this belief in the necessity for justification, which, of course, weakens the position considerably—if there can be one exception to the general rule, why should there not be others?

Judging the rationality of beliefs

> [R]ationality of belief involves two aspects: support by reasons that make the belief credible, and generation by a process that reliably produces true beliefs. (Nozick, 1993, p. 176)

How, in view of the range of opinions that have been expressed on the roles of doubt and trust in their formation and retention, are we to judge the rationality of beliefs? What are we to make, say, of Aristotle's belief that planetary bodies move in circular orbits because the circle is the perfect curve, a belief that persisted among astronomers until Kepler was able to demonstrate that the assumption of elliptical orbits would lead to a useful simplification of the Copernican theory of planetary motion? Or what do we say to the opposition among astronomers to Galileo's discovery in 1610 of four of the moons of Jupiter, on the grounds that the number of bodies circling the Earth (or Sun) had been assumed to equal the number of openings (seven) in the human head (Asimov, 1976)? What should we think of Euler's belief that both 1/0 and 2/0 are infinite, and that 2/0 is twice as large a 1/0? (Kline, 1980). Or, coming closer to our own age, how do we judge the belief of the editor of a prominent Philadelphia newspaper who, in 1894, "cautioned his readers not to converse by phone with ill persons for fear of contracting contagious diseases" (Marvin, 1988, p. 81)?

It is very easy to be uncharitable in judging the rationality of beliefs that once were held but no longer are. It is all too easy to forget that beliefs should be judged in terms of what people could reasonably be expected to know at the time. James Ussher, known to posterity as Bishop Ussher, and remembered primarily as the cleric who, in 1664, set the time of creation at 6:00 p.m. on October 22, 4004 BC, has been the subject of intense ridicule for propounding such a view. But, as Gould (1993) has pointed out, Ussher was a scholar—quite probably more so than many of his modern-day detractors—working within the accepted knowledge of his time and reaching conclusions not greatly different from those reached by other scholars among his contemporaries.

Gorst (2001), who has engagingly told the story of how Ussher arrived at his estimate of the moment of creation, notes that a later survey of works of the period found some 128 different dates for the event, ranging over three millennia. What set Ussher's estimate apart from those of many of his contemporaries was the painstaking research on which it was based—before the discovery of geological strata and the fossil records they contain, of the process of radioactive decay and the atomic clock it provides, and of numerous other discoveries that made possible the estimates of the ages of the earth and universe that are generally accepted today. Ussher spent 20 years, during a time of uncertainty and civil upheaval, working on his *The Annals of the World*, a heroic attempt to give a comprehensive account of the history of the world from the moment of creation to 70 AD. Gorst points out that in the course of this effort, he amassed a library of some 10,000 volumes—a remarkable feat in itself in view of the fact that at the outset of his quest, the library of Trinity College, his alma mater, contained the grand total of 40 volumes.

The Romans drained their swamps on the strength of the fact that people who lived near them tended to experience a certain type of illness more often than those who did not; they believed that the illness was caused by the bad air the swamps produced. In fact the illness, malaria, was determined much later to be caused by a protozoan transmitted by mosquitoes, which bred in the swamps. The swamps were drained for the wrong reason, but the action had the desired effect of reducing the incidence of the disease. The Romans' belief about the cause of the illness was not true, or, at best, only partially true. Does that make it irrational? But the belief led to effective action. Does that make it rational?

What about the Romans' action, as distinct from their belief? Was it rational? Suppose we judge the rationality of the draining of the swamps by Clarke's (1985) dictum: "A belief not supported by present evidence or by evidence which could be obtained cannot itself provide a basis for justifying an action as itself rational" (p. 32). To what extent should we consider the belief in bad swamp air to be supported by evidence at hand at the time? Surely it would be unreasonable of us to condemn their belief on the grounds that evidence of the role of mosquitoes in transmitting illness could have been obtained had they looked for it. Clarke makes a distinction between justifying actions on the basis of their rationality and doing so on the basis of their practicality: "What ought to have been done depends on what *in fact* were the relevant circumstances and what consequences the means had; what is rational depends on what was *believed* to have been the circumstances and the consequences of the means" (p. 33). Although in the case of the Roman swamps, their draining appears to have been the right action both in terms of what ought to have been done and what was rational, given the beliefs of the day, Clarke argues that this convergence does not always occur: "Since beliefs can often be mistaken, 'ought' and 'rational' can be used to arrive at conflicting assessments of a past action" (p. 34).

Belief justification and truth

It was noted above that for a belief to be justified is not the same as for a belief to be true. It seems reasonable to expect, however, that, other things equal, beliefs that are justified are more likely to be true than are beliefs that are not justified—or that beliefs that are justified are likely to be closer to the truth, on average, than are beliefs that are not justified. At least I find it easier to make that assumption than any conflicting alternative. Presumably, the primary motivation for wishing to justify beliefs is to increase the likelihood of holding beliefs that are true.

Some writers have taken the position that most of the beliefs that people hold must be true or else we would not have survived as a species (Goldman, 1986; Lycan, 1988; Millikan, 1984). Papineau (1987) argues that inasmuch as true beliefs are biologically advantageous, natural selection would have ensured the survival of habits of thought that correspond to deductively valid steps, which is to say habits that would have produced true new beliefs from true old beliefs. Adler (1981) supports a similar perspective in contending that we are committed to the view that we can discriminate between what is true and what is false, and our behavior is grounded in that commitment.

Certainly survival depends on possession of *some* true beliefs, or, to put it the other way round, survival would be seriously threatened by certain *false* beliefs. If all of us suddenly acquired the belief that we could defy the laws of gravity with impunity, the species would undoubtedly suffer a setback. But the fact that we can easily think of false beliefs that would be threats to survival does not prove the conjecture that survival of the species to this point has depended on most of our beliefs being true. The claim that true beliefs are, in general, more conducive to survival than are false ones is not universally accepted. Stich (1990) has made an extensive argument against it. To establish the plausibility of his position he hypothesizes two systems, an overly cautious one that leaps to the conclusion that danger is present on slight evidence and another that waits for more conclusive data. The first system may entertain more false beliefs than the second, but it may survive longer because it is less likely to make the more risky of the two possible types of misclassifications.

The association of true beliefs with rationality has not always been seen as the basis of the survival value of such beliefs. Nozick (1993) points out that two themes relating to the question of what constitutes rational belief permeate the philosophical literature. "First that rationality is a matter of reasons. A belief's rationality depends upon the reasons for holding that belief.... Second, that rationality is a matter of reliability. Does the process or procedure that produces (and maintains) the belief lead to a high percentage of true beliefs?" (p. 64). Neither theme alone, Nozick suggests, exhausts our notion of rationality: "Reasons without reliability seem empty, reliability without reasons seems blind" (p. 64). Reasons may themselves be beliefs and thus in need of support, which means that rational justification of a belief may involve justification at more than one level. Braithwaite (1953/1974) makes a similar point in contending that the reasonableness of a derived belief depends on the reasonableness of the beliefs from which it was inferred.

Judging one's own beliefs

How should one judge the rationality of one's own beliefs? Each of us has many of them—about the way the world works, about ourselves, about ethics and morality, about rationality, about questions of origin, purpose, destiny and other topics that have engaged philosophers for as long as we have any record of the subjects of their thought. We must have beliefs; we could not function without them. Clearly, not all beliefs are equally justified. Surely we must agree with Audi (1985) that a belief, or action predicated on a belief, should not be deemed rational if the person who holds it has enough evidence against it to dissuade a rational person from holding it; but how do we escape the circularity of this position? How are we to judge the justifiability of beliefs from a rational point of view? Audi's answer to this question is that beliefs are justified by being *well-grounded*, either directly, say through an appropriate personal experience or because of the self-evident nature of a proposition believed, or indirectly via other beliefs that are derivable, at least in part, from directly justified ones. Well-groundedness, Audi notes, is a criterion that admits of degrees, so a belief, an action, or a desire can be rational without necessarily being maximally rational.

Inwagen (1994), a philosopher, puts the problem of judging one's own beliefs this way. "Philosophers do not agree about anything to speak of. And why not? How can it be that equally intelligent and well-trained philosophers can disagree about the freedom of the will or nominalism or the covering-law model of scientific explanation when each is aware of all of the arguments and distinctions and other relevant considerations that the others are aware of? How can we philosophers possibly regard ourselves as justified in believing anything of philosophical significance under these conditions?" (p. 41). Inwagen points out that the dilemma is not unique to philosophers. How, he asks, can one consider a political position that one holds to be justified, given the knowledge that there are people at least as well-informed and as capable of evaluating arguments as oneself who hold diametrically opposing views? "How, then, can I maintain that the evidence and arguments I can adduce in support of my beliefs actually justify those beliefs? If this evidence and these arguments are capable of that, then why aren't they capable of convincing these other people that these beliefs are correct?" (p. 44). Good questions indeed.

Thouless (1947) notes the importance, as a first step in dealing with our own prejudices—which we usually do not see as prejudices—of recognizing the fact of their existence and of the likelihood that they play a large part in the shaping of our opinions. He advocates being distrustful of our own judgments and comparing them carefully with those of people who disagree with us, especially in matters in which our emotions are strongly involved. This seems to me to be good and useful advice, and advice that it is possible to follow, within limits. This is not to argue that we can really weigh our own beliefs with complete impartiality, but we can, perhaps, learn to do better than we typically do in this regard.

Nagel makes a similar case for the careful consideration of alternatives as a means of assessing one's beliefs. "Pursuit of truth requires more than imagination: it requires the generation and decisive elimination of alternative possibilities until, ideally, only one remains, and it requires a habitual readiness to attack one's own convictions. That is the only way real belief can be arrived at" (p. 9).

After discussing a number of "the various foolish opinions to which mankind are prone," Russell (1950) gives some advice to anyone who wishes to avoid them. The reader is referred to the original for the full benefit of this advice. Among the rules that Russell recommends, however, are the following:

- If the matter is one that can be settled by observation, make the observation yourself.

- If an opinion contrary to your own makes you angry, that is a sign that you are subconsciously aware of having no good reason for thinking as you do.... So whenever you find yourself getting angry about a difference of opinion, be on your guard; you will probably find, on examination, that your belief is going beyond what the evidence warrants.

- A good way of ridding yourself of certain kinds of dogmatism is to become aware of opinions held in social circles different from your own.

- Be very wary of opinions that flatter your self-esteem.

An approach that Keyser (1926), among others, has suggested is to expose one's ideas to external criticism. It may be too much to ask that one who holds a belief criticize it effectively oneself, but it seems not unreasonable to expect a willingness to expose one's beliefs to the criticism of people who do not hold them. It is very easy to fool oneself into thinking that one is doing just this, when in fact what one is doing is seeking further support for the belief in question. Thus, when I ask for a candid critique of a favored belief from someone who is not competent to provide such a critique, or who is not disposed to argue against it, or who, I know, would be reluctant to tell me to my face what nonsense he thinks it is, I am not really exposing my belief to the kind of criticism it may deserve, although I may fool myself into supposing that I am.

How do we know that the beliefs that most deserve to survive criticism do so? In fact we do not; all we know is that ideas that have survived are survivable and those that have not are not. We cannot rule out the possibility that better ideas than those that have survived have been discarded or forgotten, unless we wish to make survival a condition of being among the best, as a matter of definition. C. S. Lewis (1955) used the term "chronological snobbery" to refer to the uncritical acceptance of the intellectual climate of one's own age and the automatic discrediting of whatever has gone out of date. "You must find out why it went out of date. Was it ever refuted (and if so by whom, where, and how conclusively) or did it merely die away as fashions do? If the latter, this tells us nothing about its truth or falsehood. From seeing this, one passes to the realization that our own age is also 'a period,' and certainly has, like all periods, its own characteristic illusions. They are likeliest to lurk in those widespread assumptions which are so ingrained in the age that no one dares to attack or feels it necessary to defend them" (p. 207).

I think it must be admitted that it is exceedingly difficult, perhaps impossible, to judge fairly and objectively the rationality of one's own beliefs. As Alcock (1996) puts it, "In maintaining a healthy self-image, it is difficult to view our own beliefs as silly, irrational, chauvinistic, prejudiced, or unjustified; and we invest considerable effort in maintaining a belief system that is credible to ourselves" (p. 67). But if it is not possible to be completely fair and objective in assessing the rationality of one's own beliefs, there surely are degrees of closed-mindedness and there is a difference between blind dogmatism and being willing to admit that one might be wrong and to try, at least, to understand opposing views.

Justification criteria

> [T]o commend an apple or an action is one thing, to give your reasons for commending it is another; to reject a suggestion as untenable is one thing, to give your reasons for rejecting it is another. (Toulmin, 1958, p. 33)

According to the view generally known as classical rationalism, every belief should be justified through reference ultimately to an unshakable foundation, and that in order to avoid circularity or infinite regress, it is necessary to accept certain truths as given or revealed and beyond doubt. Albert (1985) argues that this view is indefensible, because what is to be considered given must be decided and any such decision is arbitrary: "all certainties in knowledge are self-made, and thus worthless for comprehending reality. In other words, through dogmatization we can at any point achieve certainty, by immunizing any particular component of our convictions against every possible criticism, thus securing it from the risk of failure" (p. 40).

The only assertions that are necessarily true and therefore certain are analytic assertions, but they do not provide grounding for empirical knowledge about the world. Albert defends the idea that foundationalism should be replaced with commitment to critical examination. The cost of this trade is the giving up of "self-produced certainties," but the gain is "the prospect of ever more closely approximating truth—though without ever attaining certainty—through trial and error, through tentative construction of testable theories and critical discussion in the light of relevant points of view" (p. 46).

Identification of analytic assertions as the only assertions that are necessarily true calls to mind a distinction that has been made, by Kant among others, between beliefs that are justified by experience (beliefs about the physical world and the way it works) and beliefs that are justified by reason alone (beliefs about logical or mathematical relationships—that 1+1=2—for example). While this distinction seems a compelling one, a problem arises in applying it in specific cases inasmuch as people differ with respect to what beliefs they are willing to consider to be justified by reason alone—to be self-evident—to use a well-worn term.

Wittgenstein (1969) also argues the futility of attempting to justify all beliefs. The very idea of belief justification presupposes justificatory criteria, which themselves beg justification. In other words, any justification must rest on other beliefs which themselves either must be justified or accepted without justification. At some point the regressive process of justification must end.

Whether or not we should feel compelled to justify established beliefs that are not under attack, there clearly are times when one must decide whether to accept or reject, whether to retain or discard, or to modify, a belief. For such occasions, there is the question of what the criteria should be in terms of which beliefs are judged.

Belief justification and logic

Justification rules cannot be derived from formal logic alone, at least if it is assumed that the rules used to form or justify beliefs should promote the formation and justification of true beliefs. This is pointed out clearly by Goldman (1986). Rules of logic are useful to belief formation, because they make explicit the implicative relationships among assertions, but they are not sufficient to the task of belief justification, because they ensure only that a conclusion is true *if* the premises from which it is drawn are true *and* the inferences are valid. When one shows that a new belief is logically implied by certain old beliefs, one has shown only that the new belief is sure to be true if the old ones are. Furthermore, the new belief contains nothing really new, inasmuch as it was implicit in the old beliefs already. If they are to have any practical value, belief justification rules should permit the justification of beliefs that are not implicated by old ones, but are really new.

Goldman argues that beliefs are justified or not depending on whether they were acquired by suitable elementary processes. The processes he has in mind are to be distinguished from algorithms, heuristics and other learnable techniques, which Goldman refers to collectively as *methods*. Methods, in his view, may be useful in providing secondary justification, but suitable processes are essential to primary justification. Suitable processes are those that yield a high ratio of true beliefs. "Beliefs are deemed justified when (roughly) they are caused by processes that are reliable in the world as it is presumed to be. Justification-conferring processes are ones that would be reliable in worlds like the presumptively actual world, that is, in normal worlds" (p. 108).

Goldman's use of the word "presume" here shows a sensitivity to the fact that we cannot check beliefs against the "way things really are" because we cannot know, for sure, how they really are. The best we can do is compare beliefs against the way things are presumed to be. But this is circular; what are presumptions but beliefs? If we choose to ignore that difficulty, we at least have to face the question of whose presumptions should be consulted. And who should make this selection, or specify the criteria on which it should be made? And who....? Again, we find ourselves forced back to our own intuitions. There is no escaping this, in my view. That is not a regretful observation, but simply another way of saying that all of us are responsible, in the final analysis, for our own beliefs.

Rationality requires only that we do as well as can be expected, given our limitations. This is not to suggest that satisfying this criterion is a natural or easy thing to do. But we are not completely in the dark as to what determines the reliability of belief-forming and belief-justifying processes. A process that takes competing explanatory hypotheses into consideration, for example, will be more reliable—will yield a higher truth ratio—than one that does not, so only the former would be considered suitable for belief justification. Of course, given that no human process is 100% reliable, false beliefs will sometimes be justified; this would be the case when a false belief is yielded by a process that generally yields true beliefs.

Reliable processes are, in Goldman's view, an antidote to error, but not necessarily an antidote to ignorance. This is because, while the beliefs that reliable processes produce are likely to be true, they are also likely to be few in number. The antidote to ignorance is not reliability, but intellectual power, cognitive processes that are capable of yielding a relatively large number of truths. This distinction between powerful processes and reliable processes, with the former being associated with belief generation and the latter with belief justification, is reminiscent of the distinction that is often made between creative and critical thinking. It is a distinction that emerges in several guises in the literature on reasoning. The distinctions between hypothesis generation and hypothesis testing in science and between conjecture and proof in mathematics are two variants of it.

Belief justification and utility

Another perspective on belief justification is given by Nozick (1993), who proposes two fundamental rules to govern rational belief: "do not believe any statement less credible than some incompatible alternative—the intellectual component—but then believe a statement only if the expected utility of doing so is greater than that of not believing it—the practical component" (p. 176). Nozick considers several other possible rules, but these are the basic ones. Unpacking these rules—probing their possible meanings—would take us into a number of vexed issues: What are the determinants—what should be the determinants—of credibility? What constitutes incompatibility? What notion of utility should be used?

There are two aspects of these rules that deserve emphasis: the importance that is attached to consistency and to desirability. The first rule explicitly prohibits entertaining incompatible beliefs of unequal credibility (although it does not rule out the holding of conflicting beliefs of equal credibility). The second one legitimizes desirability of a belief as a criterion for acceptance. Nozick argues that the latter criterion should be applied only to potential beliefs that satisfy the first rule—those that are not less credible than any incompatible statement, so he is not making desirability, or utility, the only, or even the primary, criterion; but he does see it as an important one. "Thus we have a two-stage procedure: the first weeds out lesser credibility values, and the second determines belief among the statements that remain by considering the consequences (broadly conceived) of such belief" (p. 86).

Nozick's rules are designed to guard one against holding beliefs that have low credibility (relative to incompatible alternatives) or credible beliefs that have low utility (relative to the utility of having no belief on a given matter). They do not specify the conditions under which one should feel compelled to believe anything in particular. One might argue that they imply that one should believe something, say h, if there is not a more credible statement that is incompatible with h *and* the expected utility of believing h is not less than that of having no belief about h, but inasmuch as there is nothing to rule out the possibility that the expected utility of having no belief about h will always be higher than that of believing h, one is left with the (admittedly remote) possibility of having no beliefs at all.

Nozick seems to be comfortable with this "screening out" or "filtering" quality of his rules. "It is clear that many things are irrational to believe. It is less clear that some beliefs are so credible that they are mandated by rationality, so that it is irrational not to hold them when you hold no belief about the matter at all. In some contexts a person might, without irrationality, impose more stringent standards of belief than others do and hence hold no belief where they hold some" (p. 87). The second rule permits one to decide, strictly on utilitarian grounds, not to believe something—which is not to say *to* believe the opposite. "Just as someone might avoid investigating certain subjects in a given society because of what he predicts will be the harmful social consequences of the results—some true belief but also much distortion and misapplication—so too someone might avoid believing something because of the effect he predicts this belief actually will have upon himself, upon his character and mode of behavior. This would not require him to hold the opposite belief, just not hold this one" (p. 93).

Justificatory argument

An account of rational belief put forth by Toulmin (1958) is built around a "jurisprudential analogy." Any assertion or claim that is meant to be taken seriously must be justifiable with an appropriate argument. Although we may sometimes be willing to accept a claim without insisting that its supporting argument be made explicit, the merits of the claim are understood to be the merits of the argument that *could be made* in its support. "Whatever the assertion may be.... we can challenge the assertion, and demand to have our attention drawn to the grounds (backing, data, facts, evidence, considerations, features) on which the merits of the assertion are to depend. We can, that is, demand an argument; and a claim need be conceded only if the argument which can be produced in its support proves to be up to standard" (p. 11).

An argument that is used to justify an assertion need not, in Toulmin's view, reflect the process of reasoning that led one to accept the assertion as true in the first place. It may do that, but it need not, and, in general, it probably will not. The process of constructing a justificatory argument—considering various possibilities, ruling some out on the basis of evidence, and converging on the one that the evidence most strongly supports—is the same whether the subject is physics, mathematics, ethics, law or some everyday matter. Justificatory arguments get their force from the quality of the evidence they muster. The stronger the evidence, the stronger the claim that is justified.

But if claims are to be justified by appropriate arguments, the problem presents itself of evaluating arguments that are used in this justificatory capacity. To decide whether a claim is justified, one must evaluate the argument that is advanced in its support. How do we tell whether the argument that is advanced to justify a claim is itself justified? Evaluating an argument requires judgment as does evaluating a belief; we seem simply to have moved the problem to another place, or dressed it with a different coat. Argument evaluation is a topic about which there is a substantial literature. Suffice it to note here that, generally speaking, justifying arguments involves justifying some claims in terms of other claims and that to avoid the problem of infinite regress one invariably finds it necessary to accept some claims as given; and the problem then becomes that of finding agreement on what should be taken as given and what should not.

There are many positions that can be—have been—taken with respect to justification of beliefs. Several of them—skepticism, fideism, justificatory rationalism, qualified and unqualified realism, naturalism—are discussed at length by Hauptli (1995). The range of opinions on what rationality demands by way of justification of beliefs is wide. The issue has many facets, but the key disagreement among theorists, as Hauptli puts it, "concerns the question of the rational status or standing of our rational standards—these theorists offer different responses to the question 'must our acceptance of the rational standard itself be subject to the same strictures which the rational maxim places upon our acceptance of our other theories, beliefs, and commitments?'" (p. 70). It seems unlikely that a universally agreed upon answer to this question will emerge from the debate anytime soon.

Hauptli concludes from a consideration of their arguments that proponents of the various positions regarding justification of beliefs are all in the same boat with respect to their inability to convince others of the merits of their position: "since each theorist must recognize that the others may not accept the beginning points of their therapy argument [an argument that offers an antidote to opposing views], each theorist must either attempt to provide an independent and nonquestion-begging rationale for his or her preference or beg the question" (p. 175). Hauptli argues that the first option is not really an option for anyone, so everyone in this boat must end up begging the question.

Hauptli goes on to qualify this assessment of the situation slightly, by contending that one's choice of perspective is not completely arbitrary, but may be made on pragmatic grounds. "The theory which best resolves the problems or enables the individuals in question to achieve their aims will be judged preferable, and this judgment is not made arbitrarily" (p. 189). Further, since people share many problems and aims, and one purpose of theorizing is to solve these problems and achieve these aims, "it seems that there will indeed be a weakly independent evaluative standard which will be available when we confront any actual problems posed by the phenomenon of conceptual diversity. Together these considerations undercut the presumption of the arbitrariness criticisms (p. 189).

Comment

Concern for the justifiability of beliefs, within the limitations of human cognition, seems to me to be a requirement of rationality; beliefs that one is unwilling to subject to any criteria of justifiability are unlikely to get much respect, nor do they deserve much respect, from people who do not hold them. But there are many views on what it means for a belief to be justified, only a few of which have been considered here. Although the views differ in particulars, there is wide agreement among them on the point that beliefs that have been subjected to some process of critical evaluation are more respectable than those that have not, independently of their truth status. Certain specific ideas are also common to many views—that known logical inconsistencies between beliefs should not be tolerated lightly, that beliefs should be consistent with relevant empirical evidence, that one should be able to give reasons for beliefs and especially beliefs that matter.

On any view of what it means to justify beliefs, there is a limit to how far justification can be pushed. This is, in part, because the process of assessing the degree to which any belief is justified must take place within a belief system, and one can always raise the question of what justifies the system within which the assessment is made (Ayer, 1956; Quine, 1981). Logical consistency among beliefs is one aspect of justification, it has been claimed. But what about belief in the efficacy of logic? How do we justify *it*? What justification can be given for believing the assertion "'All A are C' follows from 'All A are B' and 'All B are C'"? This is a fundamental question. For present purposes, it suffices to note that insistence that I be able to give a reason for *every* belief that I hold leads to an infinite regress: any reason I might give for believing X is itself a belief, and one can always ask, "Why do you believe *that*?" At some point this process must stop; one must come to a place at which one says, "I believe that, period."

Finally, it must be acknowledged that justification is a very subjective matter. What I consider to be strong justification of a particular belief, you may see as inadequate; and I may fail to see the merit in the argument you advance in support of a belief that you hold and I do not. Van Inwagen (1994) is undoubtedly right in claiming that "An argument may provide sufficient rational support for a belief and yet be impotent to produce that belief in some (or all) of those who hear and understand the argument" (p. 59). Implicit in this observation is recognition that what constitutes sufficient rational support is, to a non-trivial extent, a matter of personal judgment. One thing that justification of belief cannot mean is total agreement among rational and knowledgeable persons that it is true; on that standard, very few, if any, beliefs about any but the most mundane of matters could be considered justified.

Active fairmindedness and the cost of information

Probably everyone would agree with the general principle that a requirement of rationality is the fair treatment of evidence. But what does it mean to treat evidence fairly? One possible interpretation of this principle is that one should attempt to be as unbiased as possible in evaluating whatever evidence one happens to encounter. This gives fairness a relatively passive connotation. A more active interpretation would have rationality require that one put significant effort into seeking evidence, including evidence that goes against a favored hypothesis as well as evidence that supports it. Active search for evidence, especially counterindicative evidence, is a key aspect of some conceptions of what it means to reason well (Baron, 1985a, 1988; Nisbett & Ross, 1980; Nozick, 1993).

This seems to me to be an especially important point. It often is possible, even with only a modest effort, to avail oneself of more evidence than what happens to be lying in one's path. And it seems reasonable to question whether one has a right to a strong opinion on an issue if one has not made a serious attempt to seek out some of that evidence, including evidence that may weigh against one's favored view. Seeking evidence that is counter to a favored view is not something that most of us do naturally. Johnson (1987/1995) describes what appears to be the more natural tendency as follows: "People get a notion in their heads, cast about for a few bits of evidence to support it, and then settle comfortably into their position. We promote intuitions and half-truths based on partial evidence to the status of truths without bothering to consider the full body of evidence that bears on the issue" (p. 117).

Success or failure in searches for evidence should be assessed in light of the fact that some types of evidence are intrinsically much more difficult to come by than others. In particular, sometimes evidence on one side of a question is especially difficult to obtain. Consider, for example, the hypothesis that political coverups do not work. It is difficult to find evidence that would disconfirm this hypothesis, because successful coverups, by definition, are not discovered. Or consider the assertion that crime does not pay. The assertion may be true insofar as it pertains to crimes we know about. However, we have no idea how many crimes go undetected, and undetected crimes are more likely to pay, one would assume, than detected ones.

According to the *principle of total evidence* (Carnap, 1947) one should use all available evidence when estimating a probability. But "available" in this context is vague; it could be taken to mean "at hand" or "within easy reach," or it could be interpreted to include what can be obtained only with significant effort. Good (1983) recognizes this distinction and modifies Carnap's principle by taking account of the cost of obtaining and using evidence. According to his modification, "we should use all the evidence *already* available, provided that the cost of doing so is negligible" (p. 178). Swinburne (1983), who emphasizes the importance of actively seeking evidence relevant to beliefs that matter, acknowledges practical limits on what people can be expected to do: "The scope for investigation is endless; one can always go on looking for more evidence and check and recheck the process of utilizing it to form beliefs. All we can do is pursue such inquiries as seem to us adequate within the time at our disposal" (p. 69).

Such concessions to practicality can be accommodated theoretically by quantifying both the cost of acquiring information and the worth of the information that is sought. The worth of information will depend on the purpose for which it is to be used. If, for example, the information is sought for the purpose of increasing the probability of making a correct decision or forming a true belief, its worth will depend on how important it is that the decision be correct or that the belief be true, and on how much the probability that it will be so would be increased if the sought information were added to that already in hand.

Obviously, making the right decision or drawing the correct conclusion about a belief can be much more important in some instances than in others. It is also easy to see that the same amount of additional information would contribute more to a thought process if one had little information to begin with than if one had a lot. It seems reasonable then that we should work harder to acquire information in some situations than in others. Precisely how hard we should work in any particular case is a judgment call.

The general idea that I want to defend here is that although the rational requirement to seek evidence must be tempered by recognition that it is unrealistic to expect to be able to consider *all* the evidence that may be obtainable on any given issue, our tendency is to put too little effort into the discovery of information on many of the issues about which we have beliefs. Sometimes we hold beliefs that are important to us on the basis of scanty evidence, and do not make the effort necessary to obtain evidence that could be had for the digging. It seems to me irrational to be tenacious about such beliefs. It may be rational to hold a belief on scanty evidence if one is willing to acknowledge that the correctness of that belief is of no great personal importance—not worth the effort needed to provide evidentiary justification for it—but such a belief should be held lightly with keen recognition of the possibility that it may be wrong. Such an attitude about beliefs that really matter will not do.

Subjectivity in the interpretation of evidence

> Evidence is strong if it is convincing; it is convincing if it convinces somebody. (Polya, 1954a, p. 68)

Twelve people on a jury listen to precisely the same presentation of evidence for and against a disputed claim and, having done so, seven of them conclude that the claim has been substantiated while the remaining five conclude that it has not. How can this be? Are seven of the jurors using one set of criteria for judging the credibility of evidence and the other five another set? This is not a rhetorical question; most juries do not achieve unanimity on their first ballot after hearing all the evidence presented at trial (Hans & Vidmar, 1986; Kalven & Zeisel, 1966). Jurors often are surprised by the discovery, at the beginning of the deliberation process, that other jurors have come to a conclusion different from their own, when, in their view, the evidence so strongly favored the latter (Ellsworth, 1989).

One can find countless examples of differences of opinion among philosophers as to the persuasiveness of specific arguments regarding philosophical questions of long standing. Similarly there are many instances of scientific theories or hypotheses that some scientists have believed to be supported strongly by certain evidence while others have seen the same evidence as weak or irrelevant. Different people can put different interpretations on the same facts or assumptions.

Perhaps nowhere are more strongly opposing opinions regarding what constitutes evidence to be found than among proponents of different approaches to the interpretation of statistical data. The point is illustrated by the juxtaposition of opposing positions regarding the relevance to the interpretation of the outcome of an experiment of outcomes that could have been observed but were not. "The question of how often a given situation would arise is utterly irrelevant to the question how we should reason when it *does* arise. I don't know how many times this simple fact will have to be pointed out before statisticians of 'frequentist' persuasions will take note of it" (Jaynes, 1976, p. 247). In response to Jaynes's comment, which she quotes, Mayo (1996) has this to say: "What we error statisticians must rightly wonder is how many times we will have to point out that to us, reasoning from the result that did arise *is* crucially dependent upon how often it would arise. Lacking such information prevents us from ascertaining which inferences can be reliably drawn" (p. 358).

Wherever we look, we see indications of the wisdom of Polya's (1954b) admonition to not neglect the obvious fact that two people presented with the same evidence may honestly disagree. "Honestly" deserves emphasis here. That people sometimes force their interpretation of evidence to support a particular point of view or to serve a particular agenda is beyond doubt; the focus here is on the fact that people also can have *honest* differences of opinion regarding what a bit of evidence means. The best of intentions to be objective and unbiased in their views do not guarantee agreement. That there are many illustrations of the truth of this observation in science is particularly interesting inasmuch as science, perhaps more than any other area of human reasoning, emphasizes the role of evidence as the final arbiter of all questions of fact. But evidence must be interpreted; and it is probably very infrequently the case that the evidence on any complex issue admits of only one interpretation or is overwhelmingly indicative of only one answer. What is made of any bit of evidence—indeed the extent to which any bit of data can function *as* evidence—must depend, to no small degree, on what else the one who interprets it already knows or believes.

Also, it is doubtful that, in complicated situations, two individuals ever have *precisely* the same evidence with which to work. If there is a large amount of information that is germane to the issue, chances are that different individuals will have acquired different aspects of that information at different times under different conditions and to different degrees, so that their knowledge, as it relates to the issue at any given time, is unlikely to be exactly the same.

Even if it could be assumed that people were evaluating precisely the same evidence, it seems likely that they bring to any evidence evaluation problem different sets of preexisting beliefs. These would be expected to influence the interpretations individuals give to the evidence insofar as it admits of more than one. To the extent that internal consistency among one's beliefs is recognized to be desirable, even if not totally attainable, people would be expected to try to resolve inconsistencies when they become aware of them. When one evaluates evidence on a particular issue, one wants the conclusion one draws to be consistent not only with the immediate evidence in hand, but with whatever beliefs one holds that are related in a nontrivial way. Of course, one way to resolve inconsistencies between a newly formed conclusion and old established beliefs is to modify the beliefs. We know, however, that this can be very difficult to do; the more natural tendency seems to be to make the new conclusion fit the old views. This tendency helps account for the fact that preexisting attitudes are such good predictors of supreme court justices' decisions (Schubert, 1961) and senators' voting behavior (Poole, 1981).

There is also a question as to how one accesses and applies one's knowledge to an issue about which one is thinking. People often fail to access relevant knowledge that they have when drawing conclusions or making decisions. One buys a house and makes the unpleasant discovery some time later that the cellar takes in water in periods of unusually heavy rain. The buyer knew that a leaky cellar is not a plus for a house, but simply did not think of this issue when considering whether to make the purchase.

We do not find the idea of such lapses implausible because all of us have experienced them. Thus even if we were willing to assume that two individuals had precisely the same knowledge with respect to some issue, we should not find it difficult to believe that they could come to different conclusions about the issue, although we should expect that with appropriate prompting to bring to mind information that one or the other had overlooked, they would eventually converge on the same conclusion given identical knowledge bases. This expectation can never be more than conjectural, because we can never be sure that any two people have identical knowledge bases. Moreover, the plausibility of the conjecture suffers from instances, of which there are many, of experts drawing different conclusions from what appears to be the same evidence.

Hannes Alvén (1988) provides a particularly interesting illustration, not only that experts in the same problem area can interpret the same evidence differently from each other, but that they can each interpret the evidence in different ways at different times. In 1948, Alfvén attended a lecture in which Edward Teller claimed that cosmic rays are generated and contained within the sphere of influence of the sun. At the time, Alfvén believed that he had demonstrated conclusively that cosmic rays are generated by electromagnetic effects throughout the galaxy. However, in time Alfvén became convinced that Teller was right and came to accept the heliospheric view. Some years later, Teller changed his own views and accepted the standard account of cosmic radiation as a galactic phenomenon.

Alfvén describes, with some bemusement, the resulting situation: "it is a little paradoxical that I now should be one of the rather few supporters of Teller's theory, whereas the galactic theory which essentially derives from my views of the late 1930's is generally accepted. In fact, it has become so sacrosanct that all my attempts for decades to start a serious discussion have led to nothing" (p. 250). This is a striking demonstration of the importance of subjectivity in the uses of evidence: two highly knowledgeable people in the area of astrophysics starting out with opposing accounts of a phenomenon of interest, and ending up with opposing views, each having been converted to the view originally held by the other.

The importance of subjectivity is apparent in some types of analyses of statistical evidence. In Bayesian decision making, for example, subjectivity is often involved in the estimation of conditional probabilities. In many cases, the only source of such estimates is human judgment, and there is no objective way to verify them; in such cases it is not surprising that different individuals produce different estimates. Subjectivity in another form may be seen in Bayesian reasoning in the fact that the same observation or series of observations will yield different posterior probabilities depending on the prior probabilities assigned by the observer. To use new evidence impartially means, according to the Bayesian view, to apply to it the same computational formula independently of what one's existing belief state is. The outcome of the computation (the revised belief state) will not be independent of the existing view, because that view, along with the new evidence, is represented as a factor in the formula by which the revised view is derived. It is not only allowed but required that the impact that new evidence has on a decision process be influenced by one's prior beliefs.

This complicates the interpretation of some of the results of experiments that have been used to illustrate the unjustified role of biases and preconceptions in human judgment. An early study by Kelley (1950) of the effect of expectations on social perception, for example, found that students' perceptions of social qualities (e.g., relative sociability, friendliness) of a guest lecturer were influenced by what they had been led to expect from a prior description of the individual and, in particular, whether the description, which was given in terms of seven adjectives, included the descriptor "warm" or the descriptor "cold." I do not mean to suggest that the effect reported by Kelley was consistent with good Bayesian data processing, but only to argue that the mere fact that the interpretation of data is influenced by preexisting expectations is not, by itself, evidence of irrationality, at least as judged from a Bayesian perspective. Nisbett and Ross (1980) also argue that the fact that people's judgments are often biased by preconceptions and expectations does not necessarily demonstrate irrationality. When preconceptions themselves are based on legitimate evidence, they are analogous to base rates in the context of statistical decision-making. To ignore them would be to ignore relevant data.

Although any view of good reasoning would acknowledge the legitimacy of preexisting beliefs as contributing factors in the formation of new beliefs as a result of the acquisition of new evidence, research gives us grounds for suspecting that in many cases the effect of prior beliefs and expectations on our uses of evidence is stronger than it should be. While it is appropriate that such beliefs and expectations should influence our judgments, they should not be so resistant to change that whatever new information is acquired is arbitrarily interpreted to be consistent with them.

The possibility that they sometimes have this kind of influence is suggested by the results of experiments like that done by Lord, Ross, and Lepper (1979) in which they demonstrated that students with opposing views regarding the effectiveness of capital punishment as a deterrent to crime could interpret precisely the same data as not only consistent with, but supportive of, their own positions. Evidence that this phenomenon is not limited to students comes from a study by Sears and Whitney (1973) showing that following the Kennedy-Nixon debates during the 1960 presidential campaign, members of the general public thought the candidate of their choice, whoever that was, had won.

In short, there is no denying that intelligent and knowledgeable people can interpret what appears to be the same evidence in different ways and even, in some instances, draw conclusions from it that are diametrically opposed. This is not to say that it is pointless to present evidence on any question, because people will believe what they wish independently of what the evidence is. For every example that one can cite of evidence that intelligent and knowledgeable people interpret the same data in different ways, other examples can be given of data that people will interpret in the same way. This is fortunate, because if it were not the case, it is not clear how meaningful communication could occur.

The will to believe (or not)

> [H]umans readily subjugate their knowledge to their wishes, believing and doing what they want, all scientific facts and knowledge notwithstanding. (Bauer, 1994, p. 13)

Is it ever rational to believe X because one wishes to believe X, or to believe X rather than Y because one prefers X to Y? Before addressing this question, we should perhaps ask if it is even possible for one to believe X for no better reason than wanting to believe X. It may be, as some have argued, that belief is involuntary. J. S. Mill (1892/1995) expresses the view that people generally believe what they believe because they think they have good reason to do so, and that it is hard to imagine that it could be otherwise. Even a person with a weak mind is likely to find it impossible to believe X if he realizes that there is no evidence of the truth of X, no matter how very much he wants to believe it.

Perhaps, as Swinburne (1983) contends, belief is something that happens to one, not something one does. If one believes today is Monday, one cannot change one's mind to believe that it is Tuesday simply by deciding to do so. But Swinburne makes a strong argument that one has a moral obligation to submit one's beliefs to impartial investigation: "It is one thing to show that some belief is or is not probable on your present evidence. It is another thing to show that it is probable on as much evidence as you can readily obtain. The task of the investigator is to achieve a belief of the latter sort" (p. 175, footnote 1).

Granting that people can believe only what they find to be believable, it is beyond doubt that desires and preferences influence beliefs. While arguing that one cannot change one's beliefs at will, Swinburne (1983) points out that one can set oneself to change them over time, by, say, deliberately looking for evidence that is supportive of beliefs that one would like to hold and then trying to forget the selective character of the search. The question of interest here is whether it is ever appropriate that desires and preferences should influence beliefs. I suspect that most readers would agree that desires and preferences can and do influence beliefs inappropriately, and that there might be less agreement on the question of whether it is *always* inappropriate for beliefs to be influenced by these factors, irrespective of the circumstances. Are there conditions under which it is right for our desires or preferences to influence our beliefs?

One view is that the desirability of a belief should never be a factor in determining whether one accepts it. When desires cause beliefs, that is wishful thinking, says Davidson (1982), and beliefs thus caused are irrational beliefs. "For the wish to have a belief is not evidence for the truth of the belief, nor does it give it rational support in any other way" (p. 297). Wishful thinking, Davidson argues, represents the simplest kind of irrationality.

In contrast, William James (1896/1979) makes the case that one should feel free to choose among beliefs for which the evidence is equally supportive or equally inconclusive. Some choices of this sort—the choice between believing in free will or in determinism, for example—can have important consequences for one's outlook on life, and perhaps also for one's behavior as well. Of course, when the choice is between two or more competing beliefs, the evidence may be much stronger for one of the alternatives than for the other in the opinion of some people, but the question is should those for whom this is not true feel free to choose the alternative they prefer.

I noted earlier Albert's (1985) objection to classical foundationalism on the grounds that it requires the postulation of certain truths as given. A variant of foundationalism finds a way around the problem of infinite regress by halting the process with certain beliefs that are recognized as foundational—not justified by other beliefs—not because they are given or revealed, but because one *wills* to accept them. Albert attributes this view to Hugo Dingler.

I have already mentioned Nozick's rules for governing the rationality of beliefs, the second of which recognizes the utility of holding a belief as one consideration in justifying it. In describing the decision one faces upon discovering that premises that one accepts logically imply a conclusion that one has heretofore rejected, he notes that one has the choice of now accepting the conclusion, reconsidering and rejecting one of the premises, or perhaps postponing the decision and living with the inconsistency for a while. Nozick contends that the decision will depend on the degree of one's commitment to the truth of the premises and to the falsity of the conclusion, and that it is impossible that these are independent of the strength of one's desire that certain things be true.

Nozick recommends to philosophers that they favor a sort of philosophical explanation in which one brings oneself to see how something one wants to believe could be possible. Dennett (1984) approvingly cites this recommendation (p. 49, footnote 30) and passes it on in a discussion of the question of the tenability of belief in free will. "Having good reasons for wanting free will is not, of course, having good reasons for believing one has free will. It seems to be, however, that having good reasons for wanting free will *is* having good reasons for trying to get oneself to believe one has it" (p. 168).

The question of whether preferences can play a legitimate role in determining beliefs is an issue not only relative to philosophical or metaphysical beliefs but to scientific beliefs as well. Consider, for example, the belief that space is curved. This idea is widely accepted among modern-day physicists, but some have questioned whether it is meaningful. At least one has taken the position that whether or not one accepts it is strictly a matter of personal preference. "Not only can physics be described in flat Euclidean space, but indeed in any space that the scientist chooses. It may be that the theory can be expressed more succinctly in one geometry, but that does not make that geometry 'correct,' only convenient. The curvature of space is at the behest of the scientist.... Is space curved? The answer is yes or no depending on the whim of the answerer. It is therefore a question without empirical content, and has no place in physical inquiry" (Roxburgh, 1977, pp. 88, 89).

Do preferences have a legitimate role to play in determining what one believes? My sense is that most of us, philosophers, scientists and garden-variety folk alike, have preferences about what to believe on most matters of significance to us, and that looking for reasons to believe what one wants to believe is something we all do. I take some comfort in Nozick's contention that one should favor the sort of explanation in which one brings oneself to see how something one wants to believe could be possible, because that is what I see myself doing. But the risk is that the search for evidence that supports a preferred belief will give short shrift to evidence that counts against that belief—that a search for truth will give way to a confirmation bias—and that is a risk that should not be overlooked or forgotten.

When evidence does not suffice to dictate a choice between competing possible beliefs, it is rational, in my view, to make the selection on the basis of one's preferences. The question of free will and determinism seems to me to be such a question and my own strong preference is to believe that we are free to make choices and are therefore responsible for them. The question of whether existence is purposeful or simply the consequence of a meaningless accident is another one that seems to be unresolvable to everyone's satisfaction, at least on the basis of currently available objective evidence; here again, my own preference is to believe that there is a purpose to it all. I would not attempt to argue that this belief is forced by the evidence, but I do see it as at least as consistent with the evidence as any alternative view and therefore a rational belief to hold.

To say that what to believe in any particular instance is not clearly decidable on evidence is not to say that one cannot have reasons for making the selection one makes. Consider again the question of free will. Nagel (1986) struggles with this question and confesses to changing his mind every time he thinks about it. He distinguishes between an objective view of reality in which one sees the world, including oneself as a part of it, from a detached impersonal perspective and a subjective view in which one sees things from one's own perspective as a purposeful agent. The difference in the two perspectives is illustrated starkly in the following comment: "From far enough outside [from the objective perspective] my birth seems accidental, my life pointless, and my death insignificant, but from inside [from the subjective perspective] my never having been born seems nearly unimaginable, my life monstrously important, and my death catastrophic" (p. 209). The *doing* of an act is not part of the picture, Nagel notes, when we view the world objectively. "There seems no room for agency in a world of neural impulses, chemical reactions, and bone and muscle movements....there is only what happens" (p. 111). There is no place in this objective view for personal responsibility, for feelings of admiration or contempt, praise or blame. In this view, things *happen*, but no one *does* anything.

On the other hand, as experiencing persons, we believe ourselves to be free to make choices and we hold ourselves and others responsible for the choices we and they make. The belief in freedom is subjective, but compelling. We may conclude, as some do, that the belief is a compelling illusion, and that we really are robots, that our "choices" are fully determined by the laws of physics, even if we tend to pretend otherwise in our daily lives. I see the choice between belief in determinism or in free will as one of those that are undecidable on objective grounds and therefore in the category that William James argued could be made on the basis of other considerations. The choice to me is easy. I opt for belief in free will. Life would be far less interesting and attractive if I really believed that we are all automatons with an imagined sense of freedom and responsibility. I grant that the latter view is as tenable as the alternative that I have chosen, but not more so, and that being the case, I elect to exercise what I consider to be my free will in making my choice. Those who believe in determinism can hardly blame me for doing so.

It is important to note that belief in freedom of choice does not entail belief that choices cannot have explanations. It means only that the explanations must be in terms of the intentions of the choosing agents. As Nagel (1986) puts it, "A free action should not be determined by antecedent conditions, and should be fully explained only intentionally, in terms of justifying reasons and purposes" (p. 115).

☐ Revision of Beliefs

> From the point of view of the critique of ideology, one might say that the progress of knowledge consists in the revision of existing and influential prejudices, a revision that can advance only very slowly on all social areas. (Albert, 1985, p. 113)

Beliefs change, sometimes for good reasons, we assume, and sometimes not. Sometimes beliefs persist when they should have changed. Widespread belief in alchemy survived for over a thousand years, for example, despite the consistent failure of the numerous practitioners to produce the gold that their methods were intended to yield. The possibility of transmutation was so generally admitted during the 14th and 15th centuries in Europe that nearly every chemist of the time was more or less an alchemist. Scores of learned treatises were published on the art. Strathern (2000) contends that during the Middle Ages, alchemy was "the sole intellectual pursuit which sought to discover truths about the material world" (p. 54). He notes too that its dogged but unsuccessful search for a method for transforming base metals into gold and for the philosopher's stone yielded important knowledge about acids and other materials that paved the way for the emergence of chemistry and pharmacology.

As individuals, we also sometimes hold personal beliefs despite the availability of evidence against them. Having once formed a belief we often seem to adopt thereafter a defensive attitude toward that belief, selectively appropriating further evidence that supports it and ignoring or dismissing evidence that does not. Psychologists have studied this phenomenon, which is commonly referred to as belief perseverance or persistence.

Belief persistence

> One should not give up something which has seemed to one of supreme value and which has dominated one's way of life without considerable serious thought. (Swinburne, 1983, p. 98)

Investigators have demonstrated that beliefs, once formed, can be strongly resistant to change in the light of subsequently obtained counterindicative evidence (Edwards & Smith, 1996; Hayden & Mischel, 1976; Ross & Anderson, 1982; Ross & Lepper, 1980; Ross, Lepper, & Hubbard, 1975; Valins, 1974). Nisbett and Ross (1980) summarize the findings from much of the research predating 1980 on this topic as follows: "(1) When people already have a theory, before encountering any genuinely probative evidence, exposure to such evidence (whether it supports the theory, opposes the theory, or is mixed), will tend to result in more belief in the correctness of the original theory than normative dictates allow. (2) When people approach a set of evidence without a theory and then form a theory based on initial evidence, the theory will be resistant to subsequent evidence. More formally, people's response to two sets of evidence with opposite implications does not adhere to the commutativity rule which demands that the net effect of evidence A followed by evidence B must be the same as for evidence B followed by evidence A. (3) When people formulate a theory based on some putatively probative evidence and later discover that the evidence is false, the theory often survives such total discrediting" (p. 169).

These findings have obvious worrisome implications in many practical contexts. When doctors, jurists, politicians, among others, discount evidence in order to protect existing beliefs or hypotheses, bad consequences are likely to follow. Clearly, when important issues call for decisions that are dictated by the preponderance of evidence, the influence of the various bits of evidence should not depend on the order in which they were received.

The findings also relate to what appears to me to be an intuitively compelling fact, which is that few of us would be willing to give up long-held and valued beliefs on the first bit of contrary evidence we found. It is natural to be biased in favor of one's established beliefs. But is it rational? Here we are touching a complicated issue that can too easily be treated simplistically. One view would have it that a person should be sufficiently objective and open-minded to be willing to toss out any belief upon the first scrap of evidence that it is false. This view seems to me wrong for several reasons.

Many of the beliefs that matter to us as individuals are not the type that can be falsified, in the Popperian sense, by a single counterindicative bit of data. They tend rather to be beliefs for which one can find both supporting and counterindicative evidence, and the decision as to whether or not to hold them is appropriately made on the basis of the relative weights or merits of the pro and con considerations.

Second, it is possible to hold a belief for good and valid reasons without being able to produce all of those reasons on demand. Some of our beliefs are shaped over many years and the fact that one cannot articulate on demand every reason one has or has ever had for a particular one of them does not mean that it is unfounded. Also, as Nisbett and Ross (1980) point out, there are practical time constraints that often limit the amount of processing of new information that one can do. In view of these limitations, the tendency to persevere may be a stabilizing hedge against overly frequent changes of view that would result if one were obliged to hold only beliefs that one could justify explicitly at a moment's notice. This argument is not unlike the one advanced by Blackstone (1769/1962) in defense of not lightly scuttling legal traditions.

Third, being too quick to change one's mind could have one bouncing from position to position never stopping long enough to establish a point of view on anything. As Leftow (1994) points out, "*Some* commitment to hold on to a belief in the face of initially counterweighing evidence is necessary to hold on to almost any truth" (p. 201). This is simply to recognize that truths against which counterevidence, or at least counterarguments, cannot be advanced are probably relatively rare.

Finally, for assertions of the type that represent basic beliefs, there are two ways to be wrong: To believe false ones, or to disbelieve true ones. For many beliefs that people hold these two possibilities are not equally acceptable, which is to say that an individual might consider it more important to avoid one type of error than the other. This is, of course, the argument behind Pascal's famous wager. It also is the basis of the presumption-of-innocence principle that is at the core of jurisprudence in most civilized countries.

To argue that it is not necessarily irrational to refuse to abandon a belief that one has held for a long time upon encountering some evidence that appears to tell against it is not to deny that there is such a thing as holding on to cherished beliefs too tenaciously and refusing to give a fair consideration to counterindicative evidence. The line between understandable conservatism with respect to changing established beliefs and obstinate close-mindedness is not an easy one to draw. But clearly we sometimes persevere beyond reason, as when gamblers explain away their losses, thus permitting them to continue gambling despite them (Gilovich, 1983). People find it disturbingly easy to interpret evidence that is inconsistent with their beliefs in such a way as to make it consistent with them (Darley & Fazio, 1980; Duncan, 1976; Hayden & Mischel, 1976; Swann & Snyder, 1980). Moreover, when beliefs are changed, they may be moved in one direction more easily than in another; Rothbart and Park (1986) have presented evidence, for example, that favorable first impressions of people may be more easily changed to unfavorable ones than the reverse.

Ross, Lepper, and Hubbard (1975) have demonstrated that people sometimes persevere in beliefs even when the evidence on which the beliefs were initially formed has been shown to them to be fraudulent. They had people attempt to distinguish between authentic and unauthentic suicide notes. Participants were given feedback that was independent of their choices; some were informed that they performed far above average on the task while others were told that they performed far below average. Following completion of the task, participants were informed of the arbitrary nature of the feedback and of the fact that their rate of "success" or "failure" was predetermined and independent of their choices. Despite the debriefing information, when later asked to rate their ability to make such judgments, participants who had received much positive feedback on the contrived task rated themselves higher than did those who had received more negative feedback. Ross and his colleagues have also shown experimentally that people find it extremely easy to generate explanations of individuals' behavior and to persevere in those explanations even in the face of evidence that the data on which they were originally based were fictitious (Anderson, Lepper, & Ross, 1979; Ross & Anderson, 1982; Ross, Leper, Strack, & Steinmets, 1977).

One factor that may contribute to the perseverance of beliefs of the kind reported by Ross, Lepper, and Hubbard (1975), is the operation of a sort of confirmation bias (Nickerson, 1998; Nisbett & Ross, 1980). The receipt of feedback that supports the assumption that one is particularly good or particularly poor at a specific task may prompt one to search for additional information to confirm further that assumption. To the extent that such a search is successful, the belief that persists may rest not exclusively on the fraudulent feedback, but on other evidence that one has been able to find in support of it as well. Some support for this hypothesis comes from the finding that the imposition of a distracter task to occupy the time between the receipt of the false feedback and the discrediting of that feedback may reduce or eliminate the perseverance (Fleming & Arrowood, 1979). (Another possibility, in some cases, is that subjects, upon being told by experimenters that they were given false feedback during the experiment come to suspect that what they are told during the debriefing session may not be true; if the experimenters deceived them for scientific purposes once, why would they not do so again? Perhaps, they might think, the real point of the experiment is to see how easily one can be made to change one's mind.)

We see, in summary, that the tendency of people to persevere with established beliefs in the face of evidence that runs counter to those beliefs can be defended, within limits, on the grounds of the information processing limitations of human beings, and, as Lycan (1988) points out, in recognition that changing belief consumes energy and resources. We see also, however, that the tendency can be taken to unreasonable extremes and that there is a line, however difficult to draw, the crossing of which takes the tendency from being a functional safeguard against destabilizingly frequent revisions of belief to being recalcitrance against warranted change.

Dogmatism, which manifests itself as refusal to modify beliefs in the face of compelling evidence of the need for change, can be seen, in Albert's (1985) words, as "a determination to maintain our theories, regardless of what objections might be raised against them, and regardless, too, of what reality might be" (p. 45). I suspect that few people would contest the claim that when the tendency to persevere in a belief is so strong that one refuses to consider evidence that does not support that belief, it is irrational and offends our sense of intellectual honesty. That is not to say, however, that dogmatic confidence in one's own beliefs and intolerance of opposing views can never work to one's advantage. Boorstin (1958) argues, for example, that it was precisely these qualities that permitted the 17th century New England Puritans to establish a society with the ingredients necessary for survival and prosperity. "Had they spent as much of their energy in debating with each other as did their English contemporaries, they might have lacked the single-mindedness needed to overcome the dark, unpredictable perils of a wilderness. They might have merited praise as precursors of modern liberalism, but they might never have helped found a nation" (p. 9).

Contrary to the popular stereotype of the Puritans, they were not preoccupied with religious dogma but rather with more practical matters, because, as Boorstin notes, they had no doubts and allowed no dissent. They worried about such problems as how to select leaders and representatives, how to establish the proper limits of political power and to construct a feasible federal organization. As a study in contrast with the Puritans, Boorstin points to the Pennsylvania Quakers. They also were rigid in their beliefs, making "a dogma of the absence of dogma," but they maintained a tolerance for people who believed differently than they and preferred to have as little as possible to do with the practical matters of the building and governing of a society.

If we define being rational very narrowly as reasoning and acting in one's best self interest, we would probably have to consider the holding of beliefs that—independently of their truth or falsity—help one attain one's goals, and the insulation of those beliefs against opposing views, to be rational. This seems to me, however, to be an unacceptably narrow conception of rationality. Dogmatism has the practical effect of permitting one to protect one's beliefs, which is arguably beneficial for certain purposes, but it is an impediment to the pursuit of truth and the acquisition of knowledge.

Harman on belief revision

What are good reasons for revising beliefs? How much effort should we feel obliged to put into the evaluation of our own belief sets? How are we to judge whether a particular change—or a particular instance of maintaining a belief against pressures to change—should be considered rational? Harman (1986), who equates reasoning with reasoned revision of beliefs or intentions, has treated such questions in some detail.

The foundations and coherence theories

Harman distinguishes between two theories of reasoned revision of beliefs: the *foundations* theory and the *coherence* theory. As we have seen, according to the foundations theory, one's beliefs are interdependent and traceable to foundational beliefs. Certain beliefs are justified by other more fundamental beliefs, which in turn are justified by others more fundamental still. In tracing a belief to its justificatory roots, one ends finally with foundational beliefs that do not depend on others for their justification. Reasoned revision of beliefs, according to this theory, requires subtracting from one's system of beliefs any that are not justified (excepting of course foundational beliefs) or adding new beliefs that are either justified by the other beliefs that are held or are themselves foundational. This view is similar in spirit to Descartes's principle of doubt.

According to the coherence theory, an existing belief does not require justification unless one has a special reason to doubt it; the fact that one may not be able to remember or reconstruct the reasons for appropriating a certain belief in the first place is not justifiable grounds for discarding that belief. Belief revision should be guided by two principles: the principle of conservatism and the principle of coherence. The principle of conservatism prescribes that beliefs should be revised minimally in the interest of resolving conflicts that have come to light. The principle of coherence dictates that changes should be made in the interest of increasing overall coherence within one's total belief set. (Both the foundations theory and the coherence theory have to do with the conditions under which beliefs should be justified, but neither prescribes a particular method of belief justification. This is a separate issue. Both may be compatible with a variety of rightness criteria, and a given criterion might be satisfiable within both contexts [Goldman, 1986].)

Harman subscribes to the coherence theory as the normatively correct one and dismisses the foundations theory on the grounds that it requires one to keep track of the original reasons for one's beliefs, which is more than mere mortals can do. Moreover, the foundations theory requires that one be prepared to justify any of one's beliefs at any time, whereas the coherence theory requires that only changes in existing beliefs require justification. In Harman's words: "the foundations theory says one is justified in continuing to believe something only if one has a special reason to continue to accept that belief, whereas the coherence theory says one is justified in continuing to believe something as long as one has no special reason to stop believing it" (p. 32). The coherence view is very similar to the theory of minimal rationality advanced by Cherniak (1986). Something like it is also defended by Shatz (1994), who argues that the mere fact that one already believes something gives one a reason to keep believing it; *methodological conservatism*, which this view is sometimes called is, Shatz claims, now recognized as good rational practice.

Harman argues also that the foundations theory should be dismissed as a normative theory because, inasmuch as people do not typically keep track of the reasons for their beliefs and sometimes continue to retain beliefs even after the evidence for them has been discredited, without realizing that they are doing so (Ross & Anderson, 1982), it implies that almost all beliefs are unjustified. This, in his view, would be an absurd thing for a normative theory to do. Harman finds the idea that most of the beliefs that people hold are unjustified to be intuitively unacceptable. Of course anyone who is convinced that human beings are fundamentally irrational should have no difficulty accepting it.

Principles of positive and negative undermining

Closely related to the distinction between the foundations theory and the coherence theory is the distinction between the principle of positive undermining ("One should stop believing P whenever one positively believes one's reasons for believing P are no good" [Harman, 1986, p. 39]) and the principle of negative undermining ("One should stop believing P whenever one does not associate one's belief in P with an adequate justification [either intrinsic or extrinsic]") (p. 39). The first of these principles is more plausible, in Harman's view, than the second; the latter has the absurd implication that people should stop believing almost everything they believe, given that they do not keep track of the justifications of their beliefs.

A principle similar to Harman's principle of positive undermining is defended by Lycan (1988). According to the principle of conservatism, which Lycan calls it, one should hold on to a belief unless there is a positive reason to reject it. Lycan sees the warrant conferred by this principle on newly acquired beliefs to be a weak one, however, and notes that until a belief has passed tests such as those of consistency and coherence with one's existing belief system, it can be overridden easily by other evidential considerations.

Comment

Harman's model of belief revision is prescriptive in that it purports to say how beliefs should, or should not, be revised. It is pragmatic in that it explicitly takes human capabilities and limitations into account. If forced to choose between the foundations and coherence theories of belief revision, I would opt for the latter; and given the principles of positive and negative undermining, my preference is for the former, especially with Lycan's qualification. I think it a mistake, however, to consider it necessary to adopt one or another of these positions in its entirety. Although the coherence theory seems to me both more descriptive of human reasoning than the foundations theory and a more reasonable prescription as well, I want to argue that it is not inconsistent with human cognitive limitations to expect people to be able to give, if asked, *some* of their reasons—partial justification—for at least those of the beliefs they hold that are important to them. Similarly with respect to the distinction between positive and negative undermining, I see the former as both more descriptive and more acceptable as a normative principle than the latter, but I am not prepared to rule out the possibility that failure to find reasons to justify an existing belief—despite trying to do so—may be sufficient warrant, in some instances, to discard that belief, or at least temper it with some degree of doubt.

The idea of tempering a belief with some degree of doubt runs counter to Harman's view of beliefs as generally all-or-none in character. This view seems to involve the assumption that the only alternative to unlimited inquiry with limitless resources is full acceptance of conclusions as though their truth were beyond question. I do not see these two positions as the only possibilities. A third possibility is that one consider conclusions as plausible, or implausible, to varying degrees and accept some degree of certitude as adequate for practical purposes and therefore not worth trying to improve upon through further inquiry. In other words, according to this view, one may be willing to act *as though* one believed a particular conclusion certainly to be true, for the sake of practicality, even though one actually believed the conclusion to be true only with some probability less than 1.0. How much certitude is enough may depend on the particular conclusion involved, and how important it is for one to get it right.

I have devoted considerable space to Harman's views on belief revision because he has written in a focused way on this subject, and because, with the qualifications already mentioned, I find his analysis quite convincing. There are other views of belief revision, however, that need to be mentioned. Bayes's rule, for example, is essentially a prescription for updating beliefs in the light of newly acquired data. The question of how descriptive this rule is of how people actually apply new data to existing beliefs has been the subject of considerable research. Some of this research is discussed in Nickerson (2004). Suffice to say here that Bayes's rule is an equation for revising prior probabilities to take account of new data (although Bayesian decision making has often been given a much broader connotation), that its popularity among statisticians and other potential users has waxed and waned since its original formulation, that its use is less controversial in situations in which probabilities are based on objective relative frequencies than when they reflect subjective estimates, and that it can be a powerful tool when used with care under the right circumstances.

In mathematics, beliefs about relationships are established and revised by what Lakatos (1976) has referred to as the method of proofs and refutations. A proof, if it is valid, justifies the acceptance of a theorem as true, given the axioms of the system from which the proof was derived; refutation of a proof—demonstration that it is invalid—in any of a variety of ways, points up the need either to revise the theorem or to prove it in another way. Statistics has much to do with the evaluation of beliefs and, in particular, the assignment to them of quantitative indicants of certitude. Not all beliefs lend themselves to statistical evaluation, but for those that do statistical methods are powerful tools for practical decision making.

The scientific method prescribes that beliefs—theories—be modified whenever their implications fail to correspond with observations. Science, as a whole, appears to follow this prescription, although one can find numerous instances of individual scientists who have failed to do so in specific cases.

There are many ways to account for modifications of belief. My sense is that psychologists have paid less attention to the question of how beliefs are modified, however, or to that of how they should be modified, than to the attempt to understand why beliefs so often tend to persist, as they seem to do, when they might have been expected to change. Moreover, what it means, psychologically, to change a belief is not fully understood. Old beliefs may linger, like unwanted tenants, even after having been told to vacate their premises. And even when they appear to have gone, they may leave behind feelings and other effects that, although initially stemming from them, are no longer dependent on them. My dislike of flying may have originated with an incorrect belief about its safety relative to that of other modes of travel, but it does not follow that that dislike will disappear if I discover that flying is safer than I believed it to be. More generally, old beliefs leave residues—what Goldman (1986) refers to as *credal residues*—even after having been revised or "replaced" that can continue to affect cognition in a variety of ways. A better understanding of the nature of these residues and their effects is a continuing challenge to research.

☐ Propagation of Beliefs

Perhaps there are such things as unique personal beliefs—beliefs that are unique to the individuals who hold them. It seems likely, however, that a large majority of the beliefs that any one of us holds, at least those beliefs that pertain to the observable world, are held by other people as well. We would like to know how beliefs are propagated. How do beliefs become common among communities and cultures? Is it reasonable to speak of beliefs of groups? What role do groups play in the formation and retention of individuals' beliefs?

It is not surprising that some of the ideas about how beliefs spread should bear some resemblance to those relating to the occurrence of epidemics (Gladwell, 2000; Watts, 2003). Beliefs, one might say, can be contagious. But not all beliefs spread. Presumably whether a particular belief does so depends to some degree on the nature of the belief—some things are simply more believable than others, at least within a given cultural context—but beliefs that are presumably equally plausible within a given cultural context may not all spread equally rapidly or to equal extents. Whether a particular belief will spread appears to depend also on factors that are somewhat independent of its merits.

Information cascades

An *information cascade* occurs when an idea or belief spreads through a group by a process sometimes referred to as *observational* or *social* learning (Bikhchandani, Hirshleifer, & Welch, 1992, 1998; Watts, 2003). Situations that give rise to information cascades are those in which different people make choices in sequence over time and the main sources of information to individual choosers are the choices that immediately-preceding others made with respect to the same, or a similar, set of options. Under certain conditions, the choices of the first few individuals to make them are essentially imitated by subsequent choosers. A person wishing to buy a new car may be considering both a Ford and a Buick, say, and may even be leaning toward the Ford on the basis of his own knowledge of the alternatives, but may choose the Buick on the basis of being aware that acquaintances who have recently bought a new car have bought a Buick.

What is of special interest in the present context is the question of whether such copy-cat behavior can be considered rational. Bikhchandani, Hirshleifer, and Welch (1992, 1998) argue that under certain conditions, which they spell out, it can be, and people basing choices on the choices of others can yield better choices than would have been produced on the basis of one's individual knowledge. But there is no guarantee that this will always be the case; the quality of the choices made in an information cascade are sensitive to the quality of the selections of the few choosers who start the cascade. The problem with cascades, as Bikhchandani, Hirshleifer, and Welch (1992) put it, "is that they prevent the aggregation of information of numerous individuals. Ideally, if the information of many previous individuals is aggregated, later individuals should converge to the correct action. However, once a cascade has started, actions convey no information about private signals; thus an individual's action does not improve later decisions" (p. 998).

A simple thought experiment, based on a laboratory demonstration by Anderson and Holt (1997) makes clear how an information cascade may work. Two urns contain black and white balls, one (B) with a black-to-white ratio of 2-to-1 and the other (W) with the ratio reversed. Each of several observers draws, in turn, one ball from the same urn, silently notes its color and returns the ball to the urn before the next observer draws a ball. At some point each observer is asked, again in turn, to announce the urn from which he believes the balls were drawn. Imagine that the first two observers announce B, and suppose that the third observer drew a white ball. If the third observer makes her guess strictly on the basis of the color of the ball she drew, she should guess W. But having heard the two preceding observers guess B, she may reason that two of the first three draws were black, so she should guess black. If she is a good Bayesian and assumes that each of the two urns was equally likely to be chosen a priori, the posterior probabilities of the B and W urns, based on her draw alone would be 2-to-1 in favor of W, but if she assumes that the two preceding observers drew black balls and she takes that into account, the posterior probabilities are 2-to-1 in favor of B. So she can hardly be considered irrational to guess B, despite drawing a white ball.

Having heard three predecessors guess B, observer 4 might plausibly believe that each of them drew a black ball (unless he is sharp enough to realize that perhaps he is witnessing an information cascade), so he will have even more reason to guess B than did observer 3, independently of the color of the ball he drew. And here is the important point: given that the first few observers name the same urn, the information each subsequent observer gains from the color of the ball he/she draws will have little or no impact on his/her guess, because of what appears to be the weight of the cumulating evidence in favor of the urn first mentioned. It is not necessary that the information cascade begin with the first few observers; all that is necessary is that at some point in the process the evidence cumulating from the preceding guesses become (apparently) sufficiently strong to swamp the information one gets from looking at a single ball.

Information cascades may be at the base of fads, market bubbles or sell offs, medical practice, and even criminal behavior (Banerjee, 1992; Kahan, 1997; Phelps & Mooney, 1992; Sheffrin & Triest, 1992; Welch, 1992). Bikhchandani, Hirshleifer, and Welch (1998) give examples of how information cascades can be exploited in a variety of contexts, including consumer marketing and politics. Watts (2003) draws parallels between information cascades and cascades of other types—such as the 1996 North American power grid failure that was triggered by an incident involving a single transmission line in Oregon—the common feature being a self-propagating event or process that begins inauspiciously but quickly acquires epidemic proportions, and without the benefit of a coordinating agent. What information cascades have in common, Watts notes, is that once started, they become self-perpetuating, adding new adherents on the strength of already having acquired some.

Networks

Watts (2003) emphasizes the role that social networks play in the propagation of beliefs, and especially the importance of the interconnections between and among such networks. Network interconnections are made by "connectors"—individuals who belong to more than one network—(Gladwell, 2000). In Watts's view, belief propagation is facilitated when the connections between networks are neither too few nor too numerous. "Networks that are not connected enough.... prohibit global cascades because the cascade has no way of jumping from one vulnerable cluster to another. And networks that are too highly connected prohibit cascades also, but for a different reason: they are locked into a kind of stasis, each node constraining the influence of any other and being constrained itself" (p. 241).

The limitations arising from insufficient network connections are perhaps easier to see intuitively than those that arise from networks being too highly connected. The problem with highly interconnected networks, as facilitators of information cascades, is that high interconnectedness means that individuals are getting lots of cross-network inputs, and, as Watts puts it, "the more people whose actions or opinions you take into account before making a decision, the less influence any *one* of them will have over you. So when *everyone* is paying attention to many others, no single innovator, acting alone, can activate any one of them" (p. 240).

Watts argues that whether an innovation (new idea or belief) will propagate is likely to depend as much on network structure and on chance as on the inherent appeal of the innovation itself. For every innovation that has been successful in the sense that it has propagated wildly, there are many equally deserving ones that have received very little attention by comparison. A very similar argument is made by Taleb (2004).

Beliefs of groups

Sometimes we attribute beliefs to communities, groups, or categories of people as a whole. We say that Democrats believe thus and so, while Republicans believe something else, or that Catholics believe X while Protestants believe Y. Undoubtedly certain beliefs are much more likely to be held by members of some groups than by members of others, so it is not wrong to associate specific beliefs with specific groups, especially when members of groups emphasize beliefs as among the characteristics that distinguish them as groups. It is important to recognize, however, that beliefs are cognitive states of individuals, not of groups as a whole. Individuals, not groups, believe thus and so.

Beliefs are attributed to groups when large percentages of the people who belong to those groups give evidence of holding those beliefs, or at least do not object overtly when spokespersons for those groups express those beliefs in behalf of the groups. However, one would not be surprised to find, among the members of any given group, a considerable range of attitudes toward, and understanding of, specific beliefs that are associated with that group. It would be less than surprising to find within groups characterized by strong adherence to complicated belief sets individuals who profess total adherence but have little understanding of what some of the beliefs included mean.

Degree of group consensus, especially on matters that some group members may not understand very well, is difficult to measure, and we know that estimates of such consensus can be influenced by the behavior of individuals considered to be representative of the group (Zuckerman, Mann, & Bernieri, 1982). It seems likely that we tend to overestimate the degree of consensus within many groups and perceive the groups as more monolithic, with respect to the beliefs their members hold, than they really are. Two people reciting the same creed may have quite different understandings of what is being said. This does not mean that groups cannot act cohesively in the defense of the beliefs with which they are identified, but it is not necessary for one to understand a belief in any very deep sense in order to support its defense in tangible ways.

Peer influence in shaping beliefs

> When everyone is seeing flying saucers, you naturally would like to see one yourself. (Gardner, 1957, p. 187)

Peer pressure is a widely-acknowledged motivating force, and is a reality not only in the lives of impressionable teen-agers, but in those of mature members of society. The importance of peer pressure in influencing behavior is well documented and has been recognized by scientists and laypersons alike for a long time. Some of the rewards and sanctions that are used by groups to encourage or enforce conformity are explicit and obvious; others are subtle and inconspicuous. It is a simple matter of statistics that people are more likely to have their beliefs reinforced than challenged when they converse with others who share those beliefs. One does not go to a Republican (Democratic) political convention in order to expose one's Republican (Democratic) views to the harshest criticisms that can be leveled against them.

Commonality of beliefs can be a strong binding force and, conversely, incompatible beliefs among members of the same community can be highly divisive. By the same token, espousal of beliefs that are contrary to those that prevail within a community can evoke great pressure from the community to conform, especially if the beliefs involved are considered to be important and to have significant implications for behavior.

Lyttleton (1979) suggests that not only will the gregarious instinct tend to draw together people who have the same beliefs, but that the desire not to feel outside an accepted official group is so strong that most of us are willing to adopt views that are unacceptable scientifically in order to maintain our status within the group. Independence of opinion, at least to the extent that one's opinions are made public, can exact a price that many people will find unacceptably high. The desire to conform is sometimes even seen as inherent to human nature (Jones, 1984).

Albert (1985) argues that social factors can be extremely influential in the maintenance of beliefs, even to the point of overriding the effects of objective evidence. "As is now well known, convictions that in no way correspond to reality—the inadequacy of which is readily apparent to a critical observer—can prove extraordinarily stable if they are supported strongly enough by the society. Correspondence to reality can be extensively replaced by social anchoring" (p. 120).

Compelling experimental evidence of the effect of peer pressure on people's behavior was reported a half-century ago by Asch (1953). He found that a large percentage of participants in experiments could be induced to report believing something that they could see to be false (that a particular line on a display of lines was the longest, when it clearly was not) if all the other members of a small group made the same incorrect selection (the other members of the group having been secretly instructed beforehand by the experimenter to do so). An interesting, and encouraging, auxiliary finding was the need for unanimity among the collaborating group members in order for the peer pressure effect to be robust; if even a single other person in the group gave the correct answer, the unsuspecting participant was much less likely to yield to the pressure to conform to the group consensus.

A member of a relatively closed group who fails to recognize the tendency of groups to be noncritical with respect to beliefs that their members generally hold, and who communicates almost exclusively with other members of the group, is likely to be convinced that the evidence for the truth of the beliefs the group espouses is stronger than it really is. Never having been exposed to evidence that is contrary to those beliefs, or having encountered it only as interpreted by those who have a vested interest in being able to dismiss it, one is in a poor position to evaluate one's beliefs objectively, but may be completely unaware of the fact. If

Cummings (1995) is correct, even an entire profession can so insulate itself from contrasting views that it comes to believe the one that prevails among its members is the only one there is.

One need not be a member of a separatist or relatively-closed group to experience the reinforcing effects of selective communication with like-minded people. Who can doubt that all of us are more likely to talk with people who share those of our views that most define us as individuals than with people who do not? Unless we are naturally inclined to be argumentative, we probably enjoy the company of people with whom we tend to agree more than that of those with whom we have strong differences of opinion. What rationality requires, I want to argue, is that one recognize that this preference, understandable as it is, has the effect of providing some degree of shelter for one's favored views against unfriendly attack, and it can leave us thinking they are less vulnerable than they really are.

Arguably, many of us hold some of the beliefs that we do for no better reason than the fact that they are the beliefs that prevail in the culture, or subculture, to which we belong. Those beliefs, or at least a significant proportion of them, may be correct, but this does not mean that they have a rational basis in the minds of all the people who hold them. Acknowledging this is not espousing the postmodern position that beliefs are nothing more than social constructions that are unconstrained by objective reality. It is simply to recognize that even beliefs that correspond to objective reality can be held in a non-critical way and for reasons other than careful consideration of the evidence for or against them.

☐ Delusions and "Extreme" Beliefs

> Ask the average man in the street why he believes that the world is round and he will give you a set of very bad reasons. Ask the flat-earth fanatic why he thinks the world is flat and he will probably give you a much better set, for his reasoning powers have been sharpened in continual controversy with people holding the orthodox view. (Thouless, 1947, p. 149)

Delusions are often associated in our thinking with mental illness. If asked to illustrate what it means to be deluded, we might offer up examples of individuals who believe they are people other than who they really are. Without discounting the importance of this type of delusion and of understanding its basis, here I want to focus not on delusions as symptoms or effects of mental illness, but on the phenomenon as it might be observed among people who, by conventional standards at least, would be considered mentally intact and perfectly sane.

In its broadest connotation, a delusion is a false belief; in this sense it is safe to assume that we all suffer many of them. Generally the term is used in a more restricted way to connote false beliefs that would be recognized by most people—other than those who hold them—as false. Such beliefs are extreme in the sense that they lie outside the norm, at least insofar as that is defined by commonality.

No matter how we conceive of delusions or extreme beliefs, we have to acknowledge that they are delusional or extreme only within some frame of reference or from some perspective. What is a delusion from one point of view may be rock-solid truth from another. Nevertheless it is interesting to consider what causes delusions, at least as they would be seen as such from the perspective of this book, and what makes them persist.

Prescientific beliefs in prescientific times

> The truth is that we can always find previous world views lacking if we judge them in our terms. The price paid, however, is that what we actually learn about them is severely limited before the inquiry even begins. (Berman, 1984, p. 85)

Before the invention of the thermometer for taking body temperature, it was commonly believed among knowledgeable people that body temperature was an individual characteristic and differed significantly from person-to-person. It was also believed that people who lived in warmer climates tended to have higher body temperatures than those who lived in colder ones. The perpetuation of these beliefs, once they arose, is understandable because, before the thermometer, there was no effective way to show them to be wrong.

Prescientific beliefs should not be equated with atheoretical beliefs. In some cases beliefs were grounded more or less exclusively in theory, but in theory that was not subject to, or at least not put to, empirical test. The idea, for example, that consumption of walnuts could prevent or cure head illnesses because the convoluted shape of the nut resembled the brain in appearance was based on the theory that effects resemble their causes. The idea strikes us as strange in the extreme, but in the context of a mindset that had been conditioned to read significance into similarities wherever they were found, it was a natural inference to draw.

Sometimes a belief that was eventually shown to be false persisted for a long time despite the fact that observations of phenomena that related to that belief were being made, because the results of those observations were consistent with that belief. Euclid in his *Optics*, for example, espoused a theory of vision according to which the eye emits rays to perceived objects. This theory was as consistent with the mathematics of perspective as the alternative held by some people of the time according to which light travels from objects to the eye.

Before people like Galileo began to sow the seeds of the scientific revolution by attaching great importance to observation and measurement as ways to further understanding of natural phenomena, it was not uncommon even for thinkers to hold false beliefs that could have been discovered to be false by simple observation. The belief that heavier bodies fall faster than lighter ones, for example, prevailed from the time of Aristotle until that of Galileo, although the experiments that Galileo performed to demonstrate that this belief was false could have been done at any time during that 2,000-year period.

This is a particularly interesting example of a persisting false belief because it also might have been questioned strictly on the basis of reasoning, apart from any observations. Galileo posed a question that could have been asked by anybody who believed that heavier bodies fall faster than light ones: If a 10 pound weight falls faster than a 1 pound weight, what will happen when the two are tied together? Will the 11 pound combination fall faster than the 10 pound weight, or will it fall more slowly because the 1 pound weight holds back the 10 pound one?

How should we view beliefs once held that are now known to be wrong? It is natural, perhaps, for us to judge them by current standards and consider them irrational. But that is not fair. The merits of empiricism were not generally recognized before the time of the scientific revolution. The prevailing assumption was that the way to understand nature was to reason about it; the way to discover how things were was to figure out how they must be.

Baron (1985a) defines a delusion as "a belief whose strength is wildly greater than is justified by the evidence that would be available assuming unbiased—i.e., good—thinking" (p. 232). If we accept this definition, we must recognize that available evidence changes over time, as do ideas about what constitutes belief justification, so that the same belief might be considered rational if held at one time but delusional if held at another. Belief that the earth is flat, for example, might be considered rational when ascribed to people living in prescientific times or in nonscientific cultures, but not when it is held by people living today in the industrialized world.

What is rational in the sense of being consistent with available relevant evidence changes as the evidence and standards of relevancy change. To judge prescientific beliefs to be irrational generally is to apply current scientific standards to pre-scientific knowledge. If we wish to do that, we should be willing also to judge our own beliefs in terms of the knowledge of future centuries. Of course we cannot do that, but we can be reasonably confident that many of our current beliefs will seem as odd and unjustified to our successors of a few generations hence as belief in a flat world seems to us.

Prescientific and unscientific beliefs today

Nontrivial numbers of modern inhabitants of developed countries believe that the earth is flat, or that the earth is hollow and open at the poles, or that we live on the inside of a hollow sphere (Gardner, 1957). Many believe in ghosts, poltergeists, and magic in various forms (Rawcliffe, 1959). Not a few seek guidance for their decision making from professional astrologers, who outnumber astronomers by a considerable margin. According to a survey published by the National Science Foundation in 2002, 41% of the American public then believed that astrology is at least somewhat scientific (reported in Shermer, 2003, p. 247). How can people sustain such beliefs in the face of what most scientists would consider overwhelming evidence that they are wrong?

The answer is not necessarily that people who hold such beliefs lack the capacity to reason. As noted in the comment by Thouless above, in some cases they may be able to give better-reasoned rationales for their beliefs than can many people who hold more scientifically orthodox ones, because they have had more experience in defending them against attack. Although they may differ considerably with respect to criteria of relevance they apply to evidence, to the credibility they give to various information sources, and to the interpretation they put on the information they accept, within their own frame of reference they may be able to reason very well.

The question may be asked also with respect to cults. What members of a cult share is a set of beliefs. The beliefs often have behavioral effects and the behaviors are likely to be more apparent to observers than are the beliefs that underlie them, but the beliefs are basic. And these beliefs typically appear to be strange, sometimes bizarre, to people who do not hold them. How is it that they are so readily held by members?

Certainly factors that play a major role are isolation and insulation from opposing views. It is characteristic of many cults that members withdraw from larger society and establish living arrangements and life styles that tend to limit communication outside the group and exposure to ideas and beliefs that conflict with their own. Because they talk primarily with people who share their beliefs, those beliefs are continually reinforced, and any data that arrives from beyond the perimeter of the cult's domain is likely to be interpreted in such a way as to support the in-group views. Some groups go to considerable lengths to insure that members do not have easy access to outside information sources and are not readily exposed to outside influences. Sanctions against deviations from prescribed beliefs and practices can be very strong.

It is easy for outside observers to write off cultism as a simple consequence of ignorance and faulty reasoning and to see members of cults as misguided souls who lack a capacity to be critical with respect to their own beliefs. Devotees are viewed as victims of brainwashing, individuals who have traded their reason for the emotional gratification to be gained from belonging to a cohesive and supportive group. I doubt if it is as simple as this. How cults arise and why people join them are complex questions that are beyond the scope of this book.

A question that is relevant to this book is whether membership in a cult has implications for how one thinks. The answer clearly must be yes. This, in itself, in no way distinguishes cults. Being a member of a political party influences the way one thinks, as does being a member of a mainstream religion, or of a trade union, or of a particular profession. What is likely to distinguish cult membership in this regard is that the beliefs on some matters are strikingly incompatible with prevailing beliefs or opinions on those matters. Defending those beliefs often requires elaborate protective measures that can include doctrines and practices that have the effect of insulating members of the cult from outside influences by inhibiting open exchanges of ideas.

Cult beliefs can be amazingly impervious to even very strong evidence that they are wrong. Many times over the centuries, one or another group has confidently predicted the date of the end of the world and its members, after dutifully preparing for the event, have gathered, as the predicted time approached, to face it together. Failure of the world to cease to exist as predicted seldom seems to have caused a serious rethinking of the belief systems on which such predictions have been based; typically the miscalculation has been rationalized and, often, a new prediction made. Again it must be pointed out, however, that while persistence in the face of contrary indications is characteristic of cult beliefs, such persistence is seen not only in this context. The ability to accommodate counterindicative evidence may be said to be among the more impressive of the abilities that we as a species have developed. Scientists have their share of this ability and exercise it frequently.

It is easy to criticize people for holding strange beliefs. Often we find them amusing, and may, in less gracious moments, poke fun at them. We should not overlook the fact that probably all of us hold beliefs that appear strange to someone else. Moreover, probably each of us has certain prejudices and biases, some of which we may be aware of, and others of which we probably are not. Certainly all of us hold beliefs that will appear strange many years hence.

This does not mean that we should not attempt to distinguish between plausible and implausible beliefs. The human psyche is apparently very fragile. People appear to be capable of believing just about anything. Witness colonial Salem and 20th-century Jonestown. Demagogues and charlatans have never wanted for a receptive audience, no matter how bizarre their message. Attempting to evaluate beliefs, or potential beliefs, in the light of evidence that is relevant to them will not guarantee that one will never hold beliefs that are not warranted, but failing to do so surely increases the likelihood that one will hold some such beliefs.

Credulity

> Most professionals, throughout the ages, have been content to think only what they have been taught. (Cromer, 1993, p. 99)

Credulity, willingness to believe, is a property of persons as recipients of information or claims. We might wish to say that one is the more credulous, the more credence one attaches to an assertion of a given intrinsic credibility. But this would suppose that we know how to establish intrinsic credibility, and we do not. For present purposes let us simply assume that people differ with respect to how much evidence they require before being willing to treat an assertion as though it were true. Some people are willing to believe on the basis of very little evidence indeed.

There are many examples of credulity, some of which have involved entire populaces. France, with its unbridled enthusiasm for John Law's scheme to create wealth through the issuance of paper currency during the early part of the eighteenth century, provides one example of a populace infected with credulousness and avarice. A similar example of a nation gone berserk is found in England at about the same time when speculation in the South-Sea Company (a company established for the purpose of restoring public credit) and numerous other "Bubble Companies" reached inordinate heights (MacKay, 1841/1932).

The tenor of the times is captured by MacKay's characterization of the British populace as "a whole people shaking off the trammels of reason, and running wild after a golden vision, refusing obstinately to believe that it is not real, till, like a deluded hind running after an *ignis fatuus*, they are plunged into a quagmire" (p. 71). The proliferation of stock companies during a brief period around 1720 was, in retrospect, almost beyond belief; the willingness—eagerness—of people to purchase their stock is testimony to the extremes of which human credulity is capable. The dot-com craze in the U.S. stock market is a recent reminder that things have not changed a lot in this respect.

I have never been abducted by extraterrestrial aliens, or at least I do not remember having such an experience. If I ever am abducted, and remember the event, I probably will not be inclined to talk about it. But many reports of abduction experiences have been made (Clark, 1990; Jacobs, 1992). Some people believe these reports, others do not. An interesting question, for present purposes is, what distinguishes people who accept these reports at face value and those who do not. A second is *should* one believe them. Should *I* believe them?

How credible one is likely to find any particular claim to be depends strongly on how consistent that claim is with other beliefs one holds. I would be more likely to accept reports of abductions by aliens if I believed in, or at least accepted the possibility of, the existence of extraterrestrial creatures than if I did not. One's inclination to accept or reject such reports would be expected to depend also on several other factors to greater or lesser degrees. These include the perceived reliability of the sources of the abduction reports, peer influences (the known positions of others regarding the question), implications of acceptance or rejection (e.g., for one's peace of mind), the plausibility of alternative accounts of reported phenomena, and any (probably tacit) standards that one habitually applies to the weighing of evidence.

Should I believe these reports? My answer to this question involves the application of Occam's razor. It seems to me unnecessary and unwise to conclude that people are being abducted by alien beings if there are adequately plausible accounts of the reports and related phenomena that do not require the assumption of the existence of alien beings. I do not mean to suggest that all the people who have reported being abducted have intentionally lied about their experiences. I do not even want to argue that their accounts of those experiences are necessarily inaccurate. My point is that I have seen no evidence on the question that is sufficiently compelling to make me accept what, in my view, would be a fairly radical conclusion, and I find alternative accounts of the data that do not assume the involvement of extraterrestrial beings to be adequately plausible.

Of course, one can argue that *if* we are being visited by highly intelligent aliens with a technology vastly superior to our own, and *if* these visitors are intent on remaining inconspicuous to most earthlings, and so only occasionally whisk away a human or two for a closer look, and usually take steps to muddle their memories of the trip before returning them to earth, incredulous humans like me will never be convinced of their presence—unless of course, we happen to find ourselves among the abductees. All true.

☐ Rational Beliefs

What does rationality demand of the beliefs we hold? I can do no more than offer an opinion (my own belief, if you will) as to the answer to this question, but hopefully an opinion informed by the thinking and research that has been reviewed here.

One can believe only what one finds to be believable. But what one finds to be believable on any particular matter depends, to no small degree, on the extent to which one has sought whatever information is available on that matter. A high degree of rationality requires an effort on the part of the believer to ensure that beliefs are supported by evidence actively sought in an unbiased fashion and fairly evaluated. How much investigation of evidence is adequate regarding any particular belief depends on several considerations, notable among them the importance (to the holder) of the belief in question; some beliefs are worth trying very hard to get right; others are not.

Uninformed beliefs—beliefs that are held without reason; beliefs that have been sheltered from evidence that might tell against them—are not rational beliefs, even if true. Refusing to consider evidence that goes against a favored belief seems to me irrational, even if commonplace and natural.

Reluctance to change a belief, even in the face of evidence that it is not tenable, can be strong. Changing a belief with which one is identified can give the appearance of inconsistency and perhaps weakness of character; it may also require a change in one's view of the world, which can be disturbing. So the natural tendency seems to be to discount evidence that tells against an existing belief or to find a way to interpret the evidence so that it no longer does so.

Rationality requires, I believe, that one not lightly entertain beliefs that are inconsistent with each other, or with evidence that is relevant to them, when that evidence is interpreted as impartially as one can manage. It requires that one be as unbiased as one can in the assessment of evidence that is relevant to beliefs, especially with respect to evidence against existing beliefs, while recognizing that complete objectivity is difficult, if possible, to attain and that few, if any of us are as unbiased as we would prefer to think we are.

When evidence on a question is nondiscriminating with respect to which of two or more possible answers to a question is the more likely to be correct, one may decide on other grounds which, if any, of the possible answers to embrace. I choose not to believe that I am an automaton. And I believe I have that choice, which is to say that I believe strong, but inconclusive, arguments can be made either way. Finally, rationality dictates, I want to argue, that beliefs be recognized as beliefs, and consequently as fallible. One does well to believe that some of one's beliefs are false.

CHAPTER 5

Goals, Values, and Affect

☐ Goals

> Reason can be used by whoever grasps it, for whatever purpose—it does not discriminate. (Calne, 1999, p. 71)

Goals exist at many levels. And what is a goal from one vantage point may be a means to an end from another. Behavior can be seen as driven by hierarchies of means–ends relationships in which the ends at one level of a hierarchy serve as means to ends at higher levels. Structured approaches to decision making may explicitly acknowledge the multi-level nature of goals and promote the idea that an important component of decision making is explicating goal structures in hierarchical form (Keeney & Raiffa, 1976). Lower-level goals (the immediate objectives) of behavior are usually fairly easy to identify, even if they have not been made explicit. The deeper, longer-range goals and purposes that motivate behavior often are not clear, and even when one can say what they are, whether the behavior in question really serves them can be debatable.

Baron (1985a) has written of the fact that goals that relate explicitly to thinking can have a lot to do with the quality of one's thinking. Good thinking, may be fostered, he suggests, by "the goal of thinking well (as something one can take pride in); the goal of knowing the truth, of getting to the bottom of things; the goal of making good decisions; the goal of being reasonable in the sense of being likable for one's open-mindedness and receptivity to the suggestions of others; the goal of being moral or doing the right thing (since it often requires good thinking to decide what the right thing is); the goal of being a good citizen; or the goal of thinking for it's own sake, as something that is enjoyable as an activity (socially or alone)" (p. 256). On the other side of the coin are goals that work against good thinking such as "the goal of being steadfast (in sticking to one's conclusions despite counterevidence); the goal of reaching conclusions quickly; the goal of being authoritative (powerful in some sense); and the goal of honoring authority (despite counterevidence)" (p. 256).

Goal-directed thinking

The term "goal-directed thinking" is ambiguous in an interesting way: it can connote thinking that is directed *by* goals or thinking that is directed *at* goals. In the first case, the reference is to thinking that is done in the service of goals—a specific goal is given; the challenge is to figure out how to attain it. The goal might have been selected by oneself or imposed by someone else. It could be to solve a textbook mathematics problem, to improve one's performance at one's job, to accomplish some specific military objective, to rob a bank, or to destroy someone's reputation; whatever it is, one's acceptance of it defines one's task, and thinking is directed toward finding an effective way of performing that task. In the second sense of goal-directed thinking, goals are themselves the object of thought. In this case, one thinks *about* goals. Is a particular goal ethical? Is it consistent with one's personal values? Is it worth pursuing? If two goals are in conflict, which should take precedence? How does one—how should one—decide what one's goals should be?

Some writers contend that reason can tell us how to attain goals, but not what goals are worth pursuing. Russell (1954) takes this position. Allais (1979/1990) puts it this way: "It cannot be too strongly emphasized *that there are no criteria for the rationality of ends as such other than the condition of consistency*. Ends are completely arbitrary. To prefer highly dispersed random outcomes may seem irrational to the prudent, but for somebody with this penchant, there is nothing irrational about it. This area is like that of tastes: they are what they are, and differ from one person to the next" (p. 115).

Ehrenfeld (1981) contends that the assumption that pure reason suffices to distinguish what is humane and just from what is inhumane and unjust is patently false—that this is exactly what reason cannot do. Reason might reveal the conditions under which a country could expect to "win" a nuclear war by launching a first strike, but it alone could not be the basis for deciding the rightness or wrongness of starting a nuclear war. "There is no calculus of the just and the unjust" (p. 144). Simon (1983/1990) likens reason to a gun for hire that can be used in the service of whatever goals one has. The outrage we are likely to experience in reading Hitler's *Mein Kampf*, he argues, is not prompted by the quality of the reasoning we find there, but by what it alleges to be fact and by the offensive values it displays.

Calne (1999) describes reason as a tool—like language and mathematics. It helps to get what we want, but not to choose what we want. He sees a general turning against reason during recent years, which he attributes to disillusionment that resulted when quixotic hopes vested in reason and science early in the twentieth century were shaken by two world wars and a variety of other developments. Reason became discredited, he argues, because of exaggerated claims and false hopes. "Those who oppose reason have no difficulty in pointing to its failures, but these failures have all stemmed from misguided expectations. The hopes sprang from natural, if reckless, optimism—without critical thought about the nature of reason and without recognizing the need to clarify what reason can and cannot do" (p. 12). Reason, Calne contends, is an indispensable human capability, but it cannot control the purposes to which it is put.

From this perspective, reasoning serves many goals, bad as well as good. Realization of this should disabuse us of the easy assumption that making people smarter is tantamount to making them better. We appear to be obliged to admit that misanthropic or sadistic behavior can be rational for misanthropes and sadists. Behavior that most people would consider bizarre or psychopathic could be seen as rational for the individual with bizarre or psychopathic goals. While this may make us uncomfortable, what is the alternative? Clearly, we cannot require that to behave rationally one must behave in a way that is at odds with one's goals.

But what if one of our goals is to evaluate our goals—to decide which of many possible goals are worth having? Is it really the case that reason has nothing to contribute to this problem? I do not find this position plausible and doubt that this is quite what Russell or Allais or Simon meant by their cited comments. Perhaps the point that Russell and others intended to make was that reason, by itself, is not up to the task of selecting goals; in the final analysis what we consider important must derive from basic values and preferences that cannot be justified by reason alone. This interpretation seems to me to be right. On the other hand, thinking critically *about* goals is surely at least as important an aspect of rationality as is the effective pursuit *of* goals once they have been adopted.

If thinking about goals forces one to think about—evaluate—values and preferences, perhaps rationality demands that as well. Nagel (1986) illustrates the need with reference to an example given by Hume of one who prefers the destruction of the world to the scratching of his finger. Such a one, Nagel argues, "may not be involved in a contradiction or in any false expectations, but there is something the matter with him nonetheless, and anyone else not in the grip of an overnarrow conception of what reasoning is would regard his preference as objectively wrong" (p. 155). We should note that Nagel's assessment of the imaginary person's preference as objectively wrong implies the existence of another set of unstated values that Nagel considers superior to the one expressed. The implied values in this case would probably represent a strong consensus view.

But how do we deal with the fact that the consensus view in one culture may be diametrically opposed to that in another? In an age of hypersensitivity to political correctness, and wide endorsement of the idea that all values are relative, any suggestion that the values of some cultures should be changed is bound to invite rebuke. One must wonder how generally espousers of relativism with respect to values and ethics are willing to apply this view. Graham (1992) asks the question in concrete terms: "Shall we say simply that slavery, human sacrifice, or widow-burning is wrong for us but right for them?" (p. 42).

Even within a culture, goals that are widely assumed to be worth pursuing may deserve critical scrutiny from time to time. Wealth, leisure, and many options regarding how to spend one's time are certainly among the goals that are widely accepted within western civilization as worthy of pursuit. What is the evidence that their attainment is satisfying? Sapolsky (2002) notes that, despite the progress that has been made in realizing such goals in developed countries, major depression has become increasingly common, and he speculates that the upward trend is likely to continue. Technology, he contends, is not likely to help reduce our stress. "We will continue to come up with inventions that save us time, and then, as usual, we will readjust upward our expectation of how much there is to get done. We will fashion more material luxuries, but then we will recalibrate our baseline sense of entitlement. We have our zillions of gadgets and our leisure-filled lifestyles, but often these options are empty ones, as we struggle to decide which breakfast cereal, plastic surgeon, new-model car, or new-model spouse will be the one that finally makes us happy" (p. 116). It is not necessary to agree uncritically with this dour prediction to believe that even goals that have been taken for granted for some time may prove questionable on reflection.

One finds in the psychological literature many descriptions of thinking directed at the accomplishment of specific goals but very little discussion of thinking critically *about* goals. The distinction between thinking in the service of goals and thinking directed at goals has not been made sharply by most investigators of thinking. Exceptions to this observation are Einhorn and Hogarth (1981a), Moser (1990) and Reyna, Lloyd, and Brainerd (2003). Einhorn and Hogarth distinguish between *instrumental* rationality (the efficiency by which means secure ends) and *moral* rationality (the goodness of the ends themselves). Moser makes a similar distinction between the *instrumentalist* conception of rationality, according to which rationality is taken to be "a minister without portfolio," not requiring specific substantive goals of its own, but consisting in the optimal pursuit of one's preferred ends, whatever they happen to be, and the *substantialist* conception of rationality, according to which rationality is seen as a "minister with portfolio," because it holds that certain ends are essential to it. The latter view, Moser contends, originated with Aristotle and held sway among Western philosophers until losing influence with the rise of decision theory in recent times.

These distinctions are reminiscent of one made by Horkheimer (1947/1974) between subjective and objective reason. Subjective reason, in his terms, "is essentially concerned with means and ends, with the adequacy of procedures for purposes more or less taken for granted and supposedly self-explanatory. It attaches little importance to the question whether the purposes as such are reasonable" (p. 3). This view of reason, Horkheimer claims, is prevalent in modern Western thinking, but was not always so. The prevailing view for a long time was that reason existed as a force in the world, and great philosophical systems were founded on an objective theory of reason. Horkheimer contends that objective and subjective conceptions of reason have co-existed from the beginning but that while the former was prevalent for many centuries, the latter is so today; and he leaves little doubt regarding his assessment of this change: "The more the concept of reason becomes emasculated, the more easily it lends itself to ideological manipulation and to propagation of even the most blatant lies" (p. 24). Subjective reason, he argues, lends itself to the uses of the adversaries of traditional humanitarian values as readily as to their defenders. In Horkheimer's view, the reduction of reason to "a mere instrument" constitutes an abasement of reason the consequences of which can be, and already have been, dire.

In sum, whether reason has to do with the selection or evaluation of goals, or merely with the devising of means to attain goals once they have been established, is a question about which important differences of opinion have been expressed. In the final analysis, each of us must decide what he or she thinks about the matter. A rationality that does not consider goals in a critical and evaluative way falls short of what my intuition tells me rationality should be.

Motivation

The role of motivation in reasoning has been a subject of research and debate for some time. One of the contexts in which the interaction of motivation and cognition has been of interest is that of self-serving biases. Klaczynski and Fauth (1997) contend, for example, that people are motivated to process evidence more critically when it contradicts valued beliefs than when it supports them. Other investigators have reported similar findings (Baron, 1991, 1995; Perkins, Allen, & Hafner, 1983; Perkins, Farady, & Bushey, 1991).

On the other hand, Kunda (1990) notes that many of the phenomena that once were attributed to motivational variables have been reinterpreted more recently in cognitive terms; according to this interpretation, conclusions that appear to be drawn only because people want to draw them may be drawn because they are more consistent with prior beliefs and expectancies. She notes too that some theorists have come to believe that motivational effects are mediated by cognitive processes. Kunda defends this view, arguing that the evidence is consistent with the assumption that motivation affects reasoning, but that it does so through cognitive strategies for accessing, constructing and evaluating beliefs. Cognitive processes play a major role in producing self-serving biases by providing the mechanisms through which motivation affects reasoning. The primary cognitive operation hypothesized to mediate motivational effects is the biased searching of memory. Evidence of various types converges, Kunda argues, on desired conclusions, because those knowledge structures—memories, beliefs, and rules—that support them are accessed more readily than those that do not.

In general, when motivation has been manipulated in a controlled way in experimental situations, people who have been more highly motivated to do well—be accurate, minimize mistakes—have done better in terms of a variety of performance criteria than those who have not been so motivated (Billings & Scherer, 1988; McAllister, Mitchell, & Beach, 1979; Tetlock, 1983, 1985). Effects of differences in motivation can be mistaken for effects of differences in cognitive capacity (Kühberger, 2000).

One explanation of the beneficial effect of motivation on reasoning is that when people are highly motivated to be accurate, they are less likely to terminate their searching for, or processing of, evidence prematurely (Kruglanski, 1980; Kruglanski & Ajzen, 1983). Another is that motivation for accuracy not only decreases the likelihood of premature closure, it also beneficially influences the quality of processing that is done by eliciting more effective inferential procedures (Kunda, 1987, 1990).

Goal achievement as a criterion of rationality

> The strict decision-making criteria for rationality in the form of consistency and coherence . . . may not in practice be nearly as important as

criteria such as personal satisfaction and fulfilment. (Schneider & Barnes, 2003, p. 398)

As we have already noted, sometimes behavior is considered rational to the extent that it helps one realize one's goals. Clarke (1985) argues that the relationship between rationality and goal attainment is more complex than this simple equation suggests. Consider the following argument, which he uses to make a point:

I want E
My doing M is sufficient to attain E if C
C obtains
I ought to do M

Clarke contends that the argument is invalid, that the conclusion does not follow from the premises, because it is possible for the premises to be true and the conclusion false. "If, for example, driving my car is sufficient for getting me to work, I would not be justified in inferring that I should drive it. There may be considerations that would lead me to prefer the costs and benefits of taking the bus instead" (p. 25). More generally, rational decisions regarding what one ought to do in the pursuit of a particular goal would seem to require that one take into account the various actions that are possible, the relative costs of taking them, and so on.

Many decision situations have the characteristic that by increasing the likelihood of attaining a desired goal one also increases the likelihood of attaining a concomitant result that is not desired. This is seen clearly in situations that are well represented by the theory of signal detection, in which one can increase the probability of the desirable result of correctly detecting signals that are present by increasing also the probability of the undesirable result of incorrectly "detecting" signals that are not present (Green & Swets, 1966; Tanner & Swets, 1954). This fact is highly relevant to the evaluation of the effectiveness of diagnostic systems in medicine (Swets & Pickett, 1982) and numerous other contexts (Swets, 1988; Swets, Pickett, Whitehead, Getty, Schnur, Swets, & Freeman, 1979). The point is that any attempt to evaluate the rationality of decisions or actions on the basis of their effectiveness in achieving goals should not overlook possible consequences in addition to those that constitute goal attainment, narrowly construed.

The problem of hidden costs in decision making is well documented, as is that of the ubiquity of unanticipated tradeoffs. Sowell (1995) provides many socially significant examples. Again the point is that the use of goal attainment as a yardstick against which to measure the rationality of decisions or actions is trickier than it may appear, and an assessment that ignores hidden costs and tradeoffs can easily yield conclusions that are unlikely to stand scrutiny.

Finally, in keeping with the foregoing discussion, rationality would seem to dictate also consideration of the reasonableness of the goals themselves and of the question of whether they perhaps would best be changed. Again, Graham (1992) provides an illustration of the point. "Why would it be more rational for me to work for the money to pay for meals in more expensive restaurants than educate myself to become more conscious of the flavors of fruit, yogurt, and wholemeal bread?" (p. 281).

☐ Values

> Cognition is replete with valuations and decisions of all kinds. Its rationality is expressed precisely in the manner in which these valuations are made and these decisions are reached. (Albert, 1985, p. 84)

When we think of the uses of evidence in the abstract, our natural inclination is to focus on truth determination as the primary, if not the only, purpose for which evidence is considered. The assumption is that we use evidence in order to maximize our chances of drawing conclusions that are true. But unless the evidence one is evaluating is sufficiently strong to establish truth or falsity with certainty, there is always the possibility of drawing a wrong conclusion, and one may be more desirous of avoiding some types of errors than others. One may decide in favor of a particular conclusion, say A, even though the evidence indicates that a different conclusion, B, is more likely to be correct, because one would rather make the error of concluding A when B holds than that of concluding B when A is true. The rule that unless the guilt of a defendant in a criminal trial is proved beyond a reasonable doubt, the jury must acquit, illustrates the point. It reflects a value system that considers the erroneous conviction of an innocent person to be a more objectionable failure of justice than the erroneous acquittal of a guilty one.

There are many ways in which values may influence the uses that are made of evidence. We may require more counterindicative evidence to give up or revise beliefs that we value than to give up or revise beliefs that are of little importance to us. The value one places on protecting one's self image may influence one's treatment of evidence that relates to it. The value one attaches to knowing the answer to a particular question is likely to help determine how much time and effort one is willing to devote to finding it.

The principle of maximization of expected utility—the first principle of rationality for some theorists—takes utility, or one's value system, as given. This permits us to judge the rationality of behavior within, or relative to, a given utility set; but what about the value system itself? Does it make sense to say that one value system is more rational than another? And, if so, by what criteria do we judge the rationality of such systems?

Can questions of values be debated on rational grounds? Should rationality itself be seen as a value? Does the desire to be rational not presuppose a certain value system, and in particular a system that attaches great importance to reason? Is it not the case, as Edney (1980) suggests, that rationality is sometimes defined in terms of what is sensible and good, which is to say in value-laden terms?

Values and the representation of opposed views

Presumably most parents want their children to become independent responsible adults capable of making their own decisions and determining for themselves what they will believe. At the same time, again presumably, they wish to instill in them certain attitudes, values, and beliefs that they themselves have come to view as correct and important. In other words, one wants to teach a child to respect honest differences of opinion and to safeguard the right of all persons to their own beliefs; on the other hand, if one believes that there are certain beliefs and principles that are worth dying for, one can hardly be expected to take a laissez-faire attitude toward views that directly oppose them. I confess to being unable to understand how any parents can be indifferent to what their children believe or value or to the attitudes they develop toward their own lives, toward other people, or toward the world in which they live.

Parents (as well as teachers, preachers, and others in a position to influence the formation of people's values) often attempt to present a spectrum of views on questions of value so children, students, parishioners will be able to judge their own beliefs on their merits relative to alternative beliefs that could be held. The fact is, however, that none of us is very good at representing fairly views that we ourselves do not hold. When we attempt to explain how our own values relate to others that are inconsistent with them, we cannot be expected to do justice to the latter. What does intellectual honesty require of us in view of this fact?

How do we treat opposing beliefs and values honestly when we are not indifferent to what our children, and others as well, come to believe and to hold dear?

One possibility is to opt for indoctrination. This means presenting in the most favorable light possible the view that one wishes others to adopt, magnifying its strengths and ignoring its weaknesses. It means presenting caricatures of opposing views—representations of those views that emphasize or exaggerate aspects of them that can be criticized most easily—and then, of course, showing systematically the superiority of one's favored view to these caricatures. This is the straw man approach, widely honored in practice if not in word. The dishonesty of this approach aside, the risk in it is that later, when those who have been indoctrinated come in contact with people who hold the caricaturized views, they may discover the difference between the caricatures and the real things, and the arguments that were telling against the former may be ineffective against the latter.

Another possibility is to make an effort to present opposing views as honestly and as objectively as possible, recognizing and acknowledging one's limitations in this regard. One can and should also, I believe, point out why one considers one's own views to be worthy of being held. To present honestly views that one does not hold does not require presenting them sympathetically; it requires only that one not intentionally withhold or distort what one believes to be the facts. It requires also, however, the realization and acknowledgement that one's assessment of opposing views is very likely to be biased by virtue of the fact that they are *opposing* views.

Value-free or valueless

One myth that needs to be exploded is the idea that there is such a thing as a value-free approach to any nontrivial aspect of life. Sometimes people speak of a value-free approach to education, or of science being value free, or of the possibility of avoiding the necessity of value judgments in one's dealing with controversial issues. But avoiding making value judgments is not possible, and any serious attempt to do so quickly mires one in self contradiction and paradox. Insistence that science should be value free, for example, reflects a value judgment. Espousal of the scientific method as an effective means of acquiring useful knowledge about the world makes little sense unless some value is attached to the acquisition of such knowledge. The idea that education can or should be value-free or value-neutral is self-contradictory; acceptance of it would not make education value-free but valueless.

Even such an apparently objective and abstract subject as deductive logic is not value-free. Lewis (1990) makes this point. "Deductive logic is first of all a way of thinking, believing, and knowing; second, a way of thinking, believing and knowing about values; third, a dominant value in itself (when we place more emphasis on logic than on authority or some other mode of reasoning, we are making a crucial *value* judgment), one that precedes and colors all the other value judgments that we make" (p. 38). The idea that it is better to be logical than to be illogical is a value judgment. The attachment of importance to logical consistency rests upon this judgment; logic has no force to one for whom consistency has no worth. As Lewis also points out, discussions of the idea of value itself, even when an effort is made to keep them as fair and objective as possible, are unlikely to be free of bias and subjectivity.

One must have values. The determination that one must make, explicitly or implicitly, is what values one will have. In my view, rationality requires that we be open about this. That means attempting to understand and being willing to acknowledge what our values are; perhaps it means putting effort into the *discovery* of what they are (March, 1972). It means too being willing to reflect on them, to expose them to criticism, and to modify them when convinced that they should be modified. As to the basis on which we should be convinced of the need of modification, we are again thrown back on intuition.

Hard decisions

Many of the decisions that must be made, explicitly or implicitly, by society or by individuals, involve weighing costs and benefits, and this can only be done within the framework of some value system. Some of these decisions are very difficult, requiring forced choices among unattractive alternatives. The problem of resource allocation arises, for example, in the medical context with respect to especially expensive equipment and procedures, such as those involved in bone marrow and organ transplantation, long-term kidney dialysis, coronary artery surgery, and imaging with high-cost systems. How does society cope rationally with its inability to meet all the demands that are placed on such resources? If rationing in some form is required, how does it decide the conditions under which an individual will or will not receive a specific type of medical care?

Rationing, in this context, is a powerfully negative concept, to many a morally offensive one; we cannot escape the fact, however, that whenever the demands for medical services exceed what a society can supply, something tantamount to rationing occurs, although it may not be called by that name, or even recognized as such. And the situation, even in the most technologically advanced countries, is that the medical system is unable to meet all the demands placed upon it. Consequently choices, explicit or implicit, as to who will receive a specific service and who will not are a constant fact of life. How those choices are made should be a matter of concern. There is little evidence that they are made in a completely rational or even consistent way.

A problem closely related to that of the allocation of limited medical resources is the question of the appropriate uses of biotechnology, such as genetic testing. The rapidly increasing ability to determine through genetic testing whether a given individual is more of less likely to suffer, at some point, from a disease or disability that is at least in part of genetic origin—Huntington's chorea, Alzheimer's dementia, colon cancer—is forcing consideration of some very difficult questions (Rennie, 1994). When such information is available, who should be given access to it—individuals at risk, their spouses, other members of their families, employers, potential employers, insurers, prospective insurers? And who should answer this question? As difficult as this problem is, it shrinks in significance compared to the related, but not quite so immediate, question of the implications of sufficient knowledge of genetic engineering to make feasible a significant degree of genetic customizing of yet unborn children.

While there are likely to be many different opinions regarding the specific criteria on which decisions on such matters should be based, I suspect that many people will agree that they should be relatively objective and that personal feelings and emotions should play little, if any, role. But is it reasonable to expect that feelings and emotions can be disregarded in these situations? And why do we even wish that they could be? Would their suppression mean that the resulting decisions would be more humane? There is at least suggestive evidence that this would not be the case in the fact that physicians find it easier to decide against providing medical care to a patient on the basis of low priority or limited resources if they do not have to face the patient personally with that decision (Schwartz & Aaron, 1984/1988). Perhaps it is the case, as Ehrenfeld (1981) argues, that "dispensing with emotion because it is not rational is like rejecting one's lungs because they do not formulate thoughts" (p. 154).

Cost-benefit analyses can lead to decisions regarding medical treatment that are different from those that would be produced by clinical considerations alone (Boyle, Torrance, Sinclair, & Horwood, 1983/1988). It does not follow that decisions indicated by cost-benefit analyses are the ones that should be taken. Sometimes society may be willing to subsidize treatment in a situation in which the cost outweighs the benefit, at least from some perspective. In such cases a broadening of the concepts of cost and benefit to include such subjective factors as the value to society of perceiving itself as caring and humane, or the importance it attaches to certain ethical principles or ideals, could have the effect of making the benefits, thus redefined, outweigh the costs.

More generally, any cost-benefit analysis is done within some specific frame of reference, although the frame in which it is done may not be made explicit. A question can always be raised as to the appropriateness of the frame. If only short-term or local costs and benefits are considered, for example, it is reasonable to ask whether longer-term or more global factors should also be considered. Or if certain relevant categories of costs or benefits are omitted from the equation, perhaps because they are difficult to quantify, one may question the adequacy of an analysis that does not include them.

The relevance of these issues to societal decision making are nowhere more apparent than in the context of the problem of detrimental environmental change. The costs incurred by industries in producing material goods and those that are passed on to consumers who purchase those goods tend to be short-term costs only. Little attempt has yet been made to factor into the equation costs that may be borne by future generations that will have to deal with, say, depleted resources or the contamination of soil, water or the atmosphere from the processes involved in production. In considering cost-benefit relationships, it is very easy to discount or ignore costs that will have to be paid by generations other than one's own.

There is an unquestioned need for better ways to quantify both the costs—including lost-opportunity costs—and the benefits of specific environmental measures, and the needed techniques must take into account trade-offs involving difficult value judgments (Hammond & Coppock, 1990). The need is illustrated by an attempt by Krupnick and Portney (1991) to do a cost-benefit assessment of controls proposed for improving air quality, especially in the Los Angeles area, by decreasing the concentration of tropospheric ozone and particulates. The investigators concluded that the expected costs of the proposed controls would probably exceed their benefits, and the publication of this conclusion evoked objections both regarding the benefits mentioned (or overlooked) and the monetary values assigned to them (Chapman, 1991; Friedman, 1991; Lents, 1991; Lippert & Morris, 1991).

How does one assess the value of emotional or restorative benefits that people realize from recreational uses of wilderness areas (Kaplan & Talbot, 1983; Rossman & Ulehla, 1977; Shafer & Mietz, 1969) or to the contributions that are made to physical and mental health by trees, nature parks, and plants (Gold, 1977; Kaplan, 1983) and by birds and other wildlife (Hounsome, 1979) in urban areas? Efforts to incorporate quality-of-life assessments in economic evaluations have been made, but there is not a high degree of consensus as to how this should be done (Drummond, 1987/1988). People do not all attach the same value to any given aspect of the environment (Fischhoff, 1991; Pearce & Turner, 1990); moreover different people can value the same aspect for different, and sometimes conflicting, reasons (to wit sailors vs. power boaters, rafters vs. fishermen, snowmobilers vs. skiers).

The quantification of costs and benefits is especially difficult and controversial when it requires the attachment of numerical worth to human life, health or well-being. If one does a cost-benefit analysis as part of a process to decide whether a hospital system should acquire more dialysis machines, the cost part of this equation is straightforward, and it causes us little difficulty even when it is expressed in terms of cost per year of prolonged life (Ludbrook, 1981). But many of us are likely to find it intuitively less easy to assign a monetary value to those years, or even to think in those terms. Russell (1990) speaks of the "almost visceral reaction against the open consideration of any trade-off regarding human health and the environment [that he encountered within the EPA], even though such trade-offs are implicit in every decision" (p. 17).

The difficulty of the problem of assessing costs and benefits of various policies and practices that affect the environment is exacerbated by the fact that how things look depends on one's vantage point. Much depends not only on whether one takes a short- or long-term view, but also on whether one considers local or global effects, and in the former case, which local area is involved. The problem is illustrated by the ongoing debates in the international arena regarding the extent to which the emission of greenhouse gases should be limited in developing countries and who should bear the costs of any imposed limitations. According to one view, industrialized countries should bear most of these costs because these countries have contributed more than their fair per-capita share to the creation of the problem and have reaped the benefits of industrialization. Opinions differ as to how to translate this principle into numbers. Moreover, different countries can be expected to attach different values to the same benefit, depending on their stage of economic development and standard of living (Bhagwati, 1993).

Difficulties in quantifying costs and benefits arise too in the context of the decisions with which individuals are often faced. Sometimes quantitative values that cannot be expressed directly by people who have to make the decisions can be inferred, within limits, from the choices they make, as, for example when medical patients express a preference for a treatment with a high probability of improving their condition for a short time over a treatment that has the possibility of a longer-term effect, or more dramatic improvement but a smaller probability of providing it (Eraker & Sox, 1981; McNeil, Weichselbaum, & Pauker, 1978).

One view of what constitutes rational behavior with respect to cost-benefit analyses is that one should behave in such a way as to maximize the positive difference between benefits and costs, which is to say one should strive to get the most benefit for the least cost. But this is helpful only in the abstract. The really difficult part of the problem is determining what the benefits and costs are, and this requires the making of value judgments on which people often find it difficult to agree. The problem is further complicated by the fact that the people who realize the benefits from goods and services are not always those who pay the costs of their production and use, but this also helps establish the importance of doing such analyses. Without a reasonably accurate understanding of what the actual total benefits and costs are, and of who receives or bears them, it is hard to see what could provide a rational basis for deciding whether specific goods and services are desirable and from whose point of view they may or may not be so.

MacLean (1990) argues that, at least in the case of the assumed benefits on which environmental preservation programs are focused, the issue underlying their quantification is not strictly economic in nature, but philosophical. It is, he contends, a subject of ethics. "The appropriateness of discounting the value of future lives, the application of benefit-cost analysis as a method of setting environmental policies more generally, and other issues that remain central and contentious in the environmental policy arena are essentially moral disputes" (p. 85). Hard decisions are often like that. Again we find ourselves pushed back to fairly basic intuitions, in this case to fundamental convictions about the nature of right and wrong.

Rationality, morality and ethics

> The key notions of epistemology are normative through and through. "Justification," "warrant," "rationality," and the like are all matters of what one *ought* or *ought not* to believe. (Lycan, 1988, p. 128)

What is the relationship between rationality and morality, or ethics? Can either topic be treated independently of the other? Are despotic tyrants irrational, or just evil? Is it possible to be evil without being irrational? Can one be ethical without being rational? Rational without being ethical? Does one have a moral obligation to reason well? Or at least to attempt to do so?

Many people, the writer among them, see as essential to a meaningful concept of morality the assumption that, as individuals, we are free agents—which is to say that our belief that we have the ability to make choices is not an illusion and that the choices we make are not predetermined by the laws of physics. This is only an assumption, of course, and hardly provable, but without it the idea of moral responsibility makes little sense. Indeed, without it, it is hard to imagine any connotation that could be given to rationality that would be interesting. I find compelling Polkinghorne's (1991) argument that the denial of human freedom is incoherent, because it destroys rationality.

Rationality has to do with the question of how we *ought* to think. How we should treat evidence, how we should form and evaluate beliefs and opinions, the ways in which we should reason from premises to conclusions, are seen not as matters of taste and individual preference but as matters of obligation. The assumption is that there are certain rules or principles, not always easily articulated, that have the force of moral imperatives. That is to say there are right ways to reason and wrong ways to reason and we have an obligation to try to do it right.

Of course, this assumption can be challenged. Why should we feel an obligation to try to reason well? And if one recognizes some such obligation, are there limits to the claims of rationality upon us? To what extent should we strive to be rational? Are there situations in which rationality should not be the goal? Jungermann (1980) notes that there may be situations in which people feel the application of a rational technique for decision-making is inappropriate. Deciding whether to marry a particular person, for example, may be viewed as a decision problem that is appropriately resolved emotionally. The very thought of using a rational decision aid in such a context would appear to many to be cold and unfeeling, not to say dehumanizing, however strong a case one might make for it on logical grounds. On the other hand, few people would urge, I assume, that one should try hard in such situations to behave in an *irrational*, as distinct from an *arational*, way.

In his account of the concepts of justice and rationality in Homeric and post-Homeric Greece, MacIntyre (1988) notes that good practical reasoning, as represented in the Homeric poems, requires certain virtues in those who exhibit it. Practical reasoning arises from someone asking the question "what am I to do?" Knowing what is required of one is knowing one's role within a universe structured in terms of hierarchically ordered social rules.

A distinction that MacIntyre finds useful is between goods of excellence and goods of effectiveness. These are not presented as mutually exclusive goods; indeed the successful pursuit of goods of one type often requires obtaining, at least to some degree, goods of the other type. However, it is possible for an individual or group to subordinate the one kind of good to the other; Thucydides, for example, subordinated the goods of excellence to the goods of effectiveness, whereas Plato did the reverse. To Aristotle, virtue was fundamental to rationality; one could not make rational judgments and act in a rational way unless one had become a virtuous person: "To be uneducated in the virtues is precisely to be unable as yet to judge rightly what is good or best for one's self" (MacIntyre, 1988, p. 109). This idea is not at odds with the view that rationality is consistency with self interest; Aristotle simply says that without virtue one cannot understand what one's self-interest is.

Nagel (1986) notes that the claim that what is moral must be rational can have more than one meaning. It can mean that to be immoral is always irrational, or that to be moral is never irrational, the latter interpretation being weaker than the first. He argues that there are three possibilities regarding the rationality of a contemplated action: "Either the reasons against may be decisive enough so that the act would be irrational; or the reasons for may be decisive enough so that the act is rationally required; or there may be enough reasons both for and against so that although the act is not rationally required, it would not be irrational either—in other words, it would be rational in the weak sense: rationally acceptable" (p. 200). Nagel confesses to being strongly inclined to the view that morality must be rational at least in the weak sense, which is to say not irrational, but to prefer to be able to subscribe to a theory that showed it to be rational in a strong sense.

Calne (1999) sees a connection between rationality and morality in the need for communities to act in certain ways that are consistent with their survival. "The evidence suggests that morality is a coherent system of rational guidelines on how communities have to operate if they are to survive in an environment with limited resources. . . A rational backbone to morality (in the same sense that science has a rational backbone) becomes plausible if we recognize that ethics are not just a supercode of idealized answers to theoretical questions of what is good or bad. They have a very practical biological purpose, namely *to reconcile the needs of society with those of the individual*—and reconciliation is a necessary condition for the survival of our species" (pp. 82, 83). Reason tells us, Calne argues, that if a community is to prosper, it must have a code of ethics that encourages individual behavior that promotes the common good. A major challenge to the development of an ethical code that accomplishes this is that of recognizing the need for both competition and cooperation and for a balance between them.

Calne argues too, however, that although reason has played a central role in the development of ethical values, it is morally neutral in the sense that it is used to advantage by those who violate those values as well as by those who honor them. Criminals use reason to plead their case when caught—to attribute their criminal behavior to mitigating circumstances—while, on the other hand, society uses reason to justify holding people responsible for their actions. He might have pointed out also that criminals use reason not only to attempt to explain away crimes after having been caught, but to plot them in the first place; and it is at least a plausible hypothesis that the higher the quality of the reasoning used in planning, the higher the probability that the crime goes unsolved, or even undetected.

The objective of reconciling the needs of the community with those of the individuals who comprise it assumes the identifiability of both types of needs, which, in turn, requires that it is possible to distinguish between needs and desires. This is assuredly easier said than done. Adler (1981) makes a fairly sharp distinction, arguing that while everyone has the same human needs, individuals differ with regard to their wants. The difference between needs and wants is seen in the fact that the claim that one needs X is contestable—its truth can be evaluated objectively—whereas the claim that one wants X is not contestable—one wants what one wants. It is the affirmation of common natural needs—the means of subsistence, health, knowledge—not wants, Adler contends, that underlies the affirmation of natural rights. Adler argues too that we ought not to want what we do not need if that interferes with wanting and acquiring what we do need. The principle would be more compelling, in my view, if it were not for the fact that needs vary in degree, as Maslow (1954) has so effectively pointed out, making the line between needs and wants fuzzy. This is not to deny that some needs (food, shelter) will be widely recognized as needs, while some wants (a yacht, caviar) will be recognized by most people as less than essential.

It is also the case that what are *considered* to be needs by individuals may depend strongly on the social environment in which they exist. Many of the amenities of life that would be considered as luxuries in the poorer parts of the world (central heating, air conditioning, television) are seen as essential in the more affluent societies. And even within the same country, what one believes one needs is likely to depend on the lifestyle to which one has become accustomed.

Some people have worried that, as a species, we have advanced intellectually faster and farther than we have advanced morally. As evidence they contrast the remarkable technological achievements of the last few centuries, including the impressive array of weapons of mass destruction that have been developed, with the almost total failure to improve our ability to get along with each other. Barrow (1998), among others, notes the plausibility of the speculation that a technological society is unlikely to progress much beyond the point at which it has the means to destroy itself. This concern is heightened by the apparent disparity between the phenomenal rate of development of fundamental knowledge in the physical and biological sciences that can be used for world altering applications and the lack of progress in understanding how to ensure that the power of technology be used only for constructive ends.

The human brain differs from the brain of higher primates much more in its development of the cerebral cortex than in that of the organ's lower strata. Von Bertalanffy (1967) suggests that human evolution has been almost exclusively on the intellectual, as opposed to the instinctual, side. "The ten billion neurons of the cortex made possible the progress from stone axes to airplanes and atomic bombs, and from primitive mythology to quantum theory. However, there is no corresponding development on the instinctual side. For this reason, man's moral instincts have hardly improved over those of the chimpanzee" (p. 24). It is interesting that von Bertalanffy associates ethics with instinct, as distinct from intellect. I argue in this book that rationality rests ultimately on human intuitions regarding fundamental laws of inference and the uses of evidence. In this regard, therefore, I see a commonality and not a difference. A sense of fairness and justice and a distinction between right and wrong appear to be universal among human beings as does recognition that some inferences are valid and others are not, although in both cases, societies may differ with respect to particulars.

Reasoning about ethics

> To arrive at certain ultimate standards, by which all else can be evaluated, is the cardinal problem of reflection in ethics. It is a problem which every one, who participates in social life, must solve in some fashion, well or ill. (Columbia Associates in Philosophy, 1923, p. 302)

Whether or not there is a deep relationship between rationality and ethics, we can certainly reason *about* ethics, as attested by the writings of many philosophers from both ancient and modern times (e.g., Aristotle, 350 BC/2004; Bentham, 1789/1939; Gay, 1731/1939; Hare, 1981; Nagel, 1986; Rawls, 1971). And many of the situations that tax our reasoning ability most involve ethical issues. Most of us espouse a variety of ethical principles. One might argue that it is a requirement of rationality that one not espouse principles in an unthinking way, that one not, for example, accept a principle without reflection simply on the strength of the fact that it is espoused by one's peers, or even by one's betters.

Another requirement of rationality might arguably be that one not intentionally espouse principles that are mutually contradictory, that internal consistency is a desirable property of one's beliefs about ethics, as well as all other beliefs. This is not to suggest that rational people will never find themselves in situations in which the implications of one ethical principle seem to conflict with those of another. One may believe, for example, that the intentional infliction of physical harm on another human being is generally bad, while believing at the same time that one has a right and obligation to protect one's self and one's family from harm inflicted by others. If one embraces both of these principles, one may find oneself in a situation in which they cannot be honored simultaneously, and one must be given precedence over the other, perhaps by appeal to a more general principle that subsumes them both.

Even very general principles or goals that are widely recognized as desirable can sometimes come in conflict. Liberty, equality and justice, for example, are generally recognized as goals toward which enlightened societies should strive. And, for the most part, these goals are seen as compatible and even mutually reinforcing. But they can come in conflict in specific instances, and when they do, one or the other must take precedence. Adler (1981) argues that ultimately justice trumps liberty and equality. "No society can be too just; no individual can act more justly than is good for him or for his fellowmen" (p. 137). The same cannot be said, he argues, for liberty and equality. But what constitutes justice in specific contexts can be a matter of debate; and as St. James reminds us to our comfort, justice can be overridden by mercy (*New English Bible*, James 2:13).

One of the paradoxes of technological progress is the fact that as our ability to control various aspects of the world increases we find ourselves more and more often faced with the necessity of making decisions that we are not well prepared to make. These decisions often require value judgments involving the trading of one desirable objective for another, or containment of one undesirable event at the cost of failing to contain another. The history of war provides countless examples of decisions known in advance to result in many human deaths that were taken with the intention of preventing even more costly eventualities.

Advances in medical science have provided the means for sustaining life under conditions in which it is not clear that it should be sustained. More and more frequently, doctors and others are forced to decide whether to continue the life of a patient or to withdraw life-sustaining treatment and to permit the patient to die naturally. Such decisions can never be easy; in some instances they are exceedingly difficult, as is evidenced by the court proceedings they often prompt.

Medical science today also is increasingly able to provide information, or at least clues concerning the probable health of an unborn child. As a consequence, it has passed to expectant parents a responsibility that they once did not have the option of assuming, namely, that of deciding whether to continue or terminate the pregnancy. The societal turmoil that has been caused by differences of opinion as to the ethical or moral implications of such decisions needs no elaboration. Closely related are questions pertaining to genetic engineering and what the limits of this rapidly developing technology should be. Wilson (1999) asks starkly: "How much should people be allowed to mutate themselves and their descendants?" (p. 302). This question seems certain to become increasingly pressing.

How does one reason rationally about ethics? Can one resolve ethical dilemmas by rational argumentation? If the answer is no, then how is one to deal with these problems? By appealing to ethical principles? But how is one to decide which of the many possible ethical principles that might be applied in any case should be followed? And on what basis, if not rational argument, can one hope to justify one's choice? According to one view, while reflection on morals may never lead to general agreement on what the fundamental standards should be, reflection can at least make us cognizant of ideals different from our own (Columbia Associates in Philosophy, 1923); presumably this would be a good thing, because it could lead us either to modify our own views or give them a better informed foundation.

Harsanyi (1953, 1975a, 1975b) contends that ethics should be considered a branch of the general theory of rational behavior and that rational moral value judgments involve acting so as to maximize the average expected utility of all members of society. Ethics, in his view, is to the interests of society as a whole what game theory is to the interests of individuals. This is a modern version of the principle of "the greatest good for the greatest number," championed by the early 18th- and 19th-century British utilitarian philosophers, notably John Gay, Jeremy Bentham, and James Mill (see especially Bentham, 1789/1939). Bentham attempted to provide the rationale for a quantitative approach to ethics, based on the assumption that all behavior is motivated, and should be motivated, by the desire to obtain pleasure and avoid pain. A relatively recent paraphrase of the greatest-good principle—"the right thing to do is what will maximize the total satisfaction of the preferences of all the parties affected"—has been called *preference utilitarianism* (Nagel, 1995, p. 158). Nagel makes a case for an alternative principle of morality that does not give equal weight to everybody's preferences, but that gives priority to those of individuals most in need of help over those who are better off.

Bentham's *hedonistic calculus* or *moral arithmetic* had many critics among his contemporaries. John Stuart Mill, who defended it, in a fashion, saw its exclusive focus on quantity of pleasure and pain and its failure to recognize the importance of different qualities of experience as a serious weakness. The idea that the appropriate goal of behavior is the maximization of subjective expected utility, personal or corporate—the modern version of Bentham's calculus—has its fair share of detractors, and adherents, as well. The point on which I want to end this discussion of rationality and ethics is that ethics is an appropriate subject about which to reason, even if the reasoning leads to the conclusion, as it sometimes has, that universally applicable principles of ethics are not to be found (Williams, 1985). On the other hand, the view that ethics are at least consistent with reason, if not derivative from it, is seen, as C. S. Lewis (1947) has pointed out, in the common practice of asking people to "be reasonable" when urging them to do right. If the ability to reason does not set human beings apart from other species, the ability to reason about matters of ethics is among the better candidates for doing so.

☐ Affect

[T]he mind is more than a thinking machine; it is also a feeling machine. (Kosslyn, 1995, p. 91)

Reasoning always occurs in a context, and is bound to be influenced by that context. Albert (1985) expresses this idea in what he calls "the thesis of the *nonexistence of 'pure reason'*—that is, thought which is essentially free from all vital motivational and social influences" (p. 116). An important aspect of any context is its affective character. Who can doubt that the quality of one's reason can be influenced by one's emotional state or mood? Whether one is joyful or depressed, stressed or relaxed, angry or at peace with the world.

Most of us are well aware from experience, I suspect, that it is easier to approach a problem logically when one is unemotional and at ease than when one is angry or distraught. How many of us, when engaged in a heated argument, are as highly motivated to be rational as we are to win the dispute? Much has been written on the question of how affect of various sorts influences reasoning, and a considerable amount of empirical research has been done on the topic.

Emotion

> I suggest . . . that certain aspects of the process of emotion and feeling are indispensable for rationality. (Damasio, 1994, p. xii)

Generally, emotion is seen as antithetical to rationality. We tend to mistrust our judgment, for example, pertaining to matters in which we have a strong emotional involvement. No court would permit a jury to include close relatives or friends of the individual on trial. One's reaction to a situation may be described as irrational *because* of its apparent emotional content. A person who is emotionally upset is said to lack objectivity and is believed to be likely to view a situation in a distorted way. And who would dispute the claim that emotion often easily trumps reason in disputes?

Many philosophers have seen the relationship between emotion and reason as one of a continual struggle for control; Descartes's view that rationality requires that the passions be held in check by reason is representative. J. S. Mill (1892/1995) considered it "a psychological law, deducible from the most general laws of the mental constitution of man, that any strong passion renders us credulous as to the existence of objects suitable to excite it" (p. 87).

This perspective is not greatly different from that held by many psychologists. Emotional arousal is seen as an impediment to rational thinking, the greater the arousal the greater the impediment (Epstein, 1994). Toda (1980) suggests that emotions form a system that serves the purposes of decision making in primitive and wild environments. In his view, emotions predate cognition in general, and with modern human beings, emotional and cognitive factors often conflict in decision situations.

Emotions need not be extreme in order to affect decision making and action. Weissman (1996) points out how what he refers to as "ecosentimentalism," an overly sentimental view of nature and the past, can affect policy making in significant ways. "Not until the ecosentimentalists of our own day favored Bambi over venison, not until tick-bearing deer roamed every back yard from Falmouth to New Haven, did we have to undo the mischief of sentiment to battle the spirochete of Lyme disease. At the end of the twentieth century, rabies, tuberculosis, Lyme disease, and Hanta virus—not to speak of AIDS—are not due to industrial pollution but to a misguided choice of sentiment over reason" (p. 488).

Decision making can have emotional consequences, and the anticipation of these consequences can affect the decision-making process.

People sometimes may intentionally avoid choosing between decision alternatives and prefer to have someone else make a choice for them so they will not have to suffer regret if the decision turns out badly (Thaler, 1980).

The foregoing comments have stressed the fact that emotions can affect reasoning in deleterious ways. And, indeed, most of the research relating to the effects of emotion on reasoning, or thinking more generally, has tended to emphasize the negative impact that emotional factors can have—the ways in which emotion can undermine rationality. There is another side to the story, however. There is also good evidence that emotion is essential to rationality, at least insofar as rationality is seen to involve the ability to function effectively according to prevailing social norms. Although he notes that emotional and cognitive factors often conflict in decision making, Toda (1980), argues the necessity of emotion and points out that without it utilities could hardly exist.

The view that emotion is essential to rationality has been articulated recently by Damasio (1994), who reviews evidence—starting with the famous case of Phineas Gage—that damage to the prefrontal lobes of the brain, and other sites, often results in affective changes that, although not accompanied by the type of intellectual deficit that would be registered by standard intelligence tests, tend to be associated with a decrease in the ability to function in a rational and socially responsible way. The ability to experience normal emotions and feelings, Damasio argues, is essential to normalcy in reasoning, and often localized brain trauma that affects normalcy in the one sense does so in the other as well. It is the action of biological drives, body states, and emotions, Damasio surmises, that provides a foundation for rationality.

Studies of the role of emotions in thinking, some involving comparison of performance of people with prefrontal damage with that of normals on probabilistic learning tasks, have led to the idea that learning takes place simultaneously on two parallel tracks, one of which is largely subconscious and based on emotional responses and the other of which is conscious and based on overt recall of pertinent situational facts (Bechara, Damasio, Damasio, & Anderson, 1994; Bechara, Damasio, Tranel, & Damasio, 1997; Bechara, Tranel, Damasio, & Damasio, 1996). In the most recent of these studies, participants without prefrontal damage, but not those with such damage, gave evidence of reacting emotionally (skin conductance responses) to relatively risky choices before they had learned to distinguish overtly the riskier choices from the less risky ones.

In the *ultimatum game*, which is sometimes used to study certain aspects of decision making under uncertainty, one of two players (the proposer) is given an amount of money, say $100, with the challenge to divide the money with another player (the responder) in such a way that the other player is willing to accept what he/she is offered. If the responder accepts the offer, both players get to keep what they have; if the responder does not accept the offer, neither player gets to keep any money. Although according to some conceptions of rationality, the proposer should offer the least amount possible, $1, to the responder, and the responder should accept it, this is not what people typically do. The majority of players, when functioning as the proposer, offer to the responder something between 40 and 50 percent of what they were initially given, and such offers are generally accepted (Camerer & Thaler, 1995; Roth, 1995; Sigmund, Fehr, & Nowak, 2002).

Research with functional magnetic resonance imaging has shown that offers that are perceived as unfair elicit activity in brain areas that relate to emotion (anterior insula) and to cognition (dorsolateral prefrontal cortex) (Sanfey, Rilling, Aronson, Nystrom, & Cohen, 2003). The investigators see this result as evidence that players of the game have the emotional goal of resisting unfairness (which involves the anterior insula) and the cognitive goal of accumulating money (which involves the dorsolateral prefrontal cortex), and, more generally, of the importance of emotional influences in human decision making.

The role that emotions play in reasoning (and conversely) is clearly deserving of a lot of attention from researchers. Simon (1983/1986) argues that anything close to a complete theory of human rationality would have to contain an account of the role that emotion plays in it. While the attention the subject has received in the past is not commensurate with its importance, perhaps the situation is changing (Finucane, Peters, & Slovic, 2003; Luce, Bettman, & Payne, 1997; Mellers, Schwartz, & Ritov, 1999; Svenson, 2003).

Mood

There can be little doubt that thinking is affected by mood (Isen, 1993; Schwartz & Clore, 1983, 1988). People who are depressed can find it very difficult to focus on anything other than their own state of mind and the presumed reasons why they feel as they do. An especially cheerful mood can produce the "rose-colored glasses" phenomenon, where one interprets events more optimistically than an objective analysis would warrant.

People tend to recall better what they have recently learned if their mood at the time of recall matches what it was at the time of learning (Bower, Monteiro, & Gilligan, 1978; Bower, 1981). This is known as the mood-congruency effect on memory. Momentary mood can also affect one's retrieval of information from long-term or autobiographical memory, as when people recall more past illnesses when they are feeling sad than otherwise (Salovey & Brinbaum, 1989).

People appear to be more attentive to incoming information that matches their mood than to information that is inconsistent with it, and to have daydreams that are consistent with their mood as well (Bower, 1981, 1983, 1991). We may see these tendencies as effects of mood, but they, in turn, can contribute causally to the perpetuation or intensification of moods through a positive-feedback process. Bower (1995) gives a number of other examples of behaviors that can have the effect of prolonging or intensifying an existing mood.

Mood can affect judgments and decisions that should be made in terms of objective criteria alone. The impression that a job interviewer forms of an interviewee, for example, may be influenced by the interviewer's mood at the time of the interview, more positive impressions being associated with more positive moods (Baron, 1987). People tend also to give more positive assessments of their own behavior, attitudes, and abilities—to give evidence of greater self esteem—when in a good mood than when in a bad one (Forgas, Bower, & Krantz, 1984; Kavanaugh & Bower, 1984; Sedikides, 1992). A negative mood appears to inflate the judged frequency of mishaps (Johnson & Tversky, 1983), and the desire to maintain a positive mood may make one more than normally risk-averse (Isen & Geva, 1987; Isen, Nygren, & Ashby, 1988). Not only are people likely to behave differently when they are angry than when they are not, their perceptions and judgments of other people may be affected by anger as well; in particular they are more likely to believe they see hostility and aggression in the attitudes and behavior of others (Bandura, 1973; Zillman, 1979).

Glasser (2003, 2005) takes the provocative position that most people who are diagnosed as being mentally ill, despite no evidence of brain abnormality, are simply unhappy, and that the unhappiness more often than not stems from unsatisfying relationships with people who are important to them. Failure to recognize this, he argues, has led to widespread overprescription of psychiatric drugs—Paxil, Prozac, Zoloft—to treat the presumed illnesses. If he is right, this is a serious problem for a variety of reasons, not the least of which is that such drugs can have unwanted effects of their own. Similar concerns have been raised regarding the possible overprescription of drugs for the treatment of emotionally-based symptoms in children that have been given a variety of clinical labels, the most widely-used perhaps is Attention Deficit Disorder (ADD) or Attention Deficit Hyperactivity Disorder (ADHD) (Cummings & Wiggins, 2001; Schrag & Divoky, 1975; Wright, 2005).

Attitudes, dispositions, and perspectives

There is a keen interest among some educators and educational researchers in the possibility of improving the ability of students to reason, and to think well more generally (Baron & Sternberg, 1987; Nickerson, Perkins, & Smith, 1985; Resnick, 1987). Although attention has been directed mostly at the possibility of teaching *higher-order thinking skills*, the importance of *attitudes* and *dispositions* to good thinking has also been stressed by some writers (Baron, 1985a, 1993; Cacioppo, Petty, Feinstein, & Jarvis, 1996; Ennis, 1985, 1987; Moshman, 1994a, b; Newmann, 1991; Perkins, Jay, & Tishman, 1993; Schrag, 1987; Tishman, Jay, & Perkins, 1993). Fairmindedness, openness to evidence, a desire for clarity, respect for others' opinions, inquisitiveness, and reflectiveness are among the attitudinal qualities that have been associated with good thinking and taken as goals of efforts to teach the same. The idea that *thoughtfulness* as a habit of mind is at least as important—possibly more important—to good thinking than competence in the execution of specific thinking skills has some currency (Newmann, 1991; Schrag, 1987). Stanovich and West (1997) identify several dispositions, revealed in questionnaire studies, that they consider conducive to good reasoning; these include willingness to postpone closure, to consider alternative opinions, to consider contradictory evidence, and to engage in counterfactual thinking.

Just as some dispositions can contribute to good reasoning, others can have the opposite effect. An unwillingness to postpone closure, to consider alternative opinions, and so on can help ensure that reasoning is constrained and unreflective. A tendency to see everything in terms of black and white, to assume that every effect has a single cause, to insist that every question have a simple answer, precludes reasoning that is very deep or insightful.

Unhappily, self-confidence and a willingness to take a strong stand on an issue—whether justified or not—can be perceived as "decisiveness" and as marks of leadership. And indeed, many people who attain positions of power appear to have these traits. Taleb (2004) sees evidence of a link between leadership and a form of psychopathology in which excessive self confidence and insensitivity somehow enable the rallying of followers. Many examples of the prototype are described by Cleckley (1964).

We know less than we would like to know regarding how attitudes that are conducive to independent thinking—or attitudes that are not conducive to it—come to be. How important are early experiences in the home in the formation of attitudes that will persist into adult life? How is their development affected by formal schooling? It would be hard to believe that early experiences do not have a lot to do with the shaping of attitudes that often last throughout a lifetime, although evidence on the point is more suggestive than conclusive. If children are permitted to view the purpose of doing seatwork at school as that of completing assignments the teacher has given them rather than as that of learning something new (Anderson, 1981), is this not likely to affect developing attitudes toward authority and learning? Can children who are never permitted to question authority figures in the home or school be expected to develop an inquisitive attitude toward the world around them?

The role of perspective in conditioning beliefs is seen in the fact that how liberal and conservative one perceives political liberals and conservatives to be depends on whether one is liberal or conservative oneself (Sniderman, Brody, & Tetlock, 1991). That perspective can be a determinant of the degree of satisfaction or dissatisfaction one may experience with a situation is demonstrated poignantly by the findings of Medvec, Madey, and Gilovich (1995), who present evidence that winners of silver medals in major sports events, like the Olympic games, are likely to be less satisfied with the outcome of their performance than are winners of bronze medals. These investigators surmise that silver medal winners tend to focus on the fact that they might have won the gold (things might have been much better), whereas bronze medal winners tend to focus on the fact that they might have missed out on a medal altogether (things might have been much worse).

Stanovich (1999) notes that the attention that has been given to concepts that reside "at the borderline of cognitive psychology and personality" has been increasing generally, and that concepts that are sometimes discussed under the rubric of *thinking dispositions* are also discussed under a variety of closely related terms, such as *"intellectual style* (Sternberg, 1988, 1989), *cognitive emotions* (Scheffler, 1991), *habits of mind* (Keating, 1990), *inferential propensities* (Kitcher, 1993), *epistemic motivations* (Kruglanski, 1990), *constructive metareasoning* (Moshman, 1994a, b), and *cognitive styles* (Messick, 1984, 1994)" (p. 156). Stanovich—who prefers the term *thinking dispositions*—argues that individual differences in such dispositions must be taken into account, along with individual differences in cognitive capacities, to explain individual differences in performance of reasoning tasks. Evidence in support of this view is presented by Stanovich and West (1998c), who found that performance on a variety of reasoning and decision-making tasks varied with several indices of thinking dispositions after the effects of differences in cognitive ability had been partialed out.

Noting that it was once widely believed that positive affect impairs systematic cognitive processing and leads to poor judgment and superficial thinking, Isen and Labroo (2003) cite numerous empirical studies the results of which they interpret as evidence against this view and supportive of the conclusion that positive affect can have the opposite effect and facilitate logical thinking and problem solving. Positive affect may even, they suggest, help counter some of the biases that have been documented in the cognitive and social literature. Among several ways in which positive affect influences decision making, Isen and Labroo contend, is by increasing the flexibility that people show in making choices and their ability to respond appropriately to various aspects of a decision situation.

Esthetics

> Beauty is truth, truth beauty, that is all ye know on earth, and all ye need to know. (Keats, "Ode on a Grecian Urn")

Esthetics is sometimes considered the province of artists. But esthetics has been an extraordinarily powerful motivating factor in the thinking of many mathematicians and scientists. The importance of esthetics in mathematics is reflected in the view expressed by Bertrand Russell, as quoted in Kline (1953): "Mathematics, rightly viewed, possesses . . . supreme beauty—a beauty cold and austere, like that of sculpture, without appeal to any part of our weaker nature, without the gorgeous trappings of painting or music, yet sublimely pure, and capable of a stern perfection such as only the greatest art can show. The true spirit of delight, the exultation, the sense of being more than man, which is the touchstone of the highest excellence, is to be found in mathematics as surely as in poetry" (p. 6).

The central role that esthetics has played in the thinking of many of the greatest scientists has been documented by Holton (1973). He describes the feeling a scientist gets from attaining a view in which phenomena that had been thought to be separate are seen to be interdependent as a "quasi-aesthetic experience of the most treasured kind in the sciences" (p. 304). A similar point is made by Lerner (1959) in his identification of the quest for regularities underlying diverse events as the hallmark of scientific thinking.

A question that naturally arises is that of the role that esthetics should play in the thinking of any rational agent. Is the quest for beauty in the realm of thought appropriate only for the most creative geniuses among us? Or should it be part of the experience of us all? In my view, rationality that does not include a search for beauty is an impoverished rationality. Without denying that beauty may be, at least to some extent, in the eye of the beholder, I believe that the ability to see beauty in ideas is a human quality of the greatest value and significance.

Whether beauty is an entirely subjective quality is debatable. I find myself persuaded by Adler's (1981) argument that beauty can have an objective basis as well, but that the ability to see the beauty that is there to be seen may need to be acquired. Adler makes a distinction between *enjoyable* beauty and *admirable* beauty. Enjoyable beauty is whatever one, for whatever reason, considers beautiful. Admirable beauty is what experts in some domain agree deserves to be considered beautiful. To recognize admirable beauty, in this view, requires that one know enough about the subject—visual art, music, poetry, architecture—to appreciate the worthiness of specific instances of it. This distinction seems especially germane to the concept of beauty as it pertains to ideas. It is not reasonable to expect someone who knows no mathematics to see the beauty of a mathematical theorem that mathematicians would call elegant.

The distinction between enjoyable and admirable beauty raises the question of whether rationality requires an effort to acquire the expertise that is necessary to appreciate beauty where it may be found. It is too much, of course, to expect everyone to be sufficiently well informed in all subjects to acquire the tastes of experts in those subjects, but perhaps it is not too much to require that we recognize our limitations in this regard and to be sensitive to the fact that an inability to see the beauty that someone else sees in a particular instance may reflect a difference in knowledge on which the perception of beauty is based.

Wonderment

> If science begins in wonder, as indeed it does, it ends perforce in a sense of wonder that is greater still. (Smith, 1992, p. 118)

The last topic I want to discuss in this chapter fits less obviously, perhaps, under the general heading of affect than do those already considered. But I see it as a very important aspect of rationality, and it clearly has affective dimensions, so I will discuss it here. The topic is wonderment.

People wonder about different things. James Clerk Maxwell (1873) was fascinated by the fact that all the molecules of a particular element are identical and considered it to be unattributable to any natural cause. Salam (1992) makes the point that not only is a sense of wonder common in science, but that the deeper one's scientific knowledge, the more intense one's experience of wonderment is likely to be. Biology presents us with countless reasons for wonderment.

Here is Lewis Thomas (1979) reflecting on the process of fertilization and embryonic development: "For the real amazement, if you want to be amazed, is the process. You start out as a single cell derived from the coupling of a sperm and an egg, this divides into two, then four, then eight, and so on, and at a certain stage there emerges a single cell which will have as all its progeny the human brain. The mere existence of that cell should be one of the great astonishments of the earth. People ought to be walking around all day, all through their waking hours, calling to each other in endless wonderment, talking of nothing except that cell. It is an unbelievable thing, and yet there it is, popping neatly into its place amid the jumbled cells of every one of the several billion human embryos around the planet, just as if it were the easiest thing in the world to do" (p. 156).

Kauffman (1995) expresses a similar sentiment: "If the swarm of stars in a spiral galaxy, clustered swirling in the high blackness of space, astonishes us with the wonder of the order generated by mutually gravitating masses, think with equal wonder at our own ontogeny. How in the world can a single cell, merely some tens of thousands of kinds of molecules locked in one another's embrace, know how to create the intricacies of a human infant? No one knows. If Homo habilis wondered, if Cro-Magnon wondered how they came to be, so too must we" (p. 93).

Should a distinction be made between different types of wonderment? I think so. When I wonder about why there are 12 inches in a foot, for example, I think I have a different experience than when I wonder about why equal-radius spheres pack as precisely as they do. In the former case, I am curious as to why twelve was chosen, and can imagine several plausible reasons (Nickerson, 1999b), but reflecting on the question does not evoke in me the same sense of astonishment as does thinking about any number of mathematical relationships that seem—for no apparent reason—so incredibly elegant and useful.

Radio fascinates me. As I sit in my office, I can, with the turn of a dial, tune in to any of numerous ongoing programs originating from many different locations. If I happened to have the right kind radio, I would be able to pick up programs from around the globe. Apparently the room in which I sit contains the signals from all these stations all the time; all I need in order to pull any one of them out of the air is this little device that can be set to the necessary broadcast frequency. What I find fascinating is the fact that, at any given moment, the space that I occupy is occupied also by electromagnetic representations of countless instances of speech, music, and other kinds of sounds. Fortunately, I cannot hear them all at once, but they are all there; and my radio gives me the ability to select from among them. Moreover, if get in my car and drive off in any direction, no matter where I go, I will be in the same situation. The air, everywhere, is full of information. To me, radio is a truly remarkable technology; the more I think about it, the more amazing I find it to be. I find myself in a similar state of mind when I think about electricity. The fact that the energy that is needed to power the homes and business establishments of a community—operate the myriad tools and appliances on which modern society has become so dependent—can be transported from place over a little copper wire is remarkable, to say the very least.

As fascinating as radio, electricity, and a variety of other scientifically derived phenomena are, the kind of wonder they evoke, in me at least, differs in a subtle, but important, way from the wonder inspired by what, for want of a better term, I will call *natural elegancies*. Within limits, I can understand how radio works and how energy can be changed from one form to another and transported from place to place. At least I can read the scientific accounts of these phenomena; whether one considers these accounts to be explanations, as distinct from useful descriptions, depends on what one considers the nature of explanation to be.

In contrast, I feel a sense of awe when I think about the fact that my body is composed of atoms that have existed for billions of years, that originated in the interiors of stars long since dead, and that, during their few billion years on earth, have been the building blocks of countless other animate and inanimate forms. But what really boggles my mind is the idea that every proton in the universe is identical to every other one, or at least, so we are told; this, to me, is truly amazing. Structure, energy, consciousness—existence—the wonderment that these ideas evoke is, in my experience, quite different from curiosity about how things work.

One can, of course, have any of a variety of attitudes toward wonderment. At one extreme, one can take the view that things are as they are, and that is all there is to be said about it. Wondering why they are as they are is a waste of time, a childish indulgence. At the other extreme, one can see cause for wonder everywhere: Why is there something rather than nothing? What is consciousness, and why is there such a thing, given that it seems neither to be necessary nor to follow naturally from the physical activity that is assumed to underlie it? Who—what—am I?

Nagel (1986) notes the awe-inspiring nature of both the thought of one's own existence, and of that of the possibility that one had never been born. With respect to the former: "Almost every possible person has not been born and never will be, and it is sheer accident that I am one of the few who actually made it (p. 211). And with respect to the latter: "If you concentrate hard on the thought that you might never have been born—the distinct possibility of your eternal and complete absence from this world—I believe you too will find that this perfectly clear and straightforward truth produces a positively uncanny sensation" (p. 212).

The possibility of becoming paralyzed by wonderment seems very real to me, and I do not see that as a desirable state. What surprises me, however, is how little we wonder about truly wonderful aspects of our existence. Why are we so insensitive to the strangeness, the improbability, the utter inexplicability of it all? I suspect there is a certain fear of wonderment, stemming in part perhaps from a distaste for the type of mysticism—like number mysticism—to which it appears sometimes to have led. I suspect also, however, that the confession of wonderment is perceived sometimes as a lack of sophistication. To be awestruck by characteristics of the universe in which we find ourselves, of which we are a part, is seen as juvenile, a sign of intellectual immaturity, and no one, of course, wants to be perceived as intellectually immature. It is a pity.

It is interesting to note that Einstein attributed his formulation of the theory of relativity in part to the fact that he kept asking himself questions about space and time that only children wonder about (Holton, 1973). Bertrand Russell (1955/1994) speaks of Einstein as having "the faculty of not taking familiar things for granted" and illustrates the fact by referring to Einstein's expression of "'surprised thankfulness' that four equal rods can make a square, since, in most of the universes he could imagine, there would be no such things as squares" (p. 408).

That one of the most acclaimed and influential scientists of all time characterized his own thought processes as childlike in a significant way is a sobering thought. Is it possible that we have as few Einsteins as we do because the process of getting a formal education and learning to be what society expects intellectually mature individuals to be stifles in most of us the curiosity with which nature endowed us? "Children sometimes see things clearly that are indeed obscured in later life. We often forget the wonder that we felt as children when the cares of the activities of the 'real world' have begun to settle upon our shoulders. Children are not afraid to pose basic questions that may embarrass us, as adults, to ask. What happens to each of our streams of consciousness after we die; where was it before each was born; might we become, or have been, someone else; why do we perceive at all; why are we here; why is there a universe here at all in which we can actually be?" (Penrose, 1989, p. 448). The idea that becoming an adult means learning to be embarrassed by an inclination to wonder about the mysteriousness of our existence and that of the universe of which we are a part is a terrible thought, and—what makes it more terrible still—not beyond believing.

CHAPTER 6

Explanations

> Man differs from animals in that he has a reasoning mind, and this mind...cannot tolerate a vacuum, it finds an explanation for everything. (Gabor, 1972, p. 53)

We seem to have an intolerance for uncertainty and ambiguity and a deep need for explanations—a need, one might say, for *sense-making*. We are uneasy when we have a collection of facts that we cannot see as some consistent whole. This need is the root of superstitions as well as of scientific theories. Regularities and patterns that we observe demand explanations, as do unanticipated changes in the status quo, and coincidences. We often accept ready-made explanations uncritically and we invent them at the slightest provocation. Himsworth (1986) attributes this need for explanations to fear of the unknown: "Fear of the unknown is deeply ingrained in human beings. In consequence, faced by anything they do not understand, they cannot rest until they have given themselves an explanation of it" (p. 94). Whether or not fear is the motivating factor, we are explanation-generating entities.

The need for explanations is seen at a fundamental level in our compulsion to structure sensory input. When confronted with an ambiguous pattern—as when walking into a dimly lighted room or looking at a photograph that is unclear or of unknown scale—one struggles to make sense of it. One attempts to organize the sensory data in terms of familiar percepts; the ambiguity is not happily tolerated. Sometimes the ambiguity is resolved in favor of a plausible but incorrect interpretation. When that happens, the erroneous interpretation can be remarkably resistant to correction.

The compulsion to structure sensory input is seen also in our tendency to put concrete interpretations even on abstract patterns whenever possible. People have always seen objects and creatures when they gazed at the stars, and long ago gave them names. We see objects or animals also in clouds, in maps of islands, or in the splotches made by spilled ink. Hermann Rorschach exploited this fact to develop a test in the early 1920s that is supposed to reveal secrets about our innermost selves from what we see in ink blots. People read causality and even human intent and emotion (attraction, repulsion, anger, aggression, playfulness) into the behavior of dots moving in various ways in relation to each other on a visual display (Heider & Simmel, 1944; Michotte, 1950, 1963; Dasser, Ulbaek, & Premack, 1989). This all illustrates what Bartlett (1932) referred to as an "effort after meaning," which he believed characterized not only the act of perceiving but all cognitive activity, including imagining, remembering, and reasoning.

The need for explanations appears to be strong in children as well as in adults. A large part of the problem of getting students to understand scientific explanations of phenomena stems from the fact that they often already have explanations for those phenomena, only the explanations they have differ from those that are generally accepted by science (Anderson & Smith, 1987; Eaton, Anderson, & Smith, 1984). For this reason, much of science education requires unlearning as well as learning; Anderson (1987) describes science learning as a complex process of conceptual change, in which some beliefs about how the world works are modified while others are strengthened and reorganized.

People learning to use word-processing software spontaneously invent explanations of why the systems they are using act as they do (Carroll, 1990; Lewis & Mack, 1982; Mack, Lewis, & Carroll, 1983). The explanations they invent may bear little relationship to what is actually going on in the computer, but they serve to make sense of the interaction in the users' minds. Carroll (1990) argues that the innate need of people to make sense of novel situations should be taken into account by designers of approaches for training people to use new systems effectively, because penalizing them for making incorrect inferences in the interest of sense-making can impede the learning process.

The ease with which after-the-fact "explanations" can be found for essentially anything undermines the credibility of many of them. It appears that "I don't know" is exceedingly difficult for some people to say; so the question "why" seldom wants for an answer. One sees the need for explanations in postmortem analyses of various sorts of events. Within specific universes of discourse there may be small numbers of assertions that are standardly selected to construct such explanations. The ability of financial analysts to explain after the fact, for example, events that came as a complete surprise is remarkable. Precipitous rises or falls of unusual magnitude in stock-price averages never want for explanations after they have occurred. One has to look long and hard to find analysts who admit to being at a loss to account for unanticipated behavior. After-the-fact explanations can always be produced, and when they are produced by people who are highly conversant with the domain of interest, they can sound very convincing, especially to one whose knowledge of the domain is limited. This does not mean that they are correct in any deep sense. Distinguishing between bona fide explanations and the proffering of "reasons" that have little or no actual explanatory value is not always easy, but it is a skill worth cultivating.

Developmental psychologists, many of whom have been inspired by the work of Piaget have studied explanations of various phenomena offered by children and how the character and quality of those explanations change as children age. Some investigators have made explanation, or the idea that people naturally seek to explain what they observe, a central construct around which to develop theories of comprehension (Miller, 1979, 1986; Mooney & DeJong, 1985; Shank & Abelson, 1977).

☐ What Is an Explanation?

> At some point one has to pass from explanation to mere description. (Wittgenstein, 1972, p. 26)

What constitutes an explanation is a disarmingly easy question to ask, but an exceedingly difficult one to answer in a noncontroversial way. The following exchange between Paul Davies and David Bohm during a BBC radio interview of the latter by the former on the topic of quantum physics illustrates the difficulty.

Bohm: I think we should distinguish between explanation and systems of calculus, and quantum mechanics is a calculus that enables you to predict statistical results. But it has no explanation, and Bohr emphasized that there was no explanation of any kind.

Davies: But is there ever explanation in physics? I mean, don't we simply make models and invent language for them?

Bohm: But models explain the thing in the sense that they show how it comes about; the explanation makes it intelligible. Quantum mechanics says that nature is unintelligible except as a calculus, that all you can do is to compute with the equations and operate your apparatus and compare the results.

Davies: Can you think of another area of physics, say a simple area, where you think that we actually have an explanation?

Bohm: Well, a lot of classical physics gives an explanation in so far as it's correct.

Davies: In what way though? Isn't it just language and models relating observations? Where is the real explanation? We use the word "explanation," but it seems to me rather meaningless, and that all you're doing is relating observations together successfully.

Bohm: I don't think so..... (Davies 1986/1993, p. 131)

The dialogue continues in this vein. It is representative of wide differences of opinion among scientists as to what constitutes an explanation, at least in the context of science. The differences are especially apparent in discussions of a theory as complex as quantum mechanics, which some praise because of its extraordinary explanatory power and others see as explaining nothing at all. But throughout the scientific literature, one finds the word "explanation" used in a variety of ways. Arguably, like most words familiar from common parlance, it is used uncritically, more often than not, with the tacit assumption that everybody knows what it means.

Even when definitions are given, they often are circular. "In the language of science," Lindley (1993) offers, "to explain a problem means to account for an observation or phenomenon without recourse to arbitrariness" (p. 164). But if we consider "to explain" and "to account for" to be synonymous, we might paraphrase this definition as "to explain something is to explain it without recourse to arbitrariness." I do not expect to resolve the ambiguities surrounding the concept of explanation here, but I do hope to bring some of them to light and to note several of the ways in which the concept has been, or can be, used.

In everyday terms, to explain something—a principle, a relationship, a process, an event—is to make it plain and understandable. Explanations are enlightening answers to questions—*what* questions, *how* questions, *why* questions—and they serve a variety of purposes, ranging from the satisfaction of intellectual curiosity, to the provision of practical guidance for the performance of specific tasks, to the justification—giving "reasons" for—surprising behavior. What is the nature of existence, of space, of time, of personal identity, of consciousness? How did the universe get to be its present size? Why does an object in motion continue in motion on a straight-line path when no forces are acting on it? Why does reflected light follow the fastest path between source and observer? What keeps an automobile engine from overheating? How does one fix a leaky faucet? Why should one not use a metal dish in a microwave oven? Why has Jack been so depressed lately?

Harman (1986) distinguishes two ways in which the term "explanation" is used. Sometimes it refers to the speech act of explaining something to someone; at other times it means "something one grasps or understands that makes things more intelligible, comprehensible, or coherent, whether or not any speech act of explaining has occurred" (p. 67). The first of these meanings focuses on the process of making something clear; the second relates to the substance of the clarifying account.

Explanation as exposition or clarification

Sometimes what one does when one explains is expose or make explicit some nonobvious or hidden relationship. Many of us learned in school that a quick way to determine whether a number is divisible by 9 is to add up its integers; if the sum is a more-than-one-digit number, add its digits to get a new sum; continue in this fashion until arriving at a one-digit sum. If that digit is 9, the original number is divisible by 9; if it is not 9, the original number is not divisible by 9. Thus, 261 is divisible by 9, because 2+6+1 = 9 and so is 37,584, because 3+7+5+8+4 = 27 and 2+7 = 9, but 260 is not, because 2+6+0 = 8, nor is 37,585, because 3+7+5+8+5 = 28, 2+8 = 10, and 1+0 = 1.

One does not have to understand why this rule works to use it effectively, just as one does not have to understand why many of the algorithms we use to do simple arithmetic work in order to apply them to advantage. An inquisitive individual might seek an explanation as to why such algorithms work. An explanation of the trick for identifying numbers that are divisible by 9 might go something like this.

Given the place-notation scheme we use for representing numbers, a sequence of digits, say 261, is a short-hand way of representing the quantity $2 \times 10^2 + 6 \times 10^1 + 1 \times 10^0$, or 200+60+1. To divide one number by another, we use an algorithm that we (at least those of us in my generation) learned by rote in school, and we may never have seen through the algorithm to the logic that lies behind it. To determine how many times some number, say 9, goes into another, say 261, we need to determine see how many times it goes into 200, how many times it goes into 60 and how many times it goes into 1. (The order in which we make these determinations does not matter.) In each case there may or may not be a remainder, so we need finally to see how many times it goes into the sum of the remainders. Perhaps it will be clear, at this point, that if—and only if—the divisor, 9 in this case, goes evenly into the sum of the remainders, then it goes evenly into the original number.

Let us look again at 261 with this process in mind. Consider first the low-order digit. Inasmuch as 9 is the largest single-digit number, the only single-digit number it will go into evenly is 9. For any other digit, say d, it goes 0 times with a remainder of d, so, in this case it goes into 10 times with a remainder of 1. Now consider the *tens* digit—6. As it happens, 9 goes into 60 6 times with a remainder of 6. More generally, 9 goes into *any* 2-digit multiple of 10, say Nx10, N times with N as a remainder. This follows from the fact that 9 is 1 less than 10; thus 10/9 = 1 with a remainder of 1, 20/9 = 2 with a remainder of 2, and so on. Consequently, the *tens* digit itself indicates the remainder one gets when one divides that number of 10s by 9.

The same principle applies when we look at higher-order digits. From the fact that 9 goes evenly into 99, which is 1 less than 100, 100/9 yields a remainder of 1, 200/9 a remainder of 2 and so on. Similarly, given that 9 goes evenly into 999, which is 1 less than 1000, 1000/9 yields a remainder of 1, 2000/9 a remainder of 2, and so on. In general, division of N x 10^m by 9 yields a remainder of N. It follows that the digits of a multi-digit number *are* the remainders when the indicated multiples of the powers of 10 represented by the place-notation scheme are divided by 9. At least to the reader who understands the basic principles of place notation of the number system we use, this constitutes an explanation of why the trick of summing the digits of a number to determine whether it is divisible by 9 works. The explanation serves, in this case, to clarify what otherwise might be obscure.

Reduction as explanation

> Simplicity of explanation should not be bought at the price of eliminating the most distinctive features of the very phenomena one is trying to explain. (Ward, 1996, p. 71)

One possible view of explanation is as a description of a set of phenomena in terms of a set of concepts and principles to which those phenomena can be reduced or from which they can be derived. This is perhaps the sense in which scientific theories are explanations. A theory relates a variety of phenomena within the same conceptual framework; the larger the variety of phenomena that it can accommodate the more powerful the theory, other things equal.

A generalized form of the reductionist approach to scientific explanation has been described by Tegmark and Wheeler (2001) this way. "Theories can be crudely organized in a family tree where each might, at least in principle, be derived from more fundamental ones above it.

Almost at the top of the tree lie general relativity and quantum field theory. The first level of descendants includes special relativity and quantum mechanics, which in turn spawn electromagnetism, classical mechanics, atomic physics, and so on. Disciplines such as computer science, psychology and medicine appear far down in the lineage" (p. 74). (It is perhaps relevant to note that the proponents of this view are physicists.)

Thermodynamic and mechanical views of the world are very different, but presumably complementary. In one sense they describe the same phenomena; however, they describe it at different levels and do so in terms of qualitatively different concepts. A thermodynamic description makes use of such concepts as temperature, pressure, volume and density, which are properties of a system (e.g., gas) as a whole. A mechanical description makes use of such concepts as position and velocity, which are properties of individual molecules. There is an asymmetry in the relationship between the two types of descriptions: in theory at least, one can infer the thermodynamic behavior of a system from knowledge of the mechanics of its constituent molecules; one could not, however, infer the behavior of the individual molecules from knowledge of thermodynamic behavior. This is because a given thermodynamic state can result from many different patterns of molecular behavior, but a given pattern of molecular behavior will produce only one thermodynamic state.

This distinction illustrates one form of reductionism, which holds that a way to explain a phenomenon is to analyze it into it's constituents and describe it at a lower, or "more fundamental," level of organization. Thus heat is explained in terms of the motions of molecules; sound is explained in terms of the interaction of successions of compressed and rarified air and the action of a hearing apparatus. More generally, biological phenomena are explained by describing the chemical processes that underlie them, and chemical processes are explained in terms of the physics of molecular and atomic interactions.

As a form of explanation, reductionism is a controversial notion among scientists. Churchland and Churchland (1995) characterize the controversy this way: "For some it connotes a right-headed approach to any genuinely scientific field, an approach that seeks intertheoretic unity and real systematicity in the phenomena. It is an approach to be vigorously pursued and defended. For others, it connotes a wrong-headed approach that is narrow-minded and blind to the richness of the phenomena. It is a bullish instance of 'nothing-but-ery', insensitive to emergent complexity and higher-level organization. It is an approach to be resisted" (p. 64). Defenses of each of these positions are abundant in the literature. In what follows, I give a few examples of what has been said in support of each view.

Pro reductive explanations

Reduction has proved to be a very effective way of gaining insight into the operation of physical structures and systems. Knowledge of the interactions of various types of matter has been deepened by the discovery of the structure of atoms and the many ways in which atoms combine to make molecules. This knowledge has been deepened further by the decomposition of atoms into their subatomic particles. A current hope among many physicists is that discovery of the details of the vibrational patterns of strings—hypothesized subsubatomic particles—will provide a new explanation of the properties of what, before the appearance of strings on the scene, were considered the fundamental particles and forces of nature. Pythagoras would be proud.

The enthusiasm with which some embrace reductionistic explanations is evidenced in the description by the Columbia Associates in Philosophy (1923) of the implications of the discovery of J. P. Joules of the "mechanical equivalent" of heat, which led to his formulation of the kinetic theory of heat. Why, they ask, did physicists adopt Joules's theory? "Because they found that they could thus reduce all the different phenomena of heat to a single simple basis, the energy of motion of the molecules composing bodies, and because that motion was itself of precisely the same nature, and obeyed precisely the same laws as does any motion in the universe. It is a marvelous achievement in scientific *explanation* when we can confidently assert that the tremendous movements of the heavenly bodies and the qualitative differences in temperature of the tiniest objects are both alike, and that they are together like the simple and easily understood and predicted movements of two billiard balls striking each other. One formula will describe all three. Surely few achievements of the human mind are worthy to rank with such a feat!" (p. 135).

Reductionism is sometimes conceived as a nesting of explanations, reminiscent of Russian dolls or the peels of an onion. Open up sociology and there sits psychology; open that and one finds biology; inside biology is chemistry and inside chemistry is physics. Here, for example, is how a biologist sees the relationship between his discipline and physics. "The biologist's problem is the problem of complexity. The biologist tries to explain the workings, and the coming into existence, of complex things, in terms of simpler things. He can regard his task as done when he has arrived at entities so simple that they can safely be handed over to physicists" (Dawkins, 1986, p. 15). In describing the reductionist approach as it might apply to psychology, Lycan (1988) also ends up with the physicist. After doing what he can to analyze psychological concepts in terms of components, subcomponents, sub-subcomponents and so on, at some point he "would have to turn biologist, then chemist, and finally physicist in order to bring this explanation process to completion" (p. 33). To whom the physicist is to turn is not clear.

Wilson (1999) describes the agenda of reductionism as that of folding the laws and principles of any given level of organization into those at a more fundamental level. The strong form of reductionism, he contends, is *total consilience*, according to which all natural laws and principles can eventually be reduced to simple universal laws of physics. For Wilson, the laws of physics are the point at which reduction stops, although he notes that this view could be wrong, and undoubtedly is an oversimplification at least.

Con reductive explanations

A limitation of reductive explanations stems from the fact that in dropping to a lower level of organization one can eliminate, or "talk around," phenomena of interest. Something essential seems to be lost when one goes from one level of analysis to another. One may attempt to account for mental states, for example, by describing the behavior of the brain that accompanies changes in those states, but the language one uses to describe brain behavior is not descriptive of mental states. The language that is used to describe blood flow or electrical activity in specific regions of the brain, or the firing of particular complexes of neurons, or the biochemical processes that constitute that firing simply is not adequate to describe the experience one has when one sees a color, hears a sound, or feels happy, angry, or sad. Nowhere in the description of the physiological or physical processes that underlie thought is there any hint of what it means to *be* conscious or aware.

Weisskopf (1977) expresses his sense of the inadequacy of reductionist explanations this way.

> Beethoven's sonata is a natural phenomenon that can be analyzed physically by studying the vibrations in the air; it also can be analyzed chemically, physiologically, and psychologically by studying the processes at work in the brain of the listener. However, even if these processes are completely understood in scientific terms, this kind of analysis does not touch what we consider relevant and essential in a Beethoven sonata—the immediate and direct impression of the music. (p. 410)

In a similar vein, Jeeves (1969) uses the example of explaining a mathematical equation:

> [I]f we write 2 + 2 = 4 on the blackboard, it would be perfectly reasonable for an analytical chemist to assert that all that is on the board is so much

calcium, sulphur, oxygen, and so on. And from his viewpoint and at that level he would surely be correct. Yet to leave out altogether from a full description of the same phenomenon all reference to the mathematical equation would be to miss the point of what is written on the board. The two levels of description are related; they are necessary correlates of one another; but questions asked in the language of the one cannot meaningfully be answered in the language of the other. (p. 130)

Dyson (1995) also rejects reduction as an adequate goal of scientific explanation, arguing that progress in science requires the growth of understanding both downward from the whole to the parts and upward from the parts to the whole. In proclaiming that the growth of understanding must go only in one direction, reductionism fails to meet this requirement, in his view.

In the preceding section, I quoted the Columbia Associates in Philosophy (1923) who assessed very favorably the reductionist explanation of heat represented by the kinetic theory of that phenomenon. The same writers also caution, however, against the use of reduction in a way that denies the reality of—explains away—the phenomenon that is being explained. "Now, in so far as this process of 'reduction' means the getting rid of something with which we started, and in so far as the scientist in using the phrase means to imply that as a result of his discoveries we now know that hot objects are not really hot, but only vibrating rapidly, or that the sunset is not really a blaze of color, but only complex wave-motions, or that the man is not really manifesting the highest ethical activity, but only responding to chemical stimuli—in so far as he allows this notion to creep into his mind, he is very obviously talking nonsense" (p. 139).

These writers argue that a reductionist explanation, properly understood, does not deny the phenomenon it is intended to explain, but rather provides a more complete picture of it. Discovery that a hot body is composed of rapidly moving particles makes it no less hot, but adds to one's understanding of its heat. Explaining something is not tantamount to explaining it away. What is explained remains as real as it was before it was explained. In adding to the description of a hot object the fact that the object is composed of rapidly moving particles, one has indeed provided a more complete understanding of the object—the hot object—and its properties, but is this an explanation of why the motion of particles should give rise to the sensation of heat?

The question arises as to whether it is possible, in principle, to provide a reductionist explanation of a phenomenon without leaving out the phenomenon of interest. Nagel (1995) seems to believe that the answer is no. "A reduction is the analysis of something identified at one level of description in the terms of another, more fundamental level of description—allowing us to say that the first really is nothing but the second.... When we say heat consists of molecular motion, we mean that heat as an intrinsic property of hot objects is nothing but the motion of their molecules. Such objects produce the feeling of heat in us when we touch them, but we have expressly not identified that feeling with the molecular motion—indeed, the reduction depends on our having left it out" (p. 99).

The limitation of reductionist explanations has been stressed by some theorists, especially in the biological sciences, who have held that as matter has become organized in increasingly complex forms it has sometimes come to exhibit qualitatively different properties that are not predictable from an examination of the constituents of those forms. According to this *emergence* view, at certain levels of organization, new properties appear that are unique to that level and that cannot be explained adequately in terms of the behavior of the constituents at a lower level. Life is one example of a property that emerges unpredictably when molecules reach a certain level of complexity in their organization. Mind is seen as an emergent property that appears at a still higher organizational level. Among well-known proponents of this view are Teilhard de Chardin (1959) and Gregory Bateson (1980).

Although the idea of emergent properties is not widely promoted in contemporary scientific literature, the assumption that one can explain biological, psychological or social phenomena by looking to chemistry and physics is not universally accepted either. Dobshansky (1964) argues that even if it were possible to describe all biological, psychological, and social phenomena in chemical and physical terms, the description would be so cumbersome as to be meaningless. Life itself remains a mystery and description of the physics of living organisms does not explain it. This mystery, as one physicist puts it, "lies not so much in the nature of the forces that act on the individual molecules that make up an organism, but in how the whole assemblage operates collectively in a coherent and cooperative fashion" (Davies, 1988, p. 101).

The phenomena of embryonic development, cell specialization, and positional determination of function (How does a given cell know where it is relative to other parts of the organism, so that it can develop as the appropriate type of cell, say a neuron instead of a bit of fingernail?) suggest the operation of a blueprint or global plan for the development of the organism as a whole. Such a plan must go beyond what is encoded in the DNA of the individual cells, because it must guide different cells to implement different parts of the instructional code that they all share. The discovery of genes that are able to "switch on" other genes selectively provides a clue to the *mechanism* of morphogenesis but it does not answer the deeper question of how the mechanism is made to conform to a global plan. "The real challenge," as Davies puts it, "is to demonstrate how *localized* interactions can exercise *global* control. It is very hard to see how this can ever be explained in mechanistic terms at the molecular level" (p. 104).

The problem has been referred to as that of *causal decoupling*, the idea being that as one moves from one level of organization to another—whether one is dealing with inanimate or animate matter—one finds that the phenomena or constructs at one level often are not coupled in a causal way to those at a higher level. Pagels (1991) notes that science offers many examples of such causal decoupling. One he gives from molecular biology is the decoupling of the biological function of proteins from their representation in the genetic code.

Stressing the need for staircases or bridges between different levels of analysis, Gell-Mann (1994) defends what might be called a qualified reductionism. Different levels—physics, chemistry, biology—are distinguished by the fact that the higher (less fundamental) the level, the more restricted the conditions under which the phenomena of interest occur—chemical phenomena are a subset of physical phenomena; biological phenomena are a still further restricted subset. The higher levels are derivable from the lower ones, at least in principle, in Gell-Mann's view, but only with the assistance of information specifying the conditions under which the phenomena of the higher levels can occur. "[T]he very fact that chemistry is more special than elementary particle physics, applying only under the particular conditions that allow chemical phenomena to occur, means that information about those special conditions must be fed into the equations of elementary particle physics in order for the laws of chemistry to be derived, even in principle. Without that caveat, the notion of reduction is incomplete" (p. 112). What is important to note about this view is that the further information that is required is not itself derivable from the more fundamental science and its need becomes evident only as a consequence of the existence of the higher-level phenomena.

Morowitz (1981) argues that, at least as far as explanations of human behavior and experience are concerned, the question of the acceptability of a reductionistic view has nontrivial implications for how we think of ourselves. He characterizes uncritical reductionism not only as a weak solution to the problem of mind but as a dangerous view "since the way we respond to our fellow human beings is dependent on the way we conceptualize them in our theoretical formulations.....Radical reductionism offers very little in the area of moral imperatives" (p. 41). Boden (1995) expresses a similar view: "Given the central constructive role in our personal life of the self-concept, we should expect that people who believe (or even half-believe) they are mere machines may behave accordingly" (p. 149).

Few, if any, neuroscientists would question the belief that mental states depend on states of the brain. This is not the same, however, as believing that mental states are fully explained by brain states. Sperry (1995) argues that, while mental states are dependent on electrochemical and biophysical aspects of the brain, they differ in important ways. More generally, he dismisses the idea of fully explaining an entity at one level of organization by describing its lower-level components: a great cathedral and a sewage plant could be described in the same terms at the level of the particles of which they are made, but they are quite different at the level at which their structure and function are apparent. Sperry contends that reductionism, which experienced ups and downs during the19th century and enjoyed great popularity in the mid 1960s, has given way more recently "to a new flowering of holism and an acceptance of the concept of the irreducible whole" (p. 42). The new attitude to which Sperry refers is illustrated in Edelman's (1995) contention that "to reduce a theory of an individual's behaviour to a theory of molecular interactions is simply silly" (p. 201).

Nagel (1986) argues that the inadequacy of the explanatory power of reductionism is illustrated by the inability to account for electricity and magnetism in terms of Newtonian mechanics. Getting from Newton's universe to relativity required the development of new types of concepts. He sees a parallel between the need for qualitatively different concepts to explain the newly explored phenomena to which he refers here and the need for nonphysical concepts to explain mental phenomena. "To insist on trying to explain the mind in terms of concepts and theories that have been devised exclusively to explain nonmental phenomena is, in view of the radically distinguishing characterists of the mental, both intellectually backward and scientifically suicidal" (p. 52).

One need not accept the idea that reduction is the only, or even the best, form of scientific explanation in order to believe that reduction can often be illuminating and can serve an explanatory function—at least in the sense of making phenomena and relationships clearer than they were before. Reduction sometimes helps to unify previously disparate areas of observation. Churchland and Churchland (1995) illustrate this by pointing to the encompassment of Kepler's account of planetary motion by Newton's more comprehensive mechanics, the reduction of classical chemistry to atomic and subatomic physics, and the reduction of Newton's laws of motion to the mechanics of special relativity. The effect in all cases was to provide a new perspective in terms of which to understand the old phenomena and their relationship to phenomena not before observed. Sometimes too reduction has the consequence of actually making an old view no longer tenable, as when the oxygen theory of combustion displaced the earlier phlogiston theory.

Reductive explanations in psychology sometimes involve attempting to explain behavior in terms of unobservable constructs that represent mental of cognitive entities. Behaviorism, especially as represented in the work of Watson (1914, 1919, 1925) and Skinner (1946, 1953, 1974), rejected this approach to psychological explanation, and the use of mental constructs was essentially forbidden for a while in many psychology training programs as a result of this influence. Mentalistic explanatory concepts are now much in use again, and have been for some time since the occurrence of what is sometimes referred to as the "cognitive revolution," but their use has articulate forceful critics (Midgley, 1995; Uttal, 1998, 2000, 2003). Uttal (2003) summarizes his position as holding "that a coherent scientific psychology is only capable of *describing* the transformations that occur between stimuli and responses and not *reductively explaining* them" (p. 13).

The reductive path in psychology also sometimes is from behavior, or mental states, to biochemical processes in the brain. Rapidly growing interest in neuroscience, spurred by advances in technology that provide unprecedented possibilities of observing how activity in different parts of the brain correlate with physical and mental activity is testimony to the attractiveness of this type of reduction. Some of the assumptions that appear to underlie this interest have been challenged (Utall, 2001). And descriptions of what is occurring in the brain when one is thinking deal with qualitatively different phenomena than the thought itself. As Gelernter (1994) puts it, "Neurons are fascinating and fun, but they don't absolve us from the responsibility of understanding thought on its own terms" (p. 41).

Reduction is a widely used form of explanation. Perhaps there is such a thing as "reductive megalomania," as Midgley (1995) has called it, in which reduction is considered to be the only respectable form of explanation. (Midgley's critique of reduction in psychological theorizing, in which she sees the epitome of reductive megalomania, is particularly scathing.) But, as Midgley points out, reasoning does not require that one give the most economical account of a phenomenon that is conceivable, but only the most economical one that will provide the explanation that is needed. When reduction amounts to destroying or ignoring the phenomenon of interest, the explanation it provides can hardly be an explanation of that phenomenon. Midgley judges reductionism harshly: "reduction is never value-neutral, never just aimed at simplicity....it is always part of some positive propaganda campaign" (p. 135). The campaign, as I understand this metaphor, is aimed at making the case that description at a lower level of analysis is always to be preferred—is better, closer to reality, more satisfying—than description at a higher level. But if the phenomenon of interest is not seen at the lower level, only the died-in-the-wool reductionist is likely to be fully satisfied that it has been adequately explained.

The bottom line regarding reduction as explanation, as I see it, is that it has its place, but also its limits. Examining a phenomenon at a lower level of analysis can often provide insights into the phenomenon that could not be obtained in any other way. On the other hand, it is often the case that in going from a higher to a lower level of description, the phenomenon of primary interest is lost. That something vital can be lost in the process of decomposing something that exists as an integrated entity at one level of observation into its constituent parts is beyond question, in my view. One typically cannot infer higher-level phenomena from lower-level descriptions, and there is the problem of infinite regress, which is to say that one can never be sure that one has gotten to the bottom of the reduction hierarchy, so one can not reasonably hope to have an ultimate explanation of anything. Reduction, like the surgeon's scalpel, is to be used with care; it can be revealing, but when used with abandon it can kill what one wants most to keep alive.

Deduction as explanation

As we have seen, a limitation of reductionistic explanations is that they often seem to toss the baby out with the bathwater. The most interesting aspects of a phenomenon are nowhere to be seen in descriptions of that phenomenon in terms of concepts that are appropriate to a lower level of organization. When consciousness, for example, is reduced to biochemistry, what we have is the biochemistry of the brain; conscious experience has left the picture. To say that what is described at one level is essential to the observation of the phenomenon at the higher level is to say something important and interesting about the higher-level phenomenon, but for many people, this will not seem like a very adequate explanation of it.

One view of why reduction often fails to yield satisfying explanations is that the lower-level phenomena do not imply—or at least it is not apparent that they imply—the higher-level phenomena. Assuming that one did not already know of the higher-level phenomenon, observing the lower-level phenomena to which it is reduced would not force an inference of the existence of the higher-level one as a logical consequence.

One may have a stronger sense that A explains B if A implies B—if B can be deduced from A. A, in this case, would be seen as a sufficient cause of B. Whenever you have A, you invariably have B as a consequence. According to this view of explanation, sometimes called the deductive-nomological view, one explains a phenomenon when one deduces it from established laws and principles (Hempel, 1965).

This form of explanation is of special interest in science. Given a phenomenon, B, one may ask, from what set of plausible conditions, A, could it be deduced? If B, which I have observed to be true, is the conclusion, what are the premises from which it logically follows? The fact that I am able to identify a set of premises (or many such sets) from which B follows does not, of course, establish the truth of that set (or of any of its members), but it may provide one or more hypotheses that deserve investigation. The qualification that the set of conditions, A, from which B might be deduced be plausible is necessary to rule out the possibility of beginning with self-contradictory premises, from which anything can be deduced. As Good (1983) points out, the premise $0 = 1$ logically implies everything, but it is an extremely poor explanation of anything.

It is important here to distinguish among several types of deductive explanations. There are those that we believe to be true, because it has been possible to obtain compelling evidence, independent of B, of the truth of a set of premises, A, from which B follows. For want of a better term, let us refer to such explanations as factual explanations. There are also deductive explanations that are plausible in that their premises are consistent with what is known, but the evidence for their truth is not compelling; perhaps they represent one set among others that *could* be true, but are not assuredly so, and evidence that will help settle the issue is being sought. These are tentative explanations. There also are "explanations" that are known, or at least strongly believed, to be false.

One might think the last type of deductive explanation would be useless, or worse. But, in fact, such hypothetical explanations, or potential explanations, as Nozick (1981) calls them, can be useful in explicating alternative ways in which a phenomenon could conceivably be produced. Knowing both that *if* A were true B would follow and that A is not true can provide hints as to where to look, or not to look, for other conditions from which B would follow and that might be true.

Scientific laws and explanations

> When we explain anything we observe, it is in terms of scientific principles that are themselves explained in terms of deeper principles. Following this chain of explanations, we are led at last to laws of nature that cannot be explained within the boundaries of contemporary science. (Weinberg, 1994, p. 45)

Scientific laws express relationships between or among variables. Laws are descriptive of how nature works and they are extremely useful for both theoretical and practical purposes. Discovery of such laws is the quest of science. But scientific laws are not explanations. Knowledge that F = ma is not equivalent to knowledge of why F = ma. Moreover, although a law may be a dependable and precise description of some aspect of nature, it cannot be considered the cause of the relationship it describes.

The discovery of laws that bear some resemblance to each other despite the fact that they deal with what appear to be different and relatively independent aspects of nature can be prods to theorizing that will show the resemblance to be more than chance coincidence. The law of gravitation, as expressed by Newton, has the attractive force between two objects varying inversely with the square of the distance between the objects. Is it mere coincidence that Coulomb's laws for the attractions or repulsions between two electric charges or between two magnetic poles also have the strength of the force varying inversely with the square of the distance between the objects that carry them? Or is there a common explanation of all three phenomena?

Schrödinger's formulation of his famous wave equation is generally considered to have been a major advance in scientists' understanding of the behavior of the electron. Lederman (1993) calls Schrödinger's equation, or more specifically, Max Born's interpretation of it, the most dramatic change in our world view since Newton. But is it an explanation? Or, to ask a slightly different question, what does it explain? Miller (2003), in reflecting about the puzzling nature of quantum theory, makes this comment regarding what happens to the wave function of an electron when an observation is made, which, according to the theory, causes the state of the electron to change from being potentially everywhere to being definitely somewhere: "Before the measurement is made, the electron is in a combination of several quantum states, but the very act of measurement is believed—according to standard quantum lore—to put it in one particular state. What on earth is the underlying mechanism behind this? On this fundamental question, the Schrödinger equation and the other fundamental equations of quantum theory are silent" (p. 128). The laws of quantum mechanics, as represented by Shrödinger's equation illustrate clearly that the discovery or statement of a law can raise more questions than it answers. Polkinghorne (1991) describes as "the greatest surprise associated with quantum theory....the fact that more than sixty years after that theory's discovery, and despite its brilliant successes, we still cannot agree on how quantum mechanics should be interpreted" (p. 88).

More generally, scientific laws—which succinctly describe discovered regularities in nature—are enormously useful to an understanding of how the world works, but the laws themselves beg an explanation. In some cases laws describing relationships among physical variables can be shown to follow from the operation of other laws that describe relationships among variables at a more detailed level of observation or analysis, but this process of reduction always comes to an end and one arrives at laws for which science has no explanation. If one has no stomach for metaphysics, one, in effect, is forced to settle for the bottom-line "explanation" that that is simply the way things are.

Gardner (2003) captures this limitation of scientific laws as explanations very well. "Explanation consists of finding a general law that explains a fact or a less general law. Why does Earth go around the Sun? Because, Einstein revealed, large masses distort space-time, causing objects to move along geodesic paths. Why do objects take geodesic paths? Because they are the shortest paths through space-time. Why do objects take the shortest paths? Now we hit a stone wall. Time, space, and change are given aspects of reality. You can't define any of these concepts without introducing the concept into the definition. They are not mere aspects of human consciousness, as Kant imagined. They are 'out there,' independent of you and me. They may be unknowable in the sense that there is no way to explain them by embedding them in more general laws" (p. 328). Again, "No matter how many levels of generalization are made in explaining facts and laws, the levels must necessarily reach a limit beyond which science is powerless to penetrate" (p. 330).

Scientific theories as explanations

Scientific theories have proved to be enormously useful in a variety of ways. They provide relatively coherent and self-consistent conceptual representations of a wide range of phenomena. They sometimes show how phenomena at one level of observation arise as a natural consequence of structures and processes at a more detailed level. More often than not, they tend to be reductive in this sense. They establish a basis for prediction and control, and these abilities constitute the foundation upon which much of technology is built. Scientific theories also often are considered to be explanations of the phenomena to which they pertain. It is this function that is of interest here. We should note, however, that predictive validity—the demonstrated ability of a theory to make predictions, even surprising predictions, that prove to be accurate—is not necessarily the same as explanatory validity. As Kauffman (1995) notes, "a table of the tides predicts, but does not explain" (p. 16).

Many scientific explanations are both causal and mechanistic in the sense that they identify a mechanism that is *capable* of causing an observed effect. Darwin's theory of natural selection is a case in point. Although we usually credit Darwin with the theory of evolution, the basic idea was known to a number of his predecessors including his grandfather, Erasmus Darwin. What Charles Darwin did that went beyond the thinking of his predecessors was propose a mechanism—natural selection—that he believed to be capable of effecting the evolutionary changes that had been hypothesized. Berry (1988) draws a parallel between the role that mechanism played in establishing the theory of evolution and that which it had in the history of the theory of continental drift. The latter was proposed by Alfred Wegener in 1915 but was not widely accepted until the mechanism of plate tectonics was described in the 1960s.

Every explanation has its limitations. Each begins with some givens. Darwin's theory of natural selection, for example, provides a mechanistic account of changes in species over time; it does not explain, however, why genes mutate, why all species produce more progeny than the environment can sustain, from whence comes the will to survive, or why, if fitness for survival is the basis of selection, the direction of evolution is invariably from simpler to more complex forms—bacteria are eminently more survivable than people and no organism is as survivable as a rock. Selection may be seen as "a necessary consequence of prodigality and variability of all species," as Nogar (1966, p. 77) puts it, but what necessitates that species be so prodigal and variable? Other theories may explain what Darwin's takes as given, but they will have their own givens in turn.

Another way to make the same point is to say that theories typically answer some questions, but in so doing, raise others; they provide explanations for specific phenomena and relationships but only at the expense of introducing ideas that beg explanations themselves. In his history of atomic physics, Pais (1986) contends that progress leads to confusion, which in turn leads to progress, and on and on without respite. Every major advance creates new problems. The confusions that progress produces are not to be deplored; they provide the impetus for work that eventually leads to further advance.

According to current theory, electrons are distinguished by four quantum numbers, each of which can have a restricted set of values. In 1925 Wolfgang Pauli proposed what became known as the Pauli exclusion principle, according to which it is assumed that no two electrons of the same atom can have the same set of values of these four numbers.

This principle was proposed in order to make sense of the otherwise inexplicable behavior of atoms, for example, the fact that all electrons do not fall into the lowest possible energy orbital. The principle has considerable explanatory power. In accounting for why the electrons distribute themselves in different orbitals, as they do, it accounts also for the relationships among the atoms as revealed in the periodic table of elements and for the ways in which atoms form chemical bonds—why some atoms bond and others do not. It explains, in other words, much of chemistry. But the principle itself begs an explanation: why do electrons obey it? To make chemistry possible? Most scientists would not be happy with such a teleological explanation. But what *is* the explanation? Indeed, what would constitute one?

The second law of thermodynamics, according to which the entropy—randomness—of any closed system always increases, is at the center of one of the most intriguing enigmas of physics and cosmology. The fact that some systems become more structured in time is reconciled with this law by noting that the increase of order in one part of the universe is offset, or paid for, by a compensating decrease in another part. The form of the payment for increased order is an expenditure of energy, which is tantamount to an increase in entropy. Increases in order are seen as local phenomena, while the continuous decrease in order, or increase in entropy, pertains to the universe as a whole.

What is not accounted for is the existence of order in the first place. If the second law of thermodynamics applies to the universe as a whole, we are obliged to believe that the orderliness of the universe not only is, but always has been, decreasing. But if this is the case, how did the universe acquire order in the beginning? The odds against this happening by chance are so huge as to be unimaginable. In the words of Paul Davies (1983), "If the universe is simply an accident, the odds against it containing any appreciable order are ludicrously small. If the Big Bang was just a random event, then the probability seems *overwhelming* (a colossal understatement) that the emerging cosmic material would be in thermodynamic equilibrium at maximum entropy with zero order" (p. 167). Penrose (1979) has estimated the probability of a universe such as the one in which we live occurring by chance to be one in 10 to the 10 to the 30th. There is little point in trying to imagine the enormity of such a number.

Scientists have dealt with this problem in different ways. Some find it easy to attribute the existence of the universe to chance, despite the infinitesimally small probability; some do not. Some, in order to make room for the universe that we know, assume that during countless eons of existence, the universe has realized all possible states of order and disorder, including the one in which we find ourselves. According to this view, given infinite time, the universe will find itself in each of all possible states infinitely often. Still others assume that many, perhaps an infinity, of universes exist simultaneously. What determines which of the possible views any particular individual will find to be most plausible is very difficult to say. It is not possible to select among them on the basis of the outcomes of empirical tests.

It is not unusual in science for a hypothesis to be put forth in order to fill an explanatory vacuum. The hypothesis of an inflationary expansion of the universe—according to which the universe expanded at a rate greater than the speed of light for a period immediately following the Big Bang—is a case in point (Guth, 1981; Guth & Steinhardt, 1984); the question it was intended to answer was how parts of the universe too distantly separated from each other to have been in communication happen to have precisely the same temperature (the *horizon problem*). Another is the hypothesis that, contrary to the usual interpretation of the second law of thermodynamics, order in the universe is actually increasing, and has been from the beginning (Young, 1986). Others include the hypothesized ever-so-slight difference in the abundances of matter and antimatter produced in the Big Bang and the Higgs field that has been hypothesized to pervade the universe and to be the source of matter's mass. Lindley (1993) argues that each of these hypotheses was introduced to solve an explanatory problem, and that none of them has any independent empirical support. With respect to the Higgs mechanism, for example, Lindley contends that it was invented for the sole purpose of accomplishing a particular end. Moreover, it works, he notes, albeit at the expense of introducing some additional theoretical complications.

Scientists do not like the fact that these, and other, hypotheses have not yet been shown to be testable directly and they continue to look for ways to find evidences for or against them that are independent of the phenomena they were invoked to explain. The introduction of new concepts has often provided post hoc explanations of previously unexplained phenomena or relationships, but theories based on the ability to postdict phenomena do not have the same status in science as do those that can accurately predict previously unobserved phenomena or relationships. Nevertheless, ad hoc hypotheses can be enduring and influential even in the face of continuing failure of such efforts. For present purposes, the question of interest is the extent to which we should think of such hypotheses as explanations. Perhaps we should think of them as hypothetical explanations, which is to say that they provide *possible accounts* of certain phenomena, they give us what *could be* reasons for the phenomena of interest *if* the hypotheses are true.

Scientific explanations are limited also in the sense that there are many situations in life that we wish to understand—to be able to explain to ourselves or others—that do not lend themselves to investigation by controlled experimentation or other standard scientific techniques because they are one-time events and will never precisely recur. Nagel (1995), who makes this point, contends that this does not mean that explanation of such events is impossible, but only that it cannot be sought by usual scientific methods. In the case of human behavior, for example, an inability to run controlled experiments does not preclude trying to make internal sense of what people do, trying to see how their behavior might appear justified from their point of view.

Whatever the limits of scientific explanation are, they are not serious impediments to scientific progress, at least if progress is equated with an increasing ability to predict and control both natural and artifactual phenomena. It is not necessary to understand why the force of gravity works, or even what it *is* in any deep sense, in order to appreciate that it does work, to predict its effects in specific situations, and to apply this knowledge in many practical ways. Kline (1953) puts the matter this way: "Just as Newton's laws of motion furnished scientists with the means of working with matter and force without explaining either, so Maxwell's equations have enabled scientists to accomplish wonders with electrical phenomena despite a woefully deficient understanding of their physical nature. The quantitative laws are all we have in the way of a unifying, intelligible account. The mathematical formulas are definite and comprehensive; the qualitative interpretation is vague and incomplete" (p. 319).

In general, scientific theories have proved to be extremely effective in providing representations of phenomena, and especially of cause-effect relationships, that greatly enhance our ability to predict and control many aspects of the world. They help us understand phenomena in the sense of being able to see relationships that would be obscure if not impossible to see apart from the theoretical representations that science has produced. We may think of such theories as limited explanations of the phenomena to which they pertain, but the fact of their limitations deserves emphasis because it is easily overlooked.

Proofs as explanations

A mathematical proof is an explanation of sorts. Its effectiveness depends, as does that of all explanations, not only on its cogency, but on the ability of the individual to whom it is given to comprehend it. Some proofs seem to have more explanatory power than others. An illustration of this point comes from Steiner (1978, cited in Harman 1986, p. 73). Consider the two following proofs of the theorem that states that the sum of n consecutive positive integers beginning with 1 equals $n(n + 1)/2$.

> Proof 1. The theorem can be proved by mathematical induction if (a) the theorem can be shown to hold for $n = 1$ and (b) it can be shown that, if the theorem holds for any given number n, it also holds for the next number n+1. This can be done as follows: If n=1, the theorem holds, since $1 = (1 \times 2)/2$. Furthermore, if we assume the theorem holds for any given n, we can show it holds for n+1, for then
>
> $$\begin{aligned} 1 + 2 + \ldots + n + (n + 1) &= n(n + 1)/2 + (n + 1) \\ &= n(n + 1)/2 + 2(n + 1)/2 \\ &= (n + 1)(n + 2)/2 \end{aligned}$$
>
> QED.
>
> Proof 2: We can add the series of numbers from 1 to n to itself reversed, in the following way:
>
> $$\begin{array}{ccccccc} 1 & + & 2 & + \ldots + & (n-1) & + & n \\ n & + & (n-1) & + \ldots + & 2 & + & 1 \\ \hline (n+1) & + & (n+1) & + \ldots + & (n+1) & + & (n+1) \end{array}$$

Since the series 1 through n has been added to itself, the resulting sum, which is equivalent to (n+1) added n times, or $n(n+1)$, obviously equals twice the sum of the integers in the series, so the sum of the integers must equal $n(n + 1)/2$. As Harman points out, this proof seems more explanatory than the first; it makes the theorem intelligible in a way the first does not. Further, the second proof is structured in such a way that it could facilitate discovery of the theorem, whereas the first one can be constructed only after one knows what the theorem is.

A mathematical proof is an explanation in the sense that it answers the question of why the asserted relationship—the theorem—is true. It lays out in detail a chain of reasoning that gets one from what is already known or assumed—the axioms of the system, other previously proved theorems—to the theorem in question. Whether a proof constitutes an explanation in the sense of being "something one grasps or understands that makes things more intelligible, comprehensible, or coherent" (Harman, 1986, p. 67), depends in part of course on whether the explainee has the knowledge requisite to grasp it. Determining whether a proof has really been grasped is not always a simple matter, as is evidenced both by the many examples of proofs that have been taken to be valid by mathematicians for many years, only eventually to be shown to be faulty, and by the fact that mathematicians often disagree as to the validity of proposed proofs in specific instances.

Analogies as explanations

It is natural to try to explain what is unfamiliar in terms of what is familiar. If we know little about A and much about B, to be informed that A is like B in specific respects is to learn something about A. Descartes believed analogies to be indispensable to scientific explanation. "I claim that they [analogies] are the most appropriate way available to the human mind for explaining the truth about questions in physics; to such an extent that, if one assumes something about nature which cannot be explained by an analogy, I think that I have conclusively shown that it is false" (quoted in Barrow, 1990, p. 97).

One need not go this far to accept the idea that analogies can be very useful as aids to explanation, at least insofar as explanation is taken to connote whatever will make something more readily understandable. But their use is risky unless one is careful to make their limitations in particular instances clear. The danger is that people who are unaware of the limitations of an analogy will assume that because A and B are alike in certain specified respects, they are alike in other respects also, and such an assumption may not be justified.

Specific analogies can be compelling to some observers while appearing to others to be misleading. The point is illustrated by the analogy that has been drawn between the workings of electronic computers and those of the human mind. Many researchers have considered this analogy to be helpful in their attempt to understand cognition. There is the countervailing view that the analogy is misleading in fundamental ways. Nagel (1986), for example, takes this position: "Eventually, I believe, current attempts to understand the mind by analogy with man-made computers that can perform superbly some of the same external tasks as conscious beings will be recognized as a gigantic waste of time. The true principles underlying the mind will be discovered, if at all, only by a more direct approach" (p. 16). I quote Nagel here not to endorse the statement, but to provide an illustration of a cautionary view regarding the explanatory value of an analogy in a specific context.

Explanations and beliefs

Several investigators have shown that when people are asked to explain, or to imagine, why a hypothesis might be true or why a possible event might occur, they tend to become more convinced that the hypothesis is true or that the event will occur, especially if they have not given much thought to the hypothesis or event before (Campbell & Fairey, 1985; Fiedler, 2000; Hirt & Sherman, 1985; Sherman, Zehner, Johnson, & Hirt, 1983). In one study, people were asked to explain why a particular event had occurred, and when, after having produced an explanation, they were informed that the event did not occur; they still considered the event more "likely" than did others who were not asked to explain why it might occur (Ross, Lepper, Strack, & Steinmetz, 1977).

Koehler (1991), who has reviewed much of the work on how explanations influence beliefs, suggests that producing an explanation is not the critical factor, and that simply coming up with a focal hypothesis is enough to increase one's confidence in it. Anything, he contends, that induces one to accept the truth of a hypothesis temporarily will increase one's confidence that it is true in fact. Adoption of a *conditional reference frame*—in which a focal hypothesis is assumed to be true—influences subsequent hypothesis evaluation processes in three ways, Koehler suggests: it affects the way the problem is perceived, how relevant evidence is interpreted, and the direction and duration of information search. It appears that once having adopted a conditional reference frame, one's subsequent treatment of incoming data is biased in favor of that frame. This conclusion gets support from the finding that when people were asked to generate reasons for expecting a specified event and reasons against expecting it, those who generated the for reasons first and the against reasons later considered the event more probable than did those who generated the for and against reasons in the opposite order (Hoch, 1984). Koehler likens the phenomenon to that of *mental set* or *fixedness* that is sometimes described in discussions of problem solving.

Superstition

Superstitions, like scientific theories, are motivated by our need for explanations. And, in a perverse sort of way, superstitions, like other explanations, increase the order in one's life; they decrease the apparent uncertainty and make events seem more predictable. They help those who hold them to account for otherwise unaccountable happenings: things went badly today because it was Friday the 13th; I won the door prize because I had found a four-leaf clover.... They also can give one a sense of control over one's destiny; If I am careful to observe the right rituals, carry the proper charms, and avoid the bad luck omens, everything will be fine.

This view is difficult to discredit, because no matter what happens, good or bad, one who wishes to do so can always account for events after they happen in terms of the assumed causes of good and bad luck. If I believe that carrying a rabbit's foot will bring me good luck, I can reinforce that belief by giving special attention to those occasions on which I carried the foot and had good luck and those occasions on which I did not carry it and had bad luck. In doing this I would be biasing my observations in favor of supporting my belief. To evaluate my belief fairly, I should pay equal attention to those occasions on which I did not carry the rabbit's foot but had good luck anyway, and those occasions on which I did carry it and had poor luck; evidence suggests that we are likely to be less than completely objective about such matters When reminded that I have had good luck on days when I had left my rabbit's foot at home and bad luck on days when I had it in my pocket, I might be forced to admit that my charm does not work perfectly, but protest that I am grateful for the times it *does* work. Or, I might even take the occasion to point out that it is the exception that proves the rule.

We sometimes look condescendingly on the superstitions of our predecessors (more accurately, on those beliefs of our predecessors that we now consider to have been superstitions) and assume that our enlightened age is beyond all that, but what is the evidence that our age is any less superstitious than any preceding one? People living now probably come in contact daily with more phenomena they do not understand than did their predecessors of centuries or millennia ago. Many of the enigmas of today are the products of technology. It is doubtful that the average person understands at a very deep level how a radio works or a television or even a telephone. Electricity is a great mystery. The computer is only the latest artifact to appear on the scene the inner workings of which most people do not begin to comprehend.

To say that we do not understand these things is not to suggest that we are necessarily frightened by them or even overly impressed with them; we get used to them, learn how to use them, and come to take them for granted. More to the point, we invent our own theories (superstitions?) about how they work. We live in a more complicated world than did our forbearers. There is more to know, and, consequently, more about which to be uninformed, and perhaps superstitious.

☐ Causal Attribution

One view of what it means to explain an event or phenomenon is to identify its cause. Attribution theory has to do, at least in part, with the identification of causes of effects; we observe effects and attribute them to inferred causes (Heider, 1944; Kelley, 1967, 1971, 1972, 1973; Orvis,

Cunningham, & Kelley, 1975; Weiner, 1985; Weiner, Frieze, Kukla, Reed, Rest, & Rosenbaum, 1972). The effects to which attribution theory has been applied are primarily forms of human behavior.

Attribution theory has some relevance to moral judgments because the degree to which people are held morally responsible for their actions depends on such factors as the degree to which they, as opposed to situational variables, caused the actions and are believed to have intended the actions to have the consequences they had. Actions with desirable effects are considered praiseworthy and actions with undesirable effects blameworthy only when they are attributed to individuals rather than to external factors (Shaw & Reitan 1969; Sosis, 1974; Weiner & Kukla, 1974). The imputation of moral goodness or badness to an act involves the intentions of the actor, at least as much as the consequences of the act. Even young children use this principle in making such judgments (Suls & Gutkin, 1976).

Causal versus statistical explanation

A distinction is often made between causal and statistical explanation, and it is an especially important one as it relates to the use of explanation in science. Generally speaking, a causal explanation of a phenomenon of interest is preferred, and a statistical one is used if an adequate causal one cannot be constructed.

Whether a statistical explanation of a phenomenon is satisfying may depend on one's perspective. Consider, for example, the case of a town that notices an unusually high incidence of cancer among its residents. From the perspective of the townsfolk, it seems eminently reasonable to seek a causal explanation of the unusual rate. Is it because of pollutants in the air or water from local industries? Is it because of unusually high exposure to electromagnetic radiation in some form? Do the townsfolk, a large percentage of whom have a common ethnic heritage, have a higher than average genetic propensity to develop cancer? If a causal explanation can be found, perhaps some remedial action can be taken to lower the rate.

From the perspective of an epidemiologist, the fact that some towns have an unusually high incidence of cancer is not surprising; it would be surprising if this were not the case. If one assumes that where cancer strikes is completely random, the expected percentage of towns of a given size that will have an unusually high incidence of cancer (where unusually high is specified precisely) can be calculated. Many, if not most, of the cases of clustering of cancer that initially appear to be significant in a statistical sense turn out to be naturally occurring spikes in incidence. Kase (1996) notes that "probability theory suggests that 17 percent of the 29,000 towns or census tracts in the U. S. will have at least one of the 80 recognized types of cancer elevated in any given decade, producing 4,930 chance clusters [of cancer cases]" (p. 86). Of course, the fact that high-incidence areas are expected to occur on a chance basis may provide little comfort to people who find themselves living in one of those areas, especially if they strongly suspect that they can identify an agent that could cause an unusually high rate.

Consider the case of investing or speculating in the stock market. If one assumes that success at predicting the probable price changes in individual stocks is largely a matter of chance, one expects the performance of fund managers to be more or less randomly distributed around a mean that reflects the total market's behavior over any given period of time. In fact, this appears to be the situation (Bernstein, 1996; Malkiel, 1985; Shiller, 2000; Taleb, 2004). It is hardly surprising to find portfolio managers who happen to do well during a particular period to wish to attribute their success to insightful choices and for those who do poorly to blame bad luck. The fact that the good performance could be as easily based on chance as can the poor performance is not generally played up very much. Taleb (2004) speaks of what he calls the *survivorship bias*. People who do well as portfolio managers survive and become perceived as good managers, the assumption being that they have done well *because* they are good. Taleb argues that an alternative plausible hypothesis is that their success was the consequence of randomness in the market—some had to be on the right tail of the distribution and they happened to be the ones who were.

Explanation as identification of cause

> There are three creative ideas which, each in its turn, have been central to science. They are the idea of order, the idea of causes, and the idea of chance. (Bronowski, 1951/1982, p. 18)

During the 1990s, the rate of serious crime—homicide, burglary, and robbery—fell by over 40% in the United States (Rosenfeld, 2002, 2004). Clearly, we would like to know what caused such a dramatic and welcome decline. If the cause, or causes, could be identified, measures might be devised to perpetuate it, or at least to inhibit a reversal of the trend. Not surprisingly, several hypotheses have been offered as explanations of the phenomenon, none of which has yet carried the day. It seems likely that a compelling explanation will recognize the interplay of several factors. It is to be expected, too, that many people will see evidence in the data for the effectiveness of whatever public policies they promote or favor.

Bronowski (1951/1982), who sees cause as one of the truly great and influential ideas in science, says this about it. "Like other great principles of science, such as the principles that nature is rational and is uniform, its sanction is metaphysical. In effect this means that it is a working rule based on our experience of the past and on the way that we organize our lives on that experience in order to meet the future. Our conception of cause and effect is this: that given a definite configuration of wholly material things, there will always follow upon it the same observable event" (p. 45). In Bronowski's terms then, explaining by identifying a cause means specifying the configuration of things that will ensure the occurrence of that which is to be explained.

The idea of cause implicit in this view is that of *sufficient* cause: a sufficient cause is one that suffices to guarantee the effect; it carries the idea of inevitability. This is to be distinguished from a *necessary* cause, which is a cause that may not be sufficient, by itself, to guarantee the effect, but without which the effect cannot be obtained. We may make a further distinction to recognize also the possibility of a *contributing* cause, which would be a cause that is neither sufficient nor necessary to realize the effect but increases the probability of its occurrence. Contributing causes are easily taken to be sufficient or necessary when they are not.

The idea of cause does not solve the problem of infinite regress in explanation, because causes that are invoked to explain effects can themselves be viewed as effects that need to be explained. What causes the resistance I feel when I try to push this heavy object? Inertia. So what causes inertia?....Parents understand this phenomenon. I suspect it is an unusual one who has not on more than one occasion resorted to the imperial "because I say so" to terminate a sequence of "whats" or "whys" that got intolerably long.

Especially as a consequence of the considerable attention that has been given recently to mathematical chaos, we are coming to realize that the best of causal explanations are woefully incomplete; it is simply not possible to trace any event to the total myriad antecedent factors of which it is the confluence. Ekeland (1993) expresses this notion colorfully: "To try to isolate the causes of an event that has affected us is a necessarily limited venture; if pushed to an extreme, we might find ourselves investigating the movement of electrons on Sirius. We can only apprehend a small piece of the vast universe at a time, and we don't know when what we've forgotten is more important than what we see" (p. 122). Any causal explanation must be taken as an approximation that takes account of only the most immediate precursors of the event that is to be explained and then undoubtedly in incomplete terms.

Explaining versus naming

> A vague idea is not clarified by giving it a name. (Columbia Associates in Philosophy, 1923, p. 292)

Another problem with causal explanations is the ease with which the naming of a phenomenon can be taken as the identification of the cause of the phenomenon. When one attributes evolutionary changes in species to mutations, the combining of elements to chemical affinities, the tendency to pick fights to a quarrelsome nature, what has one done beyond putting a label on that which needs to be explained? When we say that planets maintain their orbits because of the gravitational attraction of the sun, have we done anything more than acknowledge the fact that celestial bodies attract each other? Or when we attribute the failure of the protons of an atomic nucleus to repel each other to the effect of the strong nuclear force, have we explained anything? To be sure, the strong nuclear force was postulated just so as to account for the stability of the nucleus, which was inexplicable otherwise, but in what sense does invoking this idea constitute an explanation of the phenomenon of interest?

A related problem involves appropriating a word that has acquired a relatively precise meaning in one context and using it as an explanatory construct in a different context. Evolution, for example, has a relatively precise meaning when applied to the changing of species by variation and natural selection. There is considerable converging evidence for the reality of this process in this context. The word has been used, however, to "explain" how life originated (how nonliving matter evolved into living matter), how the psychosocial properties of human beings developed, indeed, how the universe came to be what it is. All of these applications of the term require a definition that differs sufficiently from the one that is appropriate when applied to the evolution of species that one may question the advisability of even using the same term (Nogar, 1966).

Newton's law of gravitational force of attraction was a great synthesis because it applied the same law to falling bodies and tides on earth and to the motions of bodies in the heavens. By attributing such disparate motions to a common force, the law unified under a single construct phenomena that would otherwise be seen as unrelated. But in what sense is the idea of gravitational force an explanation of the phenomena to which it pertains?

Newton himself was perplexed by the concept and saw it as in need of an explanation itself. The idea of action at a distance was not acceptable to him and it appears that he assumed the eventual explanation would reveal the way in which the action is mediated: "that one body may act upon another at a distance through a vacuum, without the mediation of anything else.... is to me so great an absurdity that I believe that no man, who has in philosophical matters a competent faculty for thinking, can ever fall into it" (quoted in Bertotti, 1977, p. 93). The *force of gravity* was not in Newton's mind an explanation of anything, but was rather a generalization about the way the world works that begged to be explained. His reservations were shared by other scientists of the day, like Leibniz and Huygens, who were critical of the theory's lack of explanatory power.

Newton's specific problem with the concept of gravity was the implied principle of action apart from some medium of that action, the idea that bodies separated in space could affect each other in the absence of some material vehicle for transporting the influence from one body to the other. But suppose one had no difficulty with this idea, or suppose someone discovers the existence of particles that can mediate action between bodies separated in space, does "the force of gravity" now become a more adequate explanatory construct? One must wonder. "Gravity is what it is; and it cannot be explained in simpler terms or by an appeal to the more elementary constituents of matter. We are acquainted with gravity through its effects; we understand gravity by means of its mathematical form. Beyond this, we understand nothing" (Berlinski, 2000, p. 142). More generally, are explanations ever more than restatements of principles or relationships? Are they ever more than alternative ways of describing phenomena?

Consider the fundamental idea underlying quantum mechanics, the notion that electrons have quantized orbits, or energy levels, including minimum, or ground, levels below which they cannot fall. This idea was originally introduced to account for the stability of atoms—given that atoms have positively charged protons in their nuclei and negatively charged electrons surrounding those nuclei, the fact that they do not collapse as a consequence of the attraction between unlike charges was a great mystery. Niels Bohr dispelled the mystery by introducing the idea of quantized orbits. But is this an explanation of why atoms do not collapse? Is it more than an alternative description of the fact of their stability?

We find it easy to fool ourselves into believing that something has been explained when it has really only been labeled or described, especially if the label sounds scientific or the description is given in technical terms. We can convince ourselves that we have made progress in our understanding of nature when, in fact, all we have done is substitute in our descriptions currently acceptable words for currently unacceptable ones. Chesterton (1908/1959) has derided this particular form of self-deception. "All the terms used in the science books, 'law,' 'necessity,' 'order,' 'tendency,' and so on, are really unintellectual, because they assume an inner synthesis, which we do not possess. The only words that ever satisfied me as describing Nature are the terms used in the fairy books, 'charm,' 'spell,' 'enchantment.' They express the arbitrariness of the fact and its mystery. A tree grows fruit because it is a *magic* tree. Water runs downhill because it is bewitched. The sun shines because it is bewitched. I deny altogether that this is fantastic or even mystical..... this fairy-tale language about things is simply rational and agnostic" (p. 53).

One need not agree entirely with Chesterton's position to see the point of his comparison or to recognize the ease with which the use of terminology that is currently in fashion in science can be mistaken for deep understanding of that to which the words refer. And the fact that the words that are used to describe phenomena change over time does not necessarily demonstrate that the phenomena have become more deeply understood or better explained. "You say you want an explanation of Einstein's theory of relativity. What kind of explanation? In terms of words of the Anglo-Saxon period and therefore with very nearly the concepts prevalent at that time? In terms of the language of the 17th century and therefore with concepts prevalent about the time of Newton? In terms of the language of, say, 1900? In modern technical terms? In modern mathematical symbolism? All these would represent attempts at explanation but how successful could they possibly be?" (Calder, 1964, quoted in Dubos, 1970, p. 213). Difficulty with the idea of causal explanation was one of the motivating factors in the emergence of logical positivism. Comte (1842/1988) argued that it was futile to attempt to find causal explanations for the lawful relationships discovered by science; all one could reasonably aspire to was the discovery of the laws themselves.

If we are to take seriously the idea that to explain is to elucidate or to present something in such a way that it will be understood, we must recognize that what constitutes an explanation for one person may not serve an explanatory function for another; what constitutes an adequate explanation must depend in part on what the person to whom it is addressed already knows about the subject. We must recognize the possibility of having more than one explanation for any given thing. And we must see that one can believe one has gained an understanding of something when in fact one has not.

Independently of how close we may hope to come to getting a concept of explanation that would be satisfying from a philosophical point of view, we can recognize that, looked at pragmatically, an explanation is adequate if it serves its intended purpose. An explanation that suffices for one purpose may not do so for another. "Explaining" the constancy of the earth's orbit about the sun by attributing it to the force of gravity suffices, for example, to equate the force that has this effect with the one that causes ocean tides to rise and fall twice a day and puts a limit on how high a person can jump; and it provides a basis for dazzling technological accomplishments—but it offers little to the individual who would like to understand, in some nontrivial sense, what a force is and, in particular, the nature and basis of the one we call gravity. Perhaps description is all that can reasonably be expected of science—description in the form of generalizations expressed as laws, quantitative insofar as possible, that provide the basis for prediction and control.

The fundamental attribution error

Some causal explanations identify inanimate entities as causes; others—especially explanations of human behavior—sometimes identify as causes purposes, goals, intentions and the like. A distinction that is widely acknowledged in connection with attribution theory, is between individuals and situations as causes of behavior.

Individuals versus situations as causes of behavior

Attribution theory, in the broadest sense, is a body of ideas resulting from efforts to explain human behavior in a variety of contexts. A primary objective of attribution theorists has been to determine the conditions under which particular acts will be attributed to individuals and those under which they will be attributed to other factors, such as the situations in which the individuals find themselves. Whether an act is attributed to an individual or to a situation appears to depend on such factors as whether the individual is believed to engage consistently in the behavior in question in similar situations, and whether people in general are believed to engage in that behavior in those same situations. The individual is viewed as the cause of the behavior to the degree that that individual exhibits that behavior in a given situation while other people do not; the situation is viewed as the cause to the degree that many people would be expected to exhibit the same behavior in that situation. Success or failure on a specific undertaking may be attributed to a person's effort or lack thereof, or to situational circumstances beyond the person's control.

In many cases it is possible to view things either way and different observers will attribute effects to causes differently. However, many people seem to be more inclined, in general, to make one type of attribution than the other (Lefcourt, 1972; Rotter, 1966). What has been called the *fundamental attribution error*, or sometimes the *fundamental error of social perception*, is the tendency to attribute behavior primarily, if not exclusively, to an individual's dispositions or personality traits and to overlook possible situational determinants of that behavior (Bierbrauer, 1973; Jones, 1976, 1979; Jones & Davis, 1965; Jones & Harris, 1967; Mischel, 1968; Ross, 1978; Ross & Anderson, 1982). Nisbett and Ross (1980) believe that socialization in our culture produces a preference for dispositional over situational attributions of behavior.

As to why this should be so, one possibility is that in attributing behavior to dispositions or personality traits, we make it more predictable—at least in some instances—than it otherwise would be and thereby simplify our view of the world. The belief that behavior is largely dispositionally determined, coupled with the knowledge that a particular person has a particular disposition, provides a basis for inferring how that person will act in many specific situations. To the extent that behavior *is* dispositionally determined, such attribution-based expectations may be accurate and thus facilitate communication and social exchange. The assumption underlying the notion of a fundamental attribution error is that behavior is less dispositionally determined—is more determined by situational factors—than it is generally perceived to be. No one, to my knowledge, argues that dispositional variables are *not* determinants of behavior; the claim is only that their role is generally overweighted whereas that of situational variables is not given the weight it deserves.

Overcoming the fundamental attribution error has been seen as a major developmental challenge for adults (Blanchard-Fields, 1986); several studies have provided evidence that efforts to sensitize people to the importance of situational factors in specific cases often fail to dissuade them from electing to attribute behavior to dispositional causes (Darley & Batson, 1973; Jones, 1979; Pietromonaco & Nisbett, 1982; Safer, 1980; Snyder & Jones, 1974). Some investigators have reported success in decreasing the magnitude of the fundamental attribution error by motivating people, in one or another way, to make accurate attributions (Pittman & D'Agostino, 1985; Tetlock, 1985).

One account of the general tendency to underweight the role of situational variables as determinants of others' behavior holds that the situational variables are obscured by the salience of the behavior itself. Heider (1958) argues that, in general, behavior is so salient that it tends to obscure the field in social perception. Holland, Holyoak, Nisbett, and Thagard (1986) endorse the same idea. Increasing the visual prominence or salience of individuals in social situations appears to increase the likelihood that those individuals will be identified as causal agents when observers are asked to account for specific events (McArthur & Post, 1977; McArthur & Solomon, 1978; Taylor & Fisk, 1975, 1978; Taylor, Fisk, Close, Anderson, & Ruderman, 1979).

Holland, Holyoak, Nisbett, and Thagard (1986) contend that people tend to overestimate the stability of social behavior and to account for the behavior of individuals in terms of individuating information even when that information is weak, rather than in terms of information regarding social groups to which individuals belong. They point out the consistency of this finding with the claim that people often discount base-rate information when making probabilistic judgments. "Even useless information about an individual serves to distract people from using information about group membership that they believe to be relevant to the required judgment.... in general, it appears that individuating information, whether diagnostic or nondiagnostic, has substantial power to override default assumptions based on category membership" (Holland et al., 1986, p. 219; see also Nisbett, Zukier, & Lemley, 1981). Somewhat paradoxically, it appears that people may sometimes be even more likely to attempt to make use of nondiagnostic information that is available when they are highly motivated to be accurate (Tetlock & Boettger, 1989).

The picture may be obscured by the tendency of people to bring certain biases to the task of identifying causes of behavior and to be relatively unaffected by information regarding the commonality or rareness of the behavior in question (Kunda & Nisbett, 1986; McArthur, 1972; Miller, Gillen, Schenker, & Radlove, 1973; Nisbett, Borgida, Crandall, & Reed, 1976). Knowledge of the commonness of a specific response in a given situation does not necessarily evoke identification of the situation as its cause. Several of the experiments conducted by Nisbett, Borgida, Crandall, and Reed (1976) involved attempts to modify states of depression by providing depressed subjects with information (sometimes false) regarding the commonality of depression among other people in their same situation, and giving them a reason for the depression external to themselves. The approach did not work. The failure of people to make much use of consensus information, Nisbett et al. suggest, is analogous to the failure of people to pay much attention to base rate information in their predictions about category membership.

Nisbett and Ross (1980) take exception to much of the theorizing about attribution bias that attributes the bias to motivational as opposed to cognitive factors. They contend that, on the whole, investigators have been too quick to attribute the behavior of participants in experimental situations to motivational biases when there were equally plausible alternative interpretations of the findings. Among the cognitive sources of errors in causal attribution, they note the following: "(a) overreliance on the representativeness heuristic and on a priori theories of doubtful validity, (b) overreliance on the availability heuristic, (c) use of simplistic and 'overlyparsimonous' criteria for causal attribution, (d) absence or weakness of certain normatively appropriate causal analytic schemas, and (e) intrusion of causal theories applicable to one domain into other domains to which they are inapplicable and misleading" (p. 114–115).

Attribution in accounting for own behavior

There is some evidence that people are better at finding situational factors to account for their own behavior, or that of a member of a group to which they belong, than when it is that of others, and especially of members of groups to which they do not belong (Jones & Nisbett, 1972; Jones, 1976; Krueger, Ham, & Linford, 1996; Nisbett, Caputo, Legant, & Marecek, 1973; Pettigrew, 1979). This is sometimes referred to as the *actor-observer* bias. The tendency to attribute one's own behavior to situational factors, as distinct from character traits, is especially apparent when the behavior one is attempting to explain is behavior for which one would prefer not to take credit (Snyder & Higgins, 1988). Explanations of lateness in completing projects are more likely to cite situational factors, for example, when people are explaining their own tardiness than when they are explaining that of others (Buehler, Griffin, & Ross, 1994). When asked to produce reasons why future positive events might or might not occur, people tend to attribute positive outcomes to personal factors and negative outcomes to situational ones (Hoch, 1985).

Kipnis (1984, 1993, 1997) found evidence that the tendency of people to take responsibility for the work they do is influenced by the type of technology they use. After Faunce (1981), he distinguishes three stages of technological development—craft technology, mechanized technology, and automated technology—and argues that people are more likely to see themselves as responsible for the work they do if they use craft technology than if they use a more advanced type of technology. Use of craft technology appears also to be associated with higher feelings of competence and satisfaction (Gutek & Winter, 1990; Stern & Kipnis, 1993). The relationship between feeling of competence and satisfaction and level of technology used is not simple, however; it depends somewhat on whether the technology use is voluntary or required (Stern & Kipnis, 1993), and whether the focus is on work per se or on the outcomes of the work (Florman, 1981).

People sometimes attempt to maintain a positive self-image despite poor performance in a given situation by seeking evidence that other people have performed poorly in the same situation, so as to justify attributing their own poor showing to the situation rather than to personal inadequacies, or to find a way to discredit the poor performance evaluation (Frey, 1981; Frey & Stahlberg, 1986; Pyszczynski, Greenberg, & Holt, 1985; Pyszczynski, Greenberg, & LaPrelle, 1985). And when they are outperformed by others, they may look for ways to perceive the activity as irrelevant or inconsequential (Tesser, 1986; Tesser, & Campbell, 1983).

Such findings have led to the idea that, in addition to a fundamental attribution error, which applies primarily to attributions of other people's behavior, there exists a *self-serving attributional bias*, which reveals itself in a tendency to make dispositional attributions for one's own successes and situational attributions for one's own failures (Bowerman, 1978; Pyszczynski & Greenberg, 1987; Snyder, Stephan, & Rosenfield, 1978; Streufert & Streufert, 1969)—which is to say a tendency to credit one's successes to one's self while blaming one's failures on circumstances beyond one's control. Greenwald (1980) coined the term *beneffectance* to connote this phenomenon. The tendency is sometimes expressed in the form of behavior that appears to be intended to provide one with an excuse for performing poorly in a specific situation (say an academic test) (Arkin & Maruyama, 1979) or to make mediocre performance look good because it is above expectations (Berglas & Jones, 1978; Jones & Berglas, 78; Pyszczynski & Greenberg, 1983; Tucker, Vuchinich, & Sobell, 1981). The tendency to take more credit for successes than for failures appears to be the stronger the greater the importance of the behavior in question to the individual (Miller, 1976; Nicholls, 1978).

Probably most of us will find it easy to accept the generalization that we are likely to attribute decisions and actions that turn out well to intelligence, cleverness, carefulness, courage and other character traits and personal qualities we would like to think we possess, while blaming those that turn out poorly on circumstances beyond our control. It appears, however, that how we account for our own successes and failures can be influenced to some degree by our emotional state: when we are happy, we tend to attribute our successes to our ability and our failures to bad luck, whereas when we are sad we are more likely to do the reverse (Forgas, Bower, & Moylan, 1990). On balance, the evidence suggests that we are not very good at identifying the causes of our own behavior (Nisbett & Wilson 1977a, 1977b; Wilson & Nisbett, 1978).

Is the fundamental attribution error an error?

The heading for this major section refers to attribution "error," and I have used this term in the discussion. It must be pointed out, however, that studies of attribution typically have not included efforts to determine whether, or under what conditions, the attributions people make are empirically accurate (Ross & Fletcher, 1985); rather the focus has been on identifying the factors that determine which of various possible types of attributions they make. The fact is it is difficult in many cases to show an attribution to be wrong. Consider the common practice of asking people who have managed to live an unusually long time the secret of their longevity. Responses to this question vary considerably, but people typically come up with explanations involving one or more aspects of their lifestyles. One person will point to a life of hard work and abstinence from strong drink; another will credit the habit of consuming a quantity of liquor every day and of avoiding strenuous activities. But how does one challenge an explanation of longevity no matter what it is? People who have lived to a ripe old age are existence proofs that their lifestyles were conducive to living a long time, and if they wish to credit one or several aspects of that lifestyle as the major causes of their long lives, it is difficult to demonstrate that they are wrong.

The idea that what has been called the fundamental attribution error is fundamental, or even that it is an error, has been challenged on other grounds as well (Funder, 1982, 1987; Harvey, Town, & Yarkin, 1981; Lopes, 1976; Miller & Rorer, 1982). Lopes (1982), for example, argues that the predisposition to attribute the behavior of others to stable personality variables rather than to transient situational factors may be no error at all, when viewed from the perspective of what is conducive to survival. "Both physical and social survival require that we learn as well as we can to predict and control the effects that other people have on us. Thus, if an effect is predictable, even weakly, by the presence of some individual, then it is important that we find this out" (p. 633).

Funder (1987) points out that participants in attribution studies are often given information by the experimenter that they are expected to ignore. In terms of the assumptions that one usually makes regarding how people communicate with each other, this is a peculiar situation; normally when people volunteer some information it is because they see it as relevant to the interaction and they expect the recipient to take some note of it. So when experimenters give participants information that is considered by them (the experimenters) to be irrelevant to the task, they can hardly assume that the participants should see it as irrelevant as well; if the experimenters actually tell the participants—directly or indirectly—that the information they are providing is irrelevant, they put the participants in the position of having to ignore a basic rule of communication and leave them to wonder why, if the information is irrelevant, it was given to them at all. Moreover, in view of the fact that experimenters often mislead participants for purposes of an experiment, and that it would be naive to assume that no participants realize this, one may be forgiven for imagining that they (the participants) may, on occasion, do a little speculating as to what is really going on. Funder argues that, inasmuch as participants implicitly know the rules of social discourse, responses that look like overattribution in decontextualized experiments may make perfect sense when viewed from the perspective of the total situation, which includes the experimenter as a communicating agent. From this perspective, that the fundamental attribution error is truly an error is far from clear.

Whatever the explanation of the fundamental attribution error, or the appearance of same, even those investigators who most firmly believe there is such a thing hold it to be only a *bias* toward attributing behavior to individuals' dispositions or personality traits rather than to other factors; no one suggests that people *invariably* make this type of attribution. The importance of a variety of influences on attributions is recognized. Regan, Strauss, and Fazio (1974) found, for example, that when accounting for performance on a task requiring skill, people were likely to attribute good or poor performance to the performers' ability or lack thereof, or to external factors, depending on their liking or disliking of the performers. In particular, when liked performers did well or disliked performers did poorly, their performance tended to be attributed to their abilities; when liked performers did poorly or disliked performers did well, the tendency was to attribute performance to external situational factors. Analogous results were obtained when the behavior to be accounted for was a socially commendable act.

It could be, of course, that attributional differences that depend on whether the people whose behavior is being attributed are well-liked or disliked have some basis in fact. Perhaps likeability is highly correlated with other admirable qualities and is therefore a valid basis for making judgments of the kind noted above. It seems unlikely, however, that this is an adequate explanation for what appears to be a bias to interpret events so as to make it easy to continue to think well of people we like and to continue to dislike those whom we already dislike. A similar difference of interpretation of athletic events from fans of winning and losing teams has been described by Gilovich (1983). People find it possible also to interpret behavior that is inconsistent with their initial expectations in such a way as to make it consistent with them (Hayden & Mischel, 1976; Swann & Snyder, 1980).

Reasons for attribution

What makes attributions interesting is less their substance than their existence. We not only seem to be able to produce causal explanations for nearly everything, from cosmic events to the mundane occurrences of everyday life, but we seem to have a compulsion to do so. Why do we seem to have such a strong need to be able to identify causes?

Perhaps early educational experiences lead children to develop an oversimplified conception of cause-effect relationships. They learn to give short and simple answers to questions (What caused the First World War? The assassination of Archduke Franz Ferdinand of Austria in 1914) that do not have short simple answers. One has to wonder to what extent the early development of such a conception leads people later in life habitually to perceive things as being simpler than they really are. To look for crisp, uncomplicated answers to difficult questions, to be uncomfortable with ambiguities and uncertainties even when they are inherent to the situation, to view reflectiveness as evidence of indecisiveness or weak-mindedness.

When students object that more than one alternative on a multiple-choice test question might be considered correct, depending on how one interpreted the question, they may or may not get a sympathetic hearing. A teacher who turns a deaf ear to this type of observation may be reinforcing the idea that the world should be perceived in simple terms. Everything is either right or wrong, correct or incorrect, this or that. There are no intermediate positions or mitigating considerations, and when one insists on seeing them one is unnecessarily complicating things. Simple becomes equated with neat and good, complex with messy and bad. So people come to say with pride that they have a simple view of this or that when this or that may in reality be very complex.

These comments are conjectural, but I suspect that we early acquire overly simplistic concepts of cause-effect relationships and of explanation and understanding that stay with us in later life and make our thinking often to be shallower than it should be. If I demand very little of an explanation, I will be inclined to accept uncritically explanations that really do not explain, and I will not be motivated to challenge them. If I believe I understand concepts merely because I can use appropriately in conversation terms that relate to them, I will not be inclined to engage in the kind of probing and reflection that could lead to understanding at a more-than-superficial level.

I am not arguing that cause-effect relationships do not exist, or that it is wrong to encourage people to think in these terms. I do mean to suggest, however, that we too easily make the assumption that every effect has *an* identifiable cause—as opposed to being the result of a complex convergence of many factors. It would be useful to understand better the desire to identify causes and especially simple one-dimensional ones. It seems more than remotely possible that our intolerance of uncertainty and the assumption that we appear to make that every event has an identifiable cause may contribute to overly simplistic cause-effect views of phenomena in general and of human behavior in particular.

The possibility of overattribution

Although it has not received a lot of attention from researchers, a phenomenon that we also need to understand better is the attribution to people of hidden motives and meanings behind the things they do or say. We see this phenomenon in daily life, and also in professional analyses of literary works, government or business documents, and political speeches and communiques. Surely hidden motives and meanings sometimes exist; but just as surely, it is possible to read significance into actions or words that they do not really have. In our search for hidden motives or meanings we may sometimes invent them to satisfy our assumption that they must be there. There is, in other words, the possibility of overinterpreting words and actions, of seeing metaphors, allusions, veiled threats, prophesies, and disguised messages of various sorts that exist only in our imaginations.

Closely related to this possibility is that of attributing to people knowledge, abilities and powers they do not have. We are, perhaps, especially likely to do this with respect to people in positions of authority. Tuchman (1984) notes a tendency among political scientists to treat political power with immense, and sometimes unjustified, respect: "They fail to see it as sometimes a matter of ordinary men walking into water over their heads, acting unwisely or foolishly or perversely as people in ordinary circumstances frequently do. The trappings and impact of power deceive us, endowing the possessors with a quality larger than life. Shorn of his tremendous curled peruke, high-heels and ermine, the Sun King was a man subject to misjudgment, error, and impulse—like you and me" (p. 23).

Overattribution can contribute to the making of heroes and scapegoats as well. When a risky venture turns out well, we tend to credit whoever was in charge at the time with the foresight, skill and courage that are commensurate with our good feelings about the outcome. When it turns out poorly, we just as readily shower the leader with attributions of folly, ineptitude, and timidity (or temerity, as the case may be) that match our feelings of disappointment. I do not mean to suggest that leaders should not be held accountable for their leadership, but I do believe we find it easy to attribute to them more control over situations than they actually exercise and thus impute to them a greater responsibility for events (good and bad) than they have.

An abiding fundamental question

The problem of explaining human behavior scientifically is complicated by the fact that we view ourselves both as physical entities and as moral agents. Thus we see people's actions as the results of cause-effect relationships no different from those that govern the world of physics, but we also see them as the consequences of free choices made by purposeful and morally responsible beings. The problem of reconciling these two views is an old one, and still far from resolved. It has been debated for centuries, usually under the rubric of free will versus determinism. Some see the two notions as basically irreconcilable (Edelman, 1995). We manage, as a society, to live with a sort of schizoid approach to this question whereby we construct cause-effect explanations for specific acts but hold the individuals responsible for them all the same.

Causal explanations are often couched in terms of scientific laws. For a long time, thanks largely to Aristotle, all explanations, not just those of human behavior, were couched in terms of purpose. Clarke (1985) distinguishes between explaining (or predicting) an action on the one hand and justifying it, either as the rational thing to do or as what ought to be done, on the other. Perception of an action as justified could be part of an explanation of why it was taken, but it is not a necessary part. More generally, Clarke argues, explanations of actions need not correspond to what the actors may give as justifications of them.

Bloom (1987) makes a related distinction with respect to what he sees as a divergence between some scientific theories and the behavior of their originators. He argues that the natural and social sciences give an account of things that cannot explain the conduct of natural and social scientists. Consider, for example, Freud's claim that people are motivated by desire for sex and power. Freud, Bloom points out, did not explain his own scientific activity in terms of these motives. But if Freud, as a scientist, can be motivated by love of the truth, Bloom argues, so can others, and his description of their motives is therefore flawed.

☐ Explanation and Rationality

> The sorts of arguments put forward by explanationists are designed to show that whatever ultimately justifies a belief is a matter of the explanatory contribution of that belief. (Lycan, 1988, p. 133)

Lycan (1988) gives explanation a central role in his conception of rationality and defends a doctrine sometimes called *explanationism*, according to which "all justified reasoning is fundamentally explanatory reasoning that aims at maximizing the 'explanatory coherence' of one's total belief system" (p. 128). Explanationism holds that the goal of the rational thinker should be to accept as most probably true the hypothesis, among competing alternatives, that best explains the facts. Preference for one explanatory theory over another should be based, in Lycan's view, on such considerations as simplicity, scope, testability, minimal residual mess (how many messy questions does it raise or fail to answer), and consistency with other justified beliefs. Other things being equal, the greater the simplicity, scope, testability, and consistency, and the less the residual mess, the better.

Explanation also is central to the concept of rationality promoted by Polkinghorne (1991). "Rational inquiry is not characterized by an unwillingness to take intellectual risks, so that we cling alone to what is deductively certain, but it is bold enough to venture on the construction of a metaphysical scheme whose justification will lie in its attainment of comprehensive explanatory power" (p. 11). And he argues that this pertains whether the domain of inquiry is science or theology.

I find it easy to see explanation as a key aspect of rationality, and believe the continual search for explanations to be a defining characteristic of human nature. Explanations provide one with a sense of closure, the resolution of uncertainty, sometimes answers to vexing questions. They can facilitate thinking by permitting it to move on, as when the resolution of a specific question provides the basis for making headway on perhaps more interesting or more general ones. In science it is typically the case that whenever a satisfactory explanation of anything is given, that explanation leads to new questions and further investigations into the nature of reality.

It is important to recognize also, however, that explanations can, and sometimes do, inhibit thought. One of the most striking illustrations of this fact is the inhibition of investigations into the nature of the physical world for nearly 2000 years following Aristotle, whose ideas were accepted so widely and uncritically as to become dogma. His explanations of why things are the way they are apparently satisfied the curiosity of a hundred generations.

That the availability of a plausible explanation for some event can inhibit the production of alternative possibilities has implications for good thinking in daily life. To attempt always to think of alternative explanations before accepting a given one may be a very good rule. Consideration of more than a single possible explanation may motivate the collection of additional information that could justify a selection among the possibilities.

Arguably, all explanations are tentative; they rest not only on evidence but on assumptions—not always explicit—and they have limitations. All can be pushed back to something that must be taken as given. But we will have explanations. It is our nature to wish to know both how things are and why they are that way. The instrumental value of the kind of knowledge that many explanations represent is unquestionably great, but our desire for explanations is not limited to those that have obvious practical utility; we wish to understand for the sake of understanding, and this, in my view, is as much of a defining property of a rational being as we are likely to find.

CHAPTER 7
Preference and Judgment

> [Q]uality is much more difficult to "handle" than quantity, just as the exercise of judgment is a higher function than the ability to count and calculate. (Schumacher, 1973, p. 51)

☐ Preferences

Two assumptions that underlie much theorizing about decision making are that human beings have preferences and that those preferences can be revealed or discovered. Probably most of us would be comfortable with these assumptions, at least much of the time. We are keenly aware of liking some things, some people, some situations better than others and, in a great many instances, would have no difficulty in making those preferences explicit if asked to do so.

That is not to say that our preferences are always strong or even that we are always entirely sure, at least without some probing, what they are. As Shafir (1993) argues, we often face decisions without explicit preferences, but it is the need to decide that forces us to determine what our preferences are. Sometimes even when we are not completely indifferent to the alternatives before us, we may find it difficult to make up our minds as to what it is we want. Upon reflection, we may discover that we do not really prefer what we thought we did. We know too, from research, that the preferences people express verbally are not always consistent with those that would be inferred from their behavior (Schuman & Johnson, 1976).

What constitutes a bona fide preference? How does one measure the strength of a preference? How does one determine the basis, or bases, of a preference? How do I think about the condition of having a preference, say for cookies over carrots, while wishing that it were otherwise—in this case for carrots over cookies. I definitely prefer cookies to carrots, but I would prefer, for what seem to me legitimate reasons, to prefer carrots to cookies. Should I say that my *real* preference is for carrots, even though when given the choice, I invariably take cookies? Should I think of levels of preferences—my preference for cookies over carrots representing a relatively low-level concrete preference, and my preference for a preference for carrots over cookies representing a higher-level one? Sen (1983) makes a distinction of this sort in suggesting that it is not unreasonable for people to decide to be guided not only by their preferences but by "metarankings," which reflect what they would like their preferences to be.

Do we have preferences or do we construct them?

The fact that we often find it difficult to say, in specific instances, what our preferences are raises the question of whether the assumption that we *have* preferences in all cases is really true. Might it not be that, at least in some instances, we find it hard to say what our preferences are because we do not have them? Perhaps what we do when forced to make choices, in these cases, is *construct* preferences and fool ourselves into believing that we had those preferences all along (Payne, Bettman, & Johnson, 1992, 1993; Shafir, 1993; Shafir, Simonson, & Tversky, 1993; Slovic, 1995).

Shafir (1993) takes this position: "Preferences, as many have argued, are actually constructed—not merely revealed—during their elicitation, and the construction of preference is guided partially by the attempt to formulate coherent reasons or justifications for choosing one option rather than another" (p. 272). This helps explain, Shafir argues, how it is that Simpson's-paradox type violations of the sure-thing principle can occur (see below). The idea that preferences are constructed, at least sometimes, gets some support from the finding that the degree of satisfaction that people express with various aspects of their lives or prospects depends to some extent on their mood or emotional state when they are asked (Forgas & Moylan, 1987).

The question of whether we have preferences or construct them is similar in some respects to the question, discussed in preceding chapters, of whether we can be said to know or believe something that has never entered our mind. In the case of preferences that have never been made explicit, some may find it preferable to think of them not as preferences but as propensities for preferences of specific types.

Preference and Judgment

Even when we have no difficulty in saying what our preferences are in specific instances, we may be unable to explain, to our own satisfaction or that of others, why they are what they are. Details of a situation in which a preference is stated may *remind* one of reasons for the preference, and different situations may evoke different reasons. Or it could be the case that the situational details help one *manufacture* reasons on the spot (Shafir, Simonson, & Tversky, 1993; Tversky & Simonson, 1993). To hold the latter view, it is not necessary to assume that the reasons one manufactures are arbitrary; what reasons one finds acceptable are likely to depend on beliefs and principles that one does have and these are likely to differ from person to person.

Discovering one's preferences

Even assuming one has preferences, one may have to discover what they are. Especially is this likely to be the case when one's preferences are functions of many variables. Consider, for example, the case of the would-be purchaser of a house. Imagine that you are that would-be purchaser. You have been surveying the market and you have identified a few possibilities, each of which has some attractive and some less attractive features, but you have not been able to make up your mind about making a purchase. Imagine that a real estate agent asks you to make a list of the factors that you consider important in making comparisons among possibilities, and you generate a list, something like the following.

- Purchase price

- Style of house

- Quality of public school system

- Distance from work

- Tax rate in town

- General condition of house

- Quality of the living space

- Conveniences, amenities (patio, deck, screened porch, extra baths, garage, storage space, type of heating, fireplace(s), etc.)

- Land area (lot size)

- Neighborhood

- Availability of public transportation

Now suppose the agent asks you to assign a weight to each of the factors on your list, reflecting the importance you attach to that factor relative to all the other factors on the list. You might find that more of a struggle than you would have anticipated, but assume you could do it. Imagine further that, after you finish this assignment, the agent gives you a series of choices between pairs of hypothetical houses. Your task is to say, for each pair, which of the two you prefer. A question of considerable interest is whether your choices would be predictable from your list and the weighting of the factors on it.

In order to check for consistency between your preferences and your list of factors weighted according to relative importance, one must make some assumption about the way the factor weights are combined in the judgmental process. One possibility would be to rate each of the candidate houses with respect to each of the factors in such a way as to reflect how well the house satisfied the desideratum represented by that factor and the relative importance of the factor and then add up the scores. This procedure assumes that the factors combine linearly and that there are no interactions among them. It could be however that some factors might not count very much when considered in isolation, but would be more heavily weighted when considered in combination with other factors.

Whatever algorithm is applied to the use of factor weightings to predict preferences between specific candidate houses, one should not be surprised if the predictions often fail to prove to be correct. Our considerations so far have overlooked the fact that a given feature of a house can have both positive and negative aspects. For example, being located in a relatively isolated area may be perceived as a good thing from the point of view of privacy and perhaps the possibility of keeping pets and domesticated animals, whereas it would be an unfavorable feature from the point of view of accessibility of public transportation and other conveniences that one is likely to find in an urban area.

Another reason that a simple linear combination of weighted factors may not capture the essence of preferences among houses is that candidates may be ruled out on the basis of any one of several factors. One might be ruled out, for example, because it is too expensive, or too small, or located too close to railroad tracks. It may be that certain negative factors are deal-breakers, irrespective of how many pluses a candidate may have.

One may well discover too that in developing one's list of factors to consider, one has overlooked some that would have been considered very important if only one had thought of them: Does the cellar flood following heavy rains, or spring snow melt-off? Is the house adequately insulated? Are there serious problems that may not be obvious on casual inspection (termites, residual lead paint, radon)?

The real world has the added inconvenience that typically one does not have all the time one wants to make up one's mind. In the case of house buying, any given option will not be available indefinitely. One generally has to make a decision knowing that delay could mean the loss of an opportunity and the more attractive a given option, the greater the likelihood that it will not be available for long. In short, discovering what one's preferences are can be complicated in specific instances.

Preferences between certain and uncertain alternatives

Alternatives that must be considered in choice situations are known with certainty in some cases and only probabilistically in others. Sometimes one's alternatives may include both types—as when I have the option of spending $5 on a pair of socks or on a lottery ticket that will get me $1,000 with probability .005 and nothing with probability .995. Many experiments have been conducted to explore how people react when they have to choose between alternatives that are known with certainty and those that are known only probabilistically; one generalization that the results of such studies support is that, when the expected worth of the probabilistic alternative is about the same as the known worth of the certain alternative, people tend to prefer the certain alternative under some conditions and the probabilistic one under others.

In particular, they tend to prefer the certain alternative when the outcomes are perceived as gains and the probabilistic one when the outcomes are perceived as losses. For example, given a choice between A, a sure gain of $75, and B, a .75 probability of winning $100 coupled with a .25 probability of winning nothing, people tend to prefer A, but given a choice between C, a sure loss of $75 and D, a .75 probability of losing $100 coupled with a .25 probability of losing nothing, the same people are more likely to prefer D (Tversky & Kahneman, 1981). On the basis of this type of finding, people are said to be *risk-averse* with respect to their preferences among possible gains and *risk-seeking* with respect to their preferences among possible losses.

Determination of preferences is complicated by the fact that stated preferences among essentially the same alternatives can vary as a function of the way the alternatives are expressed (Dawes, 1988; Kahneman & Tversky, 1984). Such framing effects are commonly found in public-opinion polls (Moore, 1992; Payne, 1982; Wheeler, 1976) among other contexts (Kühberger, 1998, Levin, Schneider, & Gaeth, 1998; Schneider, 1992). They constitute a challenge to any theory that rests on the assumption that people have relatively stable preferences and that they know what those preferences are. Schneider (1992) argues that, inasmuch as different frames may communicate different contexts and different contexts may call for different actions, framing effects are not necessarily indicative of irrational behavior.

Preferences between uncertain alternatives

Much of the research on decision making has used tasks that require selecting among alternatives none of which is certain. Typically one is asked to state a preference between, or to rate the relative attractiveness of, two gambles. The gambles may differ with respect to probabilities of outcomes, payoffs associated with outcomes, or both. The participants' task may be simply to indicate which of the two gambles he or she prefers, or to adjust the parameters of one of the gambles (by adjusting probabilities or payoffs) so it is equivalent to the other gamble (so the participant sees the gambles as equally attractive or equally unattractive). The assumption is that by having an individual make lots of comparisons, one can discover the nature of the value (or utility) system that determines his or her preferences or choices. One might hope, for example, to discover that a person's behavior is consistent with some specifiable objective, such as maximization of expected value, maximization of possible gain, minimization of maximum possible loss, maximization of the probability of winning (independently of the amounts involved) or something else. An example of the discovery of such a consistency is the finding that how people rate the attractiveness of gambles is determined more by the relative probability of winning than by the size of the potential win (Slovic & Lichtenstein, 1968; Goldstein & Einhorn, 1987), which has been referred to as the *proportion dominance* phenomenon (Finucane, Peters, & Slovic, 2003).

A difficulty that can be encountered in relating choices to such rules is in the distinction between what a person might *want* to do and what he or she is capable of doing in a specific situation. One might, for example, wish to maximize the expected value of a choice, but if the situation does not permit the opportunity to do the appropriate calculation, one may not be able to do that. One might try to do it by estimating, or by using some rule of thumb that one believes would be likely to dictate the choice that would realize the desired goal, but such tactics are not likely to be as certain as actually doing the calculations. Another difficulty is that of ensuring that participants in gamble experiments take the task seriously, which is to say that they make the choices they would make if the stakes were real and they were highly motivated to make the best choices of which they are capable.

One may find consistent patterns of behavior that are suggestive of the use of rational, irrational, or arational, rules. And there is the possibility of choices showing no discernable systematicity and appearing as though they had been selected by coin tossing. A clue to rule-based behavior is consistency, as revealed, for example, in the same responses to the same pairs of gambles on different occasions or in transitive relationships in (consistent ordering of) preferences.

There are many factors that might reasonably be expected to affect people's preferences in choosing between gambles. These include their knowledge of relevant concepts, their ability to do the relevant mathematics, their ability to estimate, the effort they are willing to make, their attitude toward risk, and the context (whether the gamble is to be played many times, once, or not at all).

Efforts to find a model that is able to predict preferences with all kinds of gambles have not yet proved successful. One limiting factor has been the inability to develop a utility-based model that is descriptive of preferences between mixed gambles—those that have both gains and losses as possible outcomes (Chechile & Cooke, 1997; Chechile & Butler, 2000, 2003; Luce, 2003).

Paradoxes of preference

Suppose you are waiting to learn the outcome of some event that can go either of two ways: whether or not you are going to get a raise in pay; whether your unborn child is going to be a girl or a boy; whether or not your loan application will be approved. Suppose further that you are going to have to take one of two actions, A or B, after you learn the outcome of the uncertain event, but that you have to choose between these alternatives *before* you learn the outcome. If it is the case that you prefer action A if the first of the two possible outcomes materializes (you get the raise, the baby is a girl, the loan application is approved) *and* you prefer action A if the second outcome occurs (you do not get the raise, the baby is a boy, the loan application is disapproved), then it seems reasonable to say that you should prefer action A when the outcome is uncertain.

This idea was called by Savage (1954/1972) the *sure-thing principle* (STP), according to which, if one would prefer A to B knowing that X holds, and one would prefer A to B knowing that X does not hold, then one prefers A to B, period. When one first encounters this principle, it is hard to imagine that it could be wrong. Nevertheless, investigators have discovered a variety of instances in which the STP appears to be violated. The following example is taken from Shafir (1993).

A student who has just taken a difficult exam and not yet learned whether he passed or failed is trying to decide whether to go on vacation for the holidays. He wants to do whatever is most likely to make him happy and—having been a student for a long time and taken many examinations and vacations—he has some history that should help his deliberations. Table 7.1 and Table 7.2 show what he has done in the past and the effects of his actions on his happiness.

From this analysis it seems clear that the student should elect to go on vacation, inasmuch as, in the past he has been happy a larger percentage of the times he has gone on vacation than of the times he has stayed at home, both when he has failed exams and when he has passed them. According to the sure-thing principle, if the student prefers the vacation given one exam outcome, and he prefers the same thing given the other

TABLE 7.1 Actions and outcomes following previously failed exams

	Stayed	Went
Unhappy	6	14
Happy	1	4
% Happy	14	22

TABLE 7.2 Actions and outcomes following previously passed exams

	Stayed	Went
Unhappy	4	1
Happy	14	6
% Happy	78	86

TABLE 7.3 Actions and outcomes following all previous exams

	Stayed	Went
Unhappy	10	15
Happy	15	10
% Happy	60	40

outcome, then he prefers the vacation whatever the exam outcome, or so it would seem.

But suppose we look at the history of vacation-taking or home-staying independently of exam outcome. This we do by taking the sums of the entries in the two preceding tables as follows (Table 7.3).

Now it appears that the student should elect to stay home, because, considering all the times he has had to decide whether to go or stay following an exam, he has been happy a larger percentage of the times he has stayed than of the times he has gone. What should the student do? And what does his dilemma tell us about the sure-thing principle? Shafir (1993) summarizes the situation this way. "Based on his past experience, the student exhibits the following pattern of preferences: He decides to stay behind when he does not know whether he has passed or failed the exam, but he decides to go once he finds out that he passed and also once he finds out that he failed. This is in violation of STP" (p. 265).

Shafir points out that the student's dilemma has the form of a paradox discussed by Simpson (1951; Nickerson, 2004, chapter 6). The point that is relevant here is that surprising things can happen when data are pooled. The key to understanding the student's dilemma lies in recognizing the correlation between his choice and his state of mind, in particular the fact that he was more likely *both* to be unhappy and to go on vacation after failing an exam than after passing one.

How to interpret the relationship between the sure-thing principle and Simpson's paradox has been a matter of some debate among statisticians (Blyth, 1972a, 1972b; Good, 1972; Lindley, 1972). One position is that the sure-thing principle does not apply to situations in which the paradox can arise, and thus, technically, cannot be violated in those situations (Winkler, 1972). Messick and van de Geer (1981) argue that this position is tantamount to a claim that the sure-thing principle is not a trustworthy principle of choice under some conditions; they agree that it should not be used as a guide to choice, but reject the notion that it does not apply and therefore cannot be violated. The illustration of how the sure-thing principle might be violated that we have been considering involves a hypothetical student, and one might question whether it would be possible to construct situations in which people actually violate the principle in their choices. In fact, it has been done (Shafir & Tversky, 1992; Tversky & Shafir, 1992a).

As already noted, Shafir (1993) argues that violations of the sure-thing principle that have the structure of Simpson's paradox can occur because people often do not know what their preferences are—or may not even have preferences—until they are called upon to make them explicit by being forced to choose between specific alternatives. On this assumption, it is easy to see how the preferences one *constructs* may depend on the specifics of the context in which the construction occurs. People are likely to make choices they can justify to themselves with a *reason*. The reason for electing to go on vacation after passing a difficult exam might be to reward oneself for having done well; the reason for electing to go after failing such an exam might be to console oneself for not having done well. When the outcome is not known, one has neither reason for electing to take the vacation. One might argue that, from a purely logical point of view, if both reward for doing well and consolation for doing poorly are considered acceptable reasons for going on vacation the disjunction of these reasons—either to reward oneself for doing well or to console oneself for doing poorly—should also be an acceptable reason. This appears not to be the case, however. The fact that the disjunction of two conflicting reasons may be seen as less compelling than either of the two reasons by itself has been referred to as the *disjunction effect* (Shafir & Tversky, 1992; Tversky & Shafir, 1992a), and it is seen as implicated in some instances of violations of the sure-thing principle.

Another preference paradox involves violation of the *principle of regularity*, according to which the addition of an alternative to a choice set should not increase the attractiveness of any of the existing members of the set. It is easy to see how *deletion* of an item from a set could increase the relative attractiveness of one or more of the remaining items—if, for example, a particular item were preferred to all the other items in the set, its deletion would let one of the remaining items become the most preferred—but it is not so easy to see how the addition of an item could increase the relative attractiveness of any of the existing items.

Nevertheless, it appears that adding alternatives can have the effect of increasing the attractiveness of one or more of those that already exist. Tversky and Shafir (1992b) attribute this violation of the regularity principle to the increase in conflict that one may experience as a consequence of an increase in the size of the set among which one must make a choice—especially is the increase in conflict likely if the added alternative is very close in attractiveness to the one that, in the absence of the addition, would have been preferred—and the fact that an increase in conflict is likely to result in an increase in the tendency to opt for the status quo.

Still another type of paradox of preference involves intransitivities in preference orderings, such as situations in which A is preferred to B, B is preferred to C, and C is preferred to A. Several examples are given in Nickerson (2004) and there is evidence that such intransitivities can sometimes be seen in preferences that people express (Tversky, 1969).

While perhaps less likely to be considered a paradox, another peculiarity of preference involves anticipation of regret. I suspect that few of us would contest the notion that our behavior is often influenced by the fear of regretting a choice we are about to make if it turns out wrong. This idea has been formalized in regret theory (Bell, 1982, 1985; Loomes & Sugden, 1982), which recognizes the role of anticipated emotions, both desirable and undesirable, in motivating behavior. There is some evidence that anticipated regret regarding the consequences of actions tends to be greater than anticipated regret regarding equally serious consequences of failure to take preventive measures, i.e., that sins of commission are more regrettable than sins of omission with the same consequences (Ritov & Baron, 1990; Spranca, Minsk, & Baron, 1991). It appears that people generally feel greater responsibility for the consequences of their actions than for their failures to act.

☐ Judging Worth and Costs

It was noted at the beginning of this chapter that two of the basic assumptions underlying much theorizing about decision making are that people have preferences and that those preferences can be revealed or discovered. All structured approaches to choice or decision making rest on these assumptions. The claim was immediately qualified, however, by the observation that it may not always be the case that we are sure what our preferences are, at least without some probing.

Methods for judging worth

In a free-market economy, the value of anything is determined by the convergence of the price people who do not have it and want it are willing to pay for it and the price for which people who have it are willing to sell it. If these prices do not converge, there is no transaction, and we conclude either that those who have it put a higher value on it than those who do not, or that those who would like it do not have the means to acquire it for what they believe it to be worth. Values are contingent in the sense that what one is willing to spend to acquire X depends not only on how much one has but on the alternatives for which that might be spent and on how desirable one finds the alternatives relative to X.

How people judge the worth (value, utility) of possible decision outcomes has been the subject of considerable research. Normative models for judging worth typically call for identifying the dimensions in terms of which a meaningful comparison can be made, judging the relative merits of the items being compared with respect to each of these dimensions, and then combining the single-dimension judgments into an overall preference according to some rule—such as taking a weighted sum of their results (Fischer, 1972; Kneppreth, Gustafson, Leifer, & Johnson, 1974; MacCrimmon, 1968; Raiffa, 1968).

Although people do not always know their preferences, especially when the alternatives differ in complex ways, they do sometimes find it easy to say they prefer A to B, where A and B differ with respect to many dimensions, without being able to say precisely why they do so. Quantitative methods—multi-dimensional scaling and discriminant analysis techniques—have been developed that sometimes can be used to identify dimensions or features that appear to underlie such global preferences.

One method that has been used to determine the worth that people attach to various specific goods is to ask people how much they would be willing to pay for them if they could be purchased in a market (Kahneman & Knetsch, 1992; Kahneman, Ritov, Jacowitz, & Grant, 1993). This method is sometimes referred to as the willingness-to-pay (WTP) method and sometimes as the contingent-valuation (CV) method. It has been used to attempt to determine how much people value specific possible outcomes of governmental policies relating to public goods. One of the main findings from research in this area is that the amount people say they are willing to pay for a specific public good typically does not scale with the amount of that good. When, for example, they are asked what they would be willing to pay for a specific amount of a good, such as protection of a specific amount of federal wilderness, what they say they would be willing to pay for an amount X+Y tends not to be close to the sum of the amount they say they would be willing to pay for X and what they say they would be willing to pay for Y separately (Diamond, Hausman, Leonard, & Denning, 1993).

This is not surprising. Any indicant of value that did scale linearly with amount of good over an unlimited range would be an irrational one. If it were true in general that what we should be willing to pay to protect n acres of wilderness is n times what we are willing to pay to protect one acre, it would follow that we should be willing to pay an enormous sum to protect the entire globe as wilderness. The failure of willingness to pay for a good to scale with amount of good is consistent with the intuitively compelling notion that it is not generally the case that if having a certain amount of a good is desirable, having n times as much of it is n times as desirable. The story of King Midas makes this point in a memorable way.

Some limitations and complications

The willingness-to-pay method of determining value has some other limitations. How much people say they would be willing to pay cannot be assumed to be an accurate indication of how much they indeed *would* pay if given an opportunity actually to purchase the good with real money. And even what they say they would be willing to pay for a specific good can depend on how they are asked. If, for example, people are asked how much they would be willing to pay for a good, A, which is a natural part of a larger good, B, they are likely to give a much larger figure if they are asked about good A in isolation than if they are asked about good A after having been asked about the more inclusive good B (Kahneman & Knetsch, 1992; Kemp & Maxwell, 1993).

More generally, it is not hard to construct situations in which people assign values in contradictory ways (Irwin, Slovic, Lichtenstein, & McClelland, 1993). In the environmental context, different results may be obtained depending on whether questions are couched in terms of species lost or species saved (Tversky & Kahneman, 1981) or on whether respondents are required to reveal preferences among species by choosing some species or by rejecting some (Shafir, 1993). Shafir and Tversky (1995) discuss a number of ways in which preferences between or among choices can be affected by factors that should, theoretically, be irrelevant. They note too, however, that the fact that people sometimes make irrational choices is not compelling evidence that their intuitions are irrational, because when informed that their choices violate a principle of rationality, people typically wish to modify them so as to make them conform.

Another illustration of assigning of values, or worths, in what appear to be contradictory ways is found in what has been called the *endowment effect*, according to which people sometimes are unwilling to sell something for X when they would also be unwilling to purchase it for Y, $X > Y$, if they did not own it already (Thaler, 1985; Kahneman, Knetsch, & Thaler, 1990). This phenomenon has sometimes been called the *status-quo bias* (Samuelson & Zeckhauser, 1988).

The problem of determining worth is illustrated also in the context of national policy establishment by some of the issues—like health care, national security, and environmental change—that are topics of heated debate in the United States. Everyone wants better health care, good security and environmental protection, but there are costs involved in obtaining these objectives, and presumably rationality dictates that what we are willing to spend to get them should be commensurate with the perceived worth of the benefits. The worth of the benefits turns out to be a very subjective thing. Although it has been possible in some instances to get plausible estimates of the consequences of health care programs and services (e.g., broad-based screening for specific diseases, vaccination programs) in terms of number of years of life saved or prolonged, the translation of these estimates into financial terms is, not surprisingly, very tenuous (Leutwyler, 1995).

Moreover, some of the variables used as measures of worth are controversial. Consider, for example, number of years of prolonged life. It seems simple enough in concept—if life expectancy can be increased by, say, 5 years, surely that is unquestionably a good thing. On the other hand, while some people believe that life should always be prolonged if at all possible, this is by no means a unanimous view. Many people express the belief in living wills that life under certain conditions should not be prolonged. In deciding what course to take in the treatment of a terminal illness, one may be faced with selecting among options that involve considerations of tradeoffs between expected years of survival and quality of life during those years. Attempts have been made to quantify quality of life in ways that take into account expected benefits and adverse effects of possible treatments (Holland, 1996), but this is a very delicate and controversial matter.

Comparable difficulties are encountered in efforts to quantify the worth of measures intended to enhance national security or to protect the environment from detrimental change. With respect to national security, or public safety more generally, the issue typically boils down to the problem of comparing the value of human life with the costs (not only monetary costs but those represented by inconveniences or constraints on civil liberties) of protecting it. How much is society—or should society be—willing to pay in order to increase the security of its citizens by some unknown, but presumably estimateable, amount? And how much should individuals be willing to give up of conveniences or liberties in trade for the extra security?

Environmental protection involves the same types of issues. How much are clean air and clean water worth? How clean is clean enough? How does one quantify the benefits of climate stabilization (Nordhaus, 1992; Peck & Teisberg, 1992)? How does one attach a value to the avoidance of chronic stress and stress-related disorders that have been observed among people who live with the reality or threat of industrial or agricultural toxins in their neighborhoods (Fowlkes & Miller, 1982; Gatchel & Newberry, 1991; Gibbs, 1986)? How do we attach numbers to the worth of the pleasure that people derive from the various recreational uses they make of wilderness areas?

However worth is determined, theoretical treatments of choice and decision making—both normative and descriptive—invariably take it as a given that different possible outcomes are desirable, or undesirable, to the same individual to different degrees. If this were not the case, there would be no problem of choice. The most obvious way to identify what people value in specific situations is to see what they choose, but if we want to attribute their choices to their values, this is obviously circular. The problem is compounded by the finding that the worth one attaches to an object may increase as a consequence of having chosen that object, at least relative to the judged worth of objects not chosen; the act of choosing appears to bolster the worth of what is chosen (Janis & Mann, 1977). How to determine values and preferences independently of the choices people make remains a challenging problem.

Social factors as determinants of perceived worth

According to most economic views of rationality, what something is worth to me should be independent of what it is worth, or of what I think it is worth, to you. But there can be little doubt that the value that individuals attach to things is often greatly influenced by their perceptions of what other people consider them to be worth. What parent has not been frustrated by the fact that a particular toy can be of little interest to a toddler until a playmate appropriates it, at which time it suddenly acquires immense value in the eyes of toddler number one. Does not a similar process of socially acquired worth lie under the behavior-shaping power of fads and fashions?

Watts (2003) distinguishes two types of buyers of common stock and other financial assets—value investors and trend followers. Value investors buy assets on the basis of their judgment of their real value as represented by their expected future earnings. Trend followers are indifferent to real value; they buy and sell on the basis of whether they believe the market price of the asset is likely to go up or down, for whatever reason. Watts notes that, ironically, the market requires the activity of trend followers in order to function. Because a transaction requires a seller (who believes the asset is overpriced) and a buyer (who believes it is underpriced), if everyone behaved rationally, taking all pertinent information into account, they would all converge on the same value for a given asset and there would be no trading. Of course, one can argue that the trend follower is being rational by taking account of the fact that many people do not buy and sell on the basis of objective indicants of value and is using this knowledge in the pursuit of the goal of making money.

Determining what something costs is considerably more straightforward than determining what something is worth, or so it would seem. But is it really? What one pays, immediately, for a good or service may be obvious, but often there are other costs incurred in obtaining that good or service that are not apparent, at least to casual observation. The point is illustrated by an analysis by Illich (1974) of the cost-effectiveness of the American automobile. According to this analysis, when all the time the average American male spends each year working to purchase, insure, license, maintain, and operate a car is divided into the average number of miles driven, one gets an average travel speed of 4.7 miles per hour.

☐ Judging Information

We are inundated with information. It comes at us incessantly from all directions and in a bewildering variety of forms. Much of the information that is offered to us—through newspapers, magazines, television, radio, billboards, books, private correspondence, conversations—is of little or no interest and we ignore it, or process it only very lightly, and it does not affect our lives. But some of the information we receive, either unsolicited or as a result of an active search, is of great interest because of the implications it may have for what we decide to believe or do. So, on the compelling assumption that all the information we receive is unlikely to be of equal interest or use, we have the problem of information evaluation.

Relevance and importance

We might expect general agreement on the principle that information that is relevant—and only information that is relevant—to a decision should be considered in the making of that decision; but we should not assume that everyone will agree on what is and what is not relevant in any particular case. (See Cohen [1981] and accompanying commentary for examples of differing opinions regarding the relevance of specific base rates in Bayesian decision situations.)

One way to define relevance would be in terms of influence on one's thinking. An item of information would be said to be relevant in a particular context to the degree that possession of that information influences what one thinks or does in that context. But this is not very satisfactory; relevance, as we typically use the term, seems to convey the notion of what *should* influence one's thinking or behavior rather than of what *does* so in fact.

That irrelevant information can be influential is illustrated by an experiment in which participants were told that a container contained either 70 red, 30 white, and 50 blue beads or 30 red, 70 white, and 50 blue. The task was to determine which of these combinations was the correct one by sampling beads from the container. Drawing blue beads sometimes had the effect of reducing participants' confidence in a working hypothesis, despite the fact that the drawing of blue beads was equally likely under both possibilities and therefore irrelevant to the choice (Troutman & Shanteau, 1977). In fact, judgments are influenced by what appears to be irrelevant information under a wide variety of circumstances (Gaeth & Shanteau, 1981, 1984/1986).

Conversely, information that really is relevant may be ignored because its relevance is not recognized. Consider the problem of judging whether a particular individual in attendance at a party is a professor, given the knowledge that he is either a professor or an executive and that he is a member of the Bears Club. Most of the people faced with this problem in an experiment by Beyth-Marom and Fischhoff (1983) recognized that information regarding the percentage of the professors at the party who are members of the Bears Club would be relevant to the problem, but only about half of them saw the same information about the executives in attendance as relevant.

As already noted, consistency is often taken as the fundamental requirement of logically sound thinking. But consistency apart from relevance is a weak criterion by which to judge the quality of thought. The belief that hydrogen is the most common element in the universe is perfectly consistent with the belief that chicken pox is caused by a virus. However, holding one of these beliefs does not help me to decide whether I should hold the other as well. They simply are not sufficiently closely related for one to be relevant to the other. Although being very precise about general principles for judging relevance is difficult, we, in fact, make relevance judgments all the time without necessarily being aware of doing so.

The rule "if some is good, more is better" seems to be applied somewhat uncritically in many contexts. In the context of decision making, one sometimes hears the claim that the more information one has that is relevant to a decision, the better the decision is likely to be. The idea is tempered, however, by two caveats. First is the realization that there is a limit, possibly surprisingly small, to how much information an individual is able to assimilate and effectively use (Davis, Lohse, & Kottemann, 1994; Fleming, 1970; Hayes, 1964; Hoepfl & Huber, 1970; Kanarick, Huntington, & Petersen, 1969). Second is the fact that information often can be obtained only at some cost, so the question of whether the incremental value of additional information pertaining to some decision that is to be made justifies the cost of obtaining it becomes a significant consideration (Beach & Mitchell, 1978; Stigler, 1961).

Value

In Bayesian reasoning relevance has a quantitative connotation in the concept of *diagnosticity*, which is the extent to which a *likelihood ratio* differs from 1. A likclihood ratio is the ratio of two conditional probabilities, each of which represents the probability of a specified observation conditional on the truth of a specified hypothesis. A likelihood ratio of 1 means that the observation is equally likely under both hypotheses, so it provides no evidence that can be used to discriminate between them. An observation yielding a ratio close to 1 would be said to have little diagnostic value. In contrast, one that yielded a ratio greatly different from 1 would be said to be highly diagnostic because its effect would be to increase the probability of one of the hypotheses substantially while decreasing the probability of the other. The greater the diagnosticity of any bit of evidence, the more useful it is in helping to determine the relative plausibility of competing hypotheses.

There is evidence from studies in social cognition—in which people have had to seek information to help make judgments about personality traits—that people are fairly sensitive to diagnosticity, which is to say they tend to prefer questions the answers to which would differ depending on which of the hypotheses under consideration is true (Bassock & Trope, 1984; Trope & Bassok, 1982, 1983; Trope & Mackie, 1987). Generally, diagnosticity is not the only determinant of the questions people ask in this situation, but it is one of them.

Considerable attention has been given to the question of how well people can determine when they should gather additional information and when they should stop doing so in statistical decision-making tasks. Performance typically has been evaluated relative to normative models of behavior that have been developed to identify optimal performance when it is feasible to quantify critical aspects of the situation, such as the cost and diagnostic value of information that can be acquired (Blackwell & Girshick, 1954; Raiffa & Schlaifer, 1961; Wald, 1947, 1950). Sometimes people stop seeking information too soon, and sometimes they continue to seek it after they should have stopped; there seems to be a general trend to seek too much when little is prescribed and too little when the normative models indicate the need for a lot (Edwards, 1967; Fried & Peterson, 1969; Pitz, Reinhold, & Geller, 1969). This is reminiscent of the *contraction bias*, which refers to a tendency to overestimate relatively small magnitudes and to underestimate relatively large ones or to overestimate the frequency of low frequency events and to underestimate the frequency of high frequency ones (Attneave, 1953; Lichtenstein, Slovic, Fischhoff, Layman, & Coombs, 1978).

That it can be very difficult to determine whether information is worth the cost of obtaining it in situations of considerable importance to society is illustrated by the ongoing controversy regarding the advisability of routine mammography screening for women in their forties (Maranto, 1996) and routine PSA testing of all men for prostate cancer (Hanks & Scardino, 1996). The estimated costs in these cases are relatively easy to quantify, but the benefits are not, and thus the debate.

Unfortunately, in many—perhaps most—real life situations, neither the value of specific information nor the cost of obtaining it can be quantified very precisely. Moreover, even if the cost of obtaining further information can be computed in principle, the computation itself may be costly, and that cost, in turn, may be hard to determine, and so on. Quantitative models of behavior, whether normative or descriptive, have limited applicability when this is the case. Qualitatively, however, the principle seems clear enough; some information is worth acquiring and some is not. How good we are at telling the difference is an open question.

☐ Judging Plausibility

Weekly World News is a tabloid that, along with the *National Enquirer* and several other stalwarts of present-day journalism, graces the checkout counter at many grocery stores. Among my favorite front-page WWN stories is one that appeared in September 10, 1991, issue, the headline of which reads: "TITANIC CAPTAIN FOUND IN LIFEBOAT!". In smaller, but still bold print: "Navy ship picks up Englishman in fresh 1900s officer's uniform. He thinks it's April 15, 1912—and his pipe is still lit!" The article reveals that Captain E. J. Smith who "still looks like a man of 60 when in fact he's 139 years old" is the second nonaging survivor of the 1912 shipwreck to be found adrift in the Atlantic within 11 months. The other rescuee was a woman who appeared to be in her late 20s although her actual age was 107. Unfortunately, this lady aged rapidly after her rescue and died in about 6 months. The story quotes "a famed maritime researcher" as saying "These aren't imposters we've found—these are people who were on the Titanic and should have died when it sank..." It refers to the Saether Psychiatric Hospital where Captain Smith was undergoing a battery of tests and to Dr. Jarle Haaland, who was conducting the tests and had confirmed Captain Smith's positive identification in a news release.

This story is unusual among those that appear regularly in *Weekly World News* and similar tabloids only in its particulars; the amazing nature of its content distinguishes it not at all from countless others that appear from week to week. The same issue of *Weekly* carried an advertisement for a special-offer subscription to the paper. The headlines on the front pages of issues shown in the ad included: "JFK IS ALIVE!" "MAN FROZEN IN 1936 REVIVED!" and "ALIEN CAPTURED BY U.S. AGENTS!" The alien mentioned in the last headline was of the extraterrestrial variety; its UFO, according to the caption, had landed in the mountains of Virginia.

Probably most readers of this book find it easy to dismiss such stories as fabrications designed to exploit a particular market. I strongly suspect too, although am not aware of reliable data on the question, that there are people who accept such reports as factual. In any case, the stories mentioned in the preceding paragraphs probably represent, for most of us, something of an extreme on the dimension of plausibility. They cause us no difficulty because we are not tempted to believe them. But it is easy to find other stories, perhaps somewhat less "amazing," in mainline media and elsewhere that do give us pause; we do not know whether to believe them or not.

Importance of plausibility judgments

Every day each of us encounters numerous assertions, claims, and statements of alleged facts. These come from a variety of sources: newspaper reporters and columnists, radio and TV announcers, advertisers, employers, employees, government officials, doctors, automobile mechanics, teachers, colleagues, friends, strangers. Some of the claims are important to us because they relate to matters of personal concern; others are of little or no interest. Those in the latter category we may ignore, or process too superficially to worry about their truth or falsity. Among the assertions that matter, some we accept as true, others we reject as false, and some give us trouble on this dimension—we do not know quite what to make of them.

Sometimes we encounter clusters of related assertions, which we may refer to loosely as arguments. In the simplest form of argument we can identify two types of assertion: one conclusion or key assertion and one or more premises or supporting assertions. The conclusion or key assertion is what the originator of the argument really wants us to believe; the other assertions are offered in support of it—to implicate it in the case of formal deductive arguments, or to make it highly plausible in that of informal ones. In extended arguments the same assertion may play the role of conclusion or key assertion with respect to one portion of the argument and that of premise or supporting assertion with respect to another.

Logicians distinguish between deductive and inductive arguments. In a deductive argument, one proceeds from the more general to the more particular; one states in a conclusion only what was contained already by implication in the premises. In an inductive argument, one usually proceeds from the more particular to the more general; the conclusion in this case—a generalization—may assert more than is asserted, even by implication, by all the statements that are given in its support. Deductive inferences, if they follow the rules of logic, are said to be valid, which means that if their premises are true, their conclusions are sure to be true also. Conclusions drawn inductively can never be said to be true with certainty, only more or less plausible.

Evaluating arguments involves two kinds of judgment: (1) whether the conclusion or key assertion is implicated or made plausible by the premises or supporting assertions, and (2) whether to accept the premises or supporting assertions as true. Thus the ability to judge plausibility is doubly important: we need it both to assess claims that are of interest to us in their own right and to evaluate arguments.

There have been countless studies of various aspects of human reasoning and many books on argumentation, most from a philosophical tradition. Philosophical treatments of argumentation have dealt primarily with formal logic and deductive reasoning, although informal argumentation and "everyday" reasoning have also been receiving much attention, especially in recent years (Voss, Perkins, & Segal, 1991).

There seems to be a growing awareness that there is much more to being an effective reasoner in everyday life than being able to distinguish between valid and invalid logical forms. This is fortunate, inasmuch as most of the arguments one encounters do not fit any canonical pattern. They tend to be extended and to include both deductive and inductive components, to rely on unstated assumptions, to contain ambiguities and obscurities, to make use of various alogical stratagems, and to assume a particular knowledge base on the part of the listener or reader.

The central importance of plausibility judgments in the evaluation of everyday arguments has not received the attention it deserves. Most empirical studies of argument evaluation take the factuality of the assertions comprising an argument as given. Attention typically is focused on the question of the legitimacy of the reasoning process that gets one to the conclusion from the various assertions that comprise the argument. In real life this is an important question, but represents only part of the problem. What one wants to know is whether to accept the argument's conclusion as true, and this involves making judgments about whether or not to believe the premises.

Determinants of plausibility

The fundamental question that we need to ask is: what makes an assertion more or less plausible, or, more generally, what are the determinants of plausibility? This question suggests numerous others: Why are accurate statements of fact sometimes accepted as true and sometimes not? What determines whether specific instances of propaganda will be believed? Why are brainwashing and other types of efforts to indoctrinate sometimes effective and sometimes not? What gives rise to extremist views of different types? Why do some people readily espouse such views while others resist them? How do superstitions gain credence? What establishes the plausibility or implausibility of scientific hypotheses before they have been put to a rigorous test?

One would like both a descriptive model of plausibility (What determines plausibility?) and a normative one (What should determine plausibility?). A descriptive model should be predictive of human performance. It should tell us what makes a particular assertion more or less plausible to a particular individual. We are a long way from such a model, but we can be reasonably sure that when one is developed it will recognize a number of variables as basic determinants of plausibility, some of which are descriptive of assertions and others of which are descriptive of individuals. An adequate model will almost surely not be a strictly linear one. It will have to provide for the possibility that the effect of one variable will be contingent on the status of another.

Interperson variability with respect to the relative plausibility of specific assertions is to be expected. Assertions that are considered highly plausible by some individuals will be considered highly implausible by others. Given the fact that people differ widely in their beliefs and opinions on almost any subject, any model would be suspect that did not accommodate such individual differences. However, from the fact that people are likely to differ in what they consider plausible, it does not follow that there will be a large amount of interperson variability with respect to the factors that determine the plausibility of given assertions; the same model may predict that a given assertion will be highly plausible to one individual and highly implausible to another because of the different perspectives that the individuals bring to the situation. One hopes to find invariants, principles that hold across individuals and situations. What follows are some conjectures regarding what seem to me likely to be some of the variables that would be among the determinants of plausibility in any reasonably adequate model.

Knowledge. The more one knows about a topic, the better basis one has for making judgments about the probable truth of assertions pertaining to that topic. Assertions that follow from what one knows to be true will be seen as true. Assertions that contradict what one knows to be true will readily be recognized to be false. Of greater interest are the many assertions that fall between these extremes, namely those that neither follow from nor contradict what one knows to be true. Such assertions might be said to be consistent with one's knowledge, but consistency alone is a weak indication of truth. On the other hand, if the assertions are considered to be closely related and they are consistent, knowledge of the truth value of one may well be used as a basis for judging the probable truth value of the other.

But what about situations in which one does not have adequate knowledge on which to base a judgment? What is it, in these instances, that determines the credence one will give to an assertion? The remaining variables in this conjectural list relate to this question.

Global fit. How readily one accepts an assertion as true will depend, in part, on how well that assertion fits with one's total system of beliefs about the world. "Fits with" is an imprecise notion, but it will have to do for the present. It means more than logical consistency, but does not require logical implication. If an assertion not only is consistent with one's general system of beliefs about the world, but tends to support it in some substantive way, it is more likely to be accepted than if it does not. Conversely, if it tends to be at variance with this system of beliefs in substantive ways, it is likely to be rejected. For example, if I believe that dictatorships are more likely than most other forms of government to indulge in politically motivated imprisonments and executions, I will probably have little trouble accepting as plausible media reports of such events in countries ruled by dictators.

Credibility of source. Most of us would probably give more credence to a report of an unlikely event if we found it in a reputable mainstream newspaper than if we found it in a sensationalistic tabloid. More generally, it seems safe to assume that one is more likely to accept an assertion as true if one considers its source to be trustworthy than if one does not. Unfortunately, this observation does not help much to answer our question; it simply displaces it. What determines the credibility of a source?

Perceived trustworthiness can be based, at least in part, on data. If one has frequently received information from a particular source in the past, and if one has been able to determine, after the fact, the truth or falsity of the assertions that have come from this source, and if those assertions have usually proved to be true, then one feels justified in having a high degree of confidence in assertions from that source. Presumably something of this sort is behind newscasters' practice of noting, on occasion, that a particular news item was obtained from a "reliable source".

Confidence in a source need not have an all-or-none effect on plausibility. It seems more reasonable to assume that it increases plausibility by some amount, making an assertion more plausible than it otherwise might be. How much difference it makes is likely to depend on how much confidence one has in the source and the plausibility of the assertion independently of its origin, which is to say how plausible it would be if its source were unknown. If the assertion is highly plausible for other reasons, the fact that it came from a highly trustworthy source would not be able to have much impact. If the assertion is highly implausible a priori, then knowledge that it came from a highly trustworthy source might increase its plausibility substantially.

Clearly there are instances in which a greater weight is given to the credibility of sources than is justified. The power of demagogues comes largely from the unquestioning credence their followers give to whatever they say. Much advertising (as well as endorsements of political candidates and sundry causes) seems to be based on the assumption that many people will believe anything that a celebrity says. Some people may have a tendency to give too much credence to anything they read, on the assumption that if it is written down it must be true. One might think that any such tendency would be corrected quickly by the discovery of contradictions in print. This thought leads to the conjecture that people who read widely are less likely to accept uncritically everything they read than people who read sporadically or who restrict their attention to writers representing a narrow range of views. More research on questions of these sorts would be useful.

Preference. Philosophers and psychologists alike have observed that there appears to be a universal tendency to give more credence to assertions one would like to be true than to those one would like to be false. Most of us may find this observation to be intuitively compelling, because we see the principle at work in ourselves and in other people. And objective evidence of a positive correlation between the probability that one will believe a proposition to be true and the probability that one will consider it to be desirable is not wanting (Lefford, 1946; McGuire, 1960). Matlin and Stang (1978) see this as one manifestation of what they call the *Pollyanna principle*, according to which people tend to give preferential treatment to pleasant thoughts and memories over unpleasant ones.

Disposition. Perhaps some people are more inclined to be questioning and unwilling to accept claims uncritically than are others. One must assume that, as traits or dispositions, credulity and skepticism are, at least in part, acquired as a consequence of early experience and training. A child who has been encouraged to question is less likely to be willing to accept at face value whatever is claimed than is one whose questioning has consistently evoked authoritative rebuke. Without doubt, there are other determinants of plausibility in addition to the relatively obvious ones mentioned here. Identification of these variables and determination of their effects remain challenges for research.

Intentional criterial biases in judgment

Fairly strong biases are sometimes intentionally built into judgment and decision-making procedures, because some types of errors are more acceptable than others. In addition to medicine, another context in which this obviously is the case is that of judicial decision making. Criminal court protocol is guided by the principle that the error of letting a guilty person go free is generally more acceptable to society than that of erroneously convicting an innocent person. For that reason the point of departure for every criminal court proceeding is a presumption of the innocence of the defendant; the burden of proof rests upon the prosecution. Further, the prosecutor must prove guilt beyond reasonable doubt in order to get a conviction.

Strictly speaking, a court proceeding never results in a verdict of innocence. The verdict is either guilty or not guilty. A not-guilty verdict means literally that the prosecution failed to demonstrate the defendant's guilt beyond doubt; it does not mean that innocence was proved. This is an extremely important aspect of the judicial process in the United States and many other democracies. Defendants need not prove their innocence, they are assumed to be innocent unless the prosecution can establish their guilt.

There is an analogous bias that pertains to the method most commonly used to test hypotheses within the experimental sciences. When one applies a (Fisherian) statistical test to experimentally gathered data in order to determine whether two samples should be considered to have been drawn randomly from the same or different populations, the presumption in this case is the *null hypothesis*, the hypothesis of no difference. Typically, in order to reject this hypothesis and thereby conclude that the samples came from different populations, the outcome must be such that one could expect to obtain it by chance only infrequently, say less than 5% of the time if they did come from the same population. This rule reflects a strong preference for failing to reject the null hypothesis when it is false over rejecting it when it is true.

Scientists typically are looking for differences between sets of data, reflecting the effects of their actions, so setting the bias against rejecting the null hypothesis when there really is no difference between the samples is in the interest of conservatism. It makes it relatively difficult for scientists to conclude that they have found a difference when in fact they have not. Because of this bias, a scientist generally does not conclude that the null hypothesis has been confirmed. The conclusion either is that the null hypothesis is rejected (a difference has been found) or that the null hypothesis is not rejected (a difference has not been found).

Often socially-significant judgments must be made in light of the necessity to settle on a compromise between two undesirable possible outcomes, it being impossible to decrease the probability of one of the outcomes without increasing that of the other. Where the threshold for triggering action should be set in such cases can be a matter of debate and controversy. The possibility of identifying biological indicators of people with an unusually high potential to become violent criminals illustrates the point. Suppose such a marker, or set of markers, were discovered that could identify a subset of the population that had a much-higher-than average probability of engaging in violent crime—to be specific, suppose people with this marker, or constellation of markers, were five times as likely as those without it to do so. The incidence of violent crime could be decreased by taking some preventive measures with regard to the people so identified; however, the measures taken could be perceived as—and well might be—infringements on the rights of the individuals involved. What to do with such knowledge, if it should become available, poses a nontrivial question that society must face (Gibbs, 1995); should the bias be set so as to protect society from potentially violent people at the cost of infringing the rights of individuals who have broken no laws and may never do so, or should it be set so as to protect the rights of all individuals who have committed no crimes, at the likely expense of permitting some violent acts to occur that might have been prevented?

It is interesting to reflect on whether we make use of such criterial biases in our day-to-day judgments, perhaps without being aware of doing so. I find it easy to believe that we do and that we should. Giving one "the benefit of the doubt" seems to reflect a bias in the direction of demanding fairly compelling evidence before being willing to draw a conclusion that puts another person in an unfavorable light. (This is not to suggest, of course, that we never draw conclusions that are unfavorable to others on the basis of flimsy evidence.) Our tendency to persevere with established beliefs in the face of evidence that goes counter to those beliefs is another instance of a criterial bias that seems to operate in everyday thinking. As noted in chapter 4, this can be a functional bias, if not carried too far. How far is too far is a judgment call.

☐ Clinical Diagnosis

Clinical diagnosis is generally viewed as a demanding cognitive task requiring expertise and great skill in reasoning on the part of one who performs it well. As a consequence of increasing medical knowledge and an ever-expanding array of diagnostic procedures and treatment options, the physician's task, both as diagnostician and care giver is becoming increasingly complex (Doubilet & McNeil, 1985/1988; Garnick, 1994). Numerous investigators have studied reasoning in the specific context of clinical diagnosis. The following limited review is intended to give a glimpse of work that is representative of what has been done. More extensive reviews include Elstein and Schwartz (2002) and Wood, Garb, Lilienfeld, and Nezworski (2002).

Focusing

The results of some studies indicate that clinicians often make diagnoses on the basis of a small number of variables (e.g., three to five) even when many more are considered relevant (Fisch, Hammond, Joyce, & O'Reilly, 1981; Kirwan, Chaput de Siantonge, Joyce, & Currey, 1983). Kleinmuntz (1968) suggests that diagnosticians tend to look for a few indicators that they consider especially informative and base their judgments on those indicators. Not surprisingly, a clinician who believes that a given symptom is indicative of a specific disease is more likely to look for the disease in the presence of that symptom than in its absence (Golding & Rorer, 1972).

Investigators have emphasized the importance of pattern recognition as a way of limiting the amount of data that a clinician must keep in short term memory while working on a diagnosis. The recognition of similarity to previously-seen symptoms and cases has been identified as a major factor in diagnoses, sometimes helpful, sometimes not (Brooks, Norman, & Allen, 1991; Hatala, Norman, & Brooks, 1999). Eddy and Clanton (1982) suggest that clinicians typically aggregate the elements of a medical history into one or a few features that can be represented by a few labels. They suggest also that diagnosticians quickly select one or two findings as a "pivot" that can serve as a focus for subsequent reasoning about the case. The immediate objective then becomes to find a cause for the pivotal symptom(s).

In looking for causes, diagnosticians often generate one or a small set of hypotheses very early in the diagnostic session (Elstein, Shulman, & Sprafka,1978). A hypothesis in hand can guide the search for additional clues. It can also decrease the likelihood that alternative hypotheses will be considered, and it can bias the interpretation of subsequently acquired data (Barrows, Feightner, Neufeld, & Norman, 1978; Barrows, Norman, Neufeld, & Feightner, 1977; Elstein, Shulman, & Sprafka, 1978; Wallsten, 1978).

Accuracy and consistency in diagnosis

Studies of how much importance is attached to specific signs or symptoms in diagnosing medical problems have shown a lack of consistency among physicians in this regard (Wegton, Hoellerich, & Patil, 1986). This perhaps should not be surprising, given the fact that the reliability of many of the signs and symptoms used in medical diagnosis is not high (Koran, 1975).

Although the general unreliability of medical diagnosis is well documented (Eddy, 1984), as is the fact that physicians sometimes show low degrees of agreement among themselves in diagnoses (Garland, 1959, 1960; Hoffman, Slovic, & Rorer, 1968), the degree of uncertainty involved in the practice of medicine is probably not appreciated by lay people and perhaps not even by the medical profession (Feinstein, 1967; Fox, 1957; Katz, 1984/1988). Katz (1984/1988) discusses several reasons why physicians may resist disclosing to patients, and possibly to themselves, the degree of uncertainty that may characterize their own medical judgments.

A common finding in studies of clinical judgment has been that judgmental accuracy does not increase consistently with the amount of information at the clinician's disposable (Garb, 2005; Goldberg, 1968; Nystedt & Magnusson, 1972) or with the years of experience of the clinician (Dawes, 1989; Garb, 1989). Sisson, Schoomaker, and Ross (1976/1986) argue that the quality of clinical diagnosis can sometimes be decreased by providing the clinician with too much information. They show how the death rate might be increased as a consequence of the use of a diagnostic test that detects pancreatic cancer in 80% of people who actually have the cancer and has a 5% false-alarm rate. In their words, "additional knowledge, acquired through scientific and safe methods and no more imperfect than that available for many clinical judgments can, under some circumstances, cause more harm than good" (p. 357).

In the example used by Sisson, Schoomaker, and Ross, the incidence of the disease is assumed to be small—12 in 1,000—which means that a small false-positive rate can produce relatively large numbers. With this incidence rate, if the test were administered to 1,000 random people, it would be expected to yield positive results on about 10 of the 12 or so people who have the cancer and on about 50 of those who do not, which means that only about 1 in 6 of the positive tests would flag a real cancer. Sisson et al. give a similar illustration with the use of liver scans to help determine whether known broncogenic cancer had metastasized to the liver. Other studies have shown that many physicians find it easy to confuse the probability of the presence of a disease given a positive diagnostic test result with the probability of a positive test result given the disease (Anderson, 1990; Casscells, Schoenberger, & Grayboys, 1978), and these probabilities can be very different when dealing with a low-incidence disease and a diagnostic test with a moderate false positive rate. Generally, positive test results are likely to have relatively low positive predictive value (a small proportion of the positive results will identify true-positive cases) when the condition tested for has very low incidence in the tested population (Getty, Swets, Pickett, & Gonthier, 1995).

Actuarial statistics and clinical judgment

Diagnoses and predictions of success based on statistical methods (typically the weighted average of several predictor variables) consistently have been shown to be at least as accurate, and often more accurate, than diagnoses and predictions based on diagnosticians' judgments (Dawes, 1971, 1979; Dawes, Faust, & Meehl, 1989; Goldberg, 1970; Leli & Filskov,

1984; Meehl, 1954, 1986; Sawyer, 1966; Wedding, 1983). Essentially the same finding has been obtained with diagnoses of psychiatric disorders (Goldberg, 1965), predictions of success or failure in school (Dawes, 1971) and predictions of success or failure in business (Libby, 1975, 1976). An advantage that statistical prediction rules have over clinical judgment is that the rules will give precisely the same prediction under the same circumstances time after time. Judgment however will vary and yield different predictions even in identical cases. Meehl (1954, 1956, 1960) was an early and effective spokesman for the use of actuarial data for diagnosis.

Practitioners have been reluctant to use statistically based formulas for interpreting the results of diagnostic tests even in the face of evidence that formulas consistently do better than human interpreters (de Dombal, Leapar, Horrocks, Staniland, & McCann, 1974; Goldberg, 1968; Wade & Baker, 1977). Griffin and Tversky (1992) refer to the tendency to prefer an individual or inside view to a statistical or outside one as "one of the major departures of intuitive judgment from normative theory" (p. 432). Explaining this preference is an important question for research. The somewhat cynical view that diagnosticians reject statistically-based predictive techniques only because the use of them would devalue their own expertise is surely an overly simplistic explanation. While this consideration may be a factor, experts performing diagnoses undoubtedly sincerely believe that they can do better than the averages, whether or not they can.

Dawes (1988) points out that clinical judgment remains important despite such findings as those mentioned above because it is the clinician or judge who selects the variables used by the statistical diagnoses or prediction formulas. He notes too the importance of this selection because the statistical methods work best when each of the predictor variables has a monotonic relationship with the variable being predicted. Dawes and Corrigan (1974) present convincing evidence that the selection of an appropriate set of variables is more important than getting precisely the right weights on them. In their study a random assignment of weights produced almost as good results as did an optimal assignment. In some cases, randomly weighted linear models have done better than the experts (Dawes, 1979).

Some investigators have argued for diagnostic approaches that combine clinical judgment and statistical methods (Ægisdóttir et al., 2006; Meehl, 1996; Pankoff & Roberts, 1968; Sawyer, 1966; Swets, Dawes, & Monahan, 2000 a, b; Westen & Weinberger, 2004). Experimentation has been done with approaches in which certain judgments, estimations, or predictions made by a person regarding specific variables that relate to the problem are fed into a computational model or process that produces, or at least proposes, the solution algorithmically (Ahlers, 1966; Wendt, 1965). Westen and Weinberger (2004) defend the belief that, notwithstanding the validity of claims regarding the relative accuracy of statistical prediction, clinicians can make reliable and useful observations and inferences. They argue that clinical observation and statistical prediction are better thought of as marking the ends of a continuum of diagnostic methods than as representing a dichotomy.

Bayesian diagnosis

The possibility of applying a Bayesian approach to diagnosis has been a focus of much research. This approach involves estimating the *prior* probabilities of occurrence of specific diseases, and, for each possible disease, the probability of the specific symptoms observed, given that disease, and then using these estimates to compute, with Bayes's rule, the probabilities of specific diseases given the symptoms observed. The approach is the same in other diagnostic contexts, given appropriate substitutions for diseases and symptoms.

Debate over the usefulness of this approach has been going on for some time (Eddy & Clanton, 1982; Feinstein, 1977; Gigerenzer & Hoffrage, 1995; Harris, 1981; Jones, 1979; Krauss, Martignon, & Hoffrage, 1999; Lewis & Keren, 1999; Mellers & McGraw, 1999). Apparently, physicians do not, as a rule, use a Bayesian reasoning process spontaneously to perform a diagnosis. Eddy and Clanton (1982), who make this observation, note how difficult it is to apply the Bayesian approach in the clinical situation. The problem of estimating both the probability of occurrence of *every possible* disease (a requirement of the Bayesian approach is that the set of hypotheses be exhaustive) and the probability of the symptom set conditional upon each disease can be a daunting task indeed. Fischhoff and Beyth-Marom (1983) argue that there are a number of potential sources of bias in the use of a Bayesian approach and that bias can affect essentially any aspect of it.

On the other hand, some investigators have argued that independently of the calculation of probabilities, simply understanding the logic underlying the Bayesian approach may itself be helpful in improving systematic diagnoses. Wolf, Gruppen, and Billi (1985) suggest that the fact that application of Bayes's rule forces one to relate explicitly each of the symptoms being considered to all of the hypothesized diseases before making a judgment imposes a useful discipline on the diagnostic process. This discipline has been referred to as the *competing-hypotheses heuristic* (Elstein, Shulman, & Sprafka, 1978). Use of it should decrease the likelihood of premature closure. The need for such a heuristic is seen in evidence that medical students often tend to seek information about several symptoms for a single disease rather than evaluating one symptom across many diseases (Wolf, 1983).

The failure to consider the same symptom across alternative disease possibilities is sometimes referred to as the problem of *pseudodiagnosticity* (Kern & Doherty, (1982). The preference for evaluating several pieces of data against a single hypothesis over evaluating a single datum against several hypotheses has been found in other contexts as well (Doherty, Mynatt, Tweney, & Schiavo, 1979; Tweney, Doherty, Worner, Pliske, & Mynatt, 1980). One explanation of this preference is that people have difficulty in coping with more than one mental model of a situation—one hypothesized disease—simultaneously (Girotto, Evans, & Legrenzi, 1996).

The argument that subjecting a problem of diagnosis to a Bayesian analysis can be useful somewhat independently of the calculations involved may be made with respect to analytic techniques more generally. The benefits from use of these techniques may sometimes come primarily from the discipline of thinking about diagnostic problems in a structured way (Watson & Brown, 1975).

8 Decision and Choice

The subject of this chapter is very closely related to that of the immediately preceding one. Judgment and decision making are more often than not discussed together in the psychological literature, and it is difficult to make a sharp distinction between the two concepts. Decision making was referred to several times in the preceding chapter and sometimes when the word "judgment" or "diagnosis" was used, "decision" undoubtedly would have done just as well. A defensible rationale for separating the subjects is that the preceding chapter on preference and judgment emphasizes states of mind whereas this one on decision and choice emphasizes the process of choosing among options for action, but in fact this split was more than anything a matter of organizational convenience.

☐ Decision and Choice in Natural Settings

For most of us, selecting what to wear on any given day, what to have for lunch, whether to take in a movie after dinner, or to mow the lawn are decisions, but not momentous ones. We may give so little thought to them that we are hardly conscious of making them at all. In contrast, we are likely to be acutely aware of the effort involved in trying to decide whether or not to accept a particular job offer, how to attempt to repair a damaged relationship, or which of two possible courses of treatment for a serious illness to elect. Probably most of the decisions we make on a day-to-day basis fall somewhere between these extremes. Part of what it means to be rational is having a sense of how much thought a given decision is worth. Clearly it is possible to put too little effort into very serious decisions and too much effort into inconsequential ones.

Psychological experimentation on decision making and choice has been extensive, but despite a very large literature, surprisingly little is known about how decisions are made in nonlaboratoy situations. Most of the experimental work that has been done on choice or decision making in the laboratory has focused on the question of how people choose among alternatives and what variables affect their choices. Typically, options are provided by the experimenter and it is clear what they are. In life outside the laboratory, the most difficult aspect of choice behavior may be determining what options one has. Outside the laboratory, many of the choices people make are consequential in the sense that people have to live with their outcomes and the quality of their lives may be affected by them in nontrivial ways. Seldom is this the case in experimental situations. Not surprisingly, there is some evidence that people may perform differently in decision situations when the pressure is high (e.g., there is a potential for real personal loss) than when it is not (Einhorn, 1971; Wright, 1974).

Real-life choice problems vary over an enormous range with respect to both complexity and the seriousness of the stakes. Selecting a meal from a restaurant menu is a choice problem and, in the abstract, not unlike the problem of choosing among possible treatments for a life-threatening illness. To the individual faced with these decisions, however, there is a world of difference between them, especially in terms of the seriousness of the consequences of making a poor choice. It would be less than surprising if rules that describe behavior in the one situation reasonably well were inadequate to describe it in the other. Relatively little is known about how the rules of choice behavior depend on such factors as complexity and stakes, but what little information there is on the subject suggests that these are important variables.

This is not to suggest that laboratory studies of decision making can reveal nothing about decision making in the day-to-day world, but only that in applying findings outside the context of the situations in which they were obtained, it is important to bear the limitations of laboratory studies in mind. Moreover, although it is still true that most of the laboratory research on choice and decision making is focused on the act of choosing among alternatives, the alternatives being given, this situation may be changing. Some thinking in decision theory has been directed at the process by which the decision alternatives are initially admitted for consideration (Beach, Smith, Lundell, & Mitchell, 1988).

Making choices is not something that we can elect to do or not, choices are forced upon us and we make them, if only by default, constantly. Many of the choices one faces in daily life must be made with less than complete certainty regarding what the consequences of the choices will be. And the uncertainties often involve tradeoffs. In a democratic society, citizens are called on to make various kinds of decisions periodically via the voting booth. Often these decisions involve, at least indirectly through elections of leaders and policy makers, tradeoffs that must be made between conflicting objectives. How to strike an acceptable balance between safeguarding the freedom and liberty of the individual on the one hand and promoting the stability, safety and humaneness of society and general welfare of the citizenry on the other is a perennial challenge to rational choice.

Dynamic and naturalistic decision making

Clancy, Elliot, Ley, Omodei, Wearing, McLennan, and Thorsteinsson (2003) criticize laboratory research on decision making for being focused, for the most part, on single decisions. "The bulk of this laboratory research," they contend, "has typically employed highly artificial tasks, and as such has yielded mostly trivial outcomes" (p. 588). Real-world decision situations, they argue, tend to be dynamic in the sense that they require that a sequence of related decisions be made. Decision making, in this view, is seen more as an on-going process of interacting with one's environment, which is changing—in part as a consequence of the decisions that are made—continuously in time.

Clancy et al. give special attention to situations in which the decision making responsibility is distributed over several people functioning within a hierarchical command structure. In such a structure, the time and space horizons may differ for decision makers at different levels of the hierarchy and there may be tradeoffs between realizing more global and more local goals. Clancy et al. consider, in particular, the question of the relative effectiveness of two different styles of distributing the control of decision making across levels of a hierarchy: an *action command* style in which specific action commands are issued by the highest level, and an *intent command* style in which a top-level commander's intentions are distributed to subordinates who are relatively free to choose actions to attempt to realize those intentions. The results of a simulation study with a forest-fire control scenario were interpreted as showing the intent-command style to be superior to the action-command style in this instance. Given the prevalence of hierarchically organized authority structures in society—business, government, military—the finding seems an important one; however, having been obtained with college students without experience in the problem domain, it bears investigation with experienced decision makers in a variety of domains to determine how generally it holds.

Dynamic decision making is difficult to study in real-world situations, because typically there are many variables that cannot be controlled, and the study can interfere with the ability of the decision makers to perform their function adequately. Consequently, much of the research that has been done in this area has made use of games or simulations. Prominent among dynamic decision situations that have been studied in the laboratory with the help of gaming methods are those involving bargaining and negotiation (Morely, 1978; Morley & Stephenson, 1977). Bargaining and negotiation have in common the aim of resolving a conflict of interests or goals—convergence on a position that the parties involved, whose interests or goals differ at the outset, can both (or all) accept. Bargaining and negotiation situations can be formal or informal, and the rules that appear to apply in the one case do not necessarily hold in the other. Topics of interest to researchers include cooperation, competition, compromise, concession, and mediation. Other dynamic situations that have been studied with the help of games or simulations include such widely ranging subjects as stock purchasing (Ebert, 1972) and fire fighting (Brehmer & Allard, 1991).

Fire fighting is prototypical of many dynamic decision-making situations in which decision makers must respond to critical situations under pressing time constraints that do not permit the luxury of unlimited reflection and analysis before taking action (Kerstholt & Raaijmakers, 1997). Such situations are often encountered in the contexts of accidents, or natural disasters, and emergencies of sundry kinds (Brehmer, 1992). One objective of such research is to determine kinds of support that decision makers need to function well in such situations (Gonzalez, 2005). Another is to study how performance changes with experience and whether what is learned transfers from one dynamic situation to another (Gonzalez, 2004; Gonzalez & Quesada, 2003). Recent reviews of work on dynamic decision making include those of Sterman (1994), Kerstholt & Raaijmakers (1997), and Busemeyer (2002).

A prominent attempt to study decision making as it occurs in the world outside the laboratory—or in simulations of real world contexts—has been spearheaded by Klein and colleagues (Cannon-Bowers, Salas, & Pruitt, 1996; Klein, 1998; Klein, Orasanu, Calderwook, & Zsambok, 1993; Zsambok & Klein, 1997). Generally referred to as the Naturalistic Decision Making (NDM) approach or perspective, this line of inquiry represents an alternative to the more traditional laboratory study by acquiring some measure of realism at the cost of the loss of some measure of control. An overview of the NDM perspective and a brief history of its emergence are given by Pliske and Klein (2003). NDM researchers tend to be motivated more by the objective of finding ways to improve performance on real decision tasks than by that of developing better theories of decision making. Much of the work involves observation of experienced professionals (fire fighters, air traffic controllers, military commanders) functioning in their normal roles.

Although the NDM approach is not primarily theory driven, it is not antitheoretical. Pliske and Klein note that many of the applications developed by NDM researchers are broadly based on cognitive and social psychological theories and they consider a greater application of cognitive and social psychological theories to problems of training and system design to be desirable. Citing Lipshitz (1993), who describes nine models that relate to the NDM perspective, they identify the Recognition-Primed Decision (RPD) model first proposed by Klein, Calderwood, and Clinton-Cirocco (1986) as the one most closely associated with NDM.

In keeping with an emphasis of the NDM perspective on the importance of experience in judgment and decision-making performance, the RPD model stresses the role of memory of similar situations as the first resource to which decision makers turn in dealing with decision problems. According to this model, seasoned decision makers use their experience to generate a reasonable—not necessarily optimal—option quickly, without considering lots of alternatives. The model is descriptive and does not prescribe what decision makers should do. Pliske and Klein describe interview data supporting the contention that experienced decision makers in stressful situations typically adopt a course of action without any deliberative evaluation of alternatives and that when evaluation does occur it tends to consist of mentally simulating the possible outcomes of the proposed course of action.

Pliske and Klein deal with several criticisms that have been leveled at the NDM perspective. They point out that, in contrast to much of the work on decision making that has emphasized how heuristics have degraded the quality of decision making, NDM researchers have tended to examine the strengths of heuristics and how experts have learned to use them to advantage. The perspective is similar to that of Gigerenzer (references below) and colleagues in emphasizing the effectiveness with which simple heuristics can sometimes be applied to complex decision situations.

Everyday decisions

Decisions can be classified in a variety of ways, but a major way in which they differ from each other is in terms of their significance to the decision maker. At one extreme are life-altering decisions, such as the choice of school, vocation or profession, marriage partner, and place of residence; at the other are "everyday" decisions, examples of which include deciding what time to get up in the morning, what to wear, what to eat for breakfast, and how to use a bit of discretionary time. This is not a dichotomy; decisions can vary along a continuum of importance or practical significance.

Another distinction that has been made is based on the amount of thought that a decision requires. Again, there is not a sharp dichotomy; how much thought a decision requires can vary from next to none at all to as much as one can muster. Svenson (1999, 2003) distinguishes four levels of decisions on the basis of the amount of energy they require. He suggests that most decision making takes place at the lowest, or most mundane, level and is accomplished by such simple heuristics as doing what one has done in the same situation before or imitating what others do. In contrast, decisions at the highest level require focused attention and problem solving. Probably many, if not most, of the choices of lesser importance are made by habit with a minimum of conscious consideration of alternatives (Berger & Luckmann, 1966/1990), but people are likely to approach decisions differently if the consequences affect them personally than if they do not (Wagenaar, Keren, & Lichtenstein, 1988).

Decisions that require little, if any, thought include everyday decisions, like the decision to brush one's teeth after eating, which have become routine and automated with repetition, although they may have required thought the first few times they were made (Bargh & Chartrand, 1999; Wegner & Bargh, 1998). Such routine decisions have sometimes been referred to as *policies* (Redelmeier & Tversky, 1992; Schneider & Barnes, 2003). Schneider and Barnes note a paucity of research on their origin, despite their fundamental significance in people's daily lives.

Gigerenzer and colleagues have identified a number of *fast and frugal* heuristics that people appear to use to facilitate choice in a variety of situations (Gigerenzer & Goldstein, 1996, 1999; Gigerenzer & Todd, 1999a, b; Goldstein & Gigerenzer, 1999; Todd & Gigerenzer, 1999, 2003). One that has attracted much attention is the "Take the Best" rule, which prescribes that when one has to judge which of two alternatives beats the other with respect to some specified criterion (the larger of two cities, the more promising of two possible investments), one should compare the two alternatives with respect to properties that have some relevance to the criterion (in the case of cities, whether either has a professional sports team, a university, an airport, . . .), doing so one property at a time until a property is found on which the alternatives differ and then make the choice on the basis of that single difference.

Martignon and Krauss (2003) present evidence suggesting that whether people take a Bayesian approach to a decision problem, use a fast and frugal heuristic such as "Take the Best," or switch from one approach to the other, may depend on the particulars of the situation. They had people make buy or sell decisions with respect to a company's stock on the basis of evaluations published by three stock-trade magazines, each of which had a validity rating. If one of the validity ratings was much larger than the other two, people tended to use the Take-the-Best strategy, whereas if the ratings were close in value, they were more likely to use a Bayesian approach.

Important among the factors that influence decision making in everyday contexts are affective variables—emotion, mood, disposition (Damasio, 1994; Finucane, Alhakami, Slovic, & Johnson, 2000; Finucane, Peters, & Slovic, 2003; Hsee, 1998; Zajonc, 1980). Finucane and colleagues suggest that affect influences judgment and decision making by means of positive and negative feelings that are attached to mental representations of decision options. Such feelings depend on characteristics of the individual as well as on the decision options; the same options will evoke different feelings in different people. Making a decision on the basis of an affective reaction to the options can be faster and less cognitively demanding than weighing the pros and cons of the alternatives; for this reason, Finucane and colleagues call this use of affect the *affect heuristic*.

Finucane, Peters and Slovic (2003) describe their model of affect and decision making as having much in common with proposals put forth by Epstein (1994), Sloman (1996), and Loewenstein, Weber, Hsee, and Welsh (2001), among others. They do not argue that people invariably make decisions on the basis of affective reactions alone. They suggest that the tendency to resort to the affect heuristic increases under conditions that reduce one's capacity for deliberation, as when a decision must be made under time pressure or distracting circumstances. Citing Hess (2000) and Hess, Pullen, and McGee (1996), they note that aging also may increase reliance on affect as a basis for choice.

The "tyranny of choice"

People living today in the United States and other developed countries have more alternatives from which to choose—whether considering what to have for dinner, what to read for enjoyment, where to spend the next vacation, or what to do to make a living—than people have had at any other time in history. It seems natural to assume that greater choice means greater satisfaction, as a general rule; the greater the range of alternatives from which one can make a selection, the more likely one should be to find among those alternatives some that suit one's preferences.

The idea that the more freedom one has to choose the happier one is likely to be is challenged by Fromm (1942/1963) in *Fear of Freedom*, the main thesis of which is that people sometimes willfully give up their freedom of choice so as to be rid of the responsibility of choosing well that goes with it. Jaspers (1952) captures a similar idea in his claim of an "urge to be freed from freedom" (p. 36).

More recently, psychologists have obtained evidence that abundant choice can be a burden and can make for dissatisfaction (Lane, 2001; Schwartz, 2004a; Schwartz, Ward, Monterosso, Lyubomirsky, White, & Lehman, 2002). Schwartz (2004b) describes what he refers to as the *tyranny of choice*, which afflicts especially people who tend to seek to make choices that are optimal in some sense—people who are *maximizers*, as opposed to *satisficers*, to use a distinction made by Simon (1957). Such people may feel compelled to try to check out all the options in a choice situation before making a selection, and to feel short-changed if they are unable to do so. The greater the number of choice alternatives, the greater the burden of investigating them all, and the greater the likelihood of wondering, after a selection has been made, whether one could have done better. Some evidence suggests that maximizers may be prime candidates for mental depression.

Presumably, total lack of choice is a condition that few people would be likely to consider desirable, but the desire to be told what to do, to be completely relieved of the responsibility of choice, is a reason that some people have for joining cults that rigidly dictate one's every move (Appel, 1983). And people who are not cult-bound can feel overwhelmed by the range of choices they have in many situations. Total freedom can lead not only to anarchy on a societal scale but to angst for the individual. The question of where the happy medium lies between freedom and constraint, between too much structure and too little, between a degree of choice that is intimidating and one that is too restrictive has attracted the attention of researchers and is likely to hold it for some time to come.

Solutions versus tradeoffs

I have mentioned the idea that decisions and choices often involve tradeoffs several times in the foregoing, and I have argued the ubiquity of tradeoffs in decision making, choice and policy establishment elsewhere (Nickerson, 1992). "Industrial mass-production techniques have made consumer goods available on a much greater scale than otherwise would be possible, but it has also contributed to the pollution of the environment and to the depersonalization of work. The commercial nuclear reactor has provided a new source of energy, but at the expense of the prospects of nuclear accidents and the problem of disposal of nuclear wastes. The use of chlorine in drinking water has been effective in controlling organisms that cause typhoid and other infectious diseases. It has also left chloroform and other carcinogenic chlorinated hydrocarbons in the drinking water supply. Commercially canned foods have a smaller danger of botulism than did foods preserved in the home, but the lead solder in some metal cans introduced a toxin in commercially canned foods not present in those put up at home. The use of pesticides and herbicides in agriculture has increased food yields greatly and decreased the cost of food to consumers, but it has exposed agricultural workers to hazardous chemicals and contributed to a variety of water pollution problems" (p. 323).

Sowell (1995) makes a compelling case that, at least in the context of addressing socially significant problems of interest to the general public, there are no solutions—only tradeoffs. He contrasts two views regarding how such problems should be addressed. One he calls, somewhat derisively, the "vision of the anointed," and the other "the tragic vision." Those with the vision of the anointed—more specifically, self anointed, in Sowell's view—are apt to propose, or attempt to impose, what they see as "solutions" to public policy problems. Those who have the tragic vision, which Sowell considers the more realistic of the two, recognize that there are no solutions, but only tradeoffs. Unfortunately, the tradeoffs involved in decision and choice may not become apparent to decision makers even after the fact, because the unanticipated costs often are delayed for a sufficiently long time that they may be perceived as independent of the causal decisions that produced them.

Sowell (1995) illustrates how the seeking of a solution to a problem without considering the tradeoffs involved can produce unwanted consequences, including consequences that defeat the intended goal. He mentions a proposal to enact a federal law requiring infants to be strapped into their own seats on airplanes, in reaction to the death of an infant who was torn from its mother's arms and hurtled through the cabin in a plane crash in 1989. Considered in isolation, the proposal seems like a rational response to this tragedy. Sowell notes, however, that an economic study led to the conclusion that such a law, because it would mean purchase of another ticket by parents traveling with an infant, would motivate some of them to use less expensive ground transportation, most forms of which have higher mortality rates than airplanes. According to the analysis, the saving of one baby's life in airplane crashes would be offset by the loss of nine lives in ground transportation accidents, and an additional cost of $3 billion.

The plausibility of this analysis gets some empirical support from an analysis by Gigerenzer (2004a, 2006b) of U.S. traffic fatalities before and immediately following the terrorists' attack on the World Trade Center on September 11, 2001. Air travel decreased and highway travel increased for several months following the attack, presumably because of increased fear of flying. On the basis of his analysis, Gigerenzer estimated that this change in travel behavior resulted in the loss of about 1,500 more Americans lives to highway accidents than would normally have been expected over the course of the last three months of 2001 and first nine of 2002. These examples lend credence to Sowell's contention that "Nothing is easier that to increase safety in some arbitrarily defined sector in some arbitrarily chosen way, in disregard of what this does to safety elsewhere and in other ways" (p. 136).

There are numerous other illustrations of this type of tradeoff, some involving pesticides and vaccines, which have had (generally anticipated) beneficial effects in some ways and (generally unanticipated) detrimental ones in others. One argued by Sowell (2004) involves rent control. He contends that an ultimate effect of rent control is the deterioration of housing stock in the controlled area (lack of maintenance and of the construction of new units because of lack of incentive for landlords). The general point is that in focusing on the benefits that are expected to be derived from a proposed "solution" to a problem, it is excessively easy to overlook some of the costs of that solution, including potential exacerbation of the very problem for which a solution is sought. Other policies that can have—and often have had—unanticipated and undesirable consequences on which Sowell focuses include protective tariffs, job-security policies (which may protect the jobs of some workers at the expense of lost opportunities for others), subsidies, and other price regulations and special-interest restrictions on competition of various sorts, all of which, in his view, end up making goods and services to consumers less available and more costly than they otherwise would be, and having other deleterious effects as well. The point that "solutions" to problems can turn out to be "quasi solutions," because they generate unanticipated "residue" problems that are worse than the problems "solved" has been made also by Schwartz (1971).

Perhaps nowhere is the difficulty of assessing the long-term effects of choices greater than in the context of attempts to address problems of detrimental environmental change. Consider, for example, the problem of energy production. Much has been written about the environmentally destructive effects of conventional means of generating energy, especially the burning of fossil fuels. What is needed, we all seem to agree, are sources of "clean energy." The sun, wind, tides, nuclear fusion all have their proponents. Suppose the technology is developed that will make one or more of such energy sources to be economically feasible, cheaper say than the burning of fossil fuels. From a narrow and short-term perspective, one might say the problem had been solved.

But what about from a broader, longer-range point of view? As Ehrenfeld (1981) argues, "If a source of power is to be called 'clean,' that judgment can only be made if all of the consequences and effects of the power have been traced—from the time of its generation to the time the last kilowatt has been dissipated as irrecoverable heat" (p. 116). As to how the more readily available "clean" power will be used, Ehrenfeld makes a somewhat disheartening prediction: "It will be used to manufacture more snowmobiles, which will destroy more of the winter vegetation of the north and diminish the dwindling privacy and quiet that northern dwellers once enjoyed during the months of snow. . . It will be used to make more laser bombs and surface-to-surface missiles and Rome plows and anti-crop defoliants. It will be used to provide more electric outdoor billboards, which will help accelerate the destruction of the meaning of language. It will power the pumps of tube wells in the world's dry grasslands, thus permitting more cattle to be grazed, and more deserts to be formed" (p. 116). And so on. One need not subscribe without reservation to the dour view presented by Ehrenfeld here to appreciate the point that how clean a source of energy should be considered to be should depend in part on the uses to which the energy that is generated is put, insofar as they can be determined, and that the situation may appear to be quite different when viewed from a broad perspective than when viewed from a narrow one.

☐ Group Decision Making

[W]hen our imperfect judgments are aggregated in the right way, our collective intelligence is often excellent. (Surowiecki, 2004, p. xiv)

Collective wisdom, alas, is no adequate substitute for the intelligence of individuals. (Russell, 1957, p. 191)

Many cultures throughout history have used groups to make decisions. Presumably, the rationale for having groups make decisions is the assumption that they do a better job of it than individuals. Whether, in fact, they do so would seem to be an empirical question that could be answered by research. On the other hand, assuming that the question has an answer presupposes an unambiguous way of judging decision quality, and this presupposition is shaky at best. The experimental work that has been done on group decision making has addressed a variety of questions, and revealed several phenomena, that relate to the general question of the relative quality of group and individual decision making, perhaps without providing an unqualified answer, but it demonstrates the complexity of the ways in which individual and group processes interact and influence each other.

Illustrative real group decision problems

The following factual scenarios illustrate the nontriviality of structuring real-life problems in ways that make them amenable to the application of quantitative decision making procedures.

Staff selection problem

You are a member of a committee that has the responsibility of selecting and supervising the staff for a residence for women with fairly severe developmental disabilities. The residence accommodates eight women and three staff. The house has been staffed by a married couple and a single individual. The single individual functions as a relief manager and assumes responsibility for the house when the couple is away. The house is a relatively new venture, and the committee is still getting its bearings. The committee has been dissatisfied with the performance of the first couple it hired and has terminated its employment; it is now interviewing candidates to fill these positions. There is some urgency because the couple left the house immediately upon notice of termination, and the relief manager is shouldering the full responsibility of the house until a new couple is employed.

Three candidate couples—the only applicants for the job—have been interviewed. One has been dismissed from further consideration on the basis of the initial interview; however, the committee is finding it difficult to decide between the remaining two couples. Couple A, although young (about 26 years of age), appears to be relatively mature and has had some experience working with people with developmental disabilities in the past. The husband is a graduate law student and the wife is also taking graduate courses on a part-time basis. Couple B is even younger than Couple A (approximately 23 years of age). Both husband and wife appear to be extremely ambitious and intellectually keen. He expects to obtain his PhD in mathematics within a few months; she has been attending seminary while holding a full-time evening job. Both couples appear to be eager to obtain the position.

The members of the committee argue in favor of Couple A because of a somewhat longer marriage and greater experience as homemakers. Couple A has a baby approximately one year of age, a fact that some of the committee members see as a plus and others see as a complication. A negative factor relating to Couple A is the fact that the man has volunteered that he is likely to want to leave the state during the coming summer (about 9 months hence) to take advantage of a temporary employment opportunity between school years. The committee feels it would be very difficult to recruit house managers for a three-month stay, and, even if this were not the case, it wonders about the advisability of changing managers too frequently if this can be avoided.

How does one weigh the importance of these various factors to arrive at a rational decision? Does it make sense to talk about an optimal solution to this type of problem? There is concrete relevant information available to the committee but only a limited amount; there are also several elements of uncertainty. No one is quite sure, for example, what the effect of having a baby in the house will be, either on the parents, the child, or the other residents. The factual information available regarding the candidates is such as would appear on a resume; beyond this, none of the candidates is known to the committee members.

Several alternatives are open to the committee. (1) It could choose one of the couples and offer the position on the basis of the information available. (2) It could attempt to gather more information on these candidates to help resolve some of the uncertainties that remain after the first interview. (3) It might attempt to increase its number of options by interviewing additional candidates, if such can be found.

Each of these alternatives has some attractive and some unattractive aspects. The house is currently in need of staff, and the committee is eager to meet this need. One of the couples being interviewed must make a decision within a few days concerning another job offer that it has. The couple prefers the house manager position, but in the event that turns out not to be available, it does not want to lose out on the other opportunity. One of the committee members who has had experience in recruiting house managers for other similar residences in the past points out that both Couples A and B look very good compared to the average couple that she has interviewed. Moreover, applicants for such positions are not numerous. And so on.

Fund management problem

A board of trustees (five in number) for a small corporation's retirement fund is trying to make a decision concerning what to do with a portion of the fund. The fund is about $60 million in size. About $45 million is managed by a professional management firm, and the other $15 million is invested in commercial paper. Interest on the paper has recently decreased to the point where there is a consensus among the trustees that the money should be invested in another way. An option would be to add the $15 million to the $45 million that is already under management. Some of the trustees, however, are dissatisfied with the recent performance of the management firm and have suggested that alternatives be explored.

Several proposals have been made concerning what to do with the money. They include: keeping it in paper, on the assumption that interest rates are in a temporary slump; putting all of it in the hands of a second management firm (several candidate firms having been identified); distributing it among two or three additional firms with somewhat different management objectives and procedures. The last alternative would be viewed as an experiment leading to the eventual deposition of an increased proportion of the total fund with the firm that obtains the best results over a specified period of time. Several proposals have also been offered concerning exactly what kind of an apportionment of the money should be made in the event that more than one firm is retained.

Again, when one tries to force the problem into the mold of a normative decision algorithm, one finds it to be very difficult to do. Simply identifying all the reasonable decision alternatives that it has available is a major challenge to the board, and it is not clear how it would ever be sure that it had done so. In practice, it is likely that at some point the board decides (not necessarily explicitly) that it has identified enough options and goes on with what it has. There is always the possibility, however, of someone coming up with a new idea as deliberations proceed.

Being precise about its utilities is likely to be very difficult as well. The fund has a specific objective—an annual return on investment 5 percentage points better than the Standard and Poors index. But there are questions regarding how much latitude should be given to the fund managers in achieving this objective, how much short-term volatility the board is willing to accept in order to achieve the objective over the long term, precisely what durations "short-term" and "long-term" should denote, and so on.

Some questions

How should a group go about making a rational decision in situations like these? Is there a procedure it might follow that would maximize its chances of selecting the best possible action, or at least ensure a better-than-chance outcome? How does one define best possible action—or good enough action—in such situations? Is optimization a reasonable goal, or even a useful concept, in these contexts?

My suspicion is that the process by which decisions are made in such complex and loosely structured situations is rather similar, independently of the subject matter. Various members of the group state opinions on a variety of issues, often arguing in favor of one or another proposal or making points that they consider to be relevant to the decision at hand. There is much informal discussion, compromising, and modifying of proposals. Some additional proposals are made during the course of the discussion; some proposals that had been made are explicitly eliminated from further consideration. Eventually, attention focuses on two or three proposals that may or may not bear much resemblance to the ones that were initially put forward, and, finally, through a process involving debate, cajoling, and endurance, a majority of the group comes to an agreement concerning a specific proposal. The need to take some action within a limited time is often a critical reality.

Many questions come to mind when one reflects on the process. To what extent do outcomes depend on irrelevancies or other nonrational factors? How important are the social dynamics of the group—the relative assertiveness, argumentativeness, or docility, of individual members; personal friendships or animosities; explicit or tacit leader-subordinate relationships. How important are such factors as persistence, fatigue, mood, and competing demands on group members' time? Do chance circumstances play much of a role?

One likes not to think that chance plays a significant role in determining the outcomes of processes that are intended to produce rational decisions, but it is difficult to rule out the possibility that it does so. It is easy to imagine, for example, that how long people will be willing to hold out for some favored proposal will depend to some degree on what other kinds of pressures there are on their time. How easily people are persuaded to adopt a given position, how energetically they promote a point of view they favor, how much effort they are willing to put into really understanding the issues—these and many other factors may be affected by people's general state of health, how rested or tired they are, and what distractions are competing for attention.

How might group decision making in real-life situations such as those described above be improved? What does the "maximize-expected-utility" dictum imply regarding the making of decisions such as these? Would it be helpful if the group attempted to lay out explicitly its objectives at the beginning, and to put some kind of weighting on them? How does a group know that the set of proposals it has considered is sufficiently inclusive; how can it be sure that the one it would really like has been identified? Although these questions remain a serious challenge to research, much experimentation has been done and much has been learned as a consequence.

Experimentation with group decision making

Interest in group decision making, and the performance of groups on cognitively demanding tasks more generally, has waxed and waned over the past few decades. Influential early contributors to work in this area include Lewin (1958; Lewin, Lippit, & White, 1939), Deutsch (1949), Bales (1950) and Festinger (1950, 1957), among others (See Nagao, Vollrath, & Davis, 1978). Foci for research and theorizing have included cooperation and competition (Deutsch, 1949), effects of intragroup communication on members beliefs and opinions (e.g., polarization versus convergence) (Myers & Lamm, 1976), and effects of anonymity of group members on group performance (Postmes & Lea, 2000), among many other topics. A representative collection of reviews and original work through the late 1970s was compiled by Brandstätter, Davis, and Schuler (1978). More recent experimental work has been reviewed by Kerr and Tindale (2004).

Group decisions and individual preferences

A major goal of research on group decision making is the discovery of how group decisions depend on the preferences of, and the distribution of decision-relevant knowledge among, its members. In a review of recent work on group decision making, Kameda, Tindale, and Davis (2003) note that one of the more consistent and robust findings has been that majorities/pluralities win most of the time, and especially when no particular alternative can be shown to be correct during discussion. In general, the final consensus outcomes of group decision making are largely determined by the *social-sharedness* of the group members' initial preferences. Under some conditions, a simple averaging of the preferences of the members of a group can become accentuated in those representing group consensus—a form of the *group polarization effect*. Kameda et al. note, too, how the process by which group consensus is expressed (voting procedure) can be manipulated so as to affect the decision outcome.

It has been known for some time that all voting systems have flaws, which is to say that no system satisfies all the principles that one would like a voting system to satisfy. Given the same set of candidates for a public office, different systems, each of which has some claim to being able to represent the voters' preferences, may result in the election of different individuals (Arrow, 1951/1963; Black, 1958; Brams & Fishburn, 1983 Dodgson, 1876/1958; Meyerson, 2002). Arrow (1951/1963) proved that when individuals have transitive preferences, there is no way to design a voting system that will simultaneously satisfy all of a small set of specified properties that are generally recognized to be desirable. Barrow (1998) concludes from a consideration of intransitivity paradoxes of the sort that plague voting systems that rational collective choices cannot be established reliably. This is not to say that all voting systems are equally satisfactory (or equally unsatisfactory) for specific situations; arguments can be, and have been, advanced that some systems are more likely than others to represent the public will in specified situations and therefore should be used in those situations if the intent is a democratic process (Dasgupta & Maskin, 2004).

Any democratic form of government faces the challenge of simultaneously satisfying two objectives that are not entirely mutually compatible: following the will of the majority, and protecting the rights of minorities. This is addressed in the United States through the voting process and by having the protected rights of all citizens spelled out in a document—the constitution. The bicameral congress and the much-debated electoral college system place certain constraints on decision making at the national level that are arguably supportive of both objectives. Having the number of representatives from each state be proportional to its population serves the objective of majority rule, while having the number of senators from each state be the same serves that of protecting the smaller states from being completely dominated by the will of the larger ones. The set up of the electoral college, which has allowed the elections of four presidents who received a smaller percentage of the popular vote than their opponents, ensures that candidates in presidential elections cannot safely focus only on major population centers. As Meyerson (2002) puts it, "the electoral college requires any successful presidential candidate to win in numerous different parts of the country; a dominant base of localized support cannot suffice. Thus the more popular candidate will lose unless he or she has geographically widespread support" (p. 58). This is not to argue that the electoral college system used in the United States is an ideal system; it has its flaws, as do all the other systems, including run-off systems, which also permit a candidate other than the one preferred by the majority to win; but it is not at all clear that changing to a simple majority, or plurality, criterion would solve more problems than it would create.

The common-knowledge effect

One reason to expect groups to make better decisions than individuals is that groups presumably usually have more decision-relevant knowledge, in the aggregate, than does any given member, at least if one equates the knowledge of the group with the disjunction of the knowledge of all of its members. (But see comments in chapter 3 about what it means for a group to know something.) We might expect the benefit to be realized from the grouping of knowledge to be inversely proportional to the degree of commonality of the knowledge of the members—if every member knows precisely what every other member knows, the knowledge of the aggregate is no greater than that of a single member, but if different members know different things, then what they know in the aggregate surpasses what any of them knows individually. Whether groups composed of members with different knowledge bases can effectively tap their aggregate knowledge stores and, if so, under what conditions they can do so, are open questions.

A finding that runs counter to the idea that groups whose members have different knowledge bases might be more effective than groups whose members have more knowledge in common is that of a *common-knowledge effect* (Gigone & Hastie, 1997; Stasser, 1999; Stasser & Titus, 1985). The finding is that members of groups do not necessarily offer information they have that is not shared by other members in consensus-forming discussions. It appears that the likelihood that a particular piece of decision-relevant information will be mentioned in discussion increases with the number of group members who have that piece of information. The effect may be accounted for, at least in part, by recognition of the fallibility of memory and the fact that the probability that a given item of information will be recalled increases with the number of fallible memories in which it is stored (Hinsz, 1990; Stasser, 1988). Kameda et al. point out that, although the common knowledge effect is fairly robust, several experimenters have demonstrated ways to attenuate it, and to elicit the volunteering of more unshared information.

Attraction and friendliness

Not surprisingly, the attractiveness or friendliness of group members to each other appears to be a determinant of the extent to which members are influenced by each others' arguments during discussion (Back, 1951; Brandstätter, 1978; Brewer, 1968; Gerard, 1954). (Although for a counterexample, see Rüttinger, 1978.) The reactions of participants in groups and observers of group behavior can be influenced—though not always in the same way—by the friendliness or aggressiveness of speakers, even as evidenced by nonverbal behavior (Schuler & Peltzer, 1978), and their reactions can depend also on their own personality characteristics (e.g., need of social validation) in ways that are not easy to summarize (Brandstätter, 1978).

Displays of approval or disapproval of a speaker by an audience (e.g., applause or lack thereof) can affect the degree to which a listener finds a speaker to be persuasive (Landry, 1972; Kelley & Woodruff, 1956), especially when the audience is itself evaluated positively by the listener (von Rosenstiel & Stocker-Kreichgauer, 1978). There is some evidence that one is less likely to be swayed by an expert who holds an opinion that differs from one's own when there is at least one other (non-expert) person in the group whose opinion is the same as one's own than when there is no such "co-oriented" peer (Verhagen, 1978).

Sometimes discussion among group members who are originally divided on an issue has the effect of polarizing the group—making the proponents of opposing positions even more extreme in their opinions than before the discussion began (Myers & Kaplan, 1976; Moscovici & Zavalloni, 1969; Sunstein, 2003). Whether such a polarization effect is obtained appears to depend, in part, on the size of the group involved; the members of two person groups are likely to move toward compromise and agreement, while those of four-person groups are likely to move toward more extreme positions (Stephenson, 1978).

A phenomenon relating to group decision making that is of considerable interest has been dubbed by Mikula and Schwinger (1978) the *politeness ritual*. When members of a group have to allocate rewards among members, they may do so in accordance with any of several principles. Studies have shown that people who have contributed more than their fellow group members to the group's success are likely to elect to distribute on the basis of a principle of equality (to all members equally, independently of their contribution) whereas those who have contributed less than their peers are likely to prefer distribution according to a principle of contribution (to each according to the relative magnitude of his or her contribution). This appears to be magnanimous behavior in both instances, but, as Mikula and Schwinger (1978) note, psychologists have proposed explanations of the behavior that attribute it to self interest; they argue that application of the politeness ritual can even be used "as a negotiation tactic to impel one's opponent to a concession in a bargaining situation" (p. 244).

The quality of group decisions

The practice of trial by jury must rest on the assumption that a group of people is likely to evaluate evidence in a less biased and more effective way than is an individual, and justice is served by the practice only to the extent that the assumption is valid. Much attention has been given to the challenge of designing juries and jury decision-making procedures so as to ensure just and efficient verdicts. Hacking (1990) gives an account of the specific types of questions considered by eminent 18th- and 19th-century mathematicians, including Condorcet, Laplace, and Poisson, who were keen on trying to help realize this goal.

Empirical studies of group performance of cognitive tasks have yielded a mix of results: sometimes groups have been observed to perform no better (if not worse) than do their average members (Gigone & Hastie, 1997; Kerr, MacCoun, & Kramer, 1996) and sometimes they have been observed to perform at least as well as their more capable members (Laughlin & Ellis, 1986; Moshman & Geil, 1998; Moscovici & Doise, 1994).

In a study employing Wason's (1966) famous selection task (see chapter 2), Moshman and Geil (1998) found that while only 9% of students correctly performed the task while working alone on it, 75% of groups, each composed of 5 or 6 students, did it correctly and some groups did it correctly despite the fact that no member of the group initially gave the correct response. "Close examination of what happened within the groups showed a process of collaborative reasoning in which students presented, justified, criticized, compared, and combined a variety of ideas and possibilities until they achieved a structure of logical understanding that most or all members of the group understood and accepted" (Moshman, 2004, p. 234). Moshman and Geil interpreted their results as supportive of the idea that insight into the logic of falsification, which underlies correct performance of the selection task, if it is perceived as a logical inference task, was facilitated by discussion, or "collaborative reasoning," among the members of a group.

The "risky shift"

Among the more robust and interesting findings that have come out of experimentation with group decision making is that groups tend to make riskier decisions under uncertainty than do individuals and that individuals tend to be willing to accept greater risk when participating in a group decision-making process than when making decisions on their own (Bem, Wallach, & Kogan, 1965; Clark, 1971; Dion, Baron, & Miller, 1970; Kogan & Wallach, 1967; Lambert, 1978; Vinokur, 1971; Wallach & Kogan 1965; Wallach, Kogan, & Bem, 1962). The movement of individuals to greater riskiness when functioning as members of a group has been called the *risky-shift* phenomenon. It has been observed many times in laboratory experiments; whether it occurs in real functional groups is less clear.

Virtual (noninteracting) groups

In the foregoing discussion of group performance the emphasis has been on groups in which members interact with each other. There is also considerable interest in the functioning of what might be referred to as virtual groups—collectives of people who do not interact, and who may not know who the other members of a particular group to which they belong are.

A favorable account of the performance of such groups has been given engagingly by Surowiecki (2004) in a book with the attention-getting title *The Wisdom of Crowds*. Surowiecki does not contend that groups always display wisdom in their actions; he acknowledges that groups work well under some conditions and not so well under others, but he argues that in a surprisingly large variety of situations they work much better than has generally been realized, and often do better than any of their members would do individually. To be sure, "there are times—think of a riot, or a stock-market bubble—when aggregating individual decisions produces a collective decision that is utterly irrational" (p. xix), but Suroweicki sees such mistakes as "negative proofs" of the arguments he makes regarding the conditions that must hold for collective decision making to be good decision making.

The conditions that Surowiecki stresses most are diversity (of knowledge or opinions among the members of a group) and independence (of the contributions of individual members from those of other members). "Collective decisions are most likely to be good ones when they're made by people with diverse opinions reaching independent conclusions, relying on their private information" (p. 57). A group satisfying these conditions is likely to produce accurate judgments, he contends, because, "If you ask a large enough group of diverse, independent people to make a prediction or estimate a probability, and then average those estimates, the errors each of them makes in coming up with an answer will cancel themselves out" (p. 10).

Surowiecki argues that for small groups, such as organizational teams, to function best, it is essential that they be cognitively diverse—that the members bring different knowledge and expertise to the table. He notes the ease with which small groups can be unduly influenced by the biases of a few. Homogeneity within a group may make for cohesiveness, but in Surowiecki's view it stifles creativity, it makes it difficult for the group to consider alternatives. Groups that are too homogeneous run the risk of becoming locked in their own embrace, as it were. Because they hear views only very similar to their own, and do not hear those views being challenged by people who do not hold them, they can come to be believe that their views are better justified than they really are. In short, such groups may display the kind of collective cognitive behavior that Janis (1982) dubbed *groupthink*. The diversity that Surowiecki advocates is "informed diversity." One cannot expect that a diverse group of uninformed people will evidence much collective wisdom, "[b]ut if you can assemble a diverse group of people who possess varying degrees of knowledge and insight, you're better off entrusting it with major decisions rather than leaving them in the hands of one or two people, no matter how smart those people are" (p. 31).

Insuring the heterogeneity of an interacting group with respect to the knowledge that different members bring to the table is not enough, it appears, to guarantee that the group will effectively tap all the knowledge its members have. We have already noted the *common-knowledge effect*, according to which members of a group are more likely to discuss knowledge they share than knowledge that is held by only one or a small minority of members. Surowiecki notes the importance, as argued by Maier and Solem (1952), of group leaders taking an active role in making sure that all members are heard.

But even then, it is easy to see how personality differences and dominance relationships can influence the willingness of members to volunteer knowledge that only they have, and this helps explain why Surowiecki considers the independence of the contributions of a group's members to the performance of the group as a whole to be as important as heterogeneity. In Surowiecki's view, the objective should not be consensus: "the search for consensus encourages tepid, lowest-common-denominator solutions which offend no one rather than exciting everyone. Instead of fostering the free exchange of conflicting views, consensus-driven groups—especially when members are familiar with each other—tend to trade in the familiar and squelch provocative debate" (p. 203). Surowiecki points to financial market bubbles and crashes as examples of what can result when the conditions that make groups intelligent are not there; bubbles and crashes occur when people pay too much attention to what others are doing and copy the behavior they observe.

The claim that groups generally function best when their members act independently of each other suggests that the convention of having trial juries deliberate at length before reaching a verdict is likely to be less effective in arriving at justified verdicts than would be a process in which each juror got to vote on the verdict without any interaction with other jurors. This might be the case. It seems to me doubtful, but Surowiecki makes a thought-provoking argument about the general effectiveness of groups that function in a non-consensus-seeking way. The topic deserves more research.

Are groups rational?

What can be said of the rationality or irrationality of groups, on the whole? More or less the same that can be said about individuals. Sometimes they are rational—at least in the sense that they do well at decision making and problem solving—sometimes they are not. Watts (2003) contends that groups do well more often than not: "when large numbers of ordinary people get together, it seems that *most* of the time they behave quite reasonably, but *once in a while* they end up behaving like madmen" (p. 201). Watts is speaking of interacting groups. His claim seems to me to be consistent with the evidence, and it points up the importance of understanding better the conditions under which each situation holds.

As we have noted, decisions may be made, in effect, by the behavior of collections of individuals who are behaving as individuals without any intention, or even awareness, of contributing to a collective choice. Advocates of free-market economics point out, for example, that prices are established by the aggregate influence of the choices of individual consumers regarding alternative ways of spending their limited resources for needed or desired goods. Goods that are priced too high relative to other goods for which the available money could be used will not sell, so their prices will fall; goods that sell so quickly as to become hard to obtain are priced too low, so their prices will rise. There need not be any conscious corporate decision making going on, but decisions are, in effect, being made. Sowell (2004) argues that a free market works this way and that people, in effect, make collective decisions by their individual purchasing behavior.

This is another nod to the idea of the wisdom of crowds. Sowell argues that nobody can know all that must be known in order to set prices reasonably in an economy and that the advantage of a price-coordinated (free-market) economy is that nobody has to do so. The efficiency of a free market derives from the fact that it operates without requiring that the knowledge that is distributed among consumers be expressed explicitly; it is conveyed, along with their preferences, by the purchases they make. More generally, Sowell contends that governments that fail to tap the knowledge that is distributed among its citizenry do so at their peril.

☐ Evaluating Decisions

> [T]raditional decision theory cannot plausibly be thought to give us an uncontroversial account of rational action. Decision theory seems to generate at least as many controversial questions as it answers. (Moser, 1990, p. 9)

There are at least two aspects of the problem of evaluating decisions that should not be confused. One has to do with distinguishing better decisions from poorer ones. Here the question concerns the criteria in terms of which the quality of a decision is to be judged. A second aspect of the problem pertains to our ability to specify, after the fact, the reasons for which any particular decision was made.

Decision quality and decision outcomes

Yates, Veinott, and Patalano (2003) argue that, for most people, decision quality is not a unitary construct but rather a collection of imperfectly correlated facets. Decisions are seen not as simply good or bad to some degree, but as better or worse with respect to many dimensions. Citing data from a questionnaire study in which people were asked to think of good and bad decisions that they had made in the preceding year, they note that the main determinant of the participants' assessment of the quality of their decisions was their outcomes. "Our empirical results suggest that real deciders rarely acknowledge a concern with the rationality of their decision processes and certainly not in the coherence sense. Instead they are preoccupied with results—good outcomes of various kinds" (p. 31).

Introspection tells us that how happy or regretful we are with a particular decision often depends at least as much on the outcome of the decision as on the question of whether the decision was justified by the information on which it was based. And can anyone doubt that most of us are happier to take credit for decisions that turned out well than for those that turned out poorly, independently of the quality of the decisions as judged strictly in terms of the information in hand at the time they were made?

It is not uncommon for people to regret having made a rational decision, or not having made an irrational one. I might decide to gamble a small amount of money, for example, on a very risky stock that I think has some chance of doing well. When the stock doubles in price over 6 months, I may regret not having used my life's savings to buy as much of it as I could have managed, even though to have done so would have been considered by everyone, including myself, foolhardy in the extreme at the time the decision was made.

This natural tendency to focus on outcomes, and to evaluate decisions on the basis of them, is strongly reinforced by our culture in various ways. People generally are recognized and rewarded for the results they obtain, not for the quality of the thinking that went into their efforts. When the best possible decisions, given the information in hand, lead to undesirable outcomes, perhaps because of unanticipatable chance events, the people responsible for those decisions seldom are remembered favorably for their astuteness. It is not unusual, however, for people who have made rash decisions that have, by chance, turned out well to be venerated for their bold decisiveness. Society prefers its heroes to be winners.

The focus on outcomes as the criteria by which decisions should be judged has generally been seen not to be rational. Baron and Hershey (1988) refer to it as the *outcome bias*. The more widely accepted view is that good decisions can have bad outcomes and bad decisions can have good ones (Hammond, Keeney, & Raiffa, 1998). This is not to deny that a rational decision maker should take *possible* outcomes, and especially *expected* outcomes, into consideration when making a decision. Baron (1998) makes a strong case that decision making could be improved considerably if people generally gave more thought to the possible consequences of decisions—not only for themselves but for others—before making them. But *actual* outcomes cannot be known at decision time in many cases, so that knowledge cannot help determine decision makers' choices. A decision maker can work only with the information that is available at the time the decision must be made, and the rationality of a decision should be judged in terms of that information only, and not in terms of what was learned after the decision was made. Moreover, even after a decision has been made, one usually can know only the outcome of that decision; one cannot be sure what would have happened had a different alternative been chosen. One may speculate about alternative histories that might have unfolded had different choices been made, but one can never be sure where any of the paths not chosen would have led.

In arguing that "good decision" and "bad outcome" are inherently contradictory, Yates et al. (2003) seem to take issue with the idea that decisions should be judged in the light of information available at the time they were made and that, because of uncertainty, good decisions can sometimes yield bad outcomes. However, they temper their objection to the view they dismiss with the observation that "the proposed notion of a good decision process, with its focus on what the process *tends* to produce, is statistical. Thus it acknowledges the inescapable fact of sampling that not every decision made by a good real-life decision process will result in good outcomes" (p. 52). The contention appears to be that, on average, good decisions will yield good outcomes. Even theorists who promote the idea that decisions should be judged in light of information available at the time they were made would expect that decisions made by a good process (a process that uses the available information appropriately) would lead to good (desired) outcomes more often than not. That is to say they would not necessarily object to the idea that good decisions yield good outcomes, statistically speaking; but this is not inconsistent with the idea that individual decisions should be judged in terms of the process by which they were made.

Dawes (1988) suggests that a rational choice should be defined as one that meets three criteria:

1. It is based on the decision maker's *current* assets. Assets include not only money, but physiological state, psychological capacities, social relationships, and feelings.

2. It is based on the possible consequences of the choice.

3. When these consequences are uncertain, their likelihood is evaluated without violating the basic rules of probability theory (p. 8).

Dawes argues that the evidence is compelling that we often fail to measure up to each of these criteria. Our decisions are determined not only by our current state, but how we arrived at it, which is to say we irrationally let the past influence decisions—and hence the future—in ways that it should not; our decisions are determined not only by their possible consequences but how those consequences are described or "framed;" and we systematically violate the rules of probability theory in judging the likelihood of possible events.

The second criterion proposed by Dawes—that a choice be based on its possible consequences—is unlikely to be contested by anyone. What makes this criterion difficult to apply is the ease with which possible consequences can be overlooked. History is replete with decisions that were made with laudable intentions that had unanticipated consequences that turned out to be disastrous. How to identify the more probable consequences of policy decisions accurately is a continuing challenge to decision-making research.

Retrospective decision evaluation

> Every policy is a success by sufficiently low standards and a failure by sufficiently high standards. (Sowell, 1995, p. 102)

Judging the quality of other people's decisions after the fact is, of course, exceedingly easy to do, at least when the judgments are made on the basis of outcomes; we are all experts with the advantage of hindsight. Second-guessing—Monday-morning quarterbacking—is a ubiquitous means of convincing ourselves of our own superior decision-making capabilities:

we would have done it differently and had a better outcome. People in positions of leadership who have to make difficult choices can be certain that they will be second guessed when the choices they make turn out badly, especially by people who have never had the experience of making equally significant choices in comparably difficult circumstances.

How good are people at assessing objectively their own judgments and decision making processes after the fact? People are quite good at justifying decisions (Evans & Wason, 1976), which is to say that we usually are not at a loss to produce a set of "reasons" why a particular choice or decision was sensible at the time it was made. It is exceedingly easy, however, to mistake rationalizations, which are manufactured to justify a decision after the fact, for the factors that actually determined the decision at the time that it was made (Soelberg, 1967; Zajonc, 1980).

It may be that we even fool ourselves, in some cases, into believing that a decision was made at all. There is something to be said for the assumption that we make many fewer genuine decisions in life than we are likely to give ourselves credit for. Henle (1962a) gives the following unflattering assessment of human decision making in the aggregate. "Although it would be hard to establish quantitatively, experience suggests that we fall into an occupation, fall into marriage and other relations, fall into a way of living with alarming frequency, not stopping to ask ourselves: Is this the way of living for me? When we do think creatively in relation to our own lives, it seems most frequently to be in the sense of overcoming obstacles which stand between us and these so often unexamined goals. Even the creativeness of such thinking is limited by being in the service of an end which has not been thought out" (p. 47).

Wason and Evans (1975) argue that people are generally not aware of processes that underlie their reasoning, such as the matching bias (Evans & Lynch, 1973; Platt & Griggs, 1995) that is hypothesized to affect performance in Wason's (1960) selection task, and that the introspective accounts that people give of their performance on reasoning tasks constitute (not necessarily witting) efforts to construct justifications of their behavior. Either of these factors would suffice to make introspective reports unreliable, together they make them doubly so.

Evans (1989) cautions that even when people are successful in their attempts to solve reasoning problems, one is not entitled to assume that verbal accounts they give of unobservable aspects of their performance are necessarily accurate. "Retrospective reporting generally appears to produce new explicit reasoning from the subject who joins the experimenter in theorizing about his behaviour, rather than a recollection of the method actually used" (p. 108), which is not to suggest that introspective reports are useless in the context of reasoning research.

A case can be made for the idea that we often assess the quality of decisions strictly on the basis of intentions. One may *feel* good about a decision one made with the intention of being helpful to people who had suffered some misfortune, without the benefit of evidence as to whether the effect was in fact beneficial. And retrospective analysis of intentions may be vulnerable to coloration by a decision's outcome. The decision maker who made a decision in the pursuit of goal A may, upon learning that the decision produced B, make himself feel better about his decision by discovering that B was his goal all along. There can be little doubt that outcome-motivated redefinitions of goals occur, and it seems likely that their occurrence is fostered by such factors as the need not only to feel good about one's decisions, but to be able to justify them to others.

There is also the view that choice—even the experience of intention—is an illusion. The idea is that the sense of intending to do something—e.g., move a finger or other body part—is a retrospective consequence of having observed the action (van den Bos & Jeannerod, 2002). Results of some brain localization studies have been taken as evidence that neural activity preparatory to voluntary motion can precede the feeling of intention by as much as a second, although the feeling of intention tends to precede the actual movement by a fraction of a second (Eagleman, 2004; Haggard & Elmer, 1999). That people can selectively attend either to the intention to do something or to the intended act itself, and evidence suggesting that different brain areas may be differentially involved in the two cases (Lau, Rogers, Haggard, & Passingham, 2004), illustrate the complexity of the neural dynamics of choice.

It would be difficult to demonstrate that we are very good at retrospectively assessing the quality of our own decisions, except perhaps in terms of their outcomes, or what we perceive to be their outcomes. Even evaluations based on outcomes may be suspect, because outcomes themselves may gain perceived value through "bolstering" simply by having followed from one's choices (Janis & Mann, 1977). I find it easy to believe, and no good evidentiary reason not to, that we tend to be more kind to ourselves in those assessments than an objective and disinterested analysis would justify.

On the other hand there is something to be said for the opinion that nature is more likely, sometimes, to remind us of our failures than of our successes. Consider, for example, the character of prevention in this regard. Blame is often much easier to assign for failure to take preventive measures than is credit for having taken them, because the effects of the former are more salient than those of the latter. If my neighbor breaks his leg as a consequence of my failure to clear ice from my walkway, the incident is very likely to be noticed and blame assigned; however, if my neighbor makes it safely to my door over a walkway from which I have cleared the ice, the fact that he did not break his leg is much less likely to be the focus of much attention or the basis of much praise for my preventive action. In general, victims of preventive acts not taken are easier to identify after the fact than are the beneficiaries of successful preventive measures. Presumably many people are alive today who would not be if an effective polio vaccine had never been developed, but those of us who are members of that group have no way of knowing that we are. This is really unfortunate, and may help explain why, despite the fact that prevention is the most cost-effective approach to many of our most serious personal and societal problems, it appears to be much easier to motivate people to respond to problems and crises after they have occurred than to try to prevent them from occurring.

Accountability and decision quality

Do people make better decisions when they are held accountable, in some way, for the decisions they make? The question naturally arises when one considers that much of the evidence that has been collected regarding people's foibles as decision makers has been obtained with college students making decisions under conditions in which accountability is not an issue. One may be forgiven for wondering to what extent the findings in these experiments are generalizable to situations outside the laboratory where people not only have to live with the consequences of their decisions but often have to justify them explicitly to themselves and others.

Citing numerous studies that have shown a variety of positive effects on judgment and decision making (e.g., Siegel-Jacobs & Yates, 1996, Simonson & Nye, 1992; Tetlock & Kim, 1987), Lerner and Tetlock (2003) distinguish two overarching hypotheses about the effects of accountability on the putative biases that have been identified in judgment and decision-making research. According to one hypothesis, accountability will attenuate such biases to the extent that it increases cognitive effort; according to the other, it will—by amplifying dominant responses—attenuate biases on easy problems and increase it on difficult ones.

Lerner and Tetlock distinguish also between predecision and postdecision accountability. Predecision accountability, in this context, is knowledge before a decision is made that a justification of the decision will be required. The justification may be given before or after the decision, but knowledge that it will be required comes before. Postdecision accountability is accountability that is required after a decision has been made, the requirement of which was not anticipated before. It is accountability in retrospect.

Lerner and Tetlock cite experimental evidence that both predecision and postdecision accountability can prompt thinking about the decision. However, whereas predecision accountability tends to prompt *exploratory* thinking, which can improve the quality of decisions (e.g., by attenuating various kinds of biases even in presumably difficult tasks), postdecision accountability tends to elicit *confirmatory* thinking aimed at rationalizing the decision that was made (Conlon & Wolf, 1980; Staw & Ross, 1989; Tetlock, Skitka, & Boettger, 1989). One of the ways in which predecision accountability has its effect is through motivating increased cognitive effort. Lerner and Tetlock note, however, that whether increased effort will improve the quality of decision making depends on a number of other factors. They present a conceptualization of the decision-making process that takes these moderating factors into account and they suggest conditions under which accountability is likely to attenuate biases and those under which it is not.

The lack of any type of accountability is a worrisome feature of much decision making in the public policy arena. When decision makers have the ability to make decisions with the realization that there will be no negative consequences for them personally if their decisions should prove to be wrong—because any negative consequences that might occur will be borne at a far future time or in a far-off place—the situation is less than ideal for maximizing decision quality broadly construed.

Sowell (1995) makes another point about accountability in arguing that it is possible for a prevailing view on a specific issue to become so pervasive in a society that decisions made with respect to that issue are never called to account. The prevailing view is treated as axiomatic and consequently not vulnerable to empirical test. Another way to put it is that, no matter what the outcomes are of decisions that are justified by the prevailing axiomatic view, they will be interpreted in such a way as to ensure the preservation of the view—at least by those among whom the view prevails. In the context of socially contentious issues, one may benefit more, Sowell suggests, by being politically correct than by being factually correct.

Applicability of normative models

The most common way in which decision theorists evaluate the decisions that people make is to compare them with the decisions that are prescribed by one or another normative model. There is then always the question of whether any particular model that is being used is appropriate to the instance to which it is being applied. Normative approaches to decision making typically prescribe decomposition of a problem into sets of possible states of the world and action alternatives, and associating with each of the state-action combinations expected outcomes. Effecting the decomposition is a matter of judgment, because a given problem typically can be decomposed in a variety of ways. In illustrating this point, Jungermann (1980) notes that a decision technique used by Pauker and Pauker (1977) in the context of birth planning requires from the user one global judgment of the utility of having a child, while another technique developed by Beach, Townes, and Campbell (1978) for use in the same context, decomposes the question of having a child into 34 specific considerations.

One of the limitations of some normative models is that they pertain only to discrete incidents in which a decision is to be made in the context of a well-defined situation. Inasmuch as much of the laboratory experimentation on judgment and choice has investigated performance in discrete situations, it seems appropriate to evaluate performance in terms of these models. But the question arises as to whether the results obtained in these situations are generalizable to many real-life situations in which decision making is part of a dynamic on-going process in which feedback and adaptation play significant roles (Clancy, Elliot, Ley, Omodei, Wearing, McLennan, & Thorsteinsson, 2003).

Hogarth (1981) argues that several of the biases that have been revealed in laboratory studies with discrete situations reflect mechanisms that can be seen as rational in the continuous situations that are prevalent outside the laboratory. Here is one of the examples he gives to illustrate the point. Ronen (1973) gave people the choice between two two-step paths to a goal state with a desirable payoff; the paths had equal probability of ending up at the goal state, but one of them had a higher probability of first-step success and a lower probability of second-step success than the other. Inasmuch as the joint probability of success on both steps was the same for both paths, people should have been indifferent to which path they took, according to a standard expected utility model. But they were not; most preferred the path with the higher probability of success on the first step. Hogarth argues that, although this may be seen as an irrational preference in the laboratory situation, many real-life environments change continuously in time, and it makes sense to opt for the alternative that is most likely to keep one in the game as long as possible.

Hogarth considers a number of other phenomena that have been taken as evidence of human irrationality, or ineffective reasoning, that may be seen as reasonable approaches to problems in a dynamically changing environment. He points out too that judgment and choice are often indistinguishable in the discrete case but separable in the continuous one. In the continuous case, "judgment can be thought of as providing a temporal background of activity that is punctuated by particular choices" (p. 201). In the case of continuous processing, judgment may have the effect of delaying choice—in the sense of committing to one of two or more possible actions—for the purpose of providing time to gather more information that is relevant to the choice that is to be made.

Luce (2003) argues for the need for distinct theories of judgment and choice. The need is shown clearly, he contends, in the fact that the *preference reversal phenomenon*, which he refers to as the most striking violation of transitivity, arises from the mixing of judgment and choice procedures in experimentation. Preference reversal refers to a situation in which one expresses a preference for one opportunity over another in one context (e.g., possible wagers in a game of chance) but attaches a higher price for the lesser preferred opportunity, if asked how much one would charge to sell either one to someone else.

☐ Theories of Decision Making

Theoretical treatments of decision making abound (Bazerman, 1990; Berger, 1997; Edwards & Tversky, 1967; Einhorn & Hogarth, 1981a; Hammond, 2000; Howard, 1966; Kahneman & Tversky, 1979b; Keeney & Raiffa, 1976; Klein, 1998; Lee, 1971; Luce & Raiffa, 1957; Payne, Bettman & Johnson, 1993; Raiffa, 1968; Raiffa & Schlaifer, 1961; Savage, 1954/1972; Slovic, Fischhoff, & Lichtenstein, 1977; von Neumann & Morgenstern, 1953; von Winterfeldt & Edwards, 1986; Watson & Buede, 1987). Here I will mention briefly only a few of them. I have discussed models of decision making under uncertainty elsewhere (Nickerson, 2004).

Linear models of choice

Linear models of choice assume that choices are made by evaluating each of the alternatives in terms of a set of independent factors, each of which is given a weight that reflects its importance or desirability relative to that of each of the other factors being considered. The alternative with the largest value—largest weighted sum—is selected. Such models are attractive because of their simplicity; in particular, they assume that the value or desirability of decision alternatives can be accounted for adequately by considering only the aggregate effects of independent factors and that interactions among those factors can be safely ignored.

Foreshadowings of this approach can be seen in the prescriptions for choice proposed in the 18th century by Benjamin Franklin and by Jeremy Bentham. Franklin (1772/1907), in an often-quoted passage from a 1772 letter responding to a request for advice from his friend, Joseph Priestly, had this to say about the problem of making a "yes-no" decision.

> I cannot, for want of sufficient premises, advise you *what* to determine, but if you please I will tell you *how*. When those difficult cases occur, they are difficult, chiefly because while we have them under consideration, all the reasons *pro* and *con* are not present to the mind at the same time; but sometimes one set present themselves, and at other times another, the first being out of sight. Hence the various purposes or inclinations that alternately prevail and the uncertainty that perplexes us.
>
> To get over this, my way is to divide half a sheet of paper by a line into two columns; writing over the one Pro, and over the other *Con*. Then, during three or four days' consideration, I put down under the different heads short hints of the different motives, that at different times occur to me, *for* or *against* the measure. When I have thus got them all together, in one view, I endeavor to estimate the respective weights, and where I find two, one on each side, that seem equal, I strike them both out. If I find a reason *pro* equal to some *two* reasons *con*, I strike out the three. If I judge some two reasons *con*, equal to some three reasons *pro*, I strike out the five; and thus proceeding I find at length where the balance lies; and if after a day or two of farther consideration, nothing new that is of importance occurs on either side, I come to a determination accordingly. And, though the weight of reasons cannot be taken with the precision of algebraic quantities, yet, when each is thus considered, separately and comparatively, and the whole lies before me, I think I can judge better, and am less liable to make a rash step; and in fact I have found great advantage for this kind of equation, in what may be called *moral* or *prudential algebra*. (p. 437)

Bentham (1789/1939) put forth a quasi-quantitative method for action selection—a *hedonistic calculus*—that was designed to reveal which of a set of alternative actions would be in the best interests of a community affected by the choice. The method involved identifying and weighting the pleasures and pains that the various alternatives would be expected to produce and the numbers of people who would be affected by them. The goodness or desirability of an act was revealed by the balance of pleasure and pain that it would cause. Pleasures (or pains) did not all count equally in Bentham's scheme, but were differentiated by their intensity, duration, certainty, and propinquity (or remoteness).

Franklin's and Bentham's prescriptions are remarkable in several respects. Both involve analysis, or identification of factors that should help determine the choice—pros and cons in Franklin's case and pleasures and pains in that of Bentham. And both involve synthesis, or the combining of the parts to derive the choice. In each case the combining approach is a calculus of a sort, involving the differential weighting of factors and a final judgment as to how they balance in the aggregate. This is very similar in spirit to the approach represented by modern linear models of choice. Franklin's approach has the additional interesting feature that it explicitly recognizes our limitations as decision makers that stem from our inability to bring immediately to mind all of what we may know that is germane to a particular decision problem. Thus his advice to not rush to a choice but to take a few days to try to access the pertinent considerations. Bentham intended that his prescription apply to decisions that have implications for communities of people and it is often referred to as representing the principle of "the greatest pleasure for the greatest number." The principle has been criticized on the grounds that it does not preclude the possibility of the many benefiting at the expense of the few.

Linear models of choice, in their modern instantiations, have been applied in many contexts, including investment decision making (Slovic, 1969), consumer behavior (Bettman & Jones, 1972), x-ray interpretation (Hoffman, Slovic, & Rorer, 1968), production scheduling (Bowman, 1963; Kunreuther,1969), product pricing (Rhim & Cooper, 2004), psychological diagnosis (Hammond, 1955; Hoffman, 1960), apartment selection (Payne, 1976), and juror decision making (Hastie, 1993b). Such models have proved to be able to predict performance relatively accurately in many of these contexts (Goldberg, 1968; Hammond & Summers, 1965).

A study by Sundstrom, Lounsbury, DeVault, and Peele (1981) illustrates the application of a linear model to the assessment of preferences in a real-life situation. These investigators took opinion polls of people living in a small community near the planned site of one of the world's largest nuclear power plants as of 1980 and related their results to an expectancy-value attitude model that assumed one's attitude toward some object, in this case the nuclear plant, is a simple sum of the values of possible consequences of the existence of the object each multiplied by the individual's expectation of its occurrence. The results supported such a model, in that expressed attitudes reflected people's opinions about the relative probabilities of positive and negative consequences of the plant's existence.

Linear models of choice have proven to be quite predictive of human choice behavior in many situations, but there is considerable controversy as to what they reveal about the nature of human choice and decision-making processes. Their predictive success has not been accepted by all theorists as evidence that people actually do something analogous to weighting independent factors in terms of which the options are to be compared and then making a selection on the basis of the sums of these weights (Klein, 1993; Slovic & Lichtenstein, 1971).

Dual-process theories

The notion that people seek to maximize subjective expected utility has been a unifying idea in theorizing about choice behavior at least since the early 18th century. Although we now know that theories based on this idea have limitations in their ability to predict the choices that people actually make, the idea still is arguably as predictively powerful as any other single principle. There appears to be a growing consensus that judgment and choice are more complicated than was once believed and that any reasonably descriptive theory is likely to have to acknowledge behavior is driven by more principles than one (Doherty, 2003; Dougherty, Gronlund, & Gettys, 2003).

I have already mentioned Martignon and Krauss's (2003) contention that people behave as Bayesians in some situations and resort to fast and frugal heuristics in others. Several other theorists have proposed theories or models of decision making that recognize two or more different types of processes that may be activated in different situations. Sloman (1996), for example, distinguishes between an associative system and a rule-based system, the former being the more holistic and automatic and the latter more analytic and controlled. The systems may not yield the same solution in all cases, and which will predominate in any given case is assumed to depend on situational specifics. Similar postulations of two processes, one primarily associative and largely automatic and the other more deliberate and consciously controlled, have been put forth by Epstein (1994), and Evans and Over (1996), among others. The distinction between automatic and controlled information processing is not new, however; notable instances of it include work of Evans and Wason (1976) and of Shiffrin and Schneider (1977). A similar distinction can be made between two kinds of memory retrieval, one of which is "passive, spontaneous, and automatic" (e.g., "assigning names to common objects during conversation, remembering one's destination while driving a car") and the other "active, effortful and consciously directed" ("trying to recall the elusive name of an acquaintance of many years ago, trying to recollect when and where one first ate pizza") (Nickerson, 1981, p. 74).

Fuzzy trace theory (Reyna, 2000; Reyna & Brainerd, 1990, 1992, 1998) postulates two types of representation with which people encode information about a situation of interest, such as a decision problem, one of which preserves only gist and the other of which preserves verbatim details. Gist and verbatim representations are seen as ends of a continuum of precision. It is assumed that people can operate anywhere on the continuum, but that they characteristically operate at the least precise level of representation the situation permits (e.g., at gist in preference to verbatim when possible) when making decisions. When multiple representations are available, the default choice for use will be the one closest to the gist end that will get the task done.

Another dual-process theory has been proposed by Svenson (1992, 1999, 2003). According to this theory, the decision maker's basic task is to find or create a decision option that is sufficiently superior to its competitors to warrant selection, and the two processes that are used in performing this task are differentiation and consolidation, hence the name Diff Con theory. Differentiation is the process by which the decision selection is initially identified. As a consequence of this process, which can involve restructuring of the decision problem, one of the choice alternatives should emerge as the preferred one. Consolidation is the process by which preference for a selected option is supported and maintained after the choice has been made. Differentiation and consolidation are pre- and post-decision processes respectively. Svenson's view of decision making is a dual-process one also in the sense that it recognizes that different decision alternatives may be processed differently—one being treated holistically and with a strong affective influence, for example, while another in the same problem is treated more analytically and with less affect.

Dual-processing theories of rationality, and cognition more generally, receive considerable attention in a recent collection of emerging perspectives on judgment and decision making (Schneider & Shanteau, 2003). Luce (2003), in this collection, shows the possibility of constructing conflicting, but equally defensible, prescriptive models of rational choice and raises the question of whether there is a deeper sense of rationality that can provide the basis for selecting between such formulations. The question is left as a challenge for future research; for the present, he suggests, "perhaps.... we simply have to live with the fact that what seems rational depends more on the formulation of the domain of study than we had previously acknowledged" (p. 81).

In keeping with Occam's dictum, we should postulate a dual-process system only if a single-process theory will not fit the data. Whether a dual-process theory is necessitated by the data is a matter of contention. Some investigators are unconvinced that it is (Gigerenzer & Reiger, 1996, MacDonald & Geary, 2000; McCain, 2000; Newstead, 2000; Oberauer, 2000). The question will undoubtedly motivate continuing research and debate. A substantial number of theorists see the dual-process idea as a means of accounting for the curious mix of automated and reflective mental activities that human cognition appears to be. Whether the character of thinking is captured better by a dichotomous distinction between two modes of processing or by recognizing a continuum anchored by holistic automated actions at one end and analytic consciously controlled actions at the other remains to be seen.

Trends in judgment and decision research

In a commentary on the various perspectives presented in Schneider and Shanteau, Doherty (2003) recounts the major trends in judgment and decision-making research from the 1950s to the present. He contrasts two opposing views, or "camps," that have been prominent in the recent history of this research, which, using terminology credited to Jungermann, he designates "the *optimists*, or the *efficiency* camp," and "the *pessimists*, or the *deficiency* camp" (p. 648). Members of the efficiency camp have a generally high regard for human decision making. They tend to judge the quality of decisions in terms of how well they turn out in the real world rather than in terms of how closely the decision process adheres to the dictates of some formal normative model. Members of the deficiency camp emphasize the many ways in which people can be shown to violate widely recognized principles of sound reasoning.

Noting that optimists must surely recognize deficiencies and that pessimists must surely recognize efficiencies, Doherty anticipates a rapprochement between the two camps, both of which have contributed substantially to our understanding of inference, judgment and choice. He imagines a camp of *realists*, in which most researchers would probably wish to claim membership, that would recognize some truth in both perspectives. As one of two trends that promise further coalescence between the efficiency and deficiency camps, Doherty sees an emerging consensus that there are two modes of cognitive operation—one that is holistic, non-deliberative and fast and another that is more analytic, deliberative and relatively slow. The other such trend is greater recognition of the importance of context and task as determinants of the quality of reasoning.

***

The need for decision making—for selecting among alternative courses of action—is a constant fact of life. To be sure, many of the "decisions" each of us makes on a daily basis we make with very little thought; often habit dictates the choice and we are hardly aware that there are alternatives to what we choose. But we are all aware, from time to time, too, of choices that give us difficulties and tax our ability to think things through—to judge the likely consequences that specific possible selections would have and to evaluate those consequences in terms of our preferences and goals. It is clear that reasoning plays a big role in decision making, but it is equally clear that decision making is involved in reasoning. Nozick (1993) makes the point well: "Our principles of decision and principles of reasoning are intertwined. We reason about which principles of decision to follow.... And we also can decide which principles of reasoning to follow" (p. 135). Few, if any, of the challenges that we face are of greater importance to us as individuals, or as a species, than that of learning to make decisions in a rational—well reasoned—way.

CHAPTER 9

Understanding and Wisdom

> Wisdom is the principle thing; therefore get wisdom: and with all thy getting, get understanding. (Proverbs 4: 7)

The two topics of this chapter—understanding and wisdom—are fundamental, in my view, to what it means to be rational. However, most of what has been written on each is largely opinion and speculation. By contrast with some of the other aspects of rationality that are discussed in this book, relatively little empirical work has been done on either of them. What does it mean to understand? Or to be wise? In considering these questions, perhaps we cannot hope to do more than run around in little circles, but they deserve to be considered nevertheless.

☐ What Does it Mean to Understand?

> Is my understanding only blindness to my own lack of understanding? It often seems so to me. (Wittgenstein, 1972, p. 54)

In preceding sections of this book, the word *understand* has been used with abandon, as though it were always perfectly clear what was meant. Perhaps this is as it should be. Maybe understanding should be treated as a primitive concept; perhaps we should simply assume that we all know what it means to understand, or to fail to understand, and let it go at that. In fact, that is what we do most of the time—at least until someone comes along and convinces us we do not know what we thought we did. And in defense of this approach we might note that raising questions about the meaning of such workhorse words often has an effect similar to that of watching our feet when we run: it changes what was an easy natural process into a more difficult and awkward one. But let us ask the question anyway.

If I say I understand something—an assertion, a concept, a structure, a process, a relationship—what might I mean? I suspect that the answer to this question depends upon, among other things, what it is that is said to be understood. When I say that I understand a poem or a piece of music, I am making a rather different claim than when I say I understand a scientific theory. The state of mind to which I am alluding is perhaps different when I say that I understand an abstract assertion, such as "Democracy is a way of life," than when I claim to understand a particular proof of a mathematical theorem. And it may be different still when I say that I understand why a block of wood floats in water whereas a stone does not. Let us consider a number of connotations that understanding is sometimes given.

Understanding as knowledge

I have argued that understanding something means putting whatever it is that is to be understood into a context of existing knowledge (Nickerson, 1985). Understanding, in this view, is a knowledge-dependent process. The more one knows that is relevant to some new concept, relationship, or process, the easier it will be for one to understand what is new. This is hardly a radical idea, but it deserves emphasis. The implication is that without the necessary existing knowledge base, understanding in specific instances is difficult if not impossible. One cannot hope to understand concepts that are derivative from others that one does not have.

It is for this reason that people who try to explain complex concepts in a specific discipline to people who lack a foundation in that discipline have such a difficult task. This is not to suggest that such efforts are useless, but a non-trivial aspect of the challenge is that of providing the missing context into which the advanced ideas can be put. And the risk of oversimplification and distortion is great; the acquisition of an understanding of complex ideas, at least an understanding of them in any very deep sense of the word, is a laborious process that has no easy shortcuts to success.

The necessity to understanding of the context of existing knowledge is especially obvious in science, where discoveries are continuously changing the existing knowledge base, and often at a rapid pace. As Smolin (2002) points out, no one at the beginning of the 20th century could have understood the words with which physicists talked with each other fifty years later.

Understanding as seeing intent

When A reads something that B has written, A's task is to understand not what B says, but what B means. The task is complicated by the fact that B himself may not understand clearly what he means. It is easy to imagine conversations between two parties in which one participant claims, in all sincerity, to understand what the other has said but really does not. Misunderstanding can occur simply as a consequence of speaker and listener putting different meanings on the same words, but it can have much more subtle origins as well, as when a listener understands what a speaker has said at a superficial level but fails to see the speaker's intent, say, to deceive, ridicule, flatter, or persuade.

Understanding as seeing implications

Can one be said to understand the assertions "A is greater than B" and "B is greater than C" if one does not understand the implicit information they carry in combination, namely that A is greater than C? Certainly, we would say that the understanding of one who does not see this relationship is less complete than is that of one who does. This question illustrates the connection between inference and language comprehension. One focus of the research on linear syllogisms has been on the question of whether the information in the individual assertions is combined into a single linear sequence during the process of comprehension. There is considerable evidence that it generally is (Evans, 1982).

It would be unreasonable to hold that to understand an assertion, or set of assertions, it is necessary to be aware of all its implications or entailments, because, by virtue of such logical relationships as x implies x or y and the possibility of substituting anything under the sun for y, any assertion implies an infinity of others. It may be reasonable, however, to hold that to understand an assertion, or set of assertions, one must understand at least some of its more obvious and meaningful entailments (Black, 1970; Davidson, 1970). It would seem strange, for example, to say that one who rejected the assertion that Fido is a mammal understood and believed the claim that all dogs are mammals and Fido is a dog.

Understanding as seeing the necessity of a relationship

Something may be understood in different ways and to different degrees. One might understand, for example, how to perform long division but not understand the basis for the rules that one applies in the process. One may solve a mathematical problem and be quite convinced that the solution is correct, because one has followed a formal procedure very carefully and, having double-checked one's work, has found no errors in any of the steps. Having solved the problem, one might then say that one understands a relationship that one did not understand before.

Understanding in this way however, is different from, and may be less satisfying than, understanding a relationship because one "sees" that it must be a certain way. Sometimes in mathematics, one may solve a problem analytically, and then, after having obtained the solution, gain some insight that will permit one to tell oneself with some confidence that the answer must be of that type, that it could not be otherwise. Poincaré makes a similar distinction in the following way. "To understand the demonstration of a theorem, is that to examine successively each syllogism composing it and ascertain its correctness, its conformity to the rules of the game? . . . For some, yes; when they have done this, they will say, I understand. For the majority, no. Almost all are much more exacting; they wish to know not merely whether all the syllogisms of a demonstration are correct, but why they link together in this order rather than another. In so far as to them they seem engendered by caprice and not by an intelligence always conscious of the end to be attained, they do not believe they understand. Doubtless they are not themselves just conscious of what they crave, and they could not formulate their desire, but if they do not get satisfaction, they vaguely feel that something is lacking" (quoted in Hadamard, 1945/1954, p. 104).

Perhaps the following problem will illustrate the difference between being convinced of the problem's solution by following a step-wise procedure for inferring it and being convinced by "seeing" what the nature of the solution must be. Consider two containers, one of which, call it A, contains 10 ounces of water from the Atlantic and the other of which, P, contains 10 ounces of water from the Pacific. Suppose that, first, 2 ounces are taken from A and mixed thoroughly with the water in P, and then 2 ounces are taken from P (which now holds a mixture of Pacific and Atlantic water) and returned to A. Which container ends up with the greater amount of "foreign" water, Atlantic water being foreign to P and Pacific water being foreign to A?

One may solve this problem in a step-wise fashion: 2 ounces of Atlantic going into 10 ounces of Pacific yields in P 12 ounces of water with Pacific and Atlantic in the ratio of 10:2. When 2 ounces of this mixture is then put into A, it leaves 10 ounces in P of the mixture in the same ratio of 10:2, which means 8 1/3 ounces of Pacific and 1 2/3 ounces of Atlantic. The 2 ounces of mixture that is going to A contains Pacific and Atlantic water in the ratio 10:2, which means it is composed of 1 2/3 ounces of Pacific and 1/3 ounce of Atlantic. When this is added to the 8 ounces of Atlantic that is in A, A will contain 8 1/3 ounces of Atlantic and 1 2/3 of Pacific; which is to say that the ratio of Atlantic to Pacific water in it will be 10:2. So when the mixing and switching is done the amount of foreign water in each container is the same.

Alternatively, one may see at once that the amount of foreign water in each container must be the same, because, inasmuch as both containers begin and end with 10 ounces of water, however much of the non-foreign water that is missing from either container must have been replaced by an equal amount of water from the other container. Looking at the problem this way makes it clear also that the same answer holds no matter how much water is in the containers at the start (as long as it is the same in both), no matter how much is transferred (as long as it is the same in both directions) and whether or not the contents of the mixture was thoroughly stirred after the first, or any subsequent, transfer. As long as we start and finish with the same amount in both containers, it matters not how many transfers are made or how much is transferred in each case.

It is not the case, of course, that all problems lend themselves so readily to such disparate analyses. I wish only to illustrate that there is a difference between accepting a solution because one is convinced of the validity of a step-wise process that yields it and of "seeing" at some deeper level why the solution is what it is. Poincaré's point is that in mathematics one often has to settle for the former, but that many, if not most, mathematicians typically strive for something closer to the latter, and it is when they attain that that they are most likely to feel that they understand.

Understanding as having an adequate mental model

One current view of what it means to understand a phenomenon is to have a *mental model* of it in mind (Johnson-Laird, 1983). A model need not be complete or completely accurate in order to be useful. Indeed, Johnson-Laird holds, really complete models for empirical phenomena do not exist; moreover the usefulness of a model is not necessarily increased when information is added to it beyond a certain level. To have a mental model of a phenomenon is to have a representation of the phenomenon that can be examined independently of the phenomenon itself; to the extent that the examination of that representation permits one to make accurate descriptive statements about the phenomenon, it seems reasonable to say that having such a representation constitutes understanding of a sort.

DeKleer and Brown (1980) also equate understanding of a system with having a mental model or "envisionment" of that system and, in particular, a dynamic representation that permits one to simulate the behavior of the system in one's imagination. One understands a system, at least in terms of its behavior, according to this view, to the degree that one's dynamic model permits one to infer how the system will act under specified conditions, including novel or faulty ones.

A major challenge to the understanding of many of the concepts and relationships that science gives us is that of getting an intuitive feel for the quantities or magnitudes involved. Measures of extent that are within a few orders of magnitude in either direction of a foot are intuitively graspable, but we find it difficult to get an intuitive feel for the ultrasmall (submicron, say) and ultralarge (light years). Similarly, we can grasp quantities that are within a few orders of magnitude of 10, but we have difficulty making intuitive sense of quantities that must be expressed in exponential form and that have large exponents, either positive or negative.

A common approach in attempting to make very large or very small magnitudes or quantities intuitively meaningful is to use analogies. Consider the cells from which our bodies are made, which average about 10 microns in length. There are lots of cells in a human body—in the neighborhood of 10^{13} or 10^{14}, by some estimates. Each cell contains roughly a billion (10^9) proteins, each of which contains on the order of five thousand (5×10^3) atoms, which means that a body has on the order of 10^{26} atoms. How does one—if one wants to—get an intuitive feel for what that means?

Goodsell (1998) suggests, for the case of the cell, imagining a typical-sized room filled with rice grains to get an idea of the number of cells (a billion or so) that make up the last joint in one's finger. The same analogy can be used to get a feel for the number of proteins in a single cell. The number of atoms in a protein, about 5,000, is perhaps a bit closer to what one can imagine without the analogical crutch. Putting all this together gives one, at least in a step-wise fashion, perhaps a slightly—but only slightly—better understanding of what it means to be composed of 10^{26} atoms than does simply staring at the number itself.

Understanding and multiple representations

McKellar (1957) also ties the idea of mental models to what it means to understand. He further suggests that one understands something to the extent that one can represent it in more than one way. McKellar's use of the concept of mental model only faintly presages Johnson-Laird's extensive development and application of it, but the point that understanding involves the ability to represent something in a variety of ways strikes me as an important insight. The idea has been promoted more recently by Stevens and Collins (1977, 1980) and Collins, Brown, and Larkin (1980).

Investigators of human problem solving have put great emphasis on the ability to find a useful representation of a problem as a critical first step in solving it and have presented evidence that the representations that problem solvers who are highly knowledgeable in the problem domain construct are often qualitatively different from the representations constructed by those who are not so knowledgeable with respect to that domain (deKleer, 1977; Greeno, 1980; Nilsson, 1971; Simon & Hayes, 1976). Collins, Brown, and K. Larkin (1980) suggest that one way of characterizing an expert is as a person who not only has multiple representations of a given system but knows how the different models relate to each other and how to use them to advantage.

There are many instances in mathematics of relationships being representable in more than one way. Understanding of a relationship that is represented one way may be facilitated by considering how the same relationship could be represented in a qualitatively different way. Often it is helpful, for example, to consider both algebraic and geometric representations of the same relationship. Understanding of the relationship $(a + b)^2 = a^2 + 2ab + b^2$ may be enriched by consideration of Figure 9.1.

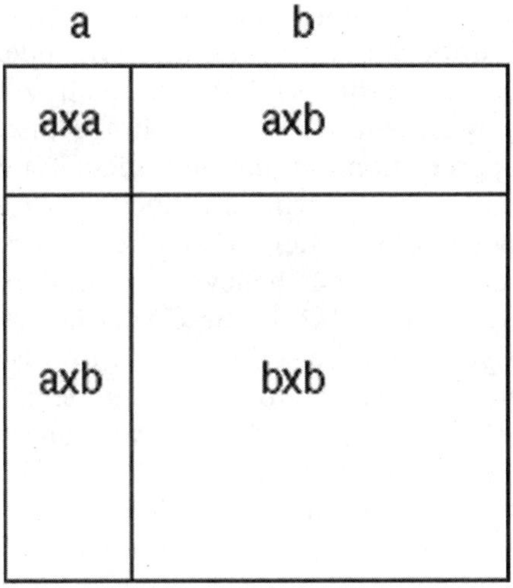

FIGURE 9.1 Illustrating the relationship $(a + b)^2 = a^2 + 2ab + b^2$.

Understanding as seeing equivalences

If I say that I understand the assertion that A is larger than B and that I understand the assertion that B is smaller than A, but then insist that these assertions are incompatible with each other, you would undoubtedly question whether I understand what I claim to understand. There are many examples in the research literature, not quite as stark as this illustration, of people failing to see the equivalence of different ways of saying the same thing. This is especially true in the area of probabilistic reasoning. For example, people, including professionals making judgments in their area of expertise, often fail to see the equivalence of claims expressed in probabilistic terms to essentially the same claims expressed in terms of relative frequencies (Slovic, Monahan, & MacGregor, 2000; Yamagishi, 1997). Similarly, they sometimes fail also to see the equivalence of relationships expressed in terms of absolute frequencies (50 out of 1,000) to the same relationships expressed as probabilities (.05) or percentages (5 percent) (Cosmides & Tooby, 1990; Gigerenzer, 1993, 1994; Gigerenzer & Hoffrage, 1995).

***

There is no simple answer, in my view, to what it means to understand. It means different things in different contexts. Whatever connotation it is given, understanding must be thought of as something that can vary in degree. There is a difference between understanding something deeply and in detail and understanding it only superficially. And there is a difference between understanding something only superficially, but correctly as far as the understanding goes, and misunderstanding, which means believing something that is not true. Perhaps what is most important for rationality is an awareness of the limits of one's understanding—an accurate appreciation of what one understands well, what one understands less than well, and what one does not understand at all.

Surely it is possible to believe that one understands something when, in fact, one does not. I may believe that I understand how to read and follow a wiring diagram, while the electrician who has to fix my botched job knows very well that I do not. Most of us probably get into trouble from time to time by believing that we understand the intentions or motivations of others when, in fact, we have them wrong.

A particularly subtle form of pseudo understanding is that that mistakes familiarity with understanding. The old saw has it that familiarity breeds contempt; what may be equally true is that familiarity breeds a false sense of understanding. The fact that one has learned to speak the jargon of a discipline is not compelling evidence that one has acquired a deep understanding of that of which one speaks. As Atkins (1994) puts it, "Names are codes; we should not let familiarity with them masquerade as understanding" (p. 15). The ease with which naming can be mistaken for explanation was discussed in chapter 6. An aspect of the confusion between naming and explaining that was not discussed there is the phenomenon of reification, or the tendency to assume that a name implies a referenced entity. Freud gave names to a variety of concepts—id, ego, superego, libido. Whether these terms refer to entities that actually exist in some sense other than as concepts that can be defined (as the concepts unicorn, tooth fairy, and Atlantis can be defined) has been a matter of considerable debate. The point I wish to make here is that it does not follow from the fact that a name exists that there exists some entity (thing, substance, essence) to which the name refers, and that overlooking this can yield a false sense of understanding.

☐ The Desire to Understand

We use effectively things and principles that we do not understand at more than a superficial level, if at that. Most of us who drive automobiles, I suspect, do not understand the operation of an internal combustion engine in any detail. Nor do those of us who daily make use of telephones, radios, televisions, computers, and a myriad of other devices electronic and otherwise, have more than the skimpiest of comprehension of the principles on which they work. Even the experts may have a much more limited understanding of some aspects of their areas of expertise than is generally recognized. Miller (2003) surmises that few of the numerous physicists who use quantum theory daily think about its interpretive subtleties. Feynman (1985) went so far as to opine that nobody understands quantum mechanics. The theory is accepted and applied by physicists not because it provides deep insights into why things are the way they are, but because it works in the sense of providing a basis for making precise predictions that prove to be true and immensely useful to practical ends. Greene (1999) makes the same point: "in a real sense those who use quantum mechanics find themselves following rules and formulas laid down by the 'founding fathers' of the theory—calculational procedures that are straightforward to carry out—without really understanding *why* the procedures work or *what* they really mean" (p. 87). "[B]eyond the fact that it is a mathematically coherent theory, the only reason we believe in quantum mechanics is because it yields predictions that have been verified to astounding accuracy" (p. 88).

Every high school student who has taken an introductory physics course—perhaps even a general science course—knows that light is believed to have properties both of waves and of particles and that which type of property one observes depends on the experiment one does. But whether anyone really understands how light can be both wave-like and particulate at the same time is doubtful. As Greene (1999) puts it: "We can utter words such as 'wave-particle duality.' We can translate these words into a mathematical formalism that describes real-world experiments with amazing accuracy. But it is extremely hard to understand at a deep, intuitive level this dazzling feature of the microscopic world" (p. 103). Learning that wave-particle duality applies to matter as well as to light does not make the idea easier to grasp.

But despite the fact that we manage to get along nicely in day-to-day life without understanding very deeply much (most?) of what we see about us, there can be no doubting that a desire to understand—curiosity—is a strong motivator of human behavior. Many have argued that it is one of the major characteristics, if not *the* characteristic, that distinguishes mankind from other species. A few examples:

- The urge to understand has differentiated man form all other creatures on the planet (Bromley, 1986, p. 622).

- The human beings were different primarily because they were the only species intensely curious about their surroundings (Lederman, 1993, p. 2).

- This tendency [to search for truth that it can represent as scientific laws], peculiar to the human race, is that which renders it superior to animals; and their progress in this respect distinguishes nations and ages and constitutes their true glory (Laplace, 1814/1956, p. 1326).

- It is intellectual curiosity and the accompanying ability to investigate the laws of nature and benefit from investigation that distinguish the human species from other forms of life (Jackson, Tigner, & Wojcicki, 1986, p. 6).

- To understand is the most human act of the human being, and all true human action is based on understanding, seeks understanding, finds understanding. Understanding is the innermost bond between humans, and the basis of all moral existence (Droysen, 1960, p. 26, quoted in Albert, 1985, p. 170, footnote 9).

What is the basis of this defining curiosity? Why do we wish to understand? Some observers have found it to be surprising that we, as a species, have not only the curiosity, but the intellectual resources that are necessary to do science. Presumably our brains evolved over millions of years, during almost all of which time the kinds of questions now addressed by science were of no consequence to us. Our main purpose, like that of any other animal, was to survive—to obtain food, avoid predators, and attain some measure of comfort. "What," asks Davies (1992), "has this got to do with discovering the laws of electromagnetism or the structure of the atom?" (p. 149). What is there in our history that can explain not only the intense desire to acquire knowledge, even that which has no practical utility, but our apparent ability to do so?

Consider the enormous effort that has been, and is being, put into understanding the origin and ultimate fate of the universe. Of what practical value, one might ask, is the knowledge of whether the universe came into existence 13 or so billion years ago, instead of, say, 5 billion or 20 billion? Of what practical relevance to our day-to-day existence is the knowledge of whether the universe will collapse many billions of years hence or go on expanding indefinitely? Why should we care a whit whether black holes really exist, or whether neutrinos have mass, or what makes pulsars pulse? Whatever the answer to why we care about such things there can be no question that we do care. Many of the best minds the species has produced have devoted themselves to trying to extend our understanding of the universe in which we find ourselves, arguably for no more compelling reason than that of extending our understanding of the universe in which we find ourselves. The urge itself is remarkable, but so, as Davies and others have noted, is the apparent ability to ask and answer questions that have little direct relevance to our survival as individuals or as a species.

☐ Evidences of Understanding

A major challenge of teaching is to get students to understand what is being taught. How can one be sure that someone else understands a concept, a relationship, a principle, a process? Perhaps one cannot. For that matter, how can one be sure that one understands such things oneself? Again, perhaps one cannot. But for practical purposes we may be willing to accept various evidences of understanding by others or ourselves. These include the ability to use concepts appropriately, which is to say, in a way that other people who presumably understand them find acceptable; the ability to communicate effectively with people who are knowledgeable with respect to a given domain; the ability to apply a principle consistently in a variety of contexts; the ability to carry out a process or procedure in such a way as to obtain consistently the desired results; the subjective confidence that one understands—"sees"—a relationship or principle; the ability to draw analogies that are considered appropriate by people who are knowledgeable with respect to the domain. Although none of these evidences is infallible, combinations of them perhaps constitute as strong evidence of understanding as we can hope to get.

The ability to paraphrase, to explain an idea "in one's own terms," or to express or represent an idea in more than one way is sometimes taken as good evidence of understanding. McKellar (1957) promotes this view in connection with his association of understanding with the construction of mental models. As he uses the term, mental models are at once vehicles for understanding and for communication. Understanding is said to be limited when one is unable to represent a given idea in more than one way. The best evidence that one indeed does understand an idea, McKellar argues, is one's ability not just to convey the idea in the words in which one encountered it, but in qualitatively different terms—to present it from a different perspective, as it were. Evidence of understanding "may be found in the ability to provide re-exposition and *alternative* models. An individual's ability to put into other words something he has been told and claims to 'understand' is convincing evidence of his genuine understanding. Furthermore, a thinker's ability to re-expound his *own* thought, to use other mental models when asked to 'explain' what he means, is good evidence that he himself knows what he means" (p. 181).

McKellar's stress on the ability to express or expound a concept in words other than those in which it was acquired is similar to the idea that if one really understands a concept, one ought to be able to apply it appropriately in unanticipated situations or in novel ways. DeKleer and Brown (1980) make a similar point in suggesting that evidence of the adequacy of one's dynamic model or envisionment of a system is its ability to provide the basis for correct answers to unanticipated questions about the behavior of the system under a variety of conditions.

Lack of understanding, especially in academic situations, can sometimes be masked by an individual's superficial knowledge of formulas and ability to manipulate them (Clement, 1982). This is an unfortunate possibility in an educational context because it means that students may be able to "do well" in certain academic situations without revealing that they do not understand at a more-than-superficial level what they are doing or why they are doing it. Clement (1981a) describes a variety of situations in which students have been found to be able to apply a mathematical procedure to get the correct answer to a problem but have shown when probed that they did not have a sufficiently good understanding of the underlying concepts to be able to apply them effectively to practical problems. Clement refers to such knowledge as "formula-centered" knowledge.

Formula-centered knowledge, thus conceived, is suggestive of the kind of knowledge that Searle (1980) made famous in his "Chinese-room" argument against the claims of "strong artificial intelligence" that suitably programmed computers can properly be said to *understand*. Searle likens a computer that gives the appearance of understanding to an individual who has learned to apply a set of rules to sets of abstract shapes to produce other sets of abstract shapes, without realizing the shapes involved are Chinese characters. If the rules are such that the sets of shapes the individual produces are interpreted by someone who understands Chinese as answers to questions represented by the shapes to which the individual responded, an observer would naturally, but wrongly, conclude that the individual understood Chinese. Searle's argument has evoked a great deal of discussion and debate, which will not be considered here; the salient point for present purposes is that the appearance of understanding can be misleading.

Formula-centered knowledge is of limited value inasmuch as formulas themselves fail to provide one with information as to when they should be used; consequently such knowledge is likely to lead to the application of formulas in inappropriate contexts. Formula-centered knowledge also would be an inadequate basis for the development of effective qualitative models of a problem situation and this helps explain why people who lack expertise in a particular area are less likely to use such models than are people who have that expertise.

☐ Degrees of Understanding

> The calculus was difficult to Newton and Weierstrass; it is easy only to those who understand it too easily. (Bell, 1945/1992, p. 150)

Certainly it is possible to be convinced that one understands something when one really does not. "We all think we know what continuity means, but some of us, surely, are inclined to wriggle uncomfortably when we learn of a function that is discontinuous at every rational number but continuous at every irrational one. (A much deeper and much more famous monster is a curve that turns continuously everywhere but has a tangent nowhere.) We are all sure we know what connectedness means, but aren't we inclined to be skeptical when we learn of a curve that consists of two pieces (such as a circle and spiral winding infinitely often around it) that is nevertheless called connected? In any event, I maintain that a student does *not* know what continuity and connectedness mean till he knows examples such as these" (Halmos, 1985, p. 63).

Marr (1982) distinguishes three levels of understanding of any information-processing device. At the most abstract level, one understands the device by being familiar with its computational theory—the theoretical account of the functional relationship between its input and its output. At the next level, understanding involves the details of how the input-output mapping is done—the process by which input gets transformed into output. At the most concrete level, one understands by knowing how the process is implemented physically. Massaro and Solso (1995) contrast Marr's levels in computer terms, likening the computational level to an abstract description of the problem to be solved, the algorithmic level to the problem-solving software, and the implementation level to the system on which the software runs.

The considerable interest among psychologists and cognitive scientists in developing computational models of various aspects of human perception and cognition reflects a pursuit of understanding at the level of computational theory (Broadbent, 1993; Meyer & Kieras, 1998). A computational model may provide an understanding of how an input-output transfer *could* be done computationally—an existence proof of the adequacy of a specific algorithmic transfer function—without demonstrating that the transfer necessarily is performed this way by humans. The ultimate goal of neuroscience research presumably is understanding at the level of how brain structures and mechanisms actually produce the phenomena of interest.

Determining whether, or the extent to which, one understands something seems likely to increase with the complexity of whatever it is that is to be understood. But what constitutes conceptual complexity, and can it be characterized in such a way that one could judge objectively and unambiguously which of any two concepts is the more complex? This is a difficult question, but one plausible answer would emphasize the importance of connections. The general notion is that the complexity of a concept is determined by the number and nature of the other concepts to which it is connected—the concepts that must be understood in order for the concept in question to be understood.

It is not necessary to have a full-blown theory of conceptual complexity to recognize that some concepts are more complex—more difficult—than others, and perhaps this is enough to justify the conjecture that complexity has something to do with our ability to determine whether something is understood. Determining whether one understands a simple command (close the door, put the book on the table, turn on the light) seems relatively straightforward. If one follows such instructions correctly, we would presumably be willing to take this as evidence that one understands them. This is not to say, however, that the fact that one can follow instructions demonstrates that one understands deeply all that is involved in doing do. I might be able to follow the instructions to identify which of several words (*mitochondria, nucleotide, quark*) is most likely to appear in a paragraph that contains also the word *gluon*, but I have only the fuzziest understanding of what a gluon is. To think of the understanding of complex concepts as an all-or-nothing affair is a great oversimplification; clearly we understand to greater or lesser degrees.

Many things can be understood at more than one level or in more than one way: metaphors, analogies, stories with morals, jokes, puns, double-entendres. When one interprets only literally what is intended to be a metaphor, or one follows a parable as a narrative account but fails to see the moral, we say that one misses the point. One can read *Gulliver's Travels* as an adventure fantasy or one can see in it also a satirical commentary on certain social phenomena of the times; we would say that the latter understanding of the work is a fuller one than the former.

One might assume that most high school graduates, certainly those who have studied mathematics through algebra would understand the meaning of the "equals" sign (=) as it is used in mathematics. But how plausible is this assumption? Realizing that the expression to the left of this sign is, in some sense, "equal to" the expression to the right of it represents some understanding of the meaning of the sign—certainly a better understanding than the assumption that it means one should add the expressions to the left and right of the sign. But a more complete understanding of the sign would recognize that it can be used to signify a tautology ($2+4 = 6$), a functional relationship ($y = 2x$), a constraint equation ($x^2+3x-10 = 0$), or a definition ($u = dy/dx$), and that the meanings in these uses are not all equivalent.

One can understand an analogy in the sense of recognizing the similarity between A and B and using one's knowledge of A to enhance one's understanding of B, without necessarily having a very deep understanding of the concept of analogy per se. In other words, it is one thing to use an analogy to facilitate understanding of one of the analogs, and it is quite another to understand what an analogy—any analogy—is. The latter should involve a realization that analogies have limits beyond which they should not be pressed and that proof by analogy is no proof at all.

☐ Common Misconceptions

It would be unrealistic to expect everyone to hold only beliefs about the world that are consistent with the latest scientific views, but a question of some practical significance is whether there are widely-shared misconceptions about natural phenomena. To the extent that failures to understand in specific instances can be attributed, at least in part, to such misconceptions, it should be possible to realize some educational leverage by focusing on ways to correct those particular misconceptions or of preventing them from arising in the first place.

That common misconceptions exist is suggested by the consistency with which certain types of errors are made when people attempt to answer questions about physical phenomena. An example for which Clement (1980, 1981a, b, 1982) has obtained evidence, is the belief that continuing motion implies the presence of a continuing force in the direction of the motion. Clement refers to this belief, which corresponds closely to the impetus theory of motion once held by Galileo and other scientists before the days of Newton, as the "motion implies force" misconception. It appears to be highly resistant to change; it has been found even among students who have successfully completed college-level courses in mechanics, which illustrates the ease with which new ideas encountered in physics courses are sometimes interpreted in such a way as to make them fit preconceptions.

Many students confuse rates with amounts, and changes in rates with rates—velocity with distance, acceleration with velocity, rate of inflation with dollar value (Lochhead, 1981; Trowbridge & McDermott, 1980, 1981). Why it is difficult to teach such distinctions is not clear. One possibility that has been suggested is that the representation of rate (and change in rate) relationships by mathematical equations is inherently static and does not facilitate an appreciation of the fact that the relationships themselves are dynamic (Clement, Lochhead, & Monk, 1981; Clement, Lochhead, & Soloway, 1980).

There is some evidence that such relationships may be conveyed more effectively in the language of computer programming than as algebraic expressions (Lochhead, 1981). The idea is that programming-language representations are more suggestive of operations performed on variables than are algebraic expressions. Lochhead also suggests that even greater facilitation in the teaching of rate concepts might be obtained from the use of computer-based dynamic representations of relationships between variables to illustrate various ways in which two functionally related variables may change together.

A number of studies have yielded results that suggest that many of the errors that students make when doing basic arithmetic are not the result of carelessness or lack of understanding of essential number facts but of the execution of incorrect procedures or "faulty algorithms" (Asklock, 1976; Bennett, 1976; Brown & Burton, 1978; Lankford, 1972; Sleeman, 1984; Woodward, & Howard, 1994; Young & O'Shea, 1981). This is not to say that faulty algorithms are the only source of errors of arithmetic, or that carelessness and lack of basic number facts are never implicated, but only that faulty algorithms appear to be a major source of difficulty.

The various evidences mentioned here of lack of understanding by students of concepts, relationships, principles or processes that they have studied are drawn from a number of different investigations. They do not constitute the results of a systematic attempt to identify the major kinds of conceptual difficulties that students have in specific subjects. However, if the problems that these investigations have identified are at all representative of the types of confusions that students carry away from formal educational programs, they represent a serious challenge to the educational establishment to find more effective ways to facilitate understanding.

☐ Limitations of Understanding

> If science is the understanding of interesting shapes in nature, how does this understanding come about? How can we tell what things not yet understood are capable of being understood? (Polyani, 1964, p. 14)

We necessarily understand the world in terms of the concepts and theories of our time. Galileo could not understand natural phenomena in terms of Newtonian mechanics and Newton could not understand them in terms of the concepts of relativity. We cannot understand them in terms of the physics of the 22nd century. Perhaps a description of our world and of ourselves will never be written in the language of "final" science; one hopes not, because that would mean that there would be nothing left to discover. In any case, our understanding can never be more than an understanding in terms of current models of, or theories about, the world.

And the understanding that theories about the world provide is bound always, one suspects, to be extremely limited. Thomas Huxley once put the matter this way: "In ultimate analysis everything is incomprehensible and the whole object of science is simply to reduce the fundamental incomprehensibilities to the smallest possible number" (quoted in Eisley, 1967, p. 18). More recently Nagel (1986) expressed a similar idea: "since we are who we are, we can't get outside of ourselves completely. Whatever we do, we remain subparts of the world with limited access to the real nature of the rest of it and of ourselves. There is no way of telling how much of reality lies beyond the reach of present or future objectivity or any other conceivable form of human understanding" (p. 6).

Nevertheless, we wish intensely to understand. We work for this goal, and we think we realize some degree of success. We believe that, as a species, we understand the universe in which we live better than did our predecessors. But we understand better too that our understanding is tenuous and woefully incomplete. The paradox is that the more we learn, the more we are made aware of the depth of our ignorance; the better we understand, the greater the mysteries that emerge from that understanding. But would we really want it any other way? The establishment of a "theory of everything" that could provide an answer to every question one might think to ask strikes me as about the most boring eventuality imaginable; I have no fear of it happening.

☐ What Is Wisdom?

> The neglect, indeed the rejection, of wisdom has gone so far that most of our intellectuals have not even the faintest idea what the term could mean. (Schumacher, 1973, p. 39)

What is wisdom? What do people think it is? Do people agree on this? Do people who study wisdom agree what it is? Can it be measured? Can it be acquired? Is it unique to old age? Is a wise person best described in terms of characteristics? Of capabilities? How does wisdom relate to knowledge, intelligence, judgment?

There are many references to wisdom in religious and philosophical literature. Wisdom is generally presented as highly desirable but rarely acquired. King Solomon pleased God by asking, upon becoming Israel's third king, not for long life or riches or victory over his enemies, but for "an understanding heart" that he might rule wisely; God gave him "a wise and understanding heart" and promised him also the riches and honor for which he had not asked. Perhaps the best known illustration of his wisdom is the account of his settling of a dispute between two women, each of whom claimed to be the mother of the same child. Solomon instructed that the child be cut in two so that each mother could have half, and when one of the mothers, upon hearing this decision, gave up her claim to the child so its life would be spared, Solomon declared that woman to be the true mother and gave the child to her (I Kings 3).

In *The Republic* Plato likens normal life to existence within a cave and perception to the watching by the cave dwellers of the shadows cast by fire against a cave wall. The cave dwellers consider these shadows to be "real" because that is all they have ever seen. A wise person, in this metaphor, is the rare individual who has emerged from the cave long enough to see the outside world in the light of the sun and to learn the difference between reality and the shadows in the cave. It is the responsibility of such a person to return to the cave with this knowledge and to help the cave dwellers understand that what they are looking at is a reflection only and that something more real exists.

The attainment of wisdom was given the highest priority by Plato and other Greek philosophers, who distinguished it from other mental abilities. Wisdom was seen less as a skill, like facility with computation, than as a character trait. It was projected in a style of living and behaving, a commitment to reasoned deliberation, reflection and choice. The rule of reason over passion figured prominently in classical views, as did self-knowledge, moderation, minimization of personal material wants, and acceptance of the inevitable (Robinson, 1990).

The perceived importance of wisdom to peace of mind is seen in the widely quoted "serenity prayer," of the 2nd-century Roman philosopher emperor, Marcus Aurelius: "God grant me the serenity to accept the things I cannot change, the courage to change the things I can, and the wisdom to tell the difference." The same thought is expressed, if somewhat more prosaically, by Birren and Fisher (1990): "Wisdom is tested in circumstances in which we have to decide what is changeable and what is not" (p. 324).

Wisdom remained a topic of considerable interest to philosophers until relatively recent times (Holliday & Chandler, 1986). However, interest in the concept appears to have waned, even among philosophers, as, partly through the influence of logical positivism, the tendency to focus on knowledge produced by the empirical methods of science became predominant. Perhaps because it has produced such tangible and obvious results, scientific thinking has become so highly valued by contemporary society that, in the view of some, legitimate alternative or complementary ways of knowing have suffered neglect (Marcel, 1951; Habermas, 1970).

As a focus of research or reflection, wisdom has never enjoyed the status among psychologists as has, say, perception, emotion, instinct, or motivation. It is not surprising, perhaps, that the concept received little attention during the decades when Watsonian behaviorism exerted its greatest influence—one looks in vain for discussions of it in general reviews of experimental psychology, such as those of Osgood (1953) and Woodworth and Schlosberg (1956)—but its neglect predates the general aversion toward mentalistic concepts shown by nearly all psychologists during this time; the word does not appear in the index of James's (1890/1983) *Principles of Psychology*, or of those of such classics as Bruner, Goodnow, and Austin's (1956) *A Study of Thinking*, Bartlett's (1958) *Thinking: An Experimental and Social Study*, or Inhelder and Piaget's (1958) *The Growth of Logical Thinking from Childhood to Adolescence*. Nor is it in the indices of such anthologies and collections of papers on thinking as those of Johnson-Laird and Wason (1977), Dillon and Sternberg (1986), Baron and Sternberg (1987), Jones and Idol (1990), or Mulcahy, Short, and Andrews (1991). But the concept has begun to receive some attention from psychologists and other social scientists. What follows is a cursory look at some relatively recent work, much of which is reported in Sternberg (1990a), and some of the conceptions of wisdom it offers.

Wisdom as a cognitive process

Csikszentmihalyi and Rathunde (1990) see three major dimensions of meaning in the treatment of the concept of wisdom by past thinkers: "It can be seen as a *cognitive* process, or a peculiar way of obtaining and processing information; as a *virtue*, or socially valued pattern of behavior; or as a *good*, or personally desirable state or condition" (p. 28). All three of these dimensions, they suggest, are relevant to an understanding of the concept. The distinctiveness of wisdom as a cognitive process, is seen, they argue, in claims that it:

a. does not deal with the appearance of fleeting phenomena but with enduring universal truths;

b. is not specialized but is an attempt to apprehend how the various aspects of reality are related to each other;

c. is not a value-free way of knowing but implies a hierarchical ordering of truths and actions directed at those truths (p. 28).

Csikszentmihalyi and Rathunde note that one major problem with this view is the lack of agreement among thinkers as to what the enduring truths are that lie behind appearances. Despite this obvious difficulty, one might still want to assume that there are such truths, that some approximations thereto are more enduring than others, and that the wise individual seeks to distinguish between the more and less enduring aspects of experience.

Wisdom as knowledge, understanding, insight, or good judgment

Baltes and Smith (1990) equate wisdom with knowledge, referring to it as "an expert knowledge system about the fundamental pragmatics of life" (p. 94). One factor analysis of words used in descriptions of wisdom or wise people yielded exceptional understanding as one key construct, among four others (Holliday & Chandler, 1986). (The other factors produced by this analysis were judgment and communication skills, general competence, interpersonal skills, and social unobtrusiveness.) Chandler and Holliday (1990) associate wisdom with a broad form of understanding that is to be contrasted with narrow forms of expertise. They react negatively to the use of expertise and specialization as key concepts in a model of wisdom, and ask whether such a model leaves any place for the concepts of wisdom and wise as ordinarily understood. Everyone knows, they contend, that there are many experts in narrowly specialized domains that no one would accuse of being wise.

Sternberg (1985) had professionals and laypersons rate each of a list of behaviors with respect to the extent to which they characterized wisdom, intelligence and creativity. A correlation analysis showed wisdom to be closer in character to intelligence than to creativity. On the basis of this analysis, Sternberg (1990a) compared and contrasted wisdom, intelligence, and creativity with respect to six aspects: knowledge, cognitive processing, intellectual style, personality, motivation, and environmental context. With respect to motivation, for example, the wise person is said to be motivated "to understand what is known and what it means," the intelligent person "to know and to use what is known," and the creative person "to go beyond what is known." The characterization of wisdom in terms of Sternberg's six aspects is striking in the fact that "understanding" appears in summarized descriptions of five of the six.

A kind of probing inquisitiveness that leads to new insights is sometimes seen as an important aspect of wisdom. Arlin (1990), for example, sees wisdom as having more to do with question asking or problem finding than with question answering or problem solving. She notes that a comparable emphasis on the importance of problem finding, as distinct from problem solving, was made by Merton (1945) and Mackworth (1965) in their accounts of original and especially productive work in science. She sees a problem-finding mind set as important not only for scientists, but for anyone who would aspire to be wise. "The questions that one asks of one's life, one's experience, and one's discipline when one has thought deeply about such matters may be the single most powerful predictor of one's decisions and judgments and of the wisdom of those decisions and judgments" (p. 240).

Judgment (good judgment, mature judgment, fair judgment) appears prominently in many conceptions of wisdom (Baltes, Dittmann-Kohli, & Dixon, 1984; Baltes & Smith,1990; Dixon, Kramer & Baltes, 1985; Holliday & Chandler, 1986; Kitchener & Brenner, 1990; Sternberg, 1985). Baltes and colleagues stress the ability to exercise good judgment especially under conditions of uncertainty as a distinctive characteristic of wise persons. Kitchener and Brenner (1990) do the same.

Wisdom as a virtue

To the classical Greeks, wisdom was not only a virtue, but was among the highest virtues to which one could aspire; it was held out as a goal toward which one should strive throughout one's entire life. The attainment of the virtue of wisdom, in some measure, qualified one to assume leadership roles in society. In Plato's *Republic*, it was to the wise, and not the merely clever, that governance was to be entrusted. Only individuals who were themselves ruled by wisdom were considered fit to rule others.

Csikszentmihalyi and Rathunde (1990) suggest that the ancient equating of wisdom with virtue not only still makes sense but that it is more relevant today than ever before. "It can be argued that the various limits on objective perception and reasoning the social sciences have revealed—repressions, defenses, bad faith, false consciousness, ethnocentricism, conditioned responses, suggestibility, and so on—are precisely the concrete 'particulars' of experience that Plato argued the philosopher must overcome in order to see the underlying truth, and thus get closer to wisdom" (p. 35).

Wisdom as self-transcendence

A common theme in the treatment of wisdom by personality theorists (e.g., Erikson, Jung, & Kohut) is the idea of self-transcendence (Orwoll &

Perlmuter, 1990). The wise person, according to this view, is characterized by an exceptionally mature personality and is less inclined than most to be preoccupied with self-referent thoughts and feelings. Although the wise person is likely to have a variety of other distinguishing characteristics as well, it is the self-transcendent aspect of personality, Orwoll and Perlmutter argue, that makes wisdom unique.

Pascual-Leone (1990) expresses a similar idea. Wisdom, in his view, involves affect and personality, as well as cognition, and its attainment is marked by an increasing ability to focus outside oneself—"a weakening of ego-centered characteristics, which leads to greater intuition and emphatic understanding of other, self, world, and nature as equally strong concerns" (p. 272). Pascual-Leone sees wisdom as an *"asymptotic state of normal human growth toward maturity,"* which, alas, "is rarely attained." Other writers who have emphasized empathy and concern for others as important aspects of wisdom include Brent and Watson (1980) and Clayton (1976).

Wisdom as balance

Labouvie-Vief (1990) defines wisdom as the "smooth and relatively balanced dialogue" between two modes of thought, one of which "provides experiential richness and fluidity, the other logical cohesion and stability" (p. 53). Labouvie-Vief refers to the first mode as *mythos* and the second as *logos*. Logos thinking, which involves knowledge that is arguable, demonstrable, precisely definable, and mechanizable, is generally given considerably more credence than mythos thinking, which is less analytical and more intuitive. Mythos thinking tends to be seen, Labouvie-Vief suggests, as an immature and degraded form of logos thinking.

Wise thinking involves both of these modes, in Labouvie-Vief's view. The wise person realizes that if thinking is limited to that which can be subjected to the strictures of logic, disembodied from a flesh-and-blood thinker and mechanized, it will yield an incomplete and impoverished result. Wisdom requires more than factual knowledge and logic, it must include emotional, ethical, expressive and mythic aspects as well. It is not to be equated with expertise. Aspects of expert cognition may mimic those of wisdom to some degree, but unlike expertise, wisdom is not specialized but integrative and organismic. Integrity (moral and spiritual), humility, compassion and insight are among the descriptors that are applied to persons considered wise according to Labouvie-Vief (1990). Wisdom involves an understanding of the relatedness of logos thinking and mythos thinking; it encompasses an understanding of moral and ethical issues, an understanding of one's own emotions and a striving for a rational attitude that seeks both objective validation and subjective significance.

Wisdom as an attitude about knowing

> An essential part of wisdom is the ability to determine what is uncertain; that is, to appreciate the limits of our knowledge and to understand its probabilistic nature in many contexts. (Dawes, 1988, p. 264)

Meacham (1983, 1990) emphasizes the importance of balance to wisdom, but in this case the balance is between knowing and doubting, and the overarching characteristic of wisdom is attitudinal. The wise person strives for knowledge, in Meacham's view, but is keenly aware of its fallibility. "Each new domain of knowledge appears uncomplicated from the vantage point of ignorance; yet the more we learn about a particular domain, the greater the number of uncertainties, doubts, questions, and complexities that arise" (1990, p. 183). The essence of wisdom, Meacham contends, is in knowing that knowledge is fallible and in striking a balance between knowing and doubting.

Meacham's sensitivity to the need for balance is seen in his caution against both of the extreme attitudes that one might have regarding what is knowable. Two people with the same knowledge might behave quite differently, depending on whether they considered what they knew to be a large or small portion of all that can be known. To be wise, Meachem argues, is to avoid both the extreme of being overly confident of one's knowledgability to the point of close-mindedness and rigidity and that of being paralyzed by a sense of one's fallibility. It is to know with neither excessive confidence nor excessive cautiousness. Wisdom is basically an attitude, to be distinguished from specialized knowledge, abilities, or skills.

Kitchener and Brenner (1990) distinguish several forms of *epistemic cognition* that, represent a progression of stages through which one might pass in the normal course of development. The perception of knowledge as relatively certain in the earlier stages gives way to the perception of knowledge as more provisional in the later ones. Individuals who have attained a late developmental stage would show a balance between knowing and recognizing the limits of their knowledge, and would avoid the extremes of over- and underconfidence in their views. Acknowledgement of the fallibility of one's own judgments does not preclude seeing those judgments as justified and more compelling and workable than alternatives. A similar emphasis on the importance of being aware of the subjective nature of knowledge is given by Kramer (1990). Wisdom, in her view, involves the ability to think "dialectically," which is to say the ability to recognize the often-contradictory and ever-changing nature of experience and to synthesize an integrated perspective through the resolution of conflict.

As the epigraph at the beginning of this section indicates, Dawes (1988) argues that understanding the uncertainty, or probabilistic nature, of much knowledge is an essential part of wisdom. I think this is a very important point. Failure to appreciate the probabilistic nature of much of what we know is the source of many reasoning difficulties. Dawes goes on to make another thought-provoking point with respect to this aspect of knowledge, namely that, despite the fact that we often find ourselves trying to reduce uncertainty in specific instances, life *without* uncertainty would be intolerable. The ability to predict the future with certainty would be a curse; it would make life boring at best and a horror at worst. People who wish for such ability are not wise.

Fortunately, such a wish is unlikely to be granted in any very general way; however, an increasing ability to predict in specific instances is a natural consequence of scientific and technological advance. Sometimes such increased ability creates difficult dilemmas, as, for example, when the daughter of a parent with Huntington's chorea is faced with the decision as to whether to be tested for the presence of the gene that will ensure that she will develop the disease. Given that there is no known cure for the disease or effective measures to forestall its onset, many people at risk for it prefer not to know whether it lies in their future (Bishop & Waldhols, 1990; Cattaneo, Rigamonti, & Zuccato, 2002). Other similar examples could be given, and their number is likely to increase steadily. Whether it is wise to want as much as possible of this type of knowledge is a debatable question.

Wisdom as a perspective

A popular model of the wise person is that of an individual who is unperturbed by circumstances, serenely content even in the midst of confusion and chaos. Consoled by philosophy, such a person is, Boethius (circa AD 523) assures us, prepared to face any eventuality with equanimity. The idea that an important aspect of wisdom is the ability to maintain a certain perspective more or less independently of one's circumstances, to remain somewhat detached from circumstances is still current (Erikson, Erikson, & Kivnik, 1986; Kramer, 1990). That wisdom involves the ability to maintain a sense of humor when one is not having an easy time of it is one version of this idea (Brent & Watson, 1980). Clayton (1976) includes peacefulness as one of the distinguishing characteristics of a wise person. Taranto (1989) sees acceptance of the limitations that stem from human finiteness as a notion that is common to all conceptualizations of wisdom.

Nagel (1986) emphasizes the importance of perspective in one's understanding of the world and one's own place in it. He considers it a major philosophical challenge to an individual to be able to view the world objectively—as a view from nowhere in particular—while at the same time seeing it subjectively, from the unique vantage point of one's own personality, interests, and circumstances. From an objective view, one is an insignificant speck in the cosmos, a speck the existence or nonexistence of which is of no consequence; but from a subjective view, one's self is of paramount importance. Reconciling these perspectives, each of which is individually compelling, is no mean feat.

Arguably the role of perspective as a determinant of human behavior and of individual well-being has been underappreciated by psychologists. An old idea in philosophy is that one's perspective on one's state—how one views one's state—is far more important that is the state itself as a determinant of one's degree of satisfaction with life. Montaigne (circa 1580/1927) expressed the idea this way: "Ease and indigence therefore depend on the opinion of each man; and neither riches nor fame and health have any more beauty and pleasure than he attributes to them by which they are possessed. Every man is well or badly off as he thinks himself to be. The man is content who believes himself to be content, not he whom the world believes to be so. And that belief alone makes it real and true" (p. 62).

The multidimensionality of wisdom

Although, as the foregoing shows, different writers have emphasized different abilities or traits as particularly indicative of wisdom, one sees considerable overlap among the aspects of wisdom mentioned. Moreover, most writers on the subject see wisdom as multidimensional; few, if any, equate it with a single characteristic. Some have stressed the multidimensional nature of the concept and have suggested how we might think of it in multidimensional terms.

On the basis of people's ratings of similarity between descriptors of wise individuals, Clayton and Birren (1980) identified three major dimensions of the concept: affective, reflective, and cognitive. Kramer (1990) stresses the interdependence of cognitive and affective aspects of wisdom, as does Roodin, Rybash, and Hoyer (1984) and Labouvie-Vief, Hakim-Larson, Devoe, and Schoeberlein (1989). Birren and Fisher (1990) see wisdom as three-dimensional, involving a balance among cognition, affect and volition, which may develop over the course of a lifetime.

A personal view

If asked to produce a set of characteristics and capabilities that are descriptive of a prototypical wise person, I would produce something like the following. Probably knows a lot, but is aware of the limitations of own knowledge. Is perceptive, can see beyond appearances. Can distinguish reasons from rationalizations. Has insightful knowledge of human beings, knows something of what motivates people, what makes them tick. Continually seeks, and finds, opportunities to learn, even from those who appear to have little to teach. Is able to see things from a variety of perspectives, including mutually contradictory ones. Is able to change the range of perspective, to take a broad inclusive view as well as to focus narrowly on details. Can anticipate probable consequences of actions, and takes them into account in making decisions. Is reflective, not easily fooled. Exercises good judgment. Is critical but constructively so. Is open to change. Has a sense of priorities and proportion, and a sense of humor. Appreciates importance of logic and aesthetics, of cerebration and emotion. Balances idealism and realism. Is aware of own capabilities and limitations. Does not greatly overestimate (or greatly underestimate) own importance. Has taste, and a strong sense of right and wrong.

Wisdom, to me, differs from knowledge and intelligence, which is to say, I find it easy to imagine an individual who knows a lot and is very clever but who would not be considered wise. Wisdom is less distinctly different, in my view, from good judgment. Of the various aspects of rationality that we have considered, wisdom, I think, comes closest to being synonymous with that concept.

☐ Why Should We Want Wisdom?

Wisdom is typically portrayed in the literature as a desirable, if rare, quality. What is it that makes wisdom desirable? Does it give one a practical advantage in life? Are wise people happier, more powerful, more likely to realize their goals, than people who are less wise? Should wisdom be considered an end in itself? Something we should seek, whether or not it has any practical significance? Even if it turned out that wise people are generally no happier—or are less happy—than unwise people?

Wisdom as a practical need

King Solomon's request for wisdom was motivated by practical concerns: he wanted to be able to rule his kingdom well. Current investigators of wisdom have stressed the practical need for a greater application of wisdom to the problems that face the modern world (Csikszentmihalyi & Rathunde, 1990; Kramer, 1990; Birren & Fisher, 1990). Kramer (1990), for example, puts it this way. "The wise person may be seen as a lay theorist who maintains a certain set of assumptions about social reality and is able to effectively apply these to a variety of domains in order to resolve problems arising in his or her own experience, advise others in resolving their problems, shape social institutions, and seek meaning and continuity in experience" (p. 280). One major function of wisdom, in her view, is to enable people to adapt effectively to the tasks of adult life—choosing a career, adjusting to various stressors, coping with illness, and the like. Other practical functions with which wisdom has been associated include offering counsel to others and managing the affairs of society.

The practical need for wisdom is seen by some to be especially great for dealing with problems that are not well-structured and in situations that are characterized by high degrees of uncertainty (Baltes & Smith, 1990; Kitchener & Brenner, 1990). Birren and Fisher (1990) undoubtedly speak for many people in expressing the hope that research on wisdom will help to develop useful tools to assist world and national leaders to deal effectively with the increasingly complex problems facing humanity.

The emphasis on making an effort to see how various aspects of reality relate to each other, which Csikszentmihalyi and Rathunde (1990) identify as one of the distinguishing characteristics of wisdom as a cognitive process, is especially thought-provoking in view of the great importance attached to specialization in our own age. As these writers point out, specialization has enabled us to gain control over specific aspects of the world, but it does not help us know how that power should be used.

A strong argument could be made that the need for wisdom is nowhere more pressing in the modern world than in the arena of deciding how to apply the considerable capability of control that scientific and technological knowledge has produced. Paradoxically, by gaining an impressive degree of control over many aspects of nature without making comparable progress in learning how to control our own impulses to use that capability for destructive purposes, we have put ourselves in a very precarious position, and more than a little wisdom is likely to be required if we are to extract ourselves from it. Russell (1957) puts it this way: "Hitherto mankind has survived because however foolish their purposes might be they had not the knowledge required to achieve them. Now that this knowledge is being acquired, a greater degree of wisdom than heretofore as regards the ends of life is becoming imperative" (p. 159). And Russell asks the obvious question: "where is such wisdom to be found in our distracted age?" (p. 159).

Some writers make a distinction between practical wisdom and philosophical wisdom (Dittmann-Kohli & Baltes, 1990). Practical wisdom helps one deal with day-to-day problems; philosophical wisdom, as the term suggests, relates to philosophical issues—questions of meaning, value, purpose—with which people often struggle. This distinction should not be drawn too sharply, however, inasmuch as how we deal with day-to-day problems is unlikely to be independent of our values or of our beliefs about meaning and purpose.

Wisdom as an intrinsic good

Wisdom was also seen by the ancients as a personal good in the sense that, independently of any other consequences of its attainment, it is its own reward. It is not only a means to other ends, but an end in itself. Although, one might see some of the arguments to this effect as more appropriately considered arguments for its importance as a means to other ends, inasmuch as they claim that its possession means joy, contentment, and fulfillment. It was also seen to be necessary for the proper appreciation and enjoyment of other goods, such as health or prosperity.

What would we think of the desirability of wisdom, as an end itself, one might ask, if we believed, or it could be shown, that its attainment meant not joy, contentment and fulfillment, but sorrow, disillusionment and a sense of the futility of it all? If one believes that wisdom involves an unusual perceptiveness, and that the truth is basically unpleasant, one might expect wisdom to lead to despair. Would it then be considered desirable, as an end in itself? My sense is that people who hold that wisdom is desirable as an end in itself assume that knowing the truth about existence, or some humanly possible approximation thereto, would not be cause for despair. This is pure conjecture, but people who urge that wisdom be sought for its own sake seem to be assuming that being wise is almost tantamount to being content.

In any case, the conceptualization of wisdom as an intrinsically rewarding good is much less in evidence in current writing on the topic than in that of the ancients, which, as Csikszentmihalyi and Rathunde (1990) point out, raises the question of whether the ancients, or we (or possibly both), have it wrong. "Is the ancient choir of praise an example of the self-delusion to which we are so prone, a whistling in the dark, an effort to seduce prospective students by praising one's craft? Or is there a genuine foundation for the claim that the pursuit of wisdom is so enjoyable?" (p. 37).

Csikszentmihalyi and Rathunde's answer to their question is that the idea that wisdom as a supreme joy in itself, and thus a personal good, is still defensible. They relate the idea to that of "intrinsically motivating" experiences, or what have sometimes been called "flow" experiences (Csikszentmihalyi, 1975), which they describe as being characterized by "egolessness, merged action and awareness, high concentration, clear feedback, control, and enjoyment of the activity for its own sake" (p. 40). The association of deep joy with certain contemplative states of mind is not completely foreign to modern literature.

Sometimes the joy appears to be evoked by experiencing an insight, by seeing some familiar thing in a new way, by gaining a new perspective on a problem, by the feeling that one understands some elusive relationship for the first time. Many scientists have described the intense joy they have experienced upon making a discovery. I do not believe that such feelings are experienced only by individuals who have made momentous discoveries; I suspect that many of us could testify to the exhilaration—almost physical pleasure—that can accompany an original thought.

☐ Wisdom and Age

Wisdom has long been associated with advanced age. Plato's assumption that the wisdom needed to make one fit to rule took time to be acquired is reflected in his restriction that only an elderly person could qualify to be a philosopher-king. The idea that wisdom is the special, if not unique, perview of elderly people persists; many psychologists see the acquisition of wisdom as a natural—not to say universal—aspect of adult development (Clayton & Birren, 1980; Erikson, 1982; Holliday & Chandler, 1986; Kitchener & Brenner, 1990; Perlmutter & Hall, 1985; Smith, Dixon, & Baltes, 1989). The idea appears to be common also among people other than those who study aging (Heckhausen, Dixon, & Baltes, 1989), and among people of all ages (Perlmutter, Adams, Nyquist, & Kaplan, 1988, reported in Orwoll & Perlmutter, 1990).

According to one view, the correlation between age and wisdom is very strong. The acquisition of wisdom is seen as the natural consequence of aging, wisdom being imputed to all people of advanced age. One becomes wise, according to this view, by virtue of living a long time and learning from many life experiences, especially, perhaps, painful ones. "Old" and "wise" are almost synonymous; one cannot get old without getting wise, and one cannot be wise unless one is old.

An alternative view that still assumes a correlation between age and wisdom sees age as a necessary but not sufficient condition for wisdom. Plato's view appears to have been of this sort. Only an elderly person could have acquired enough wisdom to be fit to rule others, but one does not necessarily become wise simply by managing to live a long time.

Although the inclination to associate wisdom with advanced age appears to be relatively pervasive among laypersons and psychologists, it is not universal. Meacham (1990), who notes that empirical support for the idea that wisdom increases with age is lacking, takes the contrary view that wisdom not only does not increase with age, but tends to decline with it: "I suggest that although the potential for wisdom is present throughout the life course, unfortunately most people lose their wisdom as they grow older" (p. 181). One cannot lose what one does not have, so implicit in this view is the assumption that people do have some amount of wisdom at some stage(s) of life, which then diminishes as they age. Meacham makes this notion explicit: "Said starkly, my hypothesis is that all people are wise to begin with, as children, but that as we grow older most people lose their wisdom" (p. 198).

As to how the idea that wisdom increases with age became so prevalent, if it is not true, Meacham suggests that its origin is the need that young people have for such a belief. Young adults, he argues, being impressed both with the complex and difficult responsibilities that adulthood has recently forced upon them and with their own inadequacies to deal as effectively as they would like with these responsibilities, find comfort in the belief that age brings wisdom and that things will get easier in the future. The belief that older people, who tend to be in positions of power and authority, are no better able to cope with the complexities of life—are no wiser—than young adults would be grounds for despair; it is better for one's peace of mind, in other words, to believe that older is wiser, whether or not it is true.

This hypothesis seems to suggest that young people should be more inclined to associate wisdom with age than are old people, who, if there is no correlation, should know better from personal experience. In fact Perlmutter, Adams, Nyquist, and Kaplan, (1988, reported in Orwoll & Perlmutter, 1990) found that old people as well as young, tended to associate wisdom with age—people older than 50 were more likely to be identified as wise by subjects in all age groups than were people younger than 50. Interestingly, however, in this study self ratings with respect to wisdom were not higher for the older people than for the younger ones, which suggests that older participants in this study, like younger ones, believed wisdom to increase with age, but they were no more likely to rate themselves as wise than were the younger ones.

Meacham (1990) notes that most of the writing that is currently being done on aging is being done by young and middle-aged people, and asks the obvious question: if the popular perspective on wisdom and aging is correct, why should middle-aged researchers be expected to be able to recognize instances of wise behavior by older persons? Perhaps, he suggests, research on wisdom should be done only by people who are certifiably old and wise.

Meacham's claim that wisdom does not increase with age needs to be qualified slightly. He argues that wisdom, as an attitude that strives for a balance between knowing and realizing the fallibility of knowledge, is not a developmental dimension, but is accessible to people of all ages. On the other hand, he acknowledges the possibility that because the amount of information and the number of experiences and insights from which one can draw is likely to increase with age, older persons who are wise can reveal their wisdom in more profound ways than can younger persons who are wise. Clearly, much remains to be learned about the relationship, if any, between age and wisdom; current understanding does not sharply distinguish between fact and lore.

☐ Approaches to the Study of Wisdom

The foregoing discussion has drawn heavily from a book edited by Sternberg (1990a). In an early chapter of that book, Baltes and Smith (1990) note that despite the apparently growing interest in the concept of wisdom among psychologists, not many empirical studies of wisdom have yet been done. In the concluding chapter, Birren and Fisher (1990) comment on the contents of the book itself and note that "the authors appeared to be more discursive than empirically oriented. Those who described research of their own described 'soft' research in which no variable was manipulated" (p. 330).

Birren and Fisher wonder whether this reflects nothing more than the fact that researchers have only recently begun to focus on wisdom and may not yet have developed sufficiently sophisticated approaches to study it effectively in the laboratory, or it indicates some deeper limitations of what can be expected from laboratory work on this complex subject. Perhaps, they speculate, real progress toward understanding wisdom will require the development of new concepts and approaches, including acknowledgment of the need for work outside the laboratory.

Much of the recent work on wisdom has involved the two approaches, as Chandler and Holliday (1990) describe them, of "rummaging through older writings on the subject of wisdom and developing systematic strategies for querying ordinary people about what they understand wisdom to mean" (p. 124). A variant on querying people about what they understand wisdom to mean is to ask people to identify others whom they consider to be wise, and then to study the identified people directly. Orwoll and Perlmutter (1990) call this the "exemplar approach," and point out that it has been used also in the study of creativity and other multidimensional attributes. Intensive studies of individuals generally considered to be wise, and cross-sectional developmental studies aimed at determining how attributes generally associated with wisdom relate to age are also possibilities noted by Orwoll and Perlmutter.

Using a distinction made by Sternberg (1990b) between intrinsic theories (private theories constructed by people, including scientists, in the natural course of their lives) and explicit theories (theories constructed by scientists on the basis of empirical data and subject to objective test), we might say that a major objective of the recent work on wisdom has been to discover what some of the intrinsic theories of wisdom are and whether there is much commonality among them. Many of the questionnaire-based studies have used factor-analytic or multidimensional-scaling techniques to identify the major factors or dimensions that make up the concept of wisdom as it is used in common discourse. The lack of consistency among the outcomes of such studies led Chandler and Holliday (1990) to the unhappy surmise that "it will likely prove always to be the case that there are exactly as many factorally distinct solutions to the structure of wisdom as there are investigative teams at work on the problem" (p. 131).

In short, wisdom has been neglected as a topic of empirical research by psychologists until quite recently. The scientific literature on the topic is scant, and there are no well-developed theories of wisdom backed by a lot of evidentiary support. The work that is currently being done on the topic must be considered exploratory, for the most part, the primary objective being not so much the testing of theories but the development of methodologies that will prove to be effective in the study of this important and neglected construct.

CHAPTER 10

The Relativity of Rationality

> Not only is belief tied to context, so is rationality. To term something rational is to make an *evaluation*: its reasons are good ones (of a certain sort), and it meets the standards (of a certain sort) that it *should* meet. These standards, we have said, may vary from area to area, context to context, time to time. (Nozick, 1993, p. 98)

One can say very little about rationality without mentioning standards, values, human cognitive limitations, and a variety of other topics. Standards and values were discussed in preceding chapters. Here I want to consider how one's conception of rationality is likely to be influenced both by what one believes about human capabilities and limitations and about "reality" and the possibility (or impossibility) of knowing it.

☐ Rationality and Finite Cognition

Conceptions of rationality as believing or behaving in accordance with one's *best* self-interest, as taking account of *all* relevant information in making decisions, or as weighing *all* the evidence properly in arriving at conclusions, assume an ideal agent and do not take into account various types of human limitations. Such conceptions preclude the possibility that human beings, given their limitations, can be rational. Writers have addressed this issue in various ways, some by making a distinction between ideal and practical rationality, and some by explicitly conceiving rationality in terms of what can be expected, given the capabilities and limitations of human beings.

Bounded rationality

Simon (1955, 1956, 1957, 1983) put forth the view that human decision making cannot satisfy economists' conception of rationality because of human cognitive limitations. People have neither the knowledge nor the reasoning ability to behave as economists' normative models say they should. They simplify decision situations in various ways to make them tractable. Simon's theory of bounded rationality holds that people construct simplified models of situations and then behave in a way that makes sense in terms of these models.

According to this conception, people do not attempt, when faced with a decision problem, to develop a payoff matrix that exhausts all possible combinations of decision options and states of the world and to assign precise values to specific combinations. Instead, they judge any particular combination as either acceptable or not. People do not seek the best possible solutions to decision problems, but only acceptable ones. They do not try to maximize expected utility but to get desirable outcomes and avoid disasters; they behave not as optimizers but as "satisficers." Also, problems are solved and decisions made as they present themselves, which typically is one at a time. For this reason, if for no other, the solutions and choices are unlikely to be optimal with respect to any global perspective, but they suffice to satisfy the individual's immediate needs for safety, shelter, food, pleasure and other basics.

Toulmin (1958) also has defended the idea that optimization, in the sense of measuring up perfectly to some analytic standard, is generally not a realistic goal in deciding what to believe. "[T]he proper course for epistemology is neither to embrace nor to armour oneself against skepticism, but to moderate one's ambitions—demanding of arguments and claims to knowledge in any field not that they shall measure up against analytic standards but, more realistically, that they shall achieve whatever sort of cogency or well-foundedness can relevantly be asked for in that field" (p. 248). Similar views have been expressed by Shackle (1958/1967), Schrenk (1969), and March (1978).

The idea of bounded rationality has been criticized for being vague: "there are so many ways in which rationality can be bounded that we can never be sure we have the right one" (Watts, 2003, p. 66). One might also argue that we should not be too quick to dismiss optimization as an objective of human reasoning, because it could be the case that people would be seen to optimize if only we could measure all the costs and values of all the variables, including time and effort, that affect behavior. If time is valuable, for example, it may be that what one gains by saving some of what would be needed to analyze a situation carefully is sometimes worth more than the information the analysis would produce. Because we cannot hope to measure all the variables involved, however, claiming that *if* we could, we would find that people do optimize is a bit of arm waving and does not contribute much to our understanding of human reasoning.

An important consequence of behaving as a satisficer is a greatly reduced cognitive burden on the individual; satisficing requires less in the way of information seeking and processing than does optimizing. The cost of this advantage is the likelihood of settling for an outcome that is less desirable than one that could have been obtained. Perhaps for the satisficer's own peace of mind, it is best to stop analyzing a situation once a decision has been taken—at least if the decision is irrevocable—because to continue analysis runs the risk of identifying other choices one will wish one had made and to experience unnecessary regret.

Among the characteristics one must have in order to be rational in this bounded sense are some way of focusing attention, a mechanism for generating alternatives, the capability to acquire facts about one's environment and to draw inferences from those facts. Such a conception of rationality recognizes computational and other types of limitations of the individual that preclude optimization as a practical objective, but that are not inconsistent with the more modest goals of surviving, of "getting along," or of doing acceptably well.

Harman (1985) argues that, as a matter of fact, in many choice situations very little analysis of alternatives takes place. One has a goal, one recognizes a means of accomplishing that goal, and that is the end of it. "In a simple case, one does not consider whether there might be some other means to E or some other end distinct from E that one might now obtain, and one disregards any other consequences of one's act. One simply forms the intention of getting E by doing M . . . The basic idea, then, is to try to keep things simple. One tries to limit oneself to considering a simple way of obtaining a simple end" (p. 106).

Toda (1980) distinguishes between decompositional (or analytical) and compositional rationality. In the former case, a decision situation is analyzed into its component elements (states and transitions) so their numerical characteristics (utilities and subjective probabilities) can be evaluated independently and the results of these evaluations can be combined to dictate a choice. The notion of compositional rationality stems from the recognition that analysis beyond some point often is not warranted by the fineness of the information available and therefore should not be attempted. Even though one might be able to conceive of a finer-grained analysis, nothing would be gained from trying to do it. it.

The general idea is that people are sensitive to the cost—in terms of time, energy, or money—of acquiring information and that they may limit what they are willing to expend in particular situations. It is possible too that people often are content with a level of judgmental confidence that is considerably below certainty, and are not highly motivated to acquire information that would be necessary to raise their confidence above that point (Chaiken, Liberman, & Eagly, 1989; Maheswaran & Chaiken, 1991).

Good (1983) makes allowances for human limitations in his distinction between Type I, or classical, rationality, which demands complete consistency with the usual axiom's of utility and probability, and Type II rationality, which takes into account the cost of theorizing and requires only that no contradiction has yet been found. Type II rationality recognizes the necessity in practical situations of deciding when to stop thinking. One cannot mull over a problem indefinitely; at some point one must act, and perhaps at the cost of sacrificing logical consistency. In Good's view, the fundamental principle of rationality is the recommendation to maximize expected utility in both cases; however, whereas Type I rationality implies complete logical consistency with the axioms of rationality, Type II is more lenient. According to the latter, "you should not normally and knowingly allow any blatant contradiction in your judgments and discernments when the axioms of rationality are taken into account; but an exception is reasonable if a decision is extremely urgent" (p. 185). Good subscribes generally to Bayesian approaches to decision making, but finds nonBayesian methods to be acceptable under some conditions.

Closely associated with the idea that the acquisition of information can be costly is the assumption that the process of acquiring information on any given issue is likely to yield diminishing returns over time. One of the requirements of rationality, in Baron's (1988) view is adequate search. Irrational behavior is seen as often the consequence of prematurely terminating the search of memory—say for reasons for and against drawing a particular conclusion, adopting a particular course of action, or holding a particular belief. But, Baron notes, thorough search is a virtue that should be practiced in moderation. Search should be thorough in proportion to the importance of the question in hand, and should not be continued beyond the point at which the gain to be expected from continuing it becomes less than the cost of doing so.

The curtailment of the search for information as soon as the cost of further search would outweigh the value of the information sought is a generally recognized principle in theories of rationality in economics (Sargent, 1993; Stigler, 1961). But because the process of determining the cost of search and the value of information can itself be costly and time-consuming, application of the principle may sometimes be impractical. It seems unlikely that many people literally compute, or estimate, the cost of search or the value of information, but one can act even on imprecise feelings of the cost getting too high or the value of information sought too low.

Nozick (1993) also emphasizes the role of search in somewhat different terms in pointing out that rationality of belief or behavior is not just a matter of mechanical weighing of given reasons or action alternatives, but also one of thinking up new and different possibilities that can be weighed. Nozick likens focusing only on *given* alternatives to a sort of cognitive myopia and argues that assessing the credibility of hypotheses is not really separable from the thinking up of new hypotheses, because in order to assess the credibility of a given hypothesis, one must compare it to the best incompatible alternative. But again the search for alternatives does not warrant unlimited effort.

Gigerenzer and his colleagues have put forth the idea of *ecological rationality*—which they define as rationality that fits with reality, rationality that is adapted to the environment (Gigerenzer, 2006a; Gigerenzer & Todd, 1999). The basis of this rationality is reasoning and decision making that make use of "fast and frugal" heuristics (Gigerenzer, 2004b; Gigerenzer & Goldstein, 1996)—principles that permit one to deal with the contingencies of life with limited time, knowledge and computational capability. Matching the heuristic to the situation or environment is important, because what works well under one set of conditions may work poorly, or not at all, under another. Gigerenzer and Todd distinguish their concept of ecological rationality from the idea of optimization under constraints, which is treated by many as synonymous with bounded rationality. They argue that ecological rationality is truer to actual human limitations than is the idea of optimization under constraints, which, having acknowledged those limitations sometimes appears to assume they do not exist: "The paradoxical approach of optimization under constraints is to model 'limited' search by assuming that the mind has essentially unlimited time and knowledge with which to evaluate the costs and benefits of further information search" (p. 11).

Minimal rationality

An extensive treatment of the question of what it means to be rational, given the cognitive capabilities and limitations of human beings, is offered by Cherniak (1986). The rationality that is required of any agent with finite cognitive resources, Cherniak suggests, is a minimal rationality. Minimal rationality is distinguished from total lack of rationality (i.e., randomness) on the one hand and ideal rationality on the other.

Cherniak takes the position that *only* minimal rationality and *at least* minimal rationality are required for an adequate theory of cognition. The conception of rationality that has been pervasively assumed in philosophy is too idealized, in his view, to be applicable to human beings.

In contrast to theories of belief that demand ideal rationality (e.g., most economic decision theories), the one proposed by Cherniak and mentioned briefly in chapter 2, takes as its point of departure the *minimal general rationality condition*, whereby one would undertake some, but not necessarily all, of those actions that are apparently appropriate to one's set of beliefs and desires, and would *not* attempt many of the actions that are *in*appropriate to it. To be minimally rational, in other words, is to be more inclined to do what is right, relative to one's beliefs and desires, than what is wrong.

This minimal-condition view is arrived at by a process of elimination. Cherniak recognizes three possibilities, two of which—null rationality (which permits a belief set to include any and all inconsistencies) and ideal rationality—are ruled out on the grounds that the former would yield no predictions about behavior (and we know that behavior is to some degree predictable) and the latter cannot be satisfied by any creature in the "finitary predicament" of having limited cognitive resources and limited time. Not only is it impossible for finite agents to realize ideal requirements, we do not use them when attributing beliefs to people in actual circumstances; we distinguish good enough from perfect. It would be irrational for a nonsuicidal creature in the finitary predicament to try to satisfy ideal conditions. It would be wasting time and resources that could be put to more productive use. Cherniak contrasts his approach of beginning with a realistic model of minimal rationality, "where the agent's ability to choose actions falls between randomness and perfection," with what he refers to as the conventional strategy of the cognitive sciences, which is "first to adopt an extreme idealization of the rationality required of an agent and then, perhaps, if they are noticed, to explain away departures of real human behavior from the ideal model" (p. 76).

The heuristic shortcuts that people use in reasoning, or something like them, are required, Cherniak suggests, to avoid computational intractability. Complexity theory shows that algorithmic approaches to even some quite simple deductive tasks are impossible in practice because they would require unavailable resources and time, and the results of recent psychological experimentation demonstrate the role of suboptimal heuristic strategies as opposed to formally correct procedures in everyday intuitive reasoning. Both of these areas of research support the idea, in this view, that the use of suboptimal heuristics may not be evidence of irrationality but of successful attempts to deal with the finitary predicament—to avoid computational paralysis and still do better than guessing.

Any conception of rationality that is intended to serve as a goal toward which it is reasonable for human beings to strive must take human capabilities and limitations into account. The ideas put forth by Simon, Harman, Good, Gigerenzer, Cherniak, and others stress not only the limits of human rationality but argue the *adequacy* of a limited rationality. The argument is that behavior that is optimal in terms of some normative standard is seldom, if ever, required for accomplishing realistic goals. Even when engaged in a competitive struggle, it usually is not necessary to do the best that is possible in order to win; one need only outdo one's opponent. Moreover, the cost of optimizing can be excessively high and the differential gain for doing so relatively small. If, for example, when I wish to buy a new car, I am determined to get the greatest possible value for my money, I have to be prepared to do a considerable amount of research, not to mention worrying about how to derive a single measure of "value" from a large number of incommensurate features. I find it more reasonable to take the attitude that there are probably many cars that are more than adequate for my needs and having identified one with which I am happy, not to worry much about whether the choice was optimal in any rigorous sense.

☐ Rationality and Reality

Realism is simply Romanticism that has lost its reason. (Chesterton, 1910, p. 13)

What does rationality have to do with truth? Does rationality guarantee that one's view of the world corresponds with reality? Or if it does not guarantee that, does it at least increase the chances of such a correspondence? This idea seems to be implicit in Blackburn's (1981) suggestion that "a feature of our cognitive lives is irrational if it increases the likelihood at arriving at false judgment" (p. 331). This sounds right.

Johnson-Laird and Byrne (1993) see truth seeking and truth preservation as definitive characteristics of rationality. "The sense of rationality that is central to life is what enables individuals to cope with its everyday exigencies. They have certain beliefs and certain desires and needs: to attain those goals, they must infer from their beliefs what they have to do to attain them and then carry out those actions. Their beliefs need to be true more often than not, and so do the conclusions that they infer from them. We therefore assume that the two central precepts of rationality are: (1) to believe what is true (the precept of rational belief); and (2) to infer what is true (the precept of rational thinking)" (p. 178). But how do we know whether what we believe is true?

Perception and reality

> We invent philosophies and scientific concepts as substitutes for the reality we cannot fully grasp. (Dubos, 1970, p. 100)

Philosophers have long been fond of pointing out that we have no way of discovering the nature of reality. Any information we have about the objective world, we have obtained through our senses. All we can know is what our senses tell us. Whether indeed there is an objective reality, independent of our perception of it, is a matter of conjecture. Redhead (1989) characterizes our situation as being imprisoned by our senses, which constitute an impenetrable wall between us and the external world. We can only know what the external world appears to be and we have no way of telling the extent to which the reality resembles the appearance.

Scientists, as a group, have been somewhat less inclined than philosophers to worry about what might be the nature of the reality that underlies our perceptual experience—or at least about the question of whether there is anything there—but some of them too have puzzled over this. And the number who do wonder about it has undoubtedly increased since quantum mechanics appeared on the scene.

Both philosophers and scientists have emphasized the importance of perception as the starting point of speculation and theorizing about the nature of reality, but they also have noted the limitations of our senses as direct detectors of reality and have cautioned that if we are not mindful of those limitations we can be seriously misled. Russell (1948) claims the primacy of perception this way: "In considering the reasons for believing in any empirical statement, we cannot escape from perception with all its personal limitations. How far the information which we obtain from this tainted source can be purified in the filter of scientific method, and emerge resplendently godlike in its impartiality, is a difficult question . . . But there is one thing that is obvious . . . Only insofar as the initial perceptual datum is trustworthy can there be any reason for accepting the vast cosmic edifice of inference which is based upon it" (p. 8). Russell contends that, because of the fundamental importance of observation to science, psychology is an essential ingredient in every part of empirical science.

But what we perceive—how we interpret what we sense—is culturally dependent to a significant degree. And who is to say what cultural context, if any, can assure that we do it right? Von Bertalanffy (1967) is severely critical of the assumption that the culture to which one belongs must surely have it right. "It is parochial and arrogant to consider the world 'As we see it'—that is, the common-sense world of the 'practical' man of modern centuries—as singular point and facsimile of the 'real' world; while relegating others no less intuitively convincing to other humans—such as the mythical, the Aristotelian, the artistic, the intuitive knowledge of the mystic—to the limbo of delusion and fancy. Rather we should recognize, in line with psychological research, linguistics, critical philosophy, modern physics, etc., that each world view is a certain *perspective* of an unknown reality, seen through the spectacles of generally human, cultural and linguistic categories" (p. 95).

What about reality as seen through the lens of scientific theory? Can we not have some confidence that this is an accurate view of what really is? Incomplete and approximate, to be sure, but accurate within the limits of the resolving power of the instruments at hand? It has been the case for a long time that the conception of the physical world that we get from science is very different from that that we construct from our direct observations, unaided by instruments. According to physics, one of the ways in which our senses deceive us is with respect to the solidity or density of things. As we view the world, it is filled with objects many of which are solid and stable. But what is a solid stable object? Objects are made of atoms and atoms are composed of ephemeral electrons swirling, in some mysterious probabilistic sense, about a nucleus of protons and neutrons. Almost all of the atom's mass is concentrated in its nucleus, the diameter of which is only about 10^{-5} the diameter of the atom as a whole. Thus all but about 10^{-15} of the volume occupied by the atom can be considered essentially empty space. And the "solidity" of even the nucleus is a matter of some debate.

While the picture of reality presented by classical physics is quite different from that supported by our direct perception, the difference is primarily one of degree—what appears to us to be solid is "in reality" largely empty space, but a comprehensible basis for the perceived solidity is there in those dense little atomic nuclei that are scattered throughout it. With the arrival of quantum mechanics, however, and especially its emphasis on the observer as a determinant not only of what is perceived but of what is there to be perceived, the difference becomes one of kind. At the heart of this theory lies, in Davies's (1983) words, "the bald question: is an atom a *thing*, or just an abstract construct of imagination useful for explaining a wide range of observations" (p. 102).

Davies (1979) closes a delightful essay on quantum mechanics entitled "Reality exists outside us?" with the following comment: "To conclude this somewhat sketchy account of what is, after all, the most successful scientific theory ever known, it would appear that the concept of an independent reality 'out there' has been discredited. We see in its place a shifting world of uncertainty in which apparent realities can come and go in seemingly random fashion, and in which even the observer himself has dissolved into something evanescent and insubstantial. The central conclusion is that if reality has any meaning at all, it is only in the context of the observer and the observation itself. There is a kind of continuous creation—a new world every moment—brought into being by our own conscious awareness. Or so it seems. In a world full of uncertainty, who can be sure?" (p. 158).

Probably most scientists assume the existence of a material universe and espouse the idea that the proper business of science is to attempt to understand it, insofar as it is possible to do so. At the same time, it is generally recognized that, quantum mechanics aside, there is a sense in which the universe, as we conceive it, is a creation of the human mind. Einstein (1961) referred to such fundamental concepts as space, time, and event as "free creations of the human intelligence, tools of thought which are to serve the purpose of bringing experiences into relation with each other, so that in this way they can be better surveyed" (p. 141).

Perhaps there is room here for more than one perspective. Morris (1987) has argued this position, pointing out that the concepts of physics can be regarded either as discoveries or inventions. "One can take the point of view that such objects as quarks, neutrinos, and quantum fields have a real existence. Alternatively, one can believe that they are only constructs that we have invented to help us make some sense out of the phenomena that are directly observed" (p. 196).

In light of all this, is our everyday belief in the reality and solidity of the world a rational one? One might answer yes on the grounds that, for most purposes of everyday life, the belief serves us very well. One might also argue that the belief in the solidity of matter is rational because, in fact, phenomenologically (much) matter *is* solid, and for most purposes the phenomenological aspects of the world are the appropriate ones on which to build models that will guide behavior. Certainly for most purposes behaving *as though* matter were solid is more likely to keep one out of difficulty than is behaving as though it were ephemeral. Even physicists who conceive of matter as fields of force are likely to behave in their daily lives as though their belief in the solidity of things was as strong as that of most of the rest of us.

One can also take the position that simultaneously believing in the solidity and the ephemerality of matter does not necessarily require holding inconsistent ideas. I see no inconsistency in believing that matter is solid in the everyday sense of solidity, which means, among other things, that if I kick a large stone hard I am likely to hurt my foot, and in believing, at the same time, that at a subatomic level matter is as ephemeral as the physicists are telling us it is. Solidity, in other words, is a property of matter viewed at a level of organization to which our senses are attuned and one that is particularly relevant to our daily lives. One could perhaps think in terms of complex organizations of fields of force and recognize that when the organization that constitutes my foot interacts in a certain way with the organization that constitutes a particular stone, I will have a sensation like the one I imagine I would have if my foot and the stone were both "solid" in the usual sense, but that seems like an impractically complicated way of thinking for everyday purposes.

How arbitrary is our current conception of reality?

Presumably most of us assume, at least tacitly, that the conceptualization of reality that we have today is *the* conceptualization that is appropriate to our current level of sophistication (or lack thereof) in studying nature. That is to say, we believe the prevailing scientific view to be the only tenable one, given knowledge accumulated over the ages and our existing investigatory tools.

But how do we know that our current conceptualization of reality is not one of many equally good possibilities? If it were, we should not be surprised to be unable to imagine what some of the other possibilities are, because our conceptualization is so much a part of us that we cannot really stand back and look at it objectively. The act of introspecting on it makes use of the very same conceptual apparatus that is the focus of attention. One can imagine, however, that at any of a number of critical points in the history of human thought, its development might have taken a turn different from the one it did, from whence it could have led to an entirely different set of concepts and representational schemes, which might be as good as or better than those we have today.

The point may be illustrated by reference to the various representational systems we use for purposes of communication, e.g. number symbols, music notation, chemistry equations and bonding diagrams, and so on. The characteristics of any given system must be constrained both by the properties—as we understand them—of whatever the system is intended to represent and by our own perceptual and cognitive capabilities and limitations. Within these constraints, however, there is a great deal of latitude as to the details of the system's design. The many schemes that have been developed in various parts of the world for representing numbers testify to this fact (Flegg, 1983; Ifrah, 1985; Menninger, 1969). When a system becomes very widely adopted, as has the Hindu-Arabic number system that is now used almost universally, we come to take it for granted and to forget the arbitrariness of some of its aspects. And, of course, by virtue of its widespread use, the arbitrary features are, for practical purposes, no longer arbitrary; the system has become a de facto standard and resistive to further significant change.

Just so, our current conceptualizations of reality are undoubtedly constrained by the trajectory of preceding thought. And there is no way to shed those constraints. We can think only what is thinkable, and what is thinkable—by us—depends to a large degree on the concepts and frames of reference we have inherited from our predecessors. Sometimes exceptionally creative people manage to provide new perspectives from which to view certain aspects of nature, but even the most revolutionary of the new ideas rest solidly on other established concepts. The most radical departures from existing views are radically different in the sense in which dogs are different from cats, but not in that in which dogs are different from clams.

☐ Rationality and Cultural Context

> Our choice of what should count as rational depends upon our conceptual frameworks and criteria for making judgments, whether we are taken as individuals or societies, and therefore any conception of *the* rational person can only collapse into at least partly personal or social preference. (Messer, 1997, p. 121)

Does rationality mean the same thing in all cultures, or do the standards of rationality vary from time to time and from place to place? Are the differences in the cognitive and ethical demands that different cultures make of their members surface differences only? Do these differences mask underlying principles that are common to all times and places, or do they represent deep and irreconcilable incompatibilities in what rationality is understood to be?

In one or another form, the question of whether the criteria for rationality are universal or only local has puzzled people who think about such things for a long time, and is very likely to continue to do so. Not surprisingly, each of the possible answers has many defendants. On one point, however, we might expect fairly general agreement: cultures differ considerably in their surface manifestations of rationality—specific beliefs and behaviors that are seen as rational in one historical or social context are considered irrational in another. If there are universal criteria of rationality, they must be in the form of principles that are sufficiently general to be applicable independently of the knowledge and customs that characterize a place and time.

Johnson-Laird and Byrne (1991) express the view that the semantic principle of validity, according to which an argument is valid only if there is no way in which its premises could be true and its conclusion false, is a central core of rationality that appears to be common to all human societies. Fundamental to Johnson-Laird and Byrne's conception of culture-free rationality is the idea that the way to test the truth of an assertion, such as the conclusion of an argument, is to search for counterexamples to its claim.

Stich (1990), who challenges the assumption that truth is an important goal of cognitive processes, does so partly on the grounds that truth is itself a culturally fashioned notion and has no universally recognized criteria of attainment. He rejects the idea that there exists any universally accepted notion of rationality. MacIntyre (1988) also argues that different traditions have their own accounts of rational justification, but he contends that this does not mean that one tradition cannot defeat or be defeated by another. Traditions are vindicated or fail to be vindicated by the adequacy or inadequacy of their responses to epistemological crises. "The rival claims to truth of contending traditions of inquiry depend for their vindication upon the adequacy and the explanatory power of the histories which the resources of each of those traditions in conflict enable their adherents to write" (p. 403).

There is, it appears, a range of opinions regarding the extent to which notions of rationality—or of what constitutes good reasoning—differ from culture to culture and regarding the prospects of arriving at culture-free standards against which the quality of reasoning can be judged. Even for one who believes that culture-free standards are possible, there can be a dilemma associated with the question of how such standards should be applied; only the most extreme chauvinist would defend applying what he or she considered to be the universal standards to cultures that did not recognize them, without some sensitivity to the opposing view(s). Gell-Mann (1994) describes the dilemma this way: "Somehow the human race has to find ways to respect and make use of the great variety of cultural traditions and still resist the threats of disunity, oppression, and obscurantism that some of those traditions present from time to time" (p. 343). A challenge indeed.

New and established ideas

Today we know that the earth rotates on its axis, making a complete revolution every 24 hours. We know also that the earth revolves about the sun once about every 365 days. We have so many evidences of these facts that it is hard to see how anyone could doubt that they are true (although, apparently there are people who do so, despite the fact that they are aware of the prevailing view). It is not surprising, however, that at one time most people believed that the sun revolved around a fixed earth. We are not immediately conscious of the rotation of the earth; we cannot feel it or otherwise perceive it directly. The sun certainly appears to rise every morning in the east and to set every evening in the west, and, in the absence of compelling evidence to the contrary, it seems reasonable to believe that things are as they appear to be.

Over the centuries careful observers noticed facts that made them wonder about whether the sun really did revolve about the earth. They noticed, for example, that the positions of the stars also changed during the course of a single night. They noticed too that the apparent shape of the moon changed regularly approximately every 28 days, going from a crescent facing in one direction, through a full disk, to a crescent facing in the other direction, and that it did this with great regularity. People who lived far away from the equator noticed also that the exact location of the rising and setting of the sun changed noticeably with the seasons, as did the length of days. In the Northern Hemisphere, for example, the sun rose and set farther north, and remained in the sky longer, during the summer than during the winter. The locations of certain stars and constellations were seen also to change with the seasons.

All of these observations could be accounted for without changing the assumption that the sun revolved about the earth. However, as more and more facts were noted about the behavior of the sun, moon and stars, explanations of that behavior that started with the assumption that everything revolved about the earth became more and more complex. Some thinkers realized that the observations could be accounted for more simply if it were assumed that the earth rotated on its axis while it, and the moon, which revolved about it, together revolved about the sun. Eventually, theories based on these assumptions replaced those that had everything revolving about the earth. It took a long time for the new type of theory to be accepted generally, however, and many people were unwilling to accept it even after the evidence in its favor had become very strong.

It is easy for us to be critical of people who were reluctant to accept the new type of theory, but we have the advantage of much more compelling evidence in its favor than they had. Because of the information that has been gathered with high-powered telescopes, and more recently as a result of space exploration, our current theory of how the sun, planets and moons in the solar system move relative to each other is as certain as one can hope for a theory to be. Doubt of this view today in the face of the overwhelming evidence for it is justifiably considered irrational; but we are hardly justified in considering people to be irrational who doubted it when it was first proposed, or those who failed to see this possibility before then.

It is difficult for us to put ourselves in the position of people who found ideas with which we are very comfortable to be highly counter-intuitive and almost impossible to accept. We tend not to think very critically about ideas that are part of our intellectual heritage and consequently tend not even to be aware of the difficulties that some of these ideas caused when they were new. We do not worry, as did thinkers in Galileo's day, for example, about how it is possible for the earth to move through its orbit around the sun at such great speed without losing its moon. We *know* that the earth revolves about the sun and that it does not leave its moon behind as it does so, and even if we do not understand the scientific explanation as to how this can be the case we are unlikely to worry about it, or even to think about it at all, for that matter. In Galileo's day, the idea that the earth revolved about the sun was not yet universally accepted, even by people who think hard about such things, and the lack of an explanation of the moon question was used as an argument against the possibility.

I said that doubt today that the earth revolves about the sun is justifiably considered irrational. However, I do not mean to suggest that belief that the earth revolves about the sun should necessarily be considered a rational belief. My own sense of what it means for a belief to be rational involves more than that the belief reflect the prevailing view. The 17th-century thinker who doubted that the earth circled the sun on the grounds that it would have left its moon behind if it did so held a more rational belief, in my view, than does a modern-day individual who believes that the earth revolves about the sun, but does so for no better reason than the fact that that is what everyone else appears to believe. In short, whether a belief is or is not rational depends not on the substance of the belief, but on the basis on which it was formed. If it was the result of a careful weighing of whatever relevant evidence was available, it should be considered rational; otherwise not. What differs from culture to culture and time to time is the evidence that is available for one to draw upon in forming beliefs. People cannot be held accountable for not considering evidence that was not produced until after they were dead, or to which they had no access.

Magic and science

In Western Europe during the Middle Ages magic and science were widely accepted among the intelligentsia as complementary endeavors and consistent aspects of a unified world view. The reality of both natural and preternatural or supernatural events was widely accepted not only among the general populace, but among many of the most learned and progressive thinkers as well. Astrology was considered an applied science rather than an occult art. Belief that human affairs are influenced by the planets was widespread at the beginning of the Renaissance and common even among the giants of science. Both Kepler and Galileo cast horoscopes for their patrons. Kepler probably did not believe in astrology, but practiced it from time-to-time as a matter of the mundane necessity of putting food on his table. Roger Bacon devoted much of his time to a search for the "philosophers stone," which alchemists believed capable of transmuting common metals into gold. One of the consequences of this search was his discovery of gunpowder. Alfred Russell Wallace was a believer in phrenology. Thomas Edison attempted, just before his death, to build a piece of apparatus for communicating with the dead (Gardner, 1957).

When we think of beliefs that would be considered rational at one time and not at another, we tend to focus on beliefs that were widely held in the past that would be seen as irrational if held today. It is possible also, however, to identify beliefs that are held by knowledgeable people today that probably would have been seen as irrational if advanced by anyone in previous centuries. These include the beliefs that space may have more than three dimensions, that disease can be caused by organisms too tiny to see, that messages can be transmitted very long distances through the air; one could generate a long list.

We have no choice but to recognize the cultural dependency of what constitutes a rational belief. To fail to do so would leave us at a loss to distinguish between what is rational and what is not. Were we to insist on consistency with the views of "final" science as a criterion for rationality, we would have to acknowledge that our own prevailing beliefs are at best indeterminate with respect to rationality, because we have no way of knowing what the views of "final" science will be. In fact, we have little reason to expect there ever to be a final scientific view. It seems far more likely that scientific theories and explanations will continue to change indefinitely, or at least as long as scientists exist.

It seems also a very good possibility that many of our current views will appear irrational to future generations, judged by the standards of their own times. Even from our frame of reference, scientific theories may often be viewed as strange beliefs that (so far) have stood up to test. Some of the ideas in modern physics are sufficiently esoteric to western minds (at least to those of non-physicists) that writers have been able to promote the thesis that there is a deep correspondence between these ideas and those found in Eastern mysticism (Capra, 1975; Zukav, 1979), although many scientists take exception to some of the parallels that have been drawn.

It has been argued too that the scientific perspective, with its emphasis on experimentation, quantification, prediction and control, is itself a cultural phenomenon, and one that could not have become pervasive much sooner than it did in the history of the world. Berman (1984) takes this position, and sees science as a system of thought specific to a certain period of time rather than as independent of time and culture. Science could not have been established in a medieval social and economic order, according to this view, but was compatible with a world defined by capital accumulation.

It is not only scientific views, or beliefs about nature, that bear the stamp of the cultures that gave rise to them. The same cultural dependency is seen in beliefs about what constitutes acceptable behavior, and about right and wrong or good and evil more generally. Mackay (1852/1952) illustrates the point with his observation that at one time, poisoning an enemy was considered a venial offense in many parts of Europe. "Persons who would have revolted at the idea of stabbing a man to the heart, drugged his potage without scruple. Ladies of gentle birth and manners caught the contagion of murder, until poisoning, under their auspices, became quite fashionable" (p. xix). Making essentially the same point, Bell (1945/1992) says more bluntly, "Italy in the Renaissance without arsenic would be like veal without salt" (p. 117).

One conclusion we must come to is that human rationality, at best, is extremely fragile. People who consider themselves enlightened, objective, nonsuperstitious, and humane must be sobered by the thought that had they been born at a different time and raised in a different culture they might well have espoused beliefs and engaged in behavior that, from their current vantage point, they find unacceptable, perhaps abhorrent. It is easy for us to condemn the inquisitors of medieval Europe, the witch hunters of colonial New England, or the slave traders of the eighteenth and nineteenth centuries, but had we been born into the cultural contexts of those whom we condemn, what compelling reason is there to believe that we would have behaved very differently than did they?

☐ Situational Frame of Reference

So far the discussion has emphasized the idea that the rationality of beliefs should be assessed in relation to their cultural context, and what applies to beliefs in this regard applies to behavior as well. But even within a given culture—even assuming a given time and place—whether a particular belief or bit of behavior is considered rational may depend in part on the specific situational frame of reference in which it is viewed. In particular, behavior that appears to be irrational, or at least suboptimal, when judged in a very narrow context may be rational or even optimal when viewed from a broader perspective. A rule of behavior that works to one's advantage on the average may work to one's disadvantage in specific instances. The point may be illustrated by reference to an imaginary machine.

Suppose one wants to build a machine that can deal autonomously with a large number of situations. And suppose further that the machine's memory capacity is necessarily sufficiently limited—perhaps one has only so much building material—that one can represent within it only a relatively small number of rules of behavior. In order to give the machine the ability to cope with many situations, one would have to classify the situations it is likely to encounter as a small number of types, and then equip the machine with the means to make the same classifications and to respond to individual situations on the basis of this classification. All situations of a given type would evoke the same response. Inasmuch as situations of a given type are bound to differ from each other in some respects, the response to some members of a type is likely to be less effective than the same response to other members of the same type. Assuming that the machine's entire memory capacity has been used up in storing the rules for responding to situation types, if one wants to improve the machine's ability to optimize its response to situations of the same type, one must do so at the expense of decreasing its ability to deal with the remaining types, perhaps by doing away with the distinctions among some of them.

Possibly something of this sort can account for some of the ways in which human behavior appears to be suboptimal or irrational. Perhaps we learn to deal with all situations of Type X in a certain way. If the approach works well for most of the Type-X situations we encounter, the trouble caused by the exceptions in which the approach does not work so well may be a reasonable price to pay for not having to devote limited resources to discriminating among Type-X situations. Cherniak (1986) makes essentially this point in the context of a discussion of the implications of the structure of human memory for rationality: "A person's action may seem irrational when considered in isolation, but it may be rational when it is more globally considered as part of the price of good memory management" (p. 67). The cost of global rationality, he argues, may be some irrationality at the local level.

A similar observation is made by Lycan (1981) who contends that some of the inductive rules that guide our thinking may be overly general in the interest of simplicity and that some tendencies that appear to be irrational in isolation may be seen to serve useful purposes when viewed within a larger frame. A tendency to jump quickly to conclusions, for example, may be more useful in some situations than lengthy deliberation. False beliefs of certain types may serve important needs. "We tend to overestimate the attractiveness and other admirable qualities of our own children; we quickly forget the painfulness of certain otherwise useful activities; we habitually deceive ourselves in any number of beneficial ways" (p. 345). The point again is that beliefs or actions that would be considered irrational—or dysfunctional—when judged from a narrow perspective may be seen differently when assessed within a broader frame of reference.

What appears to be irrational behavior sometimes takes the form of misapplying approaches to problems, using specific heuristic strategies in circumstances in which they seem not to be appropriate. Many of the demonstrations of faulty reasoning and of judgmental biases that have been widely investigated can be considered from narrower or broader perspectives. Whether a particular use of a heuristic should be considered irrational may depend on the frame of reference in which the behavior is judged and on what can be assumed about the individual's capabilities and limitations. If an individual is able to acquire and retain only n heuristics, a defensible top-level strategy would be to remember those n that, as a set, would prove to be most efficacious over the individual's lifetime. One would not be surprised, given this strategy, to find many instances in which a heuristic is used in a way that would appear suboptimal when judged from a narrow perspective. According to the broader view, however, that same heuristic would be expected to be acceptably effective in most of the situations the individual is likely to encounter. Thus behavior that appears irrational in the microcosm of a specific situation may seem to be quite rational when judged by its efficacy in a larger context.

Consider the *gambler's fallacy*. In one of its many forms, this fallacy leads one to assign a greater-than-chance probability to the occurrence of an "overdue" probabilistic event. It stems from a failure to recognize the independence of independent probabilistic happenings. In the tossing of a fair coin, the probability of getting heads on any particular toss is independent of what was obtained on prior tosses. A person who believes that following a run of outcomes of a given kind the probability of an outcome of the opposite kind increases is said to display the gambler's fallacy. The fallacy is captured in the notion that a chance event that has not occurred in some time (e.g., the failure of heads to come up in several successive tosses of a coin) becomes "due" and is therefore highly likely to occur.

The gambler's fallacy is indeed a fallacy whenever one is dealing with a sequence of truly independent events. However, many of the sequences that we encounter that ostensibly are composed of independent events, in reality are not. Whenever a sequence has been constructed by a human being, the suspicion that it departs from randomness in systematic ways is likely to be correct. The sequence of numbers representing the correct answers on a multiple-choice test, for example, is very likely not to be random. A student who has just selected Item 4 as the answer three times in a row, and who is quite sure of the correctness of the answer in each case, may be forgiven for steering clear of Item 4 when guessing on the next question.

We should note too that whenever one's task is to guess among *equally-likely* alternatives, operating on the gambler's fallacy gives one no advantage, but doing so also incurs no penalty; inasmuch as every alternative is as likely as every other, selecting a particular one, even for an invalid reason, does not diminish one's chances of guessing correctly. In the larger context, if *some* of the sequences of ostensibly independent events that we encounter are not really independent, then application of the gambler's fallacy as a general rule may be a reasonable thing to do; inasmuch as it can help us with sequences that are not independent and does not hurt us with those that are, consistent use of it can, on balance, be beneficial. Many other examples could be used to illustrate the point that how rational or irrational a belief or bit of behavior is can depend on the frame of reference within which it is viewed, and especially on the scope of that frame.

☐ Individual versus Collective Rationality

> [E]ven the most dedicated and incorruptible human group is not immune from collective fallacies and mass delusions. (Ziman, 1978, p. 126)

Can we talk of the rationality or irrationality of a group, of a nation, of an age? Historians, sociologists, and other students of aggregate human behavior often use such language. I have already noted Tuchman's claim that governments sometimes work against their own interests and even under circumstances in which the folly of their policies should be obvious. Bloom (1987) speaks of the possibility of an entire society being mad and oblivious to the fact. Nazi Germany comes immediately to mind as an example of a nation gone mad, but there are numerous more recent examples of ethnic, political, or religious groups that have been sufficiently deranged to see justice in genocide and to attempt to exterminate rival groups. And, on a smaller scale, does not the madness of crowds reveal itself repeatedly in riots, lynchings, feuds, stampedes, bandwagon pile-ons, financial market bubbles, and similar forms of irrational collective behavior?

Does it make sense to talk of the rationality or irrationality of the human species as a whole? If we do think in these terms, what criteria should we apply to make a judgment? How could we possibly conclude that the species is irrational? Do not its dominance over all other species and its intellectual accomplishments give the lie to any such conclusion? On the other hand, can we consider ourselves rational when we spend enormous amounts of monetary and human capital defending ourselves against each other and willfully engage in activities that threaten our long-term well-being and perhaps even our survival as a species?

Claims of collective madness

Numerous writers have described ways in which collections of people—small groups, communities, nations—can display, and have displayed, irrational beliefs and behavior (Erasmus, 1509/1942; Evans, 1973; Gardner, 1957; Le Bon, 1895/1982; Tuchman, 1984). A common theme in these accounts is that when acting as members of collectives of one or another sort, people often do things that they would be highly unlikely to do—indeed would consider irrational—when acting alone.

In the preface to his classic account of popular delusions, Mackay (1852/1932) has this to say: "In reading the history of nations, we find that, like individuals, they have their whims and their peculiarities; their seasons of excitement and recklessness, when they care not what they do. We find that whole communities suddenly fix their minds upon one object, and go mad in its pursuit; that millions of people become simultaneously impressed with one delusion, and run after it, until their attention is caught by some new folly more captivating than the first. We see one nation suddenly seized, from its highest to its lowest members, with a fierce desire of military glory; another as suddenly becoming crazed upon a religious scruple; and neither of them recovering its senses until it has shed rivers of blood and sowed a harvest of groans and tears, to be reaped by its posterity" (p. xix). Every age, MacKay insists, has its peculiar folly.

Societies, nations, and other groups are, of course, composed of individuals and the characteristics of a collection of people reflect the characteristics of its members in the aggregate. It is equally true, however, that the beliefs and behavior of individuals can be greatly influenced by the groups (both formal and informal) to which they belong. We know from studies of the psychology of crowds that people sometimes participate in acts as members of a group that they would consider reprehensible upon reflection apart from the group context. We know too that the influence of a group can evoke acts of heroism and self sacrifice under some conditions. I am not aware of compelling evidence that the principles that govern mob, or mass, psychology have changed very much over the period of recorded history.

The tendency to resolve disputes by violence, which at the national or societal level means the tendency to wage war, seems to have been a constant at least as long as there have been such things as national or societal entities. According to Keeley (1996), wars in prehistoric times occurred at least as frequently as they have in more recent times, and killed and maimed at least as large a percentage of the involved populations—combatants and noncombatants alike.

Cultural effects on beliefs and behavior

That prevailing beliefs and values differ from place to place and from time to time raises some interesting and important questions. How do new beliefs and values, or modifications of old ones, become established within communities and propagate throughout them? What determines how widely they will become established and how long they will last? Why do beliefs that seem completely untenable to some cultures appear to be compelling to others?

To say that a belief (value, attitude, behavior pattern) characterizes a social group or an era is not to say that it necessarily characterizes every individual who belongs to that group or who lived during that era. Presumably not everyone who lived in Europe from the 15th to the 17th century believed in witchcraft. On the other hand, it is clear the beliefs and values of individuals are shaped, to some degree, by the beliefs and values that prevail in the communities to which they belong at the time during which they live. And the number of people holding a particular belief sometimes is large enough, and its prevalence sufficiently consequential, that it can reasonably be considered representative of a particular time and place.

A strong case can be made for the appropriateness of describing societies, cultures, nations or even eras as rational or irrational in this or that respect, although it is important to bear in mind that the judgment of rationality or irrationality is being made from one's own perspective, which derives from a particular culture and time, as to what that means. One can argue too the importance of applying current notions of rationality to a country's or society's current behavior. How, for example, can a country make rational decisions about the allocation of limited resources to major national endeavors? How does one judge the rationality of a decision to fund or not to fund a multi-billion dollar effort to establish a space station, or to sequence the human genome, or to build a superconducting super collider? How can it decide, rationally, when to give up on diplomacy and go to war?

Today we look back on the witch mania of preceding centuries as an unquestionably irrational episode in the history of mankind. We are beyond such irrationalities today, or at least, so we believe. But are we, as a species, more rational than our predecessors in any general sense? It is in the nature of things that the least rational people are the least likely to be aware of their irrationality. It is possible that what appears to us to be rational will seem to those who look back on us as quite the opposite. Moreover, our age does not lack observers who see our collective behavior as a species as unswervingly on a course that threatens our well-being if not our survival, and therefore irrational in the extreme. Cases in point include Harrison Brown (1954), Bertrand Russell (1954), Rachael Carson (1962), René Dubos (1970), E. F. Schumacher (1973), Barry Commoner (1991), and Alan Durning (1992). There are many others.

Determining the will of the majority

Economists have given a great deal of attention to the question of what collective rationality might mean (Arrow, 1963; Fishburn, 1973; Heller, Starr, & Starrett, 1986). Much of this attention has been focused on how to determine the will of the majority in self-consistent and nonparadoxical ways. This work finds a practical application in the design of voting procedures, which turns out to be a very complicated problem, full of surprises (Dummett, 1984; Mueller, 1979). A glimpse of the complexity of the subject is seen in one of Arrow's (1990) "impossibility theorems." Arrow identifies four conditions that seem reasonable to impose on any codification of public values, as in a constitution.

Collective rationality: "For any given set of orderings, the social choice function is derivable from an ordering" (p. 347).

Pareto principle: "If alternative x is preferred to alternative y by every single individual according to his ordering, then the social ordering also ranks x above y" (p. 347).

Independence of irrelevant alternatives: "The social choice made from any environment depends only on the orderings of individuals with respect to the alternatives in that environment" (p. 347).

Non-dictatorship: "There is no individual whose preferences are automatically society's preferences independent of the preferences of all other individuals" (p. 348).

Arrow proves that there can be no constitution that simultaneously satisfies all of these conditions. The proof is a *reductio ad absurdum*; he assumes the truth of all four conditions and shows that the assumption leads to a contradiction.

Individual and group rationality in conflict

There are many situations in which individuals acting rationally, according to certain conceptions of rationality, will collectively act against the best interests of the groups to which they belong. A well-known illustration is Hardin's (1968) metaphor of the *tragedy of the commons*, according to which the benefit that a herdsman can realize by adding an animal to his herd that is grazing on common ground far outweighs the personal cost he incurs of slightly less grazing land per animal. If individual rationality is construed as maximizing one's personal benefit/cost ratio, the herdsman's behavior in adding an animal to his public-ground-grazing herd is perfectly rational, and this is true independently of what other herdsmen do (Swap, 1991). But, of course, if every herdsman does they same, they collectively ruin the land.

Platt (1973) describes the tragedy of the commons as an example of a social trap—a situation that, because of positive short-term benefits, entices individuals, organizations, or societies to move in a direction that will eventually lead to undesirable consequences. The term *social dilemma* (Glance & Huberman, 1994; Komorita & Parks, 1996) conveys more or less the same idea. The referenced situation of interest is one in which individuals or groups seek short-term benefits by doing things that, if done by many, would eventually have undesirable consequences for all. The positive short-term consequences are typically enjoyed by individual members or subsets of some group, whereas the long-term negative consequences (costs) are shared by the group as a whole; and even the short-term benefits evaporate if the many begin to emulate the few.

It is easy to identify situations that are analogous to the herdsman-common ground metaphor, in which individuals acting in what may be considered—at least from a narrow perspective—their personal best short-term interests act against the long-term interests of the groups to which they belong. Many such situations may be described as freeloading—enjoying a shared benefit without helping to cover its expense. Users of a private road who fail to contribute to the cost of keeping it in good repair illustrate the point. Such users get the benefit of the use of the road at no expense. According to some economic theory, freeloading is rational behavior, at least to the extent that it is effective in helping one realize one's personal goals (Olson, 1965); this seems to me, however, to require a rather impoverished notion of rationality. Freeloading works only so long as the fraction of a group that practices it is relatively small; if it gets sufficiently large the freeloaded benefit will go away. Experimental studies of freeloading suggest that only about 25% of participants consistently freeload when they are given the opportunity to do so (Fehr & Gächter, 2000).

☐ Can Irrational Thinking Serve a Rational Purpose?

> The most disturbing thing about the chicken dilemma is the "advantage" an irrational player has or seems to have. (Poundstone, 1992, p. 212)

Can irrational thinking serve a rational purpose? This question is complicated by the fact that there are more conceptions than one of rationality and that what is considered rational from one point of view may not be from another. Lycan makes this point in noting that it can, on occasion, be rational in a cost-effective sense to be irrational in the textbook sense. But to say that thinking that is considered irrational from one point of view, say that of A, serves a purpose that is seen as rational from another point of view, say that of B, creates no conceptual difficulties beyond acknowledging the existence of different points of view. If A sees both the thinking and the purpose it serves as irrational, while B sees them both as rational, there is no conflict within either point of view. The interesting question is whether thinking that is considered irrational from a given point of view can serve a useful purpose as seen from the same point of view.

Lycan (1981, 1988) notes that susceptibility to false beliefs can sometimes serve important noncognitive needs. The tendency to forget the painfulness of otherwise useful activities, or to overestimate the attractiveness of one's own children are examples of useful self deception. Lycan makes a sharp distinction, however, between the methods for justifying reasonable beliefs and the adaptiveness of the beliefs themselves, and argues that a belief can be adaptive and/or psychologically compelling without being justified. Sternberg (1981) takes a position similar to Lycan's in arguing that the fact that irrational thinking may serve rational ends, if it is a fact—as for example when the belief in one's own invincibility makes a soldier willing to go to battle—does not make the thinking less irrational.

Fischhoff and Beyth-Marom (1983) note that people may deliberately act suboptimally in the short run in the interest of pursuing long-term goals. They may, for example, ask questions the answers to which are bound to be uninformative because asking questions that could yield informative answers would be seen as impolite. This illustrates that goals can sometimes be in conflict and one must choose among them; in the case of the example the goal of maintaining civility takes precedence over that of acquiring useful information. The asking of questions that cannot yield informative answers might be considered irrational when judged in terms of the goal of information acquisition, but perhaps not when judged from that of maintaining a friendly relationship.

It is certainly possible for actions motivated by false beliefs to have desirable outcomes, or at least outcomes that are desirable from some point of view. It is also the case that people can draw empirically true conclusions from invalid inferences; they can engage in behavior that is beneficial to others for purely selfish motives; and so on. There is a question, however, as to whether it is appropriate to credit—in a cause-effect sense—the false beliefs, the invalid reasoning, the selfish motives, for those desirable outcomes. Such relationships may be fortuitous. Can it be argued that the outcomes are better than they would have been had the beliefs been true and the reasoning valid? Even if one does consider the relationship to be causal, saying that irrational thinking can have desirable effects seems to me to be different from saying that irrational thinking can serve rational purposes.

In prescribing a player's optimal strategy, game theory assumes a rational opponent. An opponent that is not rational may, under certain circumstances, fare better than one that is. The game of "chicken," which is a form of the *prisoner's dilemma*, illustrates the point. In perhaps the best known form of this game, drivers race two automobiles toward each other, and the first to swerve to avoid a head-on collision is the chicken. Rationality, assuming one values one's life, dictates that one swerve in this situation, and being a live chicken is preferred by most players to being a dead nonchicken. But the preferred outcome is to emerge from the game a live nonchicken, which is to say to have one's opponent be the one to have swerved. One might argue, with some credibility, that an irrational player is more likely to realize the preferred outcome than a rational one, but this is probably true only if the irrational player is careful to play only against rational opponents, and there is some question as to whether such a player should be considered irrational.

A generalization of the prisoner's dilemma, known as the *traveler's dilemma*, represents a situation in which both inexperienced and expert players typically play in a way that is irrational according to game theoretic dictates, and, as a consequence, do better than they would by playing rationally (Basu, 1994, 2007). The obvious question that arises is that of the adequacy of any criterion of rationality that one would invariably do better to ignore.

Suppose I have a goal and I know that one way to realize that goal is to engage in behavior that I, if honest about it, would consider irrational. To be concrete, suppose I find myself in a verbal dispute that I wish to win, and I believe my chances of winning are maximized if I resort to the kinds of alogical stratagems that Schopenhauer (1896/undated) describes in his "Art of Controversy." An onlooker would say that my argumentation is irrational, and if asked, I would admit that that is so. But, to the extent that rationality is considered to be the working toward an established goal in an effective way, one might also say that I am being quite rational in my decision to argue irrationally, because I know my chances of winning the argument, in the eyes of my opponent, are better than if I argued to the point.

The first of these hypothetical cases illustrates that intentionally *appearing* to be irrational can serve a rational purpose (at least if one accepts winning the game of chicken or any of its various analogs to be a rational purpose). The second case is more subtle, because my purpose is not necessarily to appear to be irrational; I may believe that my opponent in the dispute will consider rational the behavior that I myself view as irrational but that I adopt for the sake of winning the dispute. One might say that my intention is to *be* irrational in the pursuit of the presumably rational goal of getting the better of my opponent.

The key to this puzzle lies in the recognition that the rationality of specific acts can be judged at different levels. Judged in isolation and on its own merits, my behavior—say it involves making fallacious arguments—can legitimately be called irrational, but from a broader perspective that takes my intentions into account, it can be seen as a part of a rational strategy for attaining a goal. More generally, my claim is that it can be rational to use, knowingly and intentionally, means to accomplish specific objectives that would legitimately be considered irrational if judged apart from a knowledge of the intentions and the objectives that are being pursued. Being rational in this sense is not necessarily the same as being honorable or nice.

Nozick (1993) presents a different type of situation. Consider the mother of a convicted felon. Suppose the evidence of the culprit's guilt is too strong to permit the mother, who desperately wants to believe in her son's innocence, to do so rationally. Such a belief, even for her, would be irrational, at least by Nozick's rule that one should not believe h if some alternative statement incompatible with h has a higher credibility than does h. But the belief in her son's guilt may be very destructive for the mother. Perhaps, all things considered, it would be best, from her point of view, to believe in his innocence, despite the evidence to the contrary. As Nozick puts it, "That he is innocent is not a rational thing for her to believe; but believing that might be the best, and hence the rational, thing for her to do" (p. 86).

Again, in order to make sense of this apparent contradiction, we have to recognize that rationality must be judged from some perspective, and that judgments from different perspectives may differ. The mother's belief in her son's innocence in the face of compelling evidence to the contrary is clearly irrational when judged from the frame of reference that sees rationality as having to do only with the evidential justification of beliefs. The judgment may be different, however, as Nozick's comment suggests, when made from a frame that makes rationality a function, in part, of utilitarian concerns.

Rationality is necessarily relative. What is rational for one person, living at a particular time in a specific culture, and facing specific situations with a certain profile of cognitive strengths and weaknesses, need not be rational for another individual living at a different time in a different culture and facing different situations with a different set of cognitive assets and limitations.

☐ Cognitive Pluralism

One would like to believe that there is a set of principles that makes clear what it means to be rational. The search for such a set has been the quest for many people who have thought long and hard about the subject. The failure of theorists to find a universally applicable set of principles has led some to speculate that there is no such set to be found. "Just as there is not one particular inductive policy, no one Carnapian c-function, that is best or most effective no matter what the character of the world, so there may be no one best principle of rational decision" (Nozick, 1993, p. 47).

Stich (1990) defends what he calls *cognitive pluralism*, which denies that there is only one good way to reason. He distinguishes between *descriptive* and *normative* cognitive pluralism. According to the former, different people form and revise beliefs and other cognitive states in different ways. This is a statement of empirical fact, in Stich's view. Normative cognitive pluralism makes a claim about the cognitive processes people *ought* to use. In particular, it holds that there are a variety of such processes that differ from each other but may all be equally good.

Some might see this view as perilously close to cognitive anarchy. But to hold that there are many systems of cognitive processes that are passably good is not necessarily to hold that any system is as good as any other. Stich does not make the latter claim, but he acknowledges that evaluating systems within a framework of cognitive pluralism poses a problem. The problem is that the evaluative ideas are themselves as culture-based as the cognitive processes that need to be evaluated. Even if our own evaluative notions proved to be reasonably coherent, systematic, and stable, Stich notes, they are only one set among many possibilities.

In view of the obvious circularity of the situation, it is hard to see, Stich argues, why people would care whether a cognitive system passes muster with respect to some local set of criteria, unless—this is important—doing so correlates with something that people do naturally care about. What people care about, more or less independently of cultural context, are such states of affairs as being able to predict or control nature and leading interesting and fulfilling lives. It follows that systems of cognitive processes should be viewed as cognitive tools and evaluated instrumentally, or consequentially, which is to say in terms of their effectiveness in bringing about such states of affairs. "One system of cognitive mechanisms is preferable to another if, in using it, we are more likely to achieve those things that we intrinsically value" (p. 24).

Stich sees his view as relativistic, in the sense that neither the ends—what is valued—nor the means to attain those ends need be the same for all people. It is not relativistic in every respect, however, because it proposes an invariant *principle* in terms of which cognitive systems are to be evaluated. The principle is a pragmatic one: to the extent that a system helps people obtain what they value intrinsically, it is good. More specifically, if one system is more effective than another in this regard, it is the better system of the two; the pragmatic view does not require that one be able to say whether a system is good or bad in any absolute sense. Before deciding that someone has reasoned poorly in a specific situation, one must be sure there is a humanly feasible alternative approach that is superior from a pragmatic point of view.

Stich specifically rejects both rationality and a tendency to produce true beliefs as intrinsically valuable features for cognitive processes to have. His position is that "all cognitive value is instrumental or pragmatic—that there are no intrinsic, uniquely cognitive values" (p. 21). Truth is dismissed as an important goal of cognitive processes on the grounds that what it means for a belief to be true is ambiguous. Stich's contention, as I understand it, is that truth is itself a culturally fashioned notion and, as such, has no universally recognized criteria of attainment; so it is not clear why anyone would care whether a belief is true, so long as it is instrumentally effective in helping one realize what one intrinsically values. "Since our notion of justification is just one member of a large and varied family of concepts of epistemic evaluation, it strikes most people as simply capricious or perverse to have an intrinsic preference for justified beliefs" (p. 95). It is not entirely clear what is the basis of the claim here that the view expressed is one that "most people" hold.

Stich contends that not only do cognitive states lack *intrinsic* value, there is no good reason to believe that there is *instrumental* value in holding justified or rational beliefs. "Nor is there any plausible case to be made in favor of the instrumental value of beliefs or cognitive processes that are justified or rational" (p. 93). In other words, there is no reason to expect justified or rational beliefs or cognitive processes to be more likely than other kinds to be instrumental in helping people achieve what they intrinsically value. The issue, Stich argues, is not whether true beliefs are more instrumentally valuable than false ones, but whether beliefs that are considered true by one culture-dependent set of criteria have greater instrumental value than those considered true by a different set of criteria. "What really needs to be shown is not just that true beliefs are more conducive to some independently desirable goal than false beliefs but also that true beliefs serve us better than TRUE* ones or TRUE** ones, or any of the other categories of belief picked out by interpretation functions that don't happen to be favored by intuition and tradition" (p. 121). (TRUE* beliefs and TRUE** beliefs are beliefs that are deemed to be true by some criteria other than those peculiar to our own culturally influenced intuitions and traditions.)

In summarizing his position on the instrumental value of true beliefs, Stich states a somewhat less extreme intention than the preceding quotes might seem to suggest. "My arguments about the instrumental value of true beliefs were not aimed at establishing that true beliefs are not instrumentally valuable. The goal was more modest. What I wanted to show was that the instrumental value of true beliefs is far from obvious, and thus those who think that true beliefs are instrumentally valuable owe us an argument that is not going to be easy to provide" (p. 124). He does state unequivocally that "[i]t is surely not the case that having true beliefs is *always* the best doxastic stance in pursuing our goals," and contends that "it would be no easy matter to show that believing the truth is *generally* (or even occasionally!) instrumentally optimal" (p. 124).

I have described Stich's defense of cognitive pluralism at some length, because my own argument that the basis of rationality must be human intuition and recognition that people's intuitions regarding rationality may differ to some degree might justifiably be seen as a form of cognitive pluralism. I want to take exception, however, to the idea that truth has neither intrinsic nor instrumental value. Indeed I find it somewhat ironic that one would go to the trouble of writing a book to convince the reader that truth is not an appropriate objective for cognitive processes. I suppose I should decide whether to accept what Stich says on this subject not on the basis of whether I consider it to be true, but on that of whether incorporating the idea that truth does not matter in my belief system is likely to make me more successful in attaining whatever it is that I really value. Inasmuch as truth, as I understand the concept, is something that (I think) I really value intrinsically, I should reject Stich's argument on the basis of his instrumentality criterion, if for no other reason.

Of course my rejection of Stich's position regarding the inappropriateness of truth as an objective of reasoning does not invalidate the position, except in my own view. But I find the idea that there is neither intrinsic nor instrumental value in holding, or at least in attempting to arrive at, true or justified beliefs to be a disturbing and intuitively implausible one. The quest for truth, it seems to me, is one thing—possibly the only thing—that different traditions of rationality have in common. We may not all agree on what the truth is, but the assumption that we are all seeking it is what gives us reason to hope that progress—that can be recognized as progress by all—can be made.

11 Conclusions and a View
CHAPTER

In this final chapter, I wish to return to the two questions that motivated the book: What is rationality, and are we rational? I will first review what several writers have said on the second question: whether, or the extent to which, we are rational. I will then present a view of what it means to be rational and offer an opinion as to the extent to which we measure up to that view.

☐ Some Views on Human Rationality

Recall from the first chapter of this book that some theorists make a three-way distinction among normative, prescriptive, and descriptive models of rationality (though I have played down the normative versus prescriptive distinction). Stanovich (1999) describes three positions on the question of human rationality that reflect a range of possibilities regarding the relationship among these three types of models. According to the *Panglossian* position, there is little or no difference among the models, which means that an accurate description of how people reason is actually normative—people's reasoning is rational. The *Meliorist* position sees a considerable difference between the way people reason and the way a prescriptive model indicates they should, but does not see a big difference between prescriptive and normative models. The *Apologist* position recognizes a big difference between normative and descriptive models, and locates the prescriptive model closer to a descriptive one than to a normative one; in other words, an Apologist is likely to consider human reasoning to be closer to what can reasonably be expected (prescribed), taking human cognitive limitations into account, than is the Meliorist. "In short, the Meliorist thinks that sometimes people are not reasoning very well and that they could do much better. The Apologist thinks that sometimes people are not reasoning properly, but that they are doing about as well as they could possibly do. And finally, the Panglossian feels that people are reasoning very well—indeed, as well as anyone could possibly reason in this best of all possible worlds" (Stanovich, 1999, p. 7).

Following a review of much of the relevant work, Stanovich (1999) concludes that the Meliorists have a reasonable case: "although computational limitations are certainly present, and although performance errors are no doubt implicated in the sizable residual error variance [after computational limitations have been accounted for], the remaining systematic variance in the normative/descriptive gap . . . gives empirical support to the Meliorist claim that at least part of the discrepancy is due to nonnormative thought patterns" (p. 211). He makes the interesting argument that the penchant of Panglossians to reject some "norms" as truly normative is limited to the norms that people have been shown experimentally to violate, which suggests that the Panglossian view, in effect, takes as its warrant for normativeness the empirical fact of what people in general do and do not accept as such. As for the Apologist position, according to which human reasoning is well-adapted in an evolutionary sense if not normatively rational, Stanovich suggests that people may do well with reasoning problems when they are cast in concrete ecologically familiar terms (e.g., deontic versions of Wason's selection task) because such situations may be accommodated by heuristics that require little thinking at all, which is to say that, in finding representations of problems that make them tractable, one may have, in effect, made them less demanding of logical thought.

Do people reason logically? Yes, no, and yes and no

A variation on Stanovich's three-way partitioning of views on human rationality might group writers in terms of how they answer the question of whether people naturally reason logically. One finds the full complement of answers to the question in the literature. Relatively recent writers who contend that people's logical intuitions are basically sound and influential in their thought and behavior include Braine (1978, 1990), Dennett (1978, 1981), Cohen (1979, 1981, 1982), Lycan (1981, 1988), (Levi, 1983), Rips (1983), Macnamara (1986), Rescher (1988), Hamill (1990), Noveck, Lea, Davidson, and O'Brien (1991), Stevenson (1993), and Wetherick (1993). Similar positions were taken by Kant (1787, 1788), Boole (1854), and Piaget (1928). Few, if any, would claim that people always think in accordance with the rules of logic, as formalized by, say, the predicate or propositional calculus, but several hold that people are endowed with logical competence and will intuitively appreciate logical inconsistencies when they are pointed out to them. The fundamental assumption on which this view is based is that logic gets its authority from human intuitions rather than the reverse. The rules of logic, or at least certain concepts and principles on which those rules are based, such as the concepts of truth, implication, and contradiction and the principle of the excluded middle, are considered to be intuitively obvious and compelling to the normal human mind (Goodman, 1965).

For every articulate proponent of the soundness and importance of human logical intuitions, one can find an equally articulate defender of the position that such intuitions are fundamentally unsound or that logic has little if anything to do with the way people think and behave in their everyday lives. Among the many who take this position are Mill (1892/1995), Jourdain (1956), Erickson (1978), Evans (1982), Good (1983), Cheng and Holyoak (1985), Holland, Holyoak, Nisbett, and Thagard (1986), Margolis (1987), Piattelli-Palmarini (1994), and Oaksford and Chater (1991, 1995). Here is one unflattering summary of the empirical findings regarding people's performance on reasoning tasks: "people assess probabilities incorrectly, they display confirmation bias, they test hypotheses inefficiently, they violate the axioms of utility theory, they do not properly calibrate degrees of belief, they overproject their own opinions onto others, they allow prior knowledge to become implicated in deductive reasoning, they systematically underweight information about nonoccurrence when evaluating covariation, and they display numerous other information processing biases" (Stanovich (1999, p. 1).

In the preceding paragraphs, I have put people into two camps on the basis of their positions regarding the extent to which human logical intuitions are sound, especially as evidenced by their reasoning and behavior. Such a dichotomous partitioning is admittedly overly simple. Presumably few of the writers mentioned would argue either that people invariably reason and behave logically or that they never do. Here is one "yes and no" answer to the question of whether people think and act logically that represents a middle-of-the-road position: "I see people using logic frequently, both in ordinary tasks and in laboratory-reasoning tasks. When mental logic can be applied straightforwardly, it will be. When the reasoner has available the strategic skills required to solve a complex problem, and grasps the problem's requirements, mental logic will allow solution. Otherwise, the problem solver has no other recourse but to non-logical heuristics or to pragmatic inferences" (O'Brien, 1993, p. 126). Perhaps most researchers would agree that people are sometimes logical and sometimes not, although there would be very substantial differences in positions regarding the extent to which, and the conditions under which, logic influences behavior and thought.

Competence versus performance

> Our fellow humans have to be attributed a competence for reasoning validly, and this provides the backcloth against which we can study defects in their actual performance. (Cohen, 1981, p. 317)

Another answer to the question of whether people naturally think logically rests on the distinction between competence and performance (Braine, 1978; Braine & Rumain, 1983; Cohen, 1981; Flavell & Wohlwill, 1969; Mcnamara, 1986). People are logically competent, according to this view, even though their reasoning performance sometimes makes it appear that they are not. The fact that one does not act logically invariably is not convincing evidence that one lacks the ability to be logical, just as specific failures to act ethically do not mean necessarily that one does not know how to do right. Performance that appears to be illogical could result not only from misinterpretations of language but from a variety of other factors in addition to logical incompetence; these include working memory limitations, time limitations, task misinterpretation, confusion of entailment with degree of support, and simple carelessness (Rips, 1994, 1995). The list of possible ways of attributing to alogical causes errors that might otherwise be attributed to faulty reasoning is sufficiently long that, as Rips points out, "a determined skeptic can usually explain away any instance of what seems at first to be a logical mistake" (p. 393).

Cohen (1981) argues that human rationality is safe from attack by those who would deny it because verdicts of irrationality appeal to normative criteria that are nothing more than systematized human intuitions. If the criteria are to have force, the rationality of the intuitions from which they derive must be granted. This is not to hold that people always reason inerrently, or even to deny that there may be some types of erroneous reasoning *performance* that are fairly common, but it is to deny the possibility of pervasive lack of reasoning *competence*. "[N]othing in the existing literature on cognitive reasoning, or in any possible future results of human experimental enquiry could have bleak implications for human rationality, in the sense of implications that establish a faulty competence. At best experimenters in this area may hope to discover revealing patterns of illusion. Often they will only be testing subjects' intelligence or education. At worst they risk imputing fallacies where none exist" (p. 330).

Cohen likens his use of the distinction between competence and performance in reasoning to that employed by Chomsky in the context of linguistics. Competence in both cases refers to what people can do, and performance refers to what they actually do in specific situations. Chomsky (1957, 1965) equates linguistic competence with one's knowledge of language and performance with one's use of language, and holds that competence typically is not fully revealed by performance because performance is determined not only by one's knowledge of the language but by a variety of other factors as well.

As the distinction is applied to thinking, one is said to be competent with respect to a specific principle of reasoning if one is able to apply that principle correctly in at least some everyday situations. Having the competence to apply a principle, however, does not mean that one will always be able to articulate the principle or even that one will invariably apply it correctly in every situation in which it would be appropriate. It is assumed, however, that when people of normal intelligence do something irrational and the irrationality of the behavior is explained to them, they will readily comprehend the difficulty, thanks to the competence of their intuitions.

On the face of it, the distinction between competence and performance seems an eminently reasonable one. Most of us would probably agree that people's performance does not always match their competence exactly, and that this is true no matter what their level of competence is. It seems obvious that it is possible for one to perform a task—perhaps because of lack of interest or effort—below the level of one's ability. It seems likely too, that people may be able, on occasion, to perform above their ability, perhaps by chance, at least for short periods of time. If this were the whole story regarding the distinction between competence and performance in the context of discussions of human reasoning, the distinction would not be a contentious one, but there is more to it than this.

It is not just that competence is assumed to be correlated imperfectly with performance, but that the logical competence is assumed to be high and more or less the same for everyone. This assumption is essential, it is argued, if we are to make sense of the fact that people can understand one another's reasoning: "different logics for my idiolect and yours are not coherently supposable" (Cohen, 1981, p. 322). It follows from this assumption that what might appear to be evidences to the contrary should invariably be attributed to failures of performance.

The distinction between competence and performance is made also by Macnamara (1986), who contends that it is this distinction that permits logic's errorless ideals and the fact of logical blunders to be encompassed by a single theory of mind. He defends the thesis that "a logic that is true to intuition in a certain area constitutes a competence theory for the corresponding area of cognitive psychology" (p. 22). By *competence theory* he too means something similar to what Chomsky means by the term in the area of language. As Chomsky attributes ungrammatical utterances to such factors as slips of attention or limitations of short-term memory, as opposed to linguistic incompetence, just so Macnamara attributes logical errors to performance factors as opposed to faulty mental logic.

An unusual response to the proposed distinction between competence and performance comes from Smedslund (1981) who argues that all performance should be considered rational, in the sense of being a logical consequence of one's momentary premises. The failure of an experimental task that demands logical performance should be interpreted, on this view, as resulting from inadequate communication between experimenter and subject. "An experimental procedure that results in apparent irrational behavior *must* be regarded as inadequate" (p. 352). This view resolves any difficulties that stem from the competence-performance distinction, but its tenability is doubtful in the light of the many evidences that people are capable of performing illogically even when great care has been taken to ensure the adequacy of communication between experimenter and subject—which is not to deny that inadequate communication may be the culprit in many cases.

The distinction between competence and performance, as applied to reasoning—more specifically, the idea that most or all of the claimed evidences of incompetence can be attributed to failures of performance only—has been strongly criticized (e.g., Einhorn & Hogarth, 1981b; Evans & Pollard, 1981; Stanovich & West, 2000a, b; Stich, 1990; Stich & Nisbett, 1980). (It has been criticized also as applied to linguistics where, allegedly, it has been used "to protect linguists' theories against refutation, by permitting observations contradicting the theories to be dismissed as 'performance effects,' while those that confirm the theories are taken as a true reflection of a speaker's 'competence'" [Sampson, 1981, p. 350].) Several critics have pointed out that inasmuch as any instance of defective reasoning can be attributed to some determinant of performance other than competence, a faulty competence can never be established from observation of faulty performance (Einhorn & Hogarth, 1981b; Evans & Pollard, 1981; Johnson-Laird & Byrne, 1993); this makes the distinction of little interest from a scientific point of view.

Evans and Pollard (1981) argue that it is inconsistent to refuse to take instances of illogical performance as evidence of logical incompetence but then to accept instances of logical performance as evidence of logical competence; the appearance of competence, they point out, may be as illusory as that of incompetence. And they note that if the distinction between competence and performance is accepted, one must distinguish too between rational behavior and desirable behavior, inasmuch as some of the behavior that would pass for rational by Cohen's definition is likely to have undesirable and costly effects.

Evans (1982, 1989) argues too that the evidence that people are logically competent is very slim. He suggests that the explanations that have been proposed to account for what everybody agrees is illogical *performance* on syllogistic reasoning tasks have been somewhat paradigm-specific. While consistent results may have been found within paradigms and plausible models or explanations have been proposed to account for those results, the explanations do not carry well across paradigms.

Stich (1990) also rejects the idea that people have reliably sound intuitions about rules of inference, and maintains that careful investigation of the intuitions that lie behind faulty performance will often reveal those intuitions to be faulty as well. If, for example, people who appear to reflect some version of the gambler's fallacy in their reasoning about games of chance are interrogated about the beliefs on which their performance is based, it will be found that in many cases their beliefs are consistent with their performance. Many people really believe, for example, that the likelihood of a toss of a seven with a die, say, increases with the number of consecutive nonsevens that have been tossed.

The evidence that people do, sometimes, understand the logical requirements of a reasoning task and yet fail to apply them is compelling (Wason, 1969; Wason & Johnson-Laird, 1970; Wason & Golding, 1974). Even Evans (1989), who rejects the idea that the logicality of thought can be preserved by an appeal to the distinction between competence and performance, arguing that evidence of impressive competence is sparse, acknowledges that people often understand logical principles that they fail to apply. "[R]easoning and judgmental errors are very common in observed performance relative to the competence which people can be shown to possess. People can reason out the answer to syllogisms, for example, but frequently fall prey to a syntactic or semantic source of bias. Intuitive statistical judgments can, under favorable conditions, take heed of the law of large numbers or even base rates, but all too often fail to do so. People understand the logic of falsification of hypotheses but often cannot find the appropriate strategy to achieve this, even when exhorted by instructions. People understand the essential truth conditions of conditional sentences but cannot apply this knowledge to solution of the selection task" (p. 109).

Osherson (1995) considers the possibility that, at least in the context of probabilistic reasoning, people may have the potential to reason coherently, even though they often reason in ways that are probabilistically incoherent, and cites work of Nisbett, Krantz, Jepson, and Kunda (1983) and Gigerenzer and Murray (1987), among others, as supportive of this idea. He rules out the possibility of complete probabilistic coherence, however, on the grounds that its realization would require computational capabilities far beyond what human beings have available. This being so, one has no alternative but to resort to reasoning heuristics that are easy to apply but suboptimal from a theoretical point of view" (p. 68). But, he suggests, the fact is we make use of such heuristics not only in situations that require their use but also often in those in which coherent reasoning would be possible and preferable.

Cohen (1981) attributes some of the experimental evidences of faulty reasoning to the creation by experimenters of "cognitive illusions" that prompt people to engage in forms of reasoning that they would readily recognize to be invalid upon a few moments of reflection. Diaconis and Freedman (1981) contest the claim that the cognitive illusions to which Cohen refers are dispelled by brief reflection and make the counter claim, based on experience in teaching probability and statistics to college students, that such illusions exist, are very resistive to change by education, and even occur and recur among experts. Stein (1996) contends that the idea that every possible divergence from a normative principle of reasoning can be considered simply an error of performance, as distinct from evidence of incompetence, is, in effect, an "immunization strategy" protecting the assumption of prevailing rationality from any possible empirical refutation. Stanovich (1999) argues that the evidence is inconsistent with the assumption that people have a perfect rational competence that is obscured only by performance errors and computational limitations, and favors the view that some human behavior must be considered systematically irrational when what can be attributed to such factors has been taken into account.

To be sure, many of the ostensible demonstrations of irrationality have been criticized by researchers who have found them less than compelling for a variety of—especially methodological—reasons, but, as Shafir and LeBoeuf (2002) note in their review of much of this work, the objections that have been raised to the claims that people's reasoning often is irrational in systematic ways are themselves less than compelling in many respects. "Deviations from the criteria of rational judgment and choice cannot be seen as mere 'performance errors.' These deviations are far too systematic, both within and across individuals, to be considered randomly distributed. The systematic biases persist in the face of a variety of attempts to increase incentives as well as other motivational factors. The biases are exhibited by experts as well as novices and cannot be dismissed as random artifacts attributable to trivial uninteresting, or unrepresentative tasks" (p. 503).

Implicit in the distinction between competence and performance is the assumption that we may be more competent to make rational judgments than our performance in situations that require reasoning often demonstrates. We often perform below our potential; we are less rational in our behavior than we could be if we were motivated to behave as rationally as possible. Perkins (2002) argues that people cannot reason entirely in accordance with standard logic because of limitations of computation, intelligence and understanding, but that they also often fail to attain the degree of logicality that is within their ability to attain. One of the more obvious challenges to further research on the question of how logic relates to human reasoning is that of determining why people sometimes fail to apply to reasoning tasks logical principles that they appear not only to understand but to realize are relevant to the task.

One would like to know the extent to which this failure to apply logical competence is a failure of effort—a consequence of not thinking hard enough about reasoning problems, of taking minimally-effortful paths to quick, if uncertain, solutions—as opposed to a genuine inability, despite effort, to tap one's competence in specific situations. To the extent that one's competence is inaccessible, we might question whether it should be considered competence, but we know that specific knowledge sometimes can be accessible under some conditions and not under others, and there is little reason to believe that this does not apply to knowledge of reasoning principles as well as to knowlege of other kinds. The question is an important one, because the answer has implications for how one would go about trying to increase the extent to which people apply the reasoning competence they have.

An explanation that has been proposed of why people sometimes do not reason strictly in accordance with logical principles that they understand is that they apply to reasoning problems experience-based knowledge they have about the problem situations. Oaksford and Sellen (2000) give the following example: "take the rule, *if you turn the key the car starts*. If I believe that the car won't start because it is out of fuel, or the ignition is broken, and so on, then I might be less willing to conclude that *the car starts* on learning that *the key has been turned* (MP [modus ponens]) or that the *key has not been turned* on learning that *the car has not started* (MT [modus tollens])" (p. 691). The idea that people sometimes fail to make strictly logical inferences on laboratory reasoning tasks because they know that, in real life, exceptions to the logically-determined conclusions are available gains some credence from Oaksford and Sellen's finding that people who rank high on a schizotypy scale make more MP and MT inferences than do people who rank low on such a scale, schizotypic thinking being characterized by lack of attention to exceptions.

Stanovich (1999) raises the interesting question of what would be gained, from a practical point of view, if the case for the Panglossian position that people are rational could be established and all the ostensible evidences to the contrary accounted for in terms of the competence/performance distinction. "All of the interesting practical consequences will be on the performance side of the competence/performance divide. If the

Panglossians succeed in preserving perfectly rational competence, it will be a pyrrhic victory because by the time they have abstracted away all of the differing task construals, all algorithmic limitations, all variation in epistemic goals, and a host of other things, we will indeed have identified an abstract reasoning competence with no variability—but the variability in performance factors will in fact be the primary thing that we want to explain" (p. 217). For practical purposes, it matters little whether one comes to hold false beliefs because of faulty reasoning or faulty use of language. Moreover, the kinds of difficulties in language interpretation that have been hypothesized to account for what appear to be errors of reasoning might, in some cases, be attributed to faulty habits of thought: if I consistently interpret "All A are B" to mean also "All B are A," might one not be as justified in saying that I do not reason clearly as in characterizing my problem as faulty language use?

The distinction between competence and performance, whatever its merits, makes unclear what might be taken as convincing evidence that people do *not* naturally think logically. Competence—or incompetence—is revealed only through performance, but inasmuch as lack of competence is only one of many conceivable causes of poor performance, any instance of poor performance is likely to have a variety of possible explanations. It is for this reason that O'Brien (1993) can argue that neither failure to solve complex reasoning problems nor evidence of effects of content on logical reasoning should count against mental logic.

A major methodological impediment to the study of the role that logic plays in reasoning stems from the inscrutability of the reasoning process. The fact that one has come to a conclusion that could have been inferred logically does not mean that one arrived at the conclusion through a logical inference or chain of such inferences. Conclusions that appear to be logically valid inferences can be made by the application of knowledge of content-specific or situation-specific rules (Griggs & Cox, 1982; Manktelow & Evans, 1979; Reich & Ruth, 1982). Some investigators have argued that, typically, when people draw what appear to be logically sound conclusions, they do not use logic to do so; rather they use inferential schemas that produce results that happen to coincide with those that would be produced by formal logic (Holland, Holyoak, Nisbett, & Thagard, 1986). Others have made similar arguments regarding the use of pattern recognition (Margolis, 1987) or mental models (Johnson-Laird, 1983; Johnson-Laird & Bara, 1984; Johnson-Laird & Byrne, 1991; Johnson-Laird & Steedman, 1978) to generate answers to reasoning problems that correspond to those that would be produced by the application of logic.

Do people generally have greater logical competence than their less-than-impressive performance of tasks that call for reasoning often demonstrates? The question of whether people think logically—perhaps better, the question of the extent to which their thinking is affected by logic—must be considered still an open one, despite the many studies that have been addressed to it. An alternative to the assumption of universal competence is the view that people possess a degree of competence with respect to specific aspects of reasoning, such as the ability to reason in accordance with at least some of the rules or logic or with certain principles of statistics, but that different people are competent to different degrees and that the evidence does not justify the assumption of a broad high-level competence for reasoning that is shared by all unimpaired members of the culture (Jepson, Krantz, & Nisbett, 1983). In my view, the evidence supports the conclusion that most people do have a considerable amount of logical competence, which can be tapped under the right circumstances and often simply as a consequence of induced effort. This competence is limited, but we frequently, perhaps typically, do not make the effort to exercise that which we have. How education might be used to improve upon this situation is a question of considerable practical significance.

Other researchers have made distinctions that are similar in some respects to the distinction between competence and performance. The distinction between two general types of human error, mistakes and slips, proposed by Norman (1981) is a case in point. Somewhat analogous to this distinction, in the domain of reasoning, is Kahneman and Tversky's (1982) distinction between errors of comprehension and errors of application. A failure of comprehension is said to occur when one does not recognize the validity of a rule of good reasoning; an error of application connotes failure to apply a rule as appropriate even though one understands the rule. The fact that individuals sometimes fail to apply a particular rule that they understand does not mean that they invariably will fail to do so. If people sometimes violate a specific statistical principle in a choice situation, it does not follow that they will fail to solve correctly all problems to which that principle applies.

These distinctions—between competence and performance, between mistakes and slips, between errors of comprehension and errors of application—are conceptually meaningful and empirically defensible. They do not seem to me, however, to deal adequately with the fact that people's intuitions about rationality differ. To be fair, I should note that only one of these distinctions—that between competence and performance—was put forth for that purpose. What that distinction fails to do is account for the fact that people sometimes insist that their behavior, which has been judged by someone else to be irrational, is, indeed, rational. That is to say, it does not deal with the situation in which differences in intuitions seem to persist despite efforts to reconcile them.

The practical significance of the distinction between competence and performance has been questioned on the grounds that the practical challenge is that of improving performance in any case. On the other hand, how one would go about attempting to decrease the pervasiveness of systematic reasoning errors might depend on whether one assumed the existence of an underlying competence that could be exploited or the need to create competence where it does not exist.

The distinction between competence and performance has an implication for research methodology that deserves some emphasis. Researchers should be clear as to whether their intent in any given experimental situation is to determine what people *typically do* in similar situations or what they *are capable of doing* when working at the limits of their capacity. When the latter is the intent it is imperative to ensure that people understand completely the task they are being asked to perform and that they are motivated to do their best. When these conditions are not met, there is good reason to question whether their performance should be taken as an indication of their competence with respect to that task.

Pragmatic rationality

> It is the satisfaction of very general criteria, such as comprehensiveness, simplicity, and fertility in further development, which should be the distinguishing mark of a truly rational inquiry. (Polkinghorne, 1991, p. 7)

There are several distinctions in the literature that might be considered variants of the distinction between theoretical rationality—the kind of rationality that requires adherence to some system of logic, internal consistency among beliefs, and so on—and practical or pragmatic rationality—the kind or rationality that helps human beings, with their capabilities and limitations, effectively make their way in the world. Some would argue that it is the latter type of rationality that should be our major concern. As Willard (1995) colorfully puts it: "the image of pristine logic uncontaminated by human frailties is a poor idealization of rationality. Anyone can be rational in a hypothetical state of grace—with the luxury of reflection, freed from prejudice, social pressures, time limits, and information shortages. But we live our lives shackled to these frailties. People must be rational, not in their armchairs but *amid* the swirl of society, the clamor of competing advocates" (p. 156).

Some theorists contend that we are rational in the practical sense of forming beliefs and selecting patterns of action that are generally optimal, or at least effective, in that they assure our survival and serve our own self interests about as well as possible given the limitations of our cognitive resources. Lycan (1988) is a case in point, as is Anderson (1990), and perhaps Simon (1957), Wilson (1978), Cherniak (1986), Harman (1986), Dennett (1987), and Margolis (1987). "[T]he human species would hardly have thrived if our brains routinely deceived us. So we should expect to find that our intuitive sense of a situation is usually sound . . . even though the existence of illusions shows that it is not always sound" (Margolis, 1987, p. 13).

It was noted in chapter 6 that "explanationism," as described by Lycan (1988) takes the position that the goal of the rational thinker should be to accept as most probably true the hypothesis, among competing alternatives, that best explains the facts—with maximal simplicity, explanatory scope, and testability, and minimal residual mess. As to why theories that have these characteristics should be preferred to those that do not, Lycan argues that such preferences will promote the formation of beliefs that are more useful than those that would be promoted by preferences of other kinds. Considering the constraints of our shape, size, and biochemical composition, and the fact that much of the capacity of our brains must be devoted to noncognitive processes, there are nontrivial limits to what can be used for higher brain functions. It is necessary, therefore, that the basic mechanisms that are to help us form useful beliefs about the world be few in number and efficient, even if at some cost in reliability and detail. Given these assumptions and constraints, we would expect to have been designed to prefer simpler hypotheses to more complex ones (not, Lycan notes, because nature is simple, but because simplicity is essential to our coping), to prefer hypotheses of greater explanatory power to narrower ones (one hypothesis of broad scope is easier to deal with than several of narrow scope), and so on.

The preferences with which we find ourselves—for explanatory theories that satisfy criteria like those mentioned—have survival value, according to this view. They do not guarantee that we will arrive only at true beliefs, but they ensure that, on balance, the beliefs we come to hold support our continued existence and progress as a species, or at least they have done so in the past. A similar argument is made by Anderson (1990), who holds that much can be learned about human cognition, not by looking at what is going on inside the head, but by trying to determine what would be effective behavior given human goals and the environment in which the behavior takes place.

The equating of adaptability with rationality has been contested by Stich (1985, 1990), among others, on the grounds that many species have proved to be adaptive, but we do not attribute rationality to them for that reason. On the other hand, the accomplishments of human beings that would seem to be the direct consequence of an ability to reason are qualitatively different from those of any other species. Indeed the ability of humans to do mathematics, create music, and do science are seen by some as problematic for attempts to explain cognition in strictly adaptability terms. Barrow (1991) poses the problem this way: "Why has the process of natural selection so over-endowed us with mental faculties that we can understand the whole fabric of the Universe far beyond anything required for our past and present survival?" (p. 173).

As already noted, Davies (1992) too expresses puzzlement in the fact that we are capable of doing science, given that "human intellectual powers are presumably determined by biological evolution, and have absolutely no connection with doing science" (p. 149). From where, in particular, he asks, comes our fascination with and propensity for abstract mathematics? Where is the survival value of this propensity? Davies refers to the fact that the human brain has acquired its extraordinary mathematical ability as a surprise and a deep mystery. Why the "enchanted loom," as Sherrington (1906) referred to the human brain, got to be what it is with the ability to weave the patterns it does, which appear to be much more diverse and intricate than is required for survival represents to many observers a puzzle that adaptability does not explain.

☐ How Do We Decide What Is Rational?

> [E]ven the most analytical line of argument must rely ultimately on intuition (axioms, simplifying assumptions, definitions, etc., which appeal eventually to an intuitive conviction of reasonableness). (Margolis, 1987, p. 82)

Is it rational to work against one's own self-interests, to accept uncritically what others say, to fail to discount sunk costs, to play long odds, to discount the future sharply, to behave by rule? Is it rational to hold inconsistent beliefs, or to be defensive about the beliefs one holds? Must one be intelligent or knowledgeable to be rational? Is rationality essentially the same thing as wisdom? It should be clear by now that such questions can seldom be adequately answered with an unqualified yes or no. Behavior that is irrational for one person may be rational from the perspective of another whose knowledge, beliefs or values differ.

I do not mean to suggest that there are no standards or norms, and will attempt to make a case for a specific view of what it means to be rational; however, I do want to argue that rationality is a complex concept and that the final court of appeals on the question of what constitutes rationality must be human intuition. But it is the case, is it not, that our intuitions sometimes are wrong. Certainly science has come up with many counterintuitive discoveries, especially in this century. Mathematicians have sometimes shown even quite strong intuitions to be incorrect and have used counterintuitive proofs to do so. Do these facts not undermine the claim that intuition must be the final judge of what is rational?

I think the answer must be no. When we accept a counterintuitive discovery that science has made, our intuitions are changed as a consequence of new knowledge that we have acquired. The belief that the world revolves about the sun was counterintuitive to people who knew no more about the universe than what they immediately perceived. To us who have a wealth of information available regarding the structure of the solar system, in addition to that that we get by direct observation, it is not counterintuitive at all. Many of the ideas that are entertained by modern-day particle physicists are surely counterintuitive to most of us; however, when such an idea is accepted by an individual as the best possible account of some aspect of reality, given the current state of knowledge about it, we must assume that for that individual the idea that we find counterintuitive has become more acceptable, intuitively, than any of the alternatives available.

A similar argument applies to intuitively obvious mathematical ideas that are shown, by counterintuitive proofs, to be false. How can one become convinced that a counterintuitive proof should be accepted, except by satisfying oneself that the argument is sound? And to what does one appeal, other than to one's intuitions, to make that determination? If your answer is, one must appeal not to one's intuitions but to the rules of logic, I will ask, how does one know *which* rules of logic to accept?

When presented with the question of whether there are more integers than even integers, our first intuition might be to say yes, because for any string of consecutive integers that we imagine, only every other one is even. On the other hand, we might be convinced that there are equally as many even integers as integers on the grounds that *every* integer can be multiplied by 2 to generate its double. Mathematicians readily accept the argument that the two sets are of equal size because the even integers can be put into one-to-one correspondence with the integers,

$$1, 2, 3, 4, 5, 6, 7, \ldots$$
$$2, 4, 6, 8, 10, 12, 14, \ldots$$

and that no matter how long the first sequence gets, the second one will always be able to keep up with it.

This example is, to a degree, a matter of definition. One way to define an infinite collection is as a collection that contains, as parts, other collections that have as many items as it has (as Dedekind did). Whether one finds this definition of an infinite collection acceptable is itself at least partly a matter of intuition. Infinity is a difficult concept and has been recognized to be such at least since the days of the classical Greeks and Zeno's famous paradoxes. We may define the term in various ways; what we will find acceptable may depend on the uses to which the concept is to be put. What infinity really *is* is beyond our knowing; the best we can do is attempt to come up with definitions that will be intuitively acceptable if not compelling.

But the use of mathematics can produce results, it is claimed, that are beyond our intuitions but that we believe nevertheless. Hahn (1933/1956a) argues, for example, that although a rigorous proof can be given that a trajectory of a moving point can be defined that will take the point through all the points enclosed by a square, "[t]his motion cannot possibly be grasped by intuition; it can only be understood by logical analysis" (p. 1966). Granting Hahn's claim that the defined motion cannot be grasped intuitively does not make our acceptance of the proof, assuming we accept it, any less intuitively based; we accept the proof only if doing so is more consistent with our intuitions than is rejecting it.

Hahn claims that mathematicians have lost their confidence in intuition and abolished it from their domain. "Because intuition turned out to be deceptive in so many instances, and because propositions that had been accounted true by intuition were repeatedly proved false by logic, mathematicians became more and more skeptical of the validity of intuition. They learned that it is unsafe to accept any mathematical proposition, much less to base any mathematical discipline on intuitive convictions. Thus a demand arose for the expulsion of intuition from mathematical reasoning, and for the complete formalization of mathematics. That is to say, every new mathematical concept was to be introduced through a purely logical definition; every mathematical proof was to be carried through by strictly logical means" (p. 1970). But this is tantamount to kicking intuition out the front door and then rushing around to let it in the back one, albeit without recognizing the backdoor entrant for what it is. If there were some good reason to believe that logic is not intuitively based, then the banishment of intuition from mathematics might make sense, but I know of none.

The claim that we must fall back finally on our intuitions does not entail the assumption that our intuitions are infallible, or even that they are unchangeable. It does not rule out the possibility of sometimes finding intuitive ideas in conflict and having to give one precedence over another—just as we sometimes find ethical ideas in conflict and have to decide which to observe in the situation. It involves only the recognition that there is no other court of appeal. If there were, we would have to decide whether we should avail ourselves of it, and on what basis would we do that?

One does not get away from intuition by axiomatization. In accepting an axiomatic system, one not only accepts the axioms but the logic by which the implications of the axioms are derived. If the system is intended to be used to represent reality in some way, one must decide whether one is willing to accept the axioms, which is to say, one must decide, to the best of one's ability, whether the axioms do in fact reflect reality. And, in any case, if one wishes to make the implications of the axioms explicit, one must decide, at least tacitly, what rules of logic are to be used in their explication.

The idea that intuition must be the last court of appeal for any theory of rationality has been championed by Cohen (1981), among others. The idea has many critics, some of whom recognize a role for intuition, but who qualify that role in various ways. Kahneman (1981) acknowledges the force of the argument that normative theories of rationality must derive their authority ultimately from human intuition—"one of the criteria for a norm of thought and action must be that reasonable people will want to obey it"—but he contends that "it is improper to argue, as Cohen does, from this general belief in human rationality to a belief in the rationality of any notion for which a majority can be found" (p. 340). Kyburg (1981) contends that the objective, in developing norms of rationality, should not be "to honor all intuitions indiscriminately—even in qualified form—but to reduce collections of intuitions to a relatively small number of very basic intuitions from which others can be derived" (p. 342). Richards (1996) notes that "if there is a single distinguishing characteristic of commitments to rationality and science, it is a refusal to take unrefined intuitions as the end of any matter" (p. 405).

An obvious, and powerful, objection to the idea that intuition must be the last court of appeal for any theory of rationality is based on recognition that people's intuitions differ on the question of what should be considered rational. One response to this objection is to hold that only the intuitions of people who are qualified to have an opinion should count. But there are at least two obvious objections to this proviso. First, is the problem of determining who should be considered qualified to have an opinion that counts—or regarding what the qualifications should be. Solving this problem encounters the same difficulty as does the problem that is to be solved: who is qualified to decide who is qualified? And so on ad infinitum. In practice, what seems to happen is that people who consider themselves qualified simply identify themselves as such and make pronouncements. But the second problem is that, even assuming the first problem of deciding who is qualified to have opinions that count can be identified, there is little reason to expect all the members of any such group, unless carefully self-selected on the basis of shared intuitions, to have precisely the same intuitions regarding the question of interest.

In short, one must appeal to ones' own intuitions, in the final analysis, to answer the question of what is rational, because there is nowhere else to turn. Inasmuch as people's intuitions may differ on particulars, we are each of us on his own; you must appeal to your intuitions, I must rely on mine. We may both look to experts—to those whom we believe to be experts—for help, but inasmuch as those experts are not all likely to agree, we must look to ourselves to decide which of them to believe. Even if the experts did agree, we would have to decide whether to accept their claims of being qualified to tell us what is rational and what is not. There is no escaping one's personal responsibility in this regard. Believe what you will, but justify what you believe, not by what others—parents, teachers, political leaders, philosophers—claim to believe, but by what the evidence that you personally find compelling dictates.

The idea that people's intuitions about rationality really differ, even when one looks beneath the surface of performance differences that can be attributed to carelessness or lack of adequate thought, is a problem to anyone who wants to argue, as I do, that one's intuitions must be the final court of appeal regarding questions of what constitutes rational thought or action. I suspect that people's intuitions will be found to be very similar, for the most part, when they are probed in depth, else discourse would be more difficult than it is. On the question of whether people are logically competent, my own view is that most human beings of normal intelligence share the same intuitions at a relatively deep level and that they, therefore, possess a common inherent potential for logical competence. These intuitions can be suppressed by learned patterns of illogical or alogical thinking, and if these patterns have become deeply entrenched from long use, they may be very difficult to modify; but I believe that, in most cases, even deeply buried intuitions may be activated by reflection and that people of good will have good reason to expect that honest efforts to reason together will produce some convergence of views. So even when we are convinced that fundamental differences in views exist, we can work to resolve them, with some reasonable hope of success. And if we are left with irresolvable differences, so be it; I see no way of avoiding the problem. I cannot rely on your intuitions, nor can you rely on mine; each of us must believe what we, as individuals, find believable.

☐ Principles of Good Reasoning

> Instead of taking things for granted, one begins to think for oneself, and this is the beginning of serious responsibility. (Jaspers, 1952, p. 55)

The question of what constitutes rational beliefs or behavior should be of concern not only to philosophers, anthropologists, sociologists, psychologists, or scholars of one or another stripe; it should be of central concern to each of us. How should I spend my time? What books should I read? What should I think about? What friendships should I cultivate? How should I bring up my children? (I want them to be independent and to reason for themselves—not to be clones of me—but I am far from indifferent regarding the values they acquire and the kinds of people they become.) How do I judge the credibility of what I read in, or hear from, the media? How do I decide what to believe?

Rationality is rationality *from some point of view*. To the extent that a particular view of rationality has been favored—explicitly or implicitly—in this book, it is, of course, my view. I have tried to consider and to report what many people have said about various aspects of rationality. My own view has undoubtedly been shaped, to no small degree, by this review. I wish now to try to make that view explicit. I do not claim that this is the only view that can be held, but only that it is the one that I wish to promote.

Being rational means being a good reasoner. But what does it mean to be a good reasoner? There seems to be a tacit assumption underlying much of the discussion about teaching thinking that all good thinkers can be represented by the same description. This assumption is worth some reflection. Suppose we were to attempt to come up with a set of characteristics that all good reasoners—all rational people—would have in common, which is to say a list of characteristics that, as a set, define what it means to be a good reasoner. Would this set have many characteristics or few? Given the multifaceted nature of reasoning, should we perhaps admit the possibility of finding two people both of whom we would consider to be good reasoners who share few characteristics or conceivably even none?

Can we identify a set of characteristics that we would consider necessary though perhaps not sufficient to good reasoning? Or might we identify more than one set, any of which would be sufficient but not necessary? The latter possibility is consistent with the view that different people can be good reasoners in different ways. Are there some characteristics of good reasoning that are independent of the domain in which the reasoning is done? Are there principles that are common to reasoning in mathematics, science, law, medicine, history, and everyday affairs? Are there justifiable claims that can be made about the limitations of reasoning that apply generally?

My own position on these matters is that it is possible to produce a list of characteristics that, as a set, represent a good reasoner in more or less the sense of a platonic ideal. I believe also, however, that people need not fit this ideal perfectly to be considered good reasoners in a practical sense and that not all good reasoners, again in a practical sense, will fit it in precisely the same way. I believe further that there are general principles of good reasoning that are independent of the context in which, or the purpose for which, the reasoning is done. These are principles that hold in mathematics, in science, in other disciplinary contexts, and in everyday life. In what follows, I try to articulate some of those principles, all of which have been discussed in preceding sections of this book.

The principle of local internal consistency

Contradictory beliefs should not be lightly entertained. Assurance of complete consistency among beliefs is too much to expect of finite beings, but one should attempt to resolve contradictions that one becomes aware of—especially those involving beliefs that matter. This principle rests on two assumptions: (1) that truth is consistent and (2) that we want—should want—to hold beliefs that are true. Consistency among beliefs is not a guarantee that those beliefs are true, but inconsistency, on the first assumption, guarantees that one or more are false, and this, on the second assumption, is undesirable, especially when the beliefs involved are important to us.

The principle of openness to evidence and criticism

Rationality has to do with deciding what to believe. Independently of the context—whether it be science, law, history, philosophy, religion, or a mundane matter of daily life—the problem is that of obtaining and weighing evidence. The criteria for credibility are arguably the same in every context. In all cases, one should hold a belief with whatever strength the total relevant evidence at one's disposal warrants. This is what it means to be intellectually honest.

We are responsible for doing what we can to make our beliefs consistent with reality. If we believe X because we want to believe X and have refused to consider evidence against X, our belief of X can reasonably be considered an irresponsible—and irrational—belief. And this is so independently of whether or not X is true.

Being rational means recognizing one's own fallibility. It means being open to new ideas, to new perspectives, to changes of mind—though not so open as to be swayed always by the last persuasive argument one has heard or read on any given topic. It means also giving due respect to beliefs or opinions that one has formed in a thoughtful way over time, even if all of the reasons for those beliefs or opinions cannot be articulated immediately on demand. And it means being willing to defer judgment—to acknowledge the inconclusiveness of evidence on specific matters, when it is so.

The principle of trial by exposure

A scientific hypothesis or theory gains credibility to the extent that it survives concerted efforts by competent scientists to discredit it. Acceptance of a mathematical theorem increases as attempts by competent mathematicians to show it to be invalid fail. Neither a theory not a theorem that is not exposed to scrutiny and criticism is likely to be taken very seriously by scientists or mathematicians. In general, ideas that have survived the best efforts of critics to show them to be false make more compelling claims on us than ideas that have never been put to such a test.

This principle should apply in everyday reasoning as well as in science, mathematics, and other disciplinary contexts. Application of it here means bucking what appears to be a rather strong tendency that we have to protect our beliefs against criticism. It is not enough that we be critical of the ideas of others or even that we expose our ideas to the criticism of others; good reasoning requires that we attempt to be critical of our own ideas ourselves. I see this as an especially important principle both because we seem not to be naturally predisposed to apply it and because failure to apply it may be at the root of many social and interpersonal problems.

The principle of obligatory effort

Passive rationality is a contradiction in terms. To reason well requires effort—significant effort on a continuing basis. In particular, rationality involves the obligation, not only to weigh evidence as impartially as possible, but to seek evidence that may not be ready at hand. It involves more than selection from among ready-made decision alternatives according to some normative principles of choice, more than evaluating competently the arguments one happens upon. It means accepting responsibility for the adequacy of one's own knowledge base to inform decisions one must make in the various roles one assumes. This includes knowledge about capabilities and limitations of human beings in general and about one's own idiosyncratic strengths and limitations in particular.

The phenomenon of information cascades (Bikhchandani, Hirshleifer, & Welch, 1992, 1998) and the herd behavior to which it can lead (Banerjee, 1992) should convince us of the importance of being individually well-informed with respect to decision issues that matter to us. The tendency for copy-cat behavior to vary inversely with one's confidence in one's own judgment (Deutsch & Gerard, 1955) should do the same.

Johnson-Laird (1983) emphasizes the importance of the role of counterexamples in rationality; he sees the realization that an inference is sound only if there are no counter-examples to it and the ability to put this principle into practice as major determinants of individual differences in reasoning ability. Oakhill and Johnson-Laird (1985b) point out that if one holds some false generalization to be true and one makes no effort to determine whether there exist counterexamples to it, one may never discover that the generalization is, in fact, false. Rationality, they contend, depends on a search for counterexamples.

I agree with Johnson-Laird and Oakhill's assessment of the importance of searching for counterexamples as a means of testing the plausibility of generalizations, and here I want to put the emphasis on the *active* nature of search. The need to search for evidence that is counterindicative of generalizations that are being assessed stems in part from a natural tendency that many of us seem to have to do just the opposite—search for confirmatory evidence only—and in part from the fact that the failure to find counterindicative evidence, having tried hard to do so, is the best confirmation of a generalization one can get.

Assessing the plausibility of generalizations is not all there is to reasoning, however, so emphasis on the importance of searching for counterexamples needs to be tempered with the realization that evidence is used for other purposes—the formation of conjectures and hypotheses, the estimation of relative frequencies and probabilities, identification of possible courses of action or solutions to problems. The general point is that rationality demands that one actively seek information that is relevant to the conclusions one wants to draw, the opinions one wants to form, the decisions one has to make, the problems with which one has to deal, and that one do so in an even-handed a way as possible. In a word, being rational means being *truth seeking*.

The principle of balance

Rationality requires a balance between freedom and constraint, imagination and criticism, conjecture and refutation. Optimization, or maximization, seldom is a practical goal. Although much evidence suggests that we typically err in the direction of not gathering as much information as we should, there is a need to recognize that sometimes further information is not worth the cost of acquiring it.

Mumford's (1966) claim of the importance of balance more generally seems to me correct: "Living organisms can use only limited amounts of energy, as living personalities can utilize only limited quantities of knowledge and experience. 'Too much' or 'too little' is equally fatal to organic existence. Even too much abstract knowledge, insulated from feeling, from moral evaluation, from historical experience, from responsible purposeful action can produce a serious unbalance in both the personality and the community" (p. 314).

Having railed against the documented tendency of people to be defensive of their beliefs—typically by seeking evidence to support them and often by avoiding or discounting evidence that tells against them—I need now, in the interest of balance, to note again Nozick's (1993) recommendation to philosophers that they favor a sort of philosophical explanation in which one brings oneself to see how something one wants to believe could be possible. I take it to be a fact that our preferences influence our beliefs and am not prepared to argue that they should not do so, especially when evidence pro and con is less than compelling; however, when the search for confirming evidence becomes so strong as, in effect, to create a blind eye and deaf ear to contrary evidence, it is right, I think, to consider one's attitude to be sufficiently out of balance to qualify as irrational.

The principle of judicious bias

How we act upon beliefs should depend on the values and costs we associate with the various ways of being right or wrong. In some cases, the context dictates certain biases in this regard. In the criminal court proceeding, we are to start with the assumption that the defendant is innocent and to retain it until we consider guilt to have been established beyond reasonable doubt. A physician might elect to act as though a patient has a specific disease even though the evidence that that is the case is slim, on the grounds that the treatment will do no harm if the disease is not present and the lack of treatment would be disastrous if it is.

One can easily think of situations that are encountered in everyday life in which being wrong in one way would be much better (or much worse) than being wrong in another. In such cases, rationality dictates that we make decisions not only on the basis of the probability that they will have the desired effects, but with sensitivity to the nature of the unwanted possible outcomes. As Nozick (1993) puts it, "[i]f one principle is most reliable but disastrous when wrong, while another is somewhat less reliable but also not so very bad when wrong, we may well favor the latter, forgoing some reliability for other benefits" (p. 136).

The principle of intellectual accountability

Each of us has in his or her head a computer of sorts, that is up and running more-or-less continuously and that has a limited, but substantial, capacity that can be allocated and focused in a variety of ways. This computer typically runs in interrupt mode, which is to say, its moment-to-moment focus is determined largely by external events, but it is internally directable, within limits, by an executive control program. It spends a fair amount of time more-or-less idling, and a significant fraction of its capacity is wasted in the sense that it is not applied to any objective that the controller would acknowledge to be desirable. What does rationality require with respect to the management of such a resource? Or to ask the same question in nonmetaphorical terms, what kind of responsibility does rationality imply regarding the direction of the use of one's own brain? Is it rational to go through life always and only reacting? Never thinking about what to think about? Taking little or no interest in the management of one's own thought processes?

One might argue that what one tends to think about is determined by one's character, that one's character is defined, in large part, by one's long-term interests, and that those interests are what one naturally turns one's mind to in moments when it is not otherwise occupied. I believe there is some truth to that view, but I believe also that the question of what is worth thinking about is itself worth serious reflection from time to time. On the assumption that some things are more worthy of attention and thought than others, I want to argue that one aspect of rationality is the exercise of some control over one's mind and deciding on occasion that *this* is worth thinking about while *that* is not.

Others

Rationality means not letting emotions trump thought. It means trying to see things from perspectives different from one's own, while recognizing one's limitations in this regard—it is doubtful if anyone is capable of a truly objective and even-handed treatment of a view one strongly opposes. It means setting reasonable goals, and having a sense of priorities, of relative values, of what is worth doing—or worrying about—and what is not. It means being skeptical of glib or overly facile answers to difficult questions.

It means recognizing the need for presuppositions, the unattainability of certainty, the effects of cognitive limitations on reasoning and some of the ways in which we compensate for those limitations, or fail to do so. It means being cognizant of one's own abilities and limitations as a reasoner. It means too being somewhat aware of one's own biases. Some might contend that it means being free of bias, but I doubt there is such a thing as totally unbiased reasoning. Even a desire to be rational is a bias of sorts—a good one no doubt, but a bias nonetheless. Rationality is also an attitude—a commitment to truth. And it is the practice of thoughtfulness—the tendency habitually to attempt to "think things through."

☐ Are We Rational?

> A rational mind is sometimes the queerest mixture of rationality and irrationality on earth. (Bell, 1937, p. 43)

The question of whether we are rational has been asked countless times, not only by philosophers and psychologists, but by others who have wondered what kind of creature we are. I have offered a view of what it means to be rational in the broad sense of reasoning well. What can we conclude about human rationality in this sense? Are we rational? Can we tell?

There is the view that the question of human rationality is not one that we should expect to be able to answer, given the fragmentary nature of our understanding of human cognition. Griggs (1981) defends this position, arguing that it is difficult to judge a system as rational or irrational without understanding it and expressing the opinion that research on reasoning has not yet produced the degree of understanding that is necessary to support such judgments. This being the case, the main concern of researchers, Griggs contends, should not be to judge the rationality of human cognitive functioning but simply to gain an understanding of why people perform as they do on reasoning tasks.

But whether or not the question of our rationality is answerable, there can be no denying it is a question that we find compelling. We cannot help but ask it. That is itself an interesting fact. Why do we care whether we are rational or not? We are what we are. It is not surprising, perhaps, that we would like to understand better what that is, but why should it matter whether a better understanding reveals that we are—or are not—rational? That we find the question of our rationality so compelling suggests that we work on the assumption that there is a way we *ought* to be—that there are standards of reasoning to which we *should* conform—and we want to know how we measure up in this regard.

Erasmus (1514/1942), in his inimitable satire, written five centuries ago, had this to say on the question of human rationality: "For since according to the definition of the Stoicks, Wisdom is nothing else than to be govern'd by reason; and on the contrary Folly, to be giv'n up to the will of our Passions; that the life of man might not be altogether disconsolate and hard to away with, of how much more Passion than Reason has Jupiter compos'd us? putting in, as one would say, 'scarce half an ounce to a pound.' Besides, he has confin'd Reason to a narrow corner of the brain, and left all the rest of the body to our Passions; as also set up, against this one, two as it were, masterless Tyrants—Anger, that possesseth the region of the heart, and consequently the very Fountain of life, the Heart itself; and Lust, that stretcheth its Empire every where. Against which double force how powerful Reason is, let common experience declare, inasmuch as she, which yet is all she can do, may call out to us till she be hoarse again, and tell us the Rules of Honesty and Vertue; while they give up the Reins to their Governour, and make a hideous clamour, till at last being wearied, he suffer himself to be carried whither they please to hurry him" (p. 118). Was Erasmus right? Is our reason ruled by our passions, as he claimed—and as Plato had claimed nearly 2,000 years earlier?

Or consider the more recent assessment of Jaspers (1952). "There is something inside all of us that yearns not for reason but for mystery—not for penetrating clear thought but for the whisperings of the irrational—not for the prudence of unprejudiced sight and hearing but for the capricious surrender to the darkness of multifariousness—not for the insights of humility but for gnostic omniscience to the point of absurdity—not for science but for wizardry disguised as science—not for rationally founded influence, but for magic—not for loyalty, but adventure—not for the freedom which is one with reason and law and with the choice of one's own historicity, but for blind unrestraint and at the same time for blind obedience to a force that tolerates no questions" (p. 68).

One might dismiss the observations of Erasmus and Jaspers, and numerous similar ones that could be cited, on the grounds that they represent opinions only and are not necessarily backed up with objective evidence. But, as we have seen, there is a sizeable body of psychological literature that purports to document many ways in which people habitually behave less than completely rationally in a wide variety of situations calling for judgment, reasoning, or decision making. On the other hand are the numerous researchers who see evidence in their data of a basic logical competence that human beings appear to have. In short, on the question of the extent to which human beings measure up to the dictates of rationality, there is, among people who have written on the topic, a wide range of opinions.

It is certainly not difficult to compile a long list of evidences that we are, as a species, quite capable of working against our own long-term interests. Neither individuals nor groups are especially good at anticipating the long-range effects of their behavior or at giving long-range consequences adequate consideration, relative to the importance attached to immediate effects, in decision making. People clearly often hold beliefs that are demonstrably false, and accept explanations of natural phenomena that will not stand scrutiny. Researchers have discovered and demonstrated countless ways in which people exercise poor judgment, and violate generally accepted norms of logic and sound reasoning. Pointing out the fallacies, biases, and other foibles that plague human reasoning has been a main preoccupation of cognitive psychologists for several decades and of philosophers for millennia.

But, as we have seen, many of the claimed demonstrations of irrationality have been criticized by psychologists and philosophers on various grounds (Berkeley & Humphreys, 1982; Cohen, 1979, 1980, 1981, 1982; Gigerenzer & Murray, 1987; Macdonald, 1986; Von Winterfeldt & Edwards, 1986). Schum (1993) summarizes some of the criticisms this way:

1. There is more than one normative standard against which human probability judgments can be compared.

2. The experiments may simply be demonstrations of lack of formal knowledge rather than cognitive incompetence.

3. Inferential problems presented to experimental subjects are often vaguely or incompletely posed.

4. Subjects are often given vague and incomplete instructions (p. 184).

The last two items in this list lend credence to the claim that participants in experiments on reasoning may often have worked on problems other than those intended by the experimenters. Especially (but probably not only) when problem statements or instructions are vague, incomplete, or ambiguous, participants may interpret them differently from how the experimenters intended that they interpret them. When this happens and it does not become clear to the experimenter that it has happened, the participant's performance may be judged by an inappropriate standard. That such miscommunications and misunderstandings occur and go undetected has been argued by many researchers (e.g., Hilton, 1995; Margolis, 1987; Schwarz, 1996).

Stanovich and West (2000) list a similar set of arguments that have been brought against claimed demonstrations of irrationality: mistaking errors of performance—lapses of attention or memory—for irrationality; limitations in human computational ability that preclude realization of normative rationality; evaluation of human performance against an inappropriate normative model; misinterpretation by the reasoner of the intended problem. They note, as have others, that one who firmly believes that people are rational can generally find an explanation of what appears to be irrational behavior that is consistent with that belief.

Each of the criticisms of efforts to demonstrate irrationality mentioned has merit, in my view, in the sense that one can find specific experimental studies to which it applies. On the other hand, I do not believe that they collectively invalidate all the experimental demonstrations of irrational behavior that have been published. Moreover, independently of laboratory findings, one can find voluminous and compelling evidence of irrationality on the part of individuals, groups, and nations in the daily newspaper and other media, not to mention the first-hand observation of the behavior of ourselves and others.

One need only mention our inability, as a society, to distinguish media images from reality, our susceptibility to manipulation, our fascination with the bizarre, our need for larger-than-life idols, the ease with which we confuse fame or notoriety with heroism. One could point to the endless ethnic strife around the globe, or to the way in which we collectively are polluting the environment, or to our inclination to consume and reproduce as though the earth's resources were unlimited. One could note our willingness to take pride in race, nationality, family connections, intelligence, physical features, and other such characteristics over which we had no control and for which, therefore, we have no basis for pride or shame, credit, or blame. One could point to the enormous amounts of financial and intellectual capital we devote to finding ways to move money from one pocket to another while contributing nothing to the general good in the process of doing so. Or to the fact that we spend more, worldwide, on equipping ourselves to kill each other than on fighting disease, hunger, pestilence, and ignorance. One could argue that Plato's and Erasmus's claim that we are ruled not by our reason but by our passions is as true for us today as it ever was, that we have learned a lot about how the world works, but we have made remarkably little progress in figuring out how to live in peace and good will as human beings. In short, one could make a rather compelling case for the irrationality of our species on the whole.

But if humans are not rational, as a species, where do specific members of the species get their warrant to make this judgment? It is one thing for a person to say that cats cannot reason; it is quite another for a person to say that persons cannot do so. The first claim could be wrong, but it is not self-contradictory; the second undermines itself. Perhaps the claim that people are not rational is intended to be a claim that they are not reliably and consistently rational, not that they never are. Can we doubt that people often form opinions, hold beliefs, make judgments and decisions, draw conclusions, that, on careful reflection, most intelligent people—including themselves—would acknowledge to be irrational in the sense of violating norms that are widely (though not universally) considered compelling.

It would have been all too easy, in the preceding sentence, to say "rational" people instead of "intelligent" people, but that would have made the circularity of the argument too stark. But the circle is there and it is not clear that there is any way to escape it. The criteria for rational thinking and rational behavior are dictated by presumably rational people—when presumably they are at their rational best. Could it be otherwise? Surely we do not want irrational people telling us what it means to be rational.

Kahneman (1981) notes the importance of distinguishing between the claim that people are not always rational and the claim that they never are. Similarly, we should distinguish between claiming that people sometimes are rational and claiming that they always are. My guess is that few investigators would want to make either of the more extreme claims, but there are great differences of opinion on the question of where we sit on the continuum that runs from total rationality on the one end to complete irrationality on the other. Some writers emphasize the fallibility, perhaps frailty, of human reasoning, while others stress its functional logicality and effectiveness, especially in the context of dealing with real-life problems.

Osherson's (1990) *coexistence thesis* is an example of a middle-of-the-road position. According to this thesis, people's rationality is seen in the fact that they find many principles of rationality intuitively compelling and their irrationality is demonstrated by the frequency with which they violate these principles in practice. Contending that the "rational man" of classical economics and modern decision theory is a singularly implausible human being, Johnson-Laird and Byrne (1995) also state an in-between position, arguing that human reasoners are neither wholly rational nor wholly irrational—they make mistakes in reasoning, but they also can make valid deductions for the right reasons. The same authors argue in another place (Johnson-Laird & Byrne, 1991) that if it were easy always to be perfectly rational, logic would not have been invented, because there would be no need of it; but on the other hand, if we were completely irrational, no one *could* have invented it. Human beings, they conclude, are rational in principle, but err in practice.

Although many investigators have demonstrated that people often reason in less than perfectly logical ways, few would make the claim that logic plays no part in human reasoning at all. To acknowledge that various types of biases and alogical factors affect the inferences that people make is not necessarily to say that logic itself has no influence. Conversely, those who argue that people do have a mental logic do not, generally speaking, take the extreme position that they never resort to alogical approaches to reasoning problems. Perhaps the safest generalization that one can make, taking all the evidence into account, is that human reasoning displays a complicated mix of logical, illlogical and allogical influences. Of course, one wants details regarding what the various types of influences are and the conditions under which they have their effects. It is to questions of this sort that many of the studies cited in this book have been addressed.

One thing is clear: rationality is not an all-or-not-at-all affair. People cannot be divided neatly into two categories—those who are always rational and those who never are. Most people are rational on some occasions and irrational on others, are rational about some topics and not so rational about others, and so on. On the other hand, people differ with respect to their propensity to be rational. Some are more likely (able, inclined) to approach life reflectively than are others. Apparently, and not surprisingly, individuals differ in the satisfaction and pleasure they get from engaging in effortful thought. On any definition of rationality one is willing to accept, we would expect some people to be more, or less, rational than others. The topic of individual differences in rationality has not received as much attention from researchers as it undoubtedly deserves. This neglect has been highlighted recently by Stanovich (1999) and Stanovich and West (2000b), who make a compelling case for the existence of such differences.

Are we rational? As a species, we get, in my view, a passing grade, but not much more than that. We have survived, so far, and in some respects have done rather well, but we can hardly say that reason rules the day. As individuals, we display the whole range of possibilities. Some people measure up pretty well—most of the time—with respect to most of the principles mentioned above; others appear to do poorly with respect to many of them. Most of us, I suspect, do better on some dimensions than on others, observing some of the principles some of the time, but also violating them frequently.

The ability and propensity to be rational are, as most human abilities and traits, matters of both genetics and learning. Rationality presupposes a certain level of mental competence, which is, in part, a matter of heredity. But for a large range of native cognitive abilities, people can learn to be more rational than they naturally would be in the absence of learning. To a significant degree, rationality is a matter of habits of the mind. Characteristically rational people habitually respond to questions, problems, and claims analytically and reflectively; they try to understand situations, to seek information that will take them behind appearances, to see things from various perspectives, to expose their views to criticism, to reason consistently taking their own biases into account, and so on. There can be little doubt that such habits can be acquired. Presumably increasing the ability and desire of individuals to be rational is a major objective of education. The discovery of ways to realize this objective to a greater degree is a continuing challenge to research.

REFERENCES

Abelson, R. P. (1959). Modes of resolution of belief dilemmas. *Journal of Conflict Resolution, 3*, 343–352.

Abelson, R. P. (1995). *Statistics as principled argument*. Mahwah, NJ: Erlbaum.

Abelson, R. P., Aronson, E., McGuire, W. J., Newcomb, T. M., Rosenberg, M. J., & Tannenbaum, P. H. (1968). *Theories of cognitive consistency: A sourcebook*. Chicago: Rand-McNally.

Abramson, L. Y., Seligman, M. E. P., & Teasdale, J. (1978). Learned helplessness in humans: Critique and reformulation. *Journal of Abnormal Psychology, 87*, 49–74.

Adler, M. J. (1981). —*Six great ideas*. New York: Collier Books.

Ægisdóttir, S., White, M. J., Spengler, P. M., Maugherman, A. S., Anderson, L. A., Cook, R. S., Nichols, C. N., Lampropoulos, G. K., Walker, B. S., Cohen, G., & Rush, J. D. (2006). The meta-analysis of clinical judgment project: Fifty-six years of accumulated research on clinical versus statistical prediction. *The Counseling Psychologist, 34*, 341–382.

Ahlers, D. M. (1966). SEM: A security evaluation model. In K. J. Cohen & F. S. Hammer (Eds.), *Analytical methods in banking* (pp. 305–336). Homewood, IL: Irwin.

Albert, H. (1985). *Treatise on critical reason* (Translated by M. V. Rorty). Princeton, NJ: Princeton University Press.

Alcock, J. E. (1996). The propensity to believe. In P. R. Gross, N. Levitt, & M. W. Lewis (Eds.), *The flight from reason* (pp. 64–78). New York: The New York Academy of Sciences.

Alfvén, H. (1988). Memoirs of a dissident scientist. *American Scientist, 76*, 249–251.

Allais, M. (1990). Criticism of the postulates and axioms of the American School. In P. K. Moser (Ed.), *Rationality in action: Contemporary approaches* (pp. 113–139). New York: Cambridge University Press. (Original work published 1979)

Anderson, C. A., Lepper, M. R., & Ross, L. (1979). Theory perseverance. Unpublished manuscript, Stanford University.

Anderson, C. W. (1987). Strategic teaching in science. In B. F. Jones, A. S. Palincsar, D. S. Ogle, & E. G. Carr (Eds.), *Strategic teaching and learning: Cognitive instruction in the content areas* (pp. 73–91).

Anderson, C. W., & Smith, E. L. (1987). Teaching science. In V. Koehler (Ed.), *The educators' handbook: A research perspective* (pp. 84–111). New York: Longman.

Anderson, J. R. (1976). *Language, memory and thought.* Hillsdale, NJ: Erlbaum.

Anderson, J. R. (Ed.) (1981). *Cognitive skills and their acquisition.* Hillsdale, NJ: Erlbaum.

Anderson, J. R. (1990). *The adaptive character of thought.* Hillsdale, NJ: Erlbaum.

Anderson, J. R. (1991). Is human cognition adaptive? *Behavioral and Brain Sciences, 14,* 471–517.

Anderson, L., & Holt, C. (1997). Information cascades in the laboratory. *American Economic Review, 87,* 847–862.

Anderson, N. H. (1971). Integration theory and attitude change. *Psychological Review, 78,* 171–206.

Andrews, G. R., & Debus, R. I. (1978). Persistence and the causal perception of failure: Modifying cognitive attributions. *Journal of Educational Psychology, 70,* 154–166.

Appel, W. (1983). *Cults in America: Programmed for paradise.* New York: Holt, Rinehart and Winston.

Ardrey, R. (1970). *The social contract.* New York: Dell.

Aristotle (2004). *Nicomachean ethics.* Translator W. D. Ross, eBooks@Adelaide. (Original work published circa 350 BC)

Arkes, H. R., & Blumer, C. (1985). The psychology of sunk cost. *Organizational Behavior and Human Decision Processes, 35,* 124–140.

Arkin, R. M., & Maruyama, G. M. (1979). Attribution, affect, and college exam performance. *Journal of Educational Psychology, 71,* 85–93.

Arlin, P. K. (1990). Wisdom: The art of problem finding. In R. J. Sternberg (Ed.), *Wisdom: Its nature, origins, and development* (pp. 230–243). New York: Cambridge University Press.

Arrow, K. J. (1963). *Social choice and individual values* (2nd ed.). New York: Wiley. (Original work published 1951)

Arrow, K. J. (1990). Values and collective decision making. In P. K. Moser (Ed.), *Rationality in action: Contemporary approaches* (pp. 337–353). New York: Cambridge University Press.

Asch, S. E. (1953). Effects of group pressure upon the modification and distortion of judgments. In D. Cartwright & A. Zander (Eds.), *Group dynamics: Research and theory* (pp. 151–162). Evanston, IL: Row-Peterson.

Asimov, I. (1972). *Asimov's biographical encyclopedia of science and technology* (New Revised Edition).Garden City, NY: Doubleday and Company. (Original work published 1964)

Asklock, R. B. (1976). *Error patterns in computation.* London: Bell and Howell.

Atkins, P. W. (1994). *Creation revisited: The origin of space, time and the universe.* London: Penguin Books. (Original work published 1992)

Attneave, F. (1953). Psychological probability as a function of experienced frequency. *Journal of Experimental Psychology, 46,* 81–86.

Audi, R. (1982). Believing and affirming. *Mind, 91,* 115–120.

Audi, R. (1985). Rationality and valuation. In G. Seebass & R. Tuomela (Eds.), *Social action* (pp. 243–277). Dordrecht: Reidel.

Audi, R. (1989). *Practical reasoning.* New York: Routledge.

References

Ault, R. L. (1973). Problem-solving strategies of reflective, impulsive, fast-accurate, and slow-inaccurate children. *Developmental Psychology, 1,* 717–725.

Ayer, A. J. (1956). *The problem of knowledge.* New York: Penguin.

Ayton, P., & Hardman, D. (1997). Are two rationalities better than one? *Current Psychology of Cognition, 16,* 39–51.

Back, K. W. (1951). Influence through social communication. *Journal of Abnormal and Social Psychology, 46,* 9–23.

Bales, R. F. (1950). *Interaction process analysis: A method for the study of small groups.* Cambridge, MA: Addison Wesley.

Balla, J. I., Biggs, J. B., Gibson, M., & Chang, A. M. (1990). The application of basic science concepts to clinical problem solving. *Medical Education, 24,* 117–123.

Baltes, P. B., Dittmann-Kohli, F., & Dixon, R. (1984). New perspectives on the development of intelligence in adulthood: Toward a dual process conception and a model of selective optimization with compensation. In P. B. Baltes & O. G. Brim, Jr. (Eds.), *Life span development and behavior* (Vol. 6, pp. 33–76). New York: Academic Press.

Baltes, P. B., & Smith, J. (1990). Toward a psychology of wisdom and its ontogenesis. In R. J. Sternberg (Ed.), *Wisdom: Its nature, origins, and development* (pp. 87–120). New York: Cambridge University Press.

Bandura, A. (1973). *Aggression: A social learning analysis.* Englewood Cliffs, NJ: Prentice-Hall.

Banerjee, A. V. (1992). A simple model of herd behavior. *Quarterly Journal of Economics, 107,* 797–817.

Bargh, J. H., & Chartbrand, T. L. (1999). The unbearable automaticity of being. *American Psychologist, 54,* 462–479.

Barnes, A. E., Nelson, T. O., Dunlosky, J., Mazzoni, G., & Narens, L. (1999). An integrative system of metamemory components involved in retrieval. In D. Gopher & A. Koriat (Eds.), *Attention and performance XVII* (pp. 287–314). Cambridge, MA: MIT Press.

Baron, J. (1985a). *Rationality and intelligence.* New York: Cambridge University Press.

Baron, J. (1985b). What kinds of intelligence components are fundamental? In S. F. Chipman, J. W. Segal & R. Glaser (Eds.), *Thinking and learning skills, Vol. 2: Research and open questions* (pp. 365–390). Hillsdale, NJ: Erlbaum.

Baron, J. (1988). *Thinking and deciding.* New York: Cambridge University Press.

Baron, J. (1991). Beliefs about thinking. In J. F. Voss, D. N. Perkins, & J. W. Segal (Eds.) *Informal reasoning and education* (pp. 169–186). Hillsdale, NJ: Erlbaum.

Baron, J. (1993). Why teach thinking?—An essay. *Applied Psychology: An International Review, 42,* 191–214.

Baron, J. (1994). *Thinking and deciding* (2nd ed.). New York: Cambridge University Press.

Baron, J. (1995). Myside bias in thinking about abortion. *Thinking and reasoning, 1995* (221–235).

Baron, J. (1998). *Judgment misguided: Intuition and error in public decision making.* New York: Oxford University Press.

Baron, J., Badgio, P. C., & Gaskins, I. W. (1986). In R. J. Sternberg (Ed.), *Advances in the psychology of human intelligence* (Vol. 3). Hillsdale, NJ: Erlbaum.

Baron, J. & Hershey, J. C. (1988). Outcome bias in decision evaluation. *Journal of Personality and Social Psychology, 54,* 569–579.

Baron, Joan B., & Stermberg, R. J. (Eds.). (1987). *Teaching thinking skills: Theory and practice.* New York: Freeman.

Baron, R. A. (1987). Interviewers' mood and reaction to job applicants: The influence of affective states on applied social judgments. *Journal of Applied Social Psychology, 17,* 911–926.

Barrow, J. D. (1990). *The world within the world.* New York: Oxford University Press.

Barrow, J. D. (1991). *Theories of everything: The quest for ultimate explanation.* New York: Oxford University Press.

Barrow, J. D. (1992). *Pi in the sky: Counting, thinking, and being.* New York: Oxford University Press.

Barrow, J. D. (1998). *Impossibility: The limits of science and the science of limits.* New York: Oxford University Press.

Barrows, H. S., Freightner, J. W., Neufeld, V. R., & Norman, G. R. (1978). *Analysis of the clinical methods of medical students and physicians.* School of medicine, Hamilton, Ontario: McMaster University.

Barrows, H. S., Norman, G. R., Neufeld, V. R., & Feightner, J. W. (1977). Studies of the clinical reasoning process of medical students and physicians. *Proceedings of the sixteenth annual conference on research in medical education.* Washington, DC: Association of American Medical Colleges.

Bartlett, F. E. (1932). *Remembering.* Cambridge: Cambridge University Press.

Bartlett, F. E. (1958). *Thinking: An experimental and social study.* London: Allen and Unwin.

Bartley, W. W., III (1977). Appendix C: Editor's note on Carroll's "What the tortoise said to Achilles." In W. W. Bartley, III (Ed.), *Lewis Carroll's symbolic logic.* New York: Clarkson N. Potter.

Bartley, W. W. (1984). *The retreat to commitment* (2nd ed.). La Salle, IL: Open Court.

Bassock, M., & Trope, Y. (1984). People's strategies for testing hypotheses about another's personality: Confirmatory or diagnostic? *Social Cognition, 2,* 199–216.

Basu, K. (1994). The traveler's dilemma: Paradoxes of rationality in game theory. *American Economic Review, 84,* 391–395.

Basu, K. (2007). The traveler's dilemma. *Scientific American, 296*(6), 90–95.

Bateson, G. (1980). *Mind and nature: A necessary unity.* New York: Bantam.

Bazerman, M. H. (1990). *Judgment in managerial decision making.* New York: Wiley.

Beach, L. R., & Mitchell, T. R. (1978). A contingency model for the selection of decision strategies. *Academy of Management Review, 3,* 439–449.

Beach, L. R., Smith, B., Lundell, J. & Mitchell, T. R. (1988). Image theory: Descriptive sufficiency of a simple rule for the compatibility test. *Journal of Behavioral Decision Making, 1,* 17–28.

Beach, L. R., Townes, B. D., & Campbell, F. L. (1978). *The optional parenthood questionnaire: A guide to decision making about parenthood.* Washington, DC: National Alliance for Optional Parenthood.

Bechara, A., Damasio, A. R., Damasio, H., & Anderson, S. W. (1994). Insensitivity to future consequences following damage to human prefrontal cortex. *Cognition, 50,* 7–15.

Bechara, A., Tranel, D., Damasio, H, & Damasio, A. R. (1996). Failure to respond autonomically to anticipated future outcomes following damage to prefrontal cortex. *Cerebral Cortex, 6,* 215–225.

Bechara, A., Damasio, H, Tranel, D., & Damasio, A. R. (1997). Deciding advantageously before knowing the advantageous strategy. *Science, 275,* 1293–1295.

Becker, G. (1976). *The economic approach to human behavior.* Chicago: University of Chicago Press.

Beckerman, W. (1992). Economic growth and the environment. Whose growth? Whose environment? *World Development, 20,* 481–496.

Bell, D., Raiffa, H., & Tversky, A. (Eds.). (1988). *Decision making: Descriptive, normative, and prescriptive interactions.* Cambridge: Cambridge University Press.

Bell, D. E. (1982). Regret in decision making under uncertainty. *Operations Research, 30,* 961–981.

Bell, D. E. (1985). Disappointment in decision making under uncertainty. *Operations Research, 33,* 1–27.

Bell, E. T. (1934). The place of rigor in mathematics. *The American Mathematical Monthly, 41,* 599–607.

Bell, E. T. (1937). *Men of mathematics: The lives and achievements of the great mathematicians from Zeno to Poincare.* New York: Dover.

Bell, E. T. (1991). *The magic of numbers.* New York: Dover. (Original published 1946)

Bell, E. T. (1992). *The development of mathematics* (2nd ed.). New York: Dover. (Original 2nd edition published 1945)

Bem, D. J. (1970). *Beliefs, attitudes, and human affairs.* Belmont, CA: Brooks/Cole Publishing Company.

Bem, D. J., Wallach, M. A., & Kogan, N. (1965). Group decision making under risk of aversive consequences. *Journal of Personality and Social Psychology, 1,* 453–460.

Bennett, M. (1976). *SUBSTITUTOR: A teaching program.* Unpublished project report. Department of Artificial Intelligence, University of Edinburgh.

Bentham, J. (1939). An introduction to the principles of morals and legislation. In E. A. Burtt (Ed.), *The English philosophers from Bacon to Mill* (pp. 791–852). New York: Random House. (Original work published in 1789)

Bereiter, C. & Engelmann, S. (1966). *Teaching disadvantaged children in the preschool.* Englewood Cliffs, NJ: Prentice-Hall.

Bereiter, C., & Scardamalia, M. (1981). Cognitive coping strategies and the problem of "inert knowledge." In S. F. Chipman, J. W. Segal, & R. Glaser (Eds.), *Thinking and learning skills, Volume 2: Research and open questions.* Hillsdale, NJ: Erlbaum.

Bergamini, D. (1963). *Mathematics.* New York: Time Incorporated.

Berger, J. O. (1997). *Statistical decision theory and Bayesian analysis.* New York: Springer-Verlag.

Berger, P. L., & Luckmann, T. (1990). *The social construction of reality: A treatise in the sociology of knowledge.* New York: Anchor Books. (Original work published 1966)

Berglas, S., & Jones, E. E. (1978). Drug choice as a self-handicapping strategy in response to noncontingent success. *Journal of Personality and Social Psychology, 36,* 405–417.

Berkeley, D., & Humphreys, P. (1982). Structuring decision problems and the "bias heuristic." *Acta Psychologica, 50,* 201–252.

Berlinski, D. (2000). *Newton's gift: How Sir Isaac Newton unlocked the system of the world.* New York: Simon and Schuster.

Berman, M. (1984). *The reenchantment of the world.* New Yorks: Bantam Books.

Bernoulli, D. (1738). Specimen theoriae norae de mensura sortis. *Commentarii Academoae, Scientiarum Imperiales Petropolitanae, 5,* 175–192. (Translation published in 1954 by L. Sommer in *Econometrica, 22,* 23–26.)

Bernstein, J. (1993). *Cranks, quarks, and the cosmos.* New York: Basic Books.

Bernstein, P. L. (1996). *Against the gods: The remarkable story of risk.* New York: Wiley.

Berry, R. J. (1988). *God and evolution: Creation, evolution and the Bible.* London: Hodder and Stoughton.

Bertotti, B. (1977). The riddles of gravitation. In Duncan, R. & Weston-Smith, M. (Eds.), *The encyclopedia of ignorance* (pp. 91–98). New York: Pocket Books, Simon and Schuster.

Bethe, A. (1930). Studien über die Pastizität des Nerrensystems. I. Arachnoideen und Crustaceen. *Archive fur die gesamte Physiologie, 224,* 793–820.

Bettman, J. R., & Jones, J. M. (1972). Formal models of consumer behavior: A conceptual overview. *The Journal of Business, 45,* 544-562.

Beyth-Marom, R., & Fischhoff, B. (1983). Diagnosticity and pseudodiagnosticity. *Journal of Personality and Social Psychology, 45,* 1185–1195.

Bhagwati, J. (1993). The case for free trade. *Scientific American, 269(5),* 42–49.

Bierbrauer, G. (1973). *Effect of set, perspective, and temporal factors in attribution.* Unpublished doctoral dissertation, Stanford University.

Bikhchandani, S., Hirshleifer, D., & Welch, I. (1992). A theory of fads, fashion, custom, and cultural change as information cascades. *Journal of Political Economy, 100,* 992–1026.

Bikhchandani, S., Hirshleifer, D., & Welch, I. (1998). Learning from the behavior of others: Conformity, fads, and informational cascades. *Journal of Economic Perspectives, 12*(3), 151–170.

Billings, R. S., & Scherer, L. L. (1988). The effects of response mode and importance on decision-making strategies: Judgment versus choice. *Organizational Behavior and Decision Processes, 34,* 1–19.

Birnbaum, M. H., & Martin, T. (2003). Generalization across people, procedures and predictions: Violations of stochastic dominance and coalescing. In S. L Schneider & J. Shanteau (Eds.), *Emerging perspectives on judgment and decision research* (pp. 84–107). New York: Cambridge University Press.

Birnbaum, M. H., & Navarrete, J. B. (1998). Testing descriptive utility theories: Violations of stochastic dominance and cumulative independence. *Journal of Risk and Uncertainty, 17,* 49–78.

Birnbaum, M. H., Patton, J. N., & Lott, M. K. (1999). Evidence against rank-dependent utility theories: Violations of cumulative independence, interval independence, stochastic dominance, and transitivity. *Organizational Behavior and Human Decision Processes, 77,* 44–83.

Birren, J. E., & Fisher, L. M. (1990). The elements of wisdom: Overview and integration. In R. J. Sternberg (Ed.), *Wisdom: Its nature, origins, and development* (pp. 317-332). New York: Cambridge University Press.

Bishop, J. E., & Waldholz, M. (1990). *Genome.* New York: Simon and Schuster.

Black, D. (1958). *The theory of committees and elections.* Cambridge: Cambridge University Press.

Black, M. (1970). *Margins of precision.* Ithaca, NY: Cornell University Press.

Blackburn, S. (1981). Rational animal? Commentary on Cohen, 1981. *The Behavioral and Brain Sciences, 4,* 331-332.

Blackstone, W. (1962). *Commentaries on the laws of England of public wrongs.* Boston, MA: Beacon. (Original work published 1769)

Blackwell, D., & Girshick, M. (1954). *Theory of games and statistical decisions.* New York: Wiley.

Blake, M. (1973). Prediction of recognition when recall fails: Exploring the feeling-of-knowing phenomenon. *Journal of Verbal Learning and Verbal Behavior, 12,* 311-319.

Blanchard-Fields, F. (1986). Reasoning on social dilemmas varying in emotional saliency: An adult developmental perspective. *Psychology and Aging, 1,* 325-333.

Bloom, A. (1987). *The closing of the American mind.* New York: Simon and Schuster.

Blyth, C. R. (1972a). On Simpson's paradox and the sure-thing principle. *Journal of the American Statistical Association, 67,* 364-366.

Blyth, C. R. (1972b). Rejoinder. *Journal of the American Statistical Association, 67,* 379-381.

Boden, M. A. (1995). Artificial intelligence and human dignity. In J. Cornwell (Ed.), *Nature's imagination: The frontiers of scientific vision* (pp. 148-160). New York: Oxford University Press.

Boehm, V. R. (1968). Mr. Prejudice, Miss Sympathy and the authoritarian personality: An application of psychological measuring techniques to the problem of jury bias. *Wisconsin Law Review, 1968, 3,* 734-750.

Boethius (1902). *The consolation of philosophy.* (W. V. Cooper, Trans.). London: Dent. (Original work published circa 523)

Boole, G. (1854). *An investigation of the laws of thought on which are founded the mathematical theories of logic and probabilities.* London: Walton G. Maberly.

Boorstin, D. J. (1958). *The Americans: The colonial experience.* New York: Vintage Books.

Boorstin, D. J. (1985). *The discoverers: A history of man's search to know his world and himself.* New York: Vintage Books.

Bouleau, C. (1963). *The painter's secret geometry.* New York: Harcourt, Brace and World.

Bower, G. H. (1981). Mood and memory. *American Psychologist, 36,* 129-148.

Bower, G. H. (1983). Affect and cognition. *Philosophical Transactions of the Royal Society of London B, 302,* 387-402.

Bower, G. H. (1991). Mood congruity of social judgments. In J. P. Forgas (Ed.), *Emotion and social judgments* (pp. 31-53). Oxford: Pergamon.

Bower, G. H. (1995). *Emotion and social judgments.* Washington, DC: Federation of Behavioral, Psychological and Cognitive Sciences.

Bower, G. H., Monterio, K. P., & Gilligan, S. G. (1978). Emotional mood as a context for learning and recall. *Journal of Verbal Learning and Verbal Behavior, 17*, 573–585.

Bowerman, W. R. (1978). Subjective competence: The structure, process and function of self-referent causal attributions. *Journal for the Theory of Social Behavior, 8*, 45–57.

Bowman, E. H. (1963). Consistency and optimality in managerial decision making. *Management Science, 9*, 310–321.

Boyer, C. B., & Merzbach, U. C. (1991). *A history or mathematics* (2nd ed.). New York: Wiley.

Boyle, M. H., Torrance, G. W., Sinclair, J. C., & Horwood, S. P. (1988). Economic evaluation of neonatal intensive care of very-low-birth-weight infants. In J. Dowie & A. Elstein (Eds.), *Professional judgment: A reader in clinical decision making* (pp. 456–473). Cambridge: Cambridge University Press. (Original work published 1983)

Braine, M. D. S. (1978). On the relation between the natural logic of reasoning and standard logic. *Psychological Review, 85*, 351–354.

Braine, M. D. S., & Rumain, B. (1983). Logical reasoning. In J. H. Flavell & E. M. Markman (Eds.), *Handbook of child psychology* (4th ed.). Chichester: Wiley.

Brainerd, C. J. (1981). Working memory and the developmental analysis of probability judgment. *Psychological Review, 88*, 463–502.

Braithwaite, R. B. (1974). The predictionist justification of induction. In R. Swinburne (Ed.), *The justification of induction* (pp. 102–126). London: Oxford University Press. (Original work published 1953)

Brams, S. J., & Fishburn, P. C. (1983). *Approval voting.* New York: Birkhauser.

Brandstätter, H. (1978). Social emotions in discussion groups. In H. Brandstätter, J. H. Davis, & H. Schuler (Eds.), *Dynamics of group decisions* (pp. 93–111). London: Sage.

Brandstätter, H., Davis, J. H., & Schuler, H. (Eds.). (1978). *Dynamics of group decisions.* London: Sage.

Brandt, R. B. (1979). *A theory of the good and the right.* New York: Oxford University Press.

Brandt, R. B. (1990). The concept of rational action. In P. K. Moser (Ed.), *Rationality in action: Contemporary approaches* (pp. 398–415). New York: Cambridge University Press.

Brehmer, B. (1992). Dynamic decision making: Human control of complex systems. *Acta Psychologica, 81*, 211–241.

Brehmer, B., & Allard, R. (1991). Real-time dynamic decision making: Effects of task complexity and feedback. In J. Rasmussen, B. Brehmer, & J. Leplat (Eds.), *Distributed decision making: Cognitive models for cooperative work* (pp. 319-334). Chichester, UK: Wiley.

Brent, S. B., & Watson, D. (1980, November). *Aging and wisdom: Individual and collective aspects.* Paper presented at the Third Annual Meeting of the Gerontological Society, San Diego, CA.

Brentano, F. (1973). *Psychology from an empirical standpoint.* New York: Humanities Press.

Brewer, R. E. (1968). Attitude change, interpersonal attraction and communication in dyadic situations. *The Journal of Social Psychology, 75*, 127–134.

Broadbent, D. E. (1993). A word before leaving. In D. E. Meyer & S. Kornblum (Eds.). *Attention and performance XIV: Synergies in experimental psychology, artificial intelligence,a nd cognitive neuroscience* (pp. 863–879). Cambridge, MA: MIT Press.

Broadbent, D. E., Fitzgerald, P., & Broadbent, M. H. P. (1986). Implicit and explicit knowledge in the control of complex systems. *British Journal of Psychology, 77,* 33–50.

Bromley, D. A. (1986). Physics: Natural philosophy and invention. *American Scientist, 74,* 622–639.

Bronowski, J. (1982). *The common sense of science.* London: Heineman. (Original work published 1951)

Brooks, L. R., Norman, G. R., & Allen, S. W. (1991). Role of specific similarity in a medical diagnostic task. *Journal of Experimental Psychology: General, 120,* 278-287.

Brown, A. L., & French, L. A. (1979). The zone of potential development: Implications for intelligence testing in the year 2000. *Intelligence, 3,* 253–271.

Brown, H. (1954). *The challenge of man's future.* New York: Viking.

Brown, J. S., & Burton, R. R. (1978). Diagnostic models for procedural bugs in basic mathematical skills. *Cognitive Science, 2,* 155–192.

Brown, R. D. (1989). *Knowledge is power: The diffusion of information in early America, 1700–1865.* New York: Oxford University Press.

Brown, R., & McNeill, D. (1966). The "tip of the tongue" phenomenon. *Journal of Verbal Learning and Verbal Behavior, 5,* 325–337.

Bruner, J. S., Goodnow, J. J., & Austin, G. A. (1956). *A study of thinking.* New York: Wiley.

Bucci, W. (1978). The interpretation of universal affirmative propositions. *Cognition, 6,* 55–77.

Buddenbrock, W. von (1921). Der Rhythmns der Schreitbewegungen der Stabheuschrecke Dyxippus. *Biologisches Zentralblatt, 41,* 41–48.

Buehler, R., Griffin, D, & Ross, M. (1994). Exploring the "planning fallacy": Why people underestimate their task completion times. *Journal of Personality and Social Psychology, 67,* 366–381.

Bunge, M. (1966). Technology as applied science. *Technology and Culture, 7,* 329–347.

Busemeyer, J. R. (2002). Dynamic decision making. In N. J. Smelser & P. B. Baltes (Eds.) *International Encyclopedia of the Social and Behavioral Sciences* (Vol. 6, pp. 3903-3908). Oxford: Elsevier.

Butler, C. (1970). *Number symbolism.* London: Routledge and Kegan Paul.

Cacioppo, J. T., & Petty, R. E. (1982). The need for cognition. *Journal of Personality and Social Psychology, 42,* 116–131.

Cacioppo, J. T., Petty, R. E., Feinstein, J., & Jarvis, W. (1996). Dispositional differences in cognitive motivation: The life and times of individuals varying in need for cognition. *Psychological Bulletin, 119,* 197–253.

Calne, D. B. (1999). *Within reason: Rationality and human behavior.* New York: Vintage Books.

Camerer, C. & Thaler, R. H. (1995). Anomilies: Ultimatums, dictators and manners. *Journal of Economic Perspectives, 9,* 209–219.

Campbell, D. T. (1959). Systematic error on the part of human links in communication systems. *Information and control, 1,* 334–369.

Campbell, J. D., & Fairey, P. J. (1985). Effects of self-esteem, hypothetical explanations, and verbalization of expectancies on future performance. *Journal of Personality and Social Psychology, 48,* 1097–1111.

Cannon-Bowers, J. A., Salas, E., & Pruitt, J. S. (1996). Establishing the boundaries of a paradigm for decision making research. *Human Factors, 38,* 193–205.

Capra, F. (1975). *The Tao of physics.* New York: Bantam Books.

Carnap, R. (1937). *The logical syntax of language.* A. Smeaton (Trans.). London: Routledge and Kegan Paul.

Carnap, R. (1947). On the application of inductive logic. *Philosophy and Phenomenological Research, 8,* 133–148.

Carnap, R. (1962). *Logical foundations of probability* (2nd ed.). Chicago, Il: University of Chicago Press. (Original work published 1950)

Carraher, T. N, Carraher, D. W., & Schliemann, A. D. (1985). Mathematics in the streets and in schools. *British Journal of Developmental Psychology, 3,* 21–29.

Carroll, J. M. (1990). *The Nurnberg funnel: Designing minimalist instruction for practical computer skill.* Cambridge, MA: MIT Press.

Carroll, L. (1977). Symbol logic. In W. W. Bartley, III (Ed.), *Lewis Carroll's symbolic logic* (What the tortoise said to Achilles, pp. 431–434). New York: Clarkson N. Potter.

Carson, R. (1962). *Silent spring.* Boston, MA: Houghton Mifflin.

Casscells, W., Schoenberger, A., & Grayboys, T. B. (1978). Interpretation by physicians of clinical laboratory results. *New England Journal of Medicine, 299,* 999.

Cattaneo, E., Rigaminti, D., & Zuccato, C. (2002). The enigma of huntington's disease. *Scientific American, 287*(6), 92–97.

Ceci, S. J. (1993). Contextual trends in intellectual development. *Developmental Review, 13,* 403–435.

Ceci, S. J., & Liker, J. K. (1986). Academic and nonacademic intelligence: An experimental separation. In R. J. Sternberg & R. K. Wagner (Ed.), *Practical intelligence* (pp. 119–142). Cambridge: Cambridge University Press.

Chaiken, S., Liberman, A., & Eagly, A. H. (1989). Heuristic and systematic information processing within and beyond the persuasion context. In J. S. Uleman, & J. A. Bargh (Eds.), *Unintended thought* (pp. 212–252). New York: Guilford Press.

Champagne, A. B., Klopfer, L. E., & Anderson, J. H. (1980). Factors influencing the learning of classical mechanics. *American Journal of Physics, 48,* 1074–1079.

Chandler, M. J., & Holliday, S. (1990). Wisdom in the postapocalyptic age. In R. J. Sternberg (Ed.), *Wisdom: Its nature, origins, and development* (pp. 121–141). New York: Cambridge University Press.

Chanowitz & Langer (1981). Premature cognitive commitment. *Journal of Personality and Social Psychology, 41,* 1051–1063.

Chapman, D. (1991). Letter to the editor (Air pollution benefit-cost assessment). *Science, 253,* 608.

Charness, N. (1979). Components of skill in bridge. *Canadian Journal of Psychology, 33,* 1–16.

Chechile, R. A., & Butler, S. F. (2000). Is "generic utility theory" a suitable theory of choice behavior for gambles with mixed gains and losses? *The Journal of Risk and Uncertainty, 20,* 189–211.

Chechile, R. A., & Butler, S. F. (2003). Reassessing the testing of generic utility models for mixed gambles. *The Journal of Risk and Uncertainty, 26,* 55–76.

Chechile, R. A., & Cooke, A. D. J. (1997). An experimental test of a general class of utility models: Evidence for context dependency. *The Journal of Risk and Uncertainty, 14,* 75–93.

Cheng, P. W., & Holyoak, K. J. (1985). Pragmatic reasoning schemas. *Cognitive Psychology, 17,* 391–416.

Cheng, P. W., Holyoak, K. J., Nisbett, R. E., & Oliver, L. M. (1986). Pragmatic versus syntactic approaches to training deductive reasoning. *Cognitive Psychology, 18,* 293–328.

Cherniak C. (1986). *Minimal rationality.* Cambridge, MA, MIT Press.

Chesterton, G. K. (1910). *Alarms and discursions.* London: Methuen.

Chesterton, G. K. (1959). *Orthodoxy.* Garden City, NY: Doubleday. (Original work published 1908)

Chi, M. T. H., Feltovich, P .J., & Glaser, R. (1981). Categorization and representation of physics problems by experts and novices. *Cognitive Science, 5,* 121–152.

Chipman, S. F. (1992). The higher-order cognitive skills: What they are and how they might be transmitted. In T. G. Sticht, M. J. Beeler, & B. A. McDonald (Eds.), *The intergenerational transfer fo cognitive skills, Vol 2: Theory and research in cognitive science* (pp. 128–158). Norwood, NJ: Ablex.

Chomsky, N. (1957). *Syntactic structures.* The Hague: Mouton.

Chomsky, N. (1965). *Aspects of the theory of syntax.* Cambridge, MA: MIT Press.

Christensen-Szalanski, J. J., & Fobian-Willham, C. (1991). The hindsight bias: A meta-analysis. *Organizational Behavior and Human Decision Processes, 48,* 147–168.

Churchland, P. M., & Chruchland, P. S. (1995). Intertheoretic reduction: A neuroscientist's field guide. In J. Cornwell (Ed.), *Nature's imagination: The frontiers of scientific vision* (pp. 64–77). New York: Oxford University Press.

Clancy, J. M., Elliott, G. C., Ley, T., Omodei, M. M., Wearing, A. J., McLennan, J., & Thorsteinsson, E. B. (2003). Command style and team performance in dynamic decision-making tasks. In S. L. Schneider & J. Shanteau (Eds.), *Emerging perspectives on judgment and decision research* (pp. 586–619). New York: Cambridge University Press.

Clark, H. H., & Marshall, C. R. (1981). Definite referencd and mutual knowledge. In A. Joshi, B. Webber, and I. Sag (Eds.), *Elements of discourse understanding.* Cambridge: Cambridge University Press.

Clark, J. (1990). *The UFO encyclopedia, Vol 1: UFOs in the 1980s.* Detroit, MI: Apogee Books.

Clark, R. D. (1971). Group-induced shift toward risk: A criticalappraisal. *Psychological Bulletin, 76,* 251–270.

Clarke, D. S., Jr. (1985). *Practical inferences.* London: Routledge & Kegan Paul.

Clayton, V. (1976). *A multidimensional scaling analysis of the concept of wisdom.* Unpublished doctoral dissertation, the University of Southern California.

Clayton, V., & Birren, J. W. (1980). The development of wisdom across the life span: A reeximation of an ancient topic. In P. B. Baltes & O. G. Brim, Jr. (Eds.), *Life-span development and behavior,* Vol 3, (pp. 103–135). New York: Adademic Press.

Cleckley, H. (1964). *The mask of sanity* (4th ed.). Saint Louis, MO: C. V. Mosby.
Clemen, R. T. (1999). *Does decision analysis work? A research agenda.* Duke University (unpublished manuscript).
Clement, J. (November, 1981a). Solving problems with formulas: Some limitations. *Engineering Education*, pp. 158–162.
Clement, J. (1981b). Students' preconceptions in physics and Galileo's discussion of falling bodies. *Problem Solving, 3*, 3–5.
Clement, J. (1982). Students' preconceptions in introductory mechanics. *American Journal of Physics, 50*, 66–71.
Clement, J., Lochhead, J., & Monk, G. S. (1981). Translation difficulties in learning mathematics. *American Mathematical Monthly, 88*, 286–290.
Clement, J., Lochhead, J., & Soloway, E. (1980). Positive effects of computer programming on students' understanding of variables and equations. *Communications of the Association for Computing Machinery*, 467–474.
Cohen, J. E. (1995). Population growth and earth's human carrying capacity. *Science, 269*, 341–346.
Cohen, L. J. (1979). On the psychology of prediction: Whose is the fallacy? *Cognition, 7*, 385–407.
Cohen, L. J. (1980). Whose is the fallacy? A rejoinder to Daniel Kahneman and Amos Tversky. *Cognition, 8*, 89–92.
Cohen, L. J. (1981). Can human irrationality be experimentally demonstrated? *Behavioral and Brain Sciences, 4*, 317–331.
Cohen, L. J. (1982). Are people programmed to commit fallacies? Further thoughts about the interpretation of data on judgment. *Journal of the Theory of Social Behavior, 12*, 251–274.
Collins, A., Brown, J. S., & Larkin, K. (1980). Inference in text understanding. In R. J. Spiro, B. C. Bruce, & W. F. Brewer (Eds.), *Theoretical issues in reading comprehension*. Hillsdale, NJ: Earlbaum.
Collins, B. E., & Hoyt, M. E. (1972). Personal responsibility-for-consequences: An integration and extension of the "forced compliance" literature. *Journal of Experimental Social Psychology, 8*, 558–593.
Columbia Associates in Philosophy (1923). *An introduction to reflective thinking.* New York: Houghton Mifflin. (Associates: L. Buermeyer, W. F. Cooley, J. J. Coss, H. L. Friess, J. Gutmann, T. Munro, H. Peterson, J. H. Randall, Jr., & H. W. Schneider)
Commoner, B. (1991). The failure of the environmental effort. In A. B. Wolbrast (Ed.), *Environment in peril* (pp. 38–63). Washington, DC: Smithsonian Institution Press.
Comte, A (1988). *Introduction to positive philosophy.* Indianapolis, IN: Hackett. (Original work published 1842)
Conlisk, J. (1996). Why bounded rationality? *Journal of Economic Literature, 34*, 669–700.
Conlon, E. J., & Wolf, G. (1980). The moderating effects of strategy, visibility, and involvement on allocation behavior: An extension of Staw's escalation paradigm. *Organizational Behavior and Human Performance, 26*, 172–192.
Cooper, W. S. (1989). How evolutionary biology challenges the classical theory of rational choice. *Biology and Philosophy, 4*, 457–481.

Cosmides, L. (1985). *Deduction or Darwinian algorithms?: An explanation of the "elusive" content effect on the Wason selection task*. Unpublished doctoral dissertation, Harvard University: University Microfilms 86-02206.
Cosmides, L. (1989). The logic of social exchange: Has natural selection shaped how humans reason? Studies with the Wason selection task. *Cognition, 31*, 187–276.
Cosmides, L., & Tooby, J. (1987). From evolution to behavior: Evolutionary psychology as the missing link. In J. Dupre (Ed.), *The latest on the best: Essays on evolution and optimality*. Cambridge, MA: MIT Press.
Cosmides, L., & Tooby, J. (1989). Evolutionary psychology and the generation of culture, Part II. Case study: A computational theory of social exchange. *Ethology and Sociobiology, 10*, 51–97.
Cosmides, L., & Tooby, J. (1990). *Is the mind a frequentist?* Paper presented at the Second Annual Meeting of the Human Behaivor and Evolution Society, Los Angeles, CA, August.
Cosmides, L., & Tooby, J. (1992). Cognitive adaptations for social exchange. In J Barkow, L. Cosmides, & J. Tooby (Eds.), *The adapted mind: Evolutionary psychology and the generation of culture* (pp. 162–228). New York: Oxford University Press.
Costermans, J., Lories, G., & Ansay, C. (1992). Confidence level and feeling of knowing in question answering: The weight of inferential processes. *Journal of Experimental Psychology: Learning, Memory, and Cognition, 18*, 142–150.
Cournot, A. A. (1956). Mathematics of value and demand. In J. R. Newman (Ed.), *The world of mathematics, Vol 2* (pp. 1203–1216). New York: Simon and Schuster. (Original work published in French 1838, in English 1897)
Cromer, A. (1993). *Uncommon sense: The heretical nature of science*. New York: Oxford University Press.
Csikszentmihalyi, M. (1975). *Beyond boredom and anxiety*. San Francisco: Jossey-Bass.
Csikszentmihalyi, M., & Rathunde, K. (1990). The psychology of wisdom: An evolutionary interpretation. In R. J. Sternberg (Ed.), *Wisdom: Its nature, origins, and development* (pp. 25–51). New York: Cambridge University Press.
Cummings, N. A., & Wiggins, J. G. (2001). A collaborative primary care/behavioral health model for the use of psychotropic medication with children and adolescents. The report of a national retrospective study. *Issues in Interdisciplinary Care, 3*(2), 121–128.
Damasio, A. R. (1994). *Descartes' error: Emotion, reason, and the human brain*. New York: G. P. Putnam's Sons.
Darley, J. M., & Batson, C. D. (1973). From Jerusalem to Jericho: A study of situational and dispositional variables in helping behavior. *Journal of Personality and Social Psychology, 27*, 100–119.
Darley, J. M., & Fazio, R. H. (1980). Expectancy confirmation processes arising in the social interaction sequence. *American Psychologist, 35*, 867–881.
Dasgupta, P., & Maskin, E. (2004). The fairest vote of all. *Scientific American, 290*(3), 92–97.
Dasser, V., Ulbaek, I., & Premack, D. (1989). The perception of intention. *Science, 243*, 365–367.

Daston, L. J. (1980). Probabilistic expectation and rationality in classical probability theory. *Historia Mathematica, 7,* 234–260.
David, F. N. (1962). *Games, gods, and gambling: The origins and history of probability.* New York: Hafner.
Davidshofer, I. O. (1976). Risk-taking and vocational choice: A reevaluation. *Journal of Counseling Psychology, 23,* 151–154.
Davidson, D. (1970). Mental events. In L. Foster & J. W. Swanson (Eds.), *Experience and theory.* Amherst: University of Massachusetts Press.
Davidson, D. (1982). Paradoxes of irrationality. In R. Wollheim & J. Hopkins (Eds.), *Philosophical essays on Freud* (pp. 289–305). Cambridge: Cambridge University Press.
Davidson, D. (1995). The representativeness heuristic and the conjunction fallacy effect in children's decision making. *Merrill-Palmer Quarterly, 41,* 328–346.
Davidson, D., Suppes, P., & Siegel, S. (1957). *Decision making: An experimental approach.* Stanford, CA: Stanford University Press.
Davidson, N. E. (1996). Is hormone replacement therapy a risk? *Scientific American, 275*(3), 101.
Davies, P. C. W. (1983). *God and the new physics.* New York: Simon and Schuster.
Davies, P. (1988). *The cosmic blueprint: New discoveries in nature's creative ability to order the universe.* New York: Simon and Schuster.
Davies, P. C. W. (1992). *The mind of God: The scientific basis for a rational world.* New York: Simon and Schuster.
Davies P. C. W. (1993). Interview of Bohm, In P. C. W. Davies, & J. R. Brown (Eds.), *The ghost in the atom: A discussion of the mysteries of quantum mechanics.* New York: Cambridge University Press. (Original work published 1986)
Davis, F. D., Lohse, G. L., & Kotteman, J. E. (1994). Harmful effects of seemingly helpful information on forecasts of stock earnings. *Journal of Economic Psychology, 15,* 253–267.
Dawes, R. M. (1971). A case study of graduate admissions: Application of three principles of human decision making. *American Psychologist, 26,* 180–188.
Dawes, R. M. (1979). The robust beauty of improper linear models in decision making. *American Psychologist, 34,* 571–582.
Dawes, R. M. (1988). *Rational choice in an uncertain world.* New York: Harcourt Brace Jovanovich.
Dawes, R. M. (1989). Experience and validity of clinical judgment: The illusory correlation. *Behavioral Sciences and the Law, 7,* 457–467.
Dawes, R. M., & Corrigan, B. (1974). Linear models in decisionmaking. *Psychological Bulletin, 81,* 95–106.
Dawes, R. M., Faust, D., & Meehl, P. E. (1989). Clinical versus actuarial judgment. *Science, 243,* 1668–1674.
Dawkins, R. (1986). *The blind watchmaker.* New York: W. W. Norton and Company.
De Avila, E. A., & Duncan, S. (1985). The language minority child: A psychological, linguistic, and social analysis. In J. W. Segal, S. F. Chipman, & R. Glaser (Eds.), *Thinking and learning skills, Vol 2: Research and open questions.* Hillsdale, NJ: Erlbaum.
De Chardin, T. (1959). *The phenomenon of man.* (B. Wall, Trans.) New York: Harper and Row.

Deci, E. L., & Ryan, R. M. (1985). *Intrinsic motivation and self-determination in human behavior.* New York: Plenum Press.

De Dombal, F. T. (1988). Computer-aided diagnosis of acute abdominal pain: The British experience. In J. Dowie & A. Elstein (Eds.), *Professional judgment: A reader in clinical decision making* (pp. 190–199). Cambridge: Cambridge University Press. (Original work published 1984)

De Dombal, F. T., Leaper, D. J., Horrocks, J. C., Staniland, J. R., & McCann, A. P. (1974). Human and computer-aided diagnosis of abdominal pain: Further report with emphasis on performance of clinicians. *British Medical Journal, 1,* 376–380.

DeGroot, A. D. (1965). *Thought and choice in chess.* The Hague: Mouton.

DeKay, W. T., Haselton, M. G., & Kirkpatrick, L. A. (2000). Reversing figure and ground in the rationality debate: An evolutionary perspective. *Behavioral and Brain Sciences, 23,* 670–671.

De Kleer, J. (1977). Multiple representations of knowledge in a mechanics problem solver. *International Joint Conference on Artificial Intelligence, 5,* 299–304.

DeKleer, J., & Brown, J. S. (1980). Mental models of physical mechanisms. *Cognitive and Instructional Sciences.* Palo Alto Research Center Report No. 6. Palo Alto, CA.

Dennett, D. C. (1978). *Brainstorms.* Cambridge, MA: MIT Press.

Dennett, D. C. (1984). *Elbow room: Varieties of free will worth having.* Cambridge, MA: MIT Press.

Dennet, D. C. (1987). *The intentional stance.* Cambridge, MA: MIT Press.

Dennett, D. C. (1995). *Darwin's dangerous idea: Evolution and the meanings of life.* New York: Simon and Schuster.

Descartes, R. (1950). *Meditations on first philosophy* (L. J. Lafleur, Trans.). New York: Liberal Arts Press. (Original work published 1641)

Deutsch, M. (1949). A theory of cooperation and competition. *Human Relations, 2,* 129–152.

Deutsch, M., & Gererd, H. B. (1955). A study of normative and informational influences upon individual judgment. *Journal of Abnormal and Social Psychology, 51,* 629–636.

Dewey, J. (1933). *How we think: A restatement of the relation of reflective thinking to the educative process.* Boston, MA: Heath.

Diaconis, P., & Freedman, D. (1981). The persistence of cognitive illusions. Commentary on Cohen, 1981. *The Behavioral and Brain Sciences, 4,* 333–334.

Diamond, P. A., Hausman, J. A., Leonard, G. K., & Denning, M. A. (1993). Does contingent valuation measure preferences? Some experimental evidence. In J. A. Hausman (Ed.), *Contingent valuation L A critical assessment.* Amsterdam: North Holland.

Diener, C. I., & Dweck, C. S. (1978). An analysis of learned helplessness: Continuous changes in performance, strategy and achievement cognitions following failure. *Journal of Personality and Social Psychology, 39,* 940–952.

Dillon, R. F., & Sternberg, R. J. (Eds.) (1986). *Cognition and instruction.* New York: Academic Press.

Dimnet, E. (1928). *The art of thinking.* New York: Simon and Schuster.

Dion, K. L., Baron, R. S., & Miller, N. (1970). Why do groups make riskier decisions than individuals? Om L. Berkowitz (Ed.), *Advances in experimental social psychology* (Vol. 5). New York: Academic Press.

Dittmann-Kohli, F. & Baltes, P. B. (1990). Toward a neofunctionalist conception of adult intellectual development: Wisdom as a prototypical case of intellectual growth. In C. Alexander & E. Langer (Eds.), *Higher stages of human development* (pp. 54–78). New York: Oxford University Press.

Dixon, R. A., Kramer, D. A., & Baltes, P. B. (1985). Intelligence: A life-span developmental perspective. In B. B. Wolman (Ed.), *Handbook of intelligence: Theories, measurements, and applications* (pp. 301–350). New York: Wiley.

Dobshansky, T. (1964). Heredity and the nature of man. New York: Harcourt, Brace and World.

Dodgson, C. L. (1958). A method of taking votes on more than two issues. In D. Black (Ed.), *Theory of committees and elections*. Cambridge: Cambridge University Press. (Original work published 1876)

Doherty, M. E. (2003). Optimists, pessimists, and realists. In S. L. Schneider & J. Shanteau (Eds.), *Emerging perspectives on judgment and decision research* (pp. 643–679). Cambridge: Cambridge University Press.

Doherty, M. E., Mynatt, C. R., Tweney, R. D., & Schiavo, M. D. (1979). Pseudodiagnosticity. *Acta Psychologica, 43*, 111–121.

Doubilet, P. & McNeil, B. J. (1988). Clinical decision making. In J. Dowie & A. Elstein (Eds.), *Professional judgment. A reader in clinical decision making* (pp. 255–276). Cambridge: Cambridge University Press. (Reprinted from *Medical Care*, 1985, 23, 648–662.)

Dougherty, M. R. P., Gronlund, S. D., & Gettys, C. F. (2003). Memory as a fundamental heuristic for decision making. In S. L. Schneider & J. Shanteau (Eds.), *Emerging perspectives on judgment and decision research* (pp. 125–164). Cambridge: Cambridge University Press.

Droysen, J. G. (1960). *Historik, Vorlesungen über Enzyklopädie und Methodologie der Geschichte* (4th ed.). Munich: Oldenburg.

Drummond, M. F. (1988). Resource allocation decisions in health care: A role for quality of life assessments? In J. Dowie & A. Elstein (Eds.), *Professional judgment. A reader in clinical decision making* (pp. 436–455). Cambridge: Cambridge University Press. (Reprinted from *Journal of Chronic Diseases*, 1987, 40, 605–616.)

Dummett, M. (1984). *Voting procedures*. Oxford: Clarendon Press.

Duncan, B. L. (1976). Differential social perception and attribution of intergroup violence: Testing the lower limits of stereotyping of blacks. *Journal of Personality and Social Psychology, 34*, 590–598.

Dunlap, R. A. (1997). *The golden ratio and Fibonacci Numbers*. Singapore: World Scientific.

Durning, A. (1992). *How much is enough?* New York: W. W. Norton.

Dweck, C. S. (1975). The role of expectations and attributions in the alleviation of learned helplessness. *Journal of Personality and Social Psychology, 45*, 165–171.

Dweck, C. S., & Bempechat, J. (1983). Children's theories of intelligence. In S. Paris, G. Olsen, & H. Stevenson (Eds.), *Learning and motivation in the classroom* (pp. 239–256). Hillsdale, NJ: Erlbaum.

Dweck, C. S. & Eliott, E. S. (1983). Achievement motivation. In P. H. Mussen (Ed.), *Handbook of child psychology, Vol.4*. New York: Wiley.

Dweck, C. S., & Leggett, E. L. (1988). A social-cognitive approach to motivation and personality. *Psychological Review, 95*, 256–273.

Eagleman, D. M. (2004). The where and when of intention. *Science, 303,* 1144–1146.

Eaton, J. E., Anderson, C., & Smith, E. L. (1984). Students' misconceptions interfere with science learning: Case studies in fifth-grade students. *Elementary School Journal, 84,* 365–379.

Ebert, R. J. (1972). Human control of a two-variable decsion system. *Organizational Behavior and Human Performance, 7,* 237-264.

Ebbesen, E. B., & Konecni, V. J. (1980). On the external validity of decision-making research: What do we know about decisions in the real world? In T. S. Wallsten (Ed.), *Cognitive processes in choice and decision behavior* (pp. 21–45). Hillsdale, NJ: Erlbaum.

Eccles, J., & Robinson, D. N. (1985). *The wonder of being human: Our brain and our mind.* Boston: New Science Library.

Eddy, D. M. (1982). Probabilistic reasoning in clinical medicine: Problems and opportunities. In D. Kahneman, P. Slovic, & A. Tversky (Eds.), *Judgment under uncertainty: Heuristics and biases* (pp. 249–267). New York: Cambridge University Press.

Eddy, D. M. (1984). Variations in physician practice. The role of uncertainty. *Health Affairs, 3.* 74–89.

Eddy, D. M., & Clanton, C. H. (1982). The art of diagnosis: Solving the clinico-pathological exercise. *New England Journal of Medicine, 306,* 1263–1268.

Edelman, G. M. (1995). Memory and the individual soul: Against silly reductionism. J. Cornwell (Ed.), *Nature's imagination: The frontiers of scientific vision* (pp. 200–206). New York: Oxford University Press.

Edney, J. J. (1980). The commons problem: Alternative perspectives. *American Psychologist, 35,* 131–150.

Edwards, K., & Smith, E. E. (1996). A disconfirmation bias in the evaluation of arguments. *Journal of Personality and Social Psychology, 71,* 5–24.

Edwards, W. (1954). The theory of decision making. *Psychological Bulletin, 51,* 380–417.

Edwards, W. (1961). Behavioral decision theory. *Annual Review of Psychology, 12,* 473–493.

Edwards, W. (1967). Dynamic decision theory and probabilistic information processing. *Human Factors, 4,* 59–73.

Edwards, W. M. (1978). Technology for Director Dubious: Evaluation and discussion in public contexts. In K. R. Hammond (Ed.), *Judgment and decision in public policy formation.* Boulder, CO: Westview Press.

Edwards, W., & Tversky, A. (1967). *Decision making.* Middlesex: Penguin.

Egan, D., & Schwartz, B. (1979). Chunking in recall of symbolic drawings. *Memory and Cognition, 17,* 147–158.

Ehrenfeld, D. (1981). *The arrogance of humanism.* New York: Oxford University Press.

Einhorn, H. J. (1971). Use of non-linear, non compensatory models as a function of task in amount of information. *Organizational Behavior and Human Performance, 6,* 1–27.

Einhorn, H. J., & Hogarth, R. M. (1981a). Behavioral decision theory: Processes of judgment and choice. *Annual Review of Psychology, 32,* 53–88.

Einhorn, H. J., & Hogarth, R. M. (1981b). Rationality and the sanctity of competence. Commentary on Cohen, 1981. *The Behavioral and Brain Sciences, 4,* 334–335.

Einstein, A. (1961). *Relativity: The special and the general theory.* New York: Bonanza books. (Original work published 1916)
Eisley, L. (1967). Introduction [to "On a piece of chalk" by T. H. Huxley]. New York: Charles Scribner.
Ekeland, I. (1993). *The broken dice.* Chicago: University of Chicago Press.
Elliott, E. S., & Dweck, C. S. (1988). Goals: An approach to motivation and achievement. *Journal of Personality and Social Psychology, 54,* 5–12.
Ellsworth, P. C. (1989). Are twelve heads better than one? *Law and Contemporary Problems, 52,* 205–224.
Elstein, A. S., & Schwarz, A. (2002). Clinical problem solving and diagnostic decision making: Selective review of the cognitive literature. *British Medical Journal, 324,* 729–732.
Elstein, A. S., Shulman, L. S., & Sprafka, S. A. (1978). *Medical problem solving: An analysis of clinical reasoning.* Cambridge, MA: Harvard University Press.
Elster, J. (1989). *Solomonic judgments.* Cambridge: Cambridge University Press.
Engle, R. W., & Bukstel, L. (1978). Memory processes among bridge players of different expertise. *American Journal of Psychology, 91,* 673–689.
Ennis, R. H. (1969). *Logic in teaching.* Englewood Cliffs, NJ: Prentice-Hall.
Ennis, R. H. (1985). Critical thinking and the curriculum. *National Forum, 65,* 28–31.
Ennis, R. H. (1987). A taxonomy of critical thinking dispositions and abilities. In J. B. Baron & R. J. Sternberg (Eds.), *Teaching thinking skills: Theory and practice* (pp. 9–26). New York: Freeman.
Epstein, S. (1994). Integration of the cognitive and the psychodynamic unconscious. *American Psychologist, 49,* 709–724.
Eraker, S. A., & Sox, H. C. (1981). Assessment of patients' preferences for therapeutic outcomes. *Medicinal Decision Making, 1,* 29–39.
Erasmus, D. (1942). *The praise of folly.* New York: Walter J. Black. (Original work published 1509)
Ericsson, K. A., & Simon, H. A. (1980). Verbal reports as data. *Psychology Review, 87,* 215–251.
Erikson, E. H. (1982). *The life cycle completed.* New York: Norton.
Erikson, E. H., Erikson, J. M., & Kivnick, H. Q. (1986). *Vital involvement in old age: The experience of old age in our time.* New York: Norton.
Estes, W. K. (1961). A descriptive approach to the dynamics of choice behavior. *Behavioral Science, 6,* 177–184.
Evans, C. E. (1973). *Cults of unreason.* New York: Farrar, Straus, and Giroux.
Evans, J. St. B. T. (1972a). On the problems of interpreting reasoning data: logical and psychological approaches. *Cognition, 1,* 373–384.
Evans, J. St. B. T. (1977a). Linguistic factors in reasoning. *Quarterly Journal of Experimental Psychology, 29,* 297–306.
Evans, J. St. B. T. (1977b). Toward a statistical theory of reasoning. *Quarterly Journal of Experimental Psychology, 29,* 621–635.
Evans, J. St. B. T. (1982). *The psychology of deductive reasoning.* London: Routledge & Kegan Paul Ltd.
Evans, J. St. B. T. (1989). *Bias in human reasoning: Causes and consequences.* Hillsdale, NJ: Erlbaum.
Evans, J. St. B. T. (1993). Bias and rationality. In K. I. Manktelow & D. E. Over (Eds.), *Rationality: Psychological and philosophical perspectives* (pp. 6–30). London: Routledge.

Evans, J. St. B. T., & Lynch, J. S. (1973). Matching bias in the selection task. *British Journal of Psychology, 64*, 391–397.

Evans, J. St. B. T., & Over, D. E. (1996). *Rationality and reasoning*. Hove: Psychology Press.

Evans, J. St. B. T., Over, D. E., & Manktelow, K. I. (1993). Reasoning, decision making and rationality. *Cognition, 49*, 165–187.

Evans, J. St. B. T., & Pollard, P. (1981). On defining rationality unreasonably. *The Behavioral and Brain Sciences, 4*, 335–336.

Evans, J. St. B. T., & Wason, P. C. (1976). Rationalization in a reasoning task. *British Journal of Psychology, 63*, 205–212.

Evans, J. St. B. T., & Wason, P. C. (1976). Rationalization in a reasoning task. *British Journal of Psychology, 63*, 205–212.

Faunce, W. (1981). *Problems of an industrial society*. New York: McGraw Hill.

Faust, D., Hart, K., & Guilmette, J. (1988). Pediatric malingering: The capacity of children to fake believable deficits on neuropsychological testing. *Journal of Counseling and Clinical Psychology, 56*, 578–582.

Fazio, R. H., Effrein, E. A., & Falender, V. J. (1981). Self-perceptions following social interaction. *Journal of Personality and Social Psychology, 41*, 232–242.

Fehr, E., & Gächter, S. (2000). Cooperation and punishment in public goods experiments. *American Economic Review, 90*, 980–994.

Feinstein, A. R. (1967). *Clinical judgment*. Baltimore: Williams & Wilkins Co.

Feinstein, A. R. (1977). Clinical biostatistics: XXXIX. The haze of Bayes, the aerial palaces of decision analysis, and the computerized Ouija board. *Clinical Parmacology and Therapeutics, 21*, 482–496.

Festinger, L. (1950). Informal social communication. *Psychological Review, 57*, 271–292.

Festinger, L. (1957). *A theory of cognitive dissonance*. Evanston, IL: Row, Peterson.

Feyman, R. P. (1985). *QED: The strange theory of light and matter*. Princeton, NJ: Princeton University Press.

Fiedler, K. (2000). On mere considering: The subjective experience of truth. In H. Bless & J. P. Forgas (Eds.), *The message within: The role of subjective experience in social cognition* (pp. 13–36). Philadelphia: Psychology Press.

Finucane, M. L., Alhakami, A., Slovic, P., & Johnson, S. M. (2000). The affect heuristic in judgments of risks and benefits. *Journal of Behavioral Decision Making, 13*, 1–17.

Finucane, M. L., Peters, E., & Slovic, P. (2003). Judgment and decision making: The dance of affect and reason. In S. L. Schneider & J. Shanteau (Eds.), *Emerging perspectives on judgment and decision research* (pp. 327–364). Cambridge: Cambridge University Press.

Fisch, H.-U., Hammond, K. R., Joyce, C. R. B., & O'Reilly, M. (1981). An experimental sltudy of the clinical judgment of general physicians in evaluating and prescribing for depression. *British Journal of Psychiatry,138*, 100–109.

Fischer, G. W. (1972). *Four methods for assessing multi-attribute utilities: An experimental validation*. University of Michigan Project No. NR 197-014.

Fischhoff, B. (1975). Hindsight ≠ foresight: The effect of outcome knowledge on judgment under uncertainty. *Journal of Experimental Psychology: Human Perception and Performance, 1*, 288–299.

Fischhoff, B. (1991). Eliciting values: Is there anything in there? *American Psychologist, 46*, 835–847.

Fischhoff, B., & Beyth-Marom, R. (1975). I knew it would happen: Rremembered probabilities of once-future things. *Organizational Behavior and Human Performance, 13,* 1–16.

Fischhoff, B., & Beyth-Marom, R. (1983). Hypothesis evaluation from a Bayesian perspective. *Psychological Review, 90,* 239–60.

Fischhoff, B., Slovic, P., & Lichtenstein, S. (1982). Lay foibles and expert fables in judgments about risks. *The American Statistician, 36,* 241–255.

Fishburn, P. C. (1973). *The theory of social choice.* Princeton, NJ: Princeton University Press.

Fiske, S. T., & Taylor, S. E. (1991). *Social cognition* (2nd edition). New York: McGraw-Hill.

Flavell, J. H., & Wohlwill, J. F. (1969). Formal and functional aspects of cognitive development. In D. Elkind & J. H. Flavell (Eds.), *Studies in cognitive development* (pp. 67–120). New York: Oxford University Press.

Flegg, G. (1983). *Numbers: Their history and meaning.* Mineola, NY: Dover.

Fleming, J., & Arrowood, A. J. (1979). Information processing and the perseverance of discredited self-perceptions. *Personality and Social Psychology Bulletin, 5,* 201–204.

Fleming, R. A. (1970). The processing of conflicting information in a simulated tactical decision-making task. *Human Factors, 12,* 375–385.

Flew, A. G. N. (1967). *Evolutionary ethics.* London: MacMillan.

Florman, S. C. (1981). *Blaming technology: The irrational search for scapegoats.* New York: St. Martin's Press.

Fodor, J. (1981). Three cheers for propositional attitudes. In J. Fodor (Ed.), *Representations.* Cambridge, MA: MIT Press.

Fong, G. T., Krantz, D. H., & Nisbett, R. E. (1986). The effects of statistical training on thinking about everyday problems. *Cognitive Psychology, 18,* 253–292.

Forgas, J. P., Bower, G. H., & Krantz, S. (1984). The influence of mood on perceptions of social interactions. *Journal of Personality and Social Psychology, 20,* 497–513.

Forgas, J. P., Bower, G. H., & Moylan, S. J. (1990). Praise or blame? Affective influences on attribution for achievement. *Journal of Personality and Social Psychology, 53,* 809–819.

Forgas, J. P, & Moylan, S. J. (1987). After the movies: Transient mood and social judgment. *Personality and Social Psychology Bulletin, 13,* 467–477.

Fowlkes, M. R., & Miller, P. (1982). *Love Canal: The social construction of disaster.* Washington, DC: Federal Emergency Management Agency.

Fox, R. (1957). *Experiment perilous: Physicians and patients facing the unknown.* Glencoe, IL: Free Press.

Franklin, B. (1907). A letter to Joseph Priestly, September 19, 1772. In A. H. Smyth (Ed.), *The writings of Benjamin Franklin* (pp. 437–438). New York: MacMillan.

Frey, D. (1981). The effect of negative feedback about oneself and cost of information on preferences for information about the source of this feedback. *Journal of Experimental Social Psychology, 17,* 42–50.

Frey, D., & Stahlberg, D. (1986). Selection of information after receiving more or less reliable self-threatening information. *Personality and Social Psychology Bulletin, 12,* 434–441.

Frick, R. W. (1996). The appropriate use of null hypothesis testing. *Psychological Methods, 1,* 379–390.

Fried, L. S., & Peterson, C. R. (1969). Information seeking: Optional versus fixed stopping. *Journal of Experimental Psychology, 80,* 525–529.

Friedman, M. (1953). *Essays in positive economics.* Chicago: University of Chicago Press.

Friedman, R. M. (1991). Letter to the editor (Air pollution benefit-cost assessment). *Science, 253,* 607.

Friedrich, J. (1993). Primary error detection and minimization (PEDMIN) strategies in social cognition: A reintrerpretation of confirmation bias phenomena. *Psychological Review, 100,* 298–319.

Fromm, E. (1963). *Fear of freedom.* London: Routledge. (Original work published 1942)

Funder, D. C. (1982). On the accuracy of dispositional vs. situational attributions. *Social Cognition, 1,* 205–222.

Funder, D. C. (1987). Errors and mistakes: Evaluating the accuracy of social judgment. *Psychological Bulletin, 101,* 79–90.

Gabor, D. (1972). *The mature society.* New York: Praeger.

Gaeth, G. J., & Shanteau, J. (1981). *A bibliography of research on the effects of irrelevance in psychology* (Applied Psychology Rep. No. 81-13). Manhattan: Kansas State University, Department of Psychology.

Gaeth, G. J., & Shanteau, J. (1986). Reducing the influence of irrelevant information on experienced decision makers. In H. R. Arkes & K. R. Hammond (Eds.), *Judgment and decision making: An interdisciplinary reader* (pp. 449–465). New York: Cambridge University Press. (Reprinted from *Organizational Behavior and Human Performance,* 1984, *33,* 263–282.)

Gallistel, C. R. (1980). From muscles to motivation. *American Scientist, 68,* 398–409.

Galotti, K. M. (1989). Approaches to studying formal and everyday reasoning. *Psychological Bulletin, 105,* 331–351.

Galotti, K. M. (1995). A longitudinal study of real-life decision making: Choosing a college. *Applied Cognitive Psychology, 9,* 459–484.

Garb, H. N. (1989). Clinical judgment, clinical training, and professional experience. *Psychological Bulletin, 105,* 387–396.

Garb, H. N. (2005). Clinical judgment and decision making. *Annual Review of Clinical Psychology, 1,* 67–69.

Gardner, H. (1983). *Frames of mind: The theory of multiple intelligences.* New York: Basic Books.

Gardner, H. (1988). Mobilizing resources for individual-centered education. In R. S. Nickerson & P. P. Zodhiates (Eds.), *Technology in education: Looking toward 2020* (pp. 25–41). Hillsdale, NJ: Erlbaum.

Gardner, H. (1995). Perennial antinomies and perpetual redrawings: Is there progress in the study of mind? In R. L. Solso & D. W. Massaro (Eds.), *The science of the mind: 2001 and beyond* (pp. 65–78). New York: Oxford University Press.

Gardner, M. (1957). *Fad and fallacies in the name of science.* New York: Dover Publications.

Gardner, M. (2003). Science and the unknowable. In P. Kurtz (Ed.), *Science and religion: Are they compatible?* (pp. 325–333). Amherst, NY: Prometheus Books.

Garland, H. (1990). Throwing good money after bad: The effect of sunk costs on the decision to escalate commitment to an ongoing project. *Journal of Applied Psycology, 75,* 728–731.

Garland, L. H. (1959). Studies of the accuracy of diagnostic procedures. *American Journal of Roentgenology, Radium Therapy, and Nuclear Medicine, 82,* 25–38.

Garland, L. H. (1960). The problem of observer error. *Bulletin of the New York Academy of Medicine, 36,* 569–584.

Garnick, M. B. (1994). The dilemmas of prostrate cancer. *Scientific American, 270(4),* 72–81.

Gatchel, R. J., & Newberry, B. (1991). Psychophysiological effects of toxic chemical contanimation exposure: A community field study. *Journal of Applied Social Psychology, 21,* 1961–1976.

Gauthier, D. (1990). Maximization constrained: The rationality of cooperation. In P. K. Moser (Ed.), *Rationality in action: Contemporary approaches* (pp. 315–334). New York: Cambridge University Press. (Original work published 1986)

Gerard, H. B. (1954). The anchorage of opinions in face to face groups. *Human Relations, 7,* 313–326.

Gettier, E. (1963). Is justified true belief knowledge? *Analysis, 23,* 121–123.

Getty, D. J., Swets, J. A., Pickett, R. M., & Gonthier, D. (1995). System operator response to warnings of danger: A laboratory investigation of the effects of the predictive value of a warning on human response time. *Journal of Experimental Psychology: Applied, 1,* 19–33.

Gettys, C. F., & Fisher, S. D. (1979). Hypothesis plausibility and hypothesis generation. *Organizational Behavior and Human Performance. 24,* 93–110.

Gibbs, M. S. (1986). Psychopathological consequences of exposure to toxins in the water supply. In A. H. Lebovits, A. Baum, & J. E. Singer (Eds.), *Advances in environmental psychology: Volume 6. Exposure to hazardous substances: Psychological parameters.* Hillsdale, NJ: Erlbaum.

Gibbs, W. W. (1995). Lost science in the third world. *Scientific American, 273(2),* 92–99.

Gick, M. L., & Holyoak, K. J. (1983). Schema induction and analogical transfer. *Cognitive Psychology, 15,* 1–38.

Giere, R. (1988). *Explaining science: A cognitive approach.* Chicago: University of Chicago Press.

Gigerenzer, G. (1991a). From tools to theories: A heuristic of discovery in cognitive psychology. *Psychological Review, 98,* 254–267.

Gigerenzer, G. (1991b). How to make cognitive illusions disappear: Beyond "heuristics and biases." In W. Stroebe & M. Hewstone (Eds.), *European review of social psychology* (Vol. 2,,pp. 83–115). London: Wiley.

Gigerenzer, G. (1993). The bounded rationality of probabilistic mental models. In K. I. Manktelow & D. E. Over (Eds.), *Rationality: Psychological and philosophical perspectives* (pp. 284–313). London: Routledge.

Gigerenzer, G. (1994). Why the distinction between single-event probabilities and frequencies is important for psychology (and vice versa). In G. Wright & P. Ayton (Eds.), *Subjective probability* (pp. 129–161). New York: Wiley.

Gigerenzer, G. (2004a). Dread risk, September 11, and fatal traffic accidents. *Psychological Science, 15*, 286–287.

Gigerenzer, G. (2004b). Fast and frugal heuristics: The tools of bounded rationality. In D. Koehler & N. Harvey (Eds.), *Handbook of judgment and decision making* (pp. 62–88). Oxford: Blackwell.

Gigerenzer, G. (2004c). The irrationality paradox. *Behavioral and Brain Sciences, 27*, 336–338.

Gigerenzer, G. (2006b). Out of the frying pan into the fire: Behavioral reactions to terrorist attacks. *Risk Analysis, 26*, 347–351.

Gigerenzer, G., & Goldstein, D. G. (1996). Reasoning the fast and frugal way: Models of bounded rationality. *Psychological Review, 103*, 650–669.

Gigerenzer, G., & Hoffrage, U. (1995). How to improve Bayesian reasoning without instruction: Frequency formats. *Psychological Review, 102*, 684–704.

Gigerenzer, G., & Murray, D. J. (1987). *Cognition as intuitive statistics*. Hillsdale, NJ: Erlbaum.

Gigerenzer, G., & Regier, T. (1996). How do we tell an association from a rule? Comment on Sloman (1996). *Psychological Bulletin, 119*, 23–26.

Gigerenzer, G., Swijtink, Z., Porter, T., Daston, L., Beatty, J., & Krüger, L. (1989). *The empire of chance: How probability changed science and everyday life*. New York: Cambridge University Press.

Gigerenzer, G., & Todd, P. M. (1999a). Fast and frugal heuristics: The adaptive toolbox. In G. Gigerenzer & P. M. Todd (Eds.), *Simple heuristics that make us smart* (pp. 3–34). New York: Oxford University Press.

Gigerenzer, G., & Todd, P. M. (Eds.) (1999b). *Simple heuristics that make us smart*. New York: Oxford University Press.

Gigone, D., & Hastie, R. (1997). Proper analysis of the accuracy of group judgments. *Psychological Bulletin, 121*, 149–167.

Gilovich, T. (1983). Biased evaluation and persistence in gambling. *Journal of Personality and Social Psychology, 44*, 1110–1126.

Gilovich, T. (1991). *How we know what isn't so: The fallibility of human reason in everyday life*. New York: The Free Press.

Ginossar, Z., & Trope, Y. (1980). The effects of base rates and individuating information on judgments about another person. *Journal of Experimental Social Psychology, 16*, 228–242.

Girotto, V., Evans, J. St. B. T., & Legrenzi, P. (1996). *Relevance of information and consideration of alternatives: Pseudodiagnosticity as a focusing phenomenon*. Paper presented at the Third International Conference on Thinking, University College, London.

Gladwell, M. (2000). *The tipping point: How little things can make a big difference*. New York: Little, Brown.

Glance, N. S., & Huberman, B. A. (1994). The dynamics of social dilemmas. *Scientific American, 279*(3), 76–81.

Glaser, E. M. (1941). *An experiment in the development of critical thinking*. New York: Teachers College, Columbia University, Bureau of Publications.

Glaser, R. (1984). Education and thinking: The role of knowledge. *American Psychologist, 39*, 93–104.

Glaser, R. (1990). Expertise. In M. W. Eysenck, A. Ellis, & E. Hunt (Eds.), *The Blackwell dictionalry of cognitive psychology* (pp. 139–142). Oxford, Eng: Basil Blackwell.

Glasser, W. (2003). *Psychiatry can be hazardous to your mental health.* New York: Harper-Collins.

Glasser, W. (2005). Warning: Psychiatry can be hazardous to your mental health. In R. H. Wright & N. A. Cummings (Eds.), *Destructive trends in mental health: The well-intentioned path to harm* (pp. 113–128). New York: Routledge.

Godkewitsch, M. (1974). The golden section: An artifact of stimulus range and measure of preference. *American Journal of Psychology, 87,* 269–277.

Goffman, E. (1963). *Behavior in public places: Notes on the social organization of gatherings.* New York: The Free Press.

Gold, S. M. (1977). Social benefits of trees in urban environments. *International Journal of Environmental Studies, 10,* 85–90.

Goldberg, L. R. (1965). Diagnosticians vs. diagnostic signs: The diagnosis of psychosis vs. neurosis from MMPI. *Psychological Monographs, 79,* (Whole, No. 9).

Goldberg, L. R. (1968). Simple models or simple processes? Some research in clinical judgment. *American Psychologist, 23,* 483–496.

Goldberg, L. R. (1970). Man versus model of man: A rationale, plus some evidence for a method of improving on clinical inferences. *Psychological Bulletin, 73,* 422–432.

Golding, S. (1981). The effect of past experience on problem solving. Paper presented at the Annual Conference of the British Psychological Society, Surrey University.

Golding, S. L., & Rorer, L. G. (1972). Illusory correlation and subjective judgement. *Journal of Abnormal Psychology, 80,* 249–260.

Goldman, A. I. (1986). *Epistemology and cognition.* Cambridge, MA: Harvard University Press.

Goldstein, D. G., & Gigerenzer, G. (1999). The recognition heuristic: How ignorance makes us smart. In G. Gigerenzer & P. M. Todd (Eds.), *Simple heuristics that make us smart* (pp. 37–58). New York: Oxford University Press.

Goldstein, W., & Einhorn, H. (1987). Expression theory and the preference reversal phenomena. *Psychological Review, 94,* 236–254.

Gonzalez, C. (2004). Learning to make decisions in dynamic environments: Effects of time constraints and cognitive abilities. *Human Factors, 46,* 449–460.

Gonzalez, C. (2005). Decision support for real-time, dynamic decision-making tasks. *Organizational Behavior and Human Decision Processes, 96,* 142–154.

Gonzalez, C., & Quesada, J. (2003). Learning in dynamic decision making: The recognition process. *Computational and Mathematical Organization Theory, 9,* 287–304.

Good, I. J. (1952). Rational decisions. *Journal of the Royal Statistical Society, Series B, 14,* 107–114.

Good, I. J. (1972). Comment. *Journal of the American Statistical Associaton, 67,* 374–375.

Good I. J. (1983). *Good thinking: The foundations of probability and its applications.* Minneapolis: University of Minnesota Press.

Goodie, A. S., & Williams, C. C. (2000). Some theoretical and practical implications of defining aptitude and reasoning in terms of each other. *Behavioral and Brain Sciences, 23,* 675–676.

Goodman, N. (1983). *Fact, fiction, and forecast* (4th ed.). Cambridge, MA: Harvard University Press. (Original work published 1954)

Goodman, N. (1966). *The structure of appearance* (2nd ed.). Indianapolis, IN: Bobbs-Merrill.

Goodsell, D. S. (1998). *The machinery of life.* New York: Copernicus/Springer-Verlag.

Gorst, M. (2001). *Measuring eternity: The search for the beginning of time.* New York: Broadway Books.

Gould, S. J. (1981). *The mismeasure of man.* New York: W. W. Norton.

Gould, S. J. (1993). *Eight little piggies.* New York: W. W. Norton Lewis

Graham, A. C. (1992). *Unreason within reason: Essays on the outskirts of rationality.* LaSalle, IL: Open Court.

Grant, J. (1989). Clinical decision making: Rational principles, clinical intuition or clinical thinking. In J. I. Balla, M. Gibson, & A. M. Chang (Eds.), *Learning in medical school: A model for the clinical professions.* Hong Kong: Hong Kong University Press.

Green, B. F., Jr. (1977). Parameter sensitivity in multivariate methods. *Multivariate Behavioral Research, 12,* 263–287.

Green, D. M., & Swets, J. A. (1966). *Signal detection theory and psychophysics.* New York: Wiley.

Greene, B. (1999). *The elegant universe: Superstrings, hidden dimensions, and the quest for the ultimate theory.* New York: Vintage Books.

Greeno, J. G. (1980). Trends in the theory of knowledge for problem solving. In D.T. Tuma and F. Reif (Eds.), *Problem solving and education: Issues in teaching and research* (pp. 9–23). Hillsdale, NJ: Erlbaum.

Greenwald, A. G. (1980). The totalitarian ego: Fabrication and revision of personal history. *American Psychologist, 35,* 603–618.

Grice, H. P. (1975). Logic and conversation. In P. Cole & J. I. Morgan (Eds.), *Syntax and semantics, Volume 3: Speech acts* (pp. 41–58). New York: Seminar Press.

Griffin, D. W., & Tversky, A. (1992). The weighing of evidence and the determinants of confidence. *Cognitive Psychology, 24,* 411–435.

Griggs, R. A. (1981). Human reasoning: Can we judge before we understand? Commentary on Cohen, 1981. *The Behavioral and Brain Sciences, 4,* 338–339.

Griggs, R. A., & Cox, J. R. (1982). The elusive thematic-materials effect in Wason's selection task. *British Journal of Psychology, 73,* 407–420.

Griggs, R. A., & Cox, J. R. (1993). Permission schemas and the selection task. In J. St. B. T. Evans (Ed.), *The cognitive psychology of reasoning* (pp. 637–651). Hillsdale, NJ: Erlbaum.

Gruneberg, M. M., & Monks, J. (1974). "Feeling of knowing" and cued recall. *Acta Psychologica, 38,* 257–265.

Gruneberg, M. M., Monks, J., & Sykes, R. N. (1977). Some methodological problems with feeling of knowing studies. *Acta Psychologica, 41,* 365–371.

Gutek, B. A., & Winter, S. J. (1990). Computer use, control over computers, and job satisfaction. In S. Oskamp & S. Spacapan (Eds.), *People's reaction to technology* (pp. 121–144). Belmont, CA: Sage.

Guth, A. (1981). The inflationary universe: A possible solution to the horizon and flatness problems. *Physical Review, 23,* 347–356.

Guth, A., & Steinhardt, P. (1984). The inflationary universe. *Scientific American, 250*(5), 116–128.

Habermas, J. (1970). *Knowledge and human interests.* Boston: Beacon Press.

Hacking, I. (1975). *The emergence of probability.* New York: Cambridge University Press.

Hacking, I. (1990). *The taming of chance.* New York: Cambridge University Press.

Hadamard, J. (1954). *The psychology of invention in the mathematical field.* New York: Dover. (Original work published 1945)

Haggard, P., & Eimer, M. (1999). On the relation between brain potentials and the awareness of voluntary movements. *Experimental Brain Research, 126,* 128–133.

Haldane, J. B. S. (1956). On being the right size. In J. R. Newman (Ed.), *The world of mathematics, Vol. 2* (pp. 952–957). New York: Simon and Schuster. (Original work published 1928)

Halmos, P. R. (1985). *I want to be a mathematician: An automathography in three parts.* New York: Springer-Verlag.

Hamill, J. F. (1990). *Ethno-logic: The anthropology of human reasoning.* Urbana: University of Illinois Press.

Hamming, R. W. (1980). The unreasonable effectiveness of mathematics. *American Mathematics Monthly, 87,* 81–90.

Hammond, K R. (2000). *Human judgment and social policy.* New York: Oxford University Press.

Hammond, J. S., Keeney, R. L., & Raiffa, H. (1998). The hidden traps in decision making. *Harvard Business Review, 16,* 47–58.

Hammond, K. R. (1955). Probabilistic functioning and the clinical method. *Psychological Review, 62,* 255–262.

Hammond, K. R., & Summers, D. A. (1965). Cognitive dependence on linear and nonlinear cues. *Psychological Review, 72,* 215–224.

Hammond, P. B., & Coppock, R. (Eds.), (1990). *Valuing health risks, costs, and benefits for environmental decision making.* Washington, DC: National Academy Press.

Hanks, G. E., & Scardino, P. T. (1996). Does screening for prostate cancer make sense? *Scientific American, 275*(3), 114–115.

Hans, V. P. & Vidmar, N. (1986). *Judging the jury.* New York: Plenum Press.

Hardin, G. (1968). The tragedy of the commons. *Science, 162,* 1243–1248.

Hardman, D. (2000). The understanding/acceptance principle: I understand it, but don't accept it. *Behavioral and Brain Sciences, 23,* 677–678.

Hare, R. M. (1981). *Moral thinking: Its levels, method, and point.* Oxford: Oxford University Press.

Harkness, A. R., DeBono, K. G., & Borgida, E. (1985). Personal involvement and strategies for making contingency judgments: A stake in the dating game makes a difference. *Journal of Personality and Social Psychology, 49,* 22–32.

Harman, G. (1986). *Change in view: Principles of reasoning.* Cambridge, MA: MIT Press.

Harman, G. (1995) Rationality. In E. E. Smith & D. N. Osherson (Eds.), *Thinking: An Invitation to Cognitive Science, Volume 3* (2nd ed., pp.175–211). Cambridge, MA: MIT Press.

Harris, D. H. (1990). Effect of human information processing on the ultrasonic detection of intergranular stress-corrosion cracking. *Materials Evaluation, 48,* 475–480.

Harris, J. M. (1981). The hazards of bedside Bayes. *Journal of American Medical Association, 246,* 2602–2605.

Harris, M. (1989, August). You may already be a victim of fraud. *Money Magazine,* pp. 74–91.

Harsanyi, J. C. (1953). Cardinal utility in the welfare economics and in the theory of risk-taking. *Journal of Political Economy, 61,* 434–435.

Harsanyi, J. C. (1975a). Can the maximum principle serve as a basis for morality? A critique of John Rawls's theory. *American Political Science Review, 59,* 594–606.

Harsanyi, J. C. (1975b). Nonlinear social welfare functions. *Theory and Decision, 7,* 61–82.

Harsanyi, J. C. (1990). Advances in understanding rational behavior. In P. K. Moser (Ed.), *Rationality in action: Contemporary approaches* (pp. 271–293). New York: Cambridge University Press. (Original work published 1977)

Hart, J. T. (1965). Memory and the feeling of knowing experience. *Journal of Educational Psychology, 56,* 208–216.

Hart, J. T. (1967). Memory and the memory-monitoring process. *Journal of Verbal Learning and Verbal Behavior, 6,* 685–691.

Harvey, J. H., Town, J. P., & Yarkin, K. L. (1981). How fundamental is the "fundamental attribution error"? *Journal of Personality and Social Psychology, 43,* 345–346.

Hastie, R. (1993). Algebraic models of juror decision processes. In R. Hastie (Ed.), *Inside the juror: The psychology of juror decision making* (pp. 84–115). New York: Cambridge University Press.

Hatala, R., Norman, G. R., & Brooks, L. R. (1999). Influence of a single example on subsequent electrocardiogram interpretation. *Teaching and learning in medicine, 11,* 110-117.

Hatcher, D. (1985). A critique of critical thinking. *Teaching Thinking and Problem Solving, 7*(10), 1, 2, 5.

Hauptli, B. W. (1995). *The reasonableness of reason: Explaining rationality naturalistically.* Chicato: Open Court Publishing.

Hawkins, S. A., & Hastie, R. (1990). Hindsight: Biased judgments of past events after the outcomes are known. *Psychological Bulletin, 107,* 311–327.

Hayden, T., & Mischel, W. (1976). Maintaining trait consistency in the resolution of behavioral inconsistency: The wolf in sheep's clothing? *Journal of Personality, 44,* 109–132.

Hayes, J. R. M. (1964). Human data processing limits in decision making. In E. Bennett (Ed.), *Information system science and engineering: Proceedings of the First Congress on the Information System Sciences.* New York: McGraw-Hill.

Heckhausen, J., Dixon, R. A., & Baltes, P. B. (1989). Gains and losses in development thoughout adulthood as perceived by different adult age groups. *Developmental Psychology, 25,* 109–121.

Heider, F. (1944). Social perception and phenomenal causality. *Psychological Review, 51,* 358–374.

Heider, F., & Simmel, M. (1944). An experimental study of apparent behavior. *American Journal of Psychology, 57,* 243–259.

Heller, W., Starr, R., & Starrett, D. (Eds.) (1986). *Essays in honor of Kenneth Arrow* (3 vols.). Cambridge: Cambridge University Press.

Hempel, C. G. (1965). *Aspects of scientific explanation.* New York: Free Press.

Henle, M. (1962a). The birth and death of ideas. In H. Gruber, G. Terrell, & M. Wertheimer (Eds.), *Contemporary approaches to creative thinking* (pp. 31–62). New York: Atherton.

Henle, M. (1962b). On the relation between logic and thinking. *Psychological Review, 69,* 366–378.

Herrnstein, R. J. (1990). Rational choice theory: Necessary but not sufficient. *American Psychologist, 45,* 356–367.

Herrnstein, R. J., & Murray, C. A. (1995). *The bell curve: Intelligence and class structure in American life.* New York: Free Press.

Hersh, R. (1997). *What is mathematics really?* New York: Oxford University Press.

Hertwig, R. (2000). The questionable utility of "cognitive ability" in explaining cognitive illusions. *Behavioral and Brain Sciences, 23,* 678–679.

Herz-Fischler, R. (1998). *A mathematical history fo the golden number.* Mineola, NY: Dover.

Hess, T. M. (2000). Aging-related constraints and adaptations in social information processing. In U. von Heckere, S. Dutke, & G. Sedek (Eds.), *Generative mental processes and cognitive resources: Integrative research on adaptation and control* (pp. 129–155) Dordrecht: Kluwer Academic.

Hess, T. M., Pullen, S. M., & McGee, K. A. (1996). Acquisition of prototype-based information about social groups in adulthood. *Psychology and Aging, 11,* 179–190.

Hilton, D. J. (1995). The social context of reasoning: Conversational inference and rational judgment. *Psychological Bulletin, 118,* 248–271.

Himsworth, H. (1986). *Scientific knowledge and philosophic thought.* Baltimore: The Johns Hopkins University Press.

Hinsz, V. B. (1990). Cognitive and consensus processes in group recognition memory performance. *Journal of Personality and Social Psychology, 59,* 705–718.

Hirt, E. R., & Sherman, S. J. (1985). The role of prior knowledge in explaining hypothetical events. *Journal of Experimental Social Psychology, 21,* 519–543.

Hoch, S. J. (1984). Availability and inference in predictive judgment. *Journal of Experimental Psychology: Learning, Memory, and Cognition, 10,* 649–662.

Hoch, S. J. (1985). Counterfactual reasoning and accuracy in predicting personal events. *Journal of Experimental Psychology: Learning, Memory, and Cognition, 11,* 719–731.

Hoepfl, R. T., & Huber, G. P. (1970). A study of self-explicated utility models. *Behavioral Science, 15,* 408–414.

Hoffman, P. J. (1960). The paramorphic representation of clinical judgments. *Psychological Bulletin, 57,* 116–131.

Hofstadter, D. R., & Dennett, D. C. (1981). *The mind's I: Fantasies and reflections on self and soul.* New York: Basic Books.

Hogarth, R. M. (1981). Beyond discrete biases: Functional and dysfunctional aspects of judgmental heuristics. *Psychological Bulletin, 90,* 197–217.

Holland, J. C. (1996). Cancer's psychological challenges. *Scientific American, 275*(3), 158–161.

Holland, J. H., Holyoak, K. J., Nisbett, R. E., & Thagard, P. R. (1986). *Induction: Processes of inference, learning, and discovery.* Cambridge, MA: MIT Press.

Holliday, S. G., & Chandler, M. J. (1986). *Wisdom: Explorations in adult competence.* Basel, Switzerland: Karger.

Holmes, J. G., & Strickland, L. H. (1970). Choice freedom and confirmation of incentive expectancy as determinants of attitude change. *Journal of Personality and Social Psychology, 14,* 39–45.

Holton, G. (1973). *Thematic origins of scientific thought.* Cambridge, MA: Harvard University Press.

Horkheimer, M. (1974). *Eclipse of reason.* New York: Seabury Press. (Original work published 1947)

Hoskin, R. E. (1983). Opportunity cost and behavior. *Journal of Accounting Research, 21,* 78–95.

Hounsome, M. (1979). Bird life in the city. In I. C. Laurie (Ed.), *Nature in cities* (pp. 179–203). Chichestire: Wiley.

Howard, R. A. (1966). Decision analysis: Applied decision theory. In D. B. Hertz & J. Melese (Eds.), *Proceedings of the Fourth International Conference on Operational Research* (pp. 55–71). New York: Wiley-Interscience.

Hsee, C. K. (1998). Less is better: When low-value options are valued more highly than high-value options. *Journal of Behavioral Decision Making, 11,* 107–121.

Hume, D. (1939). An enquiry concerning human understanding. In E. A. Burtt (Ed.), *The English philosophers from Bacon to Mill.* New York: Random House. (Original work published 1748)

Huntley, H. E. (1970). *The divine proportion: A study in mathematical beauty.* New York: Dover.

Huxley, A. (1962). Achieving a perspective on the technological order. *Technology and Culture, 3,* 636–642.

Hyman, I. E., Jr., Husband, T. H., & Billings, J. F. (1995). False memories of childhood experiences. *Applied Cognitive Psychology, 12,* 371–386.

Inhelder, B., & Piaget, J. (1958). *The growth of logical thinking from childhood to adolescence.* New York: Basic Books. (Original work published 1955)

Irwin, J. R., Slovic, P., Lichtenstein, S., & McClelland, G. H. (1993) Preference-reversals and the measurement of environmental values, *Journal of Risk and Uncertainty, 6,* 5–18.

Isen, A. M. (1993). Positive affect and decision making. In M. Lewis & J. M. Haviland (Eds.), *Handbook of emotions* (pp. 261–277). New York: Guilford Press.

Isen, A. M., & Geva, N. (1987). The influence of positive affect on acceptable level of risk: The person with a large canoe has a large worry. *Organizational Behavior and Human Decision Processes, 39,* 145–154.

Isen, A. M., & Labroo, A. A. (2003). Some ways in which positive affect facilitates decision making and judgment. In S. L. Schneider & J. Shanteau (Eds.), *Emerging perspectives on judgment and decision research* (pp. 365–393). Cambridge: Cambridge University Press.

Isen, A. M., Nygren, T. E., & Ashby, F. G. (1988). Influence of positive affect on the subjective utility of gains and losses: It is just not worth the risk. *Journal of Personality and Social Psycholgy, 55,* 710–717.

Jackson, J. D., Tigner, M., & Wojcicki, S. (1986). Letter to the Editor. *Scientific American, 225*(1), 6.

Jacobs, D. (1992). *Secret life: Firsthand accounts of UFO abductions.* New York: Simon and Schuster.

Jacobs, J. E., & Potenza, M. (1991). The use of judgment heuristics to make social and object decisions: A developmental perspective. *Child Development, 62,* 166–178.

James, W. (1979). *The will to believe and other essays.* Cambridge, MA: Harvard University Press. (Original work published 1896)

James, W. (1983). *The principles of psychology.* Cambridge, MA: Harvard University Press. (Original work published 1890)

Janis, I. (1982). *Groupthink: Psychological studies of policy decisions and fiascoes.* Boston: Houghton Mifflin.

Janis, I. L., & Mann, L. (1977). *Decision making: A psychological analysis of conflict, choice, and commitment.* New York: The Free Press.

Jaspers, K. (1952). *Reason and anti-reason in our time.* (S. Godman, Trans.). New Haven: Yale University Press.

Jaynes, E. T. (1976). Common sense as an interface. In W. L. Harper & C. A. Hooker (Eds.), *Foundations of probability theory, statistical inference and statistical theories of science* (Vol. 2). Dordrecht, The Netherlands: Reidel.

Jeeves, M. A. (1969). *The scientific enterprise and Christian faith.* Downers Grove, IL: Inter-Varsity Press.

Jeffrey, R. (1992). *Probability and the art of judgment.* Cambridge: Cambridge University Press.

Jepson, C., Krantz, D. H., & Nisbett, R. E. (1983). Inductive reasoning: Competence or skill? *Behavioral and Brain Sciences, 6,* 94–101.

Jevons, W. S. (1956). Theory of political economy. In J. R. Newman (Ed.), *The world of mathematics, Vol. 2* (pp. 1217–1237). New York: Simon and Schuster. (Original work published 1871)

Johnson, E. J., & Tversky, A. (1983). Affect, generalization, and the perception of risk. *Journal of Personality and Social Psychology, 45,* 20–31.

Johnson, M. K. (1988). Reality monitoring: An experimental phenomonological approach. *Journal of Experimental Psychology: General, 117,* 390–394.

Johnson, M. K., Foley, M. A., Suengas, A. G., & Raye, C. L. (1988). Phenomenal characteristics of memories for perceived and imagined autobiographical events. *Journal of Experimental Psychology: General, 117,* 371–376.

Johnson, M. K., & Raye, C. L. (1981). Reality monitoring. *Psychological Review, 88,* 67–85.

Johnson, R. H. (1995). The blaze of her splendors: Suggestions about revitalizing fallacy theory. In H. V. Hansen & R. C. Pinto (Eds.), *Fallacies: Classical and contemporary readings* (pp. 107–119). University Park: The Pennsylvania State University Press. (Original work published 1987)

Johnson-Laird, P. N. (1983). *Mental models.* Cambridge, MA: Harvard University Press.

Johnson-Laird, P. N., & Byrne, R. M. J. (1991). *Deduction.* Hillside, NJ: Erlbaum.

Johnson-Laird, P. N., & Byrne, R. M. J. (1993). Models and deductive rationality. In K. I. Manktelow & D. E. Over (Eds.), *Rationality: Psychological and philosophical perspectives* (pp. 177–210). London: Routledge.

Johnson-Laird, P. N., Legrenzi, P., & Legrenzi, M. S. (1972). Reasoning and a sense of reality. *British Journal of Psychology, 63,* 395–400.

Johnson-Laird, P. M., & Wason, P. C. (Eds.) (1977). *Thinking: Readings in cognitive science.* London: Cambridge University Press.

Jones, B. F., & Idol, L. (Eds.) (1990), *Dimensions of thinking and cognitive instruction: Implications for educational reform.* Hillsdale, NJ: Erlbaum.

Jones, E. E. (1976). How do people perceive the causes of behavior? *American Scientist, 64,* 300–305.

Jones, E. E. (1979). The rocky road from acts to dispositions. *American Psychologist, 34,* 107–117.

Jones, E. E., & Berglas, S. (1978). Control of attributions about the self through self-handicapping strategies: The appeal of alcohol and the role of underachievement. *Personality and Social Psychology Bulletin, 4,* 200–206.

Jones, E. E., & Davis, K. E. (1965). From acts to dispositons: The attribution process in person perception. In L. Berkowitz (Ed.), *Advances in Experimental Social Psychology* (Vol. 2). New York: Academic Press.

Jones, E. E., & Harris, V. A. (1967). The attribution of attitudes. *Journal of Experimental Social Psychology, 3,* 1–24.

Jones, E. E., & Nisbett, R. E. (1972). The actor and the observer: Divergent perceptions of the causes of behavior. In E. E. Jones, D. E. Kanouse, H. H. Kelley, R. E. Nisbett, S. Valins, & B. Weiner (Eds.), *Attribution: Perceiving the causes of behavior.* Morristown, NJ: General Learning Press.

Jones, S. R. G. (1984). *The economics of conformism.* Oxford: Blackwell.

Jou, J. (2000). Understanding/acceptance and adaptation: Is the non-normative thinking mode adaptive? *Behavioral and Brain Sciences, 23,* 680–681.

Jungermann, H. (1983). The two camps on rationality. In R. W. Scholz (Ed.), *Decision making under uncertainty* (pp. 63–86). Amsterdam: Elsevier.

Jurow, G. (1971). New data on the effect of a "death qualified" jury on the guilt determination process. *Harvard Law Review, 84,* 567–611.

Kagan, J. (1966). Reflection-impulsivity: The generality and dynamics of conceptual tempo. *Journal of Abnormal Psychology, 71,* 17–24.

Kahan, M. (1997). Social influence, social meaning, and deterrence. *Virginia Law Review, 83,* 276–304.

Kahane, H. (1984). *Logic and contemporary rhetoric: The use of reason in everyday life* (4th ed.). Belmont, CA: Wodsworth.

Kahneman, D. (1981). Who shall be the arbiter of our intuitions? Commentary on Cohen, 1981. *The Behavior and Brain Sciences, 4,* 339–340.

Kahneman, D. (2000). A psychological point of view: Violations of rational rules as a diagnostic of mental processes. *Behavioral and Brain Sciences, 232,* 681–683.

Kahneman, D, & Knetsch, J. L. (1992). Valuing public goods: The purchase of moral satisfaction. *Journal of Environmental Economics and Management, 22,* 57–70.

Kahneman, D, & Knetsch, J. L., & Thaler, R. H. (1990). Experimental tests of the endowment effect and the coase theorem. *Journal of Political Economy, 98,* 1325–1348.

Kahneman, D., Ritov, I., Jacowitz, K. E., & Grant, P. (1993). Stated willingness to pay for public goods: A psychological perspective. *Psychological Science, 4,* 310–315.

Kahneman, D., & Tversky, A. (1979a). On the interpretation of intuitive probability: A reply to Jonathan Cohen. *Cognition, 7,* 409–411.

Kahneman, D., & Tversky, A. (1979b). Prospect theory. An analysis of decision under risk. *Econometrica, 47,* 263–291.

Kahneman, D., & Tversky, A. (1982a). On the study of statistical intuitions. *Cognition, 11,* 123–141.

Kahneman, D., & Tversky, A. (1982b). Variants of uncertainty. In Kahneman, D., Slovic, P., & Tversky, A. (Eds.), *Judgment under uncertainty: Heuristics and biases* (pp. 509–520). Cambridge: Cambridge University Press.

Kahneman, D., & Tversky, A. (1984). Choices, values, and frames. *American Psychologist, 39,* 341–350.

Kalven, H., & Zeisel, H. (1966). *The American jury.* Boston: Little, Brown.

Kameda, T., Tindale, R. S., & Davis, J. H. (2003). Cognitions, preferences, and social sharedness: Past, present, and future directions in group decision making. In S. L. Schneider & J. Shanteau (Eds.), *Emerging perspectives on judgment and decision research* (pp. 458–485). Cambridge: Cambridge University Press.

Kanarick, A. F., Huntington, J. M., & Petersen, R. C. (1969). Multi-source information acquisition with optional stopping. *Human Factors, 11,* 379–386.

Kant, I. (1787). *The critique of pure reason.*

Kant, I. (1788). *The critique of practical reason.*

Kaplan, A. (1956). Sociology learns the language of mathematics. In J. R. Newman (Ed.), *The world of mathematics, Vol 2* (pp. 1294–1313). New York: Simon and Schuster.

Kaplan, R. (1983). The role of nature in the urban context. In I. Altman & J. F. Wohlwill (Eds.), *Behavior and the natural environment* (pp. 127–161). New York: Plenum.

Kaplan, S., & Talbot, J. F. (1983). Psychological benefits of a wilderness experience. In I. Altman & J. F. Wohlwill (Eds.), *Behavior and the natural environment* (pp. 163–203). New York: Plenum.

Kase, L. M. (1996). Why community cancer clusters are often ignored. *Scientific American, 275*(3), 85–86.

Katz, J. (1988). Why doctors don't disclose uncertainty. In J. Dowie & A. Elstein (Eds.), *Professional judgment. A reader in clinical decision making* (pp. 544–565). Cambridge: Cambridge University Press. (Original work published 1984)

Kauffman, S. (1995). *At home in the universe: The search for the laws of self-organization and complexity.* New York: Oxford University Press.

Kavanaugh, D., & Bower, G. H. (1984). Mood and self-efficacy: Impact of joy and sadness on perceived capabilities. *Cognitive Therapy and Research, 9,* 507–525.

Keating, D. P. (1990). Charting pathways to the development of expertise. *Educational Psychologist, 25,* 243–267.

Keeley, L. H. (1996). *War before civilization.* New York: Oxford University Press.

Keeney, R. L., & Raiffa, H. (1976). *Decisions with multiple objectives.* New York: Wiley.

Kekes, J. (1980). *The nature of philosophy*. Totowa, NJ: Rowman and Littlefield.
Kelley, H. H. (1950). The warm-cold variable in first impressions of persons. *Journal of Personality, 18*, 431–439.
Kelley, H. H. (1967). Attribution theory in social psychology. In D. Levine (Ed.), *Nebraska Symposium on Motivation* (Vol. 15; pp. 192–241). Lincoln: University of Nebraska Press.
Kelley, H. H. (1971). *Attribution in social interaction*. Morristown, NJ: General Learning Press.
Kelley, H. H. (1972). Causal schemata and the attribution process. In E. E. Jones et al. (Eds.), *Attribution: Perceiving the causes of behavior*. Morristown, NJ: General Learning Press.
Kelley, H. H. (1973). The process of causal attribution. *American Psychologist, 28*, 107–128.
Kelley, H. H., & Woodruff, C. L. (1956). Members' reactions to apparent group approval of a counternorm communication. *Journal of Abnormal and Social Psychology, 52*, 67–74.
Kemp, M. A., & Maxwell, C. (1993). Exploring a budget context for contingent valuation estimates. In J. A. Hausman (Ed.), *Contingent valuation: A critical assessment*. Amsterdam: North Holland.
Keren, G. B. (1991). Calibration and probability judgments: Conceptual and methodological issues. *Acta Psychologica, 77*, 217–273.
Kern, L., & Doherty, M. E. (1982). 'Pseudodiagnosticity' in an idealized medical problem-solving environment. *Journal of Medical Education, 57*, 100–104.
Kerr, N. L., MacCoun, R. J., & Kramer, G. P. (1996). Bias in judgment: Comparing individuals and groups. *Psychological Review, 103*, 687–719.
Kerr, N. L., & Tindale, R. S. (2004). Group performance and decision making. *Annual Review of Psychology, 55*, 623–655.
Kerstholt, J. H., & Raaijmakers, J. G. W. (1997). Decision making in dynamic task environments. In W. R. Crozier, & O. Svenson (Eds.), *Decision making: Cognitive models and explanations* (pp. 205–217). London: Routledge.
Keyser, C. J. (1926). *Thinking about thinking*. New York: E. P. Ditton and Company.
Kidd, J. B. (1970). The utilization of subjective probabilities in production planning. *Acta Psychologica, 34*, 338–347.
Kipnis, D. (1984). Technology, power, and control. In S. B. Bacharach & E. Lawler (Eds.), *Sociology of organizations* (pp. 125–156). Greenwich, CT: JAI Press.
Kipnis, D. (1993). Unanticipated consequences of using behavior technology. *Leadership Quarterly, 4*, 149–171.
Kipnis, D. (1997). Ghosts, taxonomies, and social psychology. *American Psychologist, 52*, 205–211.
Kirwan, J. R., Chaput de Saintonge, D. M., Joyce, C. R. B., & Currey, H. L. F. (1983). Clinical judgment in rheumatoid arthritis: II. Judging "current disease activity" in clinical practice. *Annals of the Rheumatic Diseases, 42*, 648–651.
Kitchener, K. S., & Brenner, H. G. (1990). Wisdom and reflective judgment: Knowing in the face of uncertainty. In R. J. Sternberg (Ed.), *Wisdom: Its nature, origins, and development* (pp. 212–229). New York: Cambridge University Press.

Kitcher, P. (1993). *The advancement of science*. New York: Oxford University Press.
Klaczynski, P. A. (2000). Is rationality really "bounded" by information processing constraints? *Behavioral and Brain Sciences, 23*, 683–684.
Klaczynski, P. A., & Fauth, J. (1997). Developmental differences in memory-based intrusions and self-serving statistical reasoning biases. *Merrill-Palmer Quarterly, 43*, 539–566.
Klaczynski, P. A., & Narasimham, G. (1998). Problem representation as mediators of adolescent deductive reasoning. *Developmental Psychology, 34*, 865–881.
Klein, G. A. (1993). A recognition-primed decision (RPD) model of rapid decision making. In G. A. Klein, J. Orasanu, & C. E. Zsambok (Eds.), *Decision making in action: Models and methods* (pp. 138–157). Norwood, NJ: Ablex.
Klein, G. A. (1998). *Sources of power: How people make decisions*. MIT Press.
Klein, G. A., Calderwood, R., & Cliinton-Cirocco, A. (1986). Rapid decision making on the fireground. *Proceedings fo the 30th Annual Human Factors Society* (Vol. 1, pp. 576–580). Dayton, OH: Human Factors Society.
Klein, G.A., Orasanu, J., Calderwood, R., & Zsambok, C. E. (Eds.) (1993). *Decision making in action: Models and methods*. Norwood, NJ: Ablex.
Kleinmuntz, B. (1968). The processing of clinical information. In B. Kleinmuntz (Ed.), *Formal representation of human judgment*. New York: Wiley.
Kline, M. (1953). *Mathematics in western culture*. New York: Oxford University Press.
Kline, M. (1980). *Mathematics: The loss of certainty*. New York: Oxford University Press.
Kneppreth, N. P., Gustafson, D. H., Leifer, R. P., & Johnson, E. M. (1974). *Techniques for assessment of worth*. U. S. Army Research Institute for Behavioral and Social Sciences Technical Paper No. 254.
Koehler, D. J. (1991). Explanation, imagination, and confidence in judgment. *Psychological Bulletin, 110*, 499–519.
Kogan, N., & Wallach, M. A. (1967). Risk taking as a function of the situation, the person, and the group. In C. Mandler, P. Mussen, N. Kogan, & M. A. (Eds.), *New directions in psychology* (vol. 3, pp. 111–278). New York: Holt, Rinehard & Winston.
Kolodner, J. (Ed.) (1993). *Case-based reasoning*. San Mateo, CA: Morgan Kaufman.
Komorita, S. S., & Parks, C. D. (1996). *Social dilemmas*. Boulder, CO: Westview Press.
Koran, L. M. (1975). The reliability of clinical methods, data, and Judgments. *New England Journal of Medicine, 293*, 642–646, 695–701.
Koriat, A., & Lieblich, I. (1977). A study of memory pointers. *Acta Psychologica, 41*, 151–164.
Kosslyn, S. M. (1995). Freud returns? In R. L. Solso & D. W. Massaro (Eds.), *The science of the mind: 2001 and beyond* (pp. 90–106). New York: Oxford University Press.
Kramer, D. A. (1990). Conceptualizing wisdom: The primacy of affect-cognition relations. In R. J. Sternberg (Ed.), *Wisdom: Its nature, origins, and development* (pp. 279–313). New York: Cambridge University Press.
Krauss, S., Martignon, L., & Hoffrage, U. (1999). Simplifying Bayesian inference: The general case. In L. Magnani, N. Nersessian, & P. Thagard (Eds.), *Model-based reasoning in scientific discovery* (pp. 165–179). New York: Plenum.

Kristiansen, C. M., Harding, C. M., & Eiser, J. R. (1983). Beliefs about the relationship between smoking and causes of death. *Basic and Applied Social Psychology, 4,* 253–261.

Krueger, J. (1998). On the perception of social consensus. In M. P. Zanna (Ed.), *Advances in experimental social psychology* (pp. 163–240). New York: Academic Press.

Krueger, J. (2000). Individual differences and Pearson's r: Rationality revealed? *Behavioral and Brain Sciences, 23,* 684–685.

Krueger, J., Ham, J. J., & Linford, K. M. (1996). Perceptions of behavioral consistency: Are people aware of the actor-observer effect? *Psychological Science, 7,* 259–313.

Kruglanski, A. W. (1980). Lay epistemology process and contents. *Psychological Review, 87,* 70–87.

Kruglanski, A. W., & Ajzen, I. (1983). Bias and error in human judgment. *European Journal of Social Psychology, 13,* 1–44.

Kruglanski, A W. (1990). Lay epistemics theory in social-cognitive psychology. *Psychological Inquiry, 1,* 181–197.

Kruglanski, A. W., & Klar, Y. (1987). A view from the bridge: Synthesizing the consistency and attribution paradigms for a lay epistemic perspective. *Europena Journal of Social Psychology, 17,* 211–241.

Kruglanski, A. W., & Webster, D. (1996). Motivated closing of the mind: "Seizing" and "freezing." *Psychological Review, 103,* 263–283.

Krupnick, A. J., & Portney, P. R. (1991). Controlling urban air pollution: A benefit-cost assessment. *Science, 252,* 522–528.

Kühberger, A. (1998). The influence of framing on risky decisions. *Organizational Behavior and Human Decision Processes, 75,* 23–55.

Kühberger, A. (2000). What about motivation? *Behavioral and Brain Sciences, 23,* 685.

Kuhn, D. (1992). Thinking as argument. *Harvard Educational Review, 62,* 155–178.

Kunda, Z. (1987). Motivation and inference: Self-serving generation and evaluation of evidence. *Journal of Personality and Social Psychology, 53,* 636–647.

Kunda, Z. (1990). The case for motivated reasoning. *Psychological Bulletin, 108,* 480–498.

Kunda, Z., & Nisbett, R. E. (1986). The psychometrics of everyday life. *Cognitive Psychology, 18,* 199–224.

Kunreuther, H. (1969). Extensions of Bowman's theory on managerial decision making. *Management Science, 15,* 415–439.

Kurtz, B. E., & Borkowski, J. G. (1987). Development of strategic skill in impulsive and reflective children: A longitudinal study of metacognition. *Journal of Experimental Child Psychology, 43,* 129–148.

Kyburg, H. E., Jr. (1981). Intuition, competence, and performance. Commentary on Cohen, 1981. *The Behavioral and Brain Sciences, 4,* 341–342.

Kyburg, H. E., Jr. (1983). Rational belief. *The Behavioral and Brain Sciences, 6,* 231–273.

Labouvie-Vief, G. (1990). Wisdom as integrated thought: Historical and developmental perspectives. In R. J. Sternberg (Ed.), *Wisdom: Its nature, origins, and development* (pp. 52–83). New York: Cambridge University Press.

Labouvie-Vief, G., Hakim-Larson, J. Devoe, M., & Schoeberlein, S. (1989). Emotions and self-regulation: A life-span view. *Human Development, 32,* 279–299.

Lachman, J. L., & Lachman, R. (1980). Age and the actualization of world knowledge. In L. W. Poon, J. L. Fozard, L. S. Cermak, D. Arenberg, & L. W. Thompson (Eds.), *New directions in memory and aging* (pp. 313–343). Hillsdale, NJ: Erlbaum.

Lakatos, I. (1976). *Proofs and refutations: The logic of mathematical discovery.* (J. Worrall & E. Zahar, Eds.). New York: Cambridge University Press.

Lambert, R. (1978). Situations of uncertainty: Social influence and decision processes. In H. Brandstätter, J. H. Davis, & H. Schuler (Eds.), *Dynamics of group decisions* (pp. 53–66). London: Sage.

Lampert, M. (1986). Teaching multiplication. *Journal of Mathematical Behavior, 5,* 241–280.

Landry, D. (1972). The effects of an overheard audience's reaction and attractiveness on opinion change. *Journal of Experimental Social Psychology, 8,* 276–288.

Lane, R. E. (2001). *The loss of happiness in market democracies.* New Haven: Yale University Press.

Lankford, F. G. (1972). *Some computational strategies for seventh-grade pupils.* ERIC Reports, School of Education, Virginia University.

Laplace, P. S. (1951). *A philosophical essay on probabilities.* F. W. Truscott & F. L. Emory (Trans.) New York: Dover. (Original work published 1814)

Laplace, P. S. (1956). Concerning probability. In J. R. Newman (Ed.), *The world of mathematics: Vol II* (pp. 1325–1333). New York: Simon and Schuster. (Original work published 1814)

Larrick, R. P., Nisbett, R. E., & Morgan, J. N. (1993). Who uses the cost-benefit rules of choice? Implications for the normative status of microeconomic theory. In R. E. Nisbett (Ed.), *Rules for reasoning* (pp. 277–294). Hillsdale, NJ: Erlbaum.

Lau, H. C., Rogers, R. D., Haggard, P., & Passingham, R. E. (2004). Attention to intention. *Science, 303,* 1208–1210.

Laughlin, P. R., & Ellis, A. L. (1986). Demonstrability and social combination processes on mathematical intellective tasks. *Journal of Experimental Social Psychology, 22,* 177–189.

Lave, J, Murtaugh, M., & de la Rocha, O. (1984). The dialectic of arithmetic in grocery shopping. In B. Rogoff & J. Lave (Eds.), *Everyday cognition: Its development in social context* (pp. 67–94). Cambridge, MA: Harvard University Press.

Lave, J., & Wenger, E. (1991). *Situated learning: Legitimate peripheral participation.* Cambridge: Cambridge University Press.

Le Bon, G. (1982). *The crowd: A study of the popular mind.* Marietta, GA: Larlin. (Original work published 1895)

Lee, W. (1971). *Decision theory and human behavior.* New York: Wiley.

Lefcourt, H. M. (1972). Internal vs. external control of reinforcement revisited: Recent developments. In B. A. Maher (Ed.), *Progress in experimental personality research* (Vol. 6). New York: Academic Press.

Lefford, A. (1946). The influence of emotional subject matter on logical reasoning. *Journal of General Psychology, 34,* 127–151.

Leftow, B. (1994). From Jerusalem to Athens. In T. V. Morris (Ed.), *God and the philosophers: The reconciliation of faith and reason* (pp. 189–207). New York: Oxford University Press.

Leli, D. A., & Filskov, S. B. (1984). Clinical detection of intellectual deterioration associated with brain damage. *Journal of Clinical Psychology, 40,* 1435–1441.

Lents, J. M. (1991). Letter to the editor (Air pollution benefit-cost assessment). *Science, 253,* 607–608.

Leonesio, R, J., & Nelson, T. O. (1990). Do different metamemory judgments tap the same underlying aspects of memory? *Journal of Experimental Psychology: Learning, Memory, and Cognition, 16,* 464–470.

Lerner, D. (1959). Introduction: On evidence and inference. In D. Lerner (Ed.), *Evidence and inference* (pp. 7–18). Glencoe, IL: The Free Press.

Lerner, J. S., & Tetlock, P. E. (2003). Bridging individual, interpersonal, and institutional approaches to judgment and decision making: The impact of accountability on cognitive bias. In S. L. Schneider & J. Shanteau (Eds.), *Emerging perspectives on judgment and decision research* (pp. 431–457). Cambridge: Cambridge University Press.

Leutwyler, K. (1995). The price of prevention. *Scientific American, 272*(4), 124–129.

Levi, I. (1980). *The enterprise of knowledge.* Cambridge, MA: MIT Press.

Levi, I. (1983). Who commits the base rate fallacy? *Behavioral and Brain Sciences, 6,* 502–506.

Levi, I. (1991). *The fixation of belief and its undoing.* Cambridge: Cambridge University Press.

Levin, I. P., Schneider, S. L., & Gaeth, G. J. (1998). All frames are not created equal: A typology and critical analysis of framing effects. *Organizational Behavior and Human Decision Processes, 76,* 149–188.

Levinson, P. (1988). *Mind at large: Knowing in the techonological age.* Greenwich, CT: Jai Press.

Levinson, S. C. (1995). Interactional biases in human thinking. In E. Goody (Ed.), *Social intelligence and interaction* (pp. 221-260). New York: Cambridge University Press.

Lewandowsky, S., Kalish, M., & Ngang, S. K. (2002). Simplified learning in complex situations: Knowledge partitioning in function learning. *Journal of Experimental Psychology: General, 131,* 163–193.

Lewicki, P. (1986). *Nonconscious social information processing.* New York: Academic Press.

Lewicki, P., Hill, T., & Bizot, E. (1988). Acquisition of procedural knowledge about a pattern of stimuli that cannot be articulated. *Cognitive Psychology, 20,* 24–37.

Lewin, K. (1958). Group decision and social change. In E. E. Maccoby, T. M. Newcomb, & R. L. Hartley (Eds.), *Readings in Social Psychology* (pp. 330-344). New York: Holt, Reinhart and Winston.

Lewin, K., Lippitt, R., & White, R. K. (1939). Patterns of aggressive behavior in experimentally created "social climates." *Journal of Social Psychology, 10,* 271–299.

Lewis, C., & Keren, G. (1999). On the difficulties underlying Bayesian reasoning: A comment on Gegerenzer and Hoffrage. *Psychological Review, 106,* 411–416.

Lewis, C. H., & Mack, R. L. (1982). Learning to use a text processing system: Evidence from "thinking aloud" protocols. *Proceedings of the Conference on Human Factors in Computer Systems* (pp. 387–392). New York: Association for Computing Machinery.

Lewis, C. S. (1955). *Surprised by joy*. New York: Harcourt, Brace and Company.

Lewis, H. (1990). *A question of values: Six ways we make the personal choices that shape our lives*. San Francisco: Harper and Row.

Libby, R. (1975). Accounting rations and the prediction of failure: Some behavioral evidence. *Journal of Accounting Research, 13*, 150–161.

Libby, R. (1976). Man versus model of man: Some conflicting evidence. *Organizational Behavior and Human Performance, 16*, 1–12.

Lichtenstein, S., Fischhoff, B., & Phillips, L. D. (1982). Calibration of probabilities: The state of the art to 1980. In D. Kahneman, P. Slovic, & A. Tversky (Eds.), *Judgment under uncertainty: Heuristics and biases* (pp. 306–334). Cambridge: Cambridge University Press.

Lichtenstein, S., Slovic, P., Fishoff, B. Layman, M., & Coombs, B. (1978). Judged frequency of lethal events. *Journal of Experimental Psychology: Human Learning and Memory, 4*, 551–578.

Linder, D. E., Cooper, J., & Jones, E. E. (1967). Decision freedom as a determinant of the role of incentive magnitude in attitude change. *Journal of Personality and Social Psychology, 6*, 245–254.

Lindley, D. V. (1972). Comment. *Journal of the American Statistical Association, 67*, 373–374.

Lindley, D. V. (1993). *The end of physics: The myth of a unified theory*. New York: Basic Books.

Lippert, F. W., & Morris, S. C. (1991). Letter to the editor (Air pollution benefit-cost assessment). *Science, 253*, 606.

Lipshitz, R. (1993). Converging themes in the study of decision making in realistic settings. In G. A. Klein, J. Orasanu, R. Calderwood, & C. E. Zsambok (Eds.), *Decision making in action: Models and methods* (pp. 103–137). Norwood, NJ: Ablex.

Livio, M. (2002). *The golden ratio: The story of phy, the world's most astonishing number*. New York: Broadway Books.

Lochhead, J. (1981). The confounding of cause and effect, change and quantity. In J. T. Robinson (Ed.), *Research in science education: New questions, new directions* (pp 73–84). Center for Educational Research and Evaluation, ERIC.

Loewenstein, G. F., Weber, E. U., Hsee, C. K., & Welch, E. S. (2001). Risk as feelings. *Psychological Bulletin, 127*, 267–286.

Lombino, P. (1993, Summer). Dial-a-scam. *Fidelity Focus* (pp. 9–11).

Loomes, G. & Sugden, R. (1982). Regret theory: An alternative theory of rational choice under uncertainty. *Economic Journal, 92*, 805–824.

Lopes, L. L. (1976). Model-based decision and inference in stud poker. *Journal of Experimental Psychology: General, 105*, 217–239.

Lopes, L.L. (1981). Performing competently. Commentary on Cohen, 1981. *The Behavioral and Brain Sciences, 4*, 343–344.

Lopes, L. L. (1982). Doing the impossible: A note on induction and the experience of randomness. *Journal of Experimental Psychology: Learning, Memory, and Cognition, 8*, 626–636.

Lopes, L. L., & Ekberg, P-H. S. (1980). Test of an ordering hypothesis in risky decision-making. *Acta Psychologica, 45*, 161–167.
Lord, C., Ross, L., & Lepper, M. R. (1979). Biased assimilation and attitude polarization: The effects of prior theories on subsequently considered evidence. *Journal of Personality and Social Psychology, 37*, 2098–2109.
Luce, M. F., Bettman, J. R., & Payne, J. W. (1997). Choice processing in emotionally difficult decisions. *Journal of Experimental Psychology: Learning, Memory, and Cognition, 23*, 384–405.
Luce, R. D. (1959). *Individual choice behavior.* New York: Wiley.
Luce, R. D. (2003). Rationality in choice under certainty and uncertainty. In S. L. Schneider & J. Shanteau (Eds.), *Emerging perspectives on judgment and decision research* (pp. 64–83). Cambridge: Cambridge University Press.
Luce, R. D., & Raiffa, H. (1957). *Games and decisions.* New York: Wiley.
Ludbrook, A. (1981). A cost-effectiveness analysis of the treatment of chronic renal failure. *Applied Economics, 13*, 337–350.
Lupker, S. J., Harbluk, J. L., & Patrick, A. S. (1991). Memory for things forgotten. Journal of *Experimental Psychology: Learning, Memory, and Cognition, 17*, 897–907.
Lusted, L. B. (1977). *A study of the efficacy of diagnostic radiologic procedures: Final report on diagnostic efficacy.* Chicago: Efficacy Study Committee of the American College of Radiology.
Lycan, W. C. (1981). Is and ought in cognitive science. Commentary on Cohen, 1981. *Behavioral and Brain Science, 4*, 344–345.
Lyttleton, R. A. (1977). The nature of knowledge. In R. Duncan & M. Weston-Smith (Eds.), *The Encyclopedia of Ignorance* (pp. 9–18). New York: Pocket Books.
MacCrimmon, K. R. (1968). *Decision making among multiple-attribute alternatives: A survey and consolidated approach.* RAND Corporation Memo RM 4823-ARPA.
Macdonald, M. (1952). The language of political theory. In A. G. N. Flew (Ed.), *Logic and language* (pp. 167–186). Oxford: Basil Blackwell.
Macdonald, R. R. (1986). Credible conceptions and implausible probabilities. *British Journal of Mathematical and Statistical Psychology, 39*, 15–27.
Macdonald, R. R., & Gilhooly, K. J. (1990). More about Linda or conjunction in context. *Eurpoean Journal of Cognitive Psychology, 2*, 57–70.
MacIntyre, A. (1988). *Whose justice? Whose rationality?* Notre Dame, IN: Notre Dame University Press.
Mack, R. L., Lewis, C. H., & Carroll, J. M. (1983). Learning to use word processors: Problems and prospects. *ACM Transactions on Office Information Systems, 1*, 254–271.
Mackay, C. (1932). *Extraordinary popular delusions and the madness of crowds* (2nd ed.). Boston: L. C. Page. (Original 2nd ed. published 1841)
Mackworth, N. H. (1965). Originality. *The American Psychologist, 20*, 51–66.
MacLean, D. E. (1990) Comparing values in environmental policies: Moral issues and moral arguments. In P. B. Hammond & R. Coppock (Eds.), *Valuing health risks, costs, and benefits for environmental decision making* (pp. 83–106). Washington, DC: National Academy Press.
Macnamara, J. (1986). *A border dispute: The place of logic in psychology.* Cambridge, MA: MIT Press.

Maheswaran, D., & Chaiken, S. (1991). Promoting systematic processing in low-motivation settings: Effect of incongruent information on processing and judgment. *Journal of Personality and Social Psychology, 61,* 13–25.

Maier, N. R. F., & Solem, A. R. (1952). The contribution of a discussion leader to the quality of group thinking: The effective use of minority opinions. *Human relations, 5,* 277–288.

Malkiel, B. G. (1985). *A random walk down Wall Street* (4th ed.). New York: W. W. Norton.

Mandelbrot, B. (1982). *The fractal geometry of nature.* New York: Freeman.

Mandler, J. M. (1995). The death of developmental psychology. In R. L. Solso & D. W. Massaro (Eds.), *The science of the mind: 2001 and beyond* (pp. 79–89). New York: Oxford University Press.

Manis, M., Dovalina, I., Avis, N. E., & Cardoze, S. (1980). Base rates can affect individual predictions. *Journal of Personality and Social Psychology, 38,* 231–240.

Manktelow, K. (1999). *Reasoning and thinking.* Hove: Psychology Press.

Manktelow, K. I., & Evans, J. St. B. T. (1979). Facilitation of reasoning by realism: Effect of non effect? *British Journal of Psychology, 70,* 477–488.

Manktelow, K. I., & Over, D. E. (1991). Social roles and utilities in reasoning with deontic conditionals. *Cognition, 39,* 85–105.

Maranto, G. (1996). Should women in their 40s have mammograms? *Scientific American, 275*(3), 113.

Marcel, G. (1951). *The decline of wisdom.* London: Harvel Press.

March, J. G. (1972). Model bias in social action. *Review of Educational Research, 42,* 413–429.

March, J. G. (1978). Bounded rationality, ambiguity, and the engineering of choice. *Bell Journal of Economics, 9,* 587–607.

Margalit, A., & Bar-Hillel, M. (1981). The irrational, the unreasonable, and the wrong. Commentary on Cohen, 1981. *The Behavioral and Brain Sciences, 4,* 346–349.

Margolis, H. (1987). *Patterns, thinking, and cognition.* Chicago: University of Chicago Press.

Marr, D. (1982). *Vision.* New York: Freeman.

Martignon, L., & Krauss, S. (2003). Can l'homme eclaire be fast and frugal? Reconciling Bayesianism and bounded rationality. In S. L. Schneider & J. Shanteau (Eds.), *Emerging perspectives on judgment and decision research* (pp. 108–122). Cambridge: Cambridge University Press.

Marvin, C. (1988). *When old technologies were new: Thinking about electric communication in the late nineteenth century.* New York: Oxford University Press.

Maslow, A. (1954). *Motivation and personality.* New York: Harper.

Massaro, D. W., & Solso, R. L. (1995). Perennial issues for the next century. In R. L. Solso & D. W. Massaro (Eds.), *The science of the mind: 2001 and beyond* (pp. 305–316). New York: Oxford University Press.

Matlin, M. W., & Stang, D. J. (1978). *The Pollyanna principle: Selectivity in language, memory and thought.* Cambridge, MA: Shenkman.

Maxwell, J. C. (1873). Molecules. In W. D. Niven (Ed.), (1890). *Scientific papers, Vol. 2* (pp. 361–377). Cambridge: Cambridge University Press.

Mayo, D. G. (1996). *Error and the growth of experimental knowledge.* Chicago: The University of Chicago Press.

Mazzoni, D. A. L., Loftus, E. F., & Kirsch, I. (2001). Changing beliefs abou t implausible autobiographical events: A little plausibility goes a long way. *Journal of Experimental Psychology: Applied, 7,* 51–59.

McAllister, D. W., Mitchell, T. R., & Beach, L. R. (1979). The contingency model for the selection of decision strategies: An empirical test of the effects of significance, accountability, and reversibility. *Organizational Behavior and Human Performance, 24,* 228-244.

McArthur, L. (1972). The how and what of why: Some determinants and consequences of causal attributions. *Journal of Personality and Social Psychology, 22,* 171–193.

McArthur, L. Z., & Post, D. (1977). Figural emphasis and person perception. *Journal of Experimental Social Psychology, 13,* 520–535.

McArthur, L. Z., & Solomon, L. K. (1978). Perceptions of an aggressive encounger as a function of the victim's salience and the perceiver's arousal. *Journal of Personality and Social Psychology, 36,* 1278–1290.

McGuigan, F. J. (1966). Covert oral behavior and auditory hallucinations. *Psychophysiology, 3,* 73–80.

McGuire, W. J. (1960). A syllogistic analysis of cognitive relationships. In M. J. Rosenberg, C. I. Hovland, W.J . McGuire, R. P. Abelson, & J. W. Brehm (Eds.), *Attitude organization and change* (pp. 65–110). New Haven: Yale University Press.

McGuire, W. J. (1966). The current status of cognitive consistency theories. In S. Feldsman (Ed.), *Cognitive consistency: Motivational antecedents and behavioral consequences* (pp. 1–46). New York: Academic Press.

McGuire, W. J. (1969). The nature of attitudes and attitude change. In G. Lindzey & E. Aronson (Eds.), *Handbook of social psychology* (2nd ed., Vol 3, pp. 136–314). Reading, MA: Addison-Wesley.

McKellar, P. (1957). *Imagination and thnking: A psychological analysis.* New York: Basic Books.

McNeil, B. J., Weichselbaum, R., & Pauker, S. G. (1978). Fallacy of the five-year survival in lung cancer. *New Journal of Medicine, 299,* 1397–1401.

McPeck, J. (1981). *Critical thinking and education.* Oxford: Martin Robinson.

Meacham, J. A. (1983). Wisdom and the context of knowledge: Knowing that one doesn't know. In D. Kuhn & J. A. Meacham (Eds.), *On the development of developmental psychology* (pp. 111–134). Basel, Switzerland: Karger.

Meacham, J. A. (1990). The loss of wisdom. In R. J. Sternberg (Ed.), *Wisdom: Its nature, origins, and development* (pp. 181–211). New York: Cambridge University Press.

Medvec, V. H., Madey, S. F., & Gilovich, T. (1995). When less is more: Counterfactual thinking and satisfaction among Olympic medalists. *Journal of Personality and Social Psychology, 69,* 603–610.

Meehl, P. E. (1954). *Clinical versus statistical prediction: A theoretical analysis and a review of the evidence.* Minneapolis: University of Minnesota Press.

Meehl, P. E. (1956). Wanted: A good cookbook. *American Psychologist, 11,* 263–272.

Meehl, P. E. (1960). The cognitive activity of the clinician. *American Psychologist, 15,* 19–27.

Meehl, P. E. (1986). Superiority of actuarial to clinical prediction. *Journal of Personality Assessment, 50,* 370–375.

Meehl, P. E. (1996). *Clinical versus statistical prediction: A theoretical analysis and review of the evidence*. Northvale, NJ: Jason Aronson.

Mellers, B. A., & McGraw, A. P. (1999). How to improve Bayesian reasoning: Comment on Gigerenzer and Hoffrage. *Psychological Review, 106*, 417–424.

Mellers, B. A., Schwarz, A., & Ritov, I. (1999). Emotion-based choice. *Journal of Experimental Psychology: General, 128*, 332–345.

Merton, R. K. (1945). Sociology of knowledge. In G. Gurvitch & W. E. Moore (Eds.), *Twentieth-century sociology* (pp. 336–405). New York: Philosophical Library.

Messer, W. S., & Griggs, R. A. (1983). Another look at Linda. *Bulletin of the Pschonomic Society, 31*, 193–196.

Messick, S. (1984). The nature of cognitive styles: Problems and promise in educational practice. *Educational Psychologist, 19*, 59–74.

Messick, S. (1994). The matter of style: Manifestations of personality in cognition, learning, and teaching. *Educational Psychologist, 29*, 121–136.

Messick, D. M., & van d Geer, J. P. (1981). A reversal paradox. *Psychological Bulletin, 90*, 582–593.

Metcalfe, J. (1986a). Feeling of knowing in memory and problem solving. *Journal of Experimental Psychology: Learing, Memory, and Cognition, 12*, 288–294.

Metcalfe, J. (1986b). Premonitions of insight predict impending error. *Journal of Experimental Psychology: Learning, Memory, and Cognition, 12*, 623–634.

Metcalfe, J., & Weibe, D. (1987). Intuition in insight and non-insight problem solving. *Memory and Cognition, 15*, 238–246.

Meyer, D. E., & Kieras, D. E. (1998). Précis to a practical unified theory of cognition and action: Some lessons from EPIC computational models of human multiple-task performance. In D. Gopher & A. Koriat (Eds.), *Attention and performance XVII: Cognition regulation and performance: Interaction of theory and application*. Cambridge, MA: MIT Press.

Meyerson, M. (2002). *Political numeracy*. New York: W. W. Norton.

Michotte, A. (1950). The emotions regarded as functional connections. In M. L. Reymert (Ed.). *Feelings and emotions* (pp. 114–126). New York: McGraw-Hill.

Michotte, A. (1963). *The perception of causality*. London: Methuen.

Midgley, M. (1995). Reductive megalomania. In J. Cornwell (Ed.), *Nature's imagination: The frontiers of scientific vision* (pp. 133–147). New York: Oxford University Press.

Mikula, G., & Schwinger, T. (1978). Intermember relations and reward allocation: Theoretical considerations of affects. In H. Brandstätter, J. H. Davis, & H. Schuler (Eds.), *Dynamics of group decisions* (pp. 229–250). London: Sage.

Mill, J. S. (1995). On fallacies. In H. V. Hansen & R. C. Pinto (Eds.), *Fallacies: Classical and contemporary readings* (pp. 85–94). University Park: The Pennsylvania State University Press. (Original work published 1892)

Miller, A. G., & Rorer, L. G. (1982). Toward an understanding of the fundamental attribution error: Essay diagnosticity in the attitude attribution paradigm. *Journal of Research in Personality, 16*, 41–59.

Miller, A. I. (2003). Erotica, aesthetics and Schrödinger's wave equation. In G. Farmelo (Ed.), *It must be beautiful: Great equations of modern science* (pp. 110–131). New York: Granta.

Miller, D. T. (1976). Ego involvement and attributions for success and failure. *Journal of Personality and Social Psychology, 34,* 901–906.

Miller, G. A., (1979). Images and models, similes and metaphors. In A. Ortony (Ed.), *Metaphor and thought.* New York: Cambridge University Press.

Miller, G. A. (1986). *Assessing explanatory skills.* Working paper submitted to The Spencer Foundation, Chicago, IL.

Miller, G. A., Gillen, B., Schenker, C., and Radlove, S. (1973). Perception of obedience to authority. *Proceedings of the 81st Annual Convention of the American Psychological Association, 8,* 127–128.

Millikan, R. G. (1984). *Language, thought, and other biological categories: New foundations for realism.* Cambridge, MA: MIT Press.

Mintz, S., & Alpert, M. (1972). Imagery vividness, reality testing and schizophrenic hallucinations. *Journal of Abnormal Psychology, 79,* 310–316.

Mischel, W. (1968). *Personality and assessment.* New York: Wiley.

Mishan, E. J. (1976). *Cost benefit analysis.* New York: Praeger.

Montaigne, M. E. (1927). *The essays of Montaigne* (translated by E. J. Trechmann). New York: Oxford University Press. (Original work published circa 1580)

Mooney, R. J., & DeJong, G. F. (1985). Learning schemata for natural language processing. *Proceedings of the Ninth International Joint Conference on Artificial Intelligence* (pp. 551–555). Los Altos, CA: Morgan Kaufman.

Moore, D. W. (1992). *The super pollsters.* New York: Four Walls Eight Windows.

Morgan, J. N., & Duncan, G. J. (1982). *Making your choices count: Economic principles for everyday decisions.* Ann Arbor: University of Michigan Press.

Morgenstern, O. (1949). The theory of games. *Scientific American, 180*(5), 22–25.

Morley, I. E., & Stephenson, G. M. (1977). *The social psychology of bargaining.* London: George Allen and Unwin.

Morowitz, H. J. (1981). Rediscovering the mind. In D. R. Hofstadter & D. C, Dennett (Eds.), *The mind's I: Fantasies and reflections on self and soul* (pp. 34–42). New York: Basic Books.

Morowitz, H. J. (1991). Balancing species preservation and economic considerations. *Science, 253,* 752–754.

Morris, R. (1987). *The nature of reality.* New York: The Noonday Press.

Moser, P. K. (1990). Rationality in action: General introduction. In P. K. Moser (Ed.), *Rationality in action: Contemporary approaches* (pp. 1–10). New York: Cambridge University Press.

Moshman, D. (1994a). Reason, reasons, and reasoning: A constructivist account of human rationality. *Theory and Psychology, 4,* 245–260.

Moshman, D. (1994b). Reasoning, metareasoning, and the promotion of rationality. In A. Demetriou & Efklides (Eds.), *Intelligence, mind, and reasoning: Structure and development* (pp. 135–150). Amsterdam: Elsevier.

Moshman, D, (1995). Reasoning as self-constrained thinking. *Human Development, 38,* 53–64.

Moshman, D. (1998). Cognitive development beyond childhood. In D. Kuhn & R. Siegler (Eds.), *Handbook of child psychology, (5th edition), Volume 2: Cognition, perception and language* (pp. 947–978). New York: Wiley.

Moshman, D. (2000). Diversity in reasoning and rationality: Metacognitive and developmental considerations. *Behavioral and Brain Sciences, 23,* 689–690.

Moshman, D. (2004). From inference to reasoning: The construction of rationality. *Thinking and Reasoning, 10,* 221–239.

Moscovici, S., & Doise, W. (1994). *Conflict and consensus: A general theory of collective decisions*. London: Sage.

Moshman, D., & Geil, M. (1998). Collaborative reasoning: Evidence for collective rationality. *Thinking and reasoning, 4*, 231–248.

Moskovici, S., & Zavalloni, M. (1969). The group as a polarizer of attitudes. *Journal of Personality and Social Psychology, 12*, 125–135.

Mueller, D. C. (1979). *Public choice*. Cambridge: Cambridge University Press.

Mulcahy R. F., Short, R. H., & Andrews, J. (Eds.). (1991). *Enhancing learning and thinking*. New York: Praeger.

Mumford, L. (1966). Technics and the nature of man. *Technology and Culture, 7*, 303–317.

Myers, D. G., & Kaplan, M. F. (1976). Group-induced polarization in simulated juries. *Personality and Social Psychology Bulletin, 2*, 63–66.

Myers, D. G. & Lamm, H. (1976). The group polarization phenomenon. *Psychological Bulletin, 83*, 602–627.

Nagao, D. H., Vollrath, D. A., & Davis, J. H. (1978). Introduction: Origins and current status of group decision-making. In H. Brandstätter, J. H. Davis, & H. Schuler, H. (Eds.), *Dynamics of group decisions* (pp. 11–27). London: Sage.

Nagel, T. (1986). *The view from nowhere*. New York: Oxford University Press.

Nagel, T. (1995). *Other minds: Critical essays 1969–1994*. New York: Oxford University Press.

Nagel, T. (1995) Chomsky: Linguistics and epistemology. In T. Nagel, *Other minds: Critical essays 1969–1994* (pp. 26–44). New York: Oxford University Press. (Essays originally published between 1969 and 1994)

Nagel, E., & Newman, J. R. (1958). *Gödel's Proof*. New York: University Press.

National Commission on Excellence in Education (1983). *A nation at risk: The imperative for educational reform*. Washington, DC: U.S. Government Printing Office.

National Educational Goals Panel. (1991). *The national educational goals report*. Washington, DC: U.S. Government Printing Office.

Neale, M. A., & Bazerman, M. H. (1991). *Cognition and rationality in negotiation*. New York: The Free Press.

Neale, M. A., & Northcraft, G. B. (1990). Experience, expertise, and decision bias in negotiation: The role of strategic conceptualization. In B. Shepard, M. Bazerman, & R. Lewicki (Eds.), *Research in negotiation in organizations* (Vol. 2). Greenwich CT: JAI Press.

Neimark, E. D., & Chapman, R. A. (1975). Development of the comprehension of logical quantifiers. In R. J. Falmagne (Ed.), *Reasoning: Representation and process*. New York: Wiley.

Nelson, T. O., Gerler, D., & Narens, L. (1984). Accuracy of feeling of knowing judgments for predicting perceptual identification and relearning. *Journal of Experimental Psychology: General, 113*, 282–300.

Nelson, T. O., Leonesio, R. J., Shimamura, A. P., Landwehr, R. S., & Narens, L. (1982). Overlearning and the feeling of knowing. *Journal of Experimental Psychology: Learning, Memory, and Cognition, 8*, 279–288.

Nelson, T. O., & Narens, L. (1990). Metamemory: A theoretical framework and new findings. In G. H. Bower (Ed.), *The psychology of learning and motivation*, (Vol. 26, pp. 125–173). New York: Academic Press.

Newell, A. (1973). Production systems: Models of control structures. In W. G. Chase (Ed.), *Visual information processing*. New York: Academic Press.

Newell, A. (1982). The knowledge level. *Artificial Intelligence, 18*, 87–127.

Newmann, F. M. (1991). Higher order thinking in the teaching of social studies: Connections between theory and practice. In J. F. Voss, D. N. Perkins, & J. W. Segal (Eds.), *Informal reasoning and education* (pp. 381–400). Hillsdale, NJ: Erlbaum.

Neyman, J., & Pearson, E. S. (1933). The testing of statistical hypotheses in relation to probability *a priori*. *Proceedings of the Cambridge Philosophical Society, 29*, 492–510.

Nicholls, J. G. (1978). Causal attributions and other achievement-related cognitions: Effects of task outcome, attainment value, and sex. *Journal of Personality and Social Psychology, 31*, 379–389.

Nickerson, R. S. (1980). Retrieval efficiency, knowledge assessment and age: Comments on some welcome findings. In L. W. Poon, J. L. Fozard, L. S. Cermak, D. Arenburg, & L. W. Thompson (Eds.), *New directions in memory and aging* (pp. 355–366). Hillsdale, NJ: Erlbaum.

Nickerson, R. S. (1981). Motivated retrieval from archival memory. In J. H. Flowers (Ed.), *1980 Nebraska symposium on motivation: Cognitive processes* (pp. 73–119). Lincoln: University of Nebraska Press.

Nickerson, R. S. (1985). Understanding understanding. *American Journal of Education, 93*, 201–239.

Nickerson, R. S. (1988). Practical Intelligence, edited by R. J. Sternberg & R. K. Wagner (Book review). *American Journal of Psychology, 101*, 293–302.

Nickerson, R. S. (1994). The teaching of thinking and problem solving. In R. J. Sternberg (Ed.), *Thinking and problem solving*, Vol. 12 of E. C. Carterette & M. Friedman (Eds.), *Handbook of perception and cognition* (pp. 409–449). San Diego, CA: Academic Press.

Nickerson, R. S. (1995). Mind mapping: Probing questions from a constructive gadfly. (Review of the new phrenology: The limits of localizing cognitive processes in the brain, by W. R. Uttal). *Journal of Mathematical Psychology, 49*, 80–83.

Nickerson, R. S. (1998). Confirmation bias: A ubiquitous phenomenon in many guises. *Review of General Psychology, 2*, 175–220.

Nickerson, R. S. (1999b). Why are there twelve inches in a foot? *Cognitive Technology, 4*(2), 18–25.

Nickerson, R. S. (2004). *Cognition and chance: The psychology of probabilistic reasoning*. Mahwah, NJ: Erlblaum.

Nickerson, R. S., Perkins, D. N., & Smith, E. E. (1985). *The teaching of thinking*. Hillsdale, NJ: Erlbaum.

Nickerson, R. S. & Zodhiates, P. (1988.) *Technology in Education: Looking toward 2020*. Hillside, NJ: Erlbaum.

Nilsson, N. J. (1971). *Problem-solving methods in artificial intelligence*. New York: McGraw-Hill.

Nisbett, R. E., Borgida, E., Crandall, R., & Reed, H. (1976). Popular induction: Information is not necessarily informative. In J. S. Carroll & J. W. Payne (Eds.), *Cognition and social behavior* (pp. 113–134). Hillsdale, NJ: Erlbaum.

Nisbett, R. E., Caputo, C., Legant, P., & Marecek, J. (1973). Behavior as seen by the actor and as seen by the observer. *Journal of Personality and Social Psychology, 27,* 154–164.

Nisbett, R. E., Krantz, D. H., Jepson, D., & Kunda, Z. (1983). The use of statistical heuristics in everyday inductive reasoning. *Psychological Review, 90,* 339–363.

Nisbett, R. E., & Ross, L. (1980). *Human inference: Strategies and shortcomings of social judgement.* Englewood Cliffs, NJ: Prentice-Hall.

Nisbett, R. E., & Wilson, T. D. (1977a). Telling more than we know: Verbal reports on mental processes. *Psychological Review, 84,* 231–259.

Nisbett, R. E., & Wilson, T. D. (1977b). The halo effect: Evidence for unconscious alteration of judgments. *Journal of Personality and Social Psychology, 35,* 250–256.

Nisbett, R. E., Zukier, H., & Lemley, R. (1981). The dilution effect: Nondiagnostic information weakens the implications of diagnostic information. *Cognitive Psychology, 13,* 248–277.

Nogar, R. J. (1966). *The wisdom of evolution.* New York: New American Library.

Nordhaus, W. D. (1992). An optimal transition path for controlling greenhouse gases. *Science, 258,* 1315–1319.

Norman, D. A. (1981). Categorization of action slips. *Psychological Review, 88,* 1–15.

Norman, D. A. (1993). *Things that make us smart.* Reading, MA: Addison-Wesley.

Norman, D. A. (1995). The future of the mind lies in technoloty. In R. L. Solso & D. W. Massaro (Eds.), *The science of the mind: 2001 and beyond* (pp. 247–257). New York: Oxford University Press.

Nozick, R. (1981). *Philosophical explanations.* Cambridge, MA: Harvard University Press.

Nozick, R. (1993). *The nature of rationality.* Princeton, NJ: Princeton University Press.

Nystedt, L., & Magnusson, D. (1972). Prediction efficiency as a function of amount of information. *Mutivariate Behavioral Research, 7,* 441–450.

Oakhill, J. V., & Johnson-Laird, P. N. (1985a). The effects of belief on the spontaneous production of syllogistic conclusions. *Quarterly Journal of Experimental Psychology, 37A,* 553–569.

Oakhill, J. V., & Johnson-Laird, P. N. (1985b). Rationality, memory and the search for counterexamples. *Cognition, 20,* 79–94.

Oaksford, M., & Chater, N. (1995). Theories of reasoning and the computational explanation of everyday inference. *Thjinking and Cognition, 1,* 121–152.

Oaksford, M., & Sellen, J. (2000). Paradoxical individual differences in conditional inference. *Behavioral and Brain Sciences, 23,* 691–692.

Oberauer, K. (2000). Do we need two systems for reasoning? *Behavioral and Brain Sciences, 23,* 692–693.

O'Connor, M. (1989). Models of human behavior and confidence in judgment: A review. *International Journal of Forecasting, 5,* 159–169.

Odean, T. (1998). Volume, volatility, price and profit when all traders are above average. *Journal of Finance, 53,* 1887–1934.

Olson, M. (1965). *The logic of collective action.* New Haven: Yale University Press.

Orvis, B. R., Cunningham, J. D., & Kelley, H. H. (1975). A closer examination of causal inference: The roles of consensus, distinctiveness, and consistency information. *Journal of Personality and Social Psychology, 32*, 605–616.

Orwoll, L, & Perlmutter, M. (1990). The study of wise persons: Integrating a personality perspective. In R. J. Sternberg (Ed.), *Wisdom: Its nature, origins, and development* (pp. 160–177). New York: Cambridge University Press.

Osgood, C. E. (1953). *Method and theory in experimental psychology.* New York: Oxford University Press.

Osherson, D. N. (1995). Probability judgment. In E. E. Smith & D. N. Osherson (Eds.), *Thinking: An Invitation to Cognitive Science, Volume 3* (2nd ed.) (pp. 35–75). Cambridge, MA: MIT Press.

Oskamp, S. (1965). Overconfidence in case-study judgments. *Journal of Consulting Psychology, 29*, 262–265.

Pacioli, L. (1988). *Divine proportion.* Paris: Librairie do Compagnonnage. (Original work published 1509)

Pagels, H. R. (1991). *Perfect symmetry: The search for the beginning of time.* New York: Bantam Books.

Pais, A. (1986). *Inward bound: Of matter and forces in the physical world.* New York: Oxford University Press.

Pankoff, L. D., & Roberts, H. V. (1968). Bayesian synthesis of clinical and statistical prediction. *Psychological Bulletin, 70,* 762–773.

Papineau, D. (1987). *Reality and representation.* Oxford: Basil Blackwell.

Pascual-Leone, J. (1990). An essay on wisdom: Toward organismic processes that make it possible. In R. J. Sternberg (Ed.), *Wisdom: Its nature, origins, and development* (pp. 244–278). New York: Cambridge University Press.

Pauker, S. P., & Pauker, S. G. (1979). The amniocentesis decision: An explicit guide for parents. In C. J. Epstein, C. J. R. Curry, S. Packman, S. Sherman, & B. D. Hall (Eds.), *Birth defects: Original article series: Volume 15, Risk, communication, and decision making in genetic counseling* (pp. 289–324). New York: The National Foundation.

Paul, R. (1992). *Critical thinking: What every person needs to know in a rapidly changing world.* Sonoma, CA: Foundation for Critical Thinking.

Payne, J. W. (1976). Task complexity and contingent processing in decision making: An information search and protocol analysis. *Organizational Behavior and Human Performance, 16,* 366–387.

Payne, J. W. (1982). Contingent decision behavior. *Psychological Bulletin, 92,* 382–402.

Payne, J., Bettman, J., & Johnson, E. (1990). The adaptive decision maker: Effort and accuracy in choice. In R. M. Hogarth (Ed.), *Insights in decision making: A tribute to Hillel J. Einhorn* (pp. 129–153). Chicago: University of Chicago Press.

Payne, J., Bettman, J., & Johnson, E. (1992). Behavioral decision research: A constructive processing perspective. *Annual Review of Psychology, 43,* 87–131.

Payne, J., Bettman, J., & Johnson, E. (1993). *The adaptive decision maker.* New York: Cambridge University Press.

Pearce, D. W., & Turner, R. K. (1990). *Economics of natural resources and the environment.* Baltimore: Johns Hopkins University Press.

Peck, S. C., & Teisberg, T. J. (1992). *Cost-benefit analysis and climate change*. Palo Alto, CA: Electric Power Research Institute.

Peirce, C. S. (1956). The essence of mathematics. In J. R. Newman (Ed.), *The world of mathematics, Vol. 2* (pp. 1773–1783). New York: Simon and Schuster. (Original work published in 1902)

Penrose, R. (1979). Singularities and time assymetry. In S. W. Hawking & W. Isreal (Eds.), *General relativity: An Einstein centenary survey*. Cambridge:: Cambridge University Press.

Penrose, R. (1989). *The emperor's new mind: Concerning computers, minds, and the laws of physics*. New York: Oxford University Press.

Perkins, D. N. (1981). *The mind's best work*. Cambridge, MA.: Harvard University Press.

Perkins, D. N. (2002). Standard logic as a model of reasoning: The empirical critique. In D. Gabbay, R. H. Johnson, H. J. Ohlbach, & J. Woods (Eds.), *Handbook of logic of argument and inference: The turn towards the practical*. Amsterdam: Elsevier.

Perkins, D. N., Allan, R., & Hafner, J. (1983). Difficulties in everyday reasoning. In W. Maxwell (Ed.), *Thinking: The frontier expands*. Hillsdale, NJ: Erlbaum.

Perkins, D. N., Farady, M., & Bushey, B. (1991). Everyday reasoning and the roots of intelligence. In J. Voss, D. N. Perkins, & J. Segal, (Eds.), *Informal reasoning* (pp. 83–105). Hillsdale, NJ: Erlbaum.

Perkins, D. N., Jay, E., & Tishman, S. (1993). Beyond abilities: A dispositional theory of thinking. *Merrill-Palmer Quarterly, 39*, 1–21.

Perlmutter, M., Adams, C., Nyquist, L., & Kaplan, C. (1988). *Beliefs about wisdom*. Unplublished data. (Reported in Orwoll & Perlmutter, 1990.)

Perlmutter, M.., & Hall, E. (1985). *Adult development and aging*. New York: Wiley.

Peterson, M. K., Miranda, S. M., & Smith, P. B. (2003). The sociocultural contexts of decision making in organizations. In S. L. Schneider & J. Shanteau (Eds.), *Emerging perspectives on judgment and decision research* (pp. 512–555). Cambridge: Cambridge University Press.

Pettigrew, T. F. (1979). The ultimate attribution error: Extending Allport's cognitive analysis of prejudice. *Personality and Social Psychology Bulletin, 5*, 461–476.

Phelps, C. E., & Mooney, C. (1993). Variations in medical practice use: Causes and consequences. In A Richard, R. Rich & W. White (Eds.), *Competitive approaches to health care reform* (pp. 140–178). Washington, DC: Urban Institute.

Piaget, J. (1928). *Judgment and reasoning in the child*. London: Routledge and Kegan Paul.

Piattelli-Palmarini, M. (1994). *Inevitable illusions: How mistakes of reason rule our minds*. New York: Wiley.

Pietromonaco, P. R., & Nisbett, R. E. (1982). Swimming upstream against the fundamental attribution error: Subjects' weak generalizations from the Darley and Batson study. *Social Behavior and Personality, 10*, 1–4.

Pittman, T. S., & D'Agostino, P. R. (1985). Motivation and attribution: The effects of control deprivation on subsequent information processing. In G. Weary & J. Harvey (Eds.), *Attribution: Basic issues and applications* (pp. 117–141). New York: Academic Press.

Pitz, G. F., Reinhold, H., & Geller, E. S. (1969). Strategies of information seeking in deferred decision making. *Organizational Behavior and Human Performance, 4*, 1–19.

Platt, J. (1973). Social traps. *American Psychologist, 28*, 641–651.

Platt, R. D., & Griggs, R. A. (1995). Facilitation and matching bias in the selection task. *Thinking and Reasoning, 1*, 55–70.

Pliske, R., & Klein, G. (2003). The naturalistic decision-making perspective. In S. L. Schneider & J. Shanteau (Eds.), *Emerging perspectives on judgment and decision research* (pp. 559–585). Cambridge: Cambridge University Press.

Polkinghorne, J. (1991). *Reason and reality: The relationship between science and theology*. Valley Forge, PA: Trinity Press International.

Polkinghorne, J. (1998). *Belief in God in an age of reason*. New Haven: Yale University Press.

Polson, P., & Jeffries, R. (1982). Problem solving and search understanding. In R. J. Sternberg (Ed.), *Advances in the psychology of human intelligence* (Vol. 1, pp. 367–411). Hillsdale, NJ: Erlbaum.

Polanyi, M. (1967). *The tacit dimension*. Garden City, NY: Anchor Books.

Polya, G. (1954a). *Mathematics and plausible reasoning, Vol. 1: Induction and analogy in mathematics*. Princeton, NJ: Princeton University Press.

Polya, G. (1954b). *Mathematics and plausible reasoning, Vol. 2: Patterns of plausible inference*. Princeton, NJ: Princeton University Press.

Polya, G. (1957). *How to solve it: A new aspect of mathematical method*. Garden City, NY: Doubleday. (Original work published 1945)

Poole, K. T. (1981). Dimensions of interest group evaluation of the U. S. Senate, 1969–1978. *American Journal of Political Science, 25*, 49–67.

Popper, K. R. (1959). *The logic of scientific discovery*. New York: Basic Books.

Popper, K. (1966). *The open society and its enemies*. Princeton, NJ: Princeton University Press.

Postmes, P., & Lea, M. (2000). Social processes and group decision making: Anonymity in group decision support systems. *Ergonomics, 43*, 1252–1274.

Poundstone, W. (1992). *Prisoner's dilemma: John von Neumann, game theory, and the puzzle of the bomb*. New York: Anchor Books.

Pyszczynski, T., & Greenberg, J. (1983). Determinants of reduction in intended effort as a strategy for coping with anticipated failure. *Journal of Research in Personality, 17*, 412–422.

Pyszczynski, T., & Greenberg, J. (1987). Toward an integration of cognitive and motivational perspectives on social inference: A biased hypothesis-testing model. In L. Berkowitz (Ed.), *Advances in experimental social psychology* (Vol. 20, pp. 297–340). New York: Academic Press.

Pyszczynski, T., Greenberg, J., & Holt, K. (1985). Maintaining consistency between self-serving beliefs and available data: A bias in evaluation following success and failure. *Personality and Social Psychology Bulletin, 11*, 179–190.

Pyszczynski, T., Greenberg, J., & LaPrelle, J. (1985). Social comparison after success and failure: Biased search for information consistent with a self-serving conclusion. *Journal of Experimental Social Psychology, 21*, 195–211.

Quine, W. V. (1969). Epistemology naturalized. In W. V. Quine (Ed.), *Ontological relativity and other essays* (pp. 69–90). New York: Columbia University Press.

Quine, W. V. (1981). *Theories and things*. Cambridge, MA: Harvard University Press.
Raiffa, H.´(1968). *Decision analysis: Introductory lectures on choices under uncertainty*. Reading, MA: Addison-Wesley.
Raiffa, H., & Schlaifer, R. O. (1961). *Applied statistical decision theory*. Cambridge, MA: Harvard Business School.
Ramsey, F. P. (1931). Truth and probability. In R. B. Braithwaite (Ed.), *The foundations of mathematics and other logical essays*. London: Routledge and Kegan Paul.
Rapoport, Anatol. (1960). *Fights, games, and debates*. Ann Arbor, MI: The University of Michigan Press.
Rawcliffe, D. H. (1959). *Illusions and delusions of the supernatural and the occult*. New York: Dover Publications.
Rawls, J. (1971). *A theory of justice*. Cambridge, MA: Harvard University Press.
Raye, C. L., Johnson, M. K., & Taylor, T. H. (1980). Is there something special about memory for internally-generated information? *Memory and Cognition, 8*, 141–148.
Read, J. D., & Bruce, D. (1982). Longitudinal tracking of difficult memory retrievals. *Cognitive Psychology, 14*, 280–300.
Redelmeier, D. A., & Tversky, A. (1992). On the framing of multiple prospects. *Psychological Science, 3*, 191–193.
Reder, L. M. (1982). Plausibility judgments versus fact retrieval: Alternative strategies for sentence verification. *Psychological Review, 89*, 250–280.
Reder, L. M. (1987). Selection strategies in question answering. *Cognitive Psychology, 19*, 90–138.
Reder, L. M. (1988). Strategic control of retrieval strategies. In G. Bower (Ed.), *The psychology of learning and motivation* (Vol. 22, pp. 227–259). San Diego, CA: Academic Press.
Reder, L. M., & Ritter, F. E. (1992). What determines initial feeling of knowing? Familiarity with question terms, not with the answer. *Journal of Experimental Psychology: Learning, Memory, and Cognition, 18*, 435–451.
Redhead, M. (1989). *Physics for pedestrians*. Cambridge, Eng: Cambridge University Press.
Regan, D. T., Strauss, E., & Fazio, R. (1974). Liking and the attribution process. *Journal of Experimental Social Psychology, 10*, 385–397.
Reich, S. S. & Ruth, P. (1982). Wason's selection task: Verification, falsification and matching. *British Journal of Psychology, 73*, 395–405.
Reichenbach, H. (1938). *Experience and prediction*. Chicago, Il: University of Chicago Press.
Reid, W. A. (1987). Institutions and practices: Professional education reports and the language of reform. *Educational Researcher, 16*(8), 10–15.
Resnick, L. B. (Ed.), (1976). *The nature of intelligence*. Hillsdale, NJ: Erlbaum.
Resnick, L. B. (1987). *Education and learning to think*. Washington, DC: National Academy Press.
Rettinger, D. A., & Hastie, R. (2003). Comprehension and decision making. In S. L. Schneider & J. Shanteau (Eds.), *Emerging perspectives on judgment and decision research* (pp. 165–200). Cambridge: Cambridge University Press.
Reyna, V. F. (1996). Conceptions of memory development, with implications for reasoning and decision making. *Annals of Child Development, 12*, 87–118.

Reyna, V. F. (2000). Fuzzy-trace theory and source monitoring: A review of theory and false-memory data. *Learning and Individual Differences, 12*, 163–175.

Reyna, V. F., & Brainerd, C. J. (1990). Fuzzy processing in transitivity development. *Annals of Operations Research, 23*, 37–63.

Reyna, V. F., & Brainerd, C. J. (1992). A fuzzy-trace theory of reasoning and remembering: Paradoxes, patterns, and parallelism. In A. Healy, S. Kosslyn, & R. Shiffrin (Eds.), *From Learning processes to cognitive processes: Essays in honor of William K. Estes* (Vol. 2, pp. 235–259). Hillsdale, NJ: Erlbaum.

Reyna, V. F., & Brainerd, C. J. (1998). Fuzzy-trace theory and false memory: New frontiers. *Journal of Experimental Child Psychology, 71*, 194–209.

Reyna, V. F., & Ellis, S. C. (1994). Fuzzy-trace theory and framing effects in children's risky decision making. *Psychological Science, 5*, 275–279.

Reyna, V. F., Lloyd, F. J., & Brainerd, C. J. (2003). Memory, development, and rationality: An integrative theory of judgment and decision making. In S. L. Schneider & J. Shanteau (Eds.), *Emerging perspectives on judgment and decision research* (pp. 201–245). Cambridge: Cambridge University Press.

Rhim, H., & Cooper, L. G. (2004). Assessing potential threats to incumbent brands: New product positioning under price competition in a multisegmented market. *International Journal of Research in Marketing, 22*, 159-182.

Richards, J. R. (1996). Why feminist epistemology isn't. In P. R. Gross, N. Levitt, & M. W. Lewis (Eds.), *The flight from reason* (pp. 385–412). New York: The New York Academy of Sciences.

Ritov, I., & Baron, J. (1990). Reluctance to vaccinate: Omission bias and ambiguity. *Journal of Behavioral Decision Making, 3*, 263–277.

Robinson, D. N. (1990). Wisdom through the ages. In R. J. Sternberg (Ed.), *Wisdom: Its nature, origins, and development* (pp. 13–24). New York: Cambridge University Press.

Rogoff, B. (1984). Introduction: Thinking and learning in social context. In B. Rogoff & J. Lave (Eds.), *Everyday cognition: Its development in social context* (pp. 1–8). Cambridge, MA: Harvard University Press.

Roland-Robinson, M. (1977). Galaxies, quasars and the universe. In Duncan, R. & Weston-Smith, M. (Eds.) *The Encyclopedia of Ignorance* (pp. 57–65). New York: Pocket Books, Simon and Schuster.

Ronen, J. (1973). Effects of some probability displays on choices. *Organizational Behavior and Human Performance, 9*, 1–15.

Roodin, P. A., Rybash, J, & Hoyer, W. J. (1984). Affect in adult cognition: A constructivist view of moral thought and action. In C. Z. Malatesta & C. E. Izard (Eds.), *Emotion in adult development* (pp. 297–316). Beverly Hills, CA: Sage.

Rosenfeld, R. (2002). The crime decline in context. *Contexts, 1*, 25–34.

Rosenfeld, R. (2004). The cae of the unsolved crime decline. *Scientific American, 290*(2), 82–89.

Ross, L. (1978). Afterthoughts on the intuitive psychologist. In L. Berkowitz (Ed.), *Cognitive theories in social psychology* (pp. 385–400). New York: Academic Press.

Ross, L., & Anderson, C.A. (1982). Shortcomings in the attribution process: On the origins and maintenance of erroneous social assessments. In D. Kahneman, P. Slovic, & A. Tversky (Eds.), *Judgment under uncertainty: Heuristics and biases* (pp. 129-152). New York: Cambridge University Press.

Ross, M., & Fletcher, G. J. O. (1985). Attribution and social perception. In G. Lindzey & E. Aronson (Eds.), *Handbook of social psychology* (3rd ed., Vol. 2, pp. 73–122). New York: Random House.

Ross, L., & Lepper, M. R. (1980). The perseverance of beliefs: Empirical and normative considerations. In R. Shweder & D. Fiske (Eds.), *New directions for methodology of social and behavioral science: Fallibel judgment in behavioral research* (Vol. 4, pp. 17–36). San Francisco: Jossey-Bass.

Ross, L., Lepper, M. R., & Hubbard, M. (1975). Perserverance in self perception and social perception: Biased attributional processes in the debriefing paradigm. *Journal of Personality and Social Psychology, 32*, 880–892.

Ross, L., Lepper, M. R., Strack, F., & Steinmetz, J. L. (1977). Social explanation and social expectation: The effects of real and hypothetical explanations upon subjective likelihood. *Journal of Personality and Social Psychology, 35*, 817–829.

Rossman, B. B., & Ulehla, Z. J. (1977). Psychological reward values associated with wilderness use: A functional-reinforcement approach. *Environment and Behavior, 9*, 41–66.

Roth, A. E. (1995). Bargaining experiments. In J. H. Kagel & A. E. Roth (Eds.), *Handbook of experimental economics* (pp. 253–348). Princeton, NJ: Princeton University Press.

Rothbart, M., & Park, B. (1986). On the confirmability and disconfirmability of trait concepts. *Journal of Personality and Social Psychology, 50*, 131–142.

Rotter, J. B. (1966). Generalized expectancies for internal versus external control of reinforcement. *Psychological Monographs, 80*, 1, Whole No. 609.

Roxburgh, I. W. (1978). Is space curved? In R. Duncan & M. Weston-Smith (Eds.), *The encyclopedia of ignorance* (pp. 85–89). New York: Pocket Books, Simon and Schuster.

Runion, G. E. (1990). *The golden section*. Palo Alto, CA: Dale Seymour.

Ruse, M. (1999). *Mystery of mysteries: Is evolution a social construction?* Cambridge, MA: Harvard University Press.

Russell, B. (1910). *Philosophical essays*. London: Longmans, Green.

Russell, B. (1948). *Human knowledge: Its scope and limits*. New York: Simon and Schuster.

Russell, B. (1954). *Human society in ethics and politics*. London: Allen and Unwin.

Russell, B. (1956). Mathematics and metaphysics. In J. R. Newman (Ed.), *The world of mathematics, Vol. 3* (pp. 1576–1590). New York: Simon and Schuster. (Original work published 1929)

Russell, B. (1957). *Why I am not a Christian*. New York: Simon and Schuster.

Russell, M. (1990). The making of cruel choices. In P. B. Hammond & R. Coppock (Eds.), *Valuing health risks, costs, and benefits for environmental decision making* (pp. 15–22). Washington, DC: National Academy Press.

Russell, B. (1994). The greatness of Albert Einstein. In M. Gardner (Ed.), *Great essays in science* (pp. 408–412). New York: Prometheus Books. (Original work published 1950)

Rüttinger, B. (1978). Friendliness and group consensus: Field study. In H. Brandstätter, J. H. Davis, & H. Schuler (Eds.), *Dynamics of group decisions* (pp. 149–153). London: Sage.

Ryan, M. P., Petty, C. R., & Wenzlaff, R. M. (1982). Motivated remembering efforts during tip-of-the tongue states. *Acta Psychologica, 51*, 137–147.

Ryle, G. (1949). *The concept of mind.* Chicago: University of Chicago Press.

Sá, W., West, R. F., & Stanovich, K. E. (1999). The domain specifity and generality of belief bias: Searching for a generalizable critical thinking skill. *Journal of Educational Psychology, 91,* 497–510.

Saarinen, T. F. (1980). Reconnaisance trip to M. St. Helens, May 18–21, 1980. *The Bridge* (National Academy of Engineering), *10,* 19–22.

Sacks, O. (1987). *The man who mistook his wife for a hat.* New York: Harper & Row.

Safer, M. A. (1980). Attributing evil to the subject, not the situation: Student reaction to Milgram's film on obedience. *Personality and Social Psychology Bulletin, 6,* 205–209.

Salam, A. (1992). Science and religion: Reflections on transcendence and secularization. In H. Margenau & R. A. Varghese (Eds.), *Cosmos, bios, theos: Scientists reflect on science, God, and the origins of the universe, life, and Homo Sapiens* (pp. 93–104). Chicago: Open Court.

Salomon, G. (Ed.). (1993). *Distributed cognitions: Psychological and educational considerations.* New York: Cambridge University Press.

Salmon, W. C. (1974c). Rejoinder to Barker and Kyburg. In R. Swinburne (Ed.). *The justification of induction* (pp. 66–73). London: Oxford University Press.

Salovey, P. & Birnbaum, D. (1989). Influence of mood on health-relevant cognitions. *Journal of Personality and Social Psychology, 57,* 539–551.

Sampson, G. (1981). Human rationality: Misleading linguistic analogies. Commentary on Cohen, 1981. *The Behavioral and Brain Sciences, 4,* 350–351.

Samuelson, W., & Zeckhauser, R. (1988). Status-quo bias in decision making. *Journal of Risk and Uncertainty, 1,* 7–59.

Sanfey, A. G., Rilling, J. K., Aronson, J. A., Nystrom, L. E., & Cohen, J. D. (2003). The neural basis of economic decision-making in the Ultimatum Game. *Science, 300,* 1755–1758.

Sapolsky, R. M. (2002). Will we still be sad fifty years from now? In J. Brockman (Ed.), *The next fifty years: Science in the first half of the twenty-first century* (pp. 105–113). New York: Vintage.

Sargent, T. J. (1993). *Bounded rationality in macroeconomics.* Oxford: Oxford University Press.

Savage, L. J. (1972). *The foundations of statistics* (2nd ed.). New York: Dover. (Original work published 1954)

Sawyer, J. (1966). Measurement and prediction: Clinical and statistical. *Psychological Bulletin, 66,* 178–200.

Schacter, D. L., & Worling, J. R. (1985). Attribute information and the feeling-of-knowing. *Canadian Journal of Psychology, 9,* 39–54.

Schacter, S. (1982). Recidivism and self-cure of smoking and obesity. *American Psychologist, 37,* 436–444.

Schank, R. C., & Abelson, R. (1977). *Scripts, plans, goals and understanding.* Hillsdale, NJ: Erlbaum.

Scheffler, I. (1991). *In praise of cognitive emotions.* New York: Routledge.

Schlaifer, R. (1959). *Probability and statistics for business decisions.* New York: McGraw-Hill.

Schlaifer, R. (1969). *Analysis of decisions under uncertainty.* New York: McGraw-Hill.

Schoenfeld, A. (1983). Episodes and executive decisions in mathematical problem solving instruction. In H. P. Ginsberg (Ed.), *The development of mathematical thinking*, New York: Academic Press.

Schooler, J. W., & Melcher, J. (1995). The ineffability of insight. In S. M. Smith, T. B. Ward, & R. A Finke (Eds.), *The creative cognition approach* (pp. 97–133). Cambridge, MA: MIT Press.

Schneider, S. L. (1992). Framing and conflict: Aspiration level contingency, the status quo, and current theories of risky choice. *Journal of Experimental Psychology: Learning, Memory, and Cognition, 18*, 1040–1057.

Schneider, S. L. (2000). An elitist naturalistic fallacy and the automatic-controlled continuum. *Behavioral and Brain Sciences, 23*, 695–696.

Schneider, S. L., & Barnes, M. D. (2003). What do people really want? Goals and context in decision making. In S. L. Schneider & J. Shanteau (Eds.), *Emerging perspectives on judgment and decision research* (pp. 394–427).

Schopenhauer, A. (Undated). The art of controversy. In *The essays of Arthur Schopenhauer* (T. B. Saunders, Trans.). New York: Willey Book Company. (Original work published 1896)

Schrag, F. (1987). Thoughtfulness: Is high school the place for thinking? *Newsletter, National Center on Effective Secondary Schools, 2*, 2–4.

Schrag, P., & Divoky, D. (1975). *The myth of the hyperactive child*. New York: Dell.

Schrenk, L. P. (1969). Aiding the decision maker: A decision process model. *Ergonomics, 12*, 543–557.

Schubert, G. (1961). A psychometric model of the Supreme Court. *The American Behavioral Scientist, 5*(3), 14–18.

Schuler, H., & Peltzer, U. (1978). Friendly versus unfriendly nonverbal behavior: The effects on partner's decision-making preferences. In H. Brandstätter, J. H. Davis, & H. Schuler (Eds.), *Dynamics of group decisions* (pp. 113–132). London: Sage.

Schumacher, E. F. (1973). *Small is beautiful*. New York: Harper and Rowe.

Schuman, H., & Johnson, M. P. (1976). Attitudes and behavior. *Annual Review of Sociology, 40*, 161–207.

Schwartz, B. (1997). Psychology, idea technology, and ideology. *Psychological Science, 8*, 21–27.

Schwartz, B. (2004a). *The paradox of choice: Why more is less*. New York: Ecco/Harper Collins.

Schwartz, B. (2004b). The tyranny of choice. *Scientific American, 290*(4), 70–75.

Schwartz, B., & Metcalfe, J. (1992). Cue familiarity but not target retrievability enhances feeling-of-knowing judgments. *Journal of Experimental Psychology: Learnning, Memory, and Cognition, 18*, 1074–1083.

Schwartz, B., Ward, A., Monterosso, J., Lyubomirsky, S., White, K., & Lehman, D. (2002). Maximizing versus satisficing: Happiness is a matter of choice. *Journal of Personality and Social Psychology, 83*, 1178–1197.

Schwartz, E. (1971). *Overskill*. New York: Ballantine.

Schwartz, N., & Clore, G. L. (1983). Mood, misattribution, and judgments of well-being: Information and directive functions of affective states. *Journal of Personality and Social Psychology, 45*, 513–523.

Schwartz, N., & Clore, G. L. (1988). How do I feel about it? Information functions of affective states. In K. Fiedler & J. Forgas (Eds.), *Affect, cognition, and social behavior* (pp. 44–62). Toronto: Hogrefe International.

Schwartz, W. B., & Aaron, H. J. (1988). Rationing hospital care: Lessons from Britain. In J. Dowie and A. Elstein (Eds.), *Professional judgment. A reader in clinical decision making* (pp.427–435). Cambridge: Cambridge University Press. (Original work published in *The New England Journal of Medicine*, 1984, *310*, 52–56)

Schwarz, N. (1996). *Cognition and communication: Judgmental biases, research methods, and the logic of conversation.* Hillsdale, NJ: Erlbaum.

Searle, J. R. (1980). Minds, brains, and programs. *The Behavioral and Brain Science, 3*, 417–457.

Sears, D. O., & Whitney, R. E. (1973). Political persuasion. In I. deS. Pool, W. Schramm, F. W. Frey, N. Maccoby, & E. B. Parker (Eds.), *Handbook of communication* (pp. 253–289). Chicago: Rand-McNally.

Sedikides, C. (1992). Changes in the valence of the self as a function of mood. In M. S. Clark (Ed.), *Emotion and social abehavior: Review of personality and social psychology, Vol 14* (pp. 271–311). Newbury Park, CA: Sage.

Seligman, M. E. P. (1975). *Helplessness: On depression, development, and death.* San Francisco: Freeman.

Sen, A. (1983). Liberty and social choice. *Journal of Philosophy, 80*, 5–28.

Shackle, G. L. S. (1967). *Time in economics.* Amsterdam: North Holland. (Original work published 1958)

Shafir, E. (1993). Intuitions about rationality and cognition. In K. I. Manktelow & D. E. Over (Eds.), *Rationality: Psychological and philosophical perspectives* (pp. 260–283). London: Routledge.

Shafir, E., & LeBoeuf, A. (2002). Rationality. *Annual Review of Psychology, 53*, 491–517.

Shafir, E., Simonson, I., & Tversky, A. (1993). Reason-based choice. *Cognition, 49*, 11–36.

Shafir, E., & Tversky, A. (1992). Thinking through uncertainty: Nonconsequential reasoning and choice. *Cognitive Psychology, 24*, 449–474.

Shafir, E., & Tversky, A. (1995). In E. E. Smith & D. N. Osherson (Eds.), *Thinking: An Invitation to Cognitive Science, Volume 3* (2nd ed., pp. 77–100). Cambridge, MA: MIT Press.

Shafer, E. L., & Meitz, J. (1969). Aesthetic and emotional experiences rate high with northeast wilderness hikers. *Environment and Behavior, 1*, 187–197.

Shaklee, H., & Fischhoff, B. (1982). Strategies of informtion search in causal analysis. *Memory and Cognition, 10*, 520–530.

Shank, R. C., & Abelson, R. (1977). *Scripts, plans, goals, and understanding.* Hillsdale, NJ: Erlbaum.

Shannon, C. E. (1948). A mathematical theory of communication. *Bell System Technical Journal, 27*, 379–422; 623–656.

Shatz, D. (1994). The overexamined life is not worth living. In T. V. Morris (Ed.), *God and the philosophers: The reconciliation of faith and reason* (pp. 263–285). New York: Oxford University Press.

Shaw, M. E., & Reitan, H. T. (1969). Attribution of responsibility as a basis for sanctioning behavior. *British Journal of Social and Clinical Psychology, 8*, 217–226.

Sheffrin, S. M., & Triest, R. K. (1992). Can brute deterrence backfire? Perceptions and attitudes in taxpayer compliance. In J. Slemrod (Ed.), *Why people pay taxes: Tax compliance and enforcement* (pp. 193–208). Ann Arbor: University of Michigan Press.

Sherman, S. J., Zehner, K. S., Johnson, J., & Hirt, E. R. (1983). Social explanation: The role of timing, set and recall on subjective likelihood estimates. *Journal of Personality and Social Psychology, 44*, 1127–1143.

Shermer, M. (2002a). Smart people believe weird things. *Scientific American, 287*(3), 35.

Shermer, M. (2002b). *Why people believe weird things* (Rev. ed.). New York: W. H. Freeman and Company.

Shermer, M. (2003). *How we believe: Science, skepticism, and the search for God* (2nd ed.). New York: Freeman.

Sherrington, C. S. (1906). *The integrative action of the nervous system.* New York: Scribner's Sons.

Shiffrin, R. M., & Schneider, W. (1977). Controlled and automatic human information processing: II. Perceptual learning, automatic attending and a general theory. *Psychological Review, 84*, 127–190.

Shiller, R. J. (2000). *Irrational exuberance.* Princeton, NJ: Princeton University Press.

Shubik, M. (1971). The dollar auction game: A paradox in non-cooperative behavior and escalation. *Journal of Conflict Resolution, 15*, 545–547.

Siegel, H. (1988). *Educating reason.* New York: Routledge.

Siegel-Jacobs, K., & Yates, J. F. (1996). Effects of procedural and outcome accountability on judgment quality. *Organizational Behavior and Human Decision Processes, 66*, 1–17.

Sigmund, K., Fehr, E., & Nowak, M. A. (2002). The economics of fair play. *Scientific American, 286*(1), 82–87.

Simon, H. A. (1955). A behavioral model of rational choice. *Quarterly Journal of Economics, 69*, 99–118.

Simon, H. A. (1956). Rational choice and the structure of the environment. *Psychological Review, 63*, 129–138.

Simon, H. A. (1957). *Models of man: Social and rational.* New York: Wiley.

Simon, H. A. (1973). The structure of ill-structured problems. *Artificial Intelligence, 4*, 181–200.

Simon, H. A. (1983). *Reason in human affairs.* Stanford, CA: Stanford University Press.

Simon, H. A. (1990). Alternative visions of rationality. In P. K. Moser (Ed.), *Rationality in action: Contemporary approaches* (pp. 189–204). New York: Cambridge University Press. (Original work published 1983)

Simon, H. A., & Hayes, J. R. (1976). The understanding process: Problem isomorphs. *Cognitive Psychology, 8*, 165–194.

Simon, H. A., & Schaeffer, J. (1992). The game of chess. In R. J. Aumann and S. Hart (Eds.), *Handbook of game theory* (Vol. 1, pp. 1–17). Amsterdam: Elsevier.

Simonson, I., & Nye, P. (1992). The effect of accountability on susceptibility to decision errors. *Organizational Behavior and Human Decision Processes, 51*, 416–446.

Simpson, E. H. (1951). The interpretation of interaction in contingency tables. *Journal of the Royal Statistical Society, Ser B, 13*, 238–241.

Sisson, J. C., Schoomaker, E. B. & Ross, J. C. (1986). Clinical decision analysis: The hazard of using additional data. In H. R. Arkes & K. R. Hammond (Eds.), *Judgment and decision making: An interdisciplinary reader* (pp. 354–363). New York: Cambridge University Press. (Original work published 1976)

Skinner, B. F. (1946). *The behavior of organisms: An experimental analysis.* New York: Appleton-Century-Crofts.

Skinner, B. F. (1953). *Science and human behavior.* New York: Macmillan.

Skinner, B. F. (1974). *About behaviorism.* New York: Knopf.

Skyrms, B. (1996). *The evolution of the social contract.* New York: Cambridge University Press.

Sleeman, D. (1984). An attempt to understand students' understanding of basic algebra. *Cognitive Science, 8,* 387–412.

Sloman, S. A., (1996). The empirical case for two systems of reasoning. *Psychological Bulletin, 119,* 3–22.

Slovic, P. (1962). Convergent validation of risk-taking measures. *Journal of Abnormal and Social Pyschology, 65,* 68–71.

Slovic, P. (1995). The construction of preference. *American Psychologist, 50,* 364–371.

Slovic, P., Fischhoff, B., & Lichtenstein, S. (1976). Cognitive processes and societal risk taking. In J. S. Carroll & J. W. Payne (Eds.), *Cognition and social behavior* (pp. 165–184). Hillsdale, NJ: Erlbaum.

Slovic, P., Fischhoff, B., & Lichtenstein, S. (1977). Behavioral decision theory. *Annual Review of Psychology, 28,* 1–39.

Slovic, P. & Lichtenstein, S. (1968). Relative importance of probabilities and payoffs in risk taking. *Journal of Experimental Psychology, 78* (Monograph 3, Part 2), 1–17.

Slovic, P., & Lichtenstein, S. (1971). Comparison of Bayesian and regression approaches to the study of information processing in judgment. *Organizational Behavior and Human Performance, 6,* 649–744.

Slovic, P., Monahan, J., & MacGregor, D. G. (2000). Violence risk assessment and risk communication: The effects of using actual cases, providing instructions, and employing probability vs. frequency formats. *Law and Human Behavior, 24,* 271–296.

Slovic, P., & Tversky, A. (1974). Who accepts Savage's axiom? *Behavioral Science, 19,* 368–373.

Slusher, M. P., & Anderson, C. A. (1987). When reality monitoring fails: The role of imagination in stereotype maintenance. *Journal of Personality and Social Psychology, 52,* 653–662.

Smedslund, J. (1970). On the circular relation between logic and understanding. *Scandinavian Journal of Psychology, 11,* 217–219.

Smedslund, J. (1981). Rationality is a necessary presupposition in psychology. Commentary on Cohen, 1981. *The Behavioral and Brain Sciences, 4,* 352.

Smith, J. M. (1982). *Evolution and the theory of games.* New York: Cambridge University Press.

Smith, J., Dixon, R. A., & Baltes, P. B. (1989). Expertise in life planning: A new research approach to investigating aspects of wisdom. In M. L. Commons, J. D. Sinnott, F. A. Richards, & C. Armon (Eds.), *Beyond formal operations II: Comparisons and applications of adolescent and adult developmental models*. New York: Praeger.

Smith, V. L., & Clark, H. H. (1993). On the course of answering questions. *Journal of Memory and Language, 32*, 25–38.

Smith, W. (1992). The universe is ultimately to be explained in terms of a metacosmic reality. In H. Margenau & R. A. Varghese (Eds.), *Cosmos, bios, theos: Scientists reflect on science, God, and the origins of the universe, life, and Homo Sapiens* (pp. 111–118). Chicago: Open Court.

Smolin, L. (2002). The future of the nature of the universe. In J. Brockman (Ed.), *The next fifty years: Science in the first half of the twenty-first century* (pp. 3–17). New York: Vintage.

Sniderman, P. M., Brody, R. A., & Tetlock, P. E. (1991). *Reasoning and choice: Explorations in political psychology*. New York: Cambridge University Press.

Snyder, C. R., & Higgins, R. L. (1988). Excuses: Their effective role in the negotiation of reality. *Psychological Bulletin, 104*, 23–35.

Snyder, M. L., & Jones, E. E. (1974). Attitude attribution when behavior is constrained. *Journal of Experimental Social Psychology, 10*, 585–600.

Snyder, M. L., Stephan, W. G., & Rosenfield, C. (1978). Attributional egotism. In J. H. Harvey, W. J. Ickes, & R. F. Kidd (Eds.), *New directions in attribution research*, (Vol. 2, pp. 91–120). Hillsdale, NJ: Erlbaum.

Snyder, M., & Swann, W. B. (1978). Behavioral confirmation in social interaction: From social perception to social reality. *Journal of Experimental Social Psychology, 14*, 148–162.

Soelberg, P. O. (1967). Unprogrammed decision making. *Industrial Management Review, 8*, 19–29.

Sokal, A., & Bricmont, J. (1998). *Fashionable nonsense: Postmodern intellectuals' abuse of science*. New York: Picador USA.

Sosis, R. (1974). Internal-external control and the perception of responsibility of another for an accident. *Journal of Personality and Social Psychology, 30*, 393–399.

Sowell, T. (1995). *The vision of the anointed: Self-congratulation as a basis for social policy*. New York: Basic Books.

Sowell, T. (2004). *Basic economics: A citizen's guide to the economy*. New York: Basic Books.

Sperry, R.W. (1995). The impact and promise of the cognitive revolution. In R. L. Solso & D. W. Massaro (Eds.), *The science of the mind: 2001 and beyond* (pp. 35–49). New York: Oxford University Press.

Spinoza, B. (1947). The foundations of the moral life. In S. Commins & R. N. Linscott (Eds.), *Man and spirit: The speculative philosophers* (pp. 171–195). New York: Random House. (Original publication date undetermined)

Spranca, M., Minsk, E., & Baron, J. (1991). Omission and commission in judgment and choice. *Journal of Experimental Social Psychology, 27*, 76–105.

Sprent, P. (1988). *Taking risks: The science of uncertainty*. New York: Viking Penguin.

Stanovich, K. E. (1994a). Reconceptualizing intelligence: Dysrationalia as an intuition pump. *Educational Researcher, 23*, 11–22.
Stanovich, K. E. (1994b). The evolving concept of rationality: A rejoinder to Sternberg. *Educational Researcher, 23*, 33.
Stanovich, K. E. (1999). *Who is rational? Studies of individual differences in reasoning.* Mahwah, NJ: Erlbaum.
Stanovich, K. E., & West, R. F. (1997). Reasoning independently of prior belief and individual differences in actively open-minded thinking. *Journal of Educational Psychology, 89*, 342–357.
Stanovich, K. E., & West, R. F. (1998a). Cognitive ability and variation in selection task performance. *Thinking and Reasoning, 4*, 193–230.
Stanovich, K. E., & West, R. F. (1998b). Individual differences in framing and conjunction effects. *Thinking and Reasoning, 4*, 289–317.
Stanovich, K. E., & West, R. F. (1998c). Individual differences in rational thought. *Journal of Experimental Psychology: General, 127*, 161–188.
Stanovich, K. E., & West, R. F. (1998d). Who uses base rates and P(D|-H)? An analysis of individual differences. *Memory and Cognition, 28*, 161–179.
Stanovich, K. E., & West, R. F. (2000a). Authors' response. *Beharioral and Brain Sciences, 23*, 701–726.
Stanovich, K. E., & West, R. F. (2000b). Individual differences in reasoning: Implications for the rationality debate? *Behavioral and Brain Sciences, 23*, 645–665.
Stasser, G. (1988). Computer simulation as a research tool: The DISCUSS model of group decision making. *Journal of Experimental Social Psychology, 24*, 393–422.
Stasser, G. (1999). The uncertain role of unshared information in collective choice. In L. L. Thompson, J. Levine, & D. Messick (Eds.), *Shared knowledge in organizations: The management of knowledge* (pp. 49–69). Mahwah, NJ: Erlbaum.
Stasser, G., & Titus, W. (1985). Pooling of unshared information in group decision making: Biased information sampling during discussion. *Journal of Personality and Social Psychology, 48*, 1467–1478.
Staw, B. M. (1976). Knee-deep in the Big Muddy: A study of escalating commitment to a chosen course of action. *Organizational Behavior and Human Performance, 16*, 27–44.
Staw, B. M., & Ross, J. (1989). Understanding behavior in escalating situations. *Science, 246*, 216–220.
Stein, E. (1996). *Without good reason: The rationality debate in philosophy and cognitive science.* Oxford: Oxford University Press.
Steiner, M., (1978). Mathematical explanation. *Philosophical Studies, 34*, 135–151.
Stephenson, G. M. (1978). Interparty and interpersonal exchange in negotiation groups. In H. Brandstätter, J. H. Davis, & H. Schuler (Eds.), *Dynamics of group decisions* (pp. 207–228). London: Sage.
Sterman, J. D. (1994). Learning in and about complex systems. *System Dynamics Review, 10*, 291–330.
Stern, S., & Kipnis, D. (1993). Technology in everyday life and perceptions of competency. *Journal of Applied Social Psychology, 23*, 1892–1902.

Sternberg, R. J. (1981). Intelligence as thinking and learning skills. *Educational Leadership, 39*, 28–20.
Sternberg, R. J. (1985). Implicit theories of intelligence, creativity, and wisdom. Journal of *Personality and Social Psychology, 49*, 607–627.
Sternberg, R. J. (1987). Implicit theories: An alternative to modeling cognition and its development. In J. Bisanz, C. Brainerd, R. Kail (Eds.), *Formal models in developmental psychology* (pp. 155–192). New York: Springer-Verlag.
Sternberg, R. J. (1988). Mental self-government: A theory of intellectual styles and their development. *Human Development, 31*, 197–224.
Sternberg, R. J. (1989). Domain-generality versus domain specificity: The life and impending death of a false dichotomy. *Merrill-Palmer Quarterly, 35*, 115–130.
Sternberg, R. J. (1990a). Wisdom and its relations to intelligence and creativity. In R. J. Sternberg (Ed.), *Wisdom: Its nature, origins, and development* (pp. 142–159). New York: Cambridge University Press.
Sternberg, R. J. (Ed.) (1990b). *Wisdom: Its nature, origins, and development*. New York: Cambridge University Press.
Sternberg, R. J. (1994). What if the construct of dysrationalia were an example of itself? *Educational Researcher, 23*, 22–23, 27.
Sternberg, R. J. (2000). The ability is not general and neither are the conclusions. *Behaviroal and Brain Sciences, 23*, 697–698.
Sternberg, R. J., Conway, B., Kenton, J., & Bernstein, M. (1981). People's conceptions of intelligence. *Journal of Personality and Social Psychology, 41*, 37–55.
Sternberg, R. J., & Wagner, R. K. (Eds.) (1986). *Practical intelligence*. Cambridge: Cambridge University Press.
Stevens, A. L., & Collins, A. (1977). The goal structure of a Socratic tutor. *Proceedings of the Association for Computing Machinery Annual Conference*, Seattle, WA.
Stevens, A. L., & Collins, A. (1980). Multiple conceptual model of a complex system. In R. E. Snow, P. A. Federico, & W. E. Montague (Eds.), *Aptitude, learning, and instruction, 2*, Hillsdale, NJ: Erlbaum.
Stevens, P. K. (1974). *Patterns in nature*. Boston, MA: Little, Brown and Company.
Stevenson. H. W., Chen, C., & Lee, S-Y. (1993). Mathematics achievement of Chinese, Japanese, and American children: Ten years later. *Science, 259*, 53–58.
Stewart, A. L., & Brook, R. H. (1983). Effect of being overweight. *American Journal of Public Health, 73*, 171–178.
Stich, S. P. (1985). Could man be an irrational animal? Some notes on the epistemology of rationality. *Synthese, 64*, 115–135.
Stich, S. P. (1990). *The fragmentation of reason*. Cambridge, MA: MIT Press.
Stigler, G.L. (1961). The economics of information. *The Journal of Political Economy, 69*, 213–225.
Stigler, J. W., & Baranes, R. (1988). Culture and mathematics learning. In E. Z. Rothkopf (Ed.), *Review of Research in Education* (Vol. 15, pp. 253–306). Washington, DC: American Educational Research Association.
Stove, D. C. (1986). *The rationality of induction*. Oxford: Clarendon Press.
Strada, G. (1996). The horror of land mines. *Scientific American, 274*(5), 40–45.

Strathern, P. (2000). *Mendeleyev's dream: The quest for the elements.* New York: Berkley Books.

Streufert, S., & Streufert, S. C. (1969). Effects of conceptual structure, failure, and success on attribution of causality and interpersonal attitudes. *Journal of Personality and Social Psychology, 11,* 138–147.

Suengas, A. G., & Johnson, M. K. (1988). Qaulitative effects of rehearsal on memories for perceived and imagined complex events. *Journal of Experimental Psychology: General, 117,* 377–389.

Suls, J. M., & Gutkin, D. C. (1976). Children's reactions to an actor as a function of expectations and of the consequences received. *Journal of Personality, 44,* 149–162.

Sunstein, C. (2003). *Why societies need dissent.* Cambridge, MA: Harvard University Press.

Sundstrom, E., Lounsbury, J. W., DeVault, R. C., & Peele, E. (1981). Acceptance of a nuclear power plant: Applications of the expectancy-value model. In A. Baum & J. E. Singer (Eds.), *Advances in environmental psychology, Vol. 3: Energy conservation: Psychological perspectives* (pp. 171–189). Hillsdale, NJ: Erlbaum.

Svenson, O. (1992). Differentiation and consolidation theory of human decision making: A frame of reference for the study of pre- and postdecision processes. *Acta Psychologica, 80,* 143–168.

Svenson, O. (1999). Differention and consolidation theory: Decision making processes before and after a choice. In P. Juslin & H. Montgomery (Eds.), *Judgment and decision making: Neo-Brunswikian and process-tracing approaches* (pp. 175–197). Mahwah, NJ: Erlbaum.

Svenson, O. (2003). Values, affect, and processes in human decision making: A differentiation and consolidation theory perspective. In S. L. Schneider & J. Shanteau (Eds.), *Emerging perspectives on judgment and decision research* (pp. 287–326). Cambridge: Cambridge University Press.

Swann, W. B., & Snyder, M. (1980) On translating beliefs into action: Theories of ability and their application in an instructional setting. *Journal of Personality and Social Psychology, 6,* 879–888.

Swets, J. A. (1988). Measuring the accuracy of diagnostic systems. *Science, 240,* 1285–1293.

Swets, J. A., Dawes, R. M., & Monahan, J. (2000a). Better decisions through science. *Scientific American, 283*(4), 82–87.

Swets, J. A., Dawes, R. M., & Monahan, J. (2000b). Psychological science can improve diagnostic decisions. *Psychological Science in the Public Interest, 1,* 1–26.

Swets, J. A., & Pickett, R. M. (1982). *Evaluation of diagnostic systems: Methods from signal detection theory.* New York: Adademic Press.

Swets, J. A., Pickett, R. M., Whitehead, S. F., Getty, D. J., Schnur, J. A., Swets, J. B., & Freeman, B. A. (1979). Assessment of diagnostic technologies. *Science, 205,* 753–759.

Swinburne, R. (1983). *Faith and reason.* New York: Oxford University Press.

Swinburne, R. (1996). *Is there a God?* New York: Oxford University Press.

Taleb, N. N. (2004). *Fooled by randomness: The hidden role of chance in life and in the markets* (2nd ed.). New York: Texere.

Tanner, W. P. Jr., & Swets, J. A. (1954). A decision-making theory of visual detection. *Psychological Review, 61,* 401–409.
Taranto, M. A. (1989). Facets of wisdom: A theoretical synthesis. *International Journal of Aging and Human Development, 29,* 1–21.
Taylor, S. E. (1981). The interface of cognitive and social psychology. In J. H. Harvey, (Ed.), *Cognition, social behavior, and the environment.* Hillsdale, NJ: Erlbaum.
Taylor, S. E., & Fiske, S. T. (1975). Point of view and perceptions of causality. *Journal of Personality and Social Psychology, 32,* 439–445.
Taylor, S. E., & Fiske, S. T. (1978). Salience, attention and attribution: Top of the head phenomena. In L. Berkowitz (Ed.), *Advances in Experimental Social Psychology* (Vol. 11). New York: Academic Press.
Taylor, S. E., Fiske, S. T., Close, M., Anderson, C. P., & Ruderman, A. (1979). *Solo status as a psychological variable: The power of being distinctive.* Unpublished manuscript, Harvard University.
Tegmark, M., & Wheeler, J. A. (2001). 100 years of quantum mysteries. *Scientific American, 284*(2), 68–75.
Tesser, A. (1986). Some effects of self-evaluation maintenance on cognition and action. In R. M. Sorrentino & E. T. Higgins (Eds.), *The handbook of motivation and cognition: Foundations of social behavior* (pp. 435–464). New York: Guilford Press.
Tesser, A., & Campbell, J. (1983). Self-definition and self-evaluation maintenance. In J. Suls & A. Greenwald (Eds.), *Social psychological perspectives on the self* (Vol. 2, 11. 1–31). Hillsdale, NJ: Erlbaum.
Tetlock, P. E. (1983). Accountability and the perseverance of first impressions. *Social Psychology Quarterly, 46,* 285–292.
Tetlock, P. E. (1985). Accountability: A social check on the fundamental attribution error. *Social Psychology Quarterly, 48,* 227–236.
Tetlock, P. E., & Boettger, R. (1989). Accountability: A social magnifier of the dilution effect. *Journal of Personality and Social Psychology, 57,* 388–398.
Tetlock, P. E., & Kim, J. I. (1987). Accountability and judgment processes in a personality prediction task. *Journal of Personality and Social Psychology, 52,* 700–709.
Tetlock, P. E., Skitka, L., & Boettger, R. (1989). Social and cognitive strategies for coping with accountability: Conformity, complexity, and bolstering. *Journal of Personality and Social Psychology, 57,* 632–640.
Thagard, P. (1989). Explanatory coherence. *Behavioral and Brain Sciences, 12,* 435–502.
Thaler, R. (1980). Toward a positive theory of consumer choice. *Journal of Economic Behavior and Organization, 1,* 39–60.
Thaler, R. (1985). Mental accounting and consumer choice. *Marketing Science, 4,* 199–214.
Thomas, L. (1979). *The medusa and the snail: More notes of a biology watcher.* New York: Viking Press.
Thomas, L. (July, 1981). Debating the unknowable. *The Atlantic Monthly,* pp. 49–50.
Thompson, D'Arcy (1961). *On growth and form.* New York: Cambridge University Press. (Original work published 1917)

Thouless, R. H. (1947). *How to think straight*. New York: Simon and Schuster.
Thrall, R. M., Coombs, C. H., & Davis, R. L. (1954). *Decision processes*. New York: Wiley.
Tishman, S., Jay, E., & Perkins, D. N. (1993). Teaching thinking dispositions: From transmission to enculturation. *Theory into practice, 32*, 147–153.
Toda, M. (1980). Emotion and decision-making. *Acta Psychologica, 45*, 133–155.
Todd, P. M., & Gigerenzer, G. (1999). What we have learned so far. In G. Gigerenzer & P. M. Todd (Eds.), *Simple heuristics that make us smart* (pp. 357–365). New York: Oxford University Press.
Todd, P. M., & Gigerenzer, G. (2003). Bounding rationality to the world. *Journal of Economic Psychology, 24*, 143–165.
Torgeson, J. K., & Licht, B. G. (1983). The LD child as an inactive learner: Retrospects and prospects. In K. D. Gadow & I. Bialer (Eds.), *Advances in learning and behavioral disabilities*. Greenwich, CT: JAI Press.
Toulmin, S. E. (1958). *The uses of argument*. Cambridge University Press.
Trichopoulos, D., Li, F. P., & Hunter, D. J. (1996). What causes cancer? *Scientific American, 275*(3), 80–87.
Trope, Y., & Bassock, M. (1982). Confirmatory and diagnosing strategies in social information gathering. *Journal of Personality and Social Psychology, 43*, 22–34.
Trope, Y., & Bassock, M. (1983). Information-gathering strategies in hypothesis-testing. *Journal of Experimental Social Psychology, 19*, 560–576.
Trope, Y., & Mackie, D. M. (1987). Sensitivity to alternatives in social hypothesis-testing. *Journal of Experimenal Social Psychology, 23*, 445–459.
Troutman, C. M., & Shanteau, J. (1977). Inferences based on nondiagnostic information. *Organizational Behavior and Human Performance, 19*, 43–55.
Trowbridge, D. E., & McDermott, L. C. (1980). Investigation of student understanding of the concept of velocity in one dimension. *American Journal of Physics, 48*, 1020–1028.
Trowbridge, D. E., & McDermott, L. C. (1981). Investigation of student understanding of the concept of acceleration in one dimension. *American Journal of Physics, 49*, 242–253.
Tuchman, B. W. (1984). *The march of folly: From Troy to Vietnam*. New York: Ballantine Books.
Tucker, J. A., Vuchinich, R. E., & Sobell, M. B. (1981). Alcohol consumption as a self-handicapping strategy. *Journal of Abnormal Psychology, 90*, 220–230.
Turnbull, H. W. (1956). The great mathematicians. In J. R. Newman (Ed.), *The world of mathematics* (Vol. 1, pp. 75–168). New York: Simon and Schuster. (Original work published 1929)
Tversky, A. (1969). Intransitivity of preferences. *Psychological Review, 76*, 31–48.
Tversky, A. (1981). L. J. Cohen, again: On the evaluation of inductive intuitions. Commentary on Cohen, 1981. *The Behavioral and Brain Sciences, 4*, 354–356.
Tversky, A., & Kahneman, D. (1974). Judgment under uncertainty: Heuristics and Biases. *Science, 185*, 1124–1131.
Tversky, A., & Kahneman, D. (1981). The framing of decisions and the psychology of choice. *Science, 211*, 453–458.

Tversky, A., & Shafir, E. (1992a). The disjunction effect in choice under uncertainty. *Psychological Science, 3,* 305–309.

Tversky, A., & Shafir, E. (1992b). Choice under conflict: The dynamics of deferred decision. *Psychological Science, 3,* 358–361.

Tversky, A., & Simonson, I. (1993). Context-dependent preferences. *Management Science, 39,* 1179–1189.

Tweney, R. D., Doherty, M. E., Worner, W. J., Pliske, D. B., Mynatt, C. R., Gross, K. A., & Arkkelin, D. L. (1980). Strategies of rule discovery in an inference task. *Quarterly Journal of Experimental Psychology, 32,* 109–123.

Urmson, J. O. (1974). Some questions concerning validity. In R. Swinburne (Ed.), *The justification of induction* (pp. 74-84). London: Oxford University Press. (Original work published 1953)

Utall, W. R. (1998). *Toward a new behaviorism: The case against perceptual reductionism.* Mahwah, NJ: Erlbaum.

Utall, W. R. (2000). *The war between mentalism and behaviorism: On the accessibility of mental processes.* Mahwah, NJ: Erlbaum.

Utall, W. R. (2001). *The new phrenology: The limits of localizing cognitive processes in the brain.* Cambridge: Cambridge University Press.

Utall, W. R. (2003). *Psychomythics: Sources of artifacts and misconceptions in scientific psychology.* Mahwah, NJ: Erlbaum.

Valins, S. (1974). Persistent effects of information about internal: Ineffectiveness of debriefing. In H. London & R. E. Nisbett (Eds.), *Thought and feeling Cognitive modification of feeling states* (pp. 116–124). Chicago: Aldine.

Van den Bos, E., & Jeannerod, M. (2002). Sense of body and sense of action both contribute to self recognition. *Cognition, 85,* 177–187.

Van Inwagen, P. (1994). Quam dilecta. In T. V. Morris (Ed.), *God and the philosophers: The reconciliation of faith and reason* (pp. 31–60). New York: Oxford University Press.

Verhagen, J. (1978). Expertness, participation, co-orientation, and social influence. In H. Brandstätter, J. H. Davis, & H. Schuler (Eds.), *Dynamics of group decisions* (pp. 155–168). London: Sage.

Vinokur, A. (1971). Review and theoretical analysis of the effects of group processes upon individual and group decisions involving risk. *Psychological Bulletin, 76,* 231–250.

Von Bertalanffy, L. (1967). *Robots, men and minds: Psychology in the modern world.* New York: George Brazilier.

Von Neumann, J., & Morgenstern, D. (1953). *The theory of games and economic behavior* (3rd. ed.). New York: John Wiley. (Original work published 1944)

Von Rosenstiel, L., & Stocker-Kreichgauer, G. (1978). Vicarious social reinforcement. In H. Brandstätter, J. H. Davis, & H. Schuler (Eds.), *Dynamics of group decisions* (pp. 133–148). London: Sage.

Von Winterfeldt, D., & Edwards, W. (1986). *Decision analysis and behavioral research.* Cambridge: Cambridge University Press.

Voss, J. F, Perkins, D. N., & Segal, J. W. (Eds.) (1991). *Informal reasoning and education.* Hillsdale, NJ: Erlbaum.

Voss, J. F., Vesonder, G., & Spilich, G. (1980). Text generation and recall by high-knowledge and low-knowledge individuals. *Journal of Verbal Learning and Verbal Behavior, 19,* 651–667.

Wade, T. C. & Baker, T. B. (1977). Opinions and use of psychological test. *American Psychologist, 32,* 874–882.

Wagenaar, W. A., Keren, G. B., Lichtenstein, S. (1988). Islanders and hostages: Deep and surface structures of decision problems. *Acta Psychologica, 67,* 175–189.

Wagenaar, W. A., Keren, G. B., & Pleit-Kuiper, A. (1984). The multiple objectives of gamblers. *Acta Psychologica, 56,* 167–178.

Wagner, R. K., & Sternberg, R. J. (1985). Practical intelligence in real-world pursuits: The role of tacit knowledge. *Journal of Personality and Social Psychology, 49,* 436–458.

Wagner, R. K., & Sternberg, R. J. (1986). Tacit knowledge and intelligence in the everyday world. In R. J. Sternberg & R. K. Wagner (Eds.), *Practical intelligence* (pp. 51–83). Cambridge: Cambridge University Press.

Wainer, H. (1976). Estimating coefficients in linear models: It don't make no nevermind. *Psychological Bulletin, 83,* 312–317.

Wald, A. (1947). *Sequential analysis.* New York: Wiley.

Wald, A. (1950). *Statistical decision functions.* New York: Wiley.

Wallace, D. F. (2003). *Everything and more: A compact history of ∞.* New York: W. W. Norton.

Wallach, M. A., & Kogan, N. (1965). The roles of information, discussion, and consensus in group risk taking. *Journal of Experimental Social Psychology, 1,* 1–19.

Wallach, M. A., Kogan, N., & Bem, D. J. (1962). Group influence on individual risk taking. *Journal of Personality and Social Psychology, 65,* 75–86.

Wallechinsky, D., Wallace, I., & Walace, A. (1977). *The book of lists.* New York: William Morrow.

Wallsten, T. S. (1978). *Three biases in the cognitive processing of diagnostic information.* Unpublished paper. Psychometric Laboratory, Chapel Hill: University of North Carolina.

Wallsten, T. S., & Budescu, D. V. (1983). Encoding subjective probabilities: A psychological and psycbometric review. *Management Science, 29,* 152–173.

Ward, K. (1996). *God, chance and necessity.* Oxford: Oneworld.

Wason, P. C. (1960). On the failure to eliminate hypotheses in a conceptual task. *Quarterly Journal of Experimental Psychology, 12,* 129–140.

Wason, P. C. (1966). Reasoning. In B. M. Foss (Ed.), *New horizons in psychology.* Hammondsworth: Penguin.

Wason, P. C. (1968). Reasoning about a rule. *Quarterly Journal of Experimental Psychology, 12,* 129–140.

Wason, P. C., & Evans, J. St. B. T. (1975). Dual processes in reasoning. *Cognition, 3,* 141–154.

Wason, P. C., & Golding, E. (1974). The language of inconsistency. *British Journal of Psychology, 65,* 537–546.

Wason, P. C., & Johnson-Laird, P. N. (1972). *Psychology of reasoning: Structure and content.* Cambridge, MA: Harvard University Press.

Watson, J. B. (1914). *Behavior: An introduction to comparative psychology.* New York: Holt.

Watson, J. B. (1919). *Psychology from the standpoint of a behaviorist.* Philadelphia: Lippincott.

Watson, J. B. (1925). *Behaviorism.* New York: The People's Institute.
Watson, S. R., & Brown, R. V. (1975). *Issues in the value of decision analysis.* McLean, VA: Decisions and Designs. (DDI Tech. Report, 75-10)
Watson, S. R., & Buede, D. M. (1987). *Decision synthesis: The principles and practice of decision analysis.* New York: Cambridge University Press.
Watts, D. (2003). *Six degrees.* New York: Norton.
Wedding, D. (1983). Clinical and statistical prediction in neuropsychology. *Clinical Neuropsychology, 5,* 49–55.
Wegner, D. M., & Bargh, J. A. (1998). Control and automaticity in social life. In D. Gilbert, S. Fiske, & G. Lindzey (Eds.), *Handbook of social psychology* (4th ed., pp. 446–496). New York: McGraw-Hill.
Wegton, R. S., Hoellerich, V. L., & Patil, K. D. (1986). How physicians use clinical information in diagnosing pulmonary embolism: An application of conjoint analysis. *Medical Decision Making, 6,* 2–11.
Weinberg, S. (1994). Life in the universe. *Scientific American, 271*(4), 44–49.
Weiner, B. (1985). An attributional theory of achievement motivation and emotion. *Psychological Review, 92,* 548–573.
Weiner, B., Frieze, I., Kukla, A., Reed, L., Rest, S., Rosenbaum, R. M. (1972). Perceiving the causes of success and failure. In E. E. Jones et al. (Eds.), *Attribution: Perceiving the causes of behavior.* Morristown, NJ: General Learning Press.
Weiner, B., & Kukla, A. (1974). An attributional analysis of achievement motivation. *Journal of Personality and Social Psychology, 15,* 1–20.
Welch, I. (1992). Sequential sales, learning and cascades. *Journal of Finance, 47,* 695-732.
Weisskopf, V. F. (1977). The frontiers and limits of science. *American Scientist, 65,* 405–411.
Weissmann, G. (1996). Ecosentimentalism: The summer dream beneath the tamarind tree. In P. R. Gross, N. Levitt, & M. W. Lewis (Eds.), *The flight from reason* (pp. 483–489). New York: The New York Academy of Sciences.
Wendt, P. F. (1965). Current growth stock valuation methods. *Financial Analysts Journal, 21,* 91–103.
Westen, D., & Weinberger, J. (2004). When clinical description becomes statistical prediction. *American Psychologist, 59,* 595–613.
Wheeler, M. (1976). *Lies, damn lies, and statistics: The manipulation of public opinion in America.* New York: Dell.
Whimbey, A. (1975). *Intelligence can be taught.* New York: E. P. Dutton.
White, P. (1984). A model of the layperson as pragmatist. *Personality and Social Psychology Bulletin, 10,* 333–348.
Willard, C. A. (1995). Failures of relevance: A rhetorical view. In H. V. Hansen & R. C. Pinto (Eds.), *Fallacies: Classical and contemporary readings* (pp. 145–158). University Park: The Pennsylvania State University Press.
Williams, B. (1985). *Ethics and the limits of philosophy.* Cambridge, MA: Harvard University Press.
Wilson, E. O. (1978). *On human nature.* Cambridge, MA: Harvard University Press.
Wilson, E. O. (1999). *Consilience: The unity of knowledge.* New York: Vintage Books.

Wilson, T. D., & Nisbett, R. E. (1978). The accuracy of verbal reports about the effects of stimuli on evaluations and behavior. *Social Psychology, 41,* 118–131.

Wilson, T. D., & Schooler, J. W. (1991). Thinking too much: Introspection can reduce the quality of preferences and decisions. *Journal of Personality and Social Psychology, 60,* 181–192.

Winkler, R. L. (1972). Comment. *Journal of the American Statistical Associaton, 67,* 376–378.

Wittgenstein, L. (1972). *On certainty.* Edited by G. E. M. Anscombe & G. H. von Wright, translated by D. Paul & G. E. M. Anscombe. New York: Harper Torchbooks. (Original work published circa 1950)

Wolf, F. M. (1983). Increasing the use of the competing hypotheses heuristic in clinical decision-making. In Herschmen, A. (Ed.), *Abstracts of papers of the 149th national meeting* (p. 127). Washington, DC: American Association for the Advancement of Science.

Wolf, F. M., Gruppen, L. D., & Billi, J. E. (1985). Differential diagnosis and the competing-hypotheses heuristic: A practical approach to judgment under uncertainty and Bayesian probability. *Journal of the American Medical Association, 243,* 2858–2862.

Wood, J. M., Garb, H. N., Lilienfeld, S. O., & Nezworski, M. T. (2002). Clinical assessment. *Annual Review of Psychology, 53,* 519-543.

Woodward, J., & Howard, L. (1994). The misconceptions of youth: Errors and their mathematical meaning. *Exceptional Children, 61,* 126–136.

Woodworth, R. S., & Schlosberg, H. (1956). *Experimental Psychology.* New York: Henry Holt and Company.

Wright, P. (1974). The harrassed decision maker: Time pressures, distractions and the use of evidence. *Journal of Applied Psychology, 59,* 555-561.

Wright, R. H. (2005). Attention deficit hyperactivity disorder: What it is and what it is not. In R. H. Wright & N. A. Cummings (Eds.), *Destructive trends in mental health: The well-intentioned path to harm* (pp. 128–141). New York: Routledge.

Yamagishi, K. (1997). When a 12.86% mortality is more dangerous than 24.14%: Implications for risk communication. *Applied Cognitive Psychology, 11,* 495–506.

Yaniv, I., & Meyer, D. E. (1987). Activation and metacognition of inaccessible stored information: Potential bases for incubation effects in problem solving. *Journal of Experimental Psychology: Learning, Memory, and Cognition, 13,* 187–205.

Young, J. Z. (1978). *Programs of the brain.* London: Oxford University Press.

Young, R. M., & O'Shea, T. (1981). Errors in children's subtraction. *Cognitive Science, 5,* 153–177.

Zajonc, R. B. (1980). Feeling and thinking: Preferences need no inferences. *American Psychologist, 35,* 151–175.

Zillman, D. (1979). *Hostility and aggression.* Hillsdale, NJ: Erlbaum.

Ziman, J. (1978). *Reliable knowledge.* Cambridge: Cambridge University Press.

Zsambok, C. E., & Klein, G. (Eds.) (1997). *Naturalistic decision making.* Mahwah, NJ: Erlbaum.

Zuckerman, M., Mann, R.W., & Bernieri, F. (1982). Determinants of consensus estimates: Attribution, salience, and representativeness. *Journal of Personality and Social Psychology, 42,* 831–852.

Zukav, G. (1979). *The dancing Wu Li masters.* New York: Bantam Books.

INDEX

A
Abstract problems, 47–48
Accountability
  decision evaluation, 313–314
  decision quality, 313–314
  intellectual, 412
  in reasoning, 412
Acquisition of information, 359–361
  active nature of search, 410
  cost of information, 359–360, 361
  curtailment, 26, 360–361
  diminishing returns over time, 360
Actor–observer bias, 244
Adaptability, 28–32
  intelligence, relationship, 72
Adaptive-sense rationality, 33
Affect, 196–207
  positive, 202–203
Affect heuristic, 291
Age, wisdom, 352–354
Ambiguity, intolerance for, 209
Analogies, explanations, 232
Analytic assertions, 134–135
Analytic epistemology, 39–40
Application, errors of, 399
Attitudes, 201–203
  wonderment, 206
Attractiveness, 302–303
Attribution bias, 243–244
Attribution theory, 234–235
Axiomatic approach, 66
  intuition, 404–405

B
Balance, 411
  wisdom, 345–346
Bayesian diagnosis, 283–284
Bayes's rule, 159
  revising prior probabilities to account for new data, 159
Beauty
  enjoyable *vs.* admirable beauty, 204
  subjective quality, 204
Behavior
  behaving by rule, 10–12
  consistency, 54–56
  cultural effects, 378–379
Beliefs
  about one's own knowledge, 122
  alternative views, 127–128
  as causal factors in thinking, 121–123
  characteristics, 114
  children, 122
  clusters, 52
  compartmentalized, 53
  consistency, 12, 65, 137–138
    internal consistency, 52–54, 161–162
    local consistency, 52
    logical consistency, 140
    mutually inconsistent, 12
  credal residues, 160
  cultural effects, 378–379
  deductively closed, 114

489

Beliefs (*continued*)
  defined, 113–114
  degrees of, 116–119
  derivation of, 119–121
  desirability, 137–138
  direct experience, 119
  dispositional, 114–115
  disposition to search for inconsistencies, 76
  evidence, 59–60, 124, 150
    active fairmindedness, 141–143
    cost of information, 141–143
    strength of, 116–117, 118–119
  explanations, relationship, 232–233
  explicit, 114–116
  extreme, 166–173
  formation, 124–125
  freedom, 150–151
  general principle of clutter avoidance, 54
  of groups, 163–164
  historical aspects, 167–169
  implicit, 114–116
  information cascades, 161–162
  internally consistent, 52–54, 115–116
  intuition, 119
  judging one's own, 131–134
    consideration of alternatives, 132–133
    difficulties, 134
    external criticism, 133–134
    guidelines, 133
  judging rationality of, 128–134
  justification of, 123–151
    by argument, 138–140
    by being well-grounded, 132
    criteria, 134–140
    by experience, 153
    limit, 140
    by logical consistency, 135–137, 140
    by reason alone, 153
    subjective matter, 140–141
    by truth, 130–131
    by utility, 137–138
  knowledge
    justified beliefs, 81
    relationship, 81–83
    truth, 82
  logic, justification, 135–137, 140
  mutually inconsistent, 12, 118
  natural selection, 130–131
  nature of, 113–123
  networks, 162–163
  over time, 65
  peer influence, 164–166
  persistence of, 152–156
    confirmation bias, 154–155
    information processing limitations of human beings, 155
    reasons for, 152–156
  perspective, 202
  preferences, 147–151
  propagation of, 160–166
  rational, 173–174
  revision of, 151–160
    Bayes's rule, 159
    coherence theory, 156–157
    foundations theory, 156–157
    Harman on, 156–160
    principle of conservatism, 158
    principle of negative undermining, 157–158
    principle of positive undermining, 157–158
    science, 159–160
    single counterindicative bit of data, 152–153
  truth, 62
  utility, 120–121, 149
  will to believe (or not), 147–151
Beneffectance, 245
Bias, 27–28, 146–147, 271, 411–412
  actor–observer bias, 244
  attribution bias, 243–244
  confirmation bias, 122–123, 154–155
  contraction bias, 271
  fundamental attribution error, 243–244, 247
  hindsight bias, 94

intelligence, 76
intentional criterial biases, 277–279
judicious, 411–412
outcome bias, 309
status-quo bias, 265
Biological sciences, reductionism, 219
emergence view, 219
Biotechnology, values, 186
Bounded rationality, 358–361
criticism, 358
Brain, 221
brain-in-the-vat image, 96
evolution, 193

C

Case-based reasoning, 103
Causality, 234–237, *see also* Explanations
causal decoupling, 220
causal *vs.* statistical explanation distinguished, 235–236
contributing cause, 273
necessary cause, 273
sufficient cause, 273
Causation, belief in, 121–123
Certainty, 117–118, 257–258
Chance, group decision making, 299
Charity, 99
Chicken dilemma, 381, 382–383
Children, 71
beliefs, 122
need for explanations, 210, 211
Choices
linear models, 316–319
in natural settings, 285–295
solutions *vs.* tradeoffs, 292–295
Chronological snobbery, 133–134
Circularity, 43–46, 66–68
intelligence, 78
irrationality, 417
Clarification, explanations, 213–214
Classical empiricism, 33
Classical intellectualism, 33
Classical rationalism, 134
Clinical diagnosis, reasoning, 279–284
accuracy, 280–281

Bayesian diagnosis, 283–284
clinical judgment, 281–283
competing-hypotheses heuristic, 283–284
consistency, 280–281
focusing, 279–280
pattern recognition, 280
pseudodiagnosticity, 284
use of actuarial statistics, 281–283
Coexistence thesis, 418
Cognition
epistemic, 346
pragmatic adaptiveness of, 28–29
rationality, 357–363
effort, 25–26
stakes, 26
Cognitive misers, 20
Cognitive pluralism, 384–387
descriptive *vs.* normative, 384–385
Cognitive process, wisdom, 342–343
Cognitive system, default hierarchies, 53
Coherence theory, 156–157
Collective madness, 377–378
Collective rationality, determining will of majority, 379–380
Common-knowledge effect, group decision making, 301–302, 306
Communication, 29
Competence, performance, distinction as applied to reasoning, 392–400
Competence theory, 393–394
Competing-hypotheses heuristic, 283–284
Comprehension, errors of, 399
Computers
expert systems, 106
intelligence, 73–74
Confirmation bias, 122–123, 154–155
Conformity to norms, 20–24
Consensus-driven groups, group decision making, 306
Conservatism, 158
Consilience, 217
Consistency, 40, 51–65
among actions, 54–56

Consistency (*continued*)
  among set of assertions, 60–62
  beliefs, 137–138
    between beliefs and
      behavior, 56–57
    with evidence, 59–60
  ideal consistency condition, 54
  indeterminacy of, 60–64
  insufficiency of, 64–65
  internal, 52–54, 408
  local internal, 408
  minimal consistency condition, 54
  principled behavior, 58–59
  resolving inconsistencies, 62–63
  science, 63–64
  as *sine qua non* of rationality, 51–52
Contraction bias, 271
Contradiction, 40
Contributing cause, 273
Cost-benefit analysis, values, 186–187
Credibility, explanations, 210–211
Credulity, 5–6, 171–173
  causes, 172
  examples, 171–172
Criticism, 408–409
  local openness, 408–409
Cults, 169–170
Cultural context
  magic, 371–373
  perception, 364–365
  rationality, 368–373
    established ideas, 369–371
    new ideas, 369–371
  science, 371–373
Cultural effects, beliefs, 378–379
Curiosity, 331–333

D

Decision evaluation, 307–316
  accountability, 313–314
  decision outcomes, 308–310
  decision quality, 308–310
  judged by consequences, 12
  normative model applicability, 314–316
  retrospective, 310–313

Decision making, 34, *see also* Group decision making
  disposition, 291
  dual-process theories, 319–321
  dynamic, 287–289
  emotion, 197–198, 291
  everyday decisions, 289–291
  fast and frugal heuristics, 290–291
  gambles, 19
  hard decisions, 185–189
  hidden costs, 181–182
  hierarchy
    action command style, 287
    intent command style, 287
  linear models of choice, 316–319
  maximizers, 292
    subjective expected utility, 319
  medical science, 194–195
  mood, 200, 291
  naturalistic, 287–289
  in natural settings, 285–295
  normative models, 20–24
    vs. prescriptive, 21–22
  norms, 20–24
  preciptive models, *vs.* normative, 21–22
  prescriptive models, 21
  satisficers, 292
  solutions *vs.* tradeoffs, 292–295
  subjective expected utility, 18
    criticism, 18–19
  Take the Best rule, 290–291
  theories of, 316
  trends in judgment and decision research, 321
  tyranny of choice, 291–292
  unanticipated tradeoffs, 181–182
Decisiveness, reflective thinking, 26
Declarative knowledge, 85–86
Deductive logic
  explanations, 223–224
  values, 185
Delusions, 166–173, 377
  defined, 167, 168
  mental illness, 166–167
Descartes, Rene, principle of

universal doubt, 125–127
Diagnosticity, 270, *see also* Clinical diagnosis
Diff Con theory, 320
Direct experience, beliefs, 119
Discounting future, 9–10
Disjunction effect, 262
Disposition, 201–203
  decision making, 291
  judging plausibility, 277
  reasoning, 201
Diversity, group decision making, 305–306
Dogmatism, 155
Dollar auction, 7–8
Domain knowledge, problem solving, 107
Doubt, 125–127
  Descartes's principle of universal doubt, 125–127
Dreaming, 95
Dysrationalia, 75, 76

E
Ecological rationality, 361
Economic decision making
  long-term effects, 9–10
  natural resources, 9–10
  short-term effects, 10
Economic growth, 10
Economic man, 23
Economics, balancing ethics, 13
Emotion, 197–199
  decision making, 197–198, 291
  functional magnetic resonance imaging, 199
  rationality
    deleterious, 197–198
    emotion essential to rationality, 198–199
    relationship, 197
Endowment effect, 265
Ends, 15
Entropy, 228
Environmental change, 187
Environmental protection

economic decision making, 9–10
judging worth, 266–267
Epistemology, 42
  epistemic cognition, 346
  epistemologists' role, 38–39
  normative values, 189
Equivalence, 330
Erasmus, human rationality, 414
Errors of application, 399
Errors of comprehension, 399
Esthetics, 203–207
  role, 203–204
Ethics
  economics, balancing, 13
  rationality, 189–193
    reconciling individual-community needs, 190–193
  reasoning, 193–196
  reflection, 193–196
Evidence, 408–409
  beliefs, 116–117, 118–119, 124, 150
    active fairmindedness, 141–143
    cost of information, 141–143
  counterindicative, 28
  evidentiary justification, 81–83
  experts, 145–146
  honest differences of opinion, 144–145
  local openness to, 408–409
  overlooking, 65
  partially, 60
  principle of total evidence, 142
  proportionalism, 117
  selectively, 60
  subjectivity, 140, 143–147
  values, 182–193
Evolution, 28–32, 227
  beliefs, 130–131
  brain, 193
  science, 402
Expected utility, 17, 18
Experience-based reasoning, 103
Expertise, 106–108
  benefits, 108
  metaknowledge, 108
Experts, evidence, 145–146

Explanationism, 250–251, 401
Explanations, 213–214, *see also* Causality
  analogies, 232
  beliefs, relationship, 232–233
  characterized, 211–250
  clarification, 213–214
  conditional reference frame, 233
  credibility, 210–211
  deduction, 223–224
  definitions, 211–213
  explaining *vs.* naming, 238–241
  fundamental attribution error, 241–247
  as identification of cause, 236–237
  mathematical proof, 230–231
  need for, 209–210
  overattribution, 249
  proofs, 230–231
  rationality, relationship, 250–252
  reasons for attribution, 247–248
  reductionism, 214–223
    con reductive explanations, 217–223
    pro reductive explanations, 216–217
  scientific laws, 224–226
    limitation, 226
  scientific theories, 226–230
    limitations, 229–230
  superstition, 233–234
  unanswered fundamental question, 249–250
Exposition, 213–214

F
Fact, 84
Failing to discount sunk costs, 6–8
Faith, *see also* Trust
  knowledge, relationship, 83–84
Fast and frugal heuristics, decision making, 290–291
Feeling-of-knowing judgments, 90–93
  basis, 92–93
  mechanisms, 92–93
  memory, 90–91
  research, 94

Fideism, 128
Fluctuation theory, 96–97
Foundationalism, 128
  variant, 148–149
Foundations theory, 156–157
Freedom, 190
  beliefs, 150–151
Friendliness, 302–303
Functional magnetic resonance imaging, emotion, 199
Fundamental attribution error, 241–247
  attribution in accounting for own behavior, 244–245
  bias, 243–244, 247
  as error, 245–247
  explanations, 241–247
  individuals *vs.* situations as causes of behavior, 241–244
  self-image, 244–245
Fund management problem, 297–298
Future, discounting, 9–10
Fuzzy trace theory, 320

G
Gambler's fallacy, 375–376
Gambles, 8–9
  decision making, 19
  mixtures of gains and losses, 19
  playing long odds, 8–9
  voting, 9
Game theory, 23–24
Gödel's proof, mathematics, 63
Goal-directed thinking, 176–179
Goals, 175–182
  critical scrutiny of, 16
  equality of thinking, 175–176
  rationality, 16
    goal achievement as criterion, 180–182
  reason, 176–179
    choice of goal, 176–179
    methods, 176–179
Good judgment, wisdom, 343–344
Goods of effectiveness, 190–191
Goods of excellence, 190–191
Governmental policy, 4–5

folly, 5
Gravity, 238–239
Greek philosophers, 341
Group consensus, 163–164
Group decision making, 295–307
  attractiveness or friendliness of group members, 302–303
  chance, 299
  common-knowledge effect, 301–302, 306
  consensus-driven groups, 306
  diversity, 305–306
  experimentation, 300–307
  fund management problem, 297–298
  group decisions and individual preferences, 300–301
  group polarization effect, 300
  heterogeneity, 305–306
  independence, 305–306
  non-consensus-seeking, 305–306
  politeness ritual, 303
  problems, 296–298
  quality of group decisions, 303
  rationality, 305–306
  riskier decisions, 304
  risky-shift phenomenon, 304
  social-sharedness, 303
  staff selection problem, 296–297
  uncertainty, 304
  virtual (noninteracting) groups, 304–306
Group madness, 377–378
Group polarization effect, 300
Groupthink, 305
Gullibility, 5–6

H

Happiness, 14, 15
Hedonistic calculus, 196, 317
Hidden costs, decision making, 181–182
Hierarchy, decision making
  action command style, 287
  intent command style, 287
Hindsight bias, 94
Hypothesis, *see* Scientific theories

I

Ignorance
  desirability of, 12
  informed *vs.* uninformed ignorance, 100
  preferred ignorance, 98–99
  unethical, 109
  varieties, 100–101
Impersonal rationality, 34
Independence, group decision making, 305–306
Indoctrination, 184
Inference, 37–38, 39
  intuition, 395
  from performance to process, 50
  from premises, 47
  process of justification, 69
  uncertainty of, from outcomes to processes, 46–50
Influence, 27
Information cascades, beliefs, 161–162
Insight, 93–94
  wisdom, 343–344
Instrumental rationality, 66, 178–179
Intellectual accountability, 412
Intelligence
  adaptability, relationship, 72
  bias, 76
  circularity, 78
  commonsense conceptions, 74
  computers, 73–74
  concept of, 71–80
  definitions, 71
  embodied in artifacts, 73
  as explanatory construct, 73
  irrationality, 79
  kinds, 73, 74–75
  rationality, 76–79, 79
    necessary but not sufficient condition, 79–80
    relationship, 76–79
  reasoning ability, relationship, 74–75
  tests for measuring, 72
Intelligent machines, 105
Intent, 325
Introspection, 50–51

Intuition, 68–69, 125, 402–405, 403–405
  axiomatization, 404–405
  change, 67
  faulty, 395
  inference, 395
  irrationality, 392
  last court of appeal, 405–406
  role, 405–406
  tutored intuition, 41–43
  untutored intuition, 39–41
Irrationality, 414–415
  circularity, 417
  demonstrations, criticisms, 396, 415–416
  intelligence, 79
  intuition, 392
  normative criteria, 392

J

Joint receipt, 19
Judging information, 268–271
  importance, 268–270
  relevance, 268–270
  value, 270
Judging plausibility, 271–279
  credibility of source, 276
  determinants of plausibility, 274–277
    interperson variability, 274–275
  disposition, 277
  generalizations, 410
  global fit, 275
  importance, 272–274
  intentional criterial biases, 277–279
  knowledge, 275
  preference, 276–277
Judging worth, 263
  environmental protection, 266–267
  methods, 263–267
    limitations, 265–267
  normative models, 264
  social factors, 267–268
  variables used as measures, 266
Jurisprudential analogy, 138

K

Knowledge, *see also* Ignorance; Metaknowledge
  abundant and easily accessible information, 110
  beliefs
    justified beliefs, 81
    relationship, 81–83
    truth, 82
  common knowledge, 108–109
  concepts, 80–94
  constraints on human learning, 97–99
  declarative *vs.* procedural, 85–86
  evidentiary justification, 81–83
  experts *vs.* novices, 107–108
  faith, relationship, 83–84
  feeling of knowing, 90–93
  first- *vs.* second-hand knowledge, 83–84
  formula-centered, 335
  fragmentary nature, 86–87
  implicit nature, 86–87
  judging information, 268–271
  judging plausibility, 271–279
  knowers and, 88–90
    groups, 89–90
  limits, 97–99
  measuring, 101–102
  motivation, 98
  preferred ignorance, 98–99
  reasoning
    case-based reasoning, 103
    complementary, 104
    declarative *vs.* procedural knowledge, 105–106
    domain-independent skills, 103
    domain-specific skills, 103, 104
    experience-based reasoning, 103
    relationship, 102–106
  responsibility for, 108–112
  rules, 87
  society's expectation, 108–110
  types, 84–86
  understanding, relationship, 324
  untapped, 87–88
  wisdom, 343–344

L

Law of contradiction, 43
Law of non-contradiction, 41
Leadership, 201
Likelihood ratio, 270
Linear models of choice, 316–319
Logic, 37–38, 39, 44–45
  beliefs, justification, 135–137
  reasoning, 418
    methodological impediment, 398
    whether people reason logically, 390–391
Logical argument, 13
Logical imperative, 37–38
Logicians, 42
Losses, 6–8

M

Magic, cultural context, 371–373
Malaria, 129–130
Mathematics, 45, 110–111, 403–405
  in explanations, 230–231
  Gödel's proof, 63
  method of proofs and refutations, 159
  understanding, 326–327
Matters of fact, 84
Means, 15
Media, 27
Medical science, *see also* Clinical diagnosis
  decision making, 194–195
Memory
  feeling-of-knowing judgments, 90–91
  reasoning, 105
  separating, 48
Mental illness
  delusions, 166–167
  mood, 200
Mental models, 49
Metaknowledge, 90–94
  expertise, 108
Methodological conservatism, 157
Methods, in belief justification, 135–137

Minimal general rationality condition, 361–363
Minimal normative rationality, 63
Misconceptions, common, 338–339
Mistakes, 399
Monetary value, 17
Mood, 199–200
  decision making, 200, 291
  mental illness, 200
  thinking, 199–200
Moral arithmetic, 196
Morality, rationality, 189–193
  reconciling individual–community needs, 190–193
Moral philosophers, 40–41
Moral rationality, 178–179
Motion implies force misconception, 338
Motivation
  knowledge, 98
  reasoning, 179–180
Multiple representations, understanding, 328–329, *329*

N

Naming, 238–241
Naturalistic Decision Making (NDM) approach, 288–289
Natural resources
  economic decision making, 9–10
  judging worth, 266–267
Necessary cause, 273
Negative evidence, 28
Networks, beliefs, 162–163
Normative decision theory, 20–24
Normative-sense rationality, 33
Normative theory, validity, 44
Normative values, epistemology, 189
Null hypothesis, 278

O

Objective reason, 179
Obligatory effect, 409–410
Observational learning, 161
Occam's razor, 172
Odds, 8–9, *see also* Gambles
Opportunity costs, 23

Optimal analytic choice
    behavior, 16–19
Optimization, satisficing,
    contrasted, 19–20
Outcome bias, 309
Overattribution, 249
Overconfidence, 94

P
Pareto principle, 379
Pattern recognition, 30, 280
Pauli exclusion principle, 227–228
Payoffs, 17
    payoff matrix, 17
    quantified in, 17
Peer influence, beliefs, 164–166
Perception
    cultural context, 364–365
    perspective, 364–366
    reality, 364–367
Performance, competence,
    distinction as applied to
    reasoning, 392–400
Personality, 55
Personality rationality, 34
Perspectives, 201–203, 347–348
    beliefs, 202
    perception, 364–366
Philosophy, 42–43
Plato, 341
Plausibility, see Judging plausibility
Politeness ritual, group decision
    making, 303
Pollyanna principle, 277
Positive affect, 202–203
Power, 201
Pragmatic rationality, 400–402
    vs. theoretical rationality, 400
Pragmatic reasoning schemas, 48–49
Preconceptions, 146–147
Preferences, 253–263
    anticipation of regret, 263
    constructed vs. revealed, 254–255
    emotion, 263
    identifying, 255–257
    judging plausibility, 276–277
    metarankings, 254

paradoxes, 259, *260, 261*, 263
preference orderings, 263
preference reversal
    phenomenon, 316
preference utilitarianism, 195–196
    between uncertain
        alternatives, 258–259
    between uncertain and certain
        alternatives, 257–258
Preferred ignorance, 98–99
Premise conversion hypothesis, 46–47
Prescientific beliefs
    contemporary, 169–171
    in prescientific times, 167–169
Pride, 12
Principled behavior, 11–12, 58–59
Principle of balance, 411
Principle of charity, 99
Principle of conservatism, 158
Principle of intellectual
    accountability, 412
Principle of judicious bias, 411–412
Principle of local internal
    consistency, 408
Principle of local openness
    to evidence and
    criticism, 408–409
Principle of maximization of
    expected utility, 183
Principle of negative
    undermining, 157–158
Principle of obligatory effect, 409–410
Principle of positive
    undermining, 157–158
Principle of regularity, 262
Principle of stochastic dominance, 19
Principle of total evidence, 142
Principle of trial by exposure, 409
Principle of universal doubt, 125–127
Prisoner's dilemma, 382–383
Probability, 8–9, 45
Problem solving
    domain knowledge, 107
    feeling of warmth
        judgments, 93–94
Procedural knowledge, 85–86
Proofs, explanations, 230–231

Index

Proportion dominance phenomenon, 258
Pseudodiagnosticity, 284
Puritans, 155–156

Q

Quantum mechanics, 63–64, 239

R

Radical Bayesianism, 116
Rational beliefs, 173–174
Rational choice, criteria, 310
Rational decision making, alternative theory, 19
Rationality
  acquisition of certain types of knowledge as requirement, 109–110
  of actions, characterized, 32
  as agreement with user, 24
  Apologist position, 389–390
  assessing, 46–51
  of beliefs, characterized, 32
  bounded, 358–361
    criticism, 358
  carefully reasoned definition, 35–36
  characterized, 1–36
  circularity, 43–46
  cognition, 357–363
  cognitive effort, 25–26
    stakes, 26
  competence *vs.* performance, 392–400
  conceptions of, 13–32, 35
  as conformity to norms, 20–24
  consensus among qualified people, 41–43
  as consistency of actions with preferences or goals, 14–16
  as consistency with self-interest, 13–14
  contexts, 35
  criteria, matters of degree, 6
  cultural context, 368–373
    established ideas, 369–371
    new ideas, 369–371
  deciding what is rational, 402–405

  decompositional (or analytical) *vs.* compositional, 359
  disposition to shape beliefs by evidence, 75
  domain-specific mechanisms, 30–31
  economic models, 23
  emotion
    deleterious, 197–198
    emotion essential to rationality, 198–199
    relationship, 197
  empirical question, 1–2
  equating of adaptability with, 400–402
  ethics, 189–193
    reconciling individual–community needs, 190–193
  explanations, relationship, 250–252
  goal achievement as criterion, 180–182
  group decision making, 305–306
  individual and group, in conflict, 380–381
  individual differences, 418–419
  instrumental conception, 15–16
  vs. common-sense views, 16
  intelligence, 79
    necessary but not sufficient condition, 79–80
    relationship, 76–79
  Meliorist position, 389–390
  minimal, 361–363
  morality, 189–193
    reconciling individual–community needs, 190–193
  normative models, intelligence, 76–79
  normative question, 1–2
  not always *vs.* never, 416, 418–419
  as optimal analytic choice behavior, 16–19
  Panglossian position, 389–390
  practical, 32–35
  pragmatic, 400–402
    vs. theoretical rationality, 400
  as pragmatic adaptiveness, 28–32

Rationality (*continued*)
  principles, 40–41
  of process, 34
  of purpose, 34
  reality, 363
  as reflectiveness, 24–27
  relativity, 357–389
    individual *vs.* collective rationality, 376–381
    situational frame of reference, 373–376
  as responsiveness to reasons, 27–28
  as satisficing, 19–20
  self-evident first principles, 45–46
  standards, 65–66, 69
  standard setters, 37–69
  substantialist conception, 179
  survival under vigorous criticism, 68
  test situations, 3–12
  theoretical, 32–35
  Type II, 360
  various connotations, 2
  whether humans are rational, 413–419
Rationing, values, 185–186
Reality
  arbitrariness of current conception, 367–368
  perception, 364–367
  rationality, 363
Reality monitoring, 95–96
Reality testing, 95–96
Reason, 25
  basis, 45–46
  goals, 176–179
    choice of goal, 176–179
    methods, 176–179
  as tool, 177
Reasoning, 34
  clinical diagnosis, 279–284
    accuracy, 280–281
    Bayesian diagnosis, 283–284
    clinical judgment, 281–283
    competing-hypotheses heuristic, 283–284
    consistency, 280–281
    focusing, 279–280
    pattern recognition, 280
    pseudodiagnosticity, 284
    use of actuarial statistics, 281–283
  cognitive illusions, 396
  competence *vs.* performance, 392–400
  dispositions, 201
  ethics, 193–196
  influence on beliefs, 123
  intelligence, relationship, 74–75
  knowledge
    case-based reasoning, 103
    complementary, 104
    declarative *vs.* procedural knowledge, 105–106
    domain-independent skills, 103
    domain-specific skills, 103, 104
    experience-based reasoning, 103
    relationship, 102–106
  logic, 418
    methodological impediment, 398
    whether people reason logically, 390–391
  memory, 105
    separating, 48
  motivation, 179–180
  nonexistence of pure reason, 196
  principle of balance, 411
  principle of intellectual accountability, 412
  principle of judicious bias, 411–412
  principle of local internal consistency, 408
  principle of local openness to evidence and criticism, 408–409
  principle of obligatory effect, 409–410
  principle of trial by exposure, 409
  standards, 1
Reductionism
  biological sciences, 219
  emergence view, 219
  explanations, 214–223
    con reductive explanations, 217–223

pro reductive explanations, 216–217
problem of mind, 220–221
qualified, 220
Reflective thinking, 24–27
decisiveness, 26
ethics, 193–196
Regularity, 262
Relativity, 63–64
rationality
  individual vs. collective rationality, 376–381
  irrational thinking serving rational purpose, 381–384
  situational frame of reference, 373–376
Retrospection, 50–51
Risk, 3–5
  of future problem, 4
Risk-averse, 257
Risk-seeking, 257
Risk-taking behavior, intra-individual consistency, 55
Risky-shift phenomenon, group decision making, 304
Rules, 10–12, 37–38
  knowledge, 87
  process of justification, 69

S
Satisficing, 19–20, 358–359
  optimization, contrasted, 19–20
Scammers, 6
Science
  consistency, 63–64
  cultural context, 371–373
  evolution, 402
  skepticism, 126
Scientific knowledge
  escalation of ignorance, 100
  explanations, 224–226
    limitation, 226
  known unknown, 100–101
  specialization, 110–111
  unknown unknown, 100–101
  wonderment, 206–207
Scientific theories, 278

explanations, 226–230
  limitations, 229–230
Self, elasticity of concept, 14
Self-contradictory, 15
Self-critical reflection, 25
Self-evident truths, tautologies, distinction, 84
Self-examination, 12
Self-image, 1
  fundamental attribution error, 244–245
Self-interest, 3–5, 13–14
  perceived vs. actual, 14
  working against one's own, 3–5
Self-serving attributional bias, 245
Self-transcendence, wisdom, 344–345
Simpson's paradox, 260–262
Skepticism, 5–6, 125–127
  alternative views, 127–128
  science, 126
Slips, 399
Social dilemma, 380
Social factors, judging worth, 267–268
Social learning, 161
Social networks, see Networks
Societal decision making, 185–189
Solipsistic predicament, 94–97, 99
Specialization, 110–111
  divisive and factious effect, 111–112
  problem for society, 111
  scientific knowledge, 110–111
Staff selection problem, 296–297
Standards, 139
  reasoning, 1
Statistical evidence
  statistical vs. causal explanation, distinguished, 235–236
  subjectivity, 143–144, 146
Status-quo bias, 265
Stochastic dominance, 19
Stock-buying schemes, 5–6
Subjective expected utility, decision making, 18
  criticism, 18–19
Subjective reason, 179

Subjectivity
  evidence, 140, 143–147
  statistical evidence, 143–144, 146
Sufficient cause, 273
Sunk costs, 6–8, 23
  anticipated future effects, 7–8
  failing to discount, 6–8
Superstition, explanations, 233–234
Sure-thing principle, 260, 261–262
Survival, 28–29

T

Take the Best rule, decision making, 290–291
Tautologies, self-evident truths, distinction, 84
Teaching of thinking, 105
Technological progress, 193, 194
Testimony principle, 83
Thermodynamics, second law, 228
Thinking
  active search, 65
  belief in causation, 121–123
  consistency, 65
  dispositions, 202
  goal-directed thinking, 176–179
  goals, 175–176
  mood, 199–200
  one-sided thinking, 121–122
  teaching of, 105
  two-sided thinking, 121–122
Thoughtfulness, as habit of mind, 201
Thought patterns, 48–49
Tip-of-the-tongue experience, 90
Topical accounting, 7
Trading, of risk of future problems for certainty of present pleasures, 4
Tragedy of the commons, 380
Traveler's dilemma, 383
Trial by exposure, 409
True beliefs, 27
Trust, 276, *see also* Faith
Truth, 84
  beliefs, 62
    justification, 130–131
  of reason, 84
Truth seeking, 409–410
Type II rationality, 360

U

Ultimatum game, 198–199
Uncertainty, 257–259
  group decision making, riskier decisions, 304
  intolerance for, 209
  wisdom, 347
Undermining, 157–158
  negative, 157–158
  positive, 157–158
Understanding
  ability to paraphrase, 334
  as adequate mental model, 327–328
  alternative models, 334
  characterized, 323–330
  degrees of, 335–337
  desire for, 331–333, 340
  evidence of, 333–335
  knowledge, relationship, 324
  lack of, 334–335, 338–339
  limitations of, 339–340
  mathematics, 326–327
  meaning of, 323–330
  multiple representations, 328–329, *329*
  as seeing equivalences, 330
  as seeing implications, 325
  as seeing intent, 325
  as seeing necessity of relationship, 325–327
  wisdom, 343–344
Universal doubt, 125–127
Universe, origin, 333
Unlimited growth, 10
Unscientific beliefs, contemporary, 169–171
Ussher, Bishop James, 129
Utility, 17
  beliefs, 149
    justification, 137–138
  maximization of expected, 183
  subjective expected, 18

V

Validity
  appeal to standard example, 66
  inference, rules of, 66
  paradigm case, 66
  principles of, 66
Value-free, valueless,
    contrasted, 184–185
Values, 182–196
  biotechnology, 186
  codification, 379–380
  cost-benefit analysis, 186–187
  deductive logic, 185
  evidence, 182–193
  hard decisions, 185–189
  presenting opposing views, 183–184
  rationing, 185–186
  representation of opposed
    views, 183–184
  wisdom, 351–352
Virtual (noninteracting)
    groups, group decision
    making, 304–306
Virtue, wisdom, 344
Voting, playing long odds, 9

W

Warranted beliefs, 123–124
Wave-particle duality, 332
Willingness to believe (or not),
    147–151, 171–173
Willingness-to-pay method of
    determining value, 264–265
  limitations, 265–267
Wisdom
  age, 352–354
  as attitude about knowing, 346–347
  balance, 345–346
  characterized, 340–349
  cognitive process, 342–343
  good judgment, 343–344
  historically, 340–341
  insight, 343–344
  as intrinsic good, 351–352
  knowledge, 343–344
  multidimensionality, 348–349
  personal view, 349
  as perspective, 347–348
  as practical need, 350–351
  reasons for desiring, 349–352
  research, 354–355
  self-transcendence, 344–345
  uncertainty, 347
  understanding, 343–344
  virtue, 344
Witchcraft, 378, 379
Wonderment, 204–207
  attitudes, 206
  importance, 204–205
  scientific knowledge, 206–207
  types, 205–206

AUTHOR INDEX

A

Aaron, H. J., 186, 475
Abelson, R., 52, 53, 103, 211, 421, 473, 475
Abramson, L. Y., 122, 421
Adams, C., 352, 353, 468
Adler, M. J., 84, 126–127, 130–131, 192, 194, 204, 421
Ægisdóttir, S., 282, 421
Ahlers, D. M., 283, 421
Ajzen, I., 180, 455
Albert, H., 33, 53, 125, 128, 134, 148–149, 151, 155, 165, 182, 196, 332, 421
Alcock, J. E., 134, 421
Alfvén, H., 145, 421
Alhakami, A., 291, 439
Allais, M., 15, 176, 421
Allan, R., 20, 180, 468
Allard, R., 288, 428
Allen, S. W., 280, 429
Alpert, M., 96, 463
Anderson, C., 437, 477
Anderson, C. A., 96, 152, 154, 157, 242, 421, 471
Anderson, C. P., 243, 482
Anderson, C. W., 210, 421, 422
Anderson, J. H., 108, 430
Anderson, J. R., 28, 30, 32, 33, 85, 202, 281, 401, 422
Anderson, L., 161, 422
Anderson, L. A., 282, 421
Anderson, N. H., 422
Anderson, S. W., 198, 425
Andrews, G. R., 122, 422
Andrews, J., 342, 464

Ansay, C., 91, 92, 433
Appel, W., 292, 422
Ardrey, R., 422
Aristotle, 193, 422
Arkes, H. R., 7, 23, 422
Arkin, P. K., 422
Arkin, R. M., 245, 422
Arkkelin, D. L., 284, 484
Arlin, P. K., 343
Aronson, E., 52, 421
Aronson, J. A., 199, 473
Arrow, K. J., 300, 379–380, 422
Arrowood, A. J., 155, 440
Asch, S. E., 165, 422
Ashby, F. G., 200, 450
Asimov, I., 129, 422
Asklock, R. B., 339, 422
Atkins, P. W., 119, 331, 422
Attneave, F., 271, 422
Audi, R., 16, 28, 33, 114, 131–132, 422
Ault, R. L., 26, 423
Austin, G. A., 342, 429
Avis, N. E., 64, 460
Ayer, A. J., 140, 423
Ayton, P., 42, 423

B

Back, K. W., 302, 423
Badgio, P. C., 26, 423
Baker, T. B., 282, 485
Bales, R. F., 300, 423
Balla, J. I., 107, 423
Baltes, P. B., 343, 344, 350, 351, 352, 354, 423, 436, 447, 478

Bandura, A., 423
Banerjee, A. V., 162, 410, 423
Bara, 398
Baranes, R., 103, 480
Bargh, J. A., 290, 486
Bargh, J. H., 423
Bar-Hillel, M., 460
Barnes, A. E., 92, 423
Barnes, M. D., 180–181, 290, 474
Baron, J., 15, 20, 21, 25, 26, 59, 65, 76, 121, 141, 168, 175, 180, 200, 201, 263, 309, 342, 360, 423, 424, 471, 478
Baron, R. S., 304, 435
Barrow, J. D., 192, 232, 301, 402, 424
Barrows, H. S., 280, 424
Bartlett, F. E., 72, 210, 342, 424
Bartley, W. W., III, 38, 45, 424
Bassock, M., 270, 424, 483
Basu, K., 383, 424
Bateson, G., 219, 424
Batson, C. D., 242, 433
Bauer, 81, 100, 147
Bazerman, M. H., 107, 316, 424, 464
Beach, L. R., 180, 270, 286, 315, 424, 461
Beatty, J., 443
Bechara, A., 198, 425
Becker, G., 23, 425
Beckerman, W., 10, 425
Bell, D., 21, 263, 335, 373, 413, 425
Bell, E. T., 75, 425
Bem, D. J., 53, 304, 425, 485
Bempechat, J., 122, 436
Bennett, M., 339, 425
Bentham, J., 193, 195, 196, 317–318, 425
Bereiter, C., 72, 87, 425
Bergamini, D., 425
Berger, J. O., 316, 425
Berger, P. L., 290, 425
Berglas, S., 245, 426, 451
Berkeley, D., 415, 426
Berlinski, D., 239, 426
Berman, M., 167, 373, 426
Bernieri, 164
Bernouilli, D., 17, 21, 426
Bernstein, J., 426
Bernstein, M., 74, 480
Bernstein, P. L., 15, 236, 426
Berry, R. J., 227, 426
Bertotti, B., 239, 426
Bethe, A., 72, 426
Bettman, J. R., 28, 199, 254, 318, 426, 459, 467
Beyth-Marom, R., 94, 283, 382, 426, 440
Bhagwati, J., 188, 426

Bierbrauer, G., 242, 426
Biggs, J. B., 107, 423
Bikhchandani, S., 161, 162, 410, 426
Billi, J. E., 283, 487
Billings, J. F., 96, 449
Billings, R. S., 180, 426
Birnbaum, D., 200, 473
Birnbaum, M. H., 19, 426
Birren, J. E., 341, 349, 350, 354, 427
Birren, J. W., 348, 352, 431
Bishop, J. E., 347, 427
Bizot, E., 106, 457
Black, D., 300, 325, 427
Blackburn, S., 363, 427
Blackstone, W., 153, 427
Blackwell, D., 21, 23, 271, 427
Blake, M., 90, 92, 427
Blanchard-Fields, F., 427
Bloom, A., 250, 376, 427
Blumer, C., 7, 23, 422
Blyth, C. R., 261, 427
Boden, M. A., 220–221, 427
Boehm, V. R., 52, 427
Boethius, 427
Boettger, R., 243, 314, 482
Bohm, D., 211–212
Boole, G., 390, 427
Boorstin, D. J., 68, 122, 155, 427
Borgida, E., 243, 446, 465
Borkowski, J. G., 26, 455
Bouleau, C., 427
Bower, G. H., 199, 200, 245, 427, 428, 440, 452
Bowerman, W. R., 245, 428
Bowman, E. H., 318, 428
Boyer, C. B., 428
Boyle, M. H., 186, 428
Braine, M. D., 390, 392, 428
Brainerd, C. J., 77, 178, 320, 428, 471
Braithwaite, R. B., 131, 428
Brams, S. J., 300, 428
Brandstätter, H., 300, 302, 428
Brandt, R. B., 16, 36, 428
Brehmer, B., 288, 428
Brenner, H. G., 344, 346, 350, 352, 453
Brent, S. B., 345, 348, 428
Brentano, F., 50, 428
Brewer, R. E., 302, 428
Bricmont, J., 97
Broadbent, D. E., 106, 336, 429
Broadbent, M. H. P., 106, 429
Brody, R. A., 59, 202, 478
Bromley, D. A., 332, 429
Bronowski, J., 236, 237, 429
Brook, R. H., 3, 480

Brooks, L. R., 280, 429, 447
Brown, A. L., 72, 429
Brown, H., 379, 429
Brown, J. R., 95
Brown, J. S., 328, 329, 334, 339, 429, 432, 435
Brown, R., 92, 429
Brown, R. D., 110, 429
Brown, R. V., 284, 486
Bruce, D., 90, 470
Bruner, J. S., 342, 429
Bryne, 49
Bucci, W., 46, 429
Buddenbrock, W. von, 72, 429
Budescu, D. V., 94
Buede, D. M., 316, 486
Buehler, R., 244, 429
Bukstel, L., 107, 438
Bunge, M., 429
Burton, R. R., 339, 429
Busemeyer, J. R., 288, 429
Bushey, B., 20, 76, 180, 468
Butler, C., 429
Butler, S. F., 259, 430, 431
Byrne, R. M. J., 363, 369, 394, 398, 418, 450, 451

C

Cacioppo, J. T., 201, 429
Calderwood, R., 288, 289, 454
Calne, D. B., 76, 175, 177, 191, 429
Camerer, C., 199, 429
Campbell, D. T., 429
Campbell, F. L., 315, 424
Campbell, J., 245, 482
Campbell, J. D., 233, 430
Cannon-Bowers, J. A., 288, 430
Capra, F., 372, 430
Caputo, C., 244, 466
Cardoze, S., 64, 460
Carnap, R., 116, 124, 142, 430
Carraher, D. W., 430
Carraher, T. N., 74, 430
Carroll, J. M., 210, 430, 459
Carroll, L., 430
Carson, R., 379, 430
Casscells, W., 281, 430
Cattaneo, E., 347, 430
Ceci, S. J., 74, 103, 430
Chaiken, S., 360, 430, 460
Champagne, A. B., 108, 430
Chandler, M. J., 341, 343, 344, 352, 355, 430, 449

Chang, A. M., 107, 423
Chanowitz, 20, 430
Chapman, D., 187, 430
Chapman, R. A., 464
Chaput de Siantonge, D. M., 279, 453
Charness, N., 107, 430
Chartbrand, T. L., 423
Chartrand, 290
Chater, N., 391, 466
Chechile, R. A., 259, 430, 431
Chen, C., 122, 480
Cheng, P. W., 48, 88, 391, 431
Cherniak, C., 54, 63, 109, 127, 157, 361–362, 363, 374, 401
Chesterton, G. K., 240, 363, 431
Chi, M. T. H., 107, 431
Chipman, S. F., 431
Chomsky, N., 392–394, 431
Christensen-Szalanski, J. J., 94, 431
Churchland, P. M., 215, 221, 431
Churchland, P. S., 215, 221, 431
Clancy, J. M., 287, 315, 431
Clanton, C. H., 280, 283, 437
Clark, H. H., 29, 90, 91, 431
Clark, J., 172, 431
Clark, R. D., 304, 431
Clarke, D. S., Jr., 56, 130, 181, 250, 431
Clayton, V., 345, 348, 352, 431
Cleckley, H., 201, 432
Clemen, R. T., 24, 432
Clement, J., 334–335, 338, 432
Clinton-Cirocco, A., 289, 454
Clore, G. L., 199, 474
Close, M., 243, 482
Cohen, G., 282, 421
Cohen, J. D., 199, 473
Cohen, J. E., 10, 432
Cohen, L. J., 39, 42, 43, 268, 390, 392, 393, 396, 405, 415, 432
Collins, A., 329, 432, 480
Collins, B. E., 57, 432
Columbia Associates in Philosophy, 193, 195, 216, 218, 238, 432
Colvin, S. S., 72
Commoner, B., 379, 432
Comte, A., 240, 432
Conlisk, J., 432
Conlon, E. J., 314, 432
Conway, B., 74, 480
Cook, R. S., 282, 421
Cooke, A. D. J., 259, 431
Coombs, B., 271, 458
Coombs, C. H., 21, 483
Cooper, J., 57, 458
Cooper, L. G., 318, 471

Cooper, W. S., 28, 29, 32, 432
Coppock, R., 187, 446
Corrigan, B., 282, 434
Cosmides, L., 30, 31, 330, 433
Costermans, J., 91, 92, 433
Cournot, A. A., 433
Cox, J. R., 47, 48, 398, 445
Crandall, R., 243, 465
Cromer, A., 171, 433
Csikszentmihalyi, M., 342–343, 344, 350, 352, 433
Cummings, N. A., 166, 200, 433
Cunningham, J. D., 235, 467
Currey, H. L., 279, 453

D

D'Agostino, P. R., 242, 468
Damasio, A. R., 197, 198, 291, 425, 433
Damasio, H., 198, 425
Darley, J. M., 154, 242, 433
Dasgupta, P., 301, 433
Dasser, V., 210, 433
Daston, L. J., 45, 434, 443
David, F. N., 45, 434
Davidshofer, I. O., 55, 434
Davidson, D., 21, 51, 77, 325, 390, 434
Davidson, N. E., 16, 434
Davies, P., 211–212, 228, 434
Davies, P. C. W., 95, 219–220, 333, 365, 402, 434
Davis, F. D., 242, 270, 434
Davis, J. H., 300, 452, 464
Davis, K. E., 451
Davis, R. L., 21, 483
Davison, 148
Dawes, R. M., 7, 109, 258, 281, 282, 310, 346, 347, 434, 481
Dawkins, R., 216, 434
De Avila, E. A., 72, 434
DeBono, K. G., 446
Debus, R. I., 122, 422
De Chardin, T., 219, 434
Deci, E. L., 122, 435
De Dombal, F. T., 282, 435
DeGroot, A. D., 107, 435
DeJong, G. F., 211, 463
DeKay, W. T., 435
DeKleer, J., 328, 329, 334, 435
De la Rocha, O., 74, 456
Dennett, D. C., 28, 96, 115, 149, 390, 401, 435, 448
Denning, M. A., 264, 435
Descartes, R., 125–126, 435

Deutsch, M., 300, 410, 435
DeVault, R. C., 318, 481
Devoe, M., 349, 456
Dewey, J., 25, 435
Diaconis, P., 396, 435
Diamond, P. A., 264, 435
Diener, C. I., 122, 435
Dillon, R. F., 342, 435
Dimnet, K. L., 24–25, 435
Dion, K. L., 304, 435
Dittmann-Kohli, F., 344, 351, 423, 436
Divoky, D., 200, 474
Dixon, R., 344, 352, 423
Dixon, R. A., 436, 447, 478
Dobshansky, T., 219, 436
Dodgson, C. L., 300, 436
Doherty, M. E., 31, 284, 319, 321, 436, 453, 484
Doise, W., 304, 464
Doubilet, P., 279, 436
Dougherty, M. R. P., 436
Dovalina, I., 64, 460
Droysen, J. G., 332, 436
Drummond, M. F., 188, 436
Dubos, R., 240, 364, 379
Dummett, M., 379, 436
Duncan, B. L., 154, 436
Duncan, G. J., 23, 463
Duncan, S., 72, 434
Dunlap, R. A., 436
Dunlosky, J., 92, 423
Durning, A., 379, 436
Dweck, C. S., 122, 435, 436, 438
Dyson, 218

E

Eagleman, D. M., 312, 437
Eagly, A. H., 360, 430
Eaton, J. E., 210, 437
Ebbesen, E. B., 437
Ebert, R. J., 288, 437
Eccles, J., 123, 437
Eddy, D. M., 280, 283, 437
Edelman, G. M., 221, 250, 437
Edney, J. J., 183, 437
Edwards, K., 152, 437
Edwards, W., 21, 271, 316, 415, 437
Edwards, W. M., 437
Effrein, E. A., 57, 439
Egan, D., 107, 437
Ehrenfeld, D., 176, 186, 295, 437
Eimer, M., 446

Einhorn, H. J., 178, 258, 286, 316, 394, 437, 444
Einstein, A., 366, 438
Eiser, J. R., 455
Eisley, L., 340, 438
Ekberg, P.-H. S., 49, 459
Ekeland, I., 121, 237, 438
Elliot, G. C., 287, 315, 431
Elliott, E. S., 122, 436, 438
Ellis, A. L., 304, 456
Ellis, S. C., 77, 471
Ellsworth, P. C., 143, 438
Elmer, M., 312
Elstein, A. S., 279, 280, 283, 438
Elster, J., 18, 438
Engelmann, S., 72, 425
Engle, R. W., 107, 438
Ennis, R. H., 26, 201, 438
Epstein, S., 197, 291, 319, 438
Eraker, S. A., 189, 438
Erasmus, D., 377, 414, 415, 438
Erickson, E. H., 391, 438
Ericsson, K. A., 51, 438
Erikson, E. H., 347, 352
Erikson, J. M., 347, 438
Estes, W. K., 21, 438
Euclid, 168
Evans, C. E., 377, 438
Evans, J. St. B. T., 34, 47, 49, 51, 284, 311, 319, 325, 391, 394, 395, 398, 438, 439, 443, 460, 485

F

Fairey, P. J., 233, 430
Falender, V. J., 57, 439
Farady, M., 20, 76, 180, 468
Faunce, W., 244, 439
Faust, D., 94, 281, 434, 439
Fauth, J., 180, 454
Fazio, R. H., 57, 154, 247, 433, 439, 470
Fehr, E., 199, 381, 439, 476
Feightner, J. W., 280
Feinstein, A. R., 280, 283, 439
Feinstein, J., 201, 429
Feltovich, P. J., 107, 431
Festinger, L., 52, 300, 439
Feynman, R. P., 331, 439
Fiedler, K., 233, 439
Filskov, S. B., 281, 457
Finucane, M. L., 199, 258, 291, 439
Fisch, H.-U., 279, 439
Fischer, G. W., 264, 439
Fischhoff, B., 42, 94, 108, 188

Fischoff, B., 20, 271, 283, 316, 382, 426, 439, 440, 458, 475, 477
Fishburn, P. C., 300, 379, 428, 440
Fisher, L. M., 341, 349, 350, 354, 427
Fisher, S. D., 20, 319, 442
Fiske, S. T., 20, 243, 440, 482
Fitzgerald, P., 106, 429
Flavell, J. H., 392, 440
Flegg, G., 367, 440
Fleming, J., 155, 440
Fleming, R. A., 270, 440
Fletcher, G. J. O., 245, 472
Flew, A. G. N., 11, 440
Florman, S. C., 244, 440
Fobian-Willham, C., 94
Fodor, J., 28, 440
Foley, M. A., 95, 450
Fong, G. T., 88, 440
Forgas, J. P., 200, 245, 254, 440
Fowlkes, M. R., 267, 440
Fox, R., 280, 440
Franklin, B., 317–318, 440
Freedman, D., 396, 435
Freeman, B. A., 181, 481
Freightner, J. W., 424
French, L. A., 72, 429
Frey, D., 245, 440
Frick, R. W., 123
Fried, L. S., 271, 441
Friedman, M., 23, 441
Friedman, R. M., 187, 441
Friedrich, J., 28, 29, 441
Frieze, I., 235, 486
Fromm, E., 292, 441
Funder, D. C., 20, 29, 246, 441

G

Gabor, D., 209, 441
Gächter, S., 381, 439
Gaeth, G. J., 258, 269, 441, 457
Galileo, 168
Gallistel, C. R., 72, 441
Galotti, K. M., 24, 74, 441
Garb, H. N., 279, 281, 441, 487
Gardner, H., 73, 80, 98, 226, 441
Gardner, M., 164, 169, 372, 377, 441, 442
Garland, H., 8, 442
Garland, L. H., 280, 442
Garnick, M. B., 279, 442
Gaskins, I. W., 26, 423
Gatchel, R. J., 267, 442
Gauthier, D., 25, 442

Gay, 193, 195
Geary, 320
Geil, M., 304, 464
Gelernter, 222
Geller, E. S., 271, 469
Gell-Mann, 220, 369
Gerard, H. B., 302, 410, 435, 442
Gerler, D., 90, 92, 464
Gettier, E., 82, 442
Getty, D. J., 181, 281, 442, 481
Gettys, C. F., 20, 319, 436, 442
Geva, N., 200, 449
Gibbs, M. S., 442
Gibbs, W. W., 277, 442
Gibson, M., 107, 423
Gick, M. L., 87–88, 106, 442
Giere, R., 13, 442
Gigerenzer, G., 28, 42, 43, 283, 290, 293–294, 320, 330, 361, 363, 395, 415, 442, 443, 444, 483
Gigone, D., 302, 304, 443
Gilhooly, K. J., 42, 459
Gillen, B., 243, 463
Gilligan, S. G., 199, 428
Gilovich, T., 42, 154, 202, 443, 461
Ginossar, Z., 64, 443
Girotto, V., 284, 443
Girshick, M., 21, 23, 271, 427
Gladwell, M., 160, 163, 443
Glance, N. S., 380, 443
Glaser, E. M., 443
Glaser, R., 103, 107, 431, 443, 444
Glasser, W., 200, 444
Godkewitsch, M., 444
Goffman, E., 11, 444
Gold, S. M., 187, 444
Goldberg, L. R., 281, 282, 318, 444
Golding, E., 485
Golding, S., 48, 280, 395, 444
Goldman, A. I., 13, 39, 64, 81, 114, 117, 125, 130, 135–136, 157, 160, 444
Goldstein, D. G., 290, 361, 443, 444
Goldstein, W., 258, 444
Gonthier, D., 281, 442
Gonzalez, C., 288, 444
Good, I. J., 21, 68, 142, 224, 261, 360, 363, 391, 444
Goodie, A. S., 78, 445
Goodman, N., 39, 68–69, 391, 445
Goodnow, J. J., 342, 429
Goodsell, D. S., 328
Gorst, M., 129, 445
Gould, S. J., 73, 129, 445
Graham, A. C., 178, 182, 445
Grant, J., 107, 445

Grant, P., 264, 452
Grayboys, T. B., 281, 430
Green, B. F., Jr., 445
Green, D. M., 181, 445
Greenberg, J., 245, 469
Greene, B., 331, 332, 445
Greeno, J. G., 329, 445
Greenwald, A. G., 245, 445
Grice, H. P., 29, 445
Griffin, D., 244, 429
Griffin, D. W., 282, 445
Griggs, R. A., 42, 47, 48, 311, 398, 413–414, 445, 462, 469
Gronlund, S. D., 319, 436
Gross, K. A., 284, 484
Gruneberg, M. M., 90, 91, 445
Gruppen, L. D., 283, 487
Guilmette, J., 94, 439
Gustafson, D. H., 264, 454
Gutek, B. A., 244, 445
Guth, A., 229, 446
Gutkin, D. C., 235, 481

H

Habermas, J., 341, 446
Hacking, I., 45, 303, 446
Hadamard, J., 326, 446
Hafner, J., 20, 180, 468
Haggard, P., 312, 446, 456
Haggerty, M. E., 72
Hahn, 404
Hakim-Larson, J., 349, 456
Haldane, J. B. S., 115, 446
Hall, E., 352, 468
Halmos, P. R., 336, 446
Ham, J. J., 244, 455
Hamill, J. F., 85, 390, 446
Hamming, R. W., 446
Hammond, J. S., 309, 316, 446
Hammond, K. R., 279, 318, 439, 446
Hammond, P. B., 187, 446
Hanks, G. E., 271, 446
Hans, V. P., 143, 446
Harbluk, J. L., 90, 459
Hardin, G., 380, 446
Harding, C. M., 455
Hardman, D., 24, 32, 42, 423, 446
Hare, R. M., 193, 446
Harkness, A. R., 446
Harman, G., 8, 12, 35, 54, 114, 117, 156, 157, 158, 212–213, 230–231, 359, 363, 401, 446
Harris, D. H., 20, 447

Harris, J. M., 283, 447
Harris, M., 6, 447
Harris, V. A., 242, 451
Harsanyi, J. C., 15, 195, 447
Hart, J. T., 90, 92, 447
Hart, K., 94, 439
Harvey, J. H., 246
Haselton, M. G., 435
Hastie, R., 19, 94, 302, 304, 318, 443, 447, 470
Hatala, R., 280, 447
Hatcher, D., 126, 447
Hauptli, B. W., 44, 128, 139, 447
Hausman, J. A., 264, 435
Hawkins, S. A.3, 94, 447
Hayden, T., 152, 154, 247, 447
Hayes, J. R., 476
Hayes, J. R. M., 270, 329, 447
Heckhausen, J., 352, 447
Heider, F., 210, 234, 242, 447, 448
Heller, W., 379, 448
Hempel, C. G., 15, 116, 224, 448
Henle, M., 42, 46, 311, 448
Herrnstein, R. J., 23, 73, 448
Hersh, R., 125, 448
Hershey, J. C., 309, 424
Hertwig, R., 77, 448
Herz-Fischler, R., 448
Hess, T. M., 291, 448
Higgins, R. L., 244, 478
Hill, T., 106, 457
Hilton, D. J., 416, 448
Himsworth, H., 122–123, 209, 448
Hinsz, V. B., 302, 448
Hirshleifer, D., 161, 162, 410, 426
Hirt, E. R., 233, 448, 476
Hoch, S. J., 233, 244, 448
Hoellerich, V. L., 280, 486
Hoepfl, R. T., 270, 448
Hoffman, P. J., 280, 318, 448
Hoffrage, U., 283, 330, 443, 454
Hofstadter, D. R., 96, 448
Hogarth, R. M., 178, 315, 316, 394, 437, 448
Holland, J. C., 266, 449
Holland, J. H., 53, 242, 243, 391, 398
Holliday, S., 341, 343, 344, 352, 355, 430
Holmes, J. G., 57, 449
Holmes, S. G., 449
Holt, C., 161, 422
Holt, K., 161, 245, 469
Holton, G., 98, 100, 111, 203, 207, 449
Holyoak, K. J., 48, 49, 53, 87–88, 88, 106, 242, 243, 391, 398, 431, 442, 449

Horkheimer, M., 179, 449
Horrocks, J. C., 282, 435
Horwood, S. P., 186, 428
Hoskin, R. E., 23, 449
Hounsome, M., 188, 449
Howard, L., 339, 487
Howard, R. A., 316, 449
Hoyer, W. J., 349, 471
Hoyt, M. E., 57, 432
Hsee, C. K., 291, 449, 458
Hubbard, M., 152, 154, 472
Huber, G. P., 270, 448
Huberman, B. A., 380
Hume, D., 84, 126–127, 449
Humphreys, P., 415, 426
Hunter, D. J., 483
Huntington, J. M., 270, 452
Huntley, H. E., 449
Husband, T. H., 96, 449
Huxley, A., 449
Hyman, I. E., Jr., 96, 449

I

Idol, L., 342, 451
Illich, 268
Inhelder, B., 342, 449
Irwin, J. R., 265, 449
Isen, A. M., 199, 200, 202–203, 449, 450

J

Jackson, J. D., 332, 450
Jacobs, D., 172, 450
Jacobs, J. E., 77, 450
Jacowitz, K. E., 264, 452
James, W., 148, 151, 342, 450
Janis, I., 267, 305, 312, 450
Jarvis, W., 201, 429
Jaspers, K., 25, 292, 407, 414, 415, 450
Jay, E., 201, 468, 483
Jaynes, E. T., 143, 450.
Jeannerod, M., 312, 484
Jeeves, M. A., 217–218, 450
Jeffrey, R., 116, 450
Jeffries, R., 104, 469
Jepson, C., 77, 399, 450
Jepson, D., 88, 395, 466
Jevons, W. S., 17, 450
Johnson, E., 28, 199, 254, 318, 467
Johnson, E. J., 200, 450
Johnson, E. M., 264, 454
Johnson, J., 233, 476

Johnson, M. K., 95, 96, 450, 470, 481
Johnson, M. P., 253, 474
Johnson, R. H., 141, 450
Johnson, S. M., 291, 439
Johnson-Laird, P. N., 20, 48, 49, 327, 342, 363, 369, 394, 395, 398, 410, 418, 450, 451, 466, 485
Jones, B. F., 342, 451
Jones, E. E., 57, 242, 244, 245, 283, 426, 451, 458
Jones, J. M., 318, 426
Jones, S. R. G., 165, 451
Jou, J., 78, 451
Jourdain, 391
Joyce, C. R. B., 279, 439, 453
Jungermann, H., 190, 315, 321, 451
Jurow, G., 52, 451

K

Kagan, J., 26, 451
Kahan, M., 162, 451
Kahane, H., 42, 451
Kahneman, D., 7, 23, 42, 87, 257, 258, 264, 265, 316, 399, 405, 417, 451, 452, 483
Kalish, M., 53, 457
Kalven, H., 143, 452
Kameda, T., 300, 302, 452
Kanarick, A. F., 270, 452
Kant, I., 28, 32, 135, 390, 452
Kaplan, A., 23, 452, 468
Kaplan, C., 352, 353, 468
Kaplan, M. F., 303, 464
Kaplan, R., 452
Kaplan, S., 187, 452
Kase, L. M., 452
Katz, J., 280, 452
Kauffman, S., 205, 227, 452
Kavanaugh, D., 200, 452
Keating, D. P., 202, 452
Keats, 203
Keeley, L. H., 378, 452
Keeney, R. L., 175, 309, 316, 446, 452
Kekes, J., 43, 453
Kelley, H. H., 146, 234, 235, 302, 453, 467
Kemp, M. A., 265, 453
Kenton, J., 74, 480
Keren, G. B., 9, 94, 283, 290, 453, 457, 485
Kern, L., 284, 453
Kerr, N. L., 300, 304, 453
Kerstholt, J. H., 288, 453
Ketron, 74
Keyser, C. J., 113, 133, 453

Kidd, J. B., 94, 453
Kieras, D. E., 336, 462
Kim, J. I., 313, 482
King, 63
Kipnis, D., 244, 453, 479
Kirkpatrick, L. A., 435
Kirsch, I., 96, 461
Kirwan, J. R., 279, 453
Kitchener, K. S., 344, 346, 350, 352, 453
Kitcher, P., 202, 454
Kivnik, H. Q., 347, 438
Klaczynski, P. A., 77, 180, 454
Klar, Y., 20, 455
Klein, G. A., 288, 289, 319, 454, 469, 487
Kleinmuntz, B., 279, 454
Kline, M., 110, 129, 203, 230, 454
Klopfer, L. E., 108, 430
Kneppreth, N. P., 264, 454
Knetsch, J. L., 264, 265, 451
Koehler, D. J., 57, 233, 454
Kogan, N., 304, 454, 485
Kolodner, J., 103, 454
Komorita, S. S., 380, 454
Konecni, V. J., 437
Koran, L. M., 280, 454
Koriat, A., 92, 454
Kosslyn, S. M., 196, 454
Kottemann, J. E., 270, 434
Kramer, D. A., 304, 344, 347, 348, 350, 436, 454
Kramer, G. P., 453
Krantz, D. H., 77, 88, 200, 395, 399, 440, 450, 466
Krantz, S., 440
Krauss, S., 283, 290, 319, 454, 460
Kristiansen, C. M., 455
Krueger, J., 77, 79, 244, 455
Krüger, L., 443
Kruglanski, A. W., 20, 180, 202, 455
Krupnick, A. J., 187
Kühberger, A., 258, 455
Kuhn, D., 123, 455
Kukla, A., 235, 486
Kunda, Z., 88, 180, 243, 395, 455, 466
Kunreuther, H., 318, 455
Kurtz, B. E., 26, 455
Kyburg, H. E., Jr., 118, 405, 455

L

Labouvie-Vief, G., 345, 349, 455, 456
Labroo, A. A., 202–203, 449
Lachman, J. L., 91, 456
Lachman, R., 91, 456

Lakatos, I., 159, 456
Lambert, M., 304, 456
Lambert, R., 456
Lamm, H., 300, 464
Lampert, 122
Lampropoulos, G. K., 282, 421
Landry, D., 302, 456
Landwehr, R. S., 90, 464
Lane, R. E., 292, 456
Langer, 20, 430
Lankford, F. G., 339, 456
Laplace, P. S., 332, 456
LaPrelle, J., 245, 469
Larkin, K., 329, 432
Larrick, R. P., 22, 77, 78, 456
Lau, H. C., 312, 456
Laughlin, P. R., 304, 456
Lave, J., 74, 103, 456
Layman, M., 271, 458
Lea, M., 300, 390, 469
Leaper, D. J., 282, 435
LeBoeuf, A., 396, 475
Le Bon, G., 377, 456
Lederman, 225, 332
Lee, S.-Y., 122, 480
Lee, W., 21, 456
Lefcourt, H. M., 242, 456
Lefford, A., 277, 456
Leftow, B., 153, 457
Legant, P., 244, 466
Leggett, E. L., 122, 436
Legrenzi, M. S., 48, 451
Legrenzi, P., 48, 284, 443, 451
Lehman, D., 292, 474
Leifer, R. P., 264, 454
Leli, D. A., 281, 457
Lemley, R., 243, 466
Lents, J. M., 187, 457
Leonard, G. K., 264, 435
Leonesio, R. J., 90, 457, 464
Lepper, M. R., 147, 152, 154, 233, 421, 459, 472
Lerner, D., 203, 457
Lerner, J. S., 313–314, 457
Leutwyler, K., 266, 457
Levi, I., 42, 117, 390, 457
Levin, I. P., 258, 457
Levinson, P., 3, 43, 457
Levinson, S. C., 73, 457
Lewandowsky, S., 53, 457
Lewicki, P., 106, 457
Lewin, K., 300, 457
Lewis, 185
Lewis, C., 283, 457
Lewis, C. H., 210, 458, 459

Lewis, C. S., 133–134, 196, 458
Lewis, H., 458
Ley, T., 287, 315, 431
Li, F. P., 483
Libby, R., 282, 458
Liberman, A., 360, 430
Licht, B. G., 122, 483
Lichtenstein, S., 42, 94, 108, 258, 265, 271, 290, 316, 319, 440, 449, 458, 477, 485
Lieblich, I., 92, 454
Liker, J. K., 74, 430
Lilienfeld, S. O., 279, 487
Linder, D. E., 57, 458
Lindley, D. V., 212, 229, 261, 458
Linford, K. M., 244, 455
Lippert, F. W., 187, 458
Lippitt, R., 300, 457
Lipshitz, R., 289, 458
Livio, M., 458
Lloyd, F. J., 178, 471
Lochhead, J., 338, 432, 458
Loewenstein, G. F., 291, 458
Loftus, E. F., 96, 461
Lohse, G. L., 270, 434
Lombino, P., 6, 458
Loomes, G., 263, 458
Lopes, L. L., 49, 246, 458
Lord, C., 147, 459
Lories, G., 91, 92, 433
Lott, M. K., 19, 426
Lounsbury, J. W., 318, 481
Luce, M. F., 23, 199, 459
Luce, R. D., 19, 21, 259, 316, 320, 459
Luckmann, T., 290, 425
Ludbrook, A., 188, 459
Lundell, J., 286, 424
Lupker, S. J., 90, 459
Lusted, L. B., 94, 459
Lycan, W. C., 28, 37, 81, 120–121, 130, 155, 158, 189, 216, 250–251, 374–375, 381–382, 390, 401, 459
Lynch, J. S., 311, 439
Lyttleton, R. A., 117–118, 165, 459
Lyubomirsky, S., 292, 474

M

MacCoun, R. J., 304, 453
MacCrimmon, K. R., 264, 459
Macdonald, M., 459
Macdonald, R. R., 22, 42, 97, 320, 415, 459
MacGregor, D. G., 330, 477

MacIntyre, A., 40, 41, 45, 67, 68, 190–191, 369, 459
Mack, R. L., 210, 458, 459
Mackay, C., 5, 171–172, 373, 377, 459
Mackie, D. M., 270, 483
Mackworth, N. H., 344, 459
MacLean, D. E., 22, 189, 459
Macnamara, J., 53, 390, 392, 393, 459
Madey, S. F., 202, 461
Magnusson, D., 281, 466
Maheswaran, D., 360, 460
Maier, N. R. F., 306, 460
Maktelow, 34
Malkiel, B. G., 236, 460
Mandelbrot, B., 40, 460
Mandler, J. M., 102, 460
Manis, M., 64, 460
Manktelow, K. I., 42, 47, 49, 398, 439, 460
Mann, L., 164, 267, 312, 450
Maranto, G., 271, 460
Marcel, G., 341, 460
March, J. G., 185, 358, 460
Marecek, J., 244, 466
Margalit, A., 460
Margolis, H., 30, 42, 52, 55, 62, 391, 401, 402, 416, 460
Marr, D., 336, 460
Marshall, C. R., 29, 431
Martignon, L., 283, 290, 319, 454, 460
Martin, T., 19, 426
Maruyama, G. M., 245, 422
Marvin, C., 129, 460
Maskin, E., 301, 433
Maslow, A., 192, 460
Massaro, D. W., 336, 460
Matlin, M. W., 277, 460
Maugherman, A. S., 282, 421
Maxwell, C., 265, 453, 460
Maxwell, J. C., 204
Mayo, D. G., 143, 460
Mazzoni, G., 92, 96, 423, 461
McAllister, D. W., 180, 461
McArthur, L., 243, 461
McCain, 320
McCann, A. P., 282, 435
McClelland, G. H., 265, 449
McDermott, L. C., 338, 483
McGee, K. A., 291, 448
McGraw, A. P., 283, 462
McGuigan, F. J., 96, 461
McGuire, W. J., 20, 52, 53, 277, 421, 461
McKellar, P., 328–329, 334, 461
McLennan, J., 287, 315, 431
McNeil, B. J., 189, 279, 436, 461
McNeill, D., 90, 92, 429

McPeck, J., 103, 461
Meacham, J. A., 346, 353, 354, 461
Medvec, V. H., 202, 461
Meehl, P. E., 281, 282, 434, 461, 462
Meitz, J., 187, 475
Melcher, J., 94, 474
Mellers, B. A., 199, 283, 462
Menninger, 367
Merton, R. K., 344, 462
Merzbach, U. C., 428
Messer, W. S., 42, 368, 462
Messick, D. M., 261, 462
Messick, S., 202, 462
Metcalfe, J., 90, 92, 93, 462, 474
Meyer, D. E., 90, 336, 462, 487
Meyerson, M., 300, 301, 462
Michotte, A., 210, 462
Midgley, M., 222, 462
Mietz, 187
Mikula, G., 303, 462
Mill, J., 195
Mill, J. S., 147, 196, 197, 391, 462
Miller, A. G., 246, 462
Miller, A. I., 225, 331
Miller, D. T., 245, 463
Miller, G. A., 211, 243, 463
Miller, N., 304, 435
Miller, P., 267, 440
Millikan, R. G., 130, 463
Minsk, E., 263, 478
Mintz, S., 96, 463
Miranda, S. M., 468
Mischel, W., 152, 154, 242, 247, 447, 463
Mishan, E. J., 23, 463
Mitchell, T. R., 180, 270, 286, 424, 461
Monahan, J., 282, 330, 477, 481
Monk, G. S., 338, 432
Monks, J., 90, 91, 445
Montaigne, M. E., 348, 463
Monterio, K. P., 199, 428
Monterosso, J., 292, 474
Mooney, C., 162, 468
Mooney, R. J., 211, 463
Moore, D. W., 258, 463
Morely, 288
Morgan, J. N., 22, 23, 77, 78, 456, 463
Morgenstern, D., 21, 23, 316
Morgenstern, O., 18, 463
Morley, I. E., 288, 463
Morowitz, H. J., 13, 220, 463
Morris, R., 366, 463
Morris, S. C., 187, 458
Moscovici, S., 304, 464
Moser, P. K., 178–179, 307, 463
Moshman, D., 201, 202, 304, 463, 464

Moskovici, D., 303, 464
Moylan, S. J., 245, 254, 440
Mueller, D. C., 379, 464
Mulcahy, R. F., 342, 464
Mumford, L., 411, 464
Murray, C. A., 448
Murray, D. J., 43, 73, 395, 415, 443
Murtaugh, M., 74, 456
Myers, D. G., 300, 303, 464
Mynatt, C. R., 284, 436, 484

N

Nagao, D. H., 300, 464
Nagel, E., 464
Nagel, T., 44, 63, 68, 84, 87, 99, 123, 132, 150, 151, 177–178, 191, 193, 206, 218–219, 221, 230, 340, 348, 464
Narasimham, G., 77, 454
Narens, L., 90, 91, 92, 423, 464
National Commission on Excellence in Education, 464
National Educational Goals Panel, 464
Navarrete, J. B., 19, 426
Neale, M. A., 107, 464
Neimark, E. D., 464
Nelson, T. O., 90, 91, 92, 423, 457, 464
Neufeld, V. R., 280, 424
Newberry, B., 267, 442
Newcomb, T. M., 52, 421
Newell, A., 15, 107, 465
Newman, J. R., 63, 464
Newmann, F. M., 26, 201, 465
Newstead, 320
Neyman, J., 21, 465
Nezworski, M. T., 279, 487
Ngang, S. K., 53, 457
Nicholls, J. G., 245, 465
Nichols, C. N., 282, 421
Nickerson, R. S., 28, 45, 60, 72, 75, 93, 105, 106, 122, 154, 159, 201, 205, 261, 263, 292, 316, 319, 324, 465
Nilsson, N. J., 329, 465
Nisbett, R. E., 22, 42, 48, 51, 53, 77, 78, 88, 141, 146, 152, 153, 154, 242, 243–244, 245, 391, 394, 395, 398, 399, 431, 440, 449, 450, 451, 455, 456, 465, 466, 468, 487
Nogar, R. J., 227, 238, 466
Nordhaus, W. D., 266, 466
Norman, D. A., 73, 399, 466

Norman, G. R., 280, 424, 429, 447
Northcraft, G. B., 107, 464
Noveck, 390
Nowak, M. A., 199, 476
Nozick, R., 1, 8, 27, 45, 58, 66, 128, 131, 137–138, 141, 149, 224, 322, 357, 361, 383–384, 411, 412, 466
Nye, P., 313, 476
Nygren, T. E., 200, 450
Nyquist, L., 352, 353, 468
Nystedt, L., 281, 466
Nystrom, L. E., 199, 473

O

Oakhill, J. V., 20, 410, 466
Oaksford, M., 391, 397, 466
Oberauer, K., 320, 466
O'Brien, 390, 391, 398
O'Connor, M., 94, 466
Odean, T., 108, 466
Oliver, L. M., 48, 431
Olson, M., 381, 466
Omodei, M. M., 287, 315, 431
Orasanu, J., 288, 454
O'Reilly, M., 279, 439
Orvis, B. R., 234, 467
Orwoll, L., 344–345, 352, 353, 355, 467
Osgood, C. E., 342, 467
O'Shea, T., 339, 487
Osherson, D. N., 395, 418, 467
Oskamp, S., 94, 467
Over, D. E., 34, 49, 439, 460

P

Pacioli, L., 467
Pagels, H. R., 220, 467
Pais, A., 97, 227, 467
Pankoff, L. D., 282, 467
Papineau, D., 130, 467
Park, B., 154, 472
Parks, C. D., 380, 454
Pascual-Leone, J., 345, 467
Passingham, R. E., 312, 456
Patalano, 308
Patil, K. D., 280, 486
Patrick, A. S., 90, 459
Patton, J. N., 19, 426
Pauker, S. G., 315, 461, 467
Pauker, S. P., 189, 315, 467
Paul, R., 26, 467
Payne, J., 467

Payne, J. W., 23, 28, 199, 254, 258, 318, 459, 467
Pearce, D. W., 188, 467
Pearson, E. S., 21, 465
Peck, S. C., 266, 468
Peele, E., 318, 481
Peirce, C. S., 44, 468
Peltzer, U., 302, 474
Penrose, R., 207, 228, 468
Perkins, D. N., 20, 51, 72, 76, 105, 180, 201, 273, 397, 468, 483, 484
Perlmutter, M., 345, 352, 353, 355, 467, 468
Peters, E., 199, 258, 291, 439
Petersen, R. C., 270, 452
Peterson, C. R., 271, 441
Peterson, J., 72
Peterson, M. K., 468
Pettigrew, T. F., 244, 468
Petty, C. R., 90, 91, 472
Petty, R. E., 201, 429
Phelps, C. E., 162, 468
Phillips, L. D., 94, 458
Piaget, J., 342, 390, 449, 468
Piattelli-Palmarini, M., 42, 391, 468
Pickett, R. M., 181, 281, 442, 481
Pietromonaco, P. R., 242, 468
Pittman, T. S., 242, 468
Pitz, G. F., 271, 469
Platt, J., 380, 469
Platt, R. D., 311, 469
Pleit-Kuiper, A., 9, 485
Pliske, D. B., 284, 469, 484
Pliske, R., 289
Polanyi, M., 87, 339, 469
Polkinghorne, J., 116, 190, 225, 251, 400, 469
Pollard, P., 394, 439
Polson, P., 104, 469
Polya, G., 85, 143, 144, 469
Poole, K. T., 145, 469
Popper, K. R., 68, 469
Porter, T., 443
Portney, P. R., 187, 455
Post, D., 243, 461
Postmes, P., 300, 469
Potenza, M., 77, 450
Poundstone, W., 23, 61, 82, 381, 469
Premack, D., 210, 433
Pruitt, J. S., 288, 430
Pullen, S. M., 291, 448
Pyszczynski, T., 245, 469

Q

Quesada, J., 288, 444

Quine, W. V., 28, 140, 469, 470

R

Raaijmakers, J. G. W., 288, 453
Radlove, S., 243, 463
Raiffa, H., 18, 21, 23, 175, 264, 271, 309, 316, 425, 446, 452, 459, 470
Ramsey, F. P., 116, 470
Rapoport, A., 23, 470
Rathunde, K., 342–343, 344, 350, 352
Rawcliffe, D. H., 169, 470
Rawls, J., 193, 470
Raye, C. L., 95, 96, 450, 470
Read, J. D., 90, 470
Redelmeier, D. A., 290, 470
Reder, L. M., 91, 92, 470
Redhead, M., 364, 470
Reed, H., 243, 465
Reed, L., 235, 486
Regan, D. T., 247, 470
Regier, T., 320, 443
Reich, S. S., 47, 398, 470
Reichenbach, H., 124, 470
Reid, W. A., 122, 470
Reinhold, H., 271, 469
Reitan, H. T., 235, 475
Rennie, 186
Rescher, 390
Resnick, L. B., 26, 71, 73, 201, 470
Rest, S., 235, 486
Rettinger, D. A., 19, 470
Reyna, V. F., 77, 178, 320, 470, 471
Rhim, H., 318, 471
Richards, J. R., 127, 405, 471
Rigaminti, D., 347, 430
Rilling, J. K., 199, 473
Rips, 390, 392
Ritov, I., 199, 263, 264, 452, 462, 471
Ritter, F. E., 91, 92, 470
Roberts, H. V., 282, 467
Robinson, D. N., 123, 341, 437, 471
Rogers, R. D., 312, 456
Rogoff, B., 74, 471
Roland-Robinson, M., 101, 471
Ronen, J., 315, 471
Roodin, P. A., 349, 471
Rorer, L. G., 246, 280, 318, 444, 462
Rosenbaum, R. M., 235, 486
Rosenberg, M. J., 52, 421
Rosenfeld, R., 236, 471
Rosenfield, C., 245, 478
Rosenstiel, 303
Ross, J., 314, 479

Ross, J. C., 281, 477
Ross, L., 42, 141, 146, 147, 152, 153, 154, 157, 233, 242, 243–244, 245, 421, 459, 466, 471, 472
Ross, M., 244, 429, 472
Rossman, B. B., 187, 472
Roth, A. E., 199, 472
Rothbart, M., 154, 472
Rotter, J. B., 242, 472
Roxburgh, I. W., 149, 472
Ruderman, A., 243, 482
Rumain, 392
Runion, G. E., 472
Ruse, M., 68, 472
Rush, J. D., 282, 421
Russell, B., 80, 94, 133, 176, 188, 203, 207, 295, 351, 364, 379, 472
Russell, M., 472
Ruth, P., 47, 398, 470
Rüttinger, B., 302, 472
Ryan, M. P., 90, 91, 472
Ryan, R. M., 122, 435
Rybash, J., 349, 471
Ryle, G., 85, 473

S

Sá, W., 79, 473
Saarinen, T. F., 4, 473
Sacks, O., 94, 473
Safer, M. A., 242, 473
Salam, A., 204, 473
Salas, E., 288, 430
Salmon, W. C., 13, 24, 473
Salomon, G., 73, 473
Salovey, P., 200, 473
Sampson, G., 394, 473
Samuelson, W., 265, 473
Sanfey, A. G., 199, 473
Sapolsky, R. M., 178, 473
Sargent, T. J., 360, 473
Savage, L. J., 18, 21, 260, 316, 473
Sawyer, J., 282, 473
Scardamalia, M., 87, 425
Scardino, P. T., 271, 446
Schacter, D. L., 92, 473
Schacter, S., 3
Schaeffer, J., 107, 476
Schank, R. C., 103, 473
Scheffler, I., 202, 473
Schenker, C., 243, 463
Scherer, L. L., 180, 426
Schiavo, M. D., 284, 436
Schlaifer, R. O., 21, 271, 316, 470, 473

Schliemann, A. D., 74, 430
Schlosberg, H., 342, 487
Schneider, S. L., 37, 180–181, 258, 290, 320, 321, 457, 474
Schneider, W., 319, 476
Schnur, J. A., 181, 481
Schoeberlein, S., 349, 456
Schoenberger, A., 281, 430
Schoenfeld, A., 108, 122, 474
Schooler, J. W., 24, 94, 474, 487
Schoomaker, E. B., 281, 477
Schopenhauer, A., 383, 474
Schrag, F., 474
Schrag, P., 26, 200, 201, 474
Schrenk, L. P., 358, 474
Schubert, G., 145, 474
Schuler, H., 300, 302, 474
Schum, 415–416
Schumacher, E. F., 10, 253, 340, 379, 474
Schuman, H., 253, 474
Schwartz, A., 199, 279, 438
Schwartz, B., 92, 107, 123, 292, 437, 474
Schwartz, E., 294, 474
Schwartz, N., 199, 416, 474
Schwartz, W. B., 186, 475
Schwarz, A., 438, 462
Schwarz, N., 475
Schwinger, T., 303, 462
Searle, J. R., 335, 475
Sears, D. O., 147, 475
Sedikides, C., 200, 475
Segal, J. W., 273, 484
Seligman, M. E. P., 122, 421, 475
Sellen, J., 397, 466
Sen, A., 254, 475
Shackle, G. L. S., 358, 475
Shafer, E. L., 187, 475
Shafir, E., 253, 254, 255, 260, 261, 262, 265, 396, 475, 484
Shaklee, H., 20, 475
Shank, R. C., 211, 475
Shannon, C. E., 475
Shanteau, J., 269, 320, 321, 441, 483
Shatz, D., 125, 157, 475
Shaw, G. B., 80
Shaw, M. E., 235, 475
Sheffrin, S. M., 162, 475
Sherman, S. J., 233, 448, 476
Shermer, M., 126, 169, 476
Sherrington, C. S., 402, 476
Shiffrin, R. M., 319, 476
Shiller, R. J., 236, 476
Shimamura, A. P., 90, 464
Short, R. H., 342, 464
Shubik, M., 7, 476

Shulman, L. S., 107, 280, 283, 438
Siegel, H., 21, 44, 476
Siegel, S., 434
Siegel-Jacobs, K., 313, 476
Sigmund, K., 199, 476
Simmel, M., 210, 448
Simon, H. A., 19, 21, 38, 51, 107, 176, 199, 292, 329, 358, 363, 401, 438, 476
Simonson, I., 254, 255, 313, 475, 476, 484
Simpson, E. H., 261, 476
Sinclair, J. C., 186, 428
Sisson, J. C., 281, 477
Skinner, B. F., 222, 477
Skitka, L., 314, 482
Skyrms, B., 28, 32
Sleeman, D., 339, 477
Sloman, S. A., 291, 319, 477
Slovic, P., 42, 55, 78, 108, 199, 254, 258, 265, 271, 280, 291, 316, 318, 319, 330, 439, 440, 449, 458, 477
Slusher, M. P., 96, 477
Smedslund, J., 47, 394, 477
Smith, B., 286, 424
Smith, E. E., 72, 105, 152, 201, 437
Smith, E. L., 210, 422, 437
Smith, J., 343, 344, 350, 352, 354, 423, 478
Smith, J. M., 23, 477
Smith, P. B., 468
Smith, V. L., 90, 91, 478
Smith, W., 204, 478
Smolin, L., 324, 478
Sniderman, P. M., 59, 202, 478
Snyder, C. R., 478
Snyder, M., 57, 154, 247, 478, 481
Snyder, M. L., 57, 242, 244, 478
Sobell, M. B., 245, 483
Soelberg, P. O., 51, 311, 478
Sokal, A., 478
Solem, A. R., 306, 460
Solomon, L. K., 243, 461
Soloway, E., 338, 432
Solso, R. L., 336, 460
Sosis, R., 235, 478
Sowell, T., 181, 293, 294, 307, 310, 314, 478
Sox, H. C., 189, 438
Spengler, P. M., 282, 421
Sperry, R. W., 221, 478
Spilich, G., 107, 484
Spinoza, B., 478
Sprafka, S. A., 107, 280, 283, 438
Spranca, M., 263, 478
Sprent, P., 478
Stahlberg, D., 245, 440

Stang, D. J., 277, 460
Staniland, J. R., 282, 435
Stanovich, K. E., 21, 75, 76, 77, 78, 79, 201, 202, 389–390, 391, 394, 396, 397, 416, 418–419, 473, 479
Starr, R., 379, 448
Starrett, D., 379, 448
Stasser, G., 302, 479
Staw, B. M., 7, 314, 479
Steedman, 398
Stein, E., 396, 479
Steiner, M., 230, 479
Steinhardt, P., 229, 446
Steinmetz, J. L., 154, 233, 472
Stephan, W. G., 245, 478
Stephenson, G. M., 288, 303, 463, 479
Sterman, J. D., 288, 479
Stern, S., 244, 479
Sternberg, R. J., 73, 74, 76, 79, 201, 202, 342, 343, 344, 354, 355, 382, 424, 435, 480, 485
Stevens, A. L., 329, 480
Stevens, P. K., 480
Stevenson, H. W., 122, 390, 480
Stewart, A. L., 3, 480
Stich, S. P., 22, 29, 39, 123, 131, 369, 384–387, 394, 395, 401, 480
Stigler, G. L., 270, 360, 480
Stigler, J. W., 103, 480
Stocker-Kreichgauer, G., 303
Stove, D. C., 45, 116, 117, 480
Strack, F., 154, 233, 472
Strada, G., 480
Strathern, P., 151, 481
Strauss, E., 247, 470
Streufert, M. S., 245, 481
Streufert, S. C., 245, 481
Strickland, L. H., 57, 449
Suengas, A. G., 95, 450, 481
Sugden, R., 263, 458
Suls, J. M., 235, 481
Summers, D. A., 318, 446
Sundstrom, E., 318, 481
Sunstein, C., 303, 481
Suppes, P., 21, 434
Surowiecki, 295, 305, 306
Svenson, O., 20, 199, 290, 320, 481
Swann, W. B., 57, 154, 247, 478, 481
Swap, 380
Swets, J. A., 181, 281, 282, 442, 445, 481, 482
Swets, J. B., 181, 481
Swinburne, R., 124, 127, 142, 148, 152, 481
Switjink, Z., 443
Sykes, R. N., 91, 445